C000195066

STREET ATLAS
Warwickshire

First published 1992 by

Philip's, a division of
Octopus Publishing Group Ltd
2–4 Heron Quays, London E14 4JP

Second colour edition 2002
First impression 2002

ISBN 0-540-08125-6 (spiral)

© Philip's 2002

This product includes mapping data licensed
from Ordnance Survey® with the permission of
the Controller of Her Majesty's Stationery Office.
© Crown copyright 2002. All rights reserved.
Licence number 100011710.

Printed and bound in Spain
by Cayfosa-Quebecor

Contents

III **Key to map symbols**

IV **Key to map pages**

VI **Route planning**

VIII **Administrative and Postcode boundaries**

1 **Street maps** at 3½ inches to 1 mile

112 **Street maps** at 1¾ inches to 1 mile

143 **Street maps** at 3½ inches to 1 mile

151 **Street map of Coventry city centre**
at 7 inches to 1 mile

152 **Town maps** of Banbury and Tamworth

153 **Index** of towns and villages

154 **Index** of streets, hospitals, industrial estates, railway
stations, schools, shopping centres, universities
and places of interest

Digital Data

The exceptionally high-quality mapping found in this atlas is available as digital data in TIFF format,
which is easily convertible to other bit mapped (raster) image formats.

The index is also available in digital form as a standard database table. It contains all the details
found in the printed index together with the National Grid reference for the map square in which
each entry is named.

For further information and to discuss your requirements, please contact Philip's on
020 7531 8439 or george.philip@philips-maps.co.uk

Symbol	Description
(22a)	**Motorway** with junction number
	Primary route – dual/single carriageway
	A road – dual/single carriageway
	B road – dual/single carriageway
	Minor road – dual/single carriageway
	Other minor road – dual/single carriageway
	Road under construction
	Pedestrianised area
DY7	**Postcode boundaries**
	County and unitary authority boundaries
	Railway, railway under construction
	Tramway, tramway under construction
	Miniature railway
	Rural track, private road or narrow road in urban area
	Gate or obstruction to traffic (restrictions may not apply at all times or to all vehicles)
	Path, bridleway, byway open to all traffic, road used as a public path
	The representation in this atlas of a road, track or path is no evidence of the existence of a right of way
231 / 84	**Adjoining page indicators** (The colour of the arrow indicates the scale of the adjoining page - see scales below)
173 / 165	**Adjoining page indicator** showing the pages adjoining the top and bottom halves of the current page
246 / 203	The map areas within the pink/blue bands are shown at a larger scale on the page, indicated by the red/blue blocks and arrows

Symbol	Description
Walsall	**Railway station**
	Private railway station
West Bromwich Central	**Metro station**
	Tram stop
	Bus, coach station
	Ambulance station
	Coastguard station
	Fire station
	Police station
	Accident and Emergency entrance to hospital
H	**Hospital**
+	**Place of worship**
i	**Information Centre** (open all year)
P	**Parking**
P&R	**Park and Ride**
PO	**Post Office**
X	**Camping site**
	Caravan site
	Golf course
	Picnic site
Prim Sch	**Important buildings, schools, colleges, universities and hospitals**
River Medway	**Water name**
	River, stream
	Lock, weir
	Water
	Tidal water
	Woods
	Built up area
Church	**Non-Roman antiquity**
ROMAN FORT	**Roman antiquity**

Abbr	Term	Abbr	Term	Abbr	Term
Acad	**Academy**	Inst	**Institute**	Recn Gd	**Recreation Ground**
Allot Gdns	**Allotments**	Ct	**Law Court**		
Cemy	**Cemetery**	L Ctr	**Leisure Centre**	Resr	**Reservoir**
C Ctr	**Civic Centre**	LC	**Level Crossing**	Ret Pk	**Retail Park**
CH	**Club House**	Liby	**Library**	Sch	**School**
Coll	**College**	Mkt	**Market**	Sh Ctr	**Shopping Centre**
Crem	**Crematorium**	Meml	**Memorial**	TH	**Town Hall/House**
Ent	**Enterprise**	Mon	**Monument**	Trad Est	**Trading Estate**
Ex H	**Exhibition Hall**	Mus	**Museum**	Univ	**University**
Ind Est	**Industrial Estate**	Obsy	**Observatory**	Wks	**Works**
IRB Sta	**Inshore Rescue Boat Station**	Pal	**Royal Palace**	YH	**Youth Hostel**
		PH	**Public House**		

■ The small numbers around the edges of the maps identify the 1 kilometre National Grid lines ■ The dark grey border on the inside edge of some pages indicates that the mapping does not continue onto the adjacent page

The scale of the maps on the pages numbered in blue is 5.52 cm to 1 km • 3½ inches to 1 mile • 1: 18103

0   ¼   ½   ¾   1 mile
0   250 m   500 m   750 m   1 kilometre

The scale of the maps on pages numbered in green is 2.76 cm to 1 km • 1¾ inches to 1 mile • 1: 36206

0   ¼   ½   ¾   1 mile
0   250m 500m 750m 1kilometre

The scale of the maps on pages numbered in red is 11.04 cm to 1 km • 7 inches to 1 mile • 1: 9051.4

0   220 yards   440 yards   660 yards   ½ mile
0   125m   250m   375m   ½ kilometre

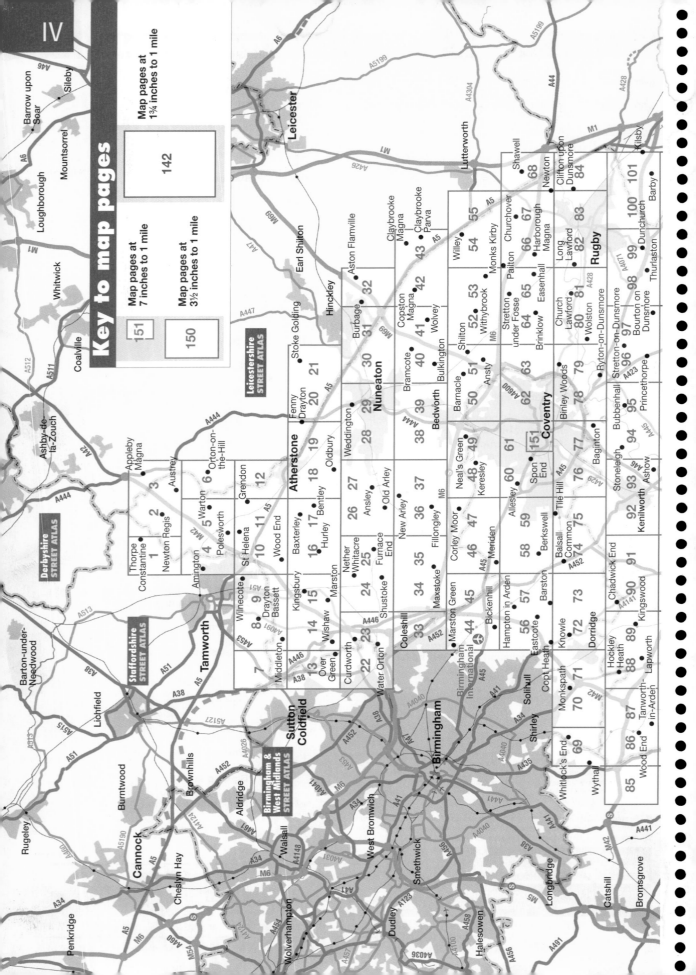

IV

Key to map pages

Map pages at
7 inches to 1 mile

151

Map pages at
3½ inches to 1 mile

150

Map pages at
1¾ inches to 1 mile

142

Leicestershire
STREET ATLAS

Derbyshire
STREET ATLAS

Staffordshire
STREET ATLAS

Birmingham &
West Midlands
STREET ATLAS

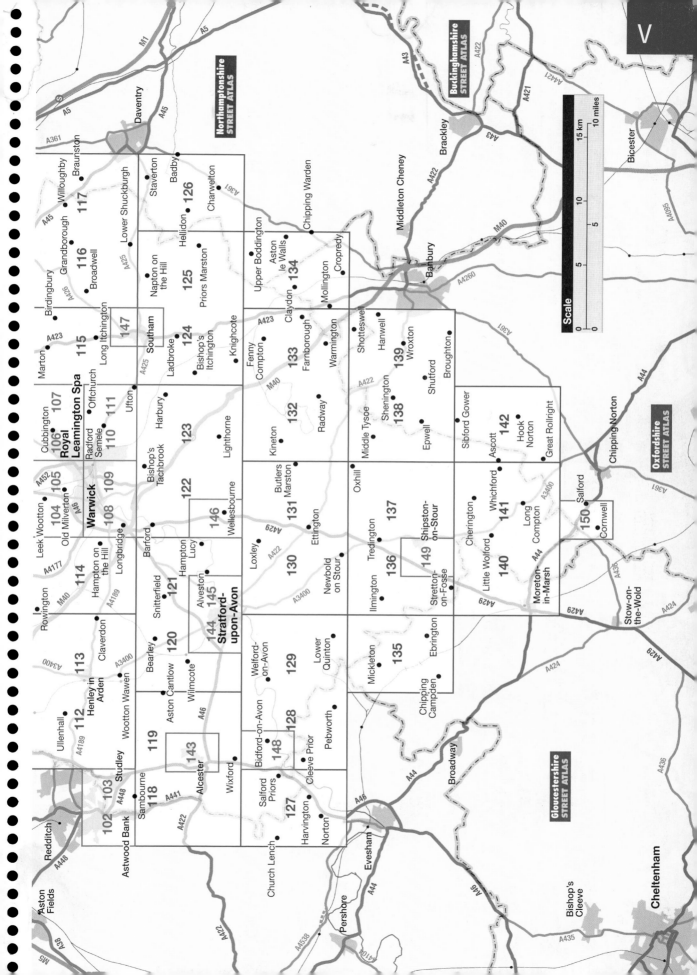

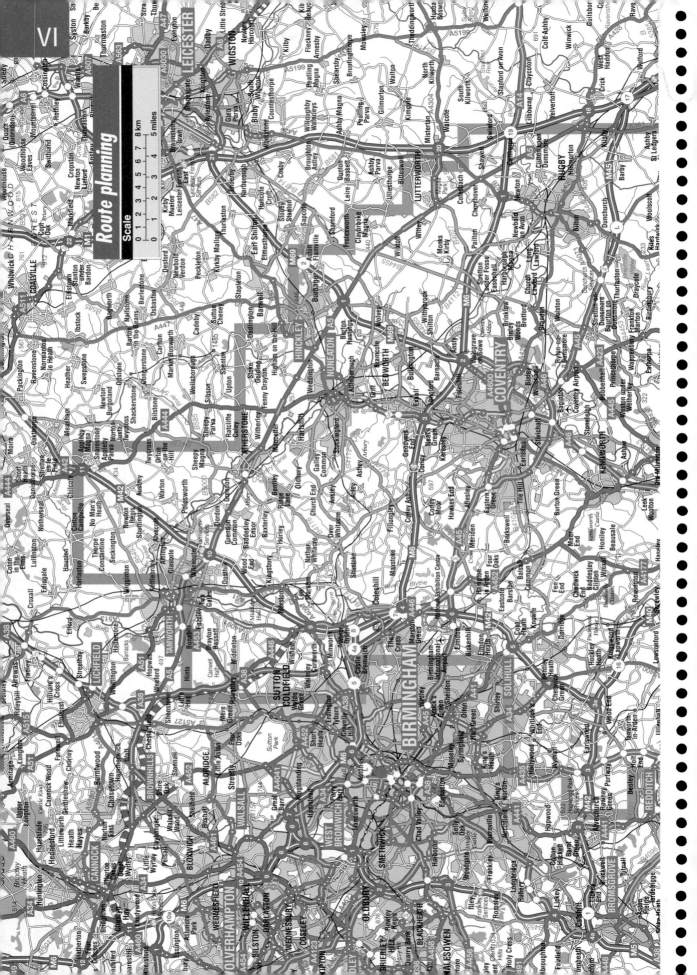

VI

Route planning

Scale

0 1 2 3 4 5 6 7 8 km
0 1 2 3 4 5 miles

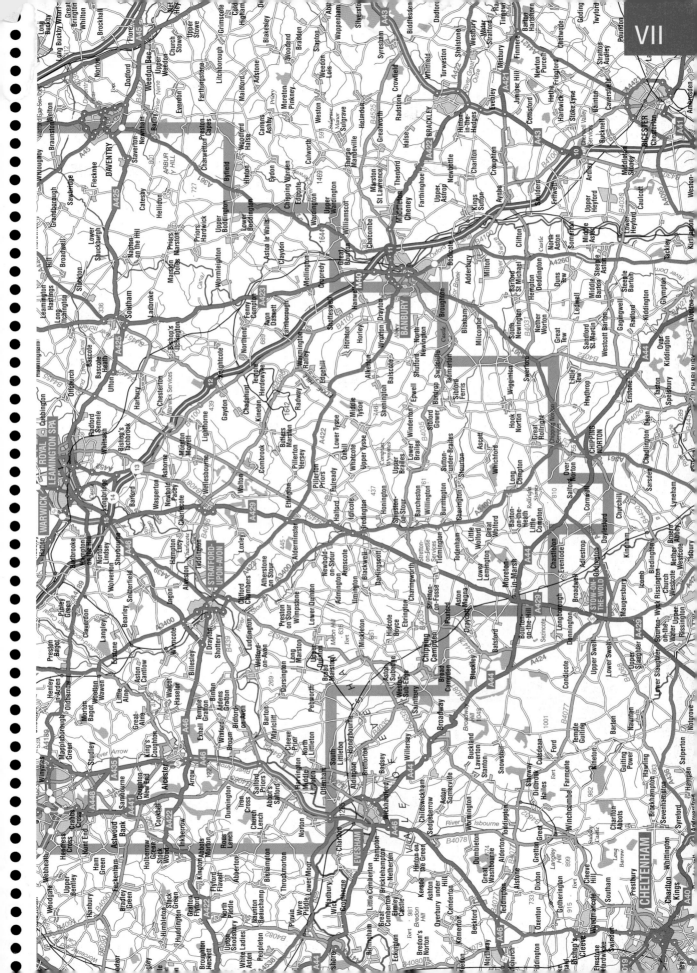

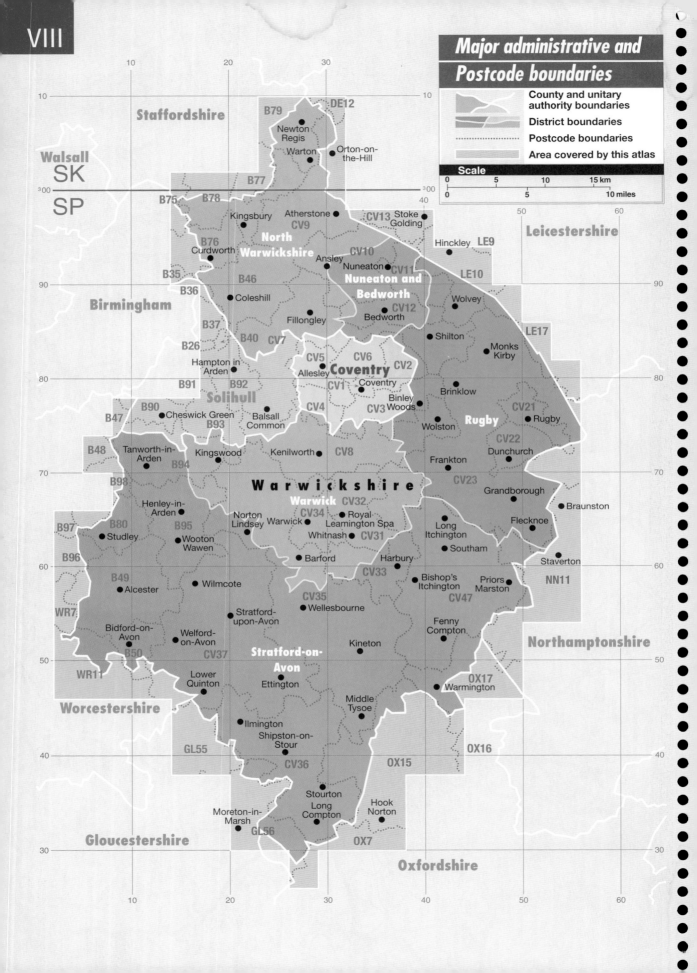

Major administrative and Postcode boundaries

County and unitary authority boundaries
District boundaries
Postcode boundaries
Area covered by this atlas

Scale
0 — 5 — 10 — 15 km
0 — 5 — 10 miles

Staffordshire

Walsall

SK
SP

B79
Newton Regis
Warton
Orton-on-the-Hill
DE12

B77

B75
B78
Atherstone
CV9
Kingsbury
CV13
Stoke Golding
Hinckley
LE9
Leicestershire

North Warwickshire
B76
Curdworth
Ansley
CV10
Nuneaton
CV11
LE10
Nuneaton and Bedworth

B35
B46
Coleshill
CV12
Bedworth
Wolvey
B36
Fillongley
LE17
Birmingham
B37
Shilton
Monks Kirby
B26
B40
CV7
CV5
CV6
CV2
Hampton in Arden
Allesley
Coventry
Shilton
Brinklow
CV21
B91
B92
CV1
Coventry
CV3
CV4
Binley Woods
Wolston
Rugby
Rugby
Solihull
B90
Cheswick Green
Balsall Common
CV8
Brinklow
B47
B93
CV22
B48
Tanworth-in-Arden
Kingswood
Kenilworth
Frankton
Dunchurch
B94
CV23

B93
W a r w i c k s h i r e
Grandborough
Braunston
Henley-in-Arden
Warwick
CV32
Flecknoe
B97
B80
B95
Norton Lindsey
CV34
Royal Leamington Spa
Long Itchington
Studley
Wooton Wawen
Whitnash
CV31
Southam
Staverton
B96
Barford
Harbury
CV33
B49
Wilmcote
Bishop's Itchington
Priors Marston
NN11
Alcester
CV35
Wellesbourne
CV47
WR7
Stratford-upon-Avon
Fenny Compton
Bidford-on-Avon
Welford-on-Avon
Kineton
Northamptonshire
B50
CV37
Stratford-on-Avon
WR11
Lower Quinton
Ettington
Middle Tysoe
OX17
Warmington
Worcestershire
Ilmington
Shipston-on-Stour
GL55
CV36
OX15
OX16
Stourton
Long Compton
Hook Norton
Moreton-in-Marsh
GL56
OX7
Gloucestershire
Oxfordshire

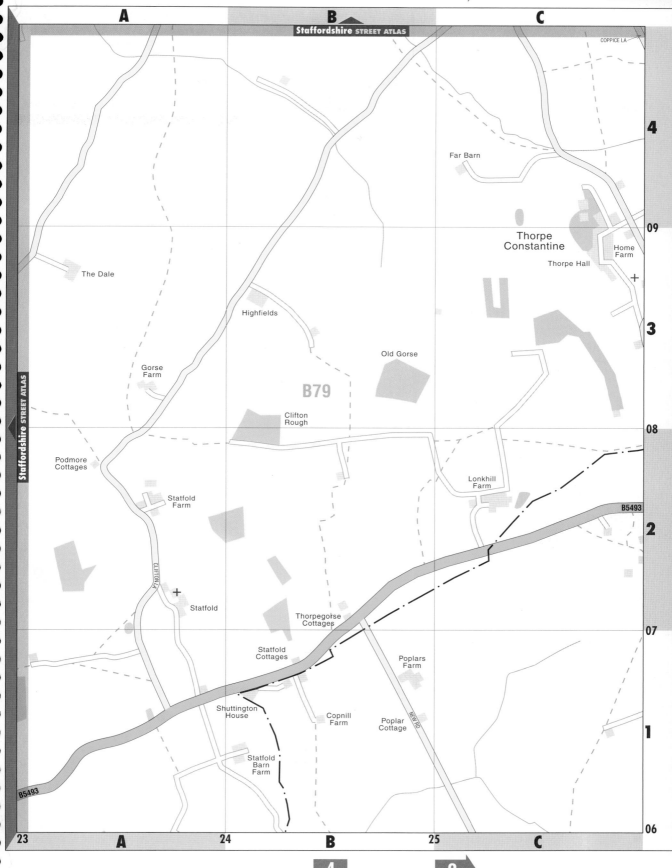

Staffordshire STREET ATLAS

Staffordshire STREET ATLAS

A B C

COPPICE LA

4

Far Barn

09

Thorpe
Constantine

The Dale

Home
Farm

Thorpe Hall

3

Highfields

Old Gorse

Gorse
Farm

B79

Clifton
Rough

08

Podmore
Cottages

Lonkhill
Farm

B5493

Statfold
Farm

2

CLIFTON LA

Statfold

Thorpegorse
Cottages

07

Statfold
Cottages

Poplars
Farm

Shuttington
House

Copnill
Farm

Poplar
Cottage

NEW RD

1

Statfold
Barn
Farm

B5493

06

23 24 25
A B C

4 2

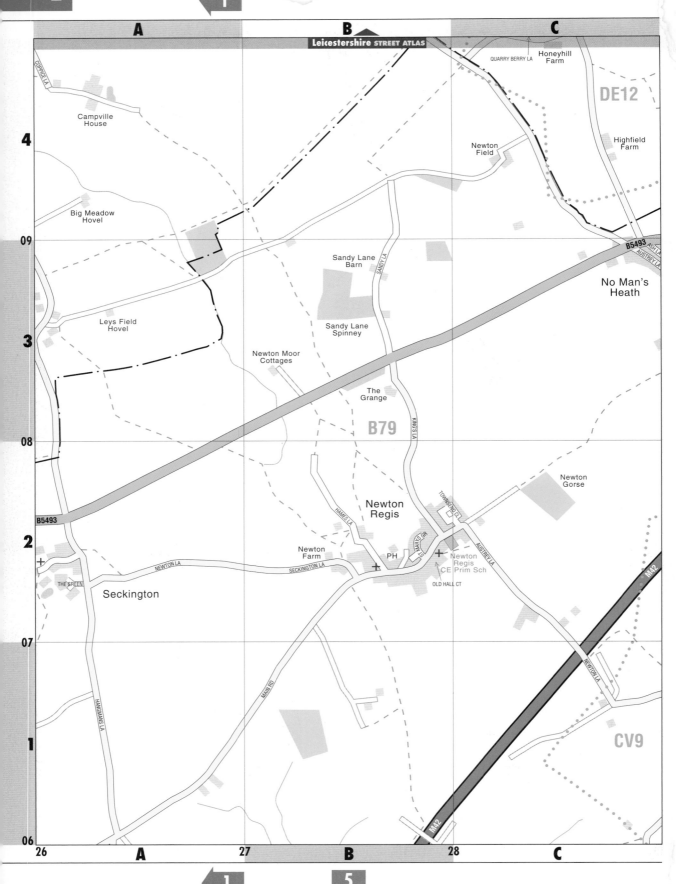

Leicestershire STREET ATLAS

A　　　　　　B　　　　　　C

DE12

QUARRY BERRY LA
Honeyhill
Farm

Campville
House

Newton
Field

Highfield
Farm

Big Meadow
Hovel

09

B5493

No Man's
Heath

Sandy Lane
Barn

SANDY LA

Leys Field
Hovel

Sandy Lane
Spinney

Newton Moor
Cottages

3

The Grange

KING'S LA

B79

08

Newton
Gorse

B5493

TOWNSEND CL

Newton
Regis

M42

THAMES LA

2

THANE'S GR

PH

Newton
Farm

Newton Regis
CE Prim Sch

AUSTREY LA

NEWTON LA

SECKINGTON LA

OLD HALL CT

Seckington

THE GREEN

NEWTON LA

07

MAIN RD

HANGMANS LA

CV9

1

M42

06

26　　A　　27　　B　　28　　C

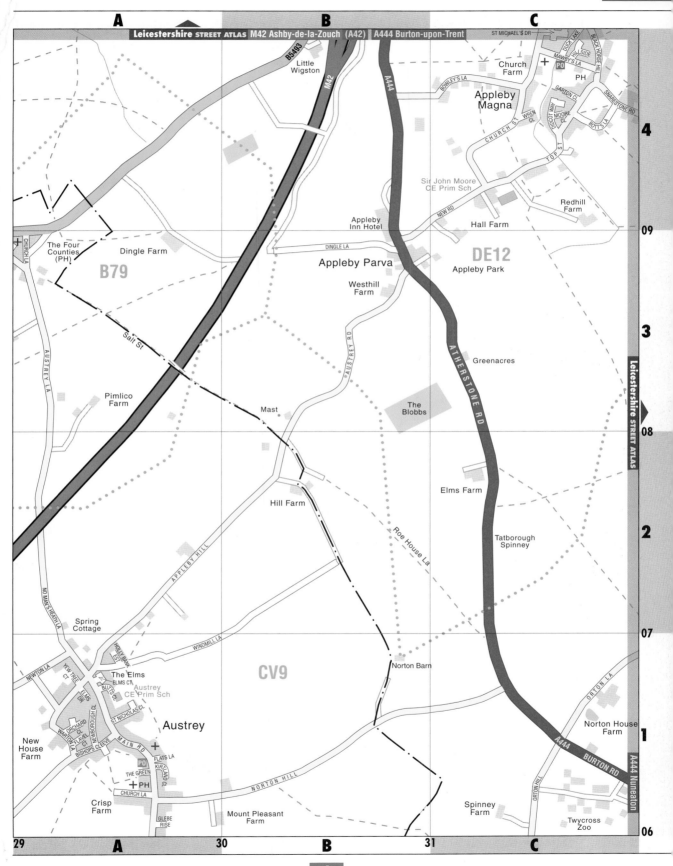

Leicestershire STREET ATLAS M42 Ashby-de-la-Zouch (A42) A444 Burton-upon-Trent

A   B   C

ST MICHAEL'S DR

B5493

Little Wigston

M42

A444

Church Farm

DUCK LAKE

BLACK HORSE HILL

MAWBY'S LA

HILLSIDE

PO

PH

Appleby Magna

BOWLEY'S LA

WREN CL

GARTON CL

SMARESTONE RD

CHURCH ST

DIDCOT WAY

MOORE CL

TOP ST

BOTT'S LA

4

The Four Counties (PH)

CHURCH LA

Dingle Farm

B79

Appleby Inn Hotel

DINGLE LA

Appleby Parva

Sir John Moore CE Prim Sch

NEW RD

Hall Farm

Appleby Park

DE12

Redhill Farm

09

Westhill Farm

AUSTREY RD

Salt St

AUSTREY LA

ATHERSTONE RD

3

Greenacres

Pimlico Farm

Mast

The Blobbs

08

Hill Farm

Elms Farm

APPLEBY HILL

Roe House La

Tatborough Spinney

2

Spring Cottage

NO MAN'S HEATH LA

WINDMILL LA

Norton Barn

07

NEWTON LA

HOLLY BANK EST

The Elms

ELMS CT

Austrey CE Prim Sch

CV9

ORTON LA

YEW TREE CT

ELMS DR

ST NICHOLAS CL

MAIN RD

Norton House Farm

Austrey

New House Farm

ORCHARD CL

HOGBOURNE CL

WARTON LA

FLAVEL CT

BISHOPS CLEVE

FLATS LA

KIRKLAND CL

1

A444

ORTON HILL

BURTON RD

PO

THE GREEN

PH

Crisp Farm

CHURCH LA

NORTON HILL

Mount Pleasant Farm

Spinney Farm

Twycross Zoo

GLEBE RISE

29   A   30   B   31   C   06

Leicestershire STREET ATLAS

A444 Nuneaton

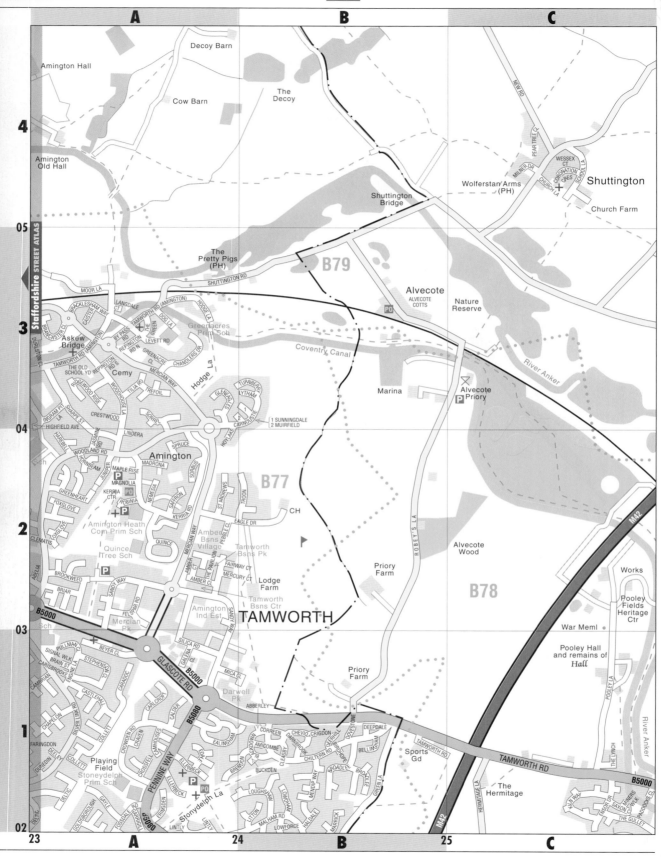

Staffordshire STREET ATLAS

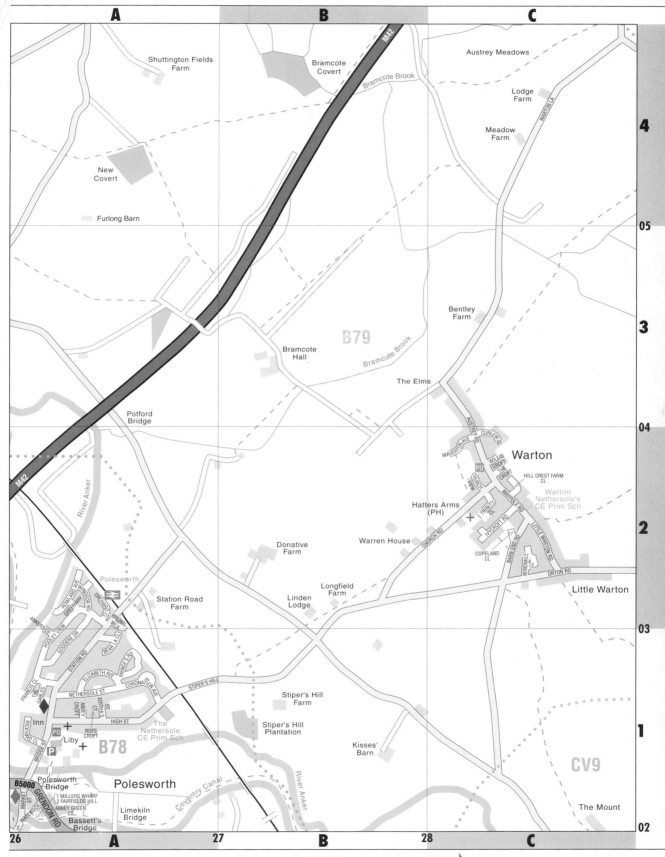

4

05

3

04

2

03

1

02

Shuttington Fields Farm

Bramcote Covert

Austrey Meadows

M42

Bramcote Brook

Lodge Farm

Meadow Farm

WARTON LA

New Covert

Furlong Barn

B79

Bentley Farm

Bramcote Brook

Bramcote Hall

The Elms

Potford Bridge

AUSTREY RD

CURLEW CL

WAVERTON AVE

WILLIS CROFT

THE CROFT

Warton

M42

River Anker

HILL CREST FARM CL

CHURCH VIEW

Warton Nethersole's CE Prim Sch

PO

Hatters Arms (PH)

TRINITY CL

MAYPOLE RD

Donative Farm

Warren House

IVYCROFT RD

LITTLE WARTON RD

Polesworth

Station Road Farm

CHURCH RD

COPELAND CL

BARN END RD

WINDMILL

Linden Lodge

Longfield Farm

ORTON RD

Little Warton

ROWLAND AVE

WINDSOR RD

GREENWAY

ORCHARD CL

BRUNEL WALK

ANKERSIDE

POOLEY VIEW

GOODERE DR

STATION RD

BEAR LA CL

ELIZABETH AVE

PRINCE'S RD

Stiper's Hill

03

FRANCIS CL

THE GABLES

NETHERSOLE ST

CORONATION AVE

ABBEY CROFT

EDITHA'S CT

HIGH ST

ST

Stiper's Hill Farm

CV9

Inn

RICKYARD CL

BRIDGE ST

PO

ROFS CROFT

Liby

P

B78

The Nethersole CE Prim Sch

Stiper's Hill Plantation

Kisses' Barn

B5000

Polesworth Bridge

GRENDON RD

MARKET ST

WATERSIDE

1 MILLERS WHARF
2 FAIRFIELDS HILL

ABBEY GREEN CT

Polesworth

Coventry Canal

River Anker

The Mount

1
2

Bassett's Bridge

Limekiln Bridge

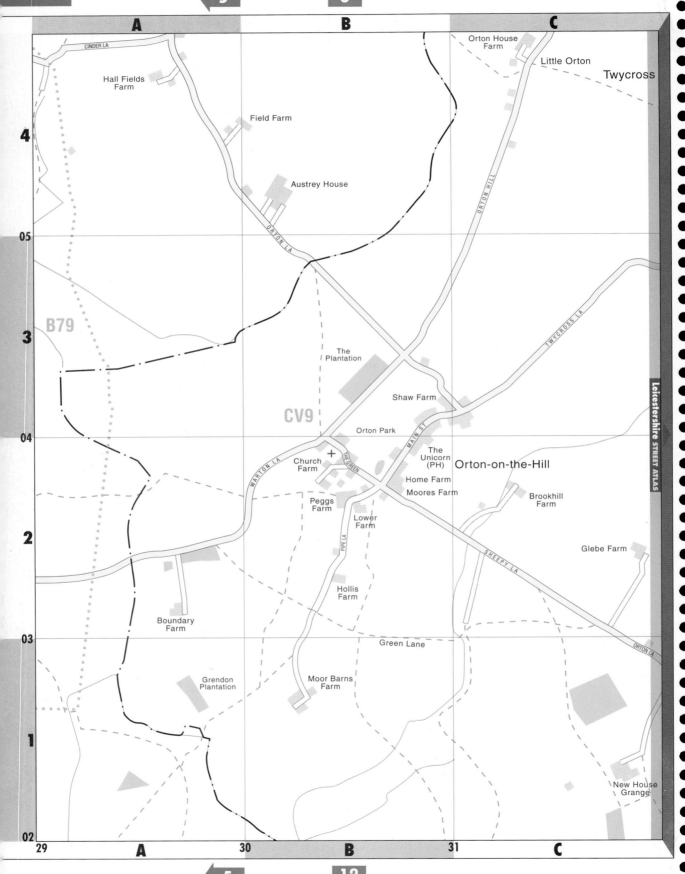

5
3

A   B   C

CINDER LA

Hall Fields
Farm

Field Farm

Austrey House

ORTON LA

4

05

B79

3

The
Plantation

CV9

Shaw Farm

Orton Park

04

WARTON LA

THE GREEN

Church
Farm

Peggs
Farm

Lower
Farm

Orton-on-the-Hill

The
Unicorn
(PH)

Home Farm

Moores Farm

MAIN ST

Brookhill
Farm

Orton House
Farm

Little Orton

Twycross

ORTON HILL

TWYCROSS LA

2

PIPE LA

Hollis
Farm

SHEEPY LA

Glebe Farm

Boundary
Farm

03

Grendon
Plantation

Moor Barns
Farm

Green Lane

ORTON LA

1

New House
Grange

02

29   A   30   B   31   C

5
12

Leicestershire STREET ATLAS

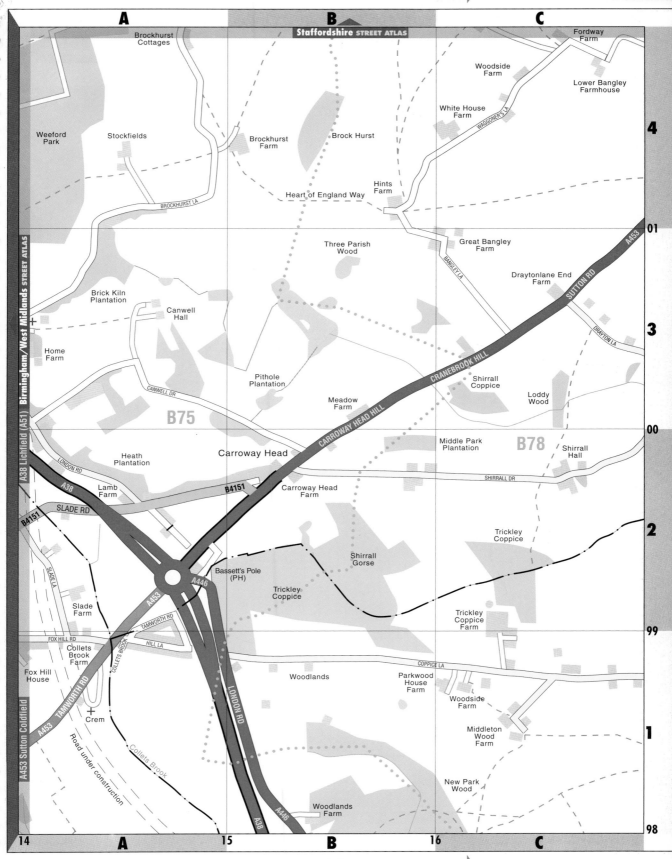

7

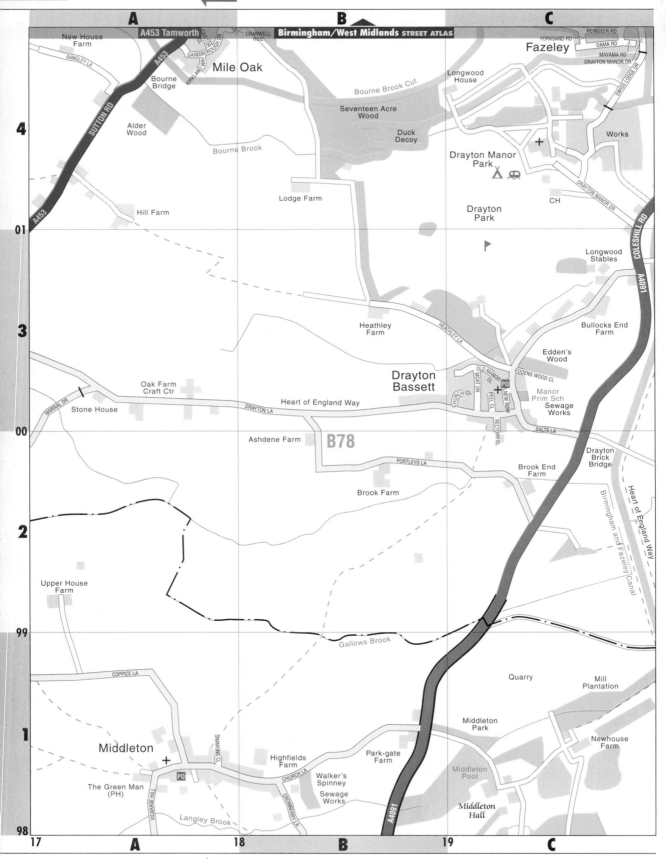

A453 Tamworth

New House Farm

Mile Oak

CRANWELL RISE

Fazeley

YORKSAND RD
REINDEER RD
DAMA RD
MAYAMA RD
DRAYTON MANOR DR

BANGLEY LA

SUTTON RD

A453

Bourne Bridge

Alder Wood

GAINSBORO GDI DR
KIRKLAND WAY
PRESTON DR

Bourne Brook Cut

Seventeen Acre Wood

Longwood House

SWISS LODGE DR

Works

Duck Decoy

Drayton Manor Park

CH

Bourne Brook

Hill Farm

Lodge Farm

Drayton Park

Longwood Stables

COLESHILL RD

A4091

DRAYTON MANOR DR

Heathley Farm

HEATHLEY LA

Bullocks End Farm

Edden's Wood

Drayton Bassett

OLD MANOR CL
MOAT DR
EDDENS WOOD CL

Oak Farm Craft Ctr

SHIRRAL DR

Stone House

Heart of England Way

DRAYTON LA

CHURCH CL
PEEL CL
NEW ROW
PO

Manor Prim Sch

Sewage Works

Ashdene Farm

B78

PORTLEYS LA

RECTORY CL

SALTS LA

Drayton Brick Bridge

Brook End Farm

Brook Farm

Birmingham and Fazeley Canal

Heart of England Way

Upper House Farm

Gallows Brook

COPPICE LA

Quarry

Mill Plantation

Middleton Park

Middleton

SIMMONS CL

Highfields Farm

CHURCH LA

Park-gate Farm

Newhouse Farm

The Green Man (PH)

PO

VICARAGE HILL

Walker's Spinney

Sewage Works

CROWBERRY LA

Middleton Pool

A4091

Middleton Hall

Langley Brook

17
A
18
B
19
C

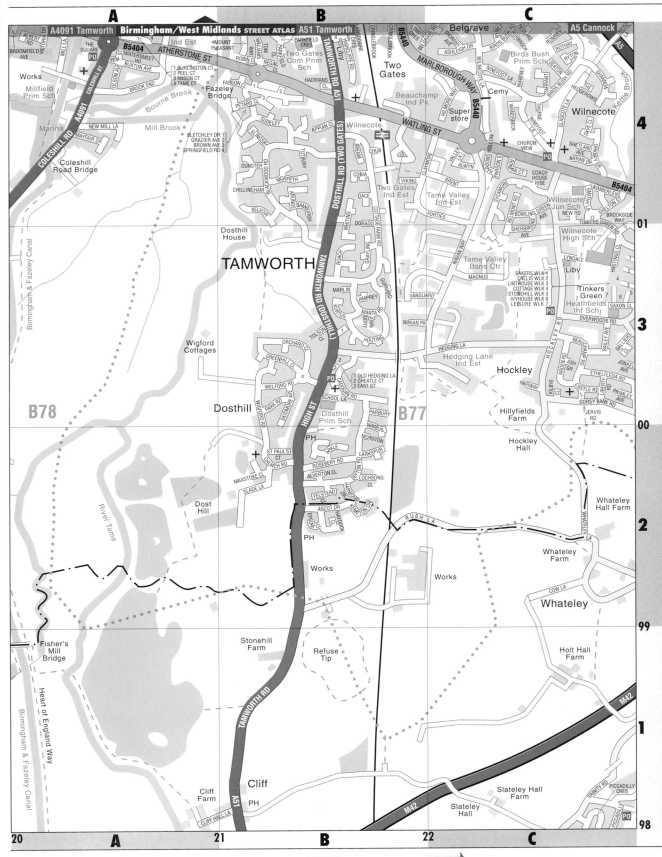

9
4

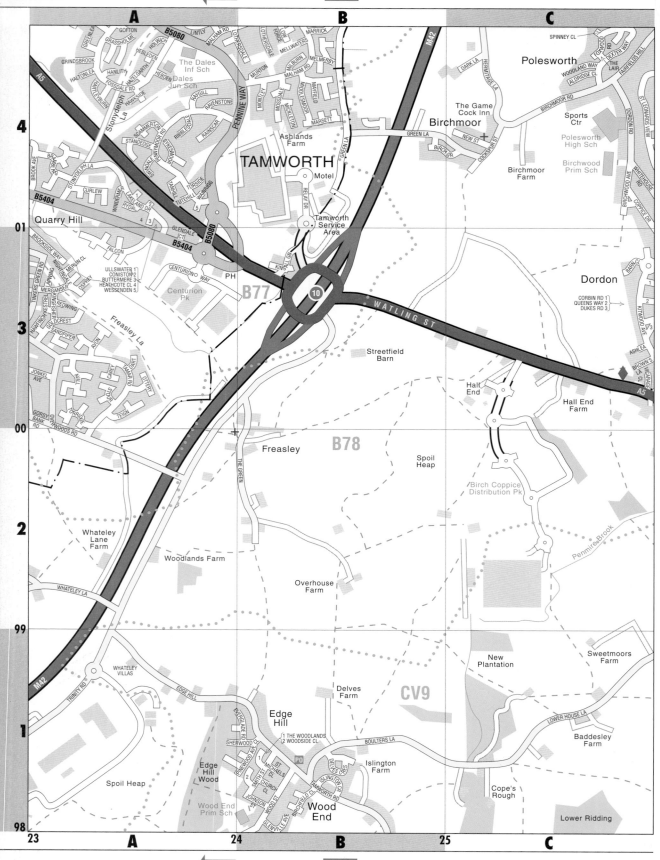

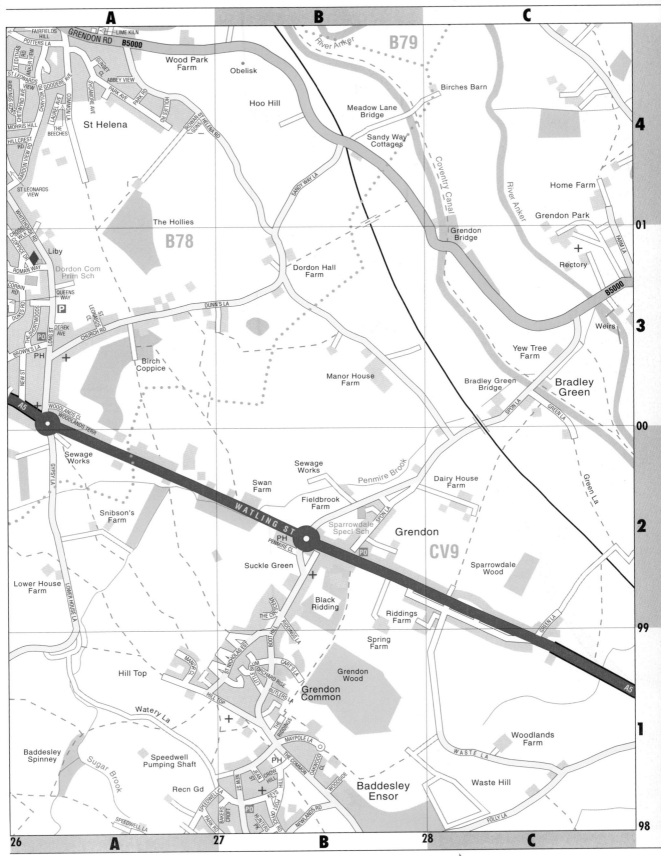

A
B
C

GRENDON RD **B5000**
FAIRFIELDS HILL
LIME KILN
POTTERS LA
River Anker
B79

Wood Park Farm
Obelisk
Birches Barn

ST EDITHS
ANKER VIEW
SURREL CL
ABBEY VIEW
SYCAMORE AVE
PARK AVE
HOLLIES RD
PARK RD

RIDDINGS
CHETWYND AVE
ST LEONARDS VIEW
GOODERE AVE
ROWAN RD
ST HELENA RD
GDNS

Hoo Hill
Meadow Lane Bridge
Sandy Way Cottages

MORRIS HILL
HILLCREST RD
THE BEECHES
LAUREL AVE
COMMON LA

St Helena
4

ST LEONARDS VIEW
SANDY WAY LA

Coventry Canal
River Anker
Home Farm
Grendon Park
01

The Hollies
B78
Grendon Bridge

WHITEHORN RD
CROSS RD
COPPICE RD
WLK RD
Liby
ROMAN WAY
Dordon Com Prim Sch

Dordon Hall Farm
HARN LA
+
Rectory
B5000

QUEENS WAY
CORBIN RD
DUKES RD
THE SHORTWOODS
ST LEONARDS CL
DEREK AVE
CHURCH RD

DUNN'S LA
Weirs
3

LONG ST
PO
BROWN'S LA
NEW ST
PH
+

Birch Coppice
Manor House Farm
Yew Tree Farm
Bradley Green Bridge
Bradley Green

A5
+
WOODLANDS CL
WOODLANDS TERR

SPON LA
GREEN LA
00

Sewage Works
Swan Farm
Sewage Works
Penmire Brook
Dairy House Farm

GYPSY LA
Snibson's Farm
Fieldbrook Farm
Sparrowdale Specl Sch
SPON LA
Grendon
Green La

WATLING ST
PH
PENMIRE CL
PO
CV9
Sparrowdale Wood
2

Lower House Farm
Suckle Green
+
Black Ridding
Riddings Farm
99

LOWER HOUSE LA
THE CRS
BOOT HILL
RIDDINGS LA
CART'S LA
Spring Farm
GREEN LA

Hill Top
MANOR CL
ST NICHOLAS EST
LITTLE BRUM
ORCHARD RISE
BUTLERS LA
Grendon Wood
Grendon Common

WATERY LA
HILL TOP
THE RIDDINGS
MAYPOLE LA
Woodlands Farm
WASTE LA
1

Baddesley Spinney
Sugar Brook
Speedwell Pumping Shaft
THE COMMON
OAKWOOD CL
WOODSIDE
Waste Hill

SPEEDWELLS
ST M'RY'N
ST JEAN
CROW HILL
KEYS
PH
Baddesley Ensor

Recn Gd
BAKERS CROFT
PARK RD
SPEEDWELL LA
HUNTERS PK
PO
NEWLANDS RD
FOLLY LA
98

26
A
27
B
28
C

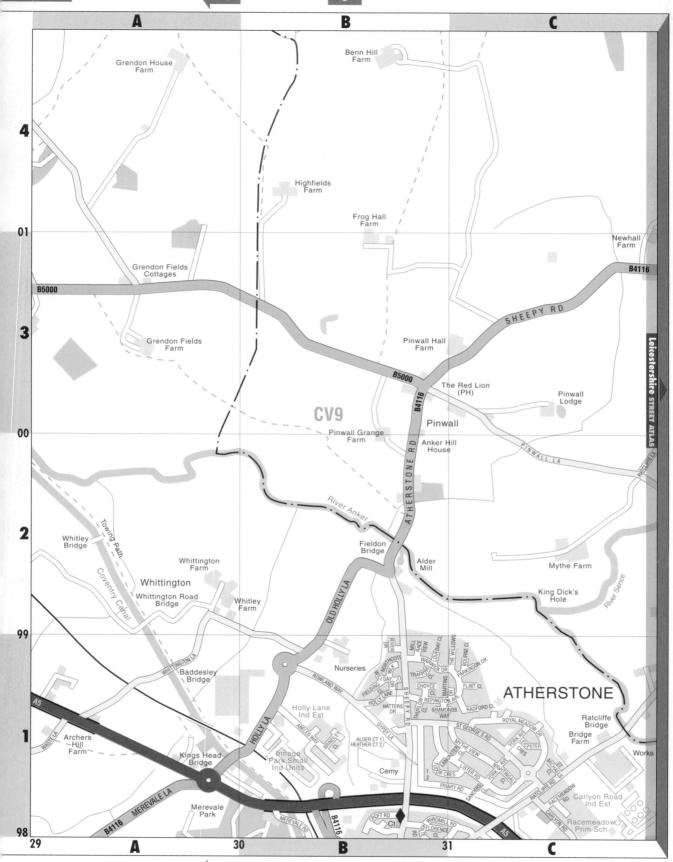

A   B   C

Grendon House Farm

Benn Hill Farm

4

Highfields Farm

Frog Hall Farm

01

Newhall Farm

B4116

Grendon Fields Cottages

B5000

SHEEPY RD

3

Grendon Fields Farm

Pinwall Hall Farm

B5000

The Red Lion (PH)

Pinwall Lodge

CV9

Pinwall

B4116

ATHERSTONE RD

00

Pinwall Grange Farm

Anker Hill House

PINWALL LA

RATCLIFFE LA

River Anker

Whitley Bridge

Towing path

2

Fieldon Bridge

Alder Mill

Mythe Farm

River Sence

Whittington Farm

Whittington

King Dick's Hole

Coventry Canal

Whittington Road Bridge

Whitley Farm

OLD HOLLY LA

WHITTINGTON LA

Baddesley Bridge

Nurseries

Rowland Way

99

A5

Holly Lane Ind Est

ATHERSTONE

Archers Hill Farm

WASTE LA

HOLLY LA

Ratcliffe Bridge

Bridge Farm

Works

1

Kings Head Bridge

ABELES WAY

Innage Park Small Ind Units

Cemy

MEREVALE LA

B4116

Merevale Park

MEREVALE RD

B4116

Croft Rd Ct

WINDMILL RD

Carlyon Road Ind Est

A5

Racemeadow Prim Sch

98

29   A   30   B   31   C

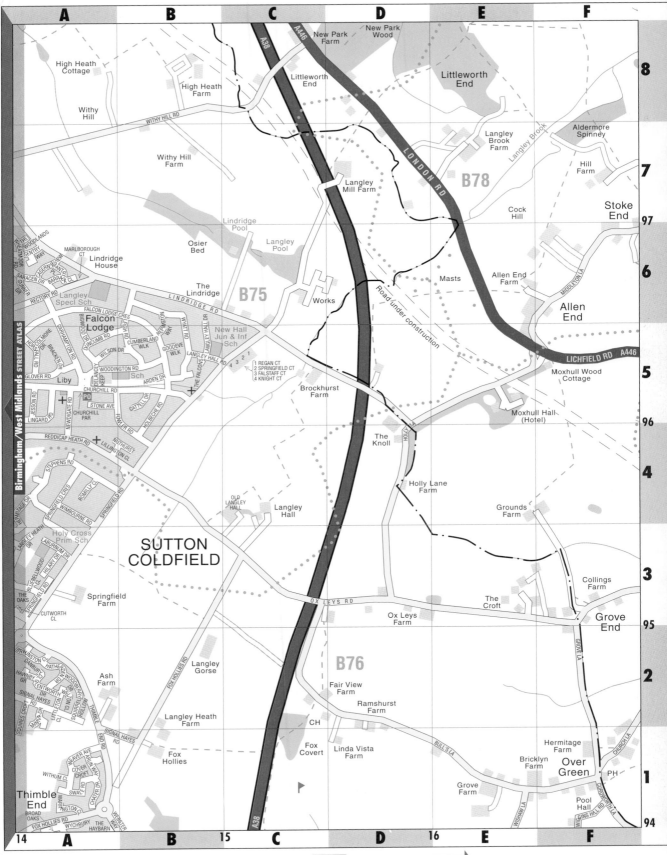

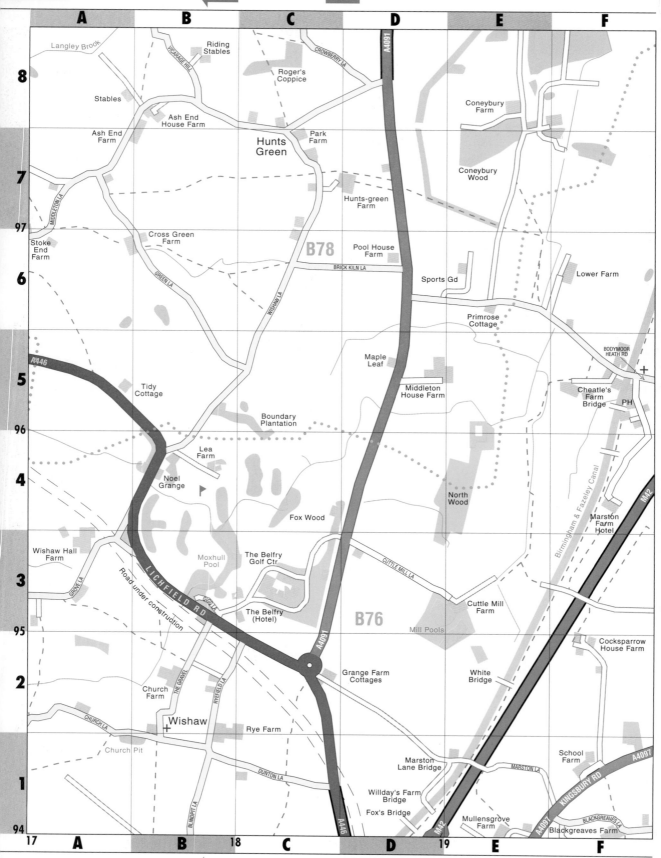

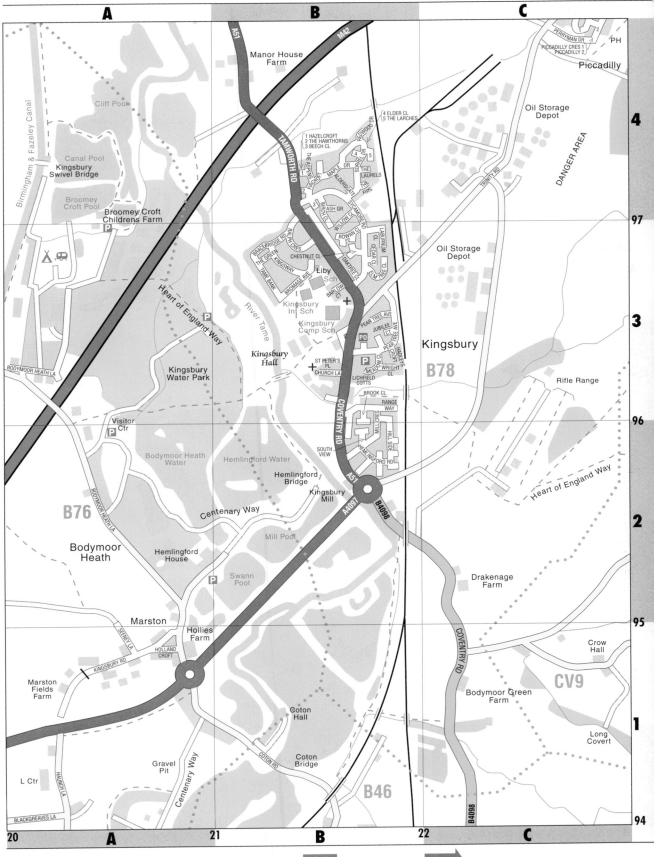

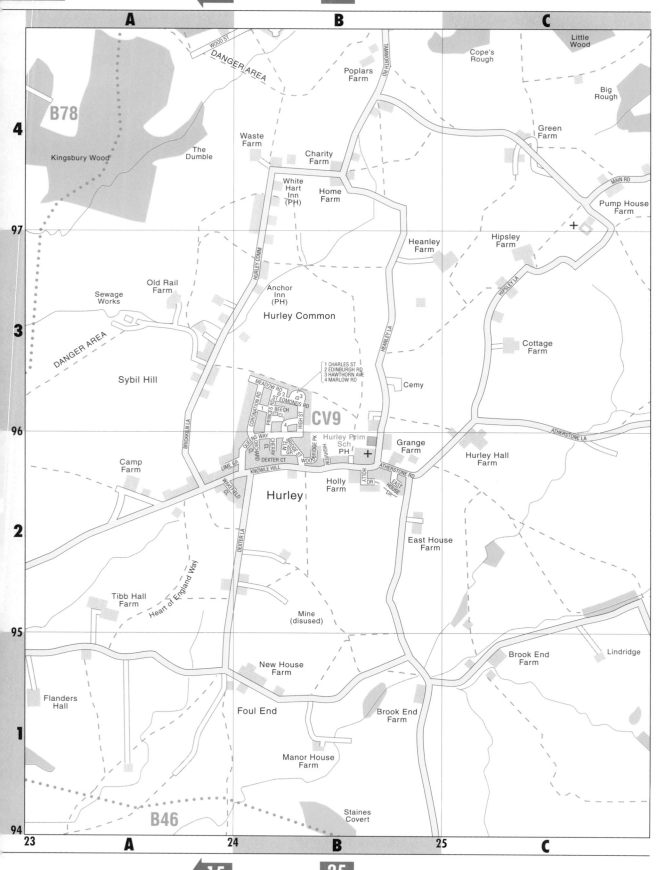

A B C

4

B78

Kingsbury Wood

The Dumble

97

DANGER AREA

WOOD ST

Poplars Farm

TAMWORTH RD

Cope's Rough

Little Wood

Big Rough

Green Farm

MAIN RD

Pump House Farm

Waste Farm

Charity Farm

White Hart Inn (PH)

Home Farm

Heanley Farm

Hipsley Farm

HURLEY COMM

Old Rail Farm

Anchor Inn (PH)

Hurley Common

HEANLEY LA

HIPSLEY LA

Cottage Farm

3

Sewage Works

DANGER AREA

Sybil Hill

BRICKKILN LA

MEADOW RD

CORONATION RD

PRINCES ROD

1 CHARLES ST
2 EDINBURGH RD
3 HAWTHORN AVE
4 MARLOW RD

EDMONDS RD

BEECH CL

HIGH ST

CV9

Cemy

ATHERSTONE LA

96

Camp Farm

LIME GR

WAKEFIELD CL

QUEENS WAY

ORCHARD RD

CHERRY

ELM GR

BRIDGE PK

HIGHWAY

WOOD

DEXTER CT

KNOWLE HILL

Hurley Prim Sch PH

Grange Farm

Hurley Hall Farm

Holly Farm

HOLLY DR

ATHERSTONE RD

EAST HOUSE DR

2

DEXTER LA

Heart of England Way

Tibb Hall Farm

East House Farm

95

Mine (disused)

Brook End Farm

Lindridge

Flanders Hall

New House Farm

Brook End Farm

1

Foul End

Manor House Farm

Staines Covert

94

B46

23 A 24 B 25 C

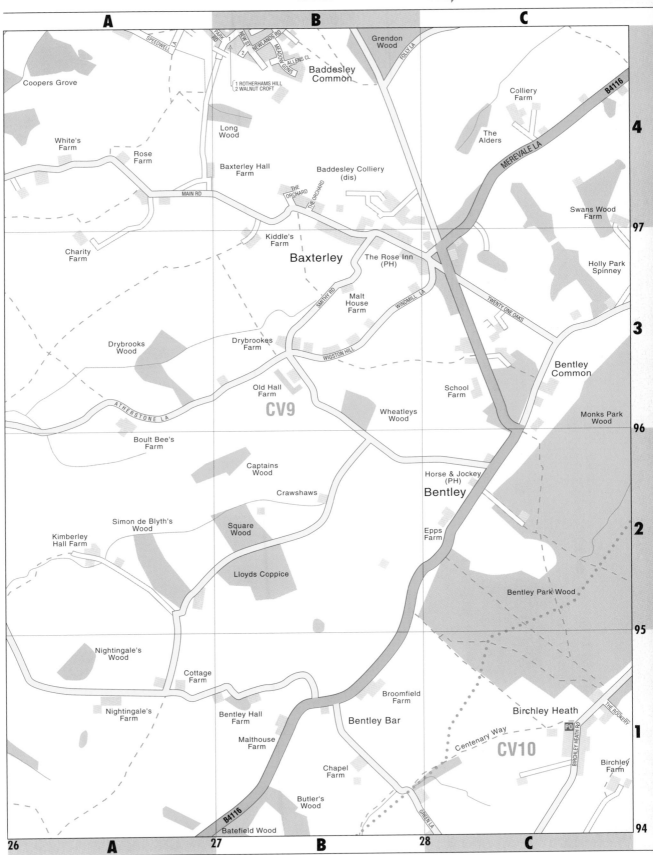

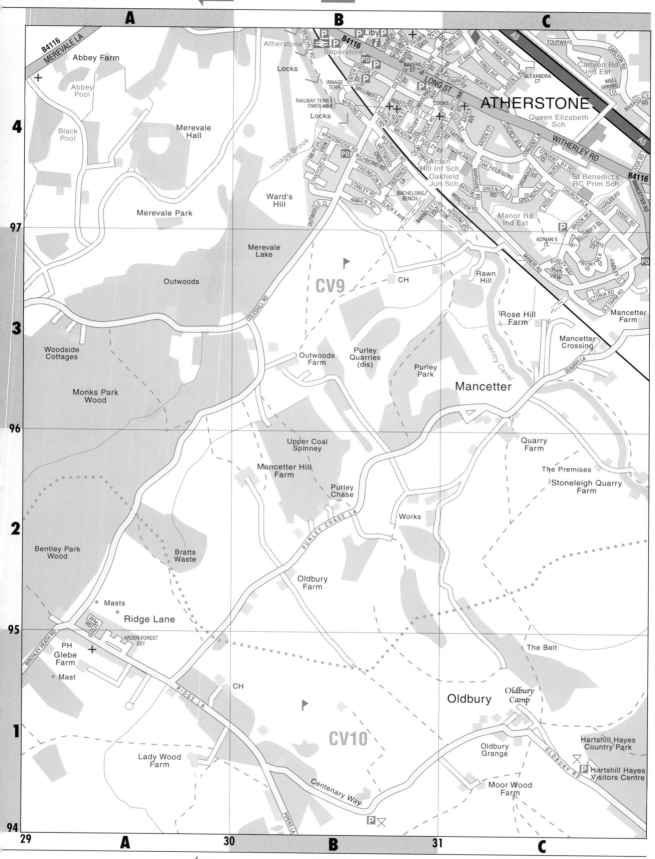

ATHERSTONE

CV9

CV10

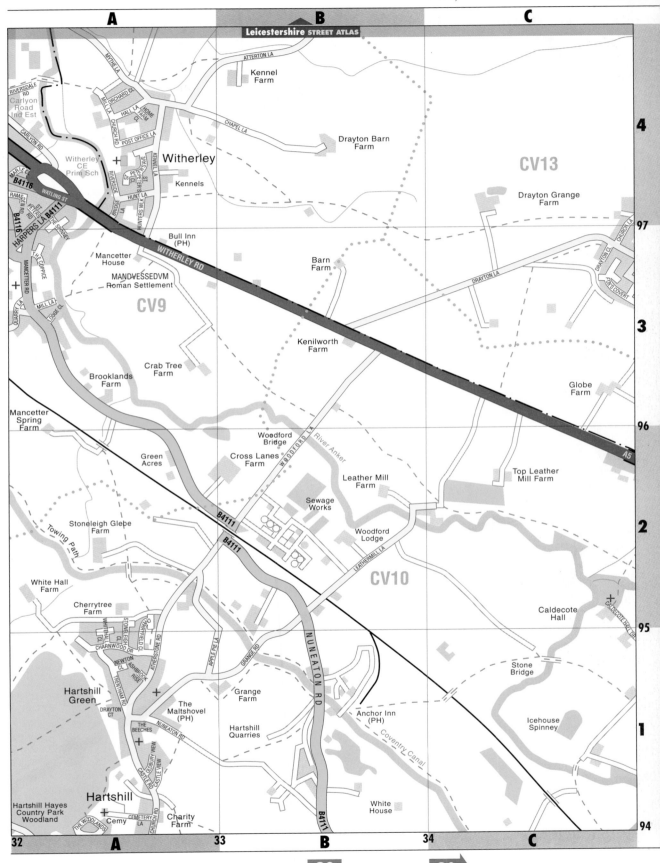

Leicestershire STREET ATLAS

A   B   C

4

3

2

1

97

96

95

94

CV13

CV9

CV10

ATTERTON LA

Kennel Farm

Drayton Barn Farm

Drayton Grange Farm

CHAPEL LA

DRAYTON LA

CHURCH LA

DRAYTON CL

FOX'S COVERT

Barn Farm

Bull Inn (PH)

Mancetter House

MANDVESSEDVM Roman Settlement

Kenilworth Farm

Globe Farm

Crab Tree Farm

Brooklands Farm

Mancetter Spring Farm

Woodford Bridge

River Anker

WOODFORD LA

Cross Lanes Farm

Leather Mill Farm

Top Leather Mill Farm

A5

Green Acres

Sewage Works

Woodford Lodge

LEATHERMILL LA

Stoneleigh Glebe Farm

Towing Path

White Hall Farm

Cherrytree Farm

Caldecote Hall

CALDECOTE HALL DR

WHITEHAL CL

STONELEIGH CL

GRANGE RD

APPLE PIE LA

NEWTON CL

ASHBROOK RISE

FRENTHAM RD

CHARNWOOD CL

ATHERSTONE RD

NUNEATON RD

Stone Bridge

Grange Farm

The Maltshovel (PH)

Hartshill Quarries

Anchor Inn (PH)

Coventry Canal

Icehouse Spinney

Hartshill Green

DRAYTON CT

THE BEECHES

AUBURY VIEW

CASTLE VIEW

CASTLE RD

White House

Hartshill

Hartshill Hayes Country Park Woodland

Cemy

CEMETERY LA

CHURCH RD

THE WOODLANDS

Charity Farm

B4111

B4111

B4111

B4116

B4116

B4111

WATLING ST

WITHERLEY RD

HARPERS LA

CARLYON RD

MANCETTER RD

QUARRY LA

MILL LA

LODGE CL

THE COPPICE

THE SPINNEY

RAMSDEN RD

MARIE CL

ST PETERS RD

Witherley CE Prim Sch

Witherley

Kennels

Carlyon Road Ind Est

RIVERSDALE RD

MYTHE LA

MILL LA

ORCHARD CL

HALL LA

CHURCH RD

INHAME FARM CL

POST OFFICE LA

KENNEL LA

ST PETER'S CL

RIVERSIDE

HUNT LA

ST WM SHENSTONE

32   33   34

A   B   C

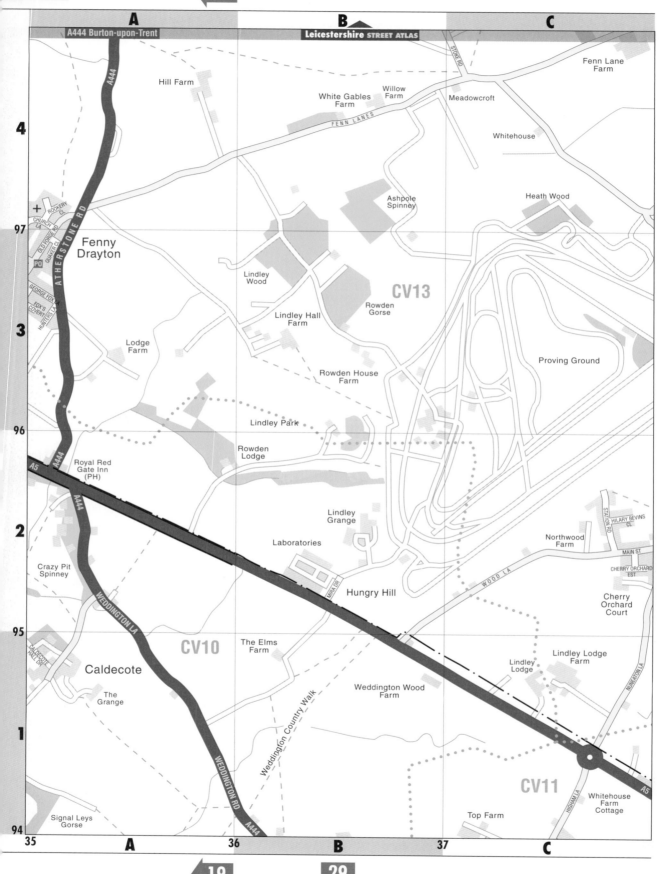

A

B

C

Hill Farm

Fenn Lane Farm

White Gables Farm

Willow Farm

Meadowcroft

Whitehouse

FENN LANES

Ashpole Spinney

Heath Wood

CV13

Fenny Drayton

Lindley Wood

Rowden Gorse

Proving Ground

Lindley Hall Farm

Lodge Farm

Rowden House Farm

Lindley Park

Rowden Lodge

Royal Red Gate Inn (PH)

Lindley Grange

Laboratories

Northwood Farm

Cherry Orchard Court

Crazy Pit Spinney

Hungry Hill

WOOD LA

CV10

The Elms Farm

Lindley Lodge

Lindley Lodge Farm

Caldecote

The Grange

Weddington Wood Farm

Weddington Country Walk

CV11

Whitehouse Farm Cottage

Signal Leys Gorse

Top Farm

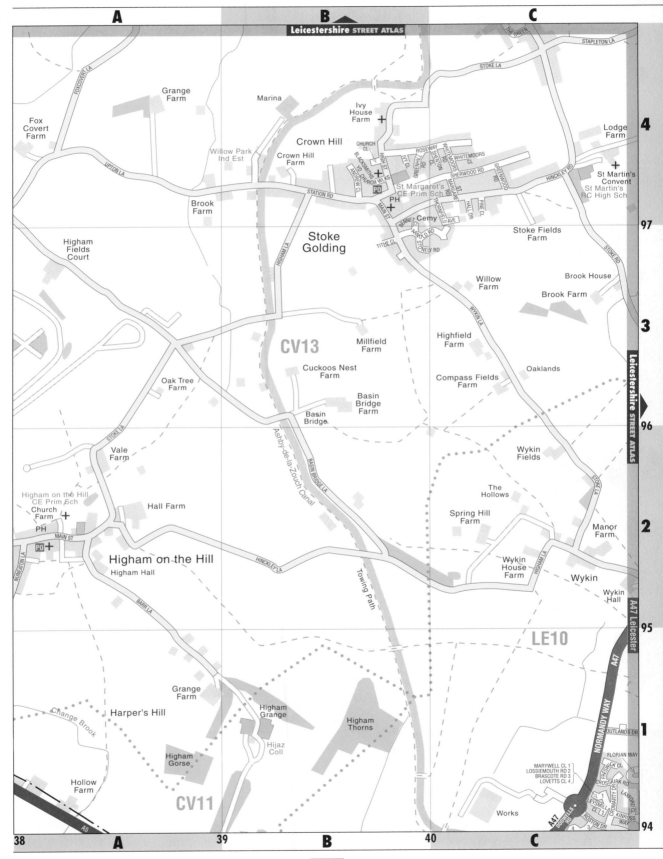

A · B · C

Map labels:

Fox Covert Farm

Grange Farm

Marina

Ivy House Farm

Lodge Farm

FOXCOVERT LA

UPTON LA

Crown Hill

Willow Park Ind Est

Crown Hill Farm

CHURCH CL
HIGH ST
OLD CHURCH WLKS
BLACKSMITHS
ST ANDREW CL
PO

ROSEWAY
GREENHILL RD
IVY CL
SHELTON
WHITMOORS CL
WHITEMOORS RD
SHERWOOD RD
GREENWOOD RD
HINCKLEY RD
ST MARGARET
THORNFIELD AVE
HALL DR
PINE CL

St Martin's Convent
St Martin's RC High Sch

STAPLETON LA
THE GREEN
STOKE LA
STOKE RD

Brook Farm

STATION RD

Higham Fields Court

HIGHAM LA

Stoke Golding

MAIN ST
PH
BENNET CL
KIRKLAND RD
ARDEN CL
TITHE CL
STONELY RD

St Margaret's CE Prim Sch
Cemy

Stoke Fields Farm

97

Willow Farm

Brook House

Brook Farm

CV13

Millfield Farm

Highfield Farm

Oaklands

3

WYKIN LA

Oak Tree Farm

Cuckoos Nest Farm

Basin Bridge Farm

Compass Fields Farm

Basin Bridge

Ashby-de-la-Zouch Canal

96

Vale Farm

STOKE LA

Wykin Fields

STOKE LA

Higham on the Hill CE Prim Sch
Church Farm
PH
PO

Hall Farm

BASIN BRIDGE LA

The Hollows

Spring Hill Farm

Manor Farm

2

HINCKLEY LA

Wykin House Farm

WYKIN LA

Wykin

Wykin Hall

NUNEATON LA

Higham on the Hill

Higham Hall

Towing Path

LE10

A47 Leicester

BARR LA

95

Change Brook

Harper's Hill

Grange Farm

Higham Grange

Higham Thorns

A47

NORMANDY WAY

1

Higham Gorse

Hijaz Coll

Hollow Farm

OUTLANDS DR
FLORIAN WAY
FESWICK CL
CROSSKIRK RD
LAWFORD CL
CROMARTY DR
KINROSS WAY

A5

CV11

Works

MARYWELL CL 1
LOSSIEMOUTH RD 2
BRASCOTE RD 3
LOVETTS CL 4

A47
DODWELLS RD
RUSTON DR

94

38 · A · 39 · B · 40 · C

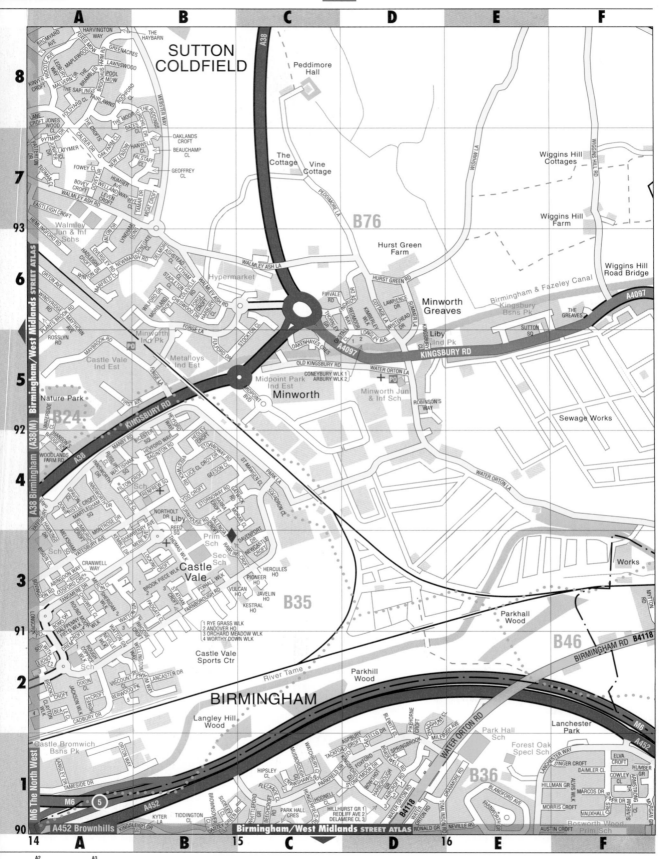

A2
1 CHIVENOR HO
2 DE HAVILLAND DR
3 HURRICANE WAY
4 KENRICK CROFT
5 SPITFIRE WAY

A3
1 LONG CLOSE WLK
2 WELLINGTON WAY
3 SQUIRES GATE WLK
4 TERNHILL HO

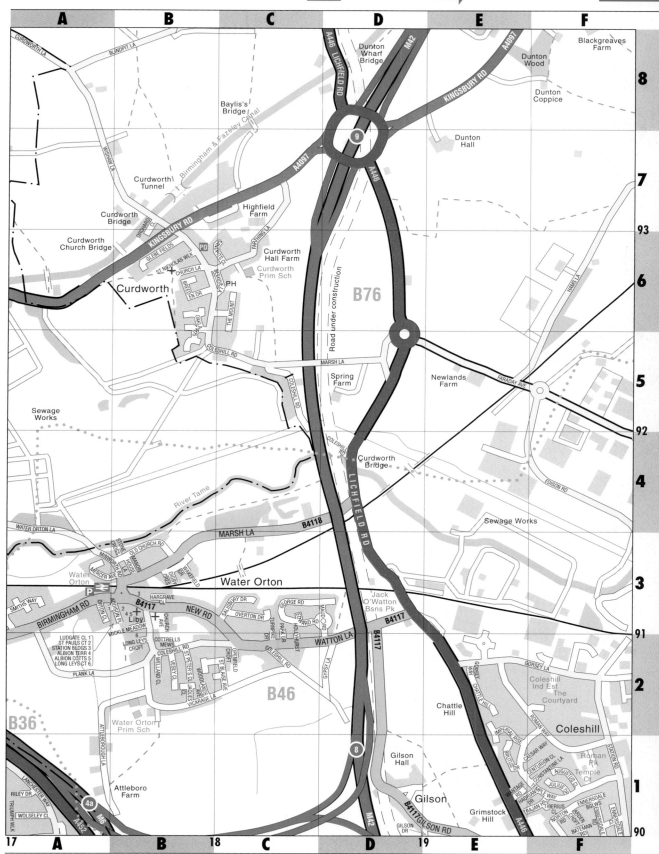

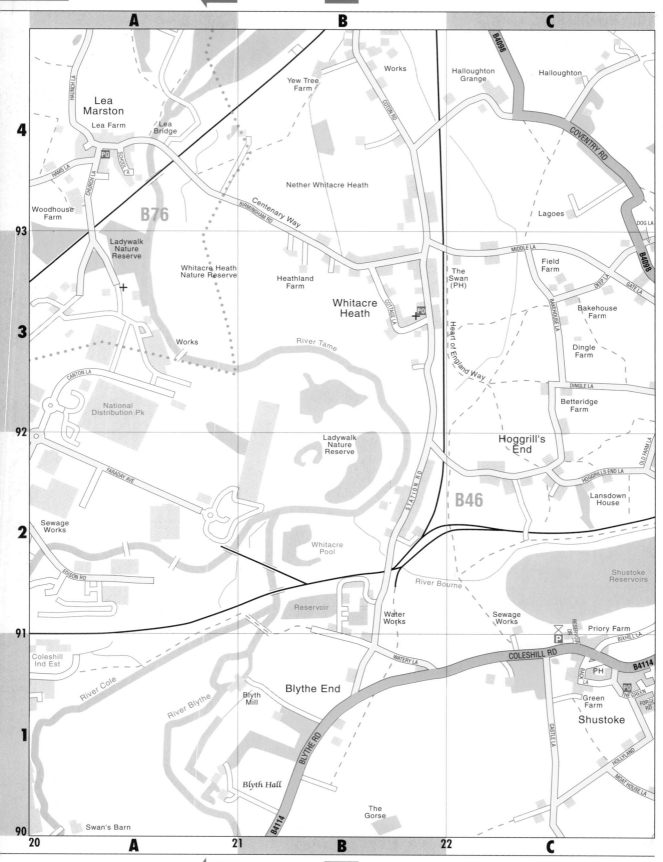

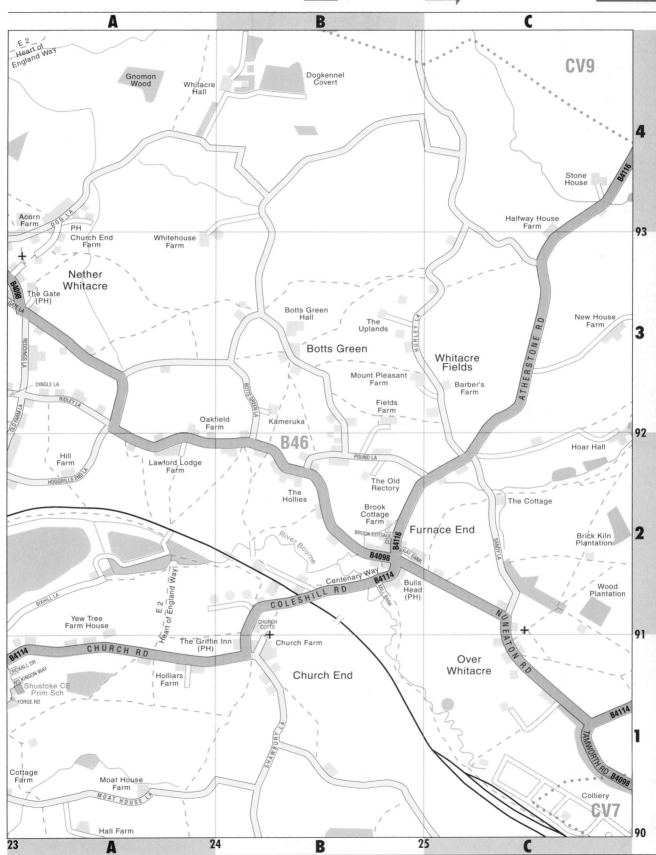

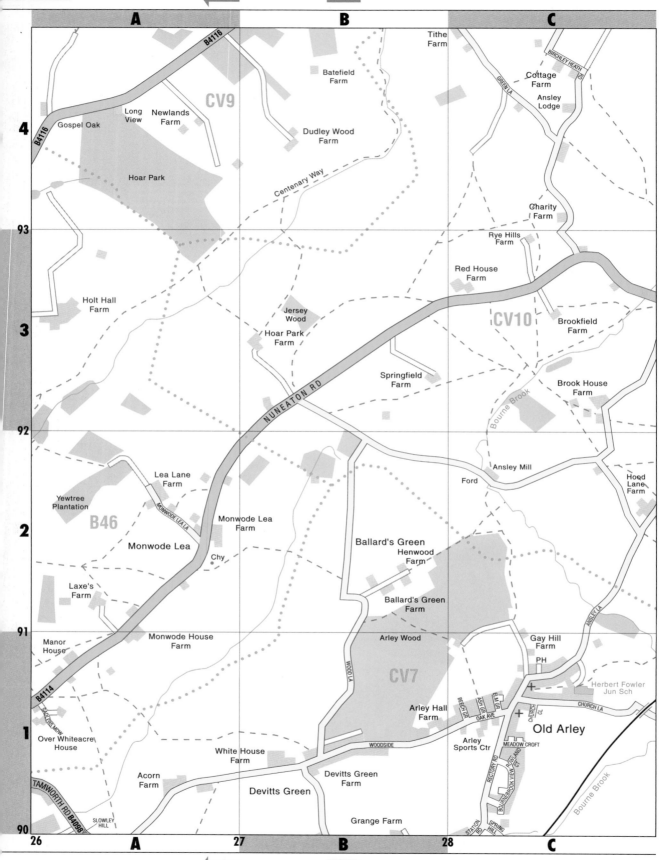

A **B** **C**

CV9

B4116

Gospel Oak
Long View
Newlands Farm

Hoar Park

Batefield Farm

Tithe Farm

Cottage Farm
Ansley Lodge

BIRCHLEY HEATH RD

GREEN LA

Dudley Wood Farm

Centenary Way

Charity Farm

Rye Hills Farm

Red House Farm

CV10

Brookfield Farm

4

93

3

Holt Hall Farm

Jersey Wood

Hoar Park Farm

NUNEATON RD

Springfield Farm

Brook House Farm

Bourne Brook

92

Lea Lane Farm

Yewtree Plantation

B46

MONWODE LEA LA

Monwode Lea Farm

Monwode Lea

Chy

Ballard's Green
Henwood Farm

Ansley Mill

Ford

Hood Lane Farm

2

Laxe's Farm

Ballard's Green Farm

91

Manor House

Monwode House Farm

Arley Wood

WOOD LA

CV7

Gay Hill Farm

PH

ANSLEY LA

Herbert Fowler Jun Sch

CHURCH LA

B4114

SADLERS MDW

Over Whiteacre House

Arley Hall Farm

WOODSIDE

BEECH GR
ASH GR
OAK AVE
ELM GR

CHURCH CL

Old Arley

1

Arley Sports Ctr

MEADOW CROFT

TAMWORTH RD B4098

SLOWLEY HILL

Acorn Farm

White House Farm

Devitts Green

Devitts Green Farm

Grange Farm

RECTORY RD
BOURNEBROOK VIEW
RUTLAND CT
STATION RD
SPRING HILL

Bourne Brook

90

A **B** **C**

26 27 28

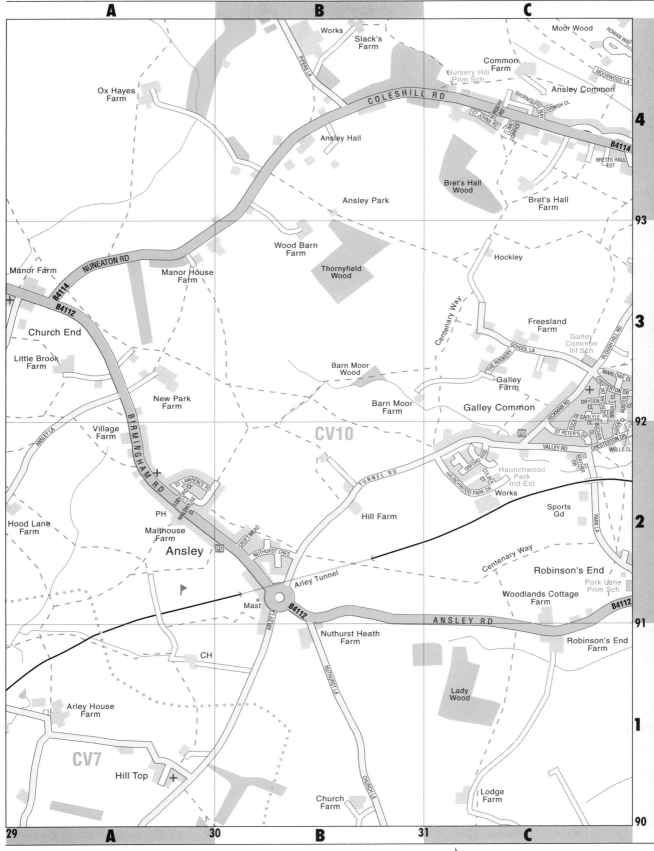

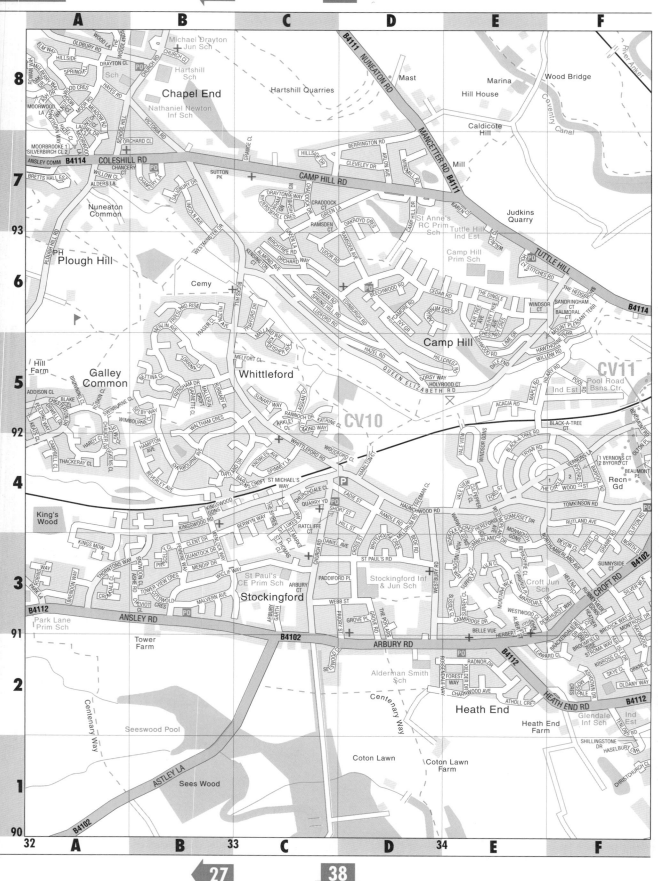

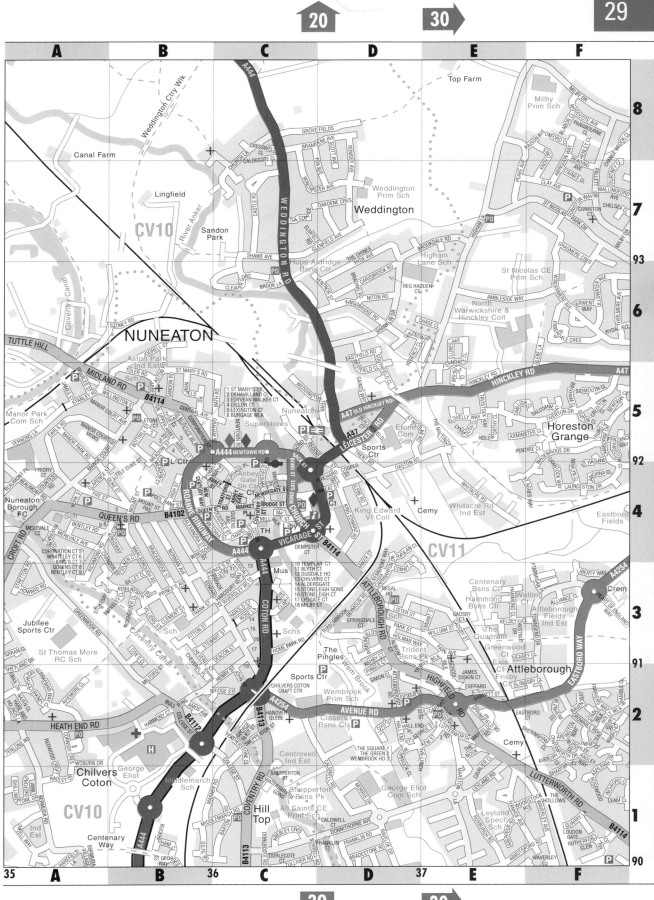

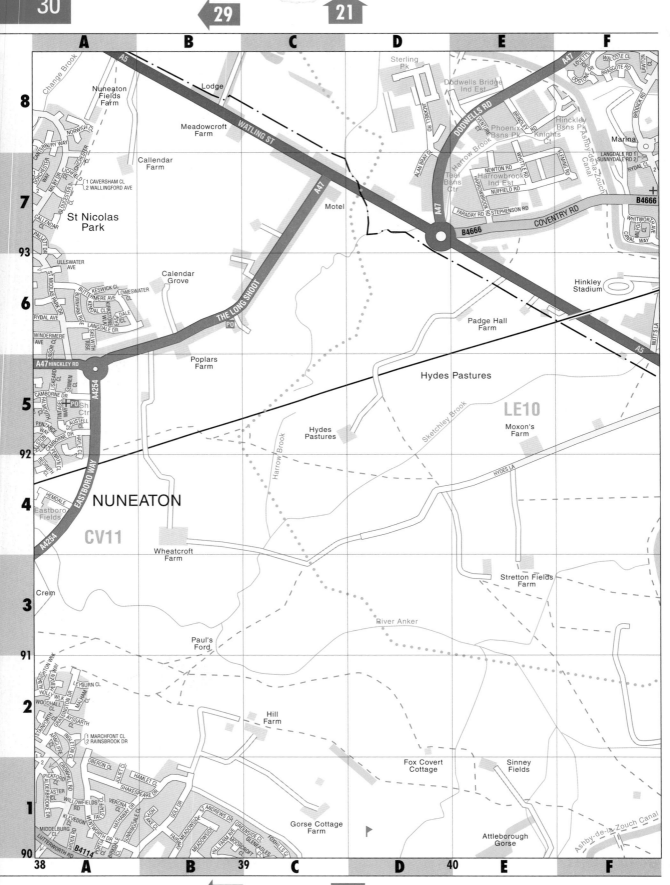

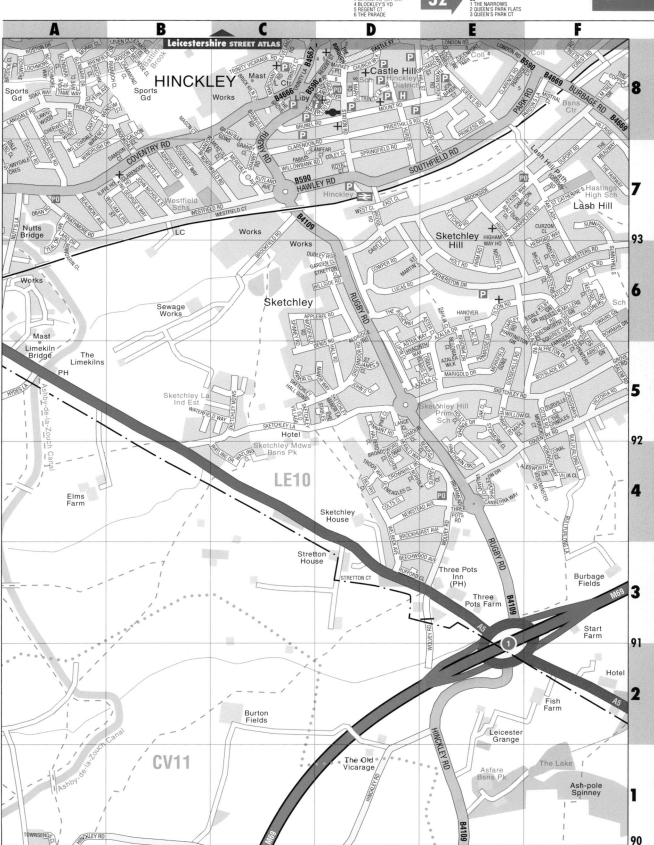

D8
1 MANSION ST
2 HANSON CT
3 Brittania Sh Ctr
4 BLOCKLEY'S YD
5 REGENT CT
6 THE PARADE

32

D8
7 EDWARDS CTR
8 THE HORSEFAIR
E8
1 THE NARROWS
2 QUEEN'S PARK FLATS
3 QUEEN'S PARK CT

4 QUEEN'S PARK TERR
5 CLARENCE CT

Leicestershire STREET ATLAS

HINCKLEY

LE10

CV11

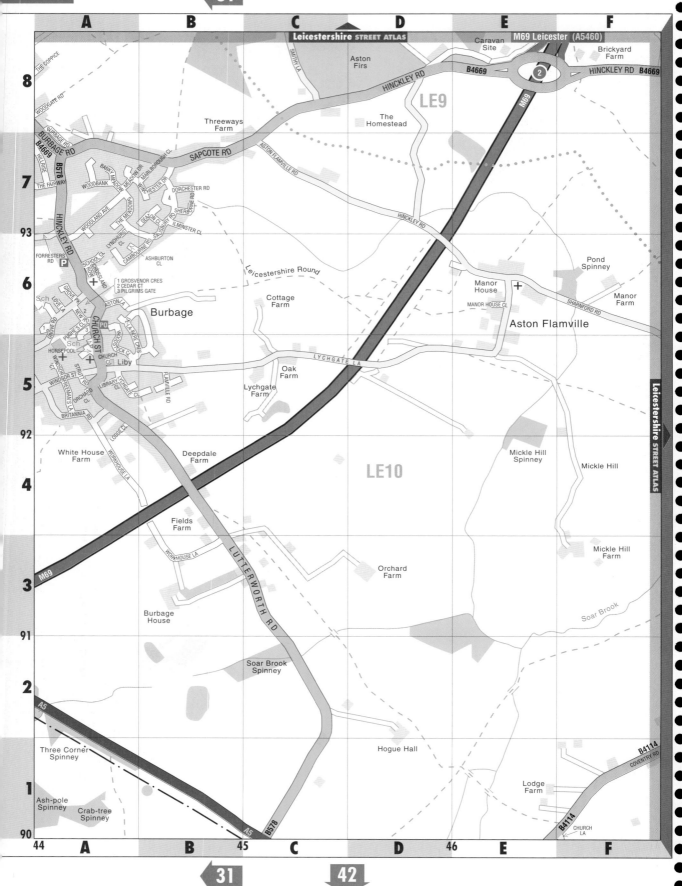

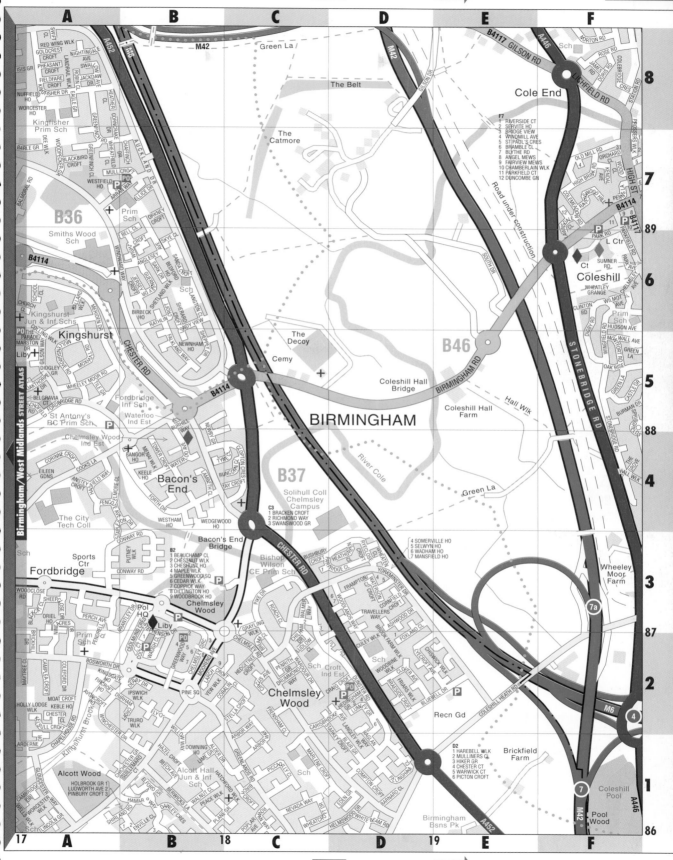

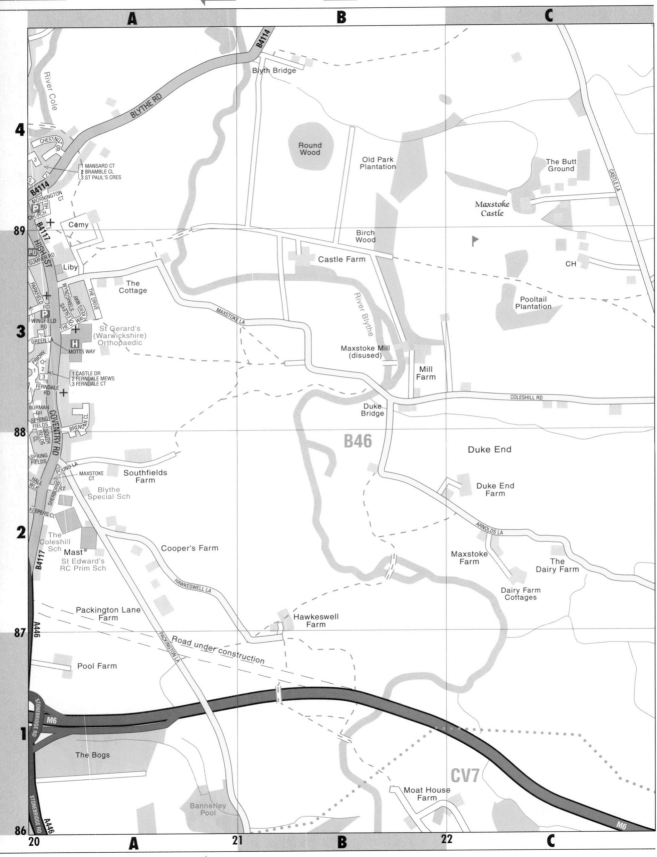

A   B   C

B4114

Blyth Bridge

River Cole

BLYTHE RD

Round Wood

Old Park Plantation

The Butt Ground

CASTLE LA

4

CHESTNUT DR
3

1 MANSARD CT
2 BRAMBLE CL
3 ST PAUL'S CRES

Maxstoke Castle

B4114
MORNINGTON CT
P
THE CHURCH

Cemy

Birch Wood

CH

89

B4117

HIGHER ST

SUMNER RD

PO

Liby

Castle Farm

Pooltail Plantation

PARKFIELD
P

WINGFIELD RD

GREEN LA

The Cottage

THE DRIVE

WINDSHIELS
ANN SMED

THE CV WAY

MAXSTOKE LA

River Blythe

3

St Gerard's (Warwickshire) Orthopaedic

H

MOTTS WAY

Maxstoke Mill (disused)

Mill Farm

PRIORY CL
1
2
3

1 CASTLE DR
2 FERNDALE MEWS
3 FERNDALE CT

FERNDALE RD

COLESHILL RD

BURMAN DR
SPRING FIELDS
SOUTH FIELDS

BREND CL

Duke Bridge

88

SPRING FIELDS

B46

Duke End

COVENTRY RD

POUND LA

MAXSTOKE CT

Southfields Farm

Duke End Farm

HALL WLK

SHERBOURNE

Blythe Special Sch

ARNOLDS LA

2

KEEPERS CL

The Coleshill Sch
Mast

St Edward's RC Prim Sch

Cooper's Farm

HAWKESWELL LA

Maxstoke Farm

The Dairy Farm

B4117

Dairy Farm Cottages

Packington Lane Farm

PACKINGTON LA

87

A446

Road under construction

Pool Farm

STONEBRIDGE RD

M6

1

The Bogs

CV7

STONEBRIDGE RD

A446

Moat House Farm

M6

86

20   21   22

A   B   C

Bannerley Pool

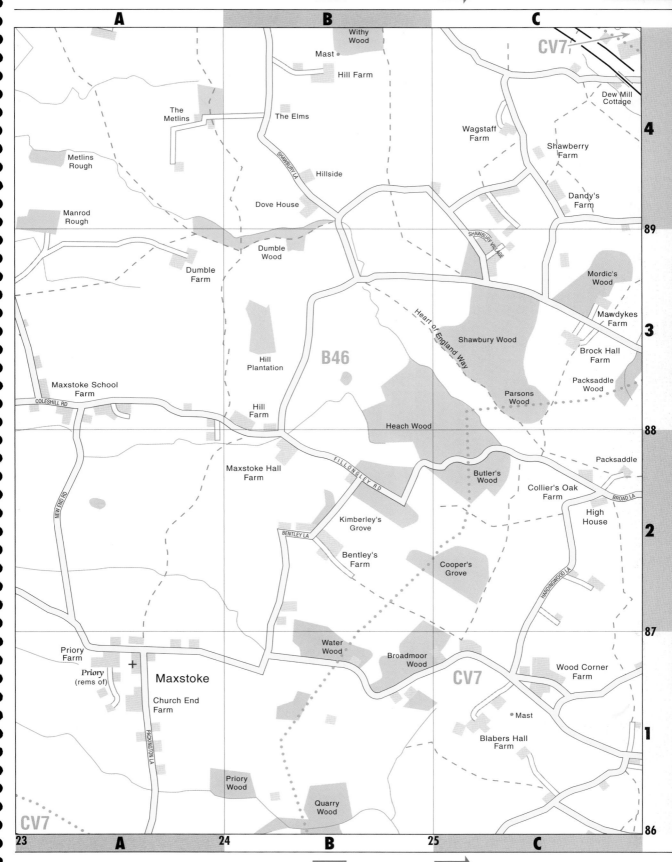

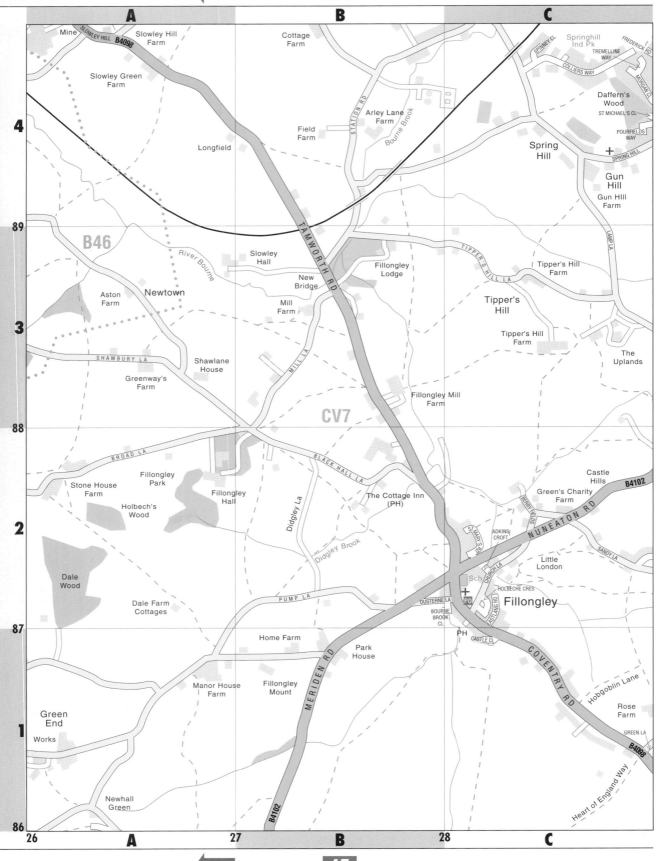

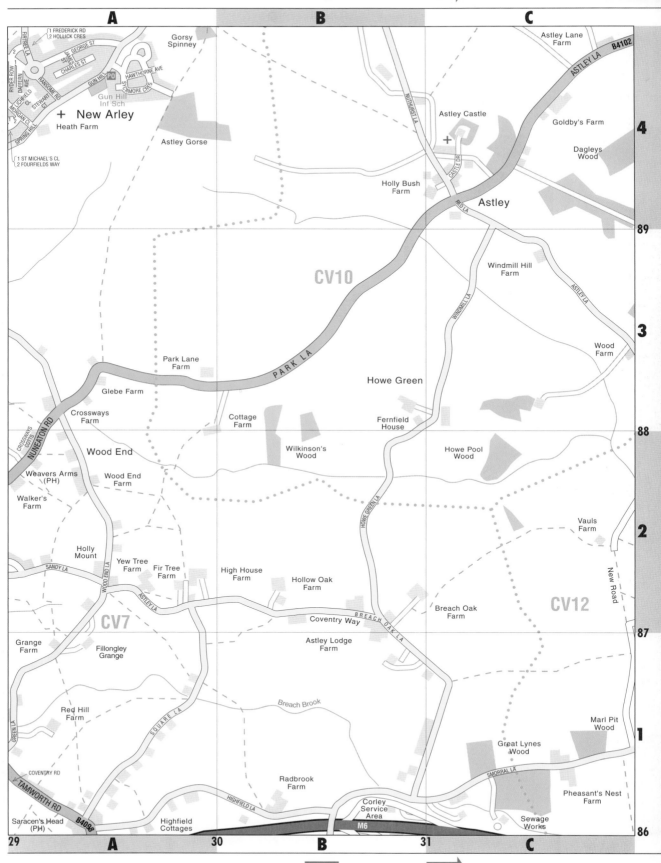

A · B · C

1 FREDERICK RD
2 HOLLICK CRES

Gorsy
Spinney

Astley Lane
Farm

ASTLEY LA

B4102

GEORGE ST

CHARLES ST

RYDER ROW

FREER LA

DAFFERN AVE

LICHFIELD RD

STEWART CT

SYCAMORE CRES

HAWTHORNE AVE

GUN HILL

RANSOME RD

MORGAN CL

SPRING HILL

PO

Gun Hill
Inf Sch

New Arley

Heath Farm

Astley Castle

Goldby's Farm

NUTHURST LA

Dagleys
Wood

4

1 ST MICHAEL'S CL
2 FOURFIELDS WAY

Astley Gorse

Holly Bush
Farm

CASTLE DR

RED LA

Astley

89

CV10

Windmill Hill
Farm

WINDMILL LA

ASTLEY LA

3

Park Lane
Farm

PARK LA

Wood
Farm

Howe Green

Glebe Farm

Crossways
Farm

NUNEATON RD

CROSSWAYS COTTS

Cottage
Farm

Fernfield
House

88

Wood End

Wilkinson's
Wood

Howe Pool
Wood

Weavers Arms
(PH)

Wood End
Farm

HOWE GREEN LA

Walker's
Farm

Vauls
Farm

2

Holly
Mount

SANDY LA

WOOD END LA

Yew Tree
Farm

Fir Tree
Farm

High House
Farm

Hollow Oak
Farm

New Road

ASTLEY LA

Breach Oak
Farm

CV12

BREACH OAK LA

CV7

Coventry Way

87

Grange
Farm

Fillongley
Grange

Astley Lodge
Farm

SQUARE LA

Red Hill
Farm

Breach Brook

GREEN LA

Marl Pit
Wood

1

Great Lynes
Wood

COVENTRY RD

Radbrook
Farm

Corley
Service
Area

SMORRAL LA

Pheasant's Nest
Farm

TAMWORTH RD

HIGHFIELD LA

M6

Sewage
Works

Saracen's Head
(PH)

B4098

Highfield
Cottages

86

B4102
ASTLEY LA

A B C D E F

8

Temple
House

Park
Farm

Spring Kidden
Wood

The
Lawns
Centenary Way
HAREFIELD LA

Mill

Tea
House

Dennis
Farm

Old Park

Arbury Park

Covents
Pool

Garners
Pool

Arbury Hall Park
and Gardens

7

High Park
Pool

Arbury

89

CV10

Works

New Park
Wood

6

Coventry
Wood

Fir Tree
Grove

GRIFF LA

South Farm

Arbury Mill
Farm

GRIFF LA

5

Cowley Wood

Soar
End

Rabbit Lane
Wood

Keeper's
Close

88

Holmes
Wood

4

Sole End
Farm

Cow
Lees

BEDWORTH LA

Colliery
Wood

Woodlands House
Farm

Bedworth
Woodlands

Norwood
Farm

DOVE CL

WOODLANDS LA

3

Taffs
Farm

Coventry Way

CV12

Woodlands
Farm

PH

WOODLANDS RD

CHARLES EATON RD

JUDD CL

87

Swain's
Wood

NEWTOWN RD

JUNIPER CL

BROOKLEA

CROFT POOL

PO

2

Astley Hall
Farm

Market End
Farm

THE LAWNS

1 BLYTH CL
2 HAMILTON CL

MARRIOTT RD

1 WILDEY RD
2 HIMLEY RD

Market
End

THE PINES
THE YEWS
THE SYCAMORES
THE WILLOWS
THE LAURELS
THE ALDERS
LABURNUM CL
CELANDINE WAY
THE LIMES
THE MAPLES
THE ELMS
THE OAKS
THE FIRS
THE CHESTNUTS
THE BEECHES
SILVER BIRCH AVE
FERN GR
HEATHER DR
ERICA
SINKINS
CROFT RD
CROFT RD

F2
1 SYDNEY CT
2 CANBERRA CT
3 MELBOURNE CT

DELAMERE RD
DALTON RD

SMORRALL LA

PH

WHITBURN RD

MARKET END CL

PEMBROKE CL

PRIMROSE DR
CROMWELL DR
BLUEBELL CL
COLUMBINE WAY
FOXGLOVE WAY

Bedworth
Heath

HOLLYHURST RD
BEECHCROFT
ALICE CL
HOLLYOAK RD

PO

1

Highfield House
Farm

ASHINGTON RD

CARDIGAN RD

TENBY CL

HOSPITAL LA

ANDERTON RD

RYHOPE CL

NEWCOMEN RD

PHEASANT CL

SAXON RD

MAYOR DR

KEENAN DR

KEENAN DR

DARK LA

DARK LA

ARTHUR
ALFORD
HO

BELLAIRS AVE

BRYONY CL

MARTINS RD

LEE AVE

KATHLEEN AVE

ROSEWORTH

SMITH ST

HEATH

ALL SAINTS RD

SMARTS RD

Liby

RIVER RD

WALKERS RD

Newdigate
Prim Sch

KEEPERS WLK 1
OAKLEY CT 2

MAYPOLE CRES
DONITY AVE
HOWELLS
CL

POTTERS RD
HESSION
RD

CASHMORE
RD

TOPPS
HEATH

HAMMERS
HEATH

A444

Church
Farm

Mast

39
30

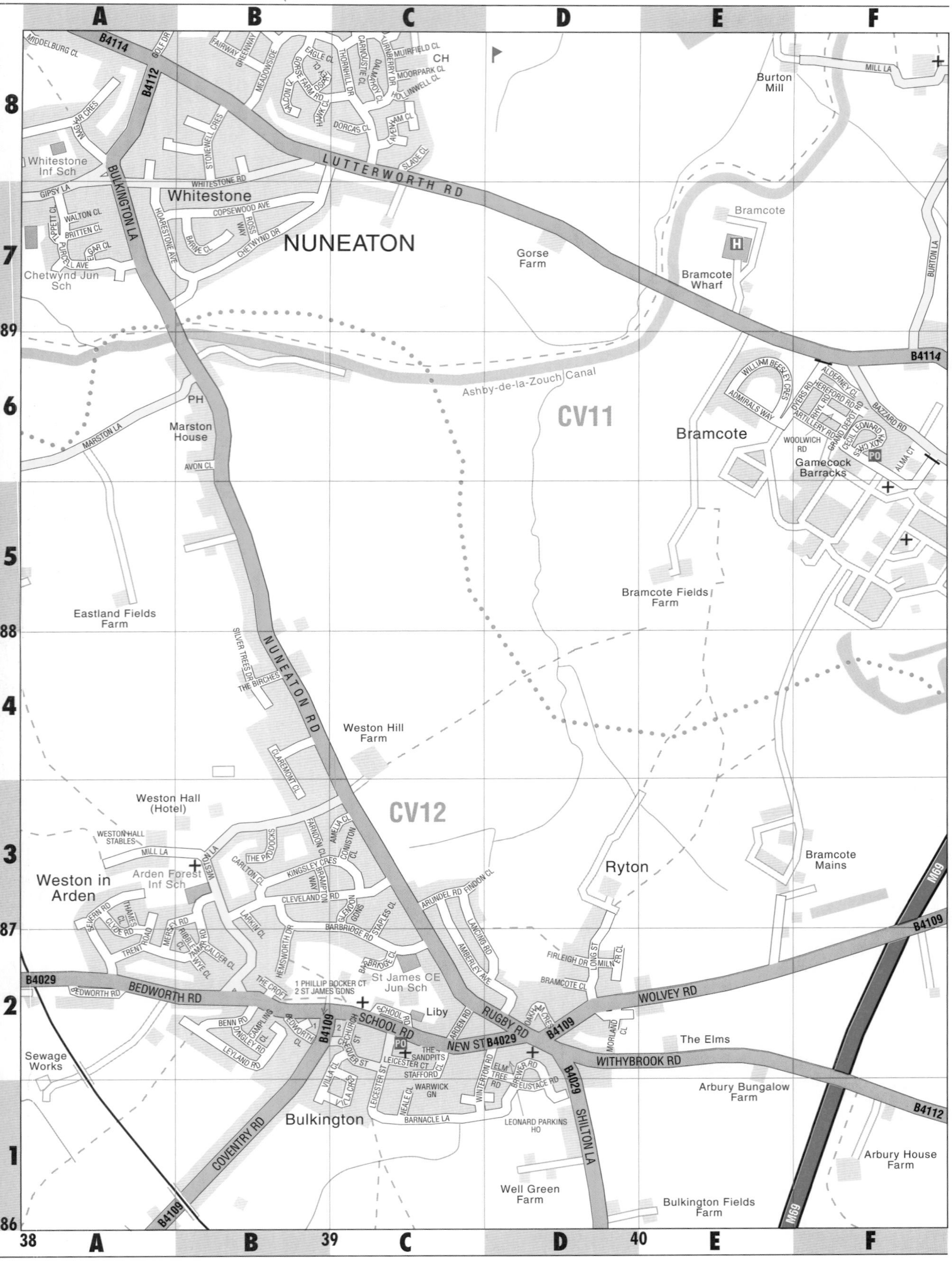
A
B
C
D
E
F
8
7
89
6
5
88
4
3
87
2
1
86
38
39
40
MIDDELBURG CL
B4114
GOLF DR
FAIRWAY
GREENWAY
MEADOWSIDE
EAGLE CL
GORSE FARM RD
FALCON CL
HAWK CL
CARNOUSTIE CL
THORNHILL DR
DALMAHOY CL
MUIRFIELD CL
CH
MOORPARK CL
HOLLINWELL CL
DORCAS CL
SLADE CL
B4112
Whitestone Inf Sch
STONEWELL CRES
WHITESTONE RD
LUTTERWORTH RD
Whitestone
GIPSY LA
WALTON CL
BRITTEN CL
COPSEWOOD AVE
ROSS WAY
CHETWYND DR
BARNE CL
NUNEATON
BULKINGTON LA
HOARESTONE AVE
Chetwynd Jun Sch
Gorse Farm
Burton Mill
MILL LA
Bramcote
Bramcote Wharf
BURTON LA
B4114
Ashby-de-la-Zouch Canal
PH
Marston House
MARSTON LA
AVON CL
CV11
WILLIAM BEESLEY CRES
ADMIRALS WAY
ALDERNEY CL
HEREFORD RD
RHYL RD
ARTILLERY RD
GRAND DEPOT RD
CECIL LEONARD KNOX CRES
BAZZARD RD
WOOLWICH RD
ALMA CT
PO
Bramcote
Gamecock Barracks
Bramcote Fields Farm
Eastland Fields Farm
SILVER TREES DR
THE BIRCHES
NUNEATON RD
Weston Hill Farm
CLAREMONT CL
CV12
Weston Hall (Hotel)
WESTON HALL STABLES
MILL LA
WESTON LA
Weston in Arden
Arden Forest Inf Sch
THE PADDOCKS
CARLTON CL
FARNDON CL
AMELIA CL
CONISTON CL
KINGSLEY CRES
BRAMPTON WAY
CLEVELAND RD
GLENDON GDNS
STAPLES CL
ARUNDEL RD
FINDON CL
LANCING RD
AMBERLEY AVE
Ryton
Bramcote Mains
M69
B4109
SEVERN RD
THAMES CL
CLYDE RD
TRENT ROAD
MERSEY RD
RIBBLE CL
TAMAR CL
WYE CL
CALDER CL
LARKIN CL
HEMSWORTH DR
BARBRIDGE RD
FIRLEIGH DR
LONG ST
MILNER CL
BRAMCOTE CL
WOLVEY RD
B4029
BEDWORTH RD
BEDWORTH RD
THE CROFT
1 PHILLIP DOCKER CT
2 ST JAMES GDNS
St James CE Jun Sch
Liby
SCHOOL RD
RUGBY RD
OAKHAM CRES
B4109
BENN RD
LAMPLING CL
DINGLEY RD
LEYLAND RD
BEDWORTH CL
CHURCH ST
CHEQUER ST
PO
THE SANDPITS
LEICESTER CT
STAFFORD CL
NEW ST
ARDEN RD
WINTERTON RD
ELM TREE RD
BREWER RD
EUSTACE RD
B4029
MORLAND CL
The Elms
WITHYBROOK RD
Sewage Works
VILLA CL
LEICESTER ST
NEALE CL
WARWICK GN
BARNACLE LA
LEONARD PARKINS HO
Bulkington
COVENTRY RD
SHILTON LA
Arbury Bungalow Farm
B4112
Arbury House Farm
Well Green Farm
Bulkington Fields Farm
B4109
M69

39
51

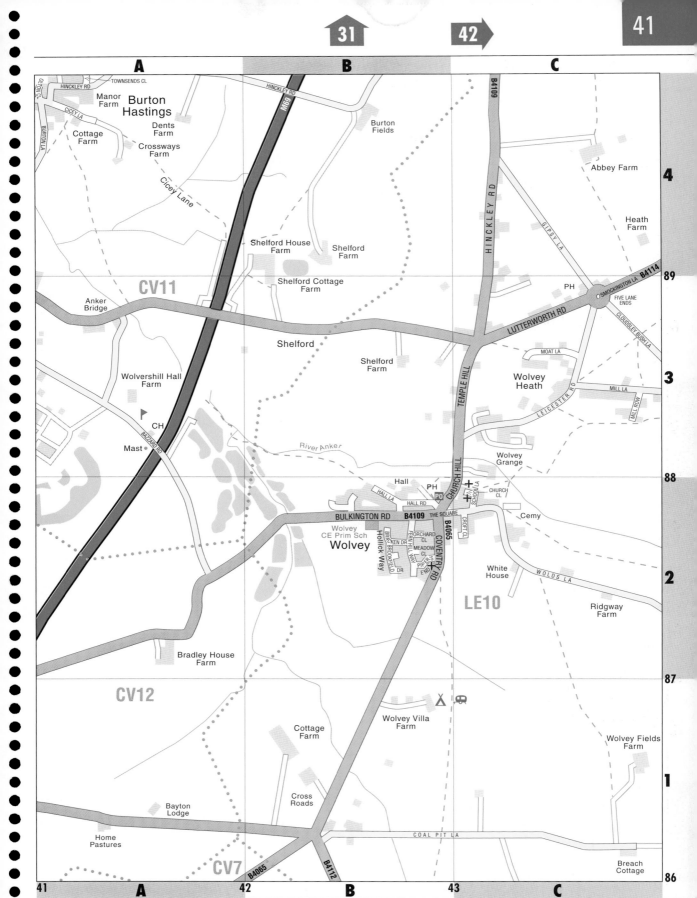

A **B** **C**

A5

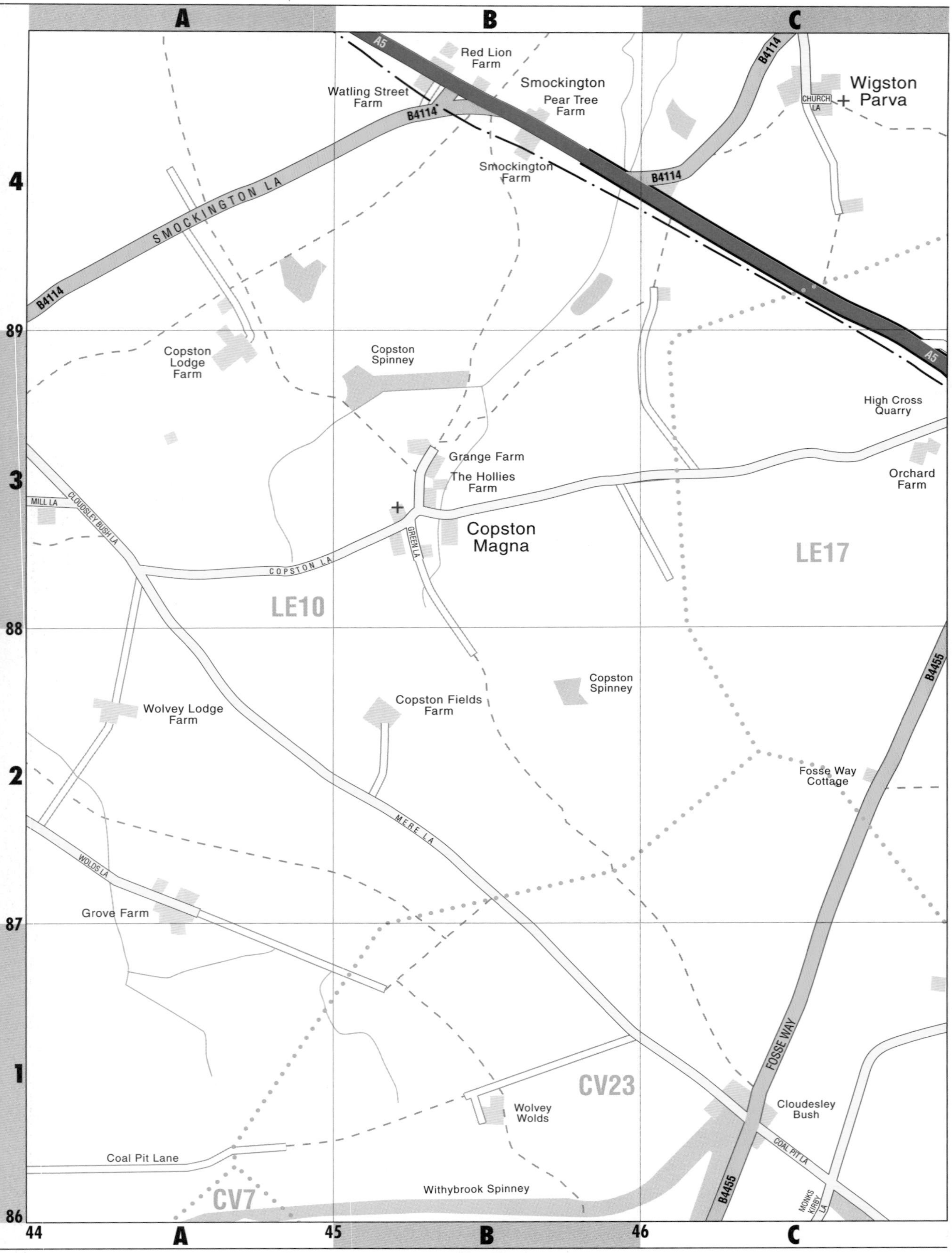

Red Lion Farm

Watling Street Farm

B4114

Smockington

Pear Tree Farm

B4114

Wigston Parva

CHURCH LA

B4114

Smockington Farm

SMOCKINGTON LA

4

B4114

89

Copston Lodge Farm

Copston Spinney

A5

High Cross Quarry

3

MILL LA

CLOUDSLEY BUSH LA

Grange Farm

The Hollies Farm

Orchard Farm

COPSTON LA

GREEN LA

Copston Magna

LE17

LE10

88

Copston Spinney

Wolvey Lodge Farm

Copston Fields Farm

B4455

2

MERE LA

Fosse Way Cottage

WOLDS LA

87

Grove Farm

1

FOSSE WAY

CV23

Wolvey Wolds

Cloudesley Bush

COAL PIT LA

Coal Pit Lane

B4455

MONKS KIRBY LA

86

CV7

Withybrook Spinney

44 **A** 45 **B** 46 **C**

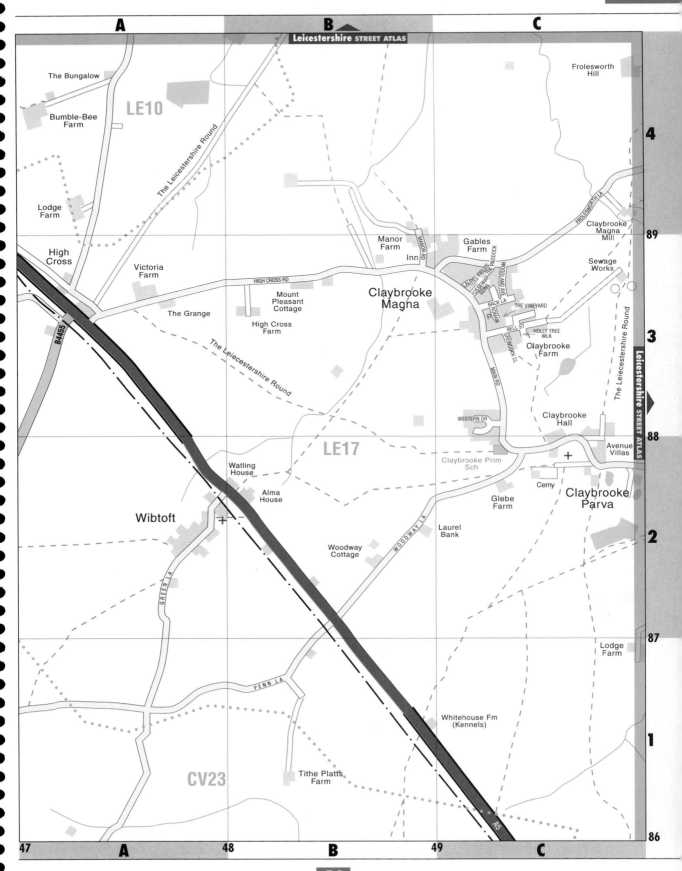

A   **B**   **C**

The Bungalow

LE10

Bumble-Bee
Farm

Lodge
Farm

Frolesworth
Hill

Claybrooke
Magna
Mill

The Leicestershire Round

High
Cross

Victoria
Farm

Manor
Farm

Inn

Gables
Farm

Sewage
Works

89

HIGH CROSS RD

The Grange

Mount
Pleasant
Cottage

High Cross
Farm

Claybrooke
Magna

LAUREL FIELDS

FOSSEWAY PL

WOODLAND AVE

PADDOCK

BACK LA

ROMAN CL

THE VINEYARD

HOLLY TREE
WLK

Claybrooke
Farm

BELL ST

GREWCOCK CL

MAIN RD

The Leicestershire Round

3

The Leicestershire Round

WESTERN DR

Claybrooke
Hall

88

LE17

Watling
House

Alma
House

Claybrooke Prim
Sch

Cemy

Avenue
Villas

Claybrooke
Parva

Wibtoft

Woodway
Cottage

WOODWAY LA

Laurel
Bank

Glebe
Farm

2

GREEN LA

87

Lodge
Farm

PENN LA

Whitehouse Fm
(Kennels)

1

A5

CV23

Tithe Platts
Farm

86

47   **A**   48   **B**   49   **C**

B4455

A B C D E F

M6

8

B37

The Bogs
Farm

Bannerley
Rough

Depot

Todd's
Rough

Mulliner's
Rough

Broadwater

7

B46

Nursery

Nursery
Farm

Ford

Golf &
Country Club

Foxes Den

85

Refuse
Tip

Little
Packington

Brook
Farm

Fish Breeding
Farm

The Ash
Beds

6

DENBIGH
CNR

Butler's
Moors

Packington
Park

Park
Meadow

Denbigh
Spinney

Church
Farm

River Blythe

Deer Park

5

Garden
Spinney

CV7

Packington
Hall

84

Park
Farm

Siding
Wood

Hall Pool

Great Pool

4

Mill
Shrubbery

The
Wilderness

Middle
Bickenhill

B92

The Mill
Farm

Little
Dayhouse
Wood

Beech
Lodge

PH

Dials
Pool

3

P

EAST WAY

COVENTRY RD

COVENTRY RD

Stonebridge

BIRMINGHAM RD

A45

83

The National
Motorcycle
Mus

Works

Pasture
Farm

Geary's
Heath

2

Mills
Gorse

Diddington
Hill

Diddington
Hall

CH

Shadow Brook

The Somers

1

Mouldings
Green Farm

Molands
Bridge

A452

B4102

82

20 A B 21 C D 22 E F

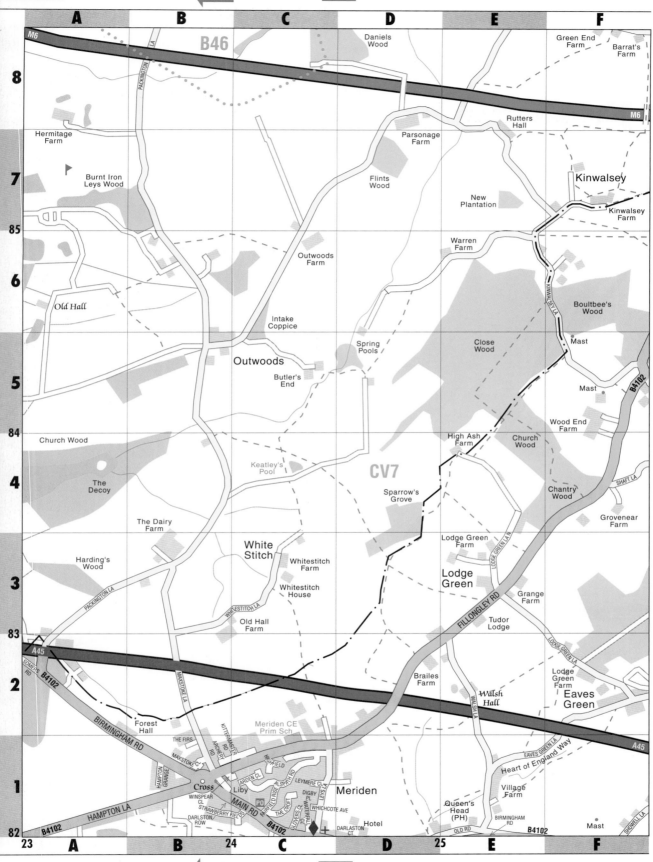

45
35
45
58

A   B   C   D   E   F

8

B46

M6
Daniels
Wood
Green End
Farm
Barrat's
Farm

M6

PACKINGTON LA

7

Hermitage
Farm

Burnt Iron
Leys Wood

Parsonage
Farm

Flints
Wood

Rutters
Hall

Kinwalsey

85

New
Plantation

Kinwalsey
Farm

Outwoods
Farm

Warren
Farm

KINWALSEY LA

6

Old Hall

Boultbee's
Wood

Mast

Intake
Coppice

Close
Wood

5

Outwoods

Butler's
End

Spring
Pools

Mast

B4102

Wood End
Farm

84

Church Wood

High Ash
Farm

Church
Wood

4

The
Decoy

Keatley's
Pool

CV7

Sparrow's
Grove

Chantry
Wood

SHAFT LA

Grovenear
Farm

The Dairy
Farm

Lodge Green
Farm

LODGE GREEN LA

3

Harding's
Wood

PACKINGTON LA

White
Stitch

Whitestitch
Farm

Lodge
Green

Grange
Farm

FILLONGLEY RD

LODGE GREEN LA

Lodge
Green
Farm

WHITESTITCH LA

Whitestitch
House

83

A45

SOMERS RD

B4102

MAXSTOKE LA

Old Hall
Farm

Tudor
Lodge

2

Brailes
Farm

Walsh
Hall

WALSH LA

Eaves
Green

BIRMINGHAM RD

Forest
Hall

THE FIRS

MAXSTOKE CL

KITTERMASTER RD

ARCHERY RD

Meriden CE
Prim Sch

EAVES GREEN LA

Heart of England Way

A45

1

HAMPTON GRANGE

Cross

WINSPEAR
CL

Liby

HIGHFIELD

ARDEN CL

ALSPATH RD

THE CROFT

LEYMERE CL

DIGBY
PL

WHITFIELD RISE

GLOVERS CL

WHITEHALL
LEYS

WHICHCOTE AVE

Meriden

Queen's
Head
(PH)

BIRMINGHAM
RD

Village
Farm

Mast

SHOWELL LA

82

HAMPTON LA

B4102

Cross

MAIN RD

PO

STRAWBERRY FIELD
DARLSTON
ROW

B4102

DARLASTON
CT

Hotel

OLD RD

B4102

23   A   B   24   C   D   25   E   F

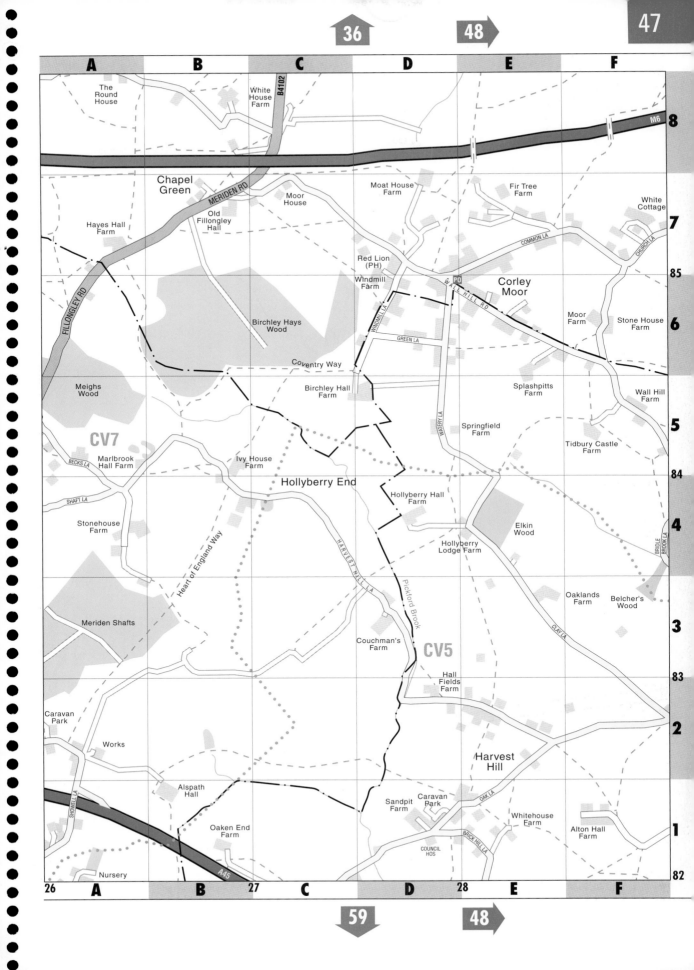

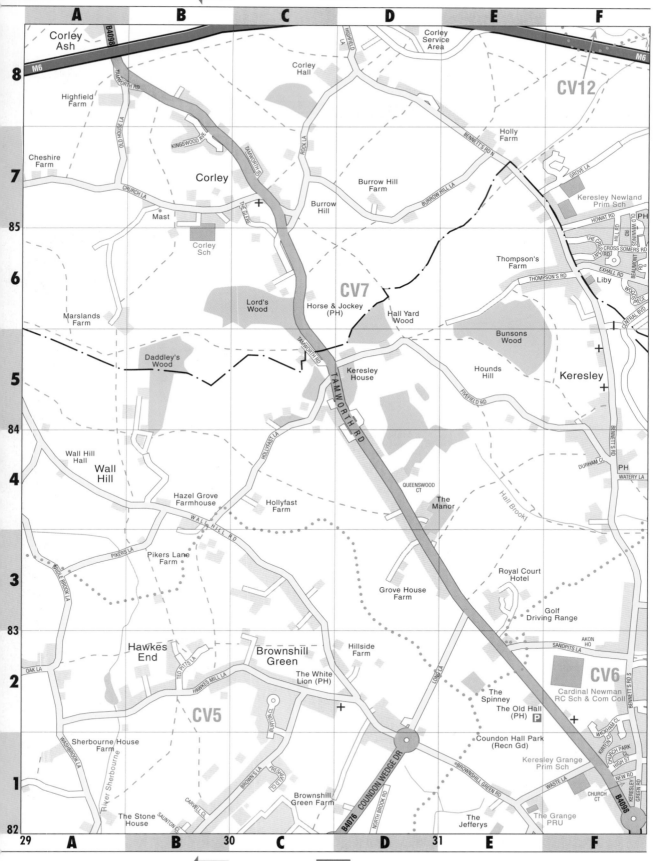

47
37
47
60

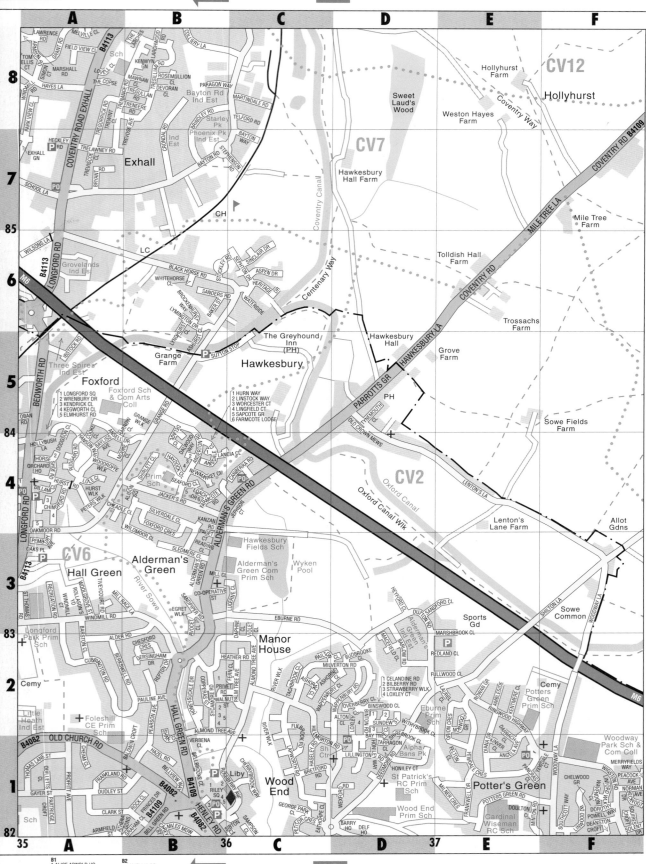

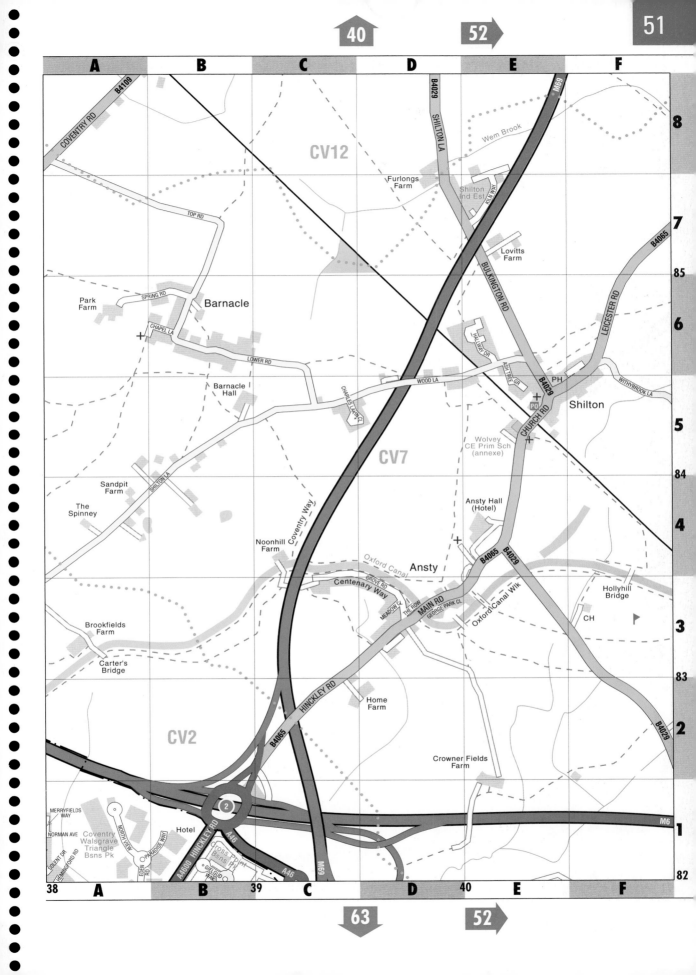

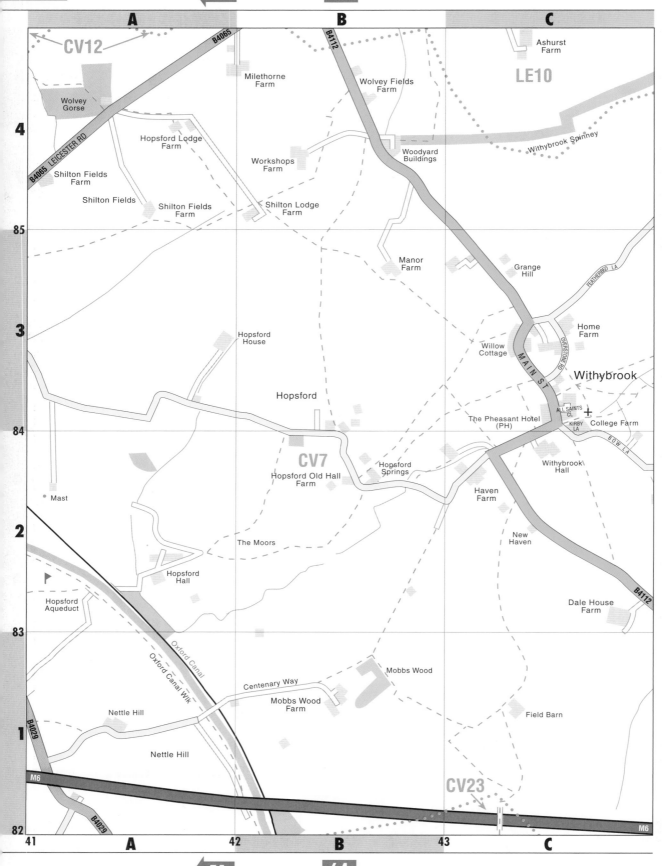

LE10

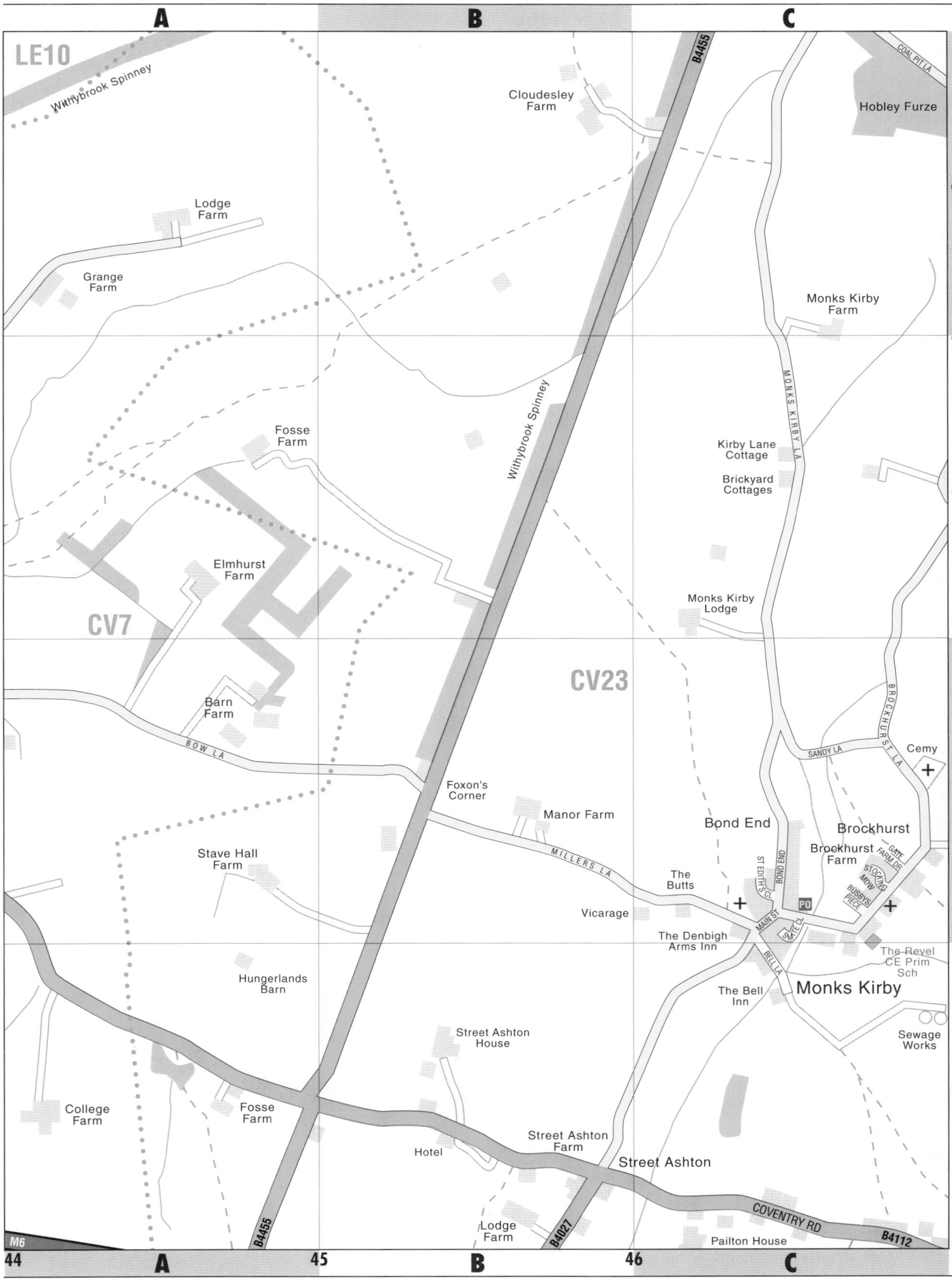

Withybrook Spinney

Cloudesley Farm

B4455

COAL PIT LA

Hobley Furze

4

Lodge Farm

Grange Farm

Monks Kirby Farm

85

Withybrook Spinney

Fosse Farm

MONKS KIRBY LA

Kirby Lane Cottage

Brickyard Cottages

3

Elmhurst Farm

CV7

Monks Kirby Lodge

84

Barn Farm

CV23

BROCKHURST LA

BOW LA

SANDY LA

Cemy

2

Foxon's Corner

Manor Farm

Bond End

Brockhurst

Brockhurst Farm

GATE FARM DR

Stave Hall Farm

MILLERS LA

The Butts

STOCKING MDW

ST EDITH'S CL

BOND END

BUSBY'S PIECE

Vicarage

MAIN ST

PO

GATE CL

83

The Denbigh Arms Inn

The Revel CE Prim Sch

Hungerlands Barn

BELL LA

Monks Kirby

The Bell Inn

Street Ashton House

Sewage Works

1

College Farm

Fosse Farm

Hotel

Street Ashton Farm

Street Ashton

Lodge Farm

B4027

COVENTRY RD

B4112

Pailton House

M6

B4455

82

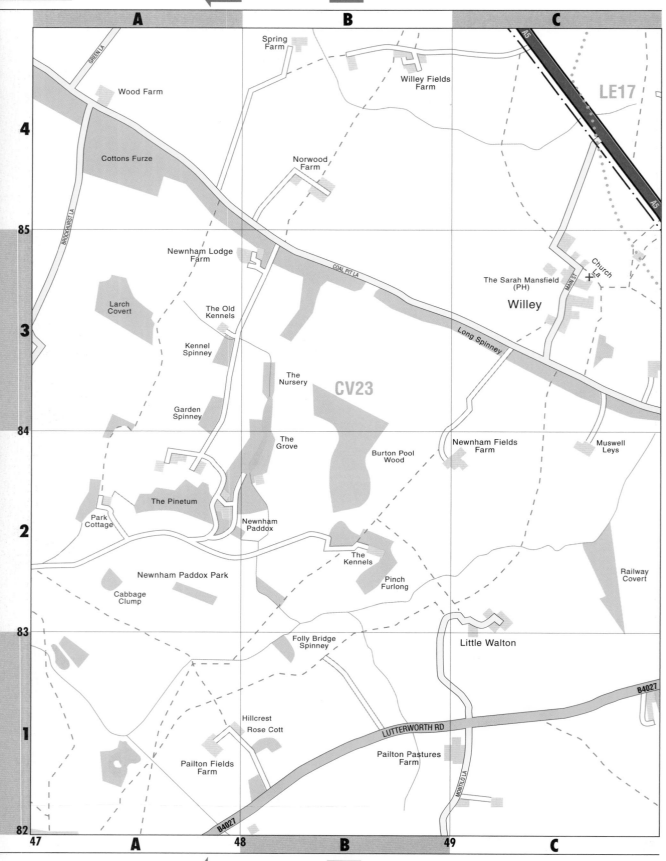

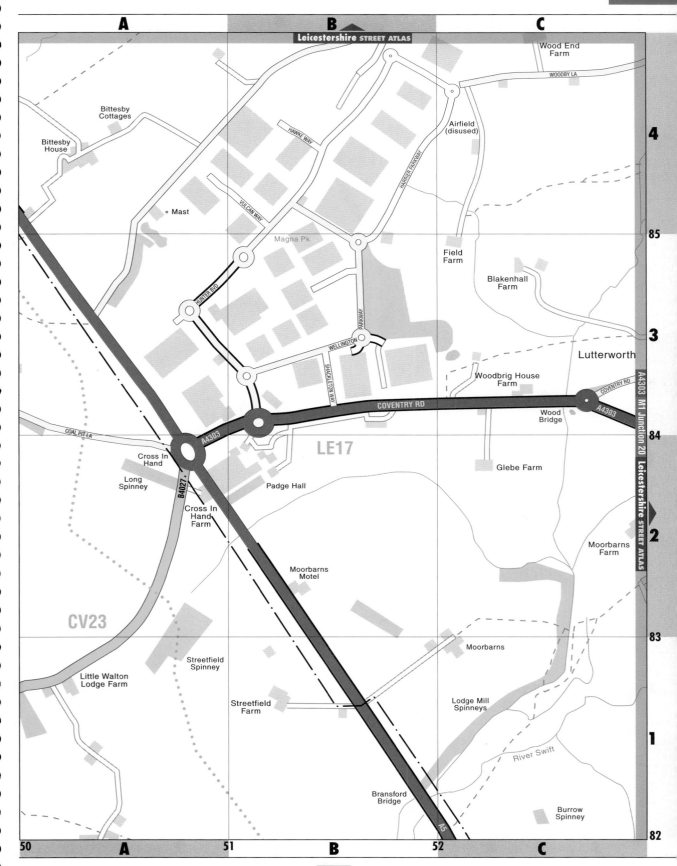

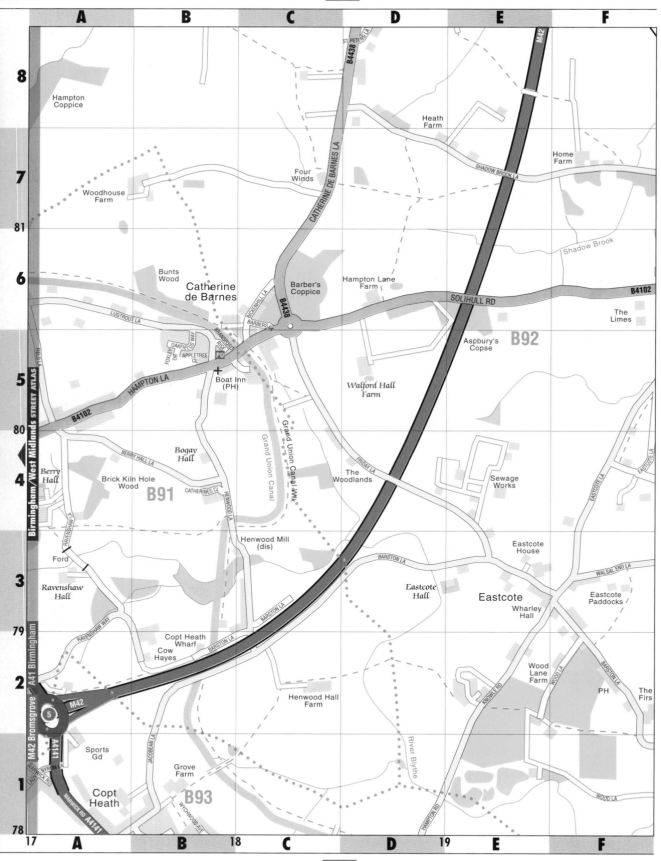

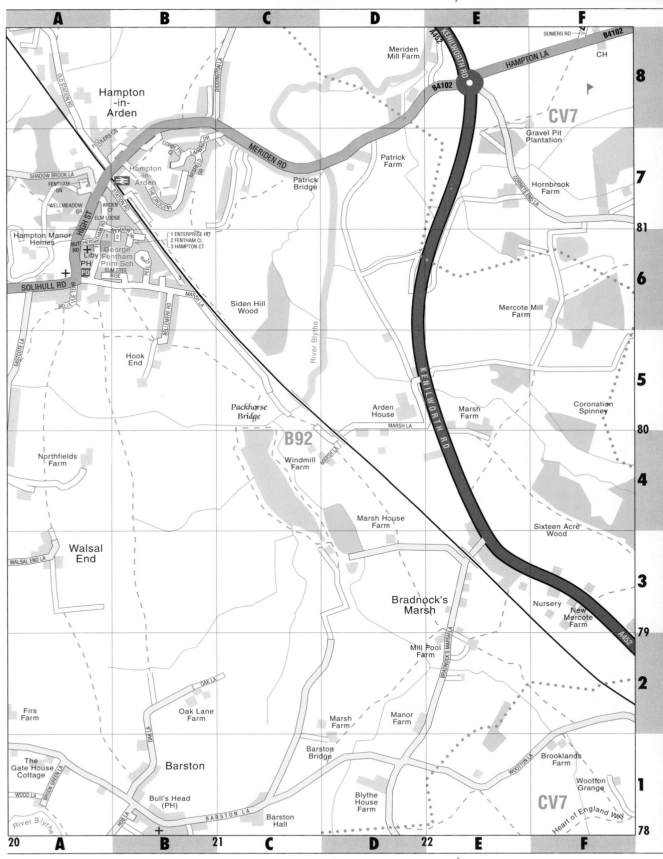

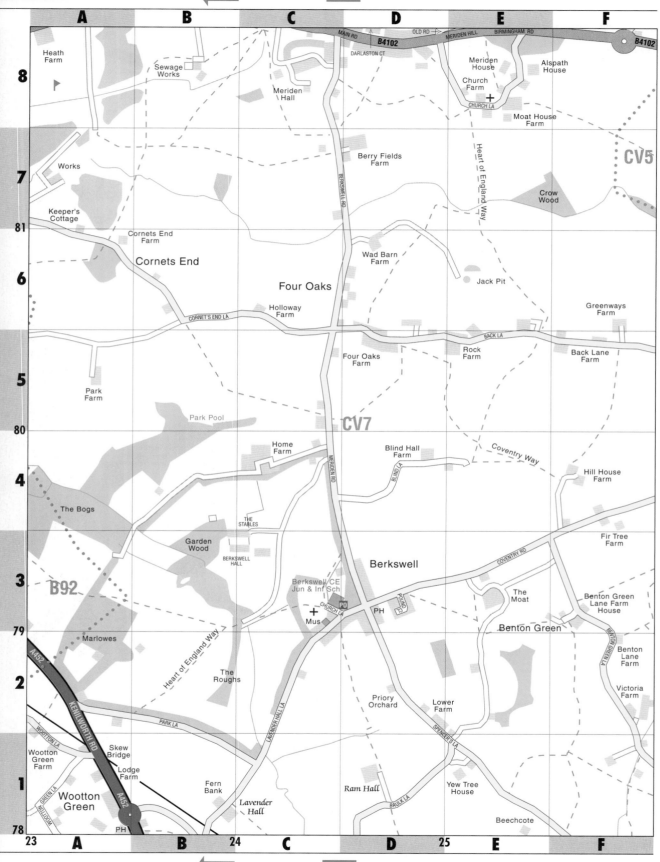

57
46

A B C D E F

8

Heath Farm

Sewage Works

Meriden Hall

B4102 Main Rd
Old Rd
Meriden Hill
Birmingham Rd
Darlaston Ct

Meriden House
Church Farm
Alspath House
Moat House Farm

7

Works

Berry Fields Farm

Heart of England Way

Crow Wood

CV5

81

Keeper's Cottage

Cornets End Farm

Cornets End

Wad Barn Farm

Jack Pit

6

Four Oaks

Holloway Farm

Greenways Farm

Cornet's End La

Back La

Four Oaks Farm

Rock Farm

Back Lane Farm

5

Park Farm

80

Park Pool

Home Farm

CV7

Blind Hall Farm

Coventry Way

Hill House Farm

4

The Bogs

The Stables

Garden Wood

Berkswell Hall

Meriden Rd
Blind La

Berkswell

Coventry Rd

Fir Tree Farm

3

B92

Berkswell CE Jun & Inf Sch

Church La
PO
PH
Pound

The Moat

Benton Green Lane Farm House

79

Marlowes

Mus

Benton Green

Benton Lane Farm

Heart of England Way

The Roughs

Priory Orchard

Lower Farm

Victoria Farm

2

A452 Kenilworth Rd

Park La

Lavender Hall La

Spencer's La

1

Wootton Green Farm

Skew Bridge

Lodge Farm

Fern Bank

Lavender Hall

Ram Hall

Baulk La

Yew Tree House

Beechcote

Wootton Green

Green La
Wootton La

A452

PH

78

23 A 24 B C 25 D E F

57
74

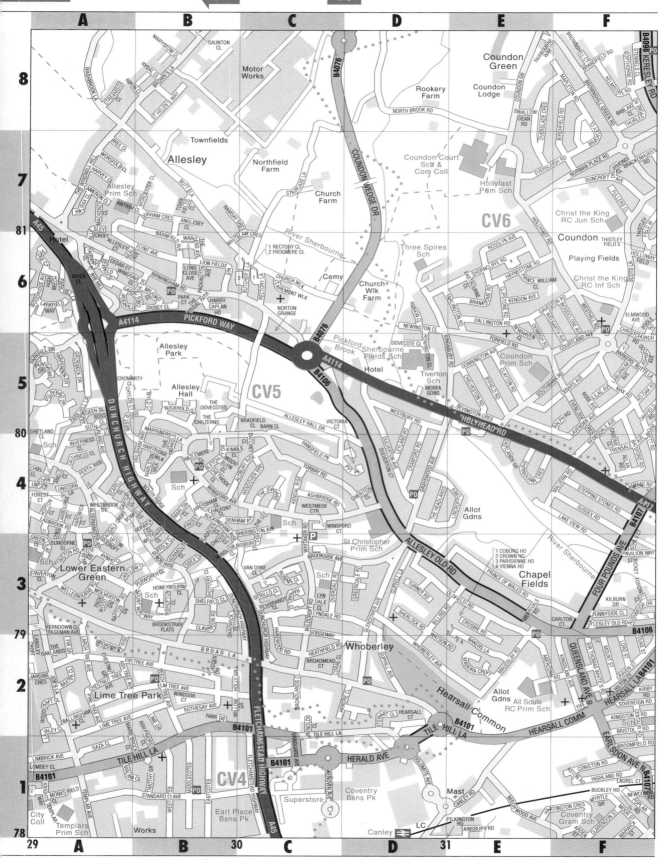

A5
1 NETHERMILL RD
2 CHILTERN CT
3 PAKE'S CROFT
4 HUMBERSTONE RD
B3
1 HAWKSWORTH DR

2 COLLETT WLK
3 RIVER CT
4 COMPASS CT
5 MEADOW HO
B2
1 WELLINGTON GDNS
2 MILESTONE HO

3 TRAFALGAR HO
4 KERRY'S HO
5 GRINDLEY HO
6 GEORGE POOLE HO
7 DRINKWATER HO
8 GARDNER HO
9 GIVENS HO

10 FENNELL HO
11 WINSLOW HO
12 ST THOMAS'S HO
13 ST THOMAS'S CT

F7
1 ADAM RD
2 WARNER ROW
3 ST NICHOLAS CT
4 PARADISE HO

For full street detail of the highlighted area see page 151.

77   62

E4
1 CAWTHORNE CL
2 PENSILVA WAY
3 JACQUARD HO
4 LEIGH ST
5 CLARENCE ST
6 THOMAS KING HO
7 NELSON ST
8 WATERLOO ST
9 VERNON CT

E3
1 HILLFIELDS HO
2 JEPHCOTT HO
3 GILBERT CL
4 VAUXHALL CL
5 VERNON CL
6 SPRING CL
7 RAGLAN CT

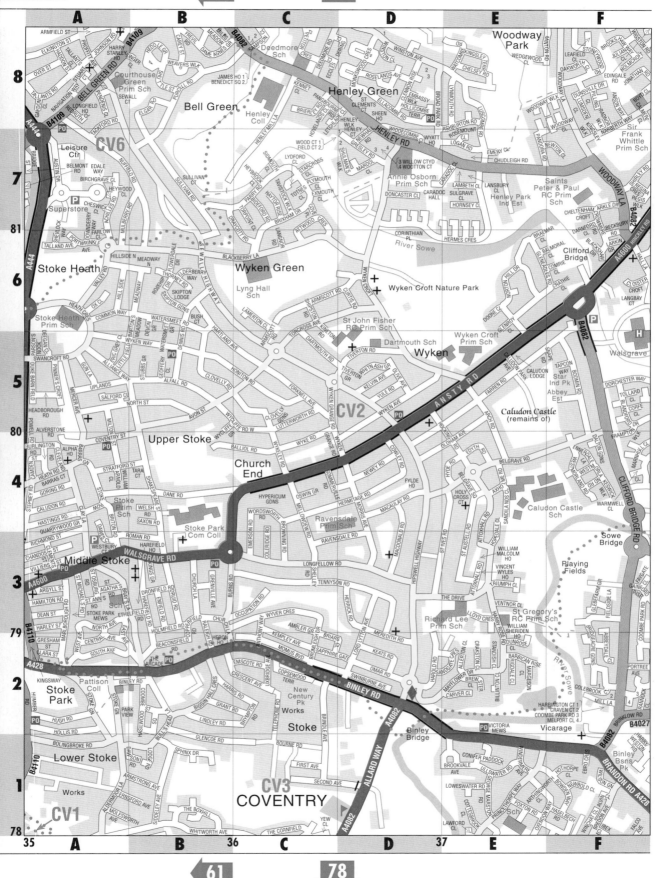

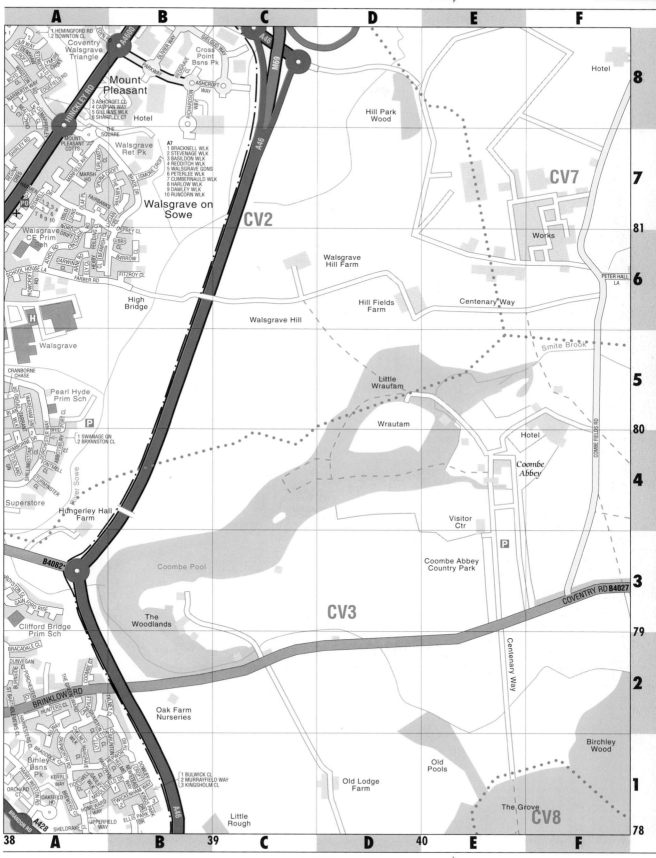

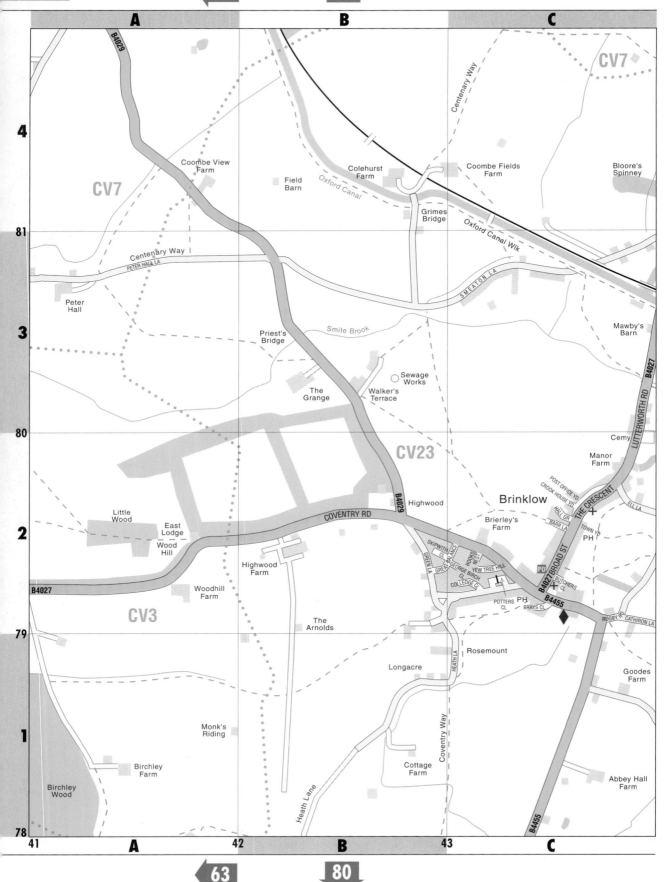

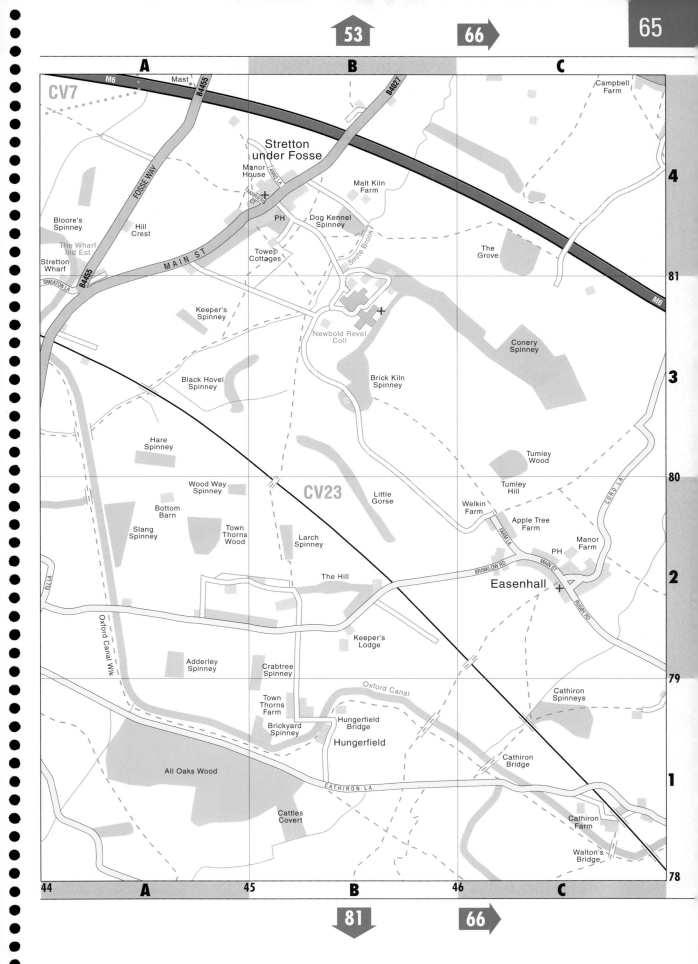

65
54

A

B

C

COVENTRY RD
B4112

FOXFIELD

BROOKSIDE AVE

Pailton
Pastures

B4027 LUTTERWORTH RD B4027

HOME FARM CL

Yews
Farm

Tythe
Farm

ST DENIS VIEW

PO

Pailton

POST
HOUSE
GDNS

RUGBY RD B4112

4

Greenway
Farm

Masts

CORD LA

81

Thwaite
Farm

Montilo
Farm

M6

MONTILO LA

Fieldgate
Farm

3

Glebe
Farm

CV23

80

Hospital
Farm

Harborough Magna

2

M6

Cosford

BACK LA

CHURCH CL

PAILTON RD

PH

Grange
Farm

THE
CRESCENT

MEADOW WAY

MAIN ST

Cosford Hall
Farm

Church
Farm

HAWTHORN TERR

Spike Lane

79

EASENHALL RD

Harborough Parva

Sandercock
Farm

Manor
Farm

Lodge
Farm

Cosford
Grounds

CV21

Chestnut
Farm

CATHIRON LA

RUGBY RD

1

Tuckey's
Farm

VALLEY DR

Oxford Canal

Swift Valley
Ind Est

Tuckey's
Bridge

Oxford Canal Wlk

SWIFT POINT

High
Oaks

CATHIRON LA

B4112

78

47   **A**   48   **B**   49   **C**

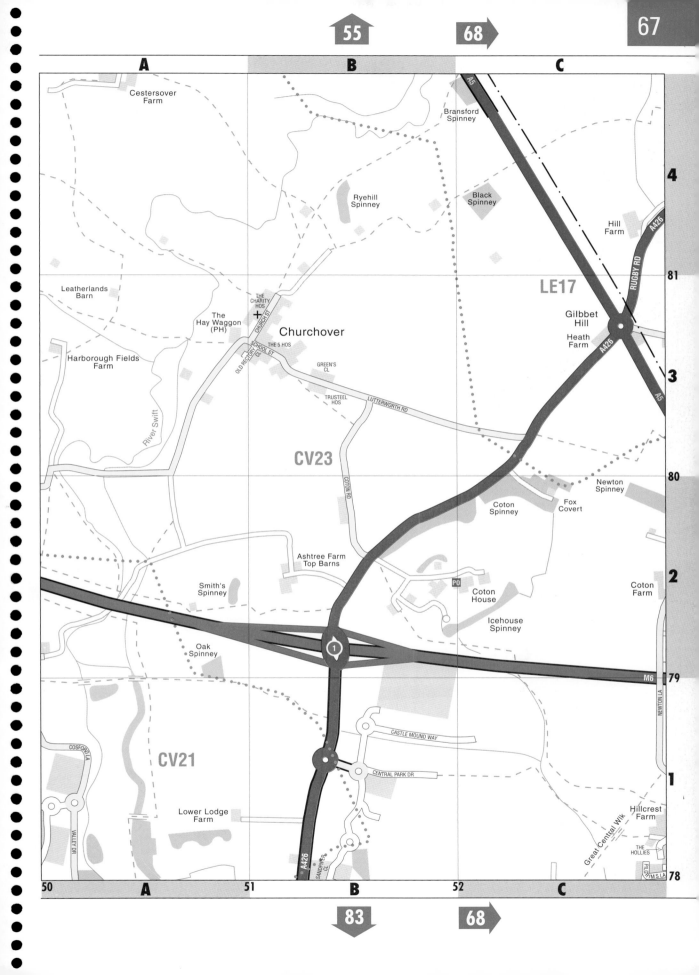

A   **B**   **C**

Leicestershire STREET ATLAS M1 Leicester (A5460)

A426 Leicester

Northamptonshire STREET ATLAS

M1 Northampton (A45)   M6 M1 Junction 19

Shawell Wood

Town End Farm

Lodge Plantations   Home Farm

Hill Farm

Spinney Farm

4

West Cottages

Hill Farm

Cotesbach Fields Farm

Shawell Lodge Farm

South Lodge

81

Green Lane Spinney

LE17

Barn Farm

GIBBET LA

Works

Middle Farm

THE GREEN

3

The White Swan (PH)

PO

Rose Farm

Shawell

80

Shawell Manor

Hill Top Farm

Stables

Hall Farm

Grange Farm

2

Depot

Tomley Hall Farm

19

79   M6

M6

Great Central Wlk

Depots

1

CV23

Old Barn Farm

THE LEYES

Manor Farm

ELM LA

Catthorpe

CATTHORPE MANOR

Newton

WATLING CRES

Works

HERMITAGE CL

PH

1 THE PADDOCK
2 THE ORCHARDS
3 PILGRIMS LA
4 SILVER ST
5 NEWTON RD

Cherry Tree (PH)

78

53   **A**   **54**   **B**   **55**   **C**

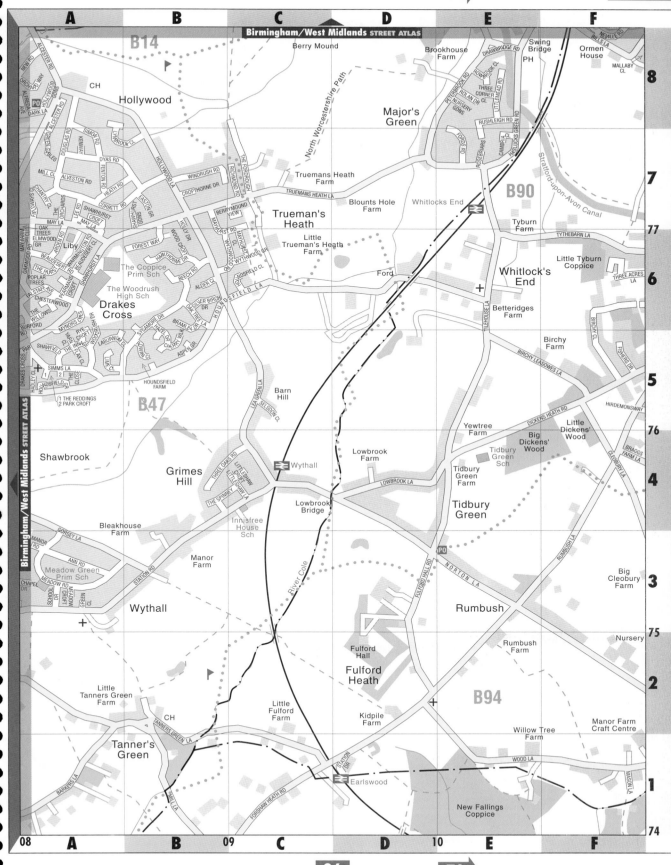

Birmingham/West Midlands STREET ATLAS

B14

Berry Mound

Brookhouse Farm

Swing Bridge PH

Ormen House

NEVILLE RD

BILLS LA

MALLABY CL

8

Hollywood

Major's Green

DRAWBRIDGE RD

ROWBROOK CL

THREE CORNER

PT NURSERY GDNS

ROLAN DR

LITTLEHEAD RD

RUSHLEIGH RD

CAMBRIA CL

HAMLOCKS GREEN RD

B90

Stratford-upon-Avon Canal

7

Truemans Heath Farm

Truemans Heath La

Blounts Hole Farm

Whitlocks End

Tyburn Farm

TYTHEBARN LA

77

Trueman's Heath

Little Trueman's Heath Farm

Ford

Whitlock's End

Little Tyburn Coppice

THREE ACRES LA

6

Liby

The Coppice Prim Sch

The Woodrush High Sch

Drakes Cross

Betteridges Farm

Birchy Farm

BIRCHY LEASOWES LA

BIRCH CL

FISHERS DR

HIRDEMONSWAY

5

Houndsfield Farm

Barn Hill

1 THE REDDINGS
2 PARK CROFT

B47

Yewtree Farm

DICKENS HEATH RD

Big Dickens' Wood

Little Dickens' Wood

CLEOBURY LA

BRAGGS FARM LA

76

Shawbrook

Grimes Hill

Wythall

Lowbrook Farm

LOWBROOK LA

Tidbury Green Farm

Tidbury Green Sch

Tidbury Green

RUMBUSH LA

Bleakhouse Farm

Innisfree House Sch

Lowbrook Bridge

Manor Farm

River Cole

PO

NORTON LA

Rumbush

Big Cleobury Farm

3

Meadow Green Prim Sch

Wythall

FULFORD HALL RD

Rumbush Farm

Nursery

75

Little Tanners Green Farm

Little Fulford Farm

Fulford Hall

Fulford Heath

Kidpile Farm

B94

Willow Tree Farm

Manor Farm Craft Centre

2

CH

Tanner's Green

TANNERS GREEN LA

Earlswood

STATION DR

WOOD LA

MASON LA

New Fallings Coppice

1

BARKERS LA

FORSHAW HEATH RD

74

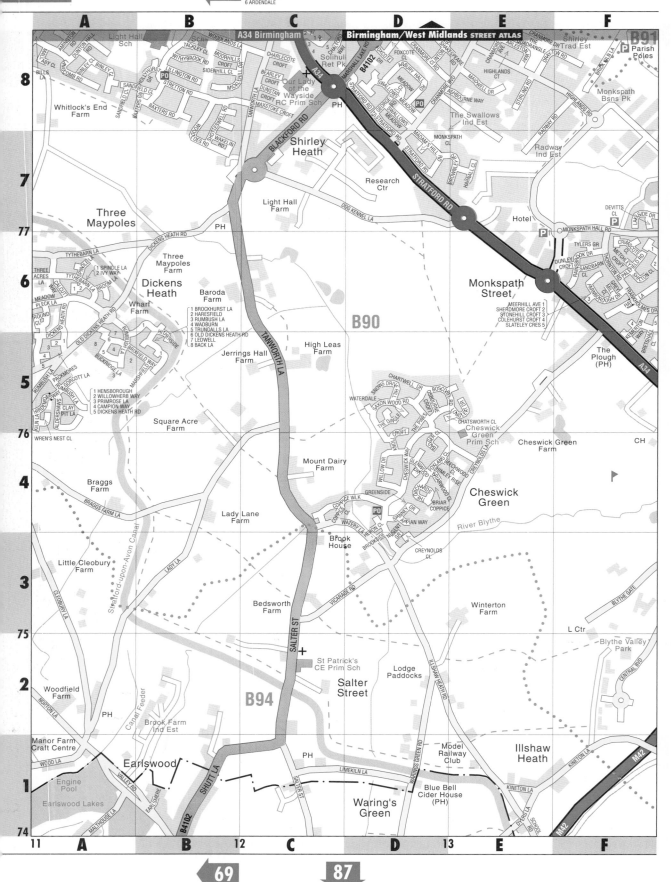

69

C8
1 HARWOOD GR 7 YARNINGDALE
2 SHIRLEYDALE
3 CHELTONDALE
4 HENLEYDALE
5 QUINTONDALE
6 ARDENDALE

A34 Birmingham

Birmingham/West Midlands STREET ATLAS

B91

Whitlock's End Farm

Three Maypoles

Three Maypoles Farm

Dickens Heath

Wharf Farm

Baroda Farm

1 BROCKHURST LA
2 HARESFIELD
3 RUMBUSH LA
4 WADBURN
5 TRUNDALLS LA
6 OLD DICKENS HEATH RD
7 LEDWELL
8 BACK LA

1 HENSBOROUGH
2 WILLOWHERB WAY
3 PRIMROSE LA
4 CAMPION WAY
5 DICKENS HEATH RD

Jerrings Hall Farm

Square Acre Farm

Braggs Farm

Little Cleobury Farm

Lady Lane Farm

Woodfield Farm

Manor Farm Craft Centre

Earlswood

Engine Pool

Earlswood Lakes

Brook Farm Ind Est

Waring's Green

Shirley Heath

Light Hall Farm

High Leas Farm

Mount Dairy Farm

Brook House

Bedsworth Farm

Salter Street

Research Ctr

B90

Monkspath Street

1 MEERHILL AVE
2 SHERDMORE CROFT
3 STONEHILL CROFT
4 COLEHURST CROFT
5 SLATELEY CRES

Waterdale

Cheswick Green Prim Sch

Cheswick Green Farm

Cheswick Green

River Blythe

Creynolds Cl

Winterton Farm

Lodge Paddocks

Model Railway Club

Blue Bell Cider House (PH)

Illshaw Heath

The Swallows Ind Est

Radway Ind Est

Hotel

The Plough (PH)

Parish Poles

Monkspath Bsns Pk

Blythe Gate

Blythe Valley Park

L Ctr

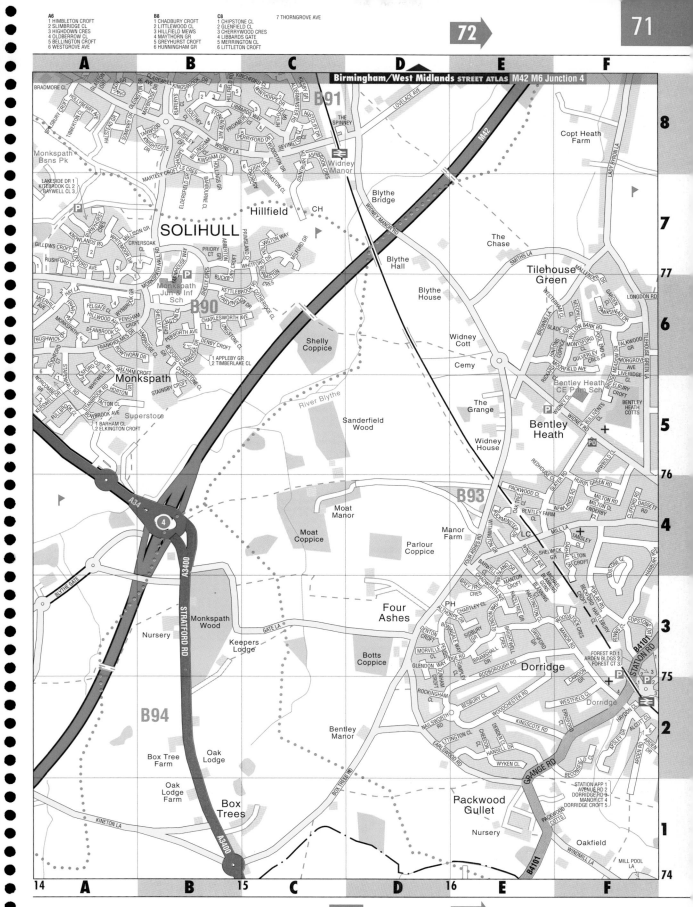

Birmingham/West Midlands STREET ATLAS M42 M6 Junction 4

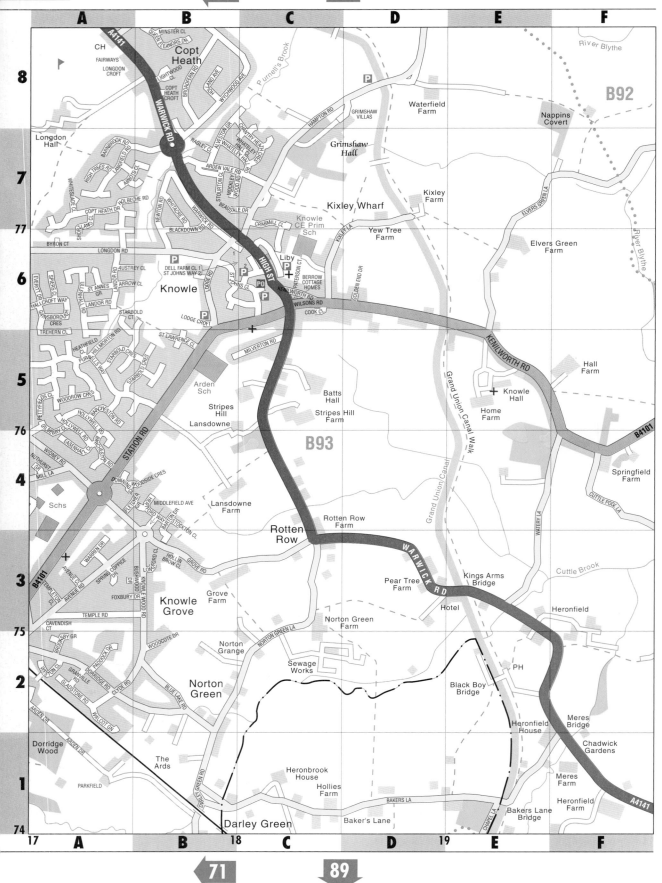

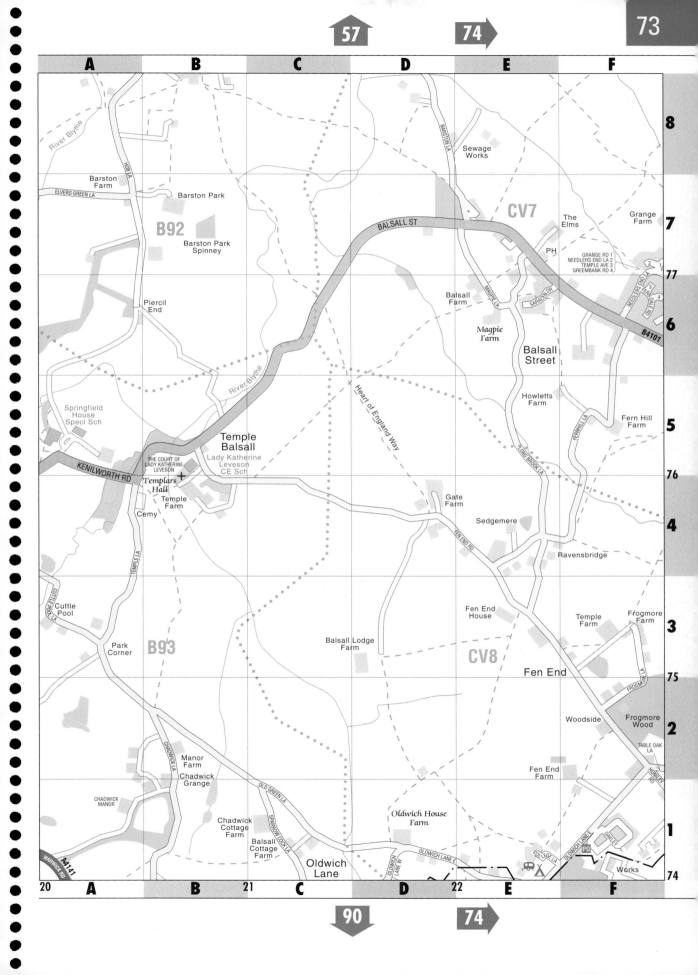

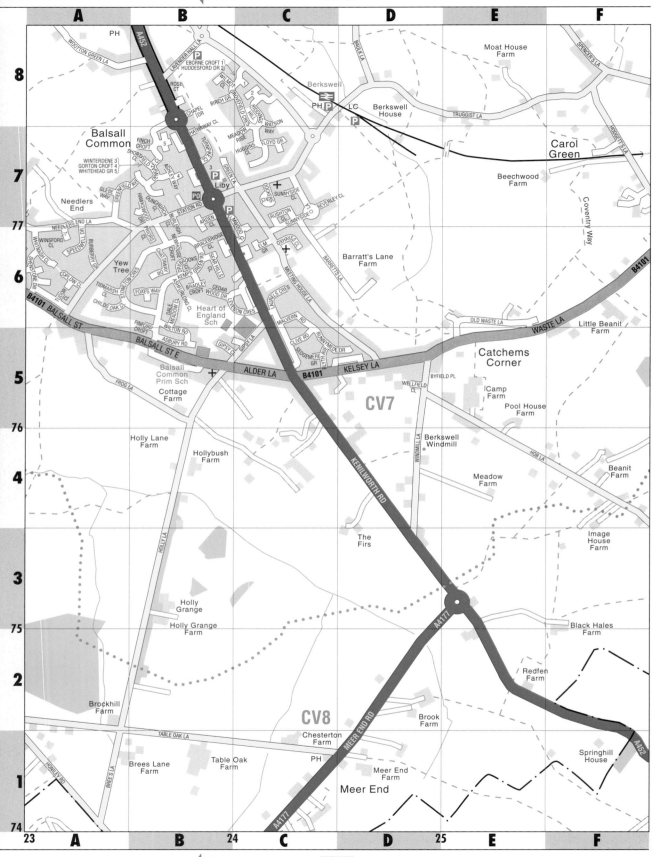

73
58

A B C D E F

8
7
77
6
5
76
4
3
75
2
1
74

23 A B 24 C D 25 E F

PH
WOOTTON GREEN LA
A452
LAVENDER HALL LA
P
EBORNE CROFT 1
HUDDESFORD DR 2
WELMOT GROVEFIELD DRES
ROSE CT
CHAPEL DR
BIRCH GR
FIELDING
WATSON
Balsall Common
FINCH CROFT
ASHLEY WAY
GREEN LA
NURNHILL
MEADOW RISE
HILL
HUGGINS CL
FLOYD GR
WINTERDENE 3
GORTON CROFT 4
WHITEHEAD GR 5
P Liby
DICKENS
SUNNYSIDE CL
Needlers End
GREENFIELD RDE
GLEBE WAY
HAWKSWOOD DR
DUNCHURCH
STATION RD
PO
P
ARDEN CL
KENILWOOD
RUSHTON CL
SUNNYSIDE RD
BEVERLEY CL
Berkswell
PH P LC
Berkswell House
TRUGGIST LA
Moat House Farm
SPENCER'S LA
HODGETTS LA
Carol Green
Beechwood Farm
Coventry Way
WINSFORD CL
WHITNASH CL
SHENSTONE DR
COPLOW CL
TUDOR
SPEEDY
BURBERRY GR
NEEDLERS END LA
HOLT
BURLEIGH
NEWHOUSE
CHATTAWAY
PRIORS
KEMPS GREEN RD
BROOKS
ASHLEIGH
BRACEBRIDGE
ELM GR
OXHAYES CL
Yew Tree
TIDMARSH CL
DALE
MEADOW CL
CHILDS OAK CL
STONECROM CRES
BRADLEY CROFT
ASHRING CL
CEDAR WOOD DR
LATSON CRES
FOXES WAY
Heart of England Sch
LAURELS CRES
MALVERN RD
BARRATTS LA
Barratt's Lane Farm
B4101
B4101 BALSALL ST
BALSALL ST E
ASBURY RD
FINFORD CROFT
MILTON CL
WILTON RD
FROG LA
GIPSY CL
GIPSY LA
CLIVE RD
RUNNYMEDE DR
SEDGEMERE GR
ALDER LA
KELSEY LA
MEETING HOUSE LA
OLD WASTE LA
WASTE LA
Little Beanit Farm
Catchems Corner
Balsall Common Prim Sch
Cottage Farm
CV7
WELLFIELD CL
BYFIELD PL
Camp Farm
Pool House Farm
Holly Lane Farm
Hollybush Farm
WINDMILL LA
Berkswell Windmill
HOB LA
Beanit Farm
HOLLY LA
KENILWORTH RD
Meadow Farm
Image House Farm
The Firs
Holly Grange
Holly Grange Farm
A4177
Black Hales Farm
Brockhill Farm
Redfen Farm
CV8
MEER END RD
Brook Farm
TABLE OAK LA
Chesterton Farm
PH
A452
Springhill House
BREES LA
Brees Lane Farm
Table Oak Farm
Meer End Farm
Meer End
HONILEY RD
A4177

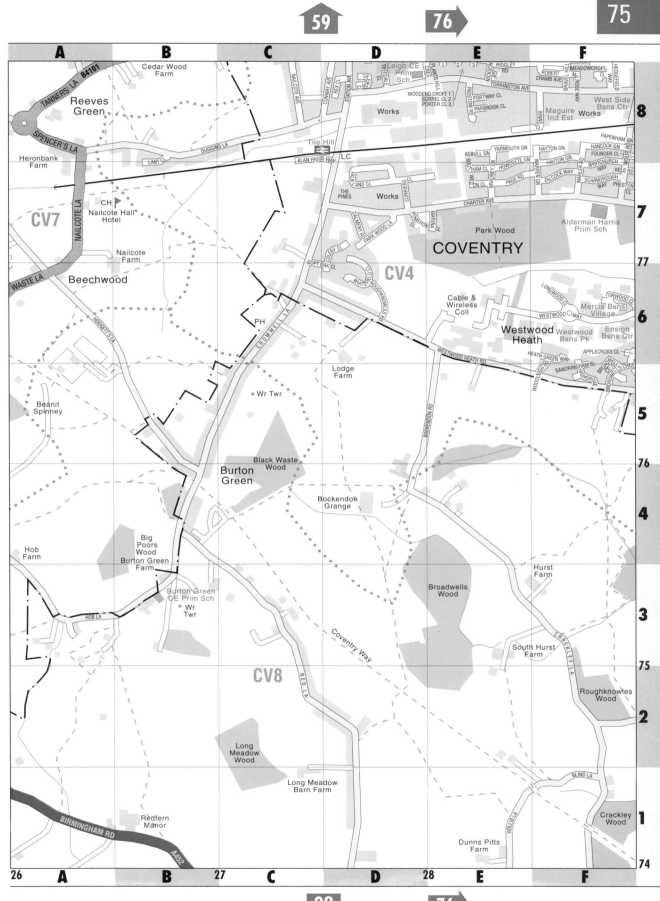

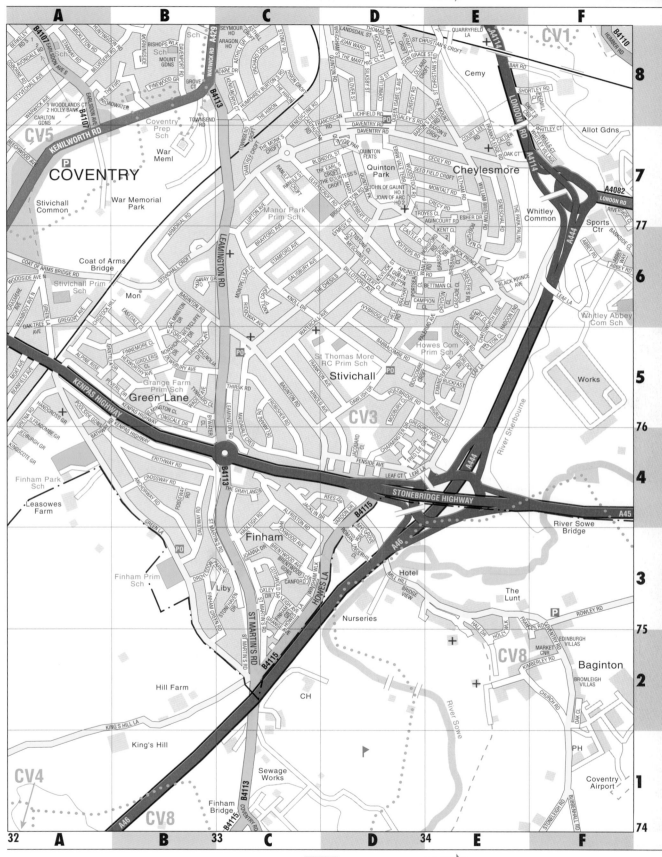

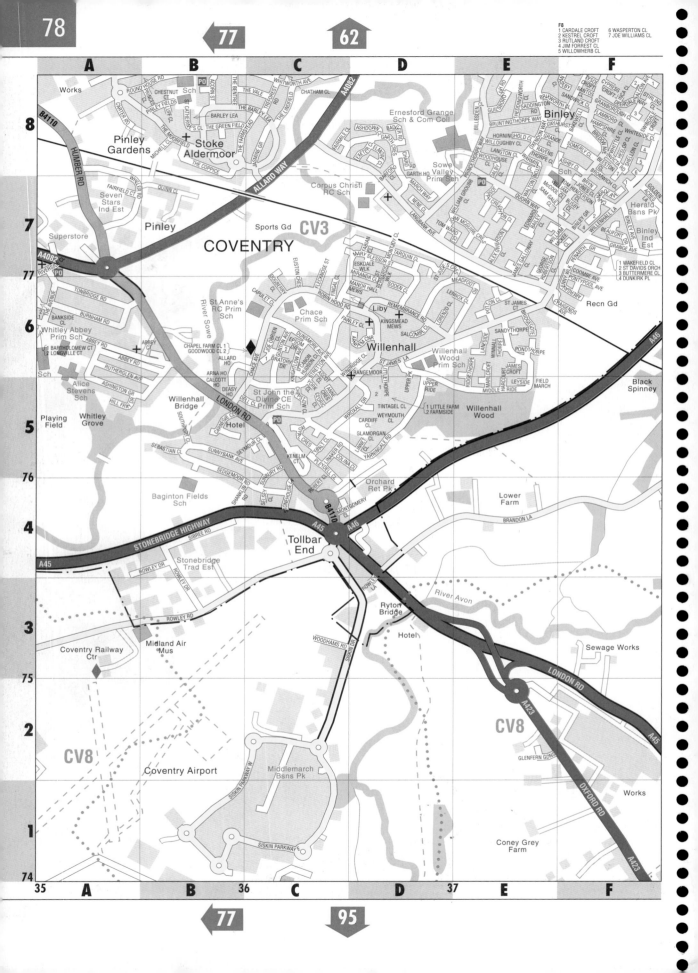

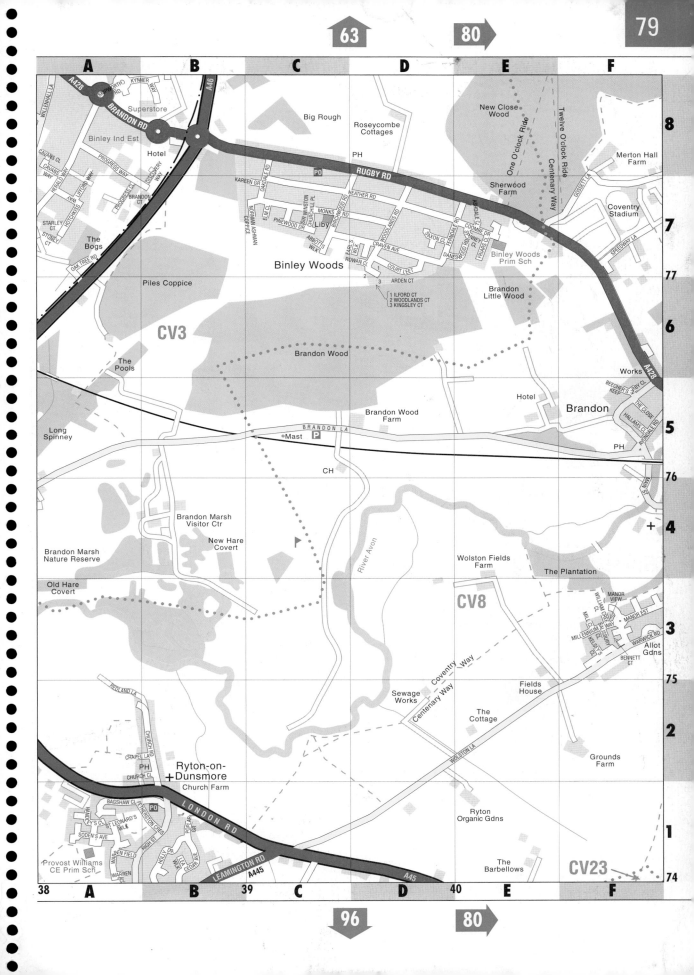

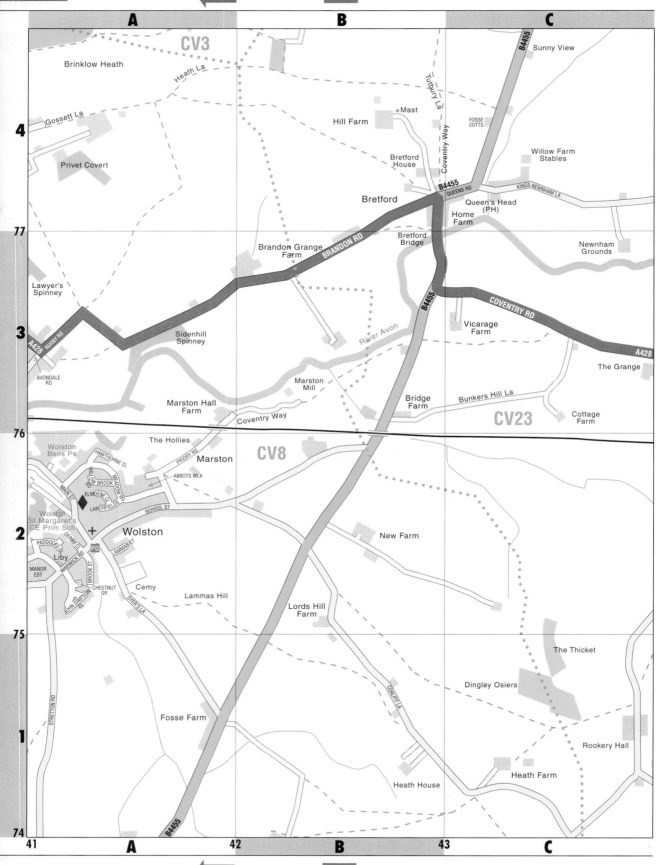

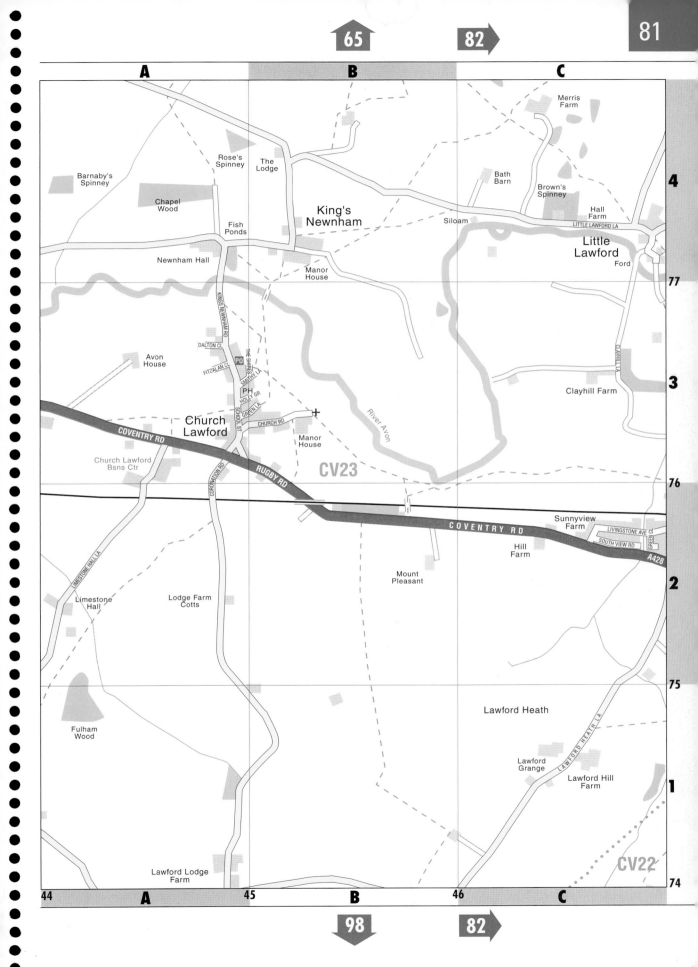

A

B

C

Merris
Farm

Rose's
Spinney

The
Lodge

Bath
Barn

Brown's
Spinney

4

Barnaby's
Spinney

Chapel
Wood

King's
Newnham

Siloam

Hall
Farm

LITTLE LAWFORD LA

Little
Lawford

Fish
Ponds

Ford

Newnham Hall

Manor
House

77

KINGS NEWNHAM RD

DALTON CL

Avon
House

FITZALAN CL

PO

THE SHIRES

SMITHY LA

CLAYHILL LA

Clayhill Farm

3

PH

HOLY GR

GREEN LA

River Avon

SCHOOL ST

Church
Lawford

CHURCH RD

Manor
House

COVENTRY RD

CORONATION RD

RUGBY RD

CV23

76

Church Lawford
Bsns Ctr

Sunnyview
Farm

LIVINGSTONE AVE CL

COVENTRY RD

SOUTH VIEW RD

GREEN CL

A428

Hill
Farm

Mount
Pleasant

2

LIMESTONE HALL LA

Limestone
Hall

Lodge Farm
Cotts

75

Lawford Heath

LAWFORD HEATH LA

Fulham
Wood

Lawford
Grange

Lawford Hill
Farm

1

CV22

Lawford Lodge
Farm

74

44

A

45

B

46

C

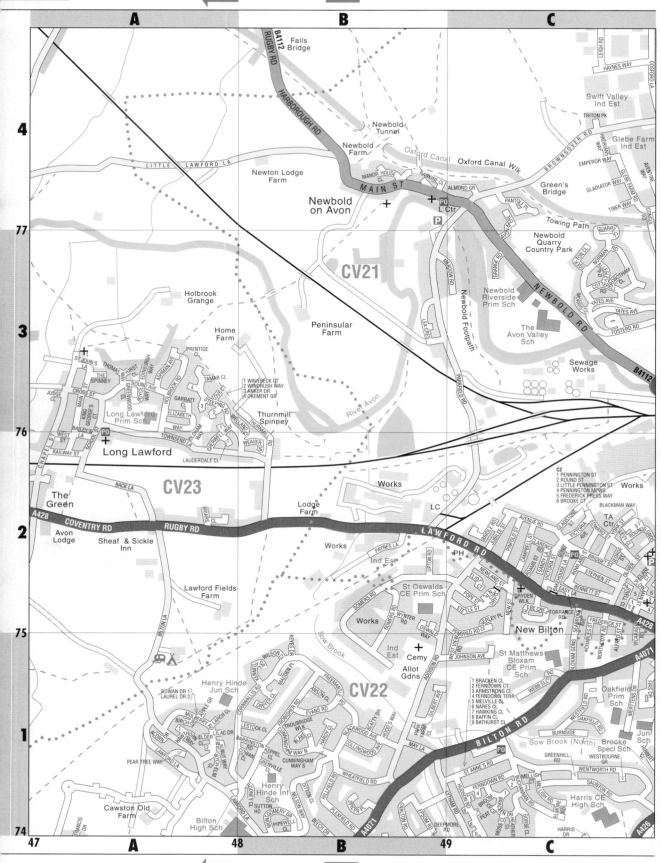

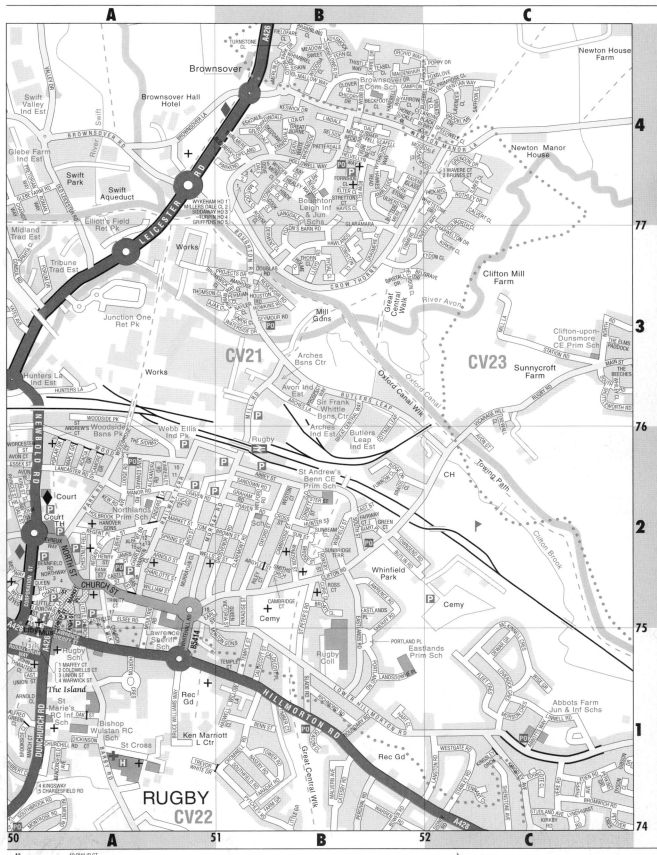

A2
1 PRINCES CT
2 DUKE ST
3 MANNING WLK
4 MARKET MALL
5 ELBOROW ST
6 BLOXAM PL
7 ST MATTHEWS ST
8 DUKES JETTY
9 WOOLL ST
10 PHILIP CT
11 OMEGA PL
12 EDWARD CT
13 PINDERS CT
14 JAMES CT
15 ALEXANDRA CT
16 CENTRAL BLDGS
17 ARNOLD VILLAS
18 CLARENDON CT

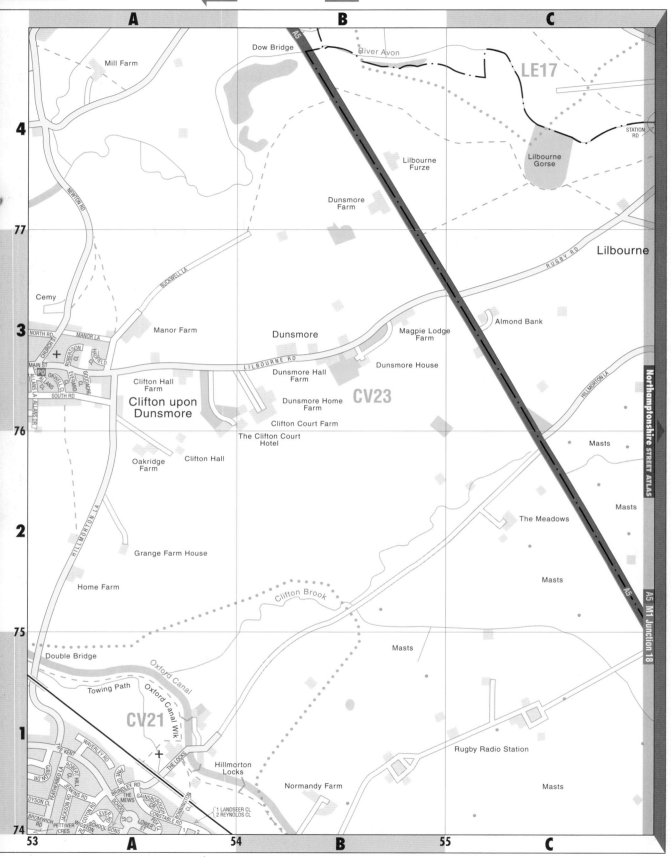

A

B

C

4

77

Mill Farm

Dow Bridge

River Avon

LE17

Lilbourne
Furze

Lilbourne
Gorse

STATION
RD

Dunsmore
Farm

NEWTON RD

Cemy

BUCKWELL LA

RUGBY RD

Lilbourne

Manor Farm

NORTH RD
MANOR LA
CHURCH ST
ROBERTSON CL
HAXFIELD
GOODACRE
EVERARD
MAIN ST
ORWELL CL
ALLANS
ALLANS LA
SOUTH RD
ALLANS DR

3

Dunsmore

Magpie Lodge
Farm

Almond Bank

Dunsmore House

HILLMORTON LA

Clifton Hall
Farm

Dunsmore Hall
Farm

LILBOURNE RD

Clifton upon
Dunsmore

Dunsmore Home
Farm

Clifton Court Farm

CV23

Masts

76

Oakridge
Farm

Clifton Hall

The Clifton Court
Hotel

Masts

HILLMORTON LA

The Meadows

2

Grange Farm House

Masts

Home Farm

Clifton Brook

75

Double Bridge

Masts

Oxford Canal

Towing Path

Oxford Canal Wlk

A5

A5 M1 Junction 18

Northamptonshire STREET ATLAS

CV21

THE LOCKS

1

AVE KENT
WAVERLEY RD
ROBERT HILL
THE GR
BRINDLEY RD
THE MEWS
MUSSON CL
FEATHERBED LA
JACKSON CL
JENKINS RD
SCHOOL
GAINSBOROUGH
CR
DYSON CL
LEVER ST
WIGSTON
SCHOOL GDNS
CONSTABLE RD
FOX CL
LOWER ST
BROMWICH RD
PETTIVER
CRES
COTTON RD
PENNINGTON

Hillmorton
Locks

Rugby Radio Station

Normandy Farm

1 LANDSEER CL
2 REYNOLDS CL

Masts

74

53

A

54

B

55

C

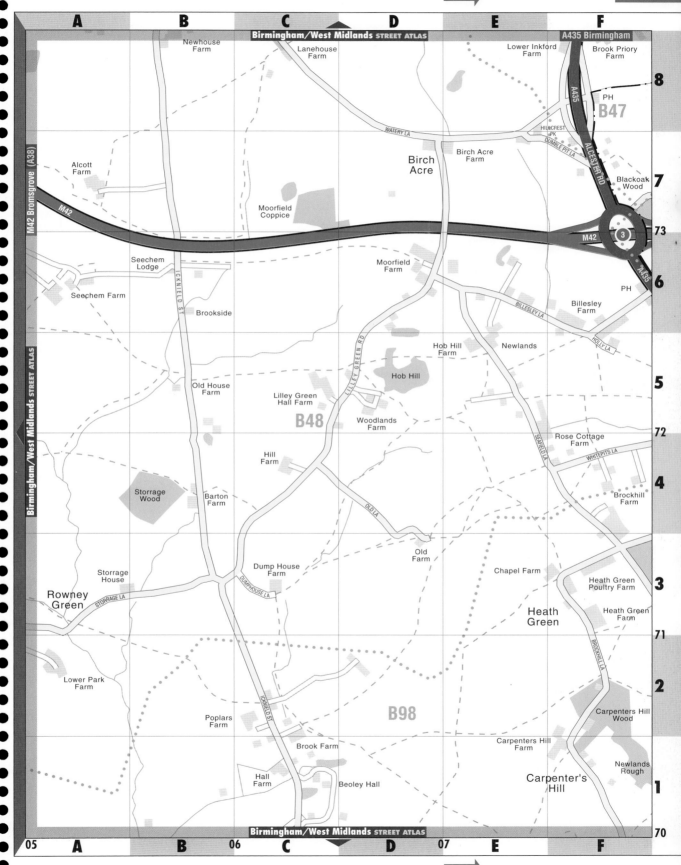

A435 Birmingham

A B C D E F

Newhouse Farm

Lanehouse Farm

Lower Inkford Farm

Brook Priory Farm

8

PH

B47

WATERY LA

Birch Acre Farm

Birch Acre

Blackoak Wood

7

Alcott Farm

M42 Bromsgrove (A38)

M42

Moorfield Coppice

HILLCREST PK

DUMBLE PIT LA

ALCESTER RD

A435

M42

3

73

A435

PH

6

Seechem Lodge

Moorfield Farm

Seechem Farm

Brookside

ICKNIELD ST

BILLESLEY LA

Billesley Farm

HOLLY LA

Moorfield Farm

LILLEY GREEN RD

Hob Hill Farm

Newlands

Old House Farm

Lilley Green Hall Farm

Hob Hill

B48

Woodlands Farm

Rose Cottage Farm

SEAFIELD LA

72

WHITEPITS LA

Hill Farm

Brockhill Farm

4

Storrage Wood

Barton Farm

OLD LA

Old Farm

Chapel Farm

Heath Green Poultry Farm

3

Storrage House

Dump House Farm

DUMPHOUSE LA

Heath Green

Heath Green Farm

Rowney Green

STORRAGE LA

71

BROCKHILL LA

Lower Park Farm

2

Carpenters Hill Wood

ICKNIELD ST

Poplars Farm

B98

Carpenters Hill Farm

Brook Farm

Newlands Rough

Hall Farm

Beoley Hall

Carpenter's Hill

1

70

85 69

River Cole

The Poplars

Clowes Wood

Terry's Pool

The Lakes

Terry's Green

Forshaw Heath

Pound Close Farm

Graves Coppice

OAKTREE FARM MOBILE HOMES PK

White House Farm

Springbrook Farm

Yew Tree Farm

Forshaw Park Farm

Glebe Farm

Checkley's Coppice

The Plantation

The Lyndons

Small Lane Farm

Earlswood Trad Est

Sewage Works

Spring Brook

Rugby Football Ground

Tyler's Grove

Windmill Naps

B48

Portway

B94

Ladbrookpark Coppice

Poolhead Farm

Pool House Farm

Holly Farm

Ladbrooke Hall Farm

Wood End

PH

Cottage Farm

Little Ladbrooke Farm

Ladbrooke Hall

CH

Lion Wood

PENN LA

Wood End

Hill Barn

Brockhill Wood

High Park Farm

Rushbrook Farm

Rushbrook

Gilbert's Green

Highpark Wood

Spring Brook

BROAD LA

B98

Branson's Cross

Aspley Heath

Park Farm

PH

Baylis Green

BEOLEY LA

BROAD LA

River Alne

Branson's Cross Farm

Pinkfield Wood

Aspley Farm

Alderhanger Wood

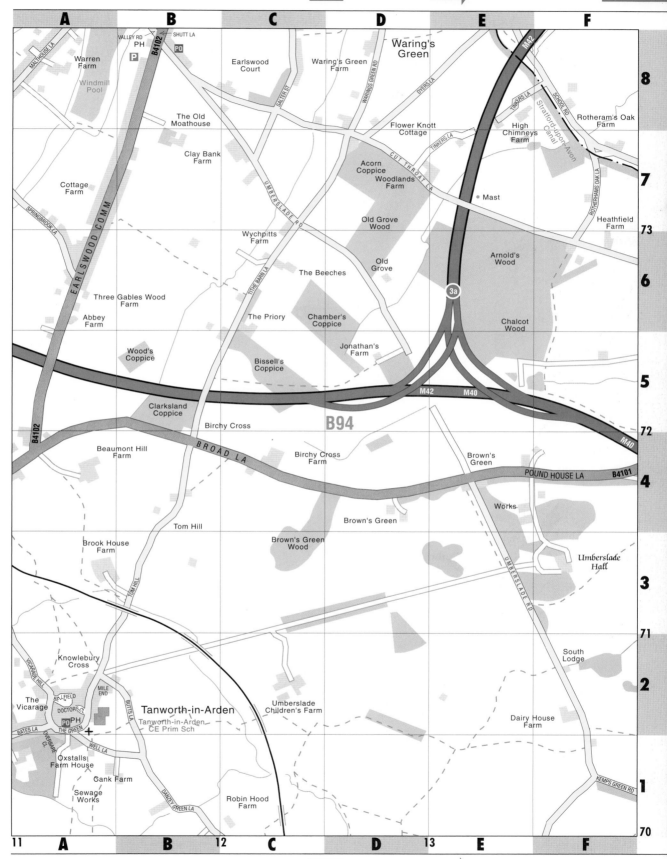

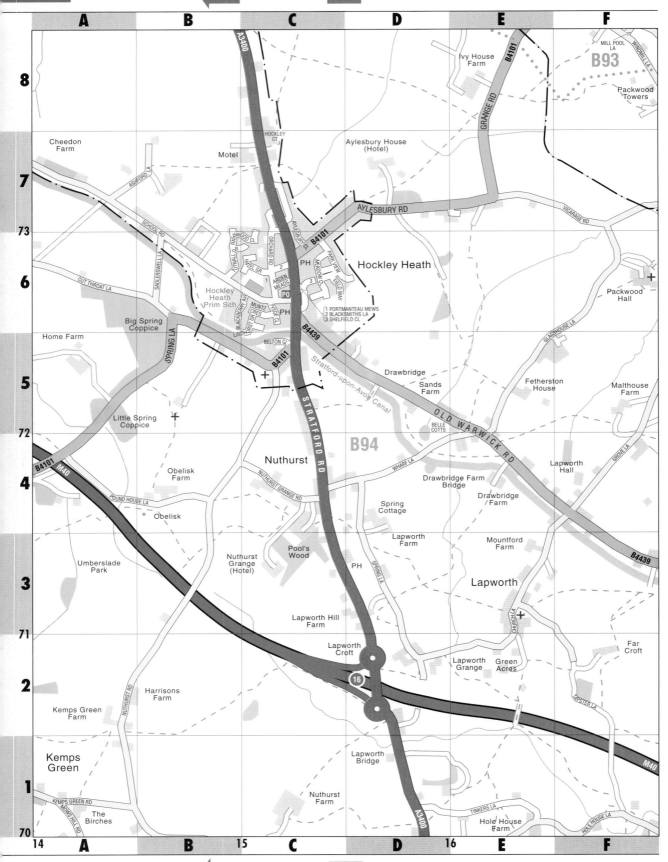

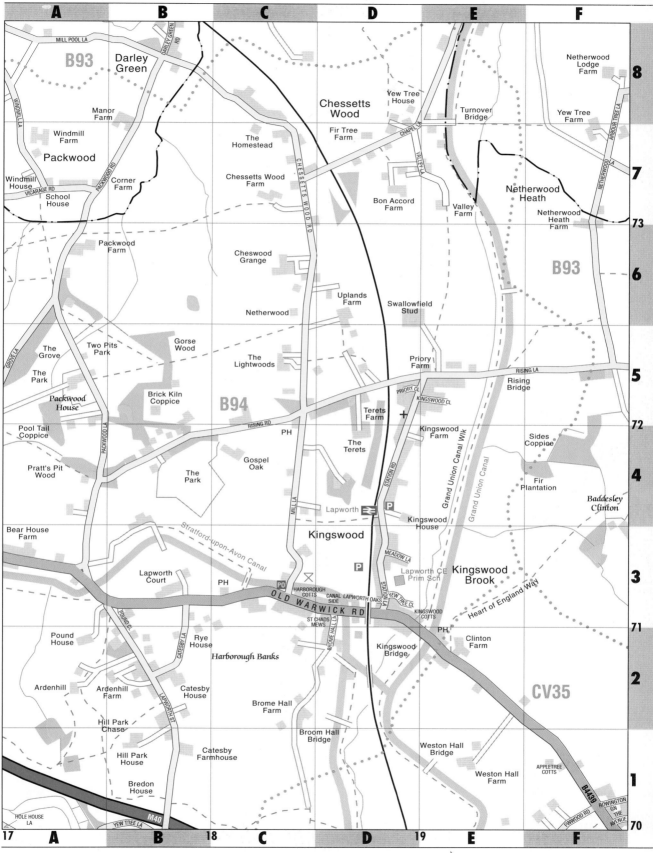

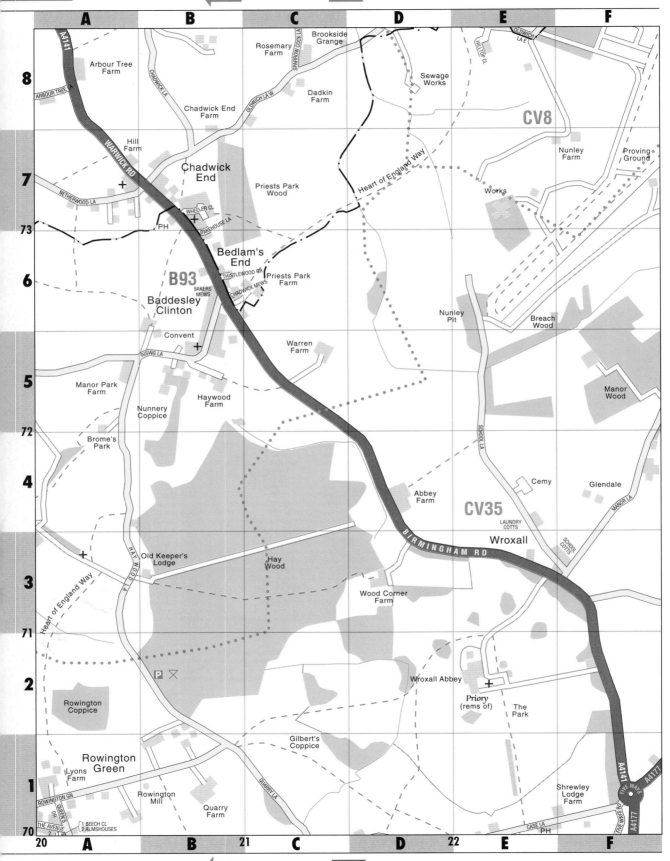

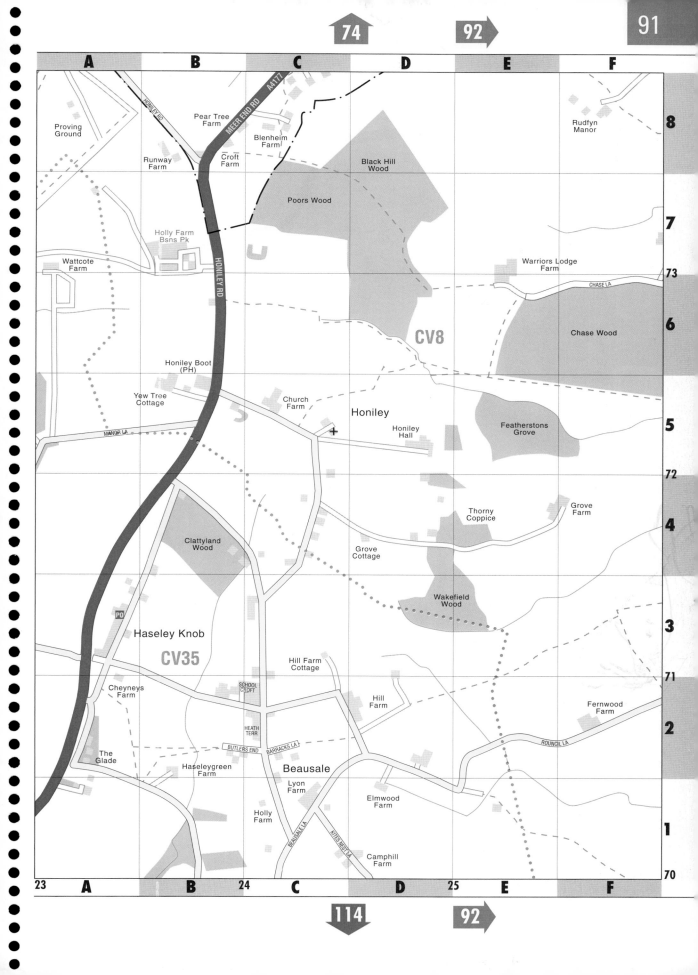

74
92
114
92

A B C D E F

8 7 73 6 5 72 4 3 71 2 1 70

Proving Ground

HONILEY RD

MEER END RD A4177

Pear Tree Farm

Blenheim Farm

Croft Farm

Runway Farm

Black Hill Wood

Rudfyn Manor

Poors Wood

Holly Farm Bsns Pk

Wattcote Farm

HONILEY RD

Warriors Lodge Farm

CHASE LA

CV8

Chase Wood

Honiley Boot (PH)

Yew Tree Cottage

Church Farm

Honiley

Honiley Hall

Featherstons Grove

MANOR LA

Thorny Coppice

Grove Farm

Clattyland Wood

Grove Cottage

Wakefield Wood

PO

Haseley Knob

CV35

Hill Farm Cottage

Cheyneys Farm

SCHOOL CROFT

Hill Farm

Fernwood Farm

ROUNCIL LA

HEATH TERR

BUTLERS END

BARRACKS LA

The Glade

Haseleygreen Farm

Beausale

Lyon Farm

Elmwood Farm

Holly Farm

BEAUSALE LA

KITES NEST LA

Camphill Farm

23 A B 24 C D 25 E F

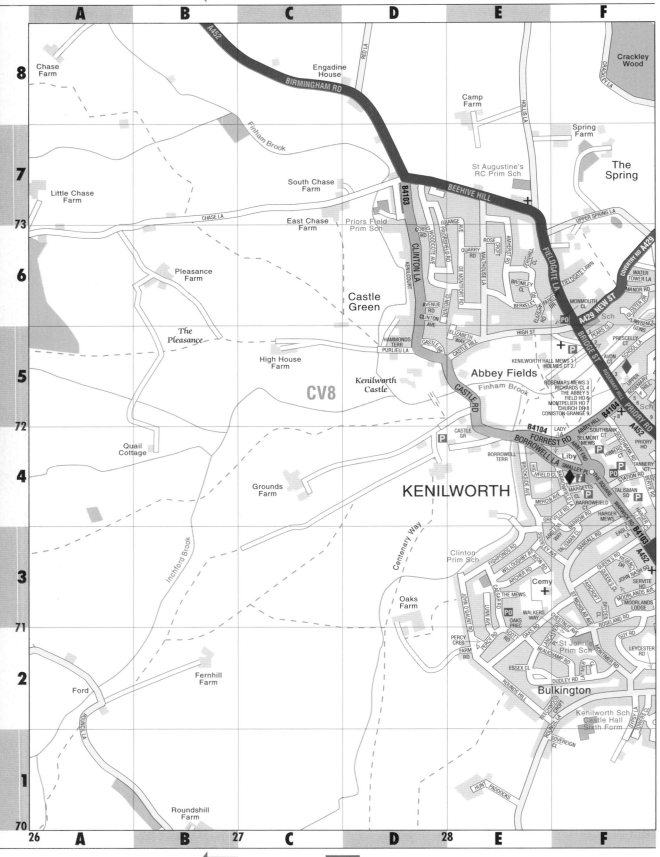

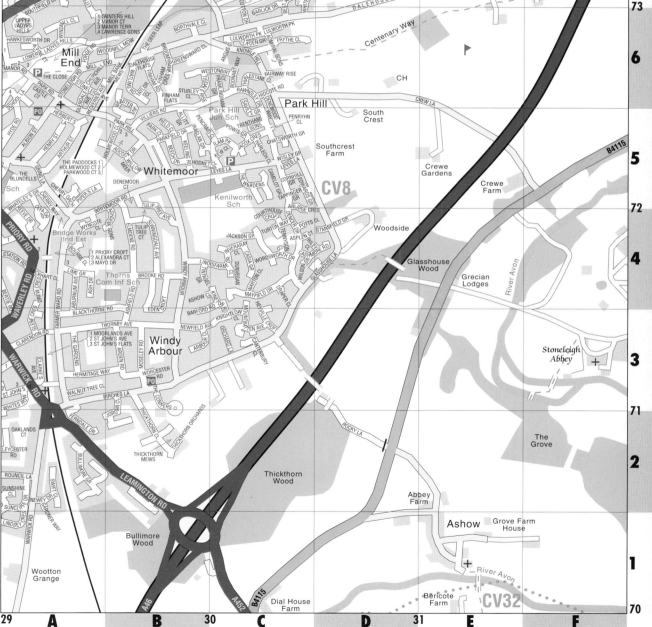

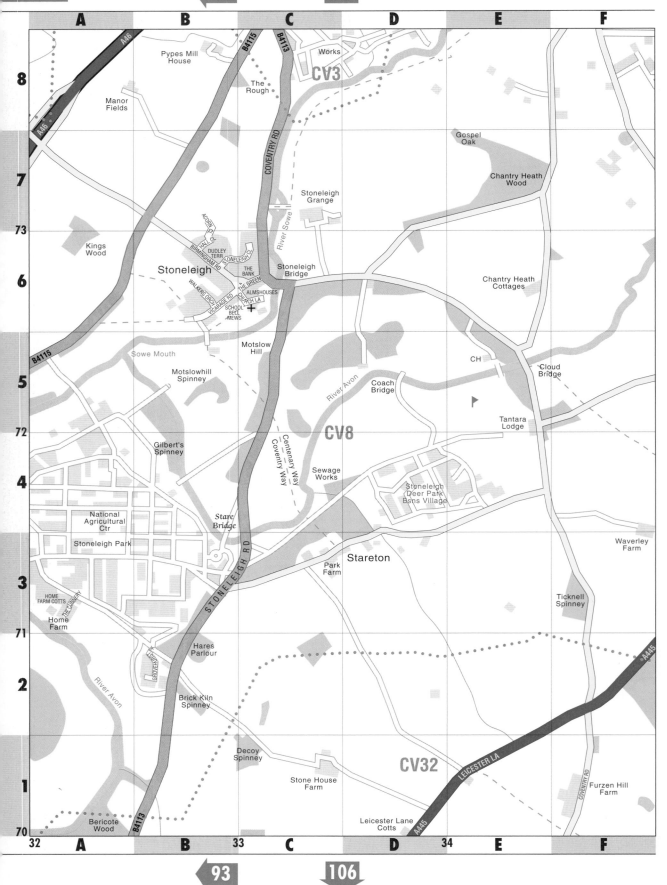

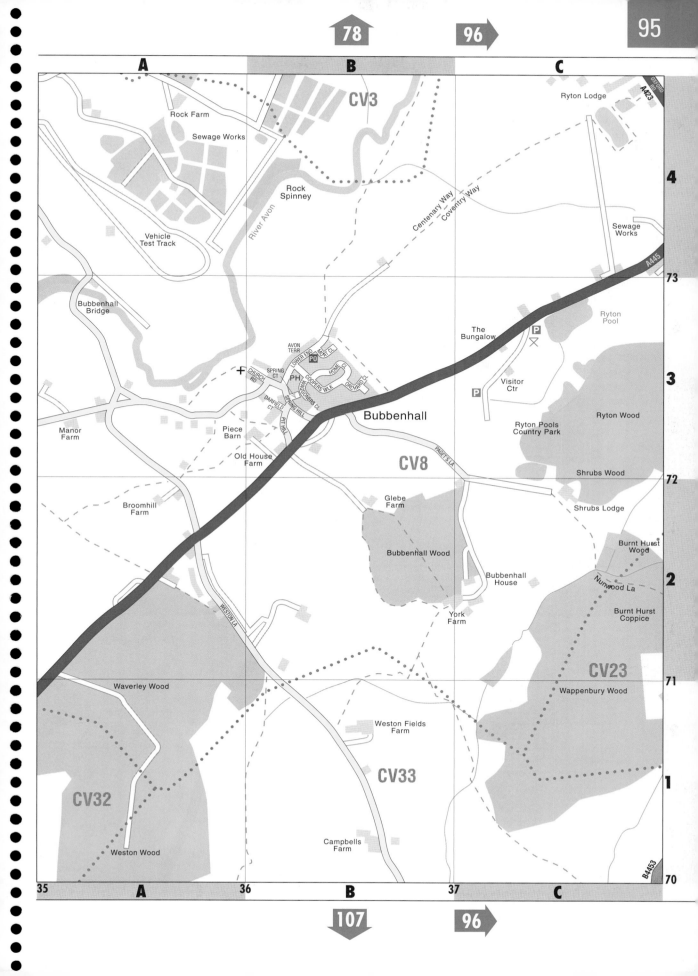

A
B
C

CV3

Rock Farm
Sewage Works

Rock Spinney

River Avon

Vehicle Test Track

4

Centenary Way
Coventry Way

Ryton Lodge

OXFORD

A423

Sewage Works

A445

73

Bubbenhall Bridge

Manor Farm

AVON TERR
LOWER END
MOAT CL
SPRING CT
PO
HOME CL
CHURCH RD
PH
COOPERS WLK
ORCHARD CL
WAGGONERS CL
DARFIELD CT
SPRING HILL
PIT HILL

Piece Barn

Old House Farm

Bubbenhall

The Bungalow

P

Visitor Ctr

P

Ryton Pool

Ryton Pools Country Park

Ryton Wood

3

CV8

PAGET'S LA

Shrubs Wood

72

Broomhill Farm

Glebe Farm

Bubbenhall Wood

Bubbenhall House

York Farm

Shrubs Lodge

Burnt Hurst Wood

Nunwood La

Burnt Hurst Coppice

2

WESTON LA

Waverley Wood

CV23

Wappenbury Wood

71

Weston Fields Farm

CV33

1

CV32

Weston Wood

Campbells Farm

B4453

70

35
A
36
B
37
C

95
79

95
115

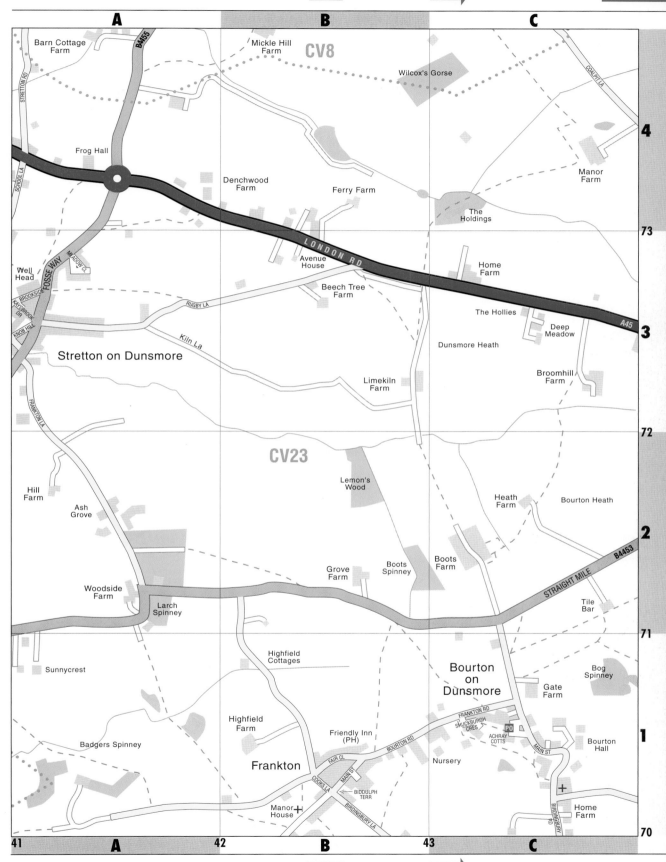

80
98

A   B   C

Barn Cottage Farm

STRETTON RD

B4455

Mickle Hill Farm

CV8

Wilcox's Gorse

COALPIT LA

4

Frog Hall

Denchwood Farm

Ferry Farm

Manor Farm

The Holdings

73

SCHOOL LA

Well Head

FOSSE WAY

MEADOW CL

LONDON RD

Avenue House

Home Farm

BROOKSIDE

RAYSBROOK DR

Beech Tree Farm

The Hollies

Deep Meadow

A45

3

KNOB HILL

Stretton on Dunsmore

RUGBY LA

Kiln La

Dunsmore Heath

Broomhill Farm

Limekiln Farm

FRANKTON LA

CV23

Lemon's Wood

Heath Farm

Bourton Heath

72

Hill Farm

Ash Grove

Grove Farm

Boots Spinney

Boots Farm

B4453

STRAIGHT MILE

2

Woodside Farm

Larch Spinney

Tile Bar

71

Sunnycrest

Highfield Cottages

Bourton on Dunsmore

Bog Spinney

Gate Farm

Highfield Farm

Friendly Inn (PH)

FRANKTON RD

SHUCKBURGH CRES

PO

Bourton Hall

BOURTON RD

ACHRAY COTTS

MAIN ST

1

Badgers Spinney

Frankton

FAIR CL

COOKS LA

MAIN ST

Nursery

BIDDULPH TERR

BIRDINGBURY LA

Manor House

BIRDINGBURY RD

Home Farm

70

41   A   42   B   43   C

115
98

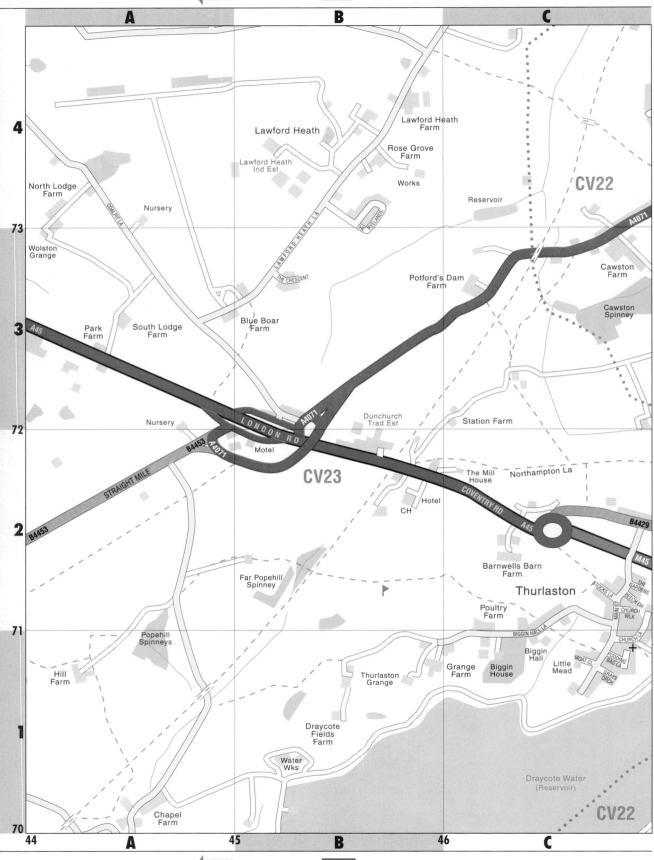

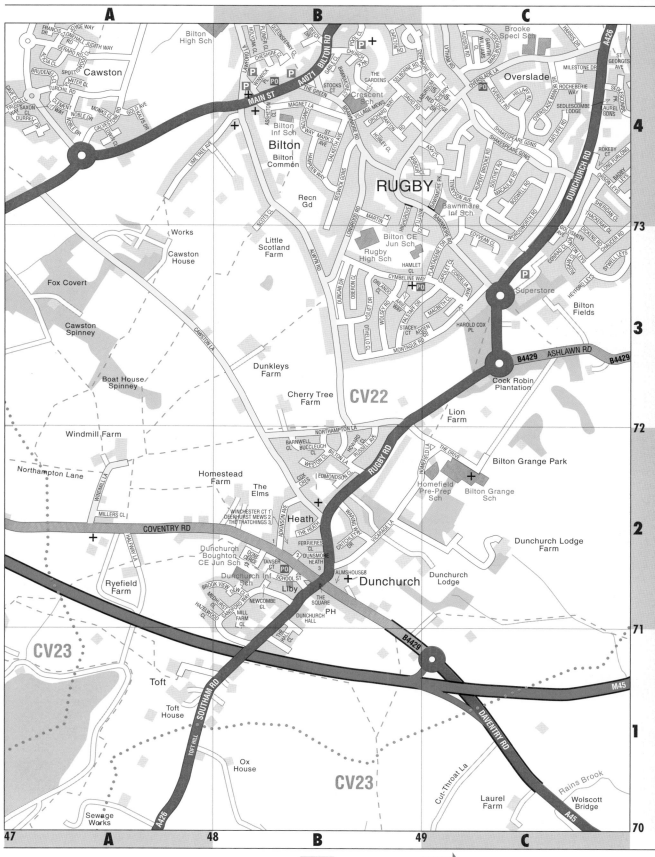

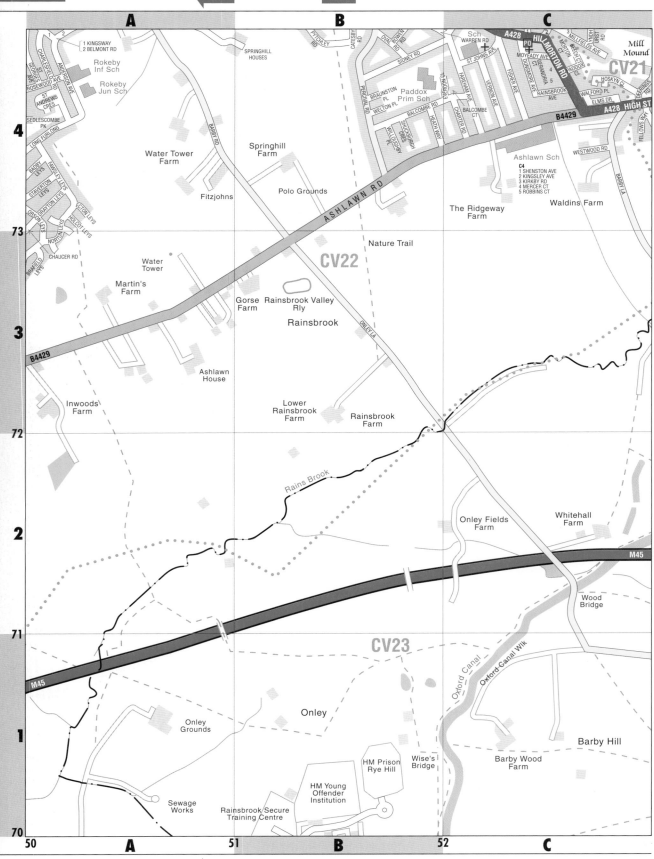

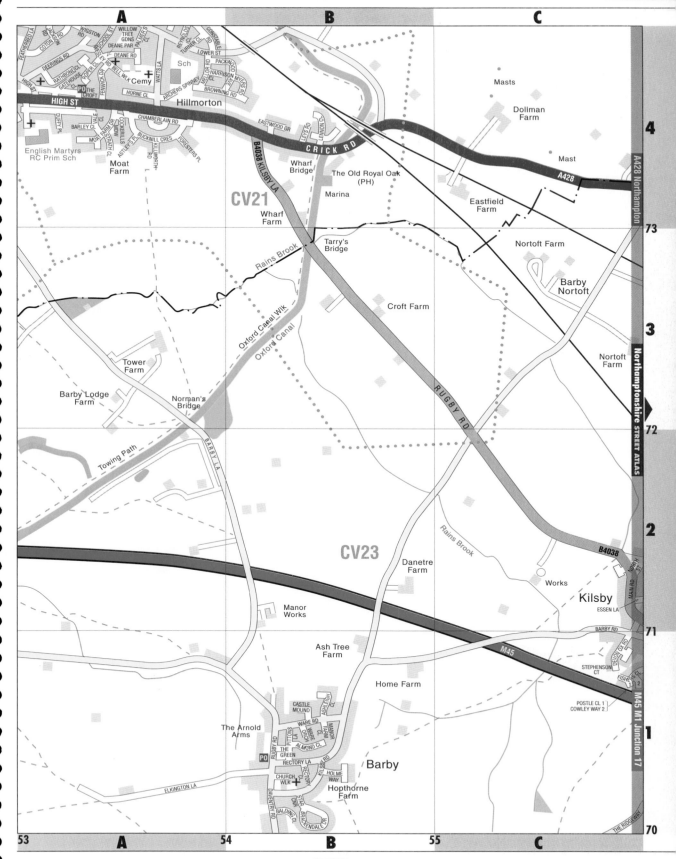

A

B

C

Featherbed La
Coton La
Wigston Rd
Hickson Rd
Willow Tree Gdns
Deane Par
Reynolds Cl
Turner Cl
Conduit St
Lower St
Packwood Cl
Myers Rd
Sch
Deerings Rd
Rathbone Cl
Gatehouse Cl
Melor Dr
Ryde Pl
Bell Wlk
Watts La
Archers Spinney
Harrison Rd
Deane Rd
High St
PO The Croft
Horne Cl
Chamberlain Rd
Browning Rd
Cemy
Hillmorton

HIGH ST

Duffy Pl
Barley Cl
Vale
Cockerills Rd
Bucknill Cres
Killworth
Foresters Pl

English Martyrs RC Prim Sch

Moat Farm

Masts

Dollman Farm

4

Mast

Eastwood Gr
Leys Rd
Lennon Cl

CRICK RD

A428

B4038 KILSBY LA

Wharf Bridge

The Old Royal Oak (PH)

Marina

Eastfield Farm

CV21

Wharf Farm

73

Rains Brook

Tarry's Bridge

Nortoft Farm

Barby Nortoft

Oxford Canal Wlk

Oxford Canal

Croft Farm

RUGBY RD

Nortoft Farm

3

Tower Farm

Barby Lodge Farm

Norman's Bridge

Northamptonshire STREET ATLAS

72

Towing Path

BARBY LA

2

Rains Brook

B4038

CV23

Danetre Farm

Works

Kilsby
ESSEN LA

Manor Works

MAIN RD
NORTH ST

Ash Tree Farm

BARBY RD

71

M45

Home Farm

STEPHENSON CT

DEVON OX RD

FISHERS CL

M45 M1 Junction 17

1

CASTLE MOUND

POSTLE CL 1
COWLEY WAY 2

The Arnold Arms

WARE RD
WARE ORCH
MANOR FARM
HIGH LEIGH CL
ALMOND CL

RUGBY RD
THE GREEN
PO
RECTORY LA
CHURCH WLK

KILSBY RD
HOLME WAY

Barby

ELKINGTON LA

DAVENTRY RD
STAR CNR
BALDING CL
BRAXENDALE CR

Hopthorne Farm

THE RIDGEWAY

70

53

A

54

B

55

C

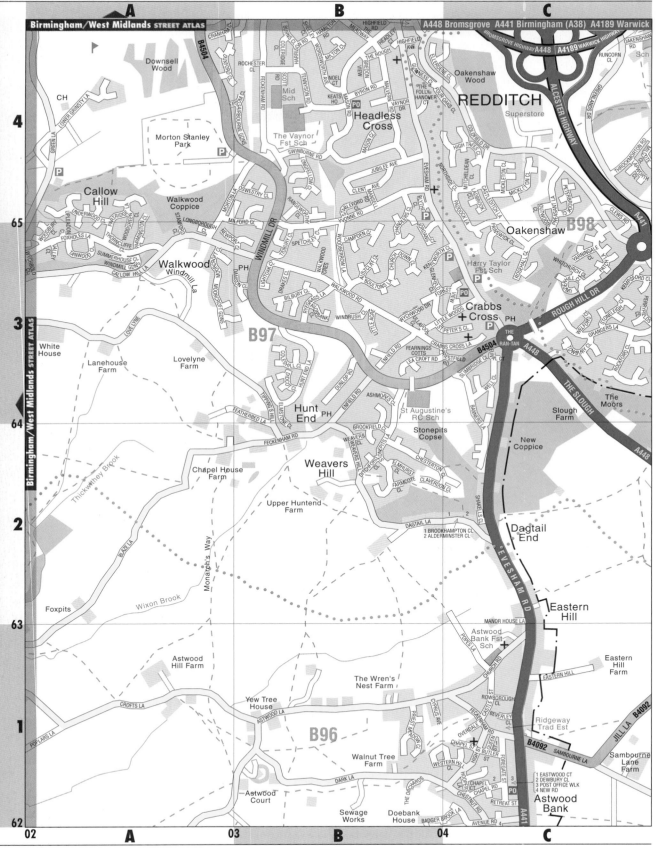

A448 Bromsgrove A441 Birmingham (A38) A4189 Warwick

REDDITCH

B98

B97

B96

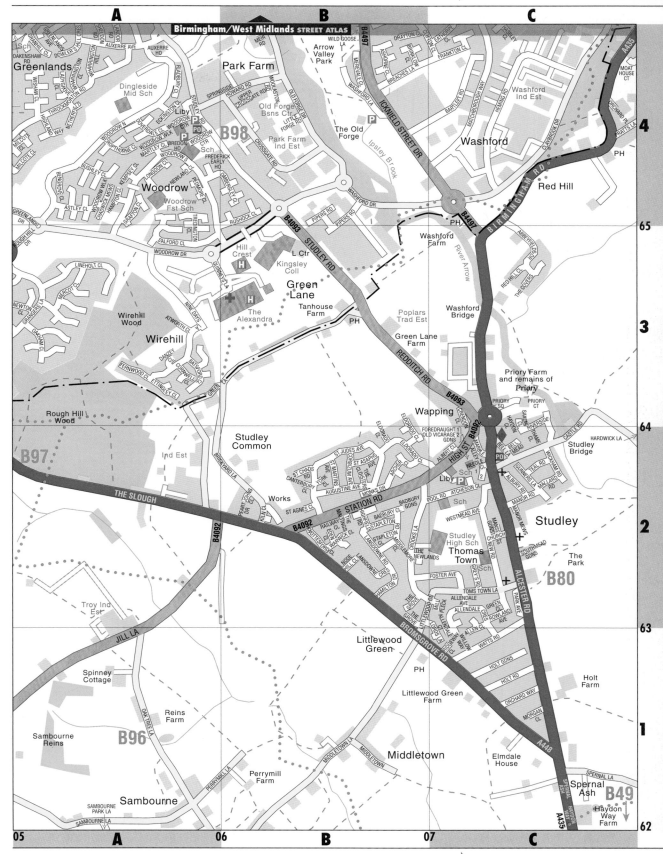

Birmingham/West Midlands STREET ATLAS

A B C D E F

8

Roundshill Farm
Abattoir
Camp Barn
Rouncil Farm
Woodcote Lodge
Little Woodcote

Bannerhill Farm

ROUNCIL LA

Goodrest Cottages

CV8

Leek Wootton

7

DANGER AREA

The Lunch
WALLER CL
WOODCOTE LA

Mast
Woodcote (County Police HQ)

Goodrest Farm

QUARRY CL
QUARRY FIELDS

69

Deer Park Farm

WOODCOTE DR
PH
HOME FARM
CHURCH LA
WARWICK RD

Stone Edge
THE ELMS

6

Terrace Hill Wood

Larch Covert

DANGER AREA

Centenary Way

Wootton Court

5

DANGER AREA

CH

68

Deer Park

Prospect Farm

CV35

Blacklow Hill

4

Wedgnock Old Park

Wedgnock Rifle Range

Gaveston's Cross

Middle Woodloes

3

Blackbrake Plantation

Woodloes Farm

Loes Farm

WOODLOES LA

67

Woodloes Park

DWARRIS WLK

CV34

2

WARWICK

WARWICK BY-PASS

1 WEALE GR
2 SHELDON GR

Nursery
A429

Wedgnock Park Farm

RIDGELEY CL
HUGHES CL
WISE GR
WELSH CL
GLEESON DR
MOORE CL
HATHAWAY DR
WADE GR
WEBB DR
LIBERTY CL
LIPSCOMB CL
KNOTT CT
CONGREVE CL
WOODLOES LA
Primrose Hill

CHANDERS RD
CROSS WLK
RAYNSFORD WLK
WARNER CL
CRANE CL
CORBISON CL
LOWES AVE N
GIFFARD WAY
BARRACK CL
LINCOLN CL
LYNTON CL
BERWICK CL
BEAUFELL CL
HINCKFORD AVE
INCHFORD AVE
WOODLOES AVE N
SUTHERLAND CL
CONRAD CL
YARDLEY CL
KIRBY AVE
COOKE CL
NICHOLSON CL
RICHARDSON CL
A429 COVENTRY RD

1

A4117 BIRMINGHAM RD
A6

WEDGNOCK LA
Wedgnock Ind Est

ROTHWELL RD
WELTON RD

Ind Est

DEANSWAY
HADLEY GR
HARMAR CL
STANTON WLK
LACELL CL
BOSWELL GR
LOWER CAPE
SMITH CL
GREENWAY
KETTLEWELL CL
AUSTWICK CL
BADEN CL
GISBURN CL
WALFORD RD
HALE AVE
BRESE AVE
NEVILLE
TOWNSEND CL
BURGES
A4177

A6

BROXELL CL
CAPE RD
LOWER CAPE
LOCK LA
LADBROKE PK
SOAR BANK

Woodloes Inf & Jun Schs
PO
WOODLOES AVE S
KINSLEY GR
MALHAM RD
THORNTON
LONGCLIFFE AVE
EDMONDSCOTE

Grand Union Canal
Grand Union Canal WLK
Grand Union Canal

Sch

26 A B 27 C D 28 E F

E1
1 NEWSHOLME CL
2 ADDINGHAM CL
3 WATSON CL
4 RYLSTONE WAY
5 KILDWICK WAY

F1
1 HETTON CL
2 BUCKDEN CL
3 LEYBURN CL
4 ARNCLIFFE WAY
5 HUDDISDON CL
6 PHILLIPPES RD

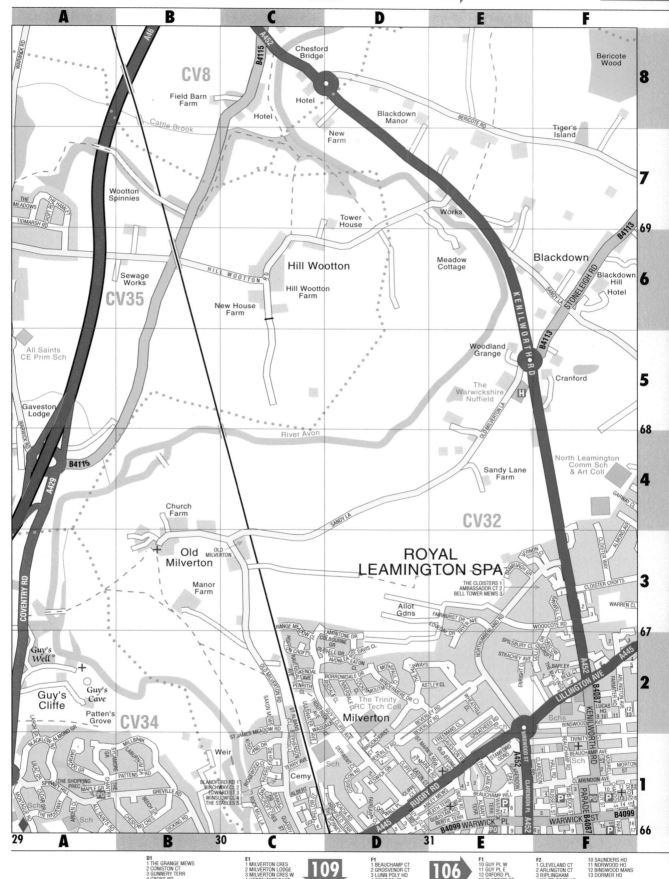

CV8

Chesford Bridge

Bericote Wood

Field Barn Farm

Hotel

Hotel

Blackdown Manor

Cattle Brook

New Farm

Tiger's Island

BERICOTE RD

Wootton Spinnies

Works

THE MEADOWS

THE HAMLET

THE CROFT RD

TIDMARSH RD

Tower House

Meadow Cottage

Blackdown

B4113

69

Blackdown Hill Hotel

HILL WOOTTON RD

Hill Wootton

STONELEIGH RD

Sewage Works

CV35

Hill Wootton Farm

SANDY LA

6

New House Farm

KENILWORTH RD

B4113

Woodland Grange

All Saints CE Prim Sch

Cranford

5

Gaveston Lodge

River Avon

OLD MILVERTON LA

The Warwickshire Nuffield

H

68

WARWICK RD

B4115

A429

Sandy Lane Farm

North Leamington Comm Sch & Art Coll

4

A46

Church Farm

SANDY LA

CV32

GARWAY CL

Old Milverton

OLD MILVERTON

ROYAL LEAMINGTON SPA

ALMOND AVE

CLOISTER WAY

3

Manor Farm

VERNON

Allot Gdns

THE CLOISTERS 1
AMBASSADOR CT 2
BELL TOWER MEWS 3

CLOISTER CROFTS

WARREN CL

COVENTRY RD

OLD MILVERTON RD

RANGE MEADOW CL

FAIRHURST DR

WOODCOTE RD

67

Guy's Well

LEAMINGTON DR
COLBOURNE GR

HOPTON CROFTS

OVERELL GR

S DAVIS CL

NORTHUMBERLAND RD

SPILSBURY CL

STRACHEY AVE

GLASGOW

A445

2

Guy's Cave

AVONLEA
EATON
CL

BEVERLEY RD

COLLEGE ST

THE MALLINS

PARMITER RD

LUCAS CT

Guy's Cliffe

Patten's Grove

CV34

KENDAL AVE

BORROWDALE DR

PENRITH CL

ASTLEY CL

WHEATHILL

BARLEY CT

BELL CT

BINSWOOD

Schs

B4087

SCHS

SCH

The Trinity RC Tech Coll

Milverton

BINSWOOD ST

TRINITY

Sch

1

THE SHOPPING PREC

MAPLE GR

ST JAMES MEADOW RD

Weir

Cemy

Sch

BEVERLEY RD

OLD STATION

STAMFORD GDNS

CLARENDON RD

HALL RD

MORETON

CLARENDON AVE

B4099

Sch

A445

RUGBY RD

A452

CLARENDON PL

WARWICK RD

A452

PARADE EAST

B4099

BLANDFORD RD 1
BIRCHWAY CL 2
EDWARD ST 3
WINSLOW CL 4
THE STABLES 5

WARWICK PL

B4087

P

P

105 94

A B C D E F

8
7
69
6
5
68
4
3
67
2
1
66

B4113

STONELEIGH RD

B4113

Bericote Fields Farm

LEICESTER LA

Cubbington Heath Farm

A445

COVENTRY RD

North Cubbington Wood

Tanner's Barn

Oakdene

WESTHILL RD

West Hill

West Hill Farm

B4453

COTTON MILL SPINNEY THORN STILE CL

WILLOW SHEETS MDW

THREE CORNERED CL

Humber Farm

Cubbington

RUGBY RD

WINDMILL CROFT

BODDINGTON RD

CHURCH LA

BRACKLEY

PRIORY RD

PH

CHURCH ST

CHURCH AUSTEN CT

STIRLING AVE

ROXBURGH CROFT

BALMORAL WAY

KENILWORTH RD

PO

KELVIN RD

BEAUFORT AVE

GIRVAN GR

DUNBLANE DR

WEST VIEW RD

WINDMILL HILL

STONEHOUSE DR

LEDBROOK RD

GRANLEIGH CT

CHURCH LA TERR

HILL CREST

HIGH ST

KINGHTLEY CL

NEW ST

Cubbington CE Prim Sch

SANDY LA

Schs

ST ANDREW'S RD

HIGH VIEW RD

SOUTH VIEW RD

Our Lady & St Teresa's RC Prim Sch

QUEEN ST

NORTH ST

PO

PRINCE RD

CROSS LA

AXE GRANGE

MILL LA

BOWERS CROFT

MONTROSE AVE

LANSDALE AVE

CRAWFORD CL

CHAMBERLAIN CL

BROOKFIELD RD

CV32

ALDWICK CL

CEDAR CL

MELTON RD

KEITH RD

HIGHLAND RD

KINROSS RD

LONSDALE RD

AVONDALE RD

Hill Farm House

Works

New Manor Farm

OFFCHURCH RD

PARK RD

BELMONT CT

ELM BANK CL

LIME AVE

MORLEY CL

CUBBINGTON RD

RIDGWAY RD

OXRIDGE RD

LEIGHTON CL

DOWNING RD

PARK AVE

CONISTON CT

MEADOW DR

EPPING WAY

DELAMERE WAY

Glebe Farm

ARBURY CT

SOUTHFIELDS

LINGTON CL

WICKHAM CT

FARM RD

MANOR RD

CROWN WAY

OLD SCHOOL MEWS

NEWNHAM RD

WALLSGROVE CL

BENTLEY RD

KELMPTON CL

SCOTT RD

AINTREE CL

WYE CL

SEVERN RD

CHESTNUT RISE

CUMBERLAND CRES

LANGCROFT CL

LILLINGTON RD

CHURCH LA

PINE CT

THE GREENWAY

PO

GRANGE RD

POUND LA

VICARAGE RD

INGLEWOOD

BORDESLEY CL

Lillington

Liby

Schs

CHARNWOOD DR

FELL GR

VALLEY RD

WICKHILL RD

NEW LAND RD

BARNARD CL

CRES

EDEN CT

Tanner's Farm

WARREN CL

WREXHAM CT

B4453

Sch

DENVILLE RD

GRANBOROUGH

HEEMSTEDE LA

LOXLEY WAY

MASON AVE

SIDBURY RD

CLASE CL

NEW LAND RD

A445

PAYNE CT

KEIR CL

CROMER RD

THURSTON CL

CRANMORE RD

WELLINGTON RD

ELDON CT

COMPTON

ROYAL

OAK TREE CL

OAK TREE CT

NAPTON DR

TAYLOR AVE

HADDON RD EAST

DENE

BRIAR CL

BUCKLEY RD

LEAMINGTON SPA

LILLINGTON RD

WATHEN RD

CAMPION RD

MILLBURY RD

WHITNASH RD

GRESHAM AVE

RAWLINSON RD

BLACK LA

Mast

Works

Ford Cotts

WELSH RD

Ford Farm

CV33

The Runghills

WALLER ST

GRANVILLE RD

PLEASANT WAY

HURLEY CL

KILN LA

FEWOOD RD

VILLIERS ST

SWAN'S GATE

LEICESTER ST

1 GRESHAM PL
2 CHESTNUT SQ
3 MARSTON CL

Campion Hills

Mast

River Leam

White House

HILL ST

NORTH VIL

NORFOLK ST

SUFFOLK

LEICESTER ST

AQUA HO

HAMPTON GR

PRINCES ST

GREENWOOD CT

St Paul's CE Prim Sch

Redhouse Farm

Offchurch Bury

CLARENDON

LANSDOWNE RD

THOMAS ST

PO

SWAN ST

QUEEN ST

DUKE

KING ST

VINCENT ST

HOLLY ST

UPPER HOLLY WLK

THE BRIDGE

FERNHILL DR

CH

CROSS ST

HOLLY WLK

B4099

TALBOT CT

CAMBRIDGE GDNS

32 A 33 B C 34 D E F

105 110

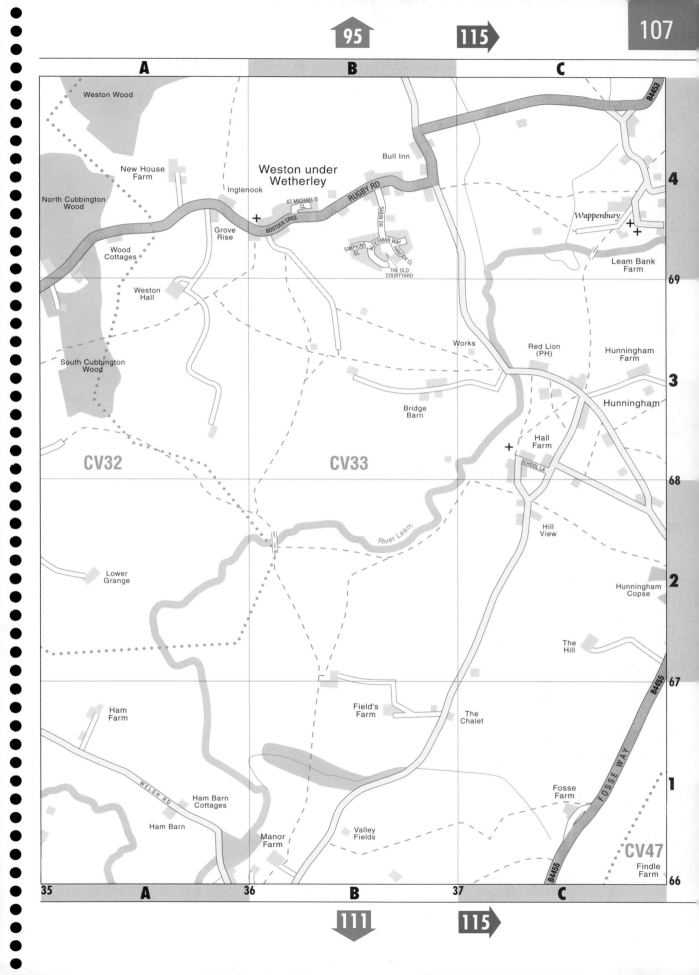

A

B

C

Weston Wood

New House Farm

North Cubbington Wood

Inglenook

Weston under Wetherley

Bull Inn

ST MICHAEL'S CL

RUGBY RD

BOSTOCK CRES

Grove Rise

SABIN DR

Wappenbury

SIMPKINS CL

ALDERMAN WAY

HANCOX CL

THE OLD COURTYARD

Leam Bank Farm

Wood Cottages

Weston Hall

69

4

South Cubbington Wood

Works

Red Lion (PH)

Hunningham Farm

CV32

CV33

Bridge Barn

Hunningham

3

Hall Farm

SCHOOL LA

River Leam

68

Hill View

Lower Grange

Hunningham Copse

2

The Hill

Field's Farm

The Chalet

67

Ham Farm

Fosse Farm

1

WELSH RD

Ham Barn Cottages

Ham Barn

Manor Farm

Valley Fields

FOSSE WAY

B4455

CV47

Findle Farm

66

B4453

B4455

35

A

36

B

37

C

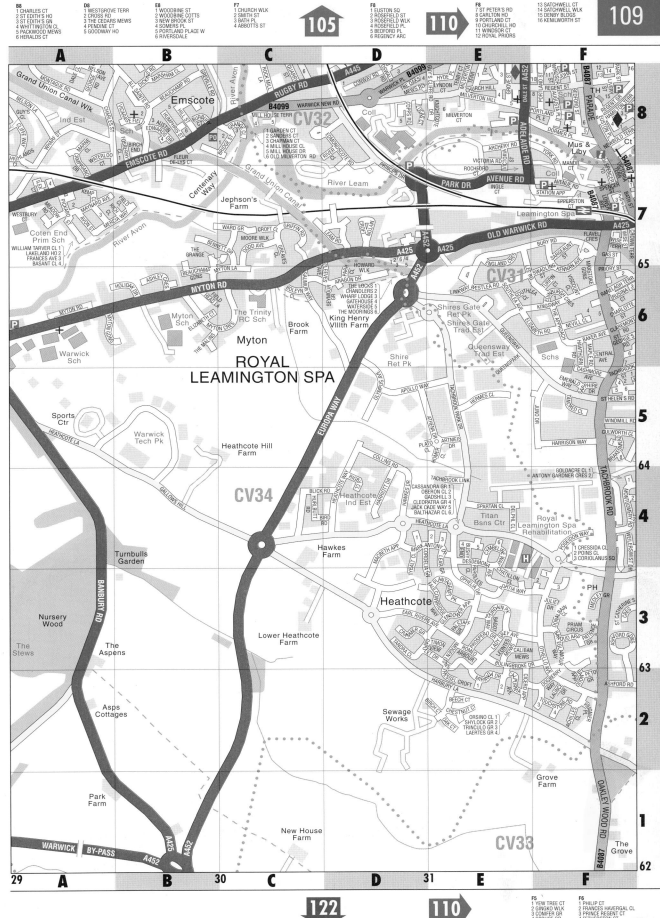

B8
1 CHARLES CT
2 ST EDITH'S HO
3 ST EDITH'S GN
4 WHITTINGTON CL
5 PACKWOOD MEWS
6 HERALDS CT

D8
1 WESTGROVE TERR
2 CROSS RD
3 THE CEDARS MEWS
4 PENDINE CT
5 GOODWAY HO

E8
1 WOODBINE ST
2 WOODBINE COTTS
3 NEW BROOK ST
4 SOMERS PL
5 PORTLAND PLACE W
6 RIVERSDALE

F7
1 CHURCH WLK
2 SMITH ST
3 BATH PL
4 ABBOTTS ST

F8
1 EUSTON SQ
2 ROSEFIELD ST
3 ROSEFIELD WLK
4 ROSEFIELD PL
5 BEDFORD PL
6 REGENCY ARC

F8
7 ST PETER'S RD
8 CARLTON HO
9 PORTLAND CT
10 CHURCHILL HO
11 WINDSOR CT
12 ROYAL PRIORS

13 SATCHWELL CT
14 SATCHWELL WLK
15 DENBY BLDGS
16 KENILWORTH ST

105
110

Emscote
CV32
Warwick New Rd
B4099
Coll
Grand Union Canal Wlk
Grand Union Canal
River Leam
River Avon
Jephson's Farm
Centenary Way
Coten End Prim Sch
WILLIAM TARVER CL 1
LAKELAND HO 2
FRANCES AVE 3
BASANT CL 4
Leamington Spa
Old Warwick Rd
CV31
Myton Rd
The Grange
The Trinity RC Sch
Myton Sch
Brook Farm
King Henry VIIIth Farm
Myton
ROYAL LEAMINGTON SPA
Shires Gate Ret Pk
Shires Gate Trad Est
Queensway Trad Est
Warwick Sch
Sports Ctr
Warwick Tech Pk
Heathcote Hill Farm
CV34
Shire Ret Pk
Heathcote Ind Est
CASSANDRA GR 1
OBERON CL 2
GADSHILL 3
CLEOPATRA GR 4
JACK CADE WAY 5
BALTHAZAR CL 6
Titan Bsns Ctr
Royal Leamington Spa Rehabilitation
1 CRESSIDA CL
2 POINS CL
3 CORIOLANUS SQ
GOLDACRE CL 1
ANTONY GARDNER CRES 2
Hawkes Farm
Heathcote
Turnbulls Garden
Nursery Wood
The Stews
The Aspens
Lower Heathcote Farm
Asps Cottages
Park Farm
New House Farm
Sewage Works
ORSINO CL 1
SHYLOCK GR 2
TRINCULO GR 3
LAERTES GR 4
Grove Farm
The Grove
CV33
BANBURY RD
WARWICK BY-PASS
A425
A452

F5
1 YEW TREE CT
2 GINGKO WLK
3 CONIFER GR
4 SPRUCE GR
5 SILVER BIRCH GR
6 WYCH ELM GR
7 BONNIKSEN CL
8 LOCKHEED CL

F6
1 PHILIP CT
2 FRANCES HAVERGAL CL
3 PRINCE REGENT CT
4 FETHERSTON CT
5 TATCHBROOK CT
6 CHARLES GARDNER RD
7 MARKET CNR

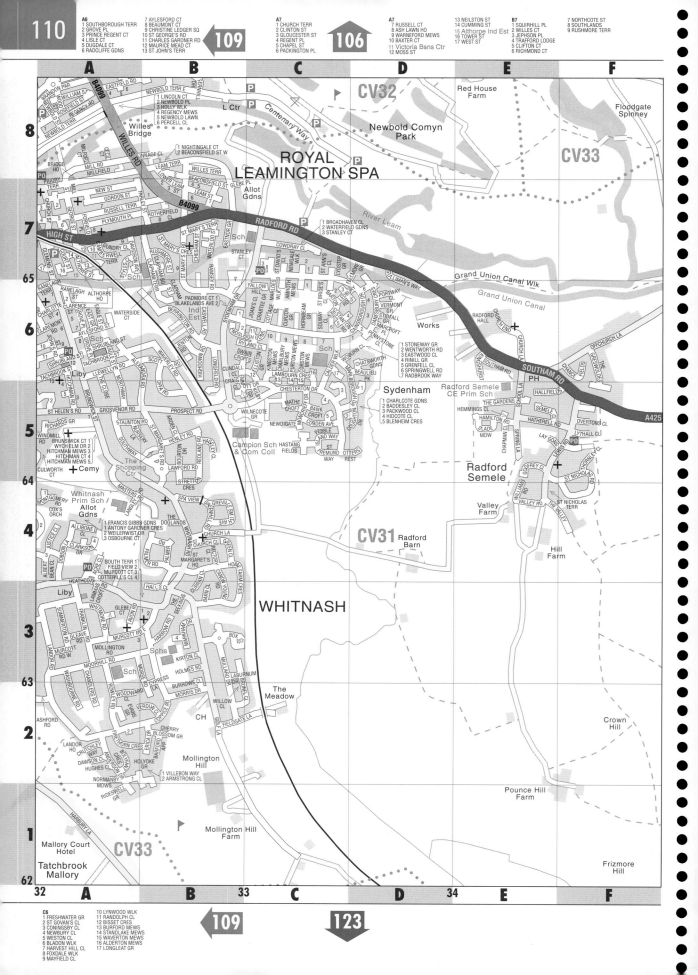

109
106

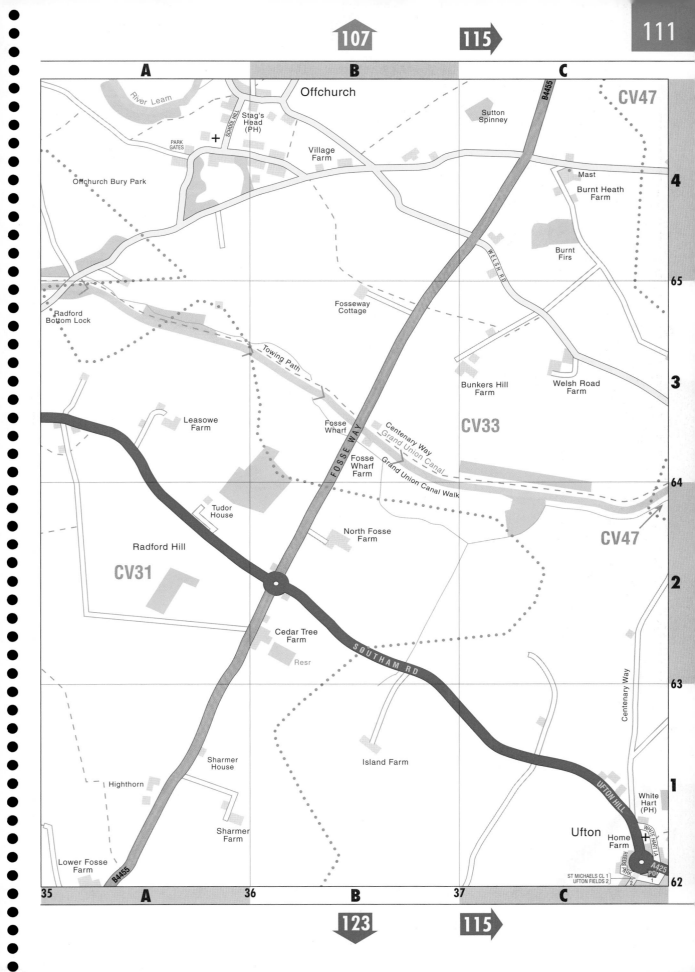

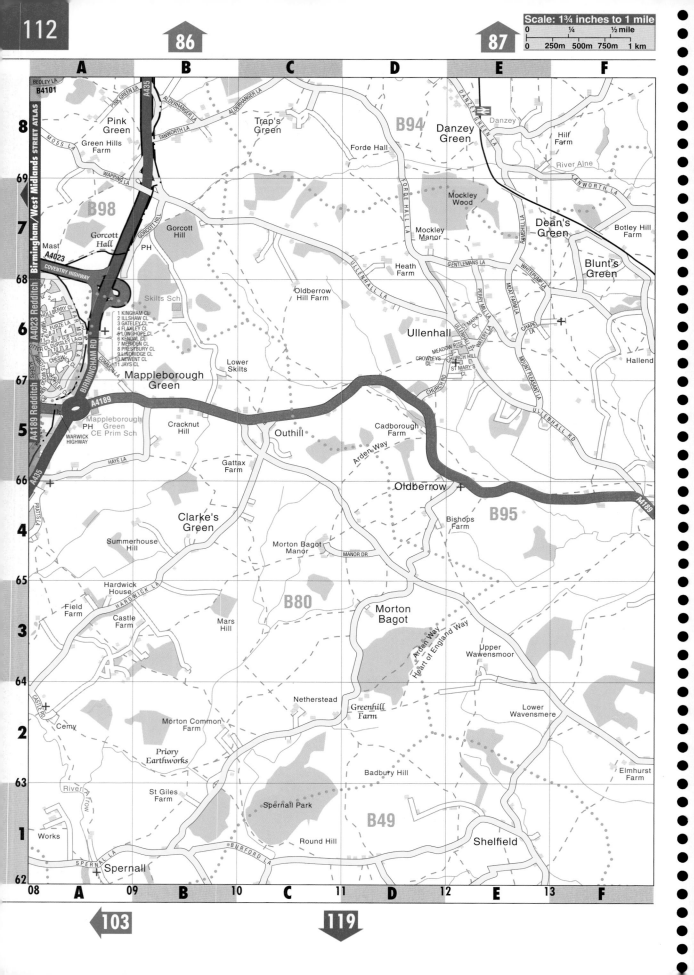

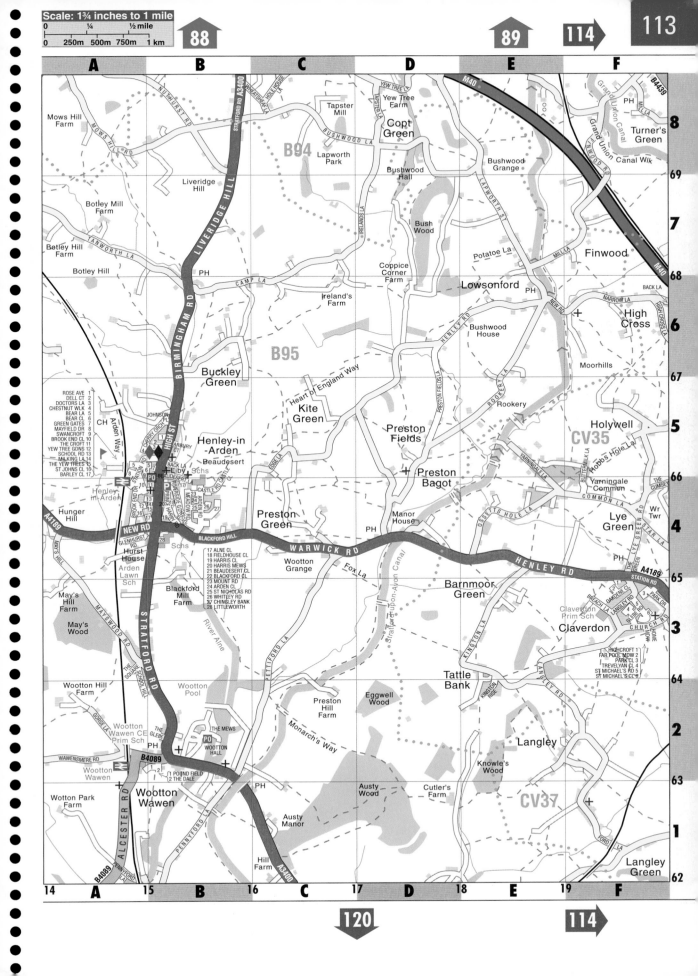

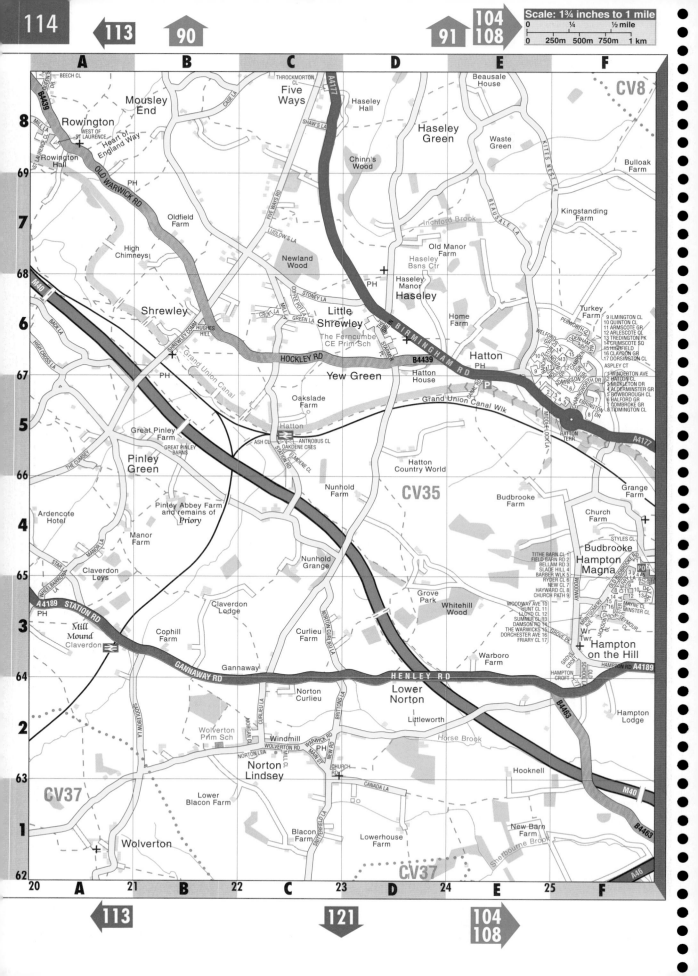

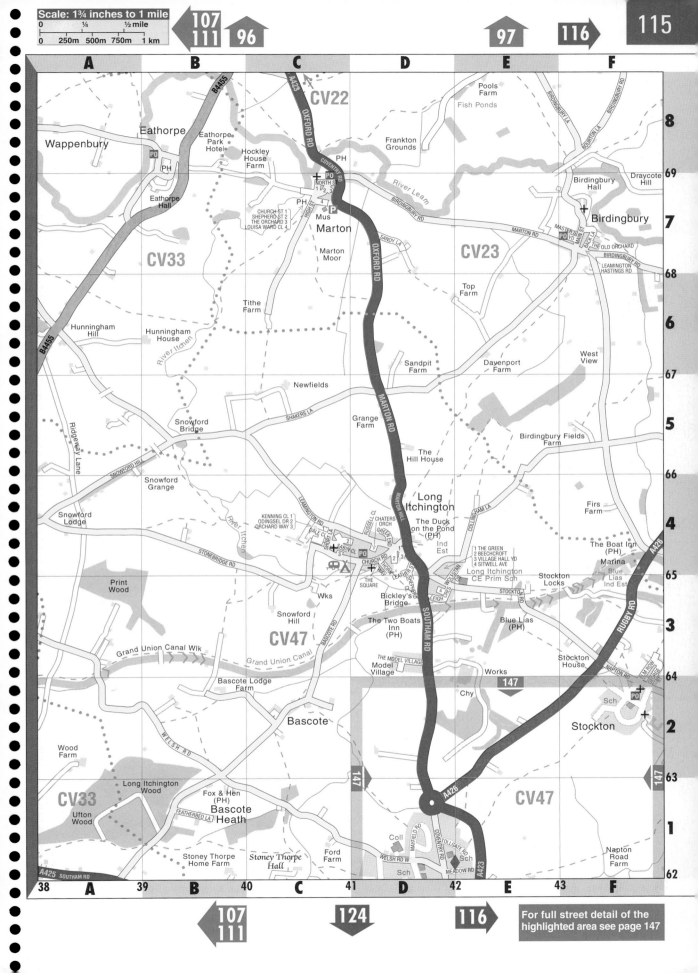

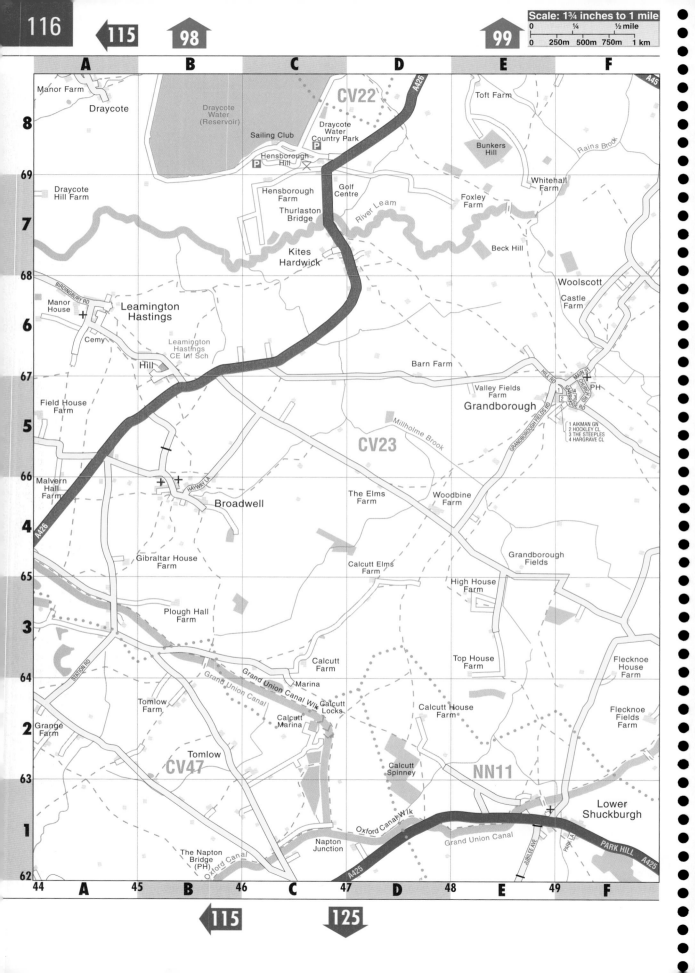

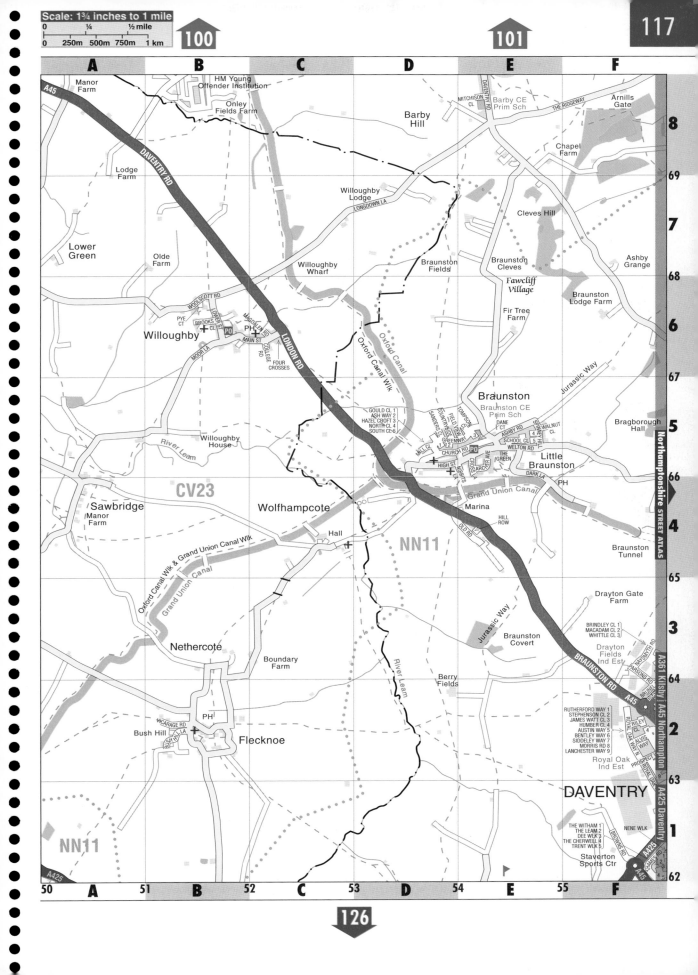

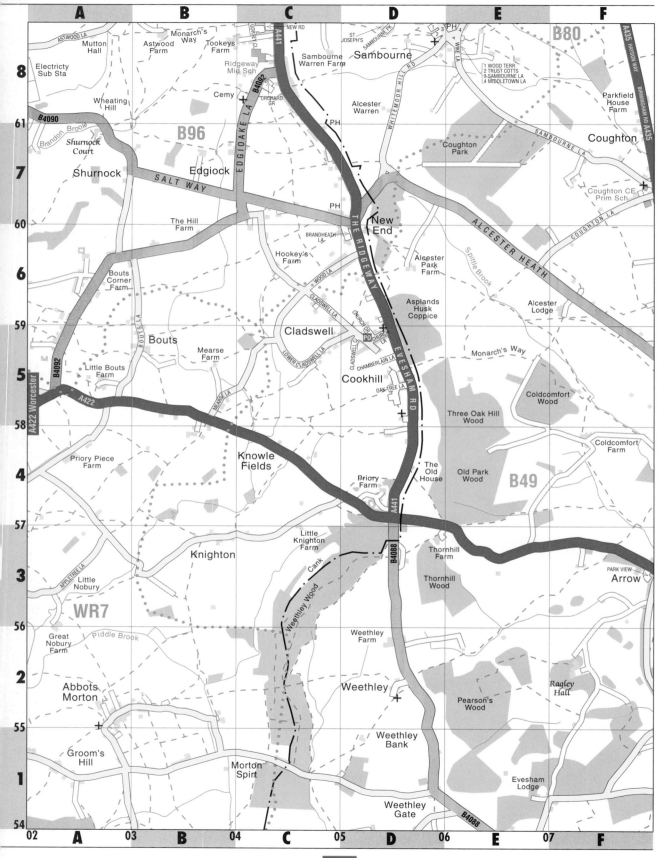
118

102

103

Scale: 1¾ inches to 1 mile
0   ¼   ½ mile
0   250m 500m 750m 1 km

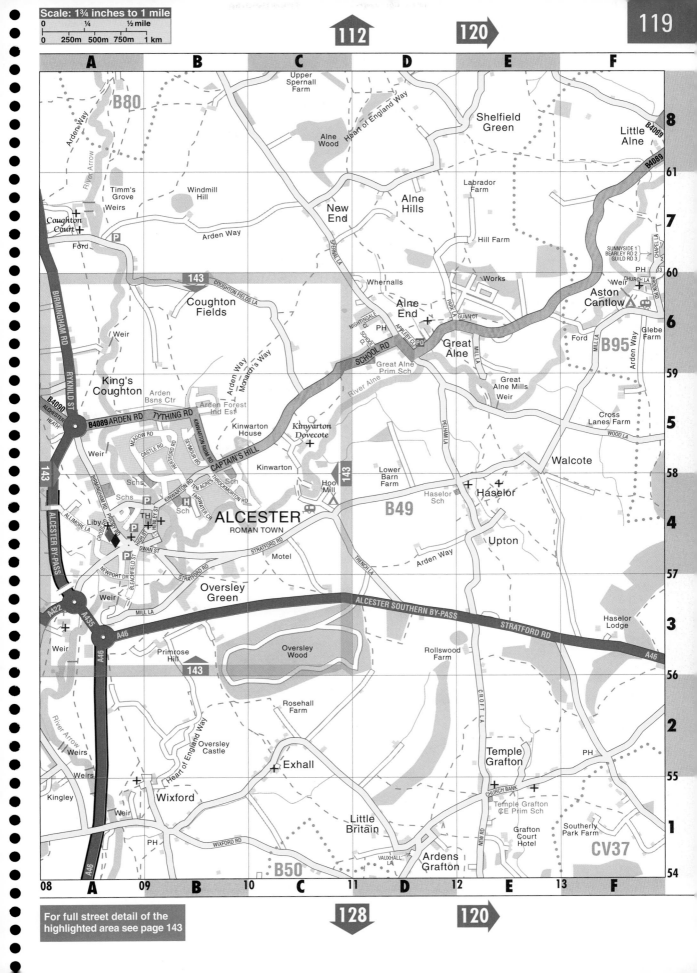

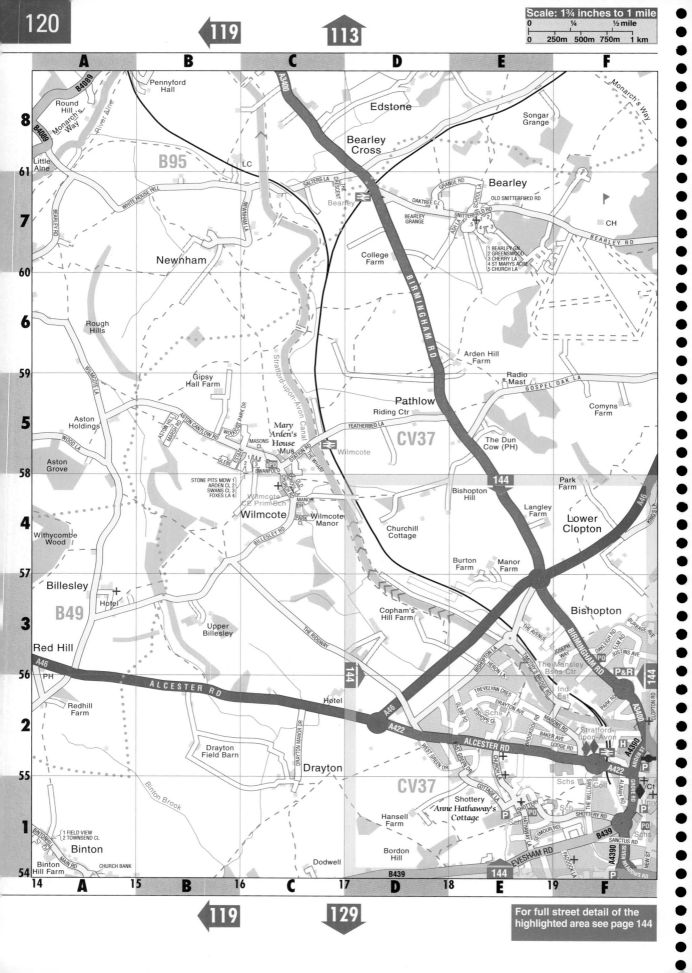

119

113

Scale: 1¾ inches to 1 mile

0 ¼ ½ mile
0 250m 500m 750m 1 km

A B C D E F

B4089
Round Hill
Monarch's Way
River Alne
Pennyford Hall
Edstone
Songar Grange
Monarch's Way

8

Little Alne
B95
LC
Bearley Cross
Bearley
Grange Rd
Old Snitterfield Rd
Oaktree C.
61

Bearley Rd
Bearley Grange
Snitterfield Rd
Ash La
School La
CH

7
Bearley Rd
Newnham
White House Hill
Newnham La
Salters La
The Crescent
Bearley
College Farm
1 BEARLEY GN
2 GREENSWOOD
3 CHERRY LA
4 ST MARYS ACRE
5 CHURCH LA

60

6
Rough Hills
Arden Hill Farm
Radio Mast
Gospel Oak La

Birmingham Rd
59
Wilmcote La
Gipsy Hall Farm
Stratford-upon-Avon Canal
Pathlow
Riding Ctr
Featherbed La
Comyns Farm

5
Aston Holdings
Wood La
Aston Cantlow Rd
Woodcot Park Dr
Aston Hill
Marsh Rd
Masons Cl
Mary Arden's House Mus
Station Rd
The Wharf
Wilmcote
CV37
The Dun Cow (PH)
Park Farm

58
Aston Grove
Glebe Estate
1 L4
2 3
3
Swanfold
STONE PITS MDW 1
ARDEN CL 2
SWANS CL 3
FOXES LA 4
Church Rd
Old School La
Manor Dr
Bishopton Hill
Langley Farm
144
A46

4
Withycombe Wood
Wilmcote CE Prim Sch
Wilmcote
Park Cl
Manor Cl
Wilmcote Manor
Churchill Cottage
Burton Farm
Manor Farm
Lower Clopton
King's La

57
Billesley
Billesley Rd
Copham's Hill Farm
Bishopton
Burbage Ave
Elm Rd

3
B49
Hotel
Upper Billesley
The Ridgway
The Avenue
Birmingham Rd
Oakleigh Rd
Justins Ave

Red Hill
A46
Joseph Way
Heron La
Timothy's Bridge Rd
The Mansley Bsns Ctr
Ind Est
P&R
144

56
PH
Alcester Rd
Hotel
Bishopton La
Trevelyan Cres
Drayton Ave
Glebe Rd
Bishops Cl
Masons Rd
Park Rd
A3400
Clopton Rd

2
Redhill Farm
Drayton Manor Dr
A422
A46
West Green Dr
East Green Dr
Brookside Rd
Baker Ave
Lodge Rd
Schs
Stratford-upon-Avon
A422
Arden St
H
Grove Rd

Drayton Field Barn
Alcester Rd
Church La
Cottage La
Schs
The Willows
Albany Rd
Ct
Univ

55
Binton Brook
Drayton
CV37
Hansell Farm
Shottery
Anne Hathaway's Cottage
Hathaway La
Seymour Rd
Shottery Rd
PO
Schs

1
Binton Hill
Main Rd
1 FIELD VIEW
2 TOWNSEND CL
Binton
Church Bank
Dodwell
Bordon Hill
Evesham Rd
A4390
Sanctus Rd
Pagock La
Seven Meadow's Rd
New St
PO
Schs

54
Binton Hill Farm
B439
144

14   A   15   B   16   C   17   D   18   E   19   F

129

For full street detail of the highlighted area see page 144

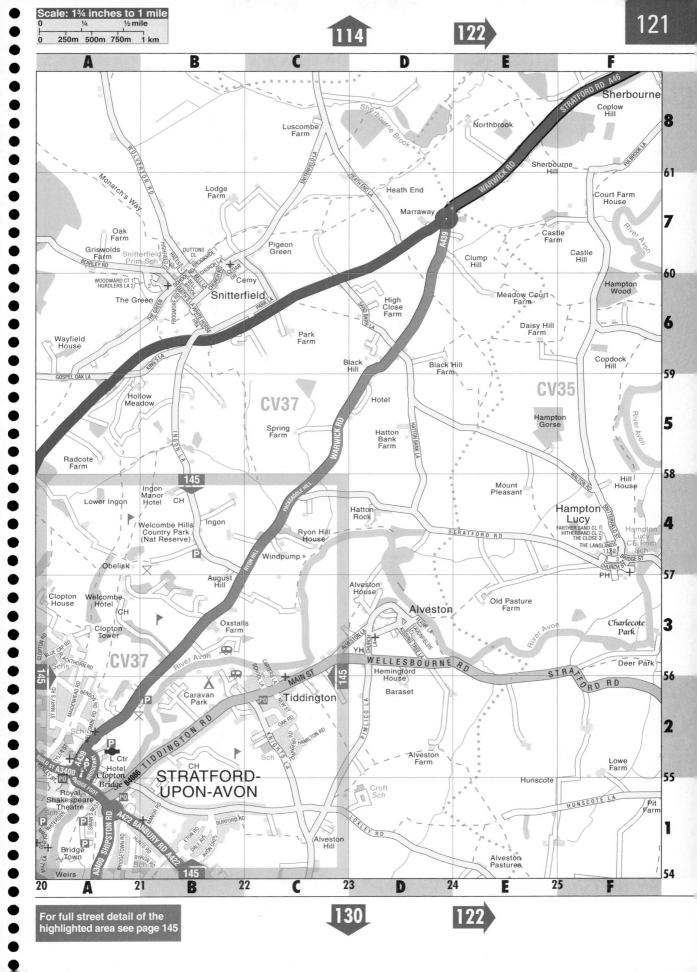

Scale: 1¾ inches to 1 mile

0   ¼   ½ mile
0 250m 500m 750m 1 km

A **B** **C** **D** **E** **F**

8
61
7
60
6
59
5
58
4
57
3
56
2
55
1
54

Sherbourne
Coplow Hill
Northbrook
STRATFORD RD A46
WARWICK RD
Sherbourne Hill
Heath End
Marraway
Court Farm House
River Avon
FULBROOK LA
A439
Castle Farm
Castle Hill
Clump Hill
Hampton Wood
Meadow Court Farm
Daisy Hill Farm
CV35
Copdock Hill
Hampton Gorse
River Avon
Mount Pleasant
WALTON RD
Hill House
Hampton Lucy
FARTHER SAND CL 1
HITHERSAND CL 2
THE CLOSE 3
THE LANGLANDS
1 1 2
SNITTERFIELD ST
Hampton Lucy CE Prim Sch
3 BRIDGE ST
CHURCH ST
PH
Charlecote Park
Old Pasture Farm
River Avon
Deer Park
STRATFORD RD
Alveston
Alveston House
WELLESBOURNE RD
Alveston Farm
Lowe Farm
Hunscote
HUNSCOTE LA
Pit Farm
Alveston Hill
LOXLEY RD
Alveston Pastures

Sherbourne Brook
Luscombe Farm
SNITTERFIELD LA
HEATH END LA
Pigeon Green
High Close Farm
WOLVERTON RD
Monarch's Way
Lodge Farm
Oak Farm
Griswolds Farm
BEARLEY RD
Snitterfield Prim Sch
DUTTONS CL
CEDAR DR
Cemy
HIGHFIELD CL
SCHOOL RD
CHURCH RD
PARK LA
Snitterfield
WOODWARD CT 1
HURDLERS LA 2
The Green
THE GREEN
FROGMORE LA
SMITH'S LA
WHITE HORSE HILL
KING'S LA
Wayfield House
GOSPEL OAK LA
Hollow Meadow
INGON LA
CV37
Spring Farm
Park Farm
SAND BARN LA
Black Hill
WARWICK RD
Hotel
Hatton Bank Farm
HATTON BANK LA
Black Hill Farm

145
Ingon Manor Hotel
CH
Lower Ingon
Ingon
Welcombe Hills Country Park (Nat Reserve)
P
Obelisk
PARKSADDLE HILL
Ryon Hill House
Hatton Rock
STRATFORD RD
RYON HILL
Windpump
August Hill
Clopton House
Welcombe Hotel
CH
Clopton Tower
CV37
Oxstalls Farm
River Avon
CLOPTON RD
BLUE CAP RD
BLACKTHORN RD
Schs
ST MARY'S RD
MAIDENHEAD RD
BENSON RD
WELCOMBE RD
Sch
P
Caravan Park
CARTER'S LA
SCHOOL LA
NEW ST
MAIN ST
145
Tiddington
PO
OAK RD
HAMILTON RD
OLD RD
KNIGHTS LA
Sch
Hemingford House
PIMLICO LA
Baraset
Alveston House
YH
ALVESTON LA
CHURCH LA
FERRY LA
AVONFIELDS
KISSING TREE LA
TIDDINGTON RD
L Ctr
Hotel
Clopton Bridge
B4086
CH
STRATFORD-UPON-AVON
MANOR RD
BURFORD RD
ETON RD
DALE AVE
AVON CRES
Alveston Hill
Croft Sch
LOXLEY RD
Alveston Farm
Royal Shakespeare Theatre
P
WATERSIDE
GUILD ST
TYLER ST
A3400
P
PO
BRIDGE ST
BRIDGE FOOT
SWAN'S NEST
A439
BRIDGEWAY
P
PO
SHIPSTON RD
A3400
A422 BANBURY RD
BRIDGETOWN RD
HUNTS RD
BYRON RD
Sch
Bridge Town
Weirs
145

20   21   22   23   24   25

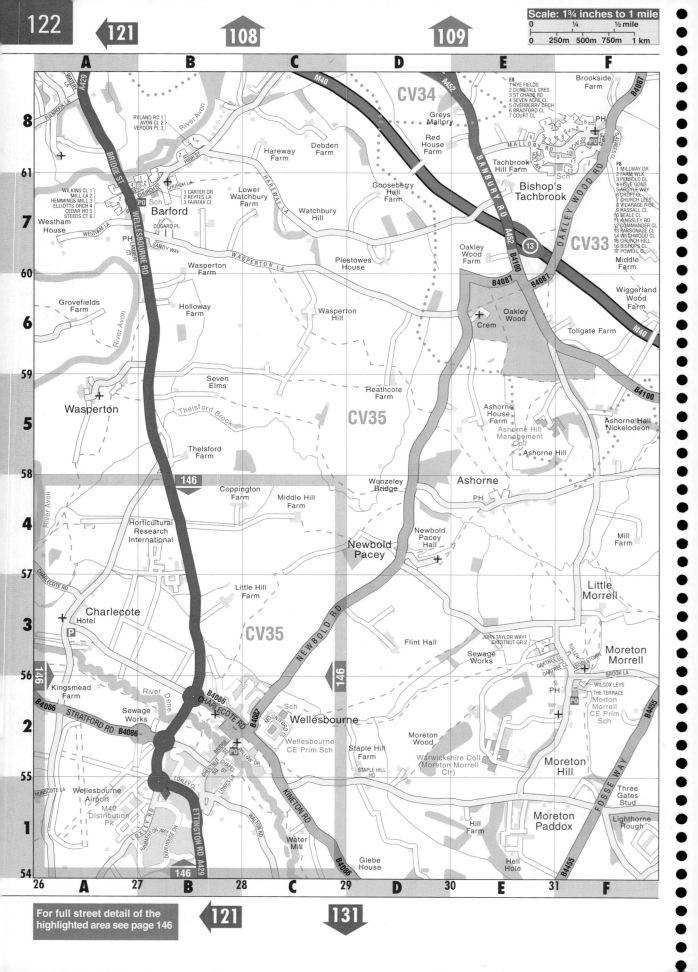

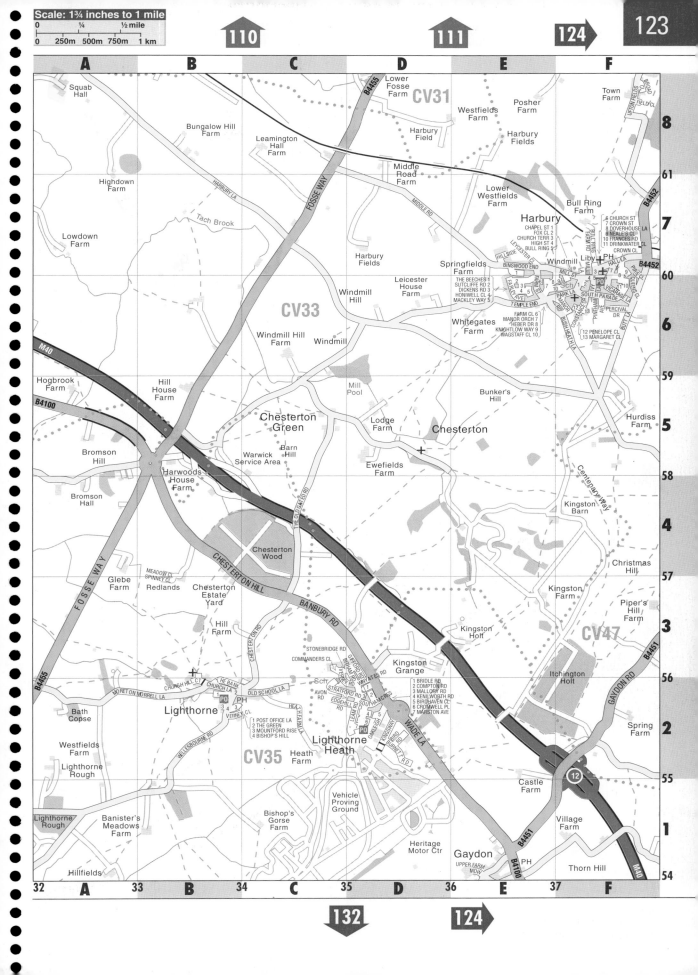

124

123

115

For full street detail of the highlighted area see page 147

Scale: 1¾ inches to 1 mile
0   ¼   ½ mile
0   250m 500m 750m 1 km

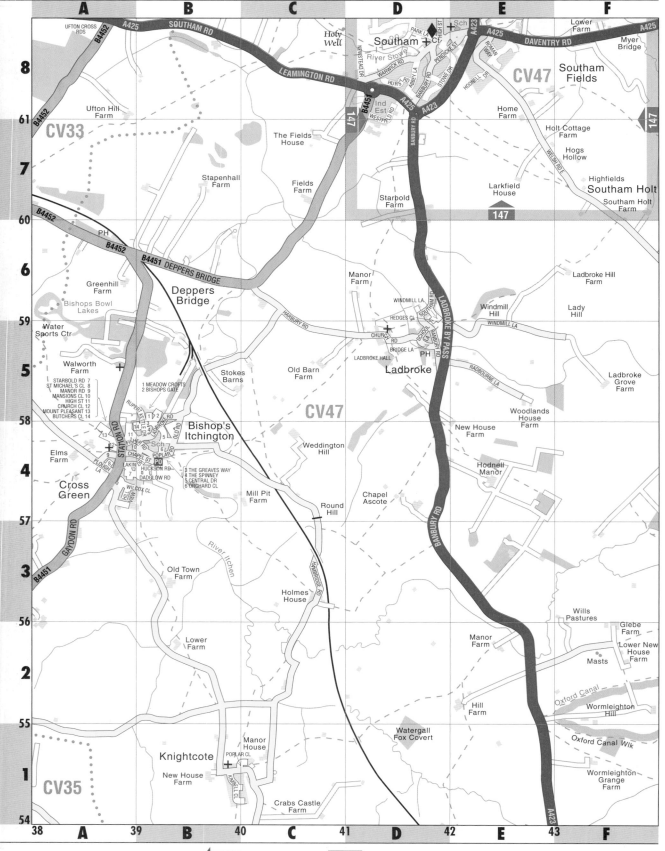

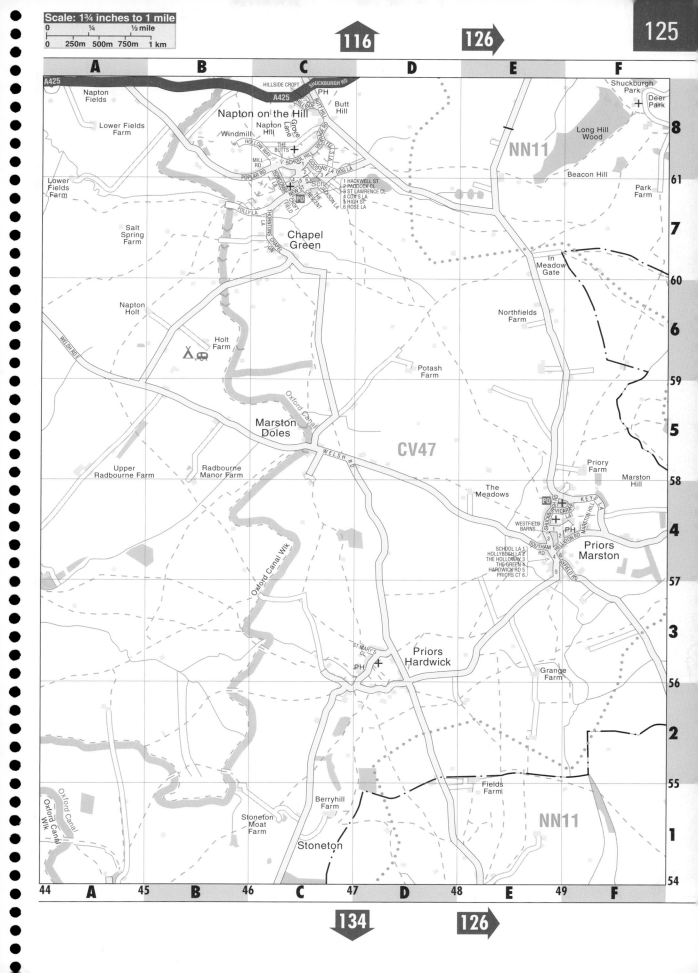

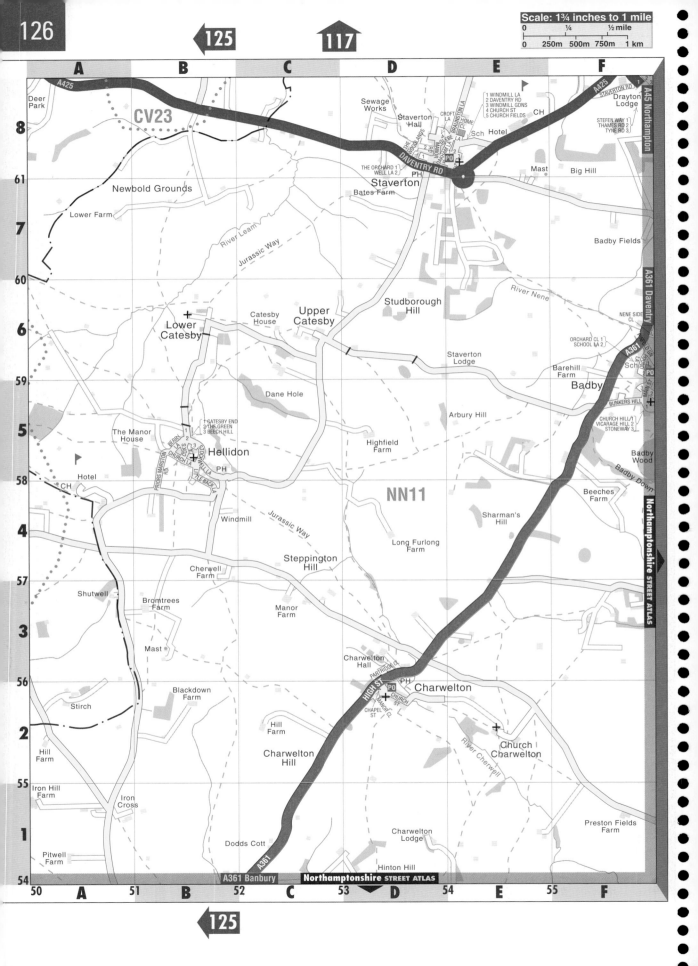

Scale: 1¾ inches to 1 mile

0   ¼   ½ mile
0   250m 500m 750m 1 km

A   B   C   D   E   F

CV23

Deer
Park

A425

8

Sewage
Works

Staverton
Hall

1 WINDMILL LA
2 DAVENTRY RD
3 WINDMILL GDNS
4 CHURCH ST
5 CHURCH FIELDS

CH

A425

STAVERTON RD

Drayton
Lodge

A45 Northampton

STEFEN WAY 1
THAMES RD 2
TYNE RD 3

Sch   Hotel

61

Newbold Grounds

DAVENTRY RD

THE ORCHARD 1
WELL LA 2

PO

PH

Staverton

Mast

Big Hill

A361 Daventry

7

Lower Farm

River Leam

Jurassic Way

Bates Farm

Badby Fields

River Nene

60

Studborough
Hill

6

Lower
Catesby

Catesby
House

Upper
Catesby

Staverton
Lodge

NENE SIDE
CL

A361

ORCHARD CL 1
SCHOOL LA 2

Barehill
Farm

Sch

PO

59

Dane Hole

Badby

5

1 CATESBY END
2 THE GREEN
3 BEECH HILL

The Manor
House

BERRY

1
2
3

Arbury Hill

Highfield
Farm

BUNKERS HILL

CHURCH HILL 1
VICARAGE HILL 2
STONEWAY 3

Badby
Wood

CHURCH LA
STOCKWELL LA

PRIORS MARSTON RD

Hellidon

PH

LT'LE BACK LA

Badby Down

Beeches
Farm

58

Hotel

CH

Windmill

Jurassic Way

NN11

4

Sharman's
Hill

57

Shutwell

Cherwell
Farm

Steppington
Hill

Long Furlong
Farm

3

Bromtrees
Farm

Manor
Farm

Mast

56

Blackdown
Farm

Charwelton
Hall

PARTRIDGE CL

PH

Charwelton

Stirch

HIGH ST

PO

CHURCH ST

2

Hill
Farm

CHAPEL ST

MANOR CL

Church
Charwelton

River Cherwell

Hill
Farm

55

Iron Hill
Farm

Iron
Cross

Charwelton
Hill

1

Pitwell
Farm

Dodds Cott

A361

Charwelton
Lodge

Preston Fields
Farm

Hinton Hill

54

A361 Banbury

Northamptonshire STREET ATLAS

50   A   51   B   52   C   53   D   54   E   55   F

Northamptonshire STREET ATLAS

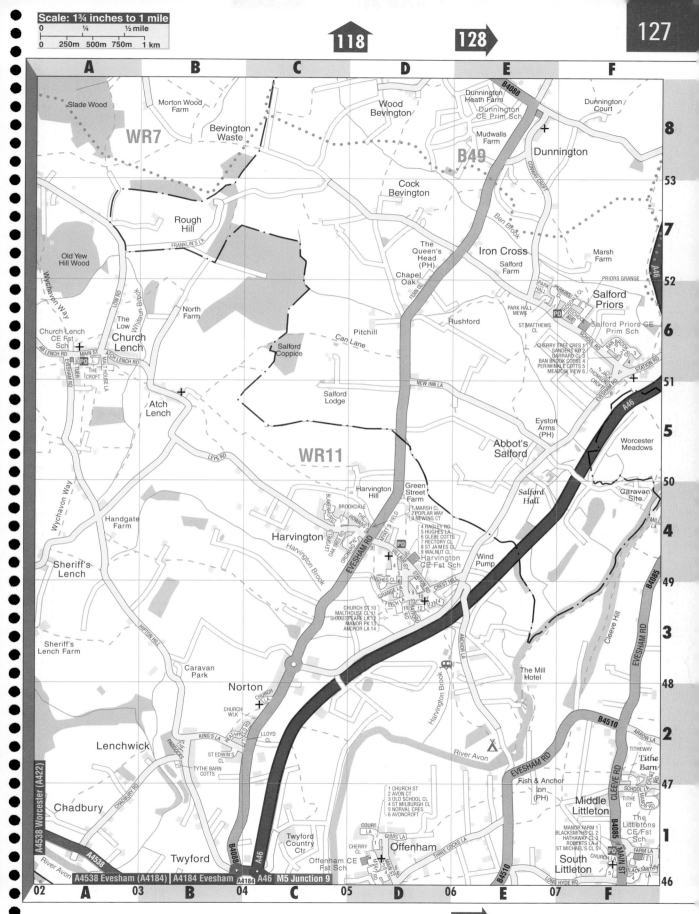

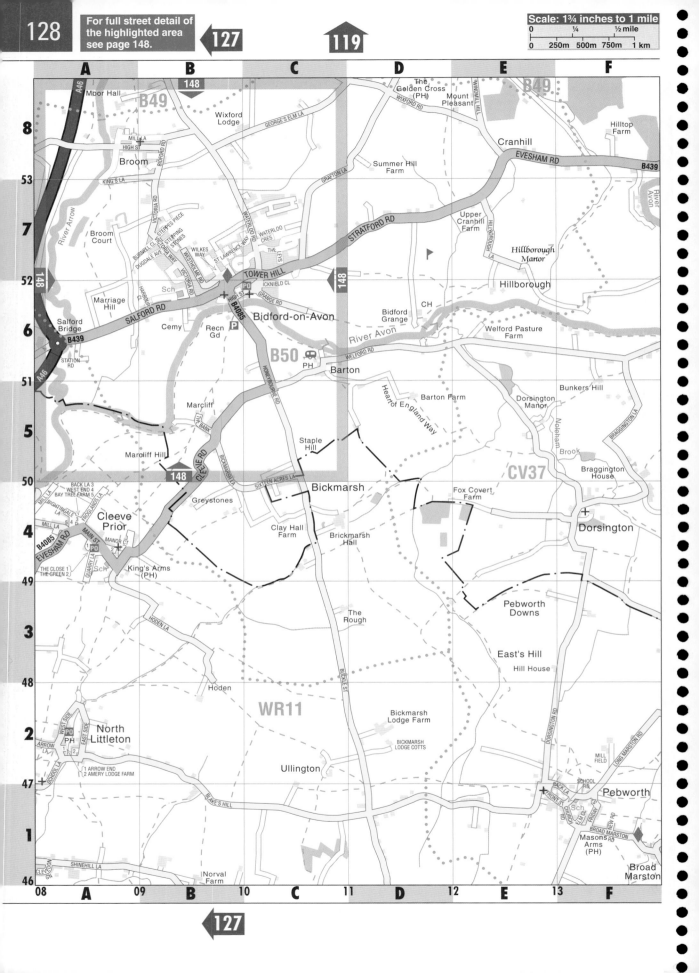

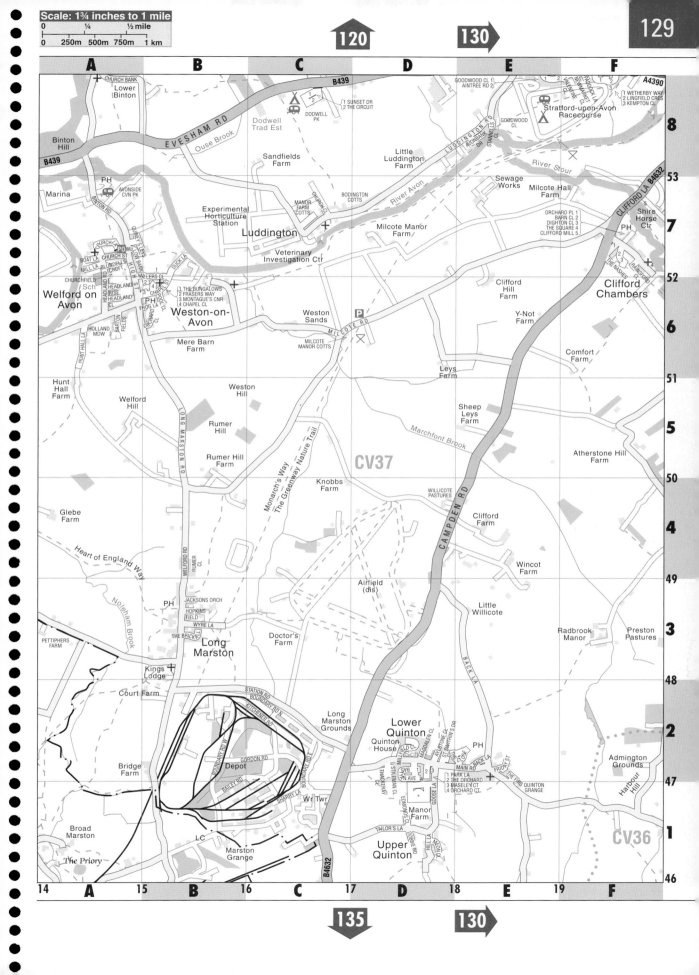

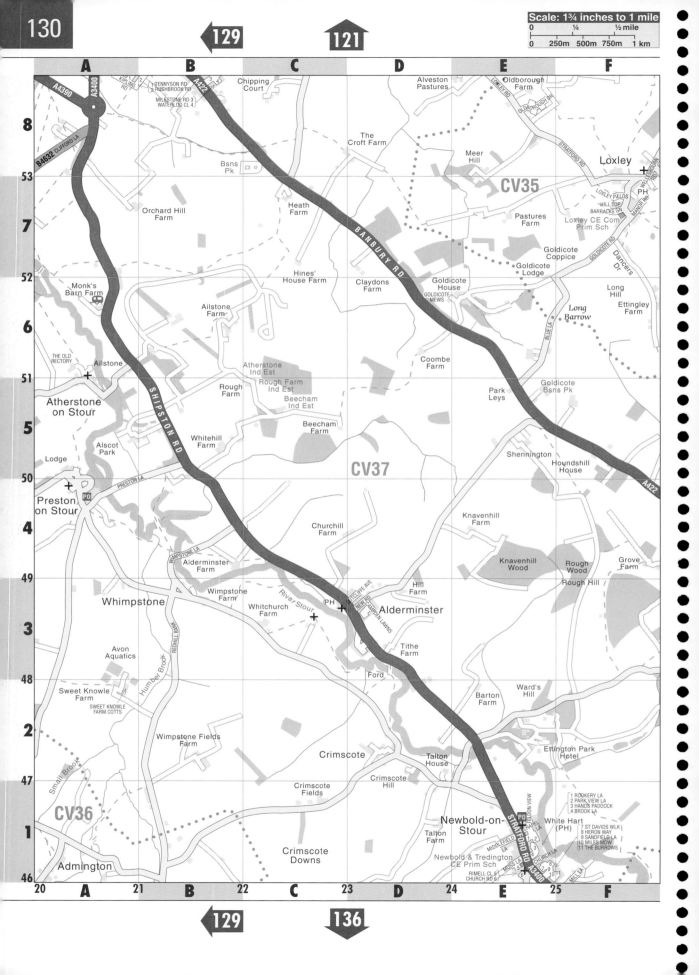

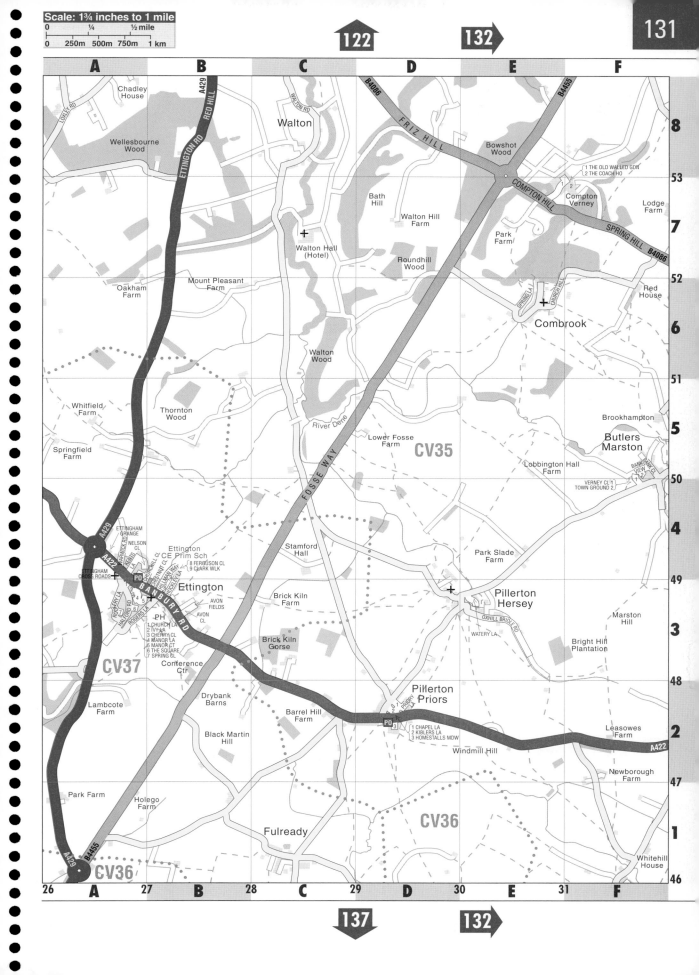

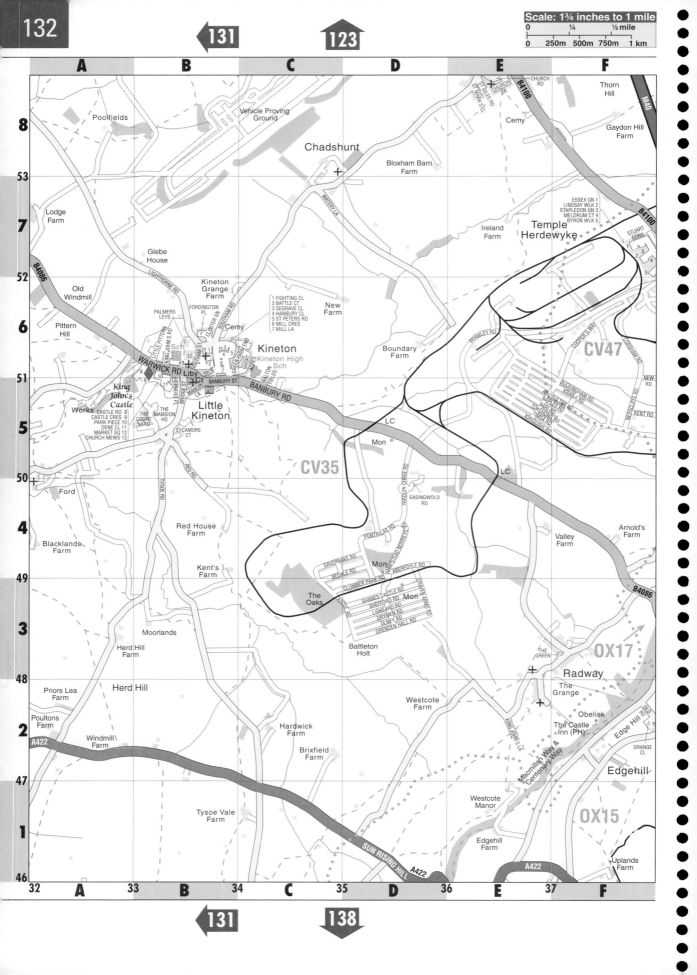

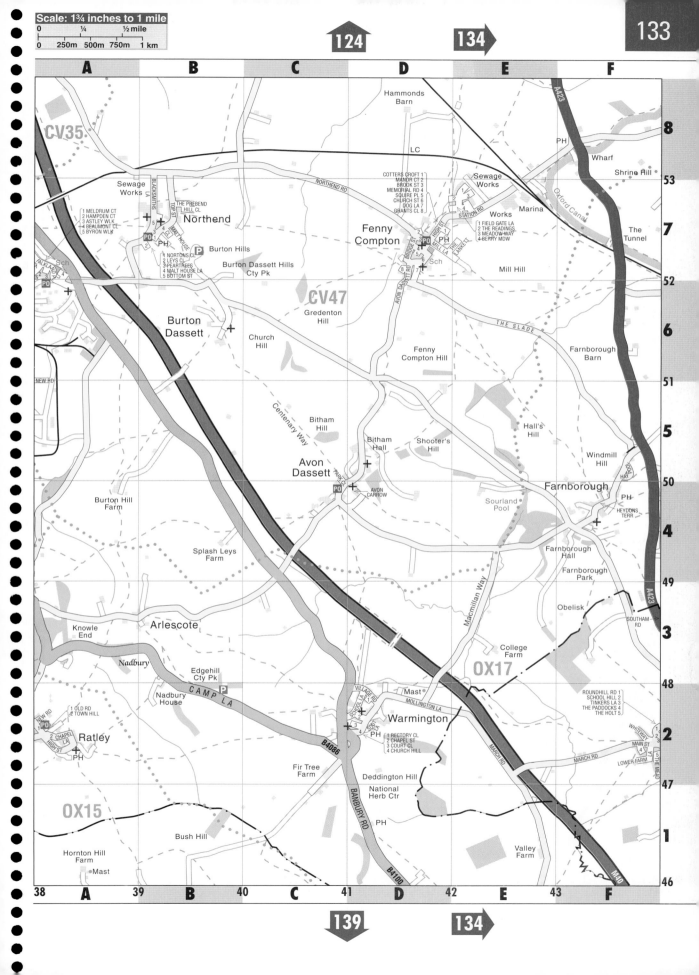

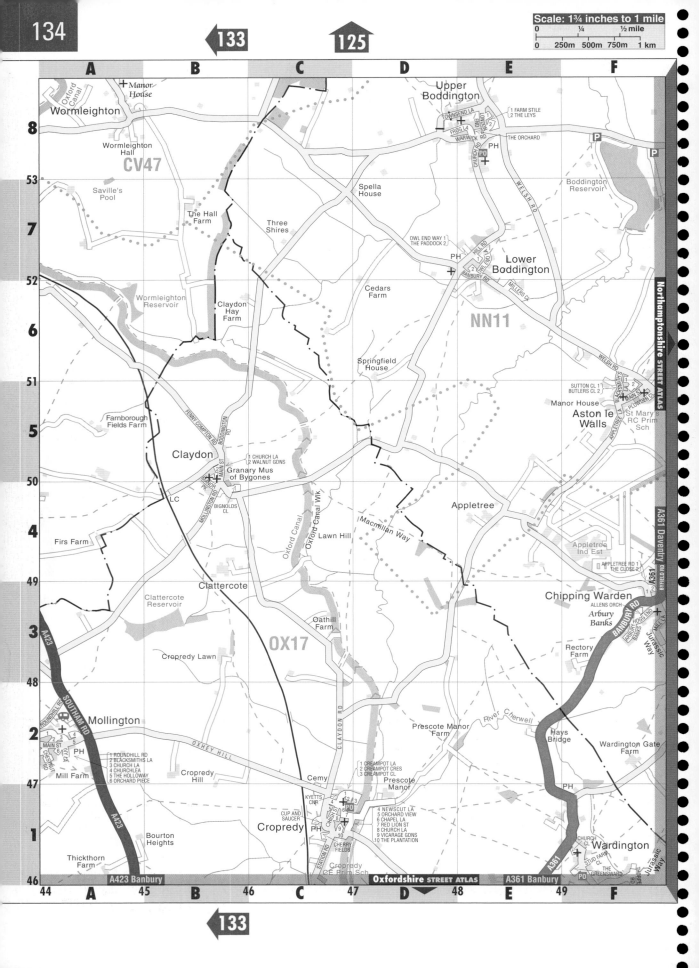

Scale: 1¾ inches to 1 mile

0   ¼   ½ mile
0   250m 500m 750m 1 km

A   B   C   D   E   F

Oxford Canal
Manor House
Wormleighton
8

Upper Boddington
TOWNSEND LA
1 FARM STILE
2 THE LEYS
FROG LA
LONDON RD
WARWICK RD
CHURCH RD
PH
THE ORCHARD
PO

P
P

Wormleighton Hall
CV47
53

Boddington Reservoir

Saville's Pool
The Hall Farm
7
Three Shires
Spella House

WELSH RD

OWL END WAY 1
THE PADDOCK 2
PH
HILL RD
OWL END LA
Lower Boddington
BANBURY RD
MILLERS CL

52
Wormleighton Reservoir
Claydon Hay Farm
Cedars Farm
NN11
WELSH RD

6
SUTTON CL 1
BUTLERS CL 2
BLACKSMITHS LA
MAIN RD
N CLOYDEN CL

51
Springfield House
Manor House
Aston le Walls
St Mary's RC Prim Sch
APPLETREE LA

Farnborough Fields Farm
FENNY COMPTON RD
BODDINGTON RD
5
1 CHURCH LA
2 WALNUT GDNS
Claydon
Granary Mus of Bygones
PRIOR
MAIN ST
LC
BIGNOLDS CL

Appletree
Appletree Ind Est
APPLETREE RD 1
THE CLOSE 2

Firs Farm
4
MOLLINGTON RD
Oxford Canal
Lawn Hill
Macmillan Way
Oxford Canal Wlk

49
Clattercote
Clattercote Reservoir
Chipping Warden
Arbury Banks
ALLENS ORCH
ARBURY BANKS
HOGG END
BANBURY RD
Jurassic Way

3
OX17
Oathill Farm
Rectory Farm
A423

Cropredy Lawn
48
SOUTHAM RD
ROUNDHILL RD

Mollington
OXHEY HILL
2
1 ROUNDHILL RD
2 BLACKSMITHS LA
3 CHURCH LA
4 CHURCHLEA
5 THE HOLLOWAY
6 ORCHARD PIECE
MAIN ST
CRES
PH
Cropredy Hill
CLAYDON RD
River Cherwell
Prescote Manor Farm
Hays Bridge
Wardington Gate Farm

Mill Farm
Cemy
KYETTS CNR
47
1 CREAMPOT LA
2 CREAMPOT CRES
3 CREAMPOT CL
Prescote Manor
PH

1
Bourton Heights
CUP AND SAUCER
STATION RD
OXHILL RD
PH
4 NEWSCUT LA
5 ORCHARD VIEW
6 CHAPEL LA
7 RED LION ST
8 CHURCH LA
9 VICARAGE GDNS
10 THE PLANTATION
CHURCH CL
Wardington
STUD FARM CL
THE GREENSWARD
Jurassic Way
THORPE

Cropredy
PH
CHERRY FIELDS
Thickthorn Farm
Cropredy CE Prim Sch
PO

46
A423 Banbury
Oxfordshire STREET ATLAS
A361 Banbury
A361

44   A   45   B   46   C   47   D   48   E   49   F

Northamptonshire STREET ATLAS
A361 Daventry

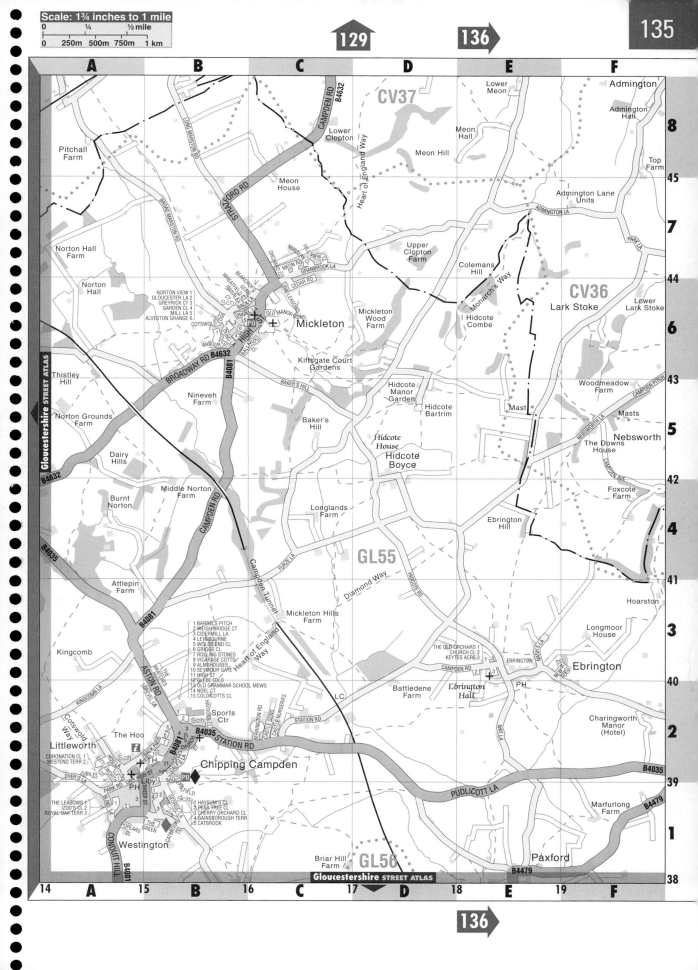

A   B   C   D   E   F

CV37

Pitchall Farm

Lower Clopton

Lower Meon

Meon Hall

Meon Hill

Admington

Admington Hall

Top Farm

8

45

Meon House

7

Meon Rd

Norton Hall Farm

Norton Hall

Upper Clopton Farm

Colemans Hill

Admington Lane Units

ADMINGTON LA

PARK LA

44

NORTON VIEW 1
GLOUCESTER LA 2
GREYRICK CT 3
GARDEN CL 4
MILL LA 5
ALVESTON GRANGE 6

Mickleton

Mickleton Wood Farm

Monarch's Way

Hidcote Combe

CV36
Lark Stoke

Lower Lark Stoke

6

BROADWAY RD B4632

B4081

Thistley Hill

Nineveh Farm

BAKER'S HILL

Kiftsgate Court Gardens

Hidcote Manor Garden

Hidcote Bartrim

Mast

Woodmeadow Farm

CAMPDEN PITCH

43

NEBSWORTH LA

Masts

Gloucestershire STREET ATLAS

Norton Grounds Farm

Baker's Hill

Hidcote House

Nebsworth

The Downs House

5

B4632

Dairy Hills

Burnt Norton

Middle Norton Farm

CAMPDEN RD

Hidcote Boyce

CAMPDEN AVE

Foxcote Farm

42

B4035

Longlands Farm

Ebrington Hill

GL55

Hoarston

4

Attlepin Farm

B4081

Campden Tunnel

FURZE LA

Diamond Way

HIDCOTE RD

41

Longmoor House

Kingcomb

Mickleton Hills Farm

Heart of England Way

1 BARRELS PITCH
2 WEIGHBRIDGE CT
3 CIDERMILL LA
4 LEYSBOURNE
5 WOLDS END CL
6 GRIGGS CL
7 ROLLING STONES
8 VICARAGE COTTS
9 ALMSHOUSES
10 SEYMOUR GATE
11 HIGH ST
12 GLEBE FOLD
13 OLD GRAMMAR SCHOOL MEWS
14 NOEL CT
15 COLDICOTTS CL

THE OLD ORCHARD 1
CHURCH CL 2
KEYTES ACRE 3

Ebrington

3

ASTON RD

LC

CAMPDEN RD

Battledene Farm

Ebrington Hall

PH

NASH LA

40

Littleworth

The Hoo

Sports Ctr

B4035 STATION RD

BERRINGTON RD

CASTLE GDNS

CASTLE NURSERIES

STATION RD

MAY LA

Charingworth Manor (Hotel)

2

Cotswold Way

CORONATION CL 1
WESTEND TERR 2

Chipping Campden

PO

B4035

39

DYER S LA

THE LEASOWS 1
IZOD'S CL 2
ROYAL OAK TERR 3

1 HAYSUM'S CL
2 PEAR TREE CL
3 CHERRY ORCHARD CL
4 GAINSBOROUGH TERR
5 CATBROOK

PUDLICOTT LA

Marfurlong Farm

B4479

Westington

CONDUIT HILL

B4081

Briar Hill Farm

GL56

Paxford

1

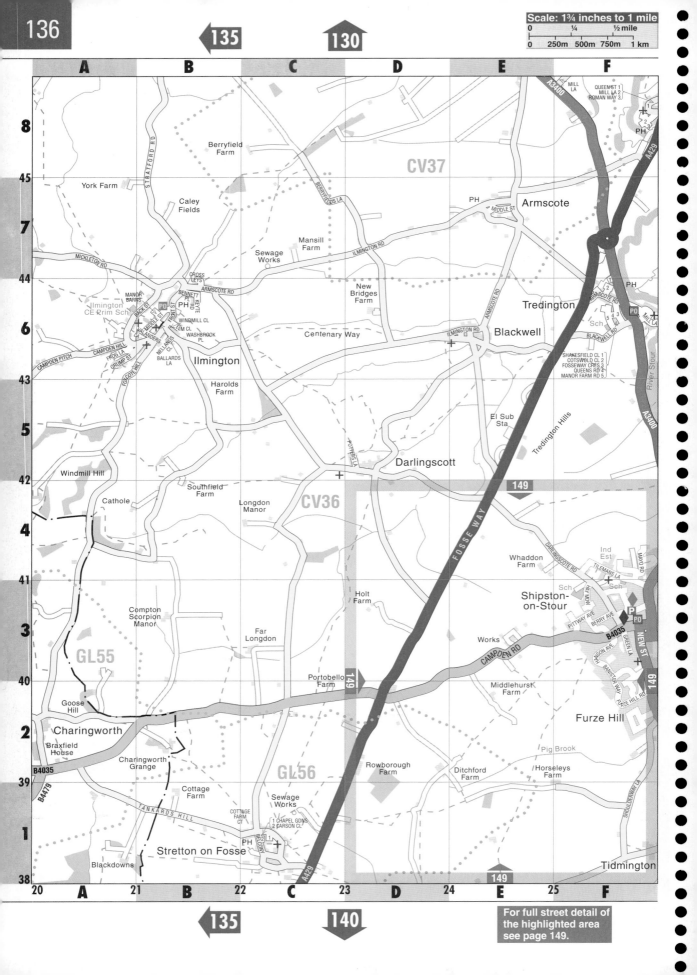

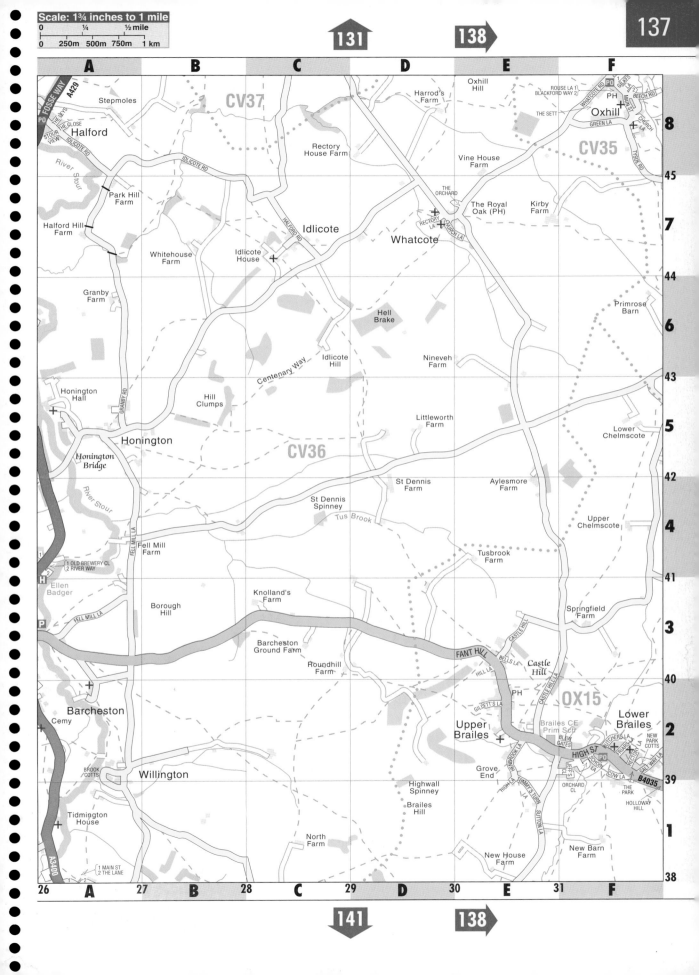

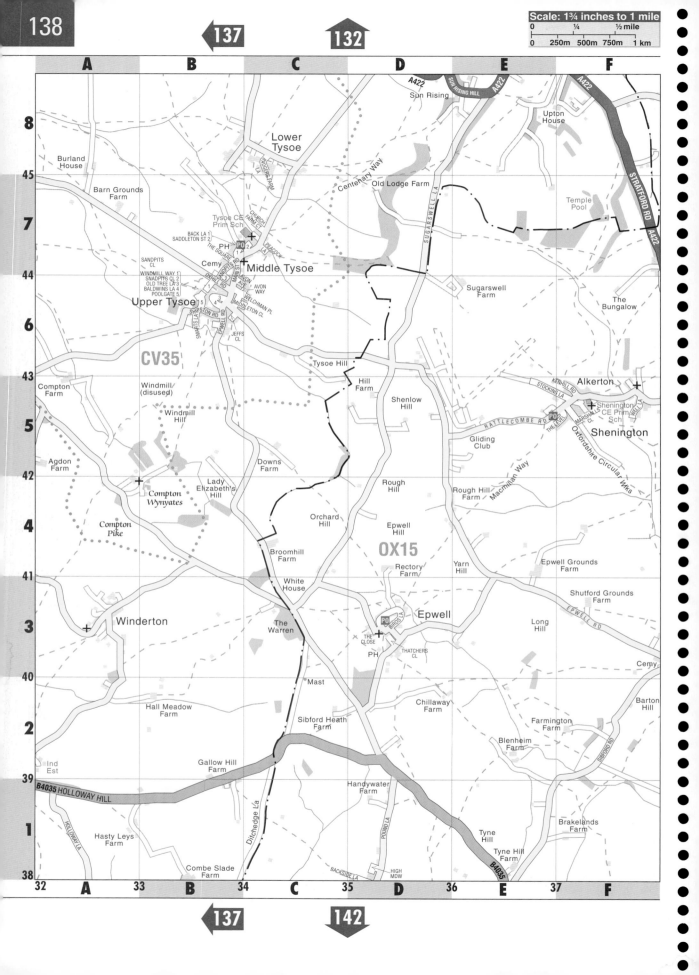

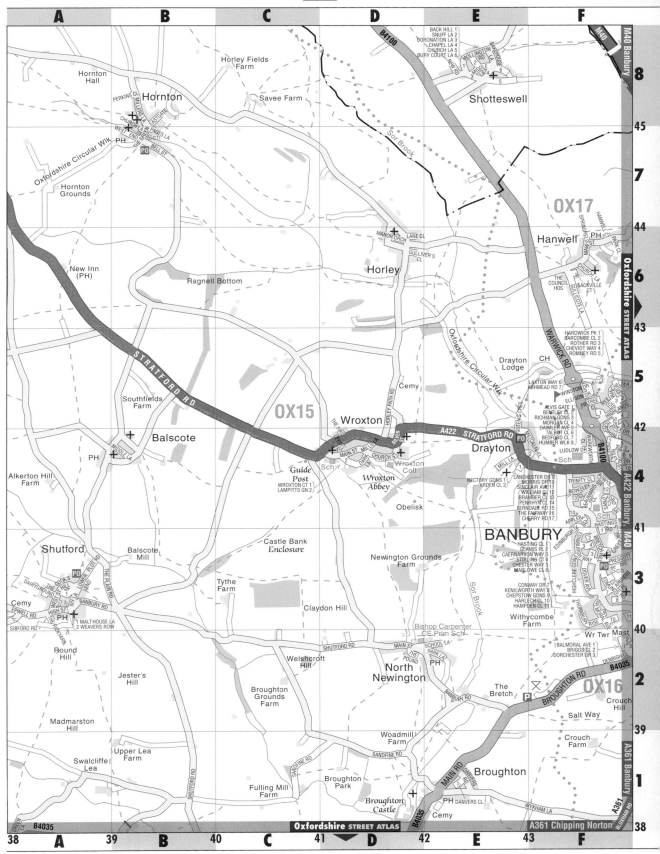

Oxfordshire STREET ATLAS

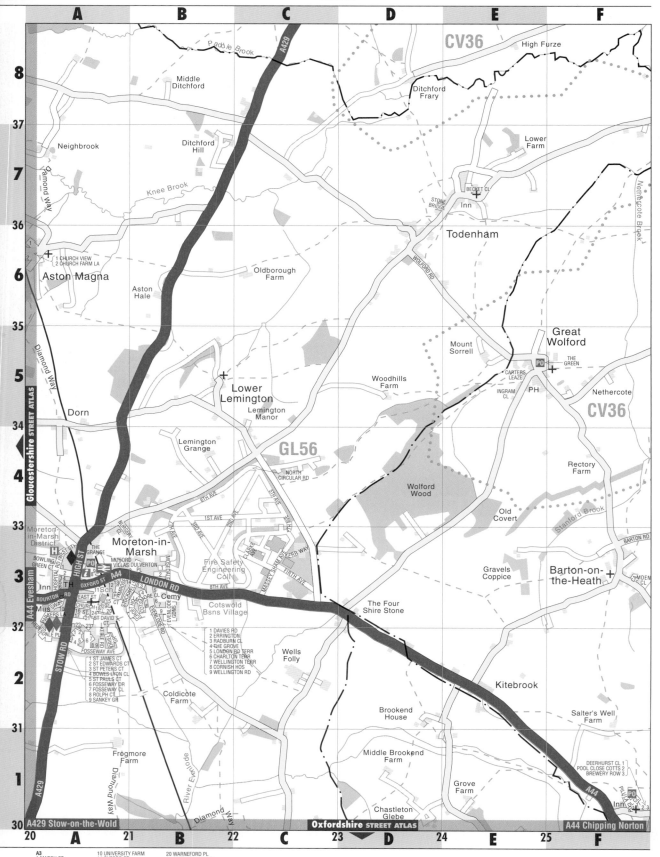

Scale: 1¾ inches to 1 mile
0   ¼   ½ mile
0   250m   500m   750m   1 km

CV36

High Furze

8

Middle
Ditchford

Ditchford
Frary

37

Neighbrook

Ditchford
Hill

Lower
Farm

7

Diamond Way

Knee Brook

STONE
BRIDGE

BECKET CL

Inn

36

Todenham

WOLFORD RD

6

Aston Magna

1 CHURCH VIEW
2 CHURCH FARM LA

Aston
Hale

Oldborough
Farm

35

Diamond Way

Great
Wolford

Mount
Sorrell

CARTERS
LEAZE

PO

THE
GREEN

5

Dorn

Lower
Lemington

Lemington
Manor

Woodhills
Farm

INGRAM
CL

PH

Nethercote

CV36

34

Lemington
Grange

NORTH
CIRCULAR RD

GL56

Wolford
Wood

Old
Covert

Rectory
Farm

Stanford Brook

4

6TH AVE

5TH AVE

2ND AVE

1ST AVE

BARTON RD

33

Moreton-
in-Marsh
District

THE GRANGE

3RD AVE

2ND AVE

CLARKE AVE

KERR WAY

Gravels
Coppice

Barton-on-
the-Heath

MDEN
CL

Moreton-in-
Marsh

MUTFORD
VILLAS DULVERTON
PL

Fire Safety
Engineering Coll

8TH AVE

MASSEY SHAW

FIRTH AVE

3

HIGH ST

HOSPITAL RD

PO
i

A44

LONDON RD

EAST ST

CORE CL

EVENLODE
GDNS

The Four
Shire Stone

A44 Evesham

Inn

BOURTON RD

Mus

CHURCH ST

Cemy

Cotswold
Bsns Village

32

STOW RD

FOSSEWAY AVE

1 DAVIES RD
2 ERRINGTON
3 RADBURN CL
4 THE GROVE
5 LONDON RD TERR
6 CHARLTON TERR
7 WELLINGTON TERR
8 CORNISH HOS
9 WELLINGTON RD

Wells
Folly

1 ST JAMES CT
2 ST EDWARDS CT
3 ST PETERS CT
4 BOWES-LYON CL
5 ST PAULS CT
6 FOSSEWAY DR
7 FOSSEWAY CL
8 ROLPH CT
9 SANKEY GR

Kitebrook

Salter's Well
Farm

2

Coldicote
Farm

Brookend
House

31

Frogmore
Farm

Middle Brookend
Farm

DEERHURST CL 1
POOL CLOSE COTTS 2
BREWERY ROW 3

1

A429

Diamond Way

River Evenlode

Grove
Farm

A44

PO

Inn

Diamond Way

Chastleton
Glebe

30

20   A   21   B   22   C   23   D   24   E   25   F

Gloucestershire STREET ATLAS

A3
1 MARSH CT
2 CORDER'S LA
3 DEVONSHIRE TERR
4 MANCHESTER CT
5 CORDER'S CL
6 REDESDALE MEWS
7 NEW RD
8 STATION RD
9 THE GREEN

10 UNIVERSITY FARM
11 OXFORD ST
12 ODDFELLOWS' TERR
13 TURNPIKE CL
14 CICESTER TERR
15 MEAD CL
16 STONEFARN CT
17 DUNSTALL HO
18 GRAY'S LA
19 ST GEORGE'S CL

20 WARNEFORD PL
21 COTSWOLD GDNS
22 JAMESON CT
23 TINKER'S CL
24 OLD TOWN

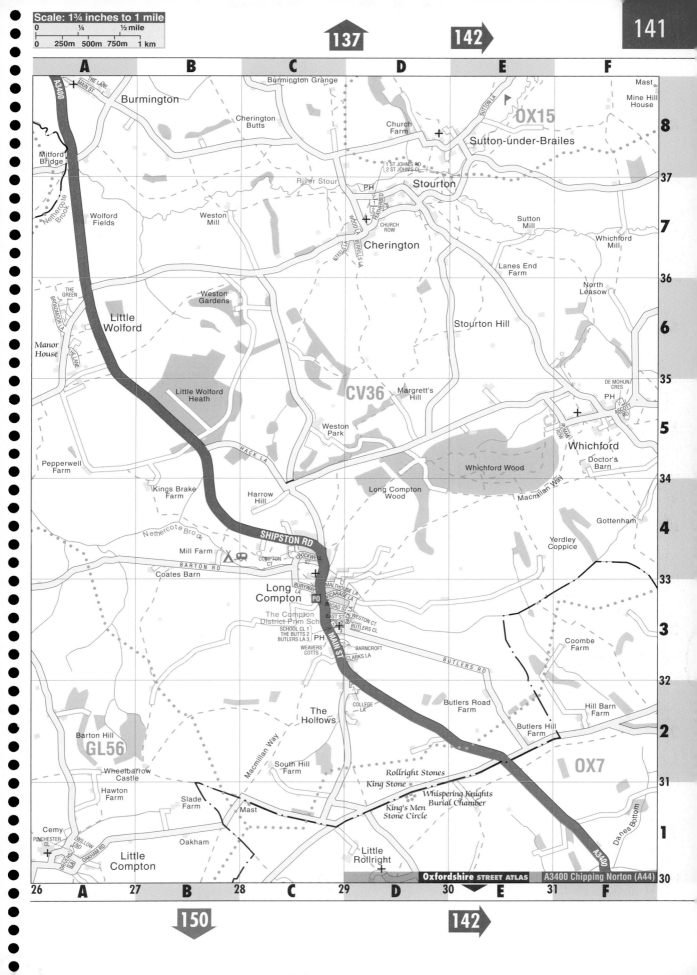

A   B   C   D   E   F

8   37   7   36   6   35   5   34   4   33   3   32   2   31   1   30

Mast
Mine Hill House

Burmington Grange

Burmington

THE LANE
MAIN ST

OX15

Cherington Butts

Church Farm

Sutton-under-Brailes

Mitford Bridge

Nethercote Brook

River Stour

1 ST JOHN'S RD
2 ST JOHN'S CL

Stourton

Wolford Fields

Weston Mill

PH

Sutton Mill

Whichford Mill

CHURCH ROW

Cherington

WOOD LA

BERRILLS LA

STEELE'S LA

Lanes End Farm

THE GREEN

Weston Gardens

Little Wolford

North Leasow

BROADMOOR LA

THE LANE

Stourton Hill

Manor House

Little Wolford Heath

CV36

Margrett's Hill

DE MOHUN CRES

PH

ASCOTT RD

ROMAN ROW

Whichford

Pepperwell Farm

HACK LA

Weston Park

Whichford Wood

Doctor's Barn

Kings Brake Farm

Harrow Hill

Long Compton Wood

Macmillan Way

Gottenham

Nethercote Brook

SHIPSTON RD

Mill Farm

BARTON RD

Coates Barn

COMPTON CT

STOCKWELL ST

Yerdley Coppice

Long Compton

BURYWAY LA

PO

MALTHOUSE LA

VICARAGE LA

BROAD ST

WESTON CT

The Compton District Prim Sch

EAST ST

BUTLERS CL

SCHOOL CL 1
THE BUTTS 2
BUTLERS LA 3

PH

WEAVERS COTTS

CLARKS LA

BARNCROFT

MAIN ST

BUTLERS RD

Coombe Farm

Hill Barn Farm

COLLEGE LA

Butlers Road Farm

Butlers Hill Farm

OX7

The Hollows

Barton Hill

GL56

Macmillan Way

South Hill Farm

Rollright Stones

King Stone

Whispering Knights Burial Chamber

Danes Bottom

Wheelbarrow Castle

Hawton Farm

Slade Farm

Mast

King's Men Stone Circle

Cemy

PINCHESTER CL

WILLOW END

DRIVER'S LA

OAKHAM RD

Little Compton

Oakham

Little Rollright

A3400

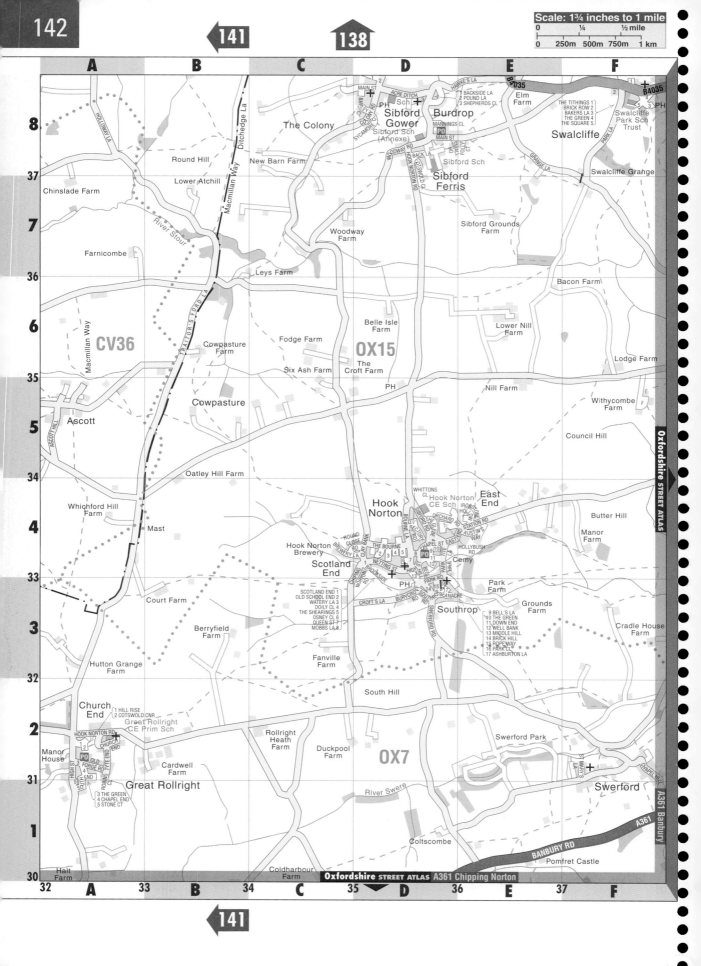

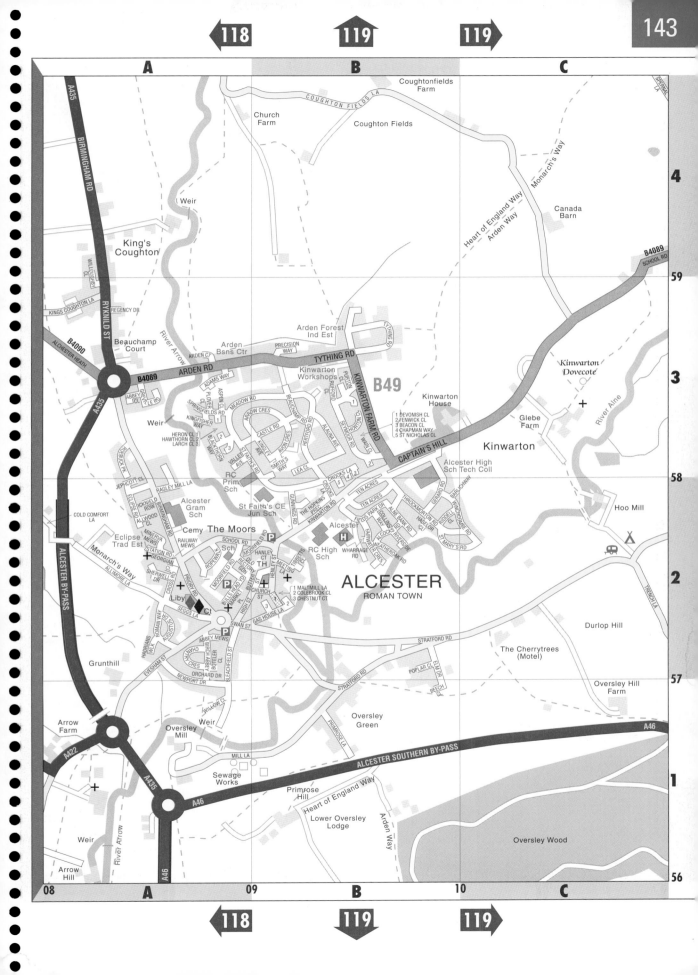

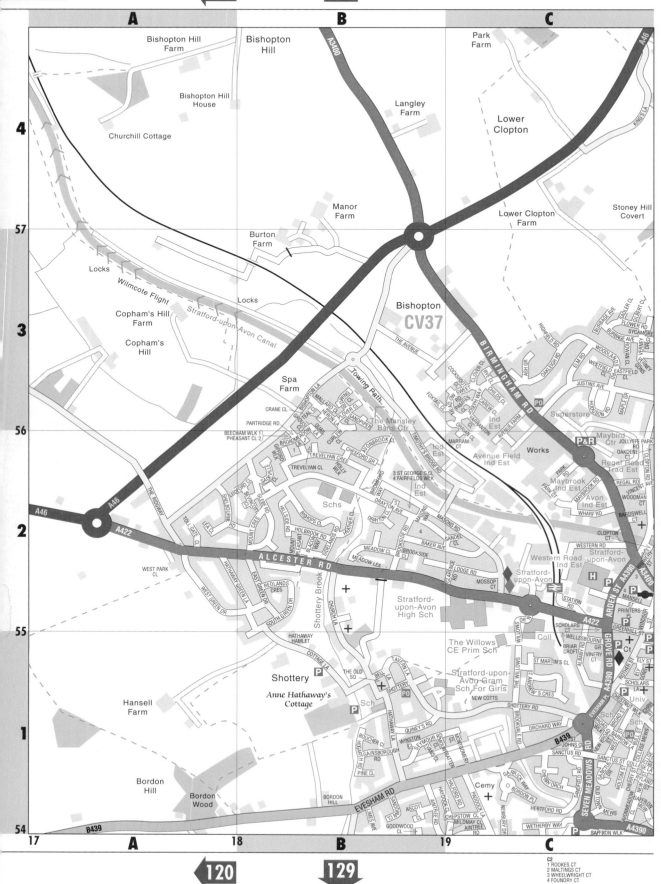

C2
1 ROOKES CT
2 MALTINGS CT
3 WHEELWRIGHT CT
4 FOUNDRY CT

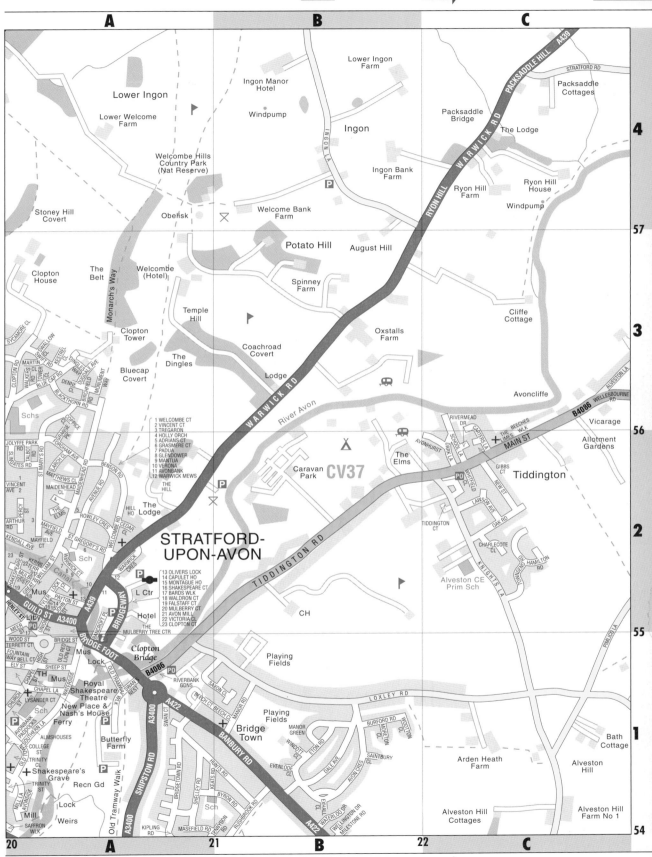

A B C

4
57
3
56
2
55
1
54

20 A 21 B 22 C

Lower Ingon
Lower Welcome Farm
Welcombe Hills Country Park (Nat Reserve)
Stoney Hill Covert
Clopton House
The Belt
Monarch's Way
Obelisk
Welcombe (Hotel)
Temple Hill
Clopton Tower
Bluecap Covert
The Dingles
Coachroad Covert
Lodge
Potato Hill
Spinney Farm
August Hill
Lower Ingon Farm
Ingon Manor Hotel
Windpump
Ingon
INGON LA
Welcome Bank Farm
Ingon Bank Farm
Oxstalls Farm
Avoncliffe
Packsaddle Hill
A439
STRATFORD RD
Packsaddle Cottages
Packsaddle Bridge
The Lodge
Ryon Hill
WARWICK RD
Ryon Hill Farm
Ryon Hill House
Windpump
Cliffe Cottage
Wellesbourne RD
B4086
Vicarage
Allotment Gardens
Tiddington
MAIN ST
Rivermead Dr
The Beeches
Avonhurst
The Elms
SCHOOL LA
CARTERS LA
LIMES WLK
DARK LA
PO
GIBBS CT
NEW ST
WHITFIELD
LAWSON AVE
OAK RD
CHARLECOTE CL
KNIGHTS LA
TIDDINGTON CT
Alveston CE Prim Sch
CH
Playing Fields
LOXLEY RD
WARWICK RD
River Avon
Caravan Park
CV37
The Lodge
HILL HO
THE HILL
STRATFORD-UPON-AVON
WARWICK CRES
Hotel
Clopton Bridge
B4086
Old Tramway Walk
Royal Shakespeare Theatre
New Place & Nash's House
Ferry
Butterfly Farm
Shakespeare's Grave
Recn Gd
Lock
Weirs
Mill
SAFFRON WLK
AVONSIDE
Bridge Town
Playing Fields
Manor Green
BURFORD RD
MORETON CL
WOOTTON CL
SAINTBURY CL
AVON CRES
DALE AVE
Arden Heath Farm
Alveston Hill
Bath Cottage
Alveston Hill Cottages
Alveston Hill Farm No 1
BANBURY RD
A422
SHIPSTON RD
A3400
TIDDINGTON RD
BRIDGE FOOT
A439
A3400
GUILD ST
BRIDGEWAY
Mus
Canal
WARWICK CT
Sch
Schs
SYCAMORE CL
SWALLOW
KESTREL
MARTIN
WALKERS CL
DINGLESIDE AVE
DUGDALE AVE
BIRCHFIELD
BLACKTHORN RD
BLUE CAP RD
DENNE CL
JOLYFFE PARK RD
LARCH CL
TALBOT RD
ST MARY'S RD
GORDON AVE
MATTHEWS CL
MAIDENHEAD CL
BENSON RD
AVENUE RD
CEDAR
WELCOMBE RD
HILL CL
ROWLEY CRES
ST GREGORY'S RD
SINGATES RD
1 VINCENT AVE 2
PERCY ST
ARTHUR RD
KENDALL AVE
MAYFIELD AVE
MAYFIELD CT
THE ELMS
SHAKESPEARE ST
MULBERRY
KERMES
PATERSON CT
WEST ST
SHEEP ST
PAYTON ST
BRIDGE ST
WOOD ST
MEER ST
ELY ST
FOUNTAIN WAY
BELL CT
TERRETT CT
OLD RED LION CT
OLD TRAMWAY WALK
WATERSIDE
CHAPEL LA
LYSANDER CT
CHURCH ST
TRINITY CL
TRINITY ST
SOUTHERN LA
AVONBANK PADDOCKS
COLLEGE ST
ALMSHOUSES
MILL LA
SWAN CT
SWAN'S NEST LA
WINDSOR ST
RIVERBANK GDNS
SAXON CT
BEECH CT
BEECH
MANOR RD
BRIDGEWAY
BRIDGETOWN RD
SHELLEY RD
KEATS RD
BYRON RD
BUSHBROOK RD
MASEFIELD RD
TENNYSON RD
KIPLING RD
WINCOTT CL
EVENLODE CL
WAVERLOO DR
WELLINGTON DR
MILESTONE RD
EXHALL CL
PIMLICO LA
ALVESTON LA
ALVESTON RD
JOHNSON CL
HAMILTON RD

1 WELCOMBE CT
2 VINCENT CT
3 TREGARON
4 HOLLY ORCH
5 ADRIANS CT
6 GRASMERE CT
7 PADUA
8 GLENDOWER
9 MANTUA
10 VERONA
11 AVONBANK
12 WARWICK MEWS

13 OLIVERS LOCK
14 CAPULET HO
15 MONTAGUE HO
16 SHAKESPEARE CT
17 BARDS WLK
18 WALDRON CT
19 FALSTAFF CT
20 MULBERRY CT
21 AVON MILL
22 VICTORIA CL
23 CLOPTON CT

THE MULBERRY TREE CTR

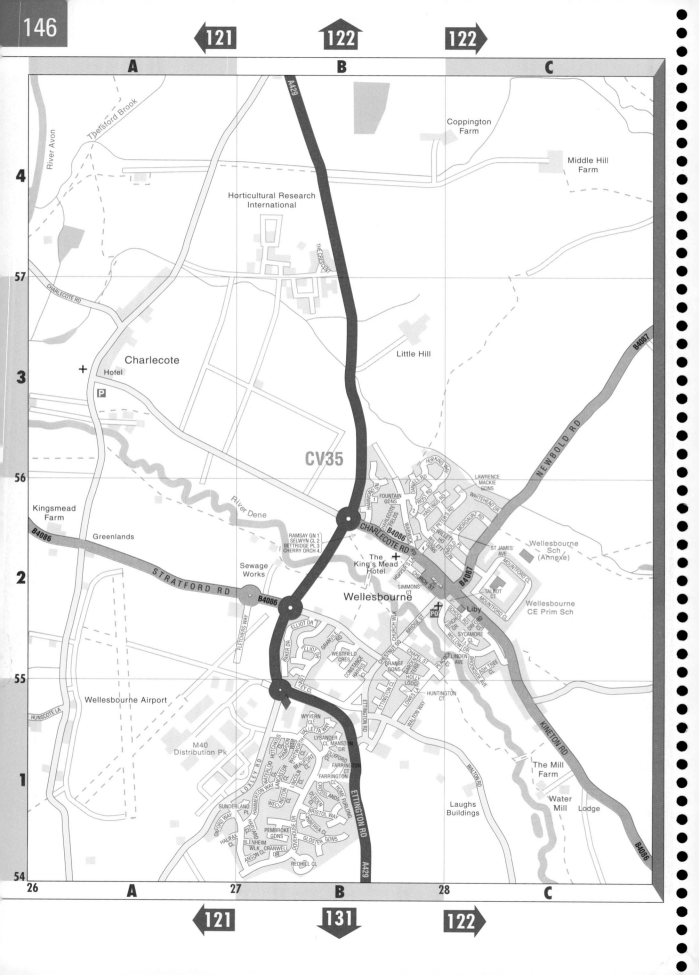

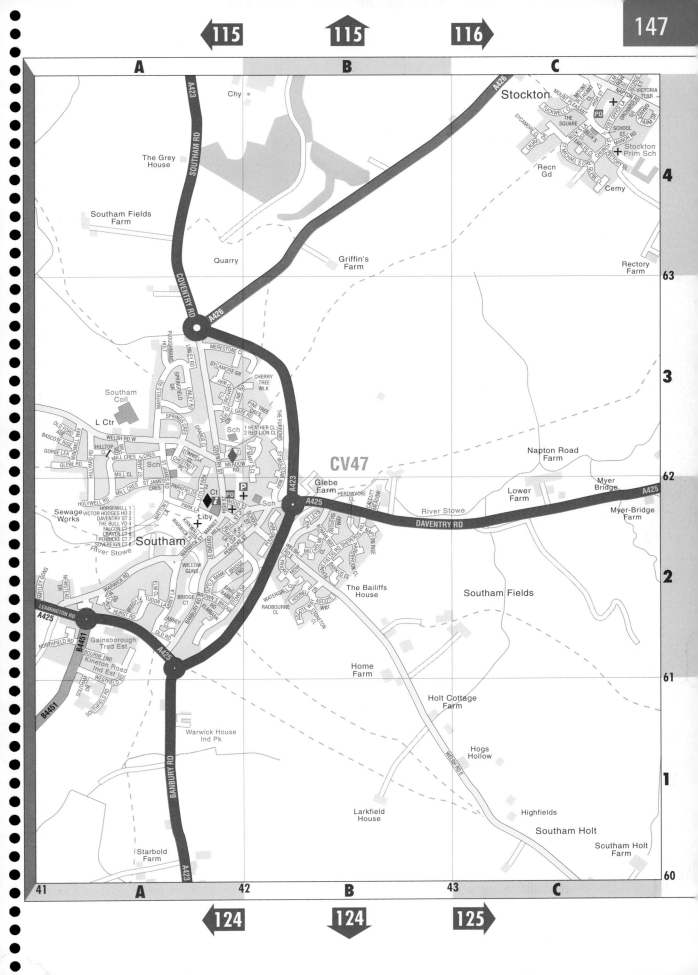

115
115
116

A   **B**   **C**

Chy

Stockton

A423

A426

SOUTHAM RD

COVENTRY RD

The Grey House

Southam Fields Farm

Quarry

Griffin's Farm

Southam Coll

L Ctr

CV47

Napton Road Farm

Myer Bridge

Lower Farm

Glebe Farm

River Stowe

DAVENTRY RD

A425

Myer-Bridge Farm

Sewage Works

River Stowe

Southam

Liby

The Bailiffs House

Southam Fields

Home Farm

Holt Cottage Farm

Hogs Hollow

Warwick House Ind Pk

BANBURY RD

A423

Larkfield House

Highfields

Southam Holt

Southam Holt Farm

Gainsborough Trad Est

Kineton Road Ind Est

LEAMINGTON RD

A425

B4451

Starbold Farm

4

63

3

62

2

61

1

60

41   42   43

A   **B**   **C**

124
124
125

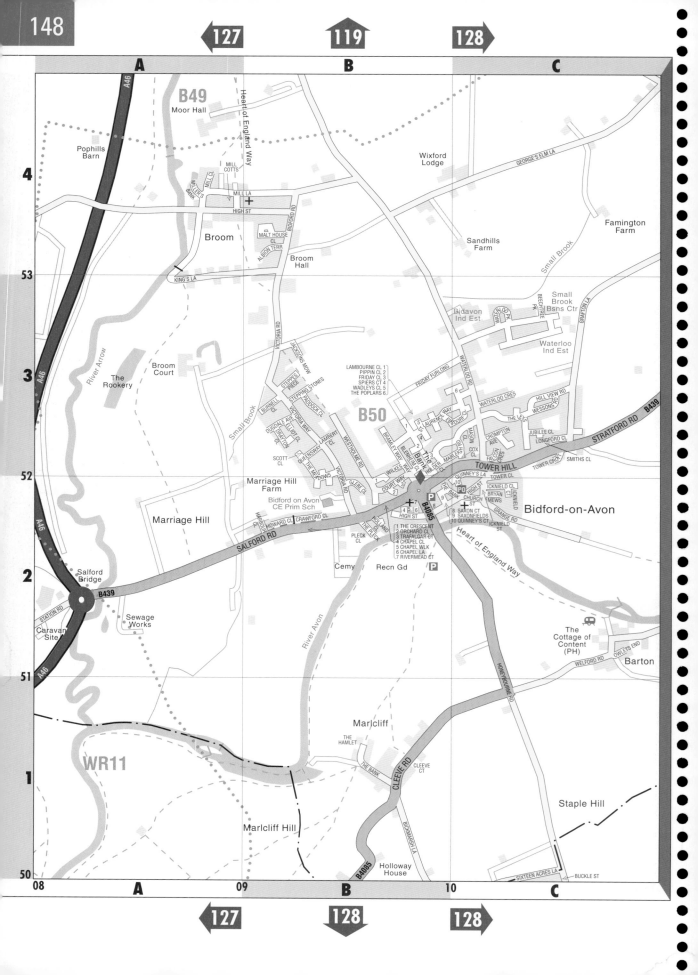

127
119
128

A **B** **C**

B49

Moor Hall

Pophills Barn

Heart of England Way

MILL CL
MILL COTTS
MILLER'S BANK
MILL LA
HIGH ST

Wixford Lodge

GEORGE'S ELM LA

Famington Farm

4

Broom

MALT HOUSE CL
ALBION TERR
Broom Hall

Sandhills Farm

Small Brook

53

KING'S LA

BIDFORD RD
VICTORIA RD

Broom Court

The Rookery

River Arrow

A46

Small Brook

JACKSONS MDW
STEPPS PIECE
STEPPING STONES
PADDOCK CL
BURNELL CL
DUGDALE AVE
ELLIOT CL
DRAYTON
VICTORIA WAY
LAMBERT CL
WESTHOLME RD
VICTORIA RD
QUEENSWAY
THE MDWS
SCOTT CL

B50

Bidavon Ind Est

WELLOT PK
BEECHTREE PK

Small Brook Bsns Ctr

Waterloo Ind Est

GRAFTON LA

LAMBOURNE CL 1
PIPPIN CL 2
FRIDAY CL 3
SPIERS CT 4
WADLEYS CL 5
THE POPLARS 6

FRIDAY FURLONG

WATERLOO RD
WATERLOO CRES

HILL VIEW RD
WESSONS RD

LAUREL WAY
MOORE
MASON
COX
MARLERS
CROMPTON AVE
JUBILEE CL
LONGFORD CL
THE LEYS

STRATFORD RD
B439

3

BRAMLEY WAY
BLEMHILL
BANK
HOLDER
COURT WAY
WILKES CL
GLEBE CL
VICTORIA RD

TOWER HILL
TOWER CRO
SMITHS CL
FALCERS

Bidford-on-Avon

52

Marriage Hill Farm

Bidford on Avon CE Prim Sch

Marriage Hill

HARBOUR
HOWARD CL
CRAWFORD CL

SALFORD RD

PLECK CL
THE PLECK
HOLLAND
HIGH ST

P
The BANK
QUINNEY'S LA
TOWER CL

CHURCH
BRYAN MEWS
ICKNIELD CL
ICKNIELD

PO
P

1 THE CRESCENT
2 ORCHARD CL
3 TRAFALGAR CT
4 CHAPEL CL
5 CHAPEL WLK
6 CHAPEL LA
7 RIVERMEAD CT

8 SAXON CT
9 SAXONFIELDS
10 QUINNEY'S CT

GRANGE RD
ICKNIELD ST

B4085

Heart of England Way

Cemy

Recn Gd

P

The Cottage of Content (PH)

WELFORD RD
OWLETS END

Barton

2

Salford Bridge

B439

Sewage Works

STATION RD
A46

Caravan Site

River Avon

HONEYBOURNE RD

51

A46

WR11

Marlcliff

THE HAMLET

THE BANK

CLEEVE RD
CLEEVE CT

Staple Hill

BUCKLE ST

1

Marlcliff Hill

BICKMARSH LA

B4085

Holloway House

SIXTEEN ACRES LA

50

08 **A** 09 **B** 10 **C**

127
128
128

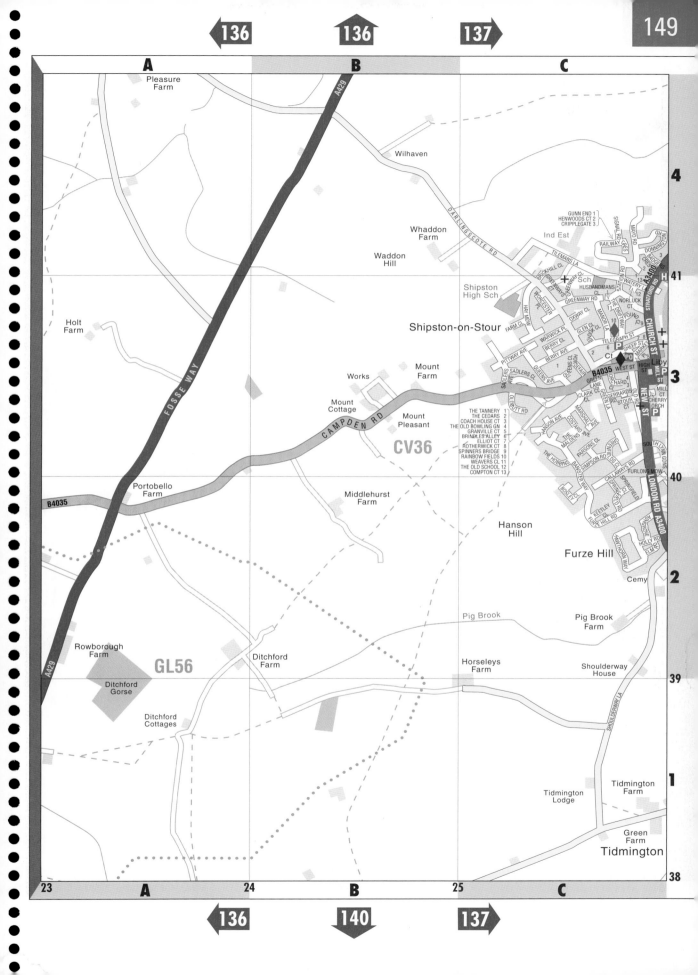

A   **B**   **C**

Pleasure Farm

A429

Wilhaven

DARLINGSCOTE RD

Whaddon Farm

4

Waddon Hill

GUNN END 1
HENWOODS CT 2
CRIPPLEGATE 3

Ind Est

SIGNAL RD
RAILWAY
MAYO RD
DONNINGTON
A3400
STRATFORD RD

Shipston High Sch

BROOKHILL CL
GREENWAYS
TILEMANS LA.
GREENWAY RD

Sch
HUSBANDMANS CL
H **41**

Holt Farm

WORCESTER
HAY MDW
FARM CL
WARWICK PL
OXWAY CL
GLEN CL
NORLUCK CT
POUND

Shipston-on-Stour

PITTWAY AVE
BERRY CL
QUEENS CL
BERRY AVE
PRIESTWAY
TELEGRAPH ST
SHEEP ST

CHURCH ST

Works

Mount Farm

SADLERS CL
SADLERS CL
QUEENS AVE

P
Ct
PO
Lib
MILL LA
3

Mount Cottage

CAMPDEN RD

Mount Pleasant

GREEN LANE
CLARK CL
GERRARDS CT
STOUR RD
WEST ST
HIGH ST
B4035
P
MILL CT
CHERRY ORCH

P

CV36

THE TANNERY 1
THE CEDARS 2
COACH HOUSE CT 3
THE OLD BOWLING GN 4
GRANVILLE CT 5
BRINDLES ALLEY 6
ELLIOT CT 7
ROTHERWICK CT 8
SPINNERS BRIDGE 9
RAINBOW FIELDS 10
WEAVERS CL 11
THE OLD SCHOOL 12
COMPTON CT 13

OLBUTT RD

HANSON AVE
COSTARD AVE
MARSHAL AVE
THE MALTINS
PARSONS CL

SOUTH LION GDNS
NEW ST

Portobello Farm

B4035

Middlehurst Farm

THE HOBBINS
SIMPSON RD
SPRINGFIELD
SPRINGCHEL
FURLONG MDW

40

Hanson Hill

CALLAWAYS RD
BINLEY
KEETLEY
FURZE HILL RD
SOUTH ROW
HOLLY CL
LONDON RD A3400
HAWTHORN WAY
ELM CL

Furze Hill

GL56

Rowborough Farm

Ditchford Farm

Pig Brook

Cemy

2

Ditchford Gorse

Horseleys Farm

Pig Brook Farm

Shoulderway House

39

Ditchford Cottages

SHOULDERWAY LA

Tidmington Farm

1

Tidmington Lodge

Green Farm

Tidmington

A429

38

23   **A**   **24**   **B**   **25**   **C**

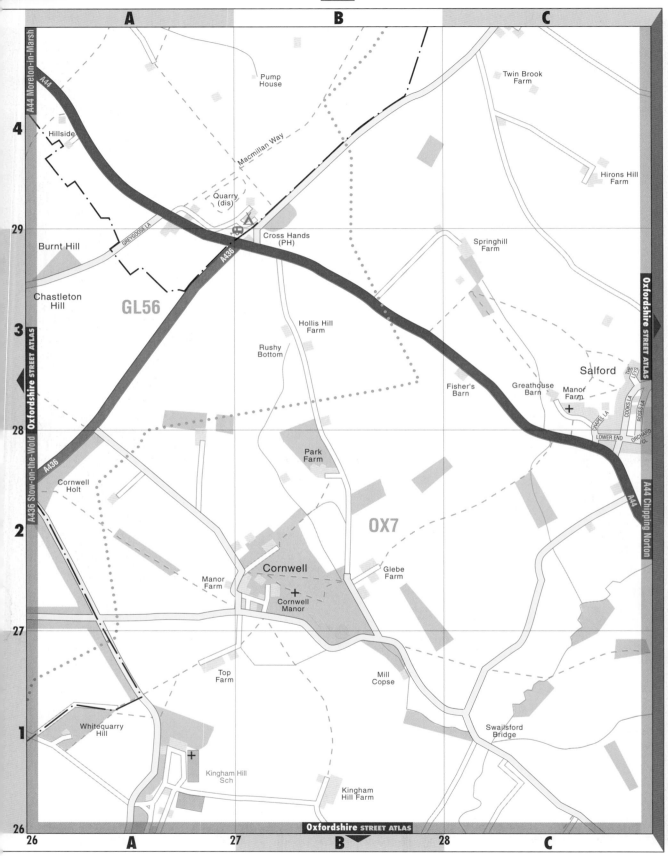

A44 Moreton-in-Marsh

A44

Oxfordshire STREET ATLAS

A436 Stow-on-the-Wold

A436

A44 Chipping Norton

4

Hillside

Pump House

Twin Brook Farm

Macmillan Way

Hirons Hill Farm

Quarry (dis)

29

Cross Hands (PH)

Burnt Hill

GREYGOOSE LA

A436

Springhill Farm

Salford

Chastleton Hill

GL56

Hollis Hill Farm

THE LEYS

3

Rushy Bottom

Fisher's Barn

Greathouse Barn

Manor Farm

CHAPEL LA

COOKS LA

ROSSES LA

ORCHARD CL

LOWER END

28

A436

Park Farm

Cornwell Holt

OX7

2

Cornwell

Manor Farm

Glebe Farm

Cornwell Manor

27

Top Farm

Mill Copse

Swailsford Bridge

1

Whitequarry Hill

Kingham Hill Sch

Kingham Hill Farm

26

26   A   27   B   28   C

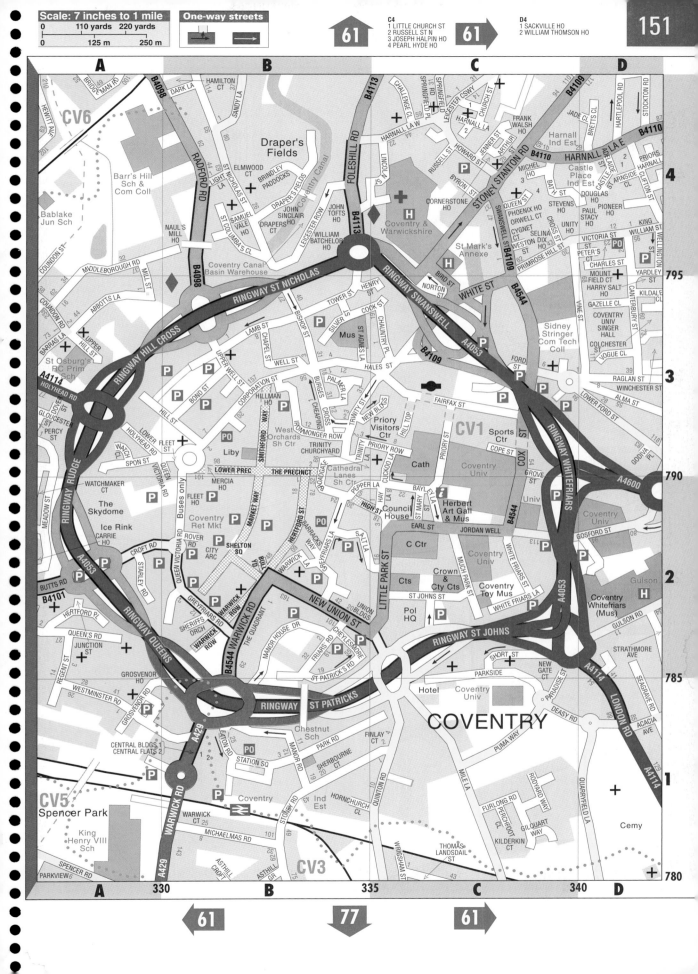

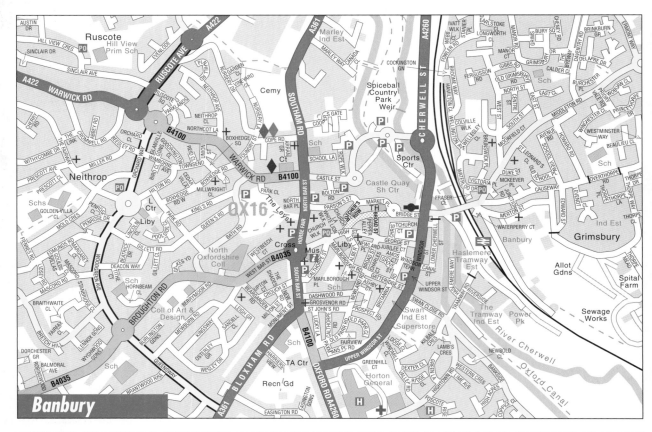

Banbury

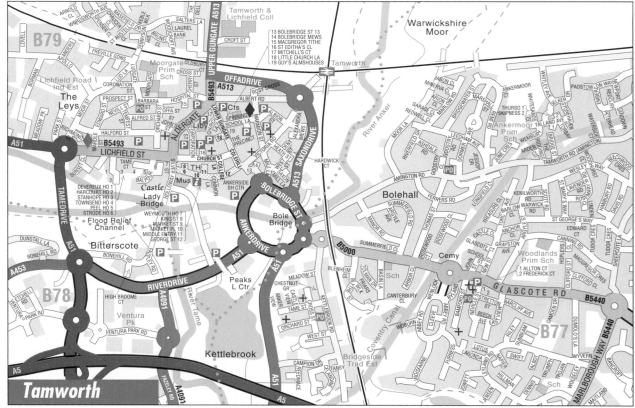

Tamworth

Index

Church Rd [6] Beckenham BR2..........**53** C6

Place name
May be abbreviated on the map

Location number
Present when a number indicates the place's position in a crowded area of mapping

Locality, town or village
Shown when more than one place has the same name

Postcode district
District for the indexed place

Page and grid square
Page number and grid reference for the standard mapping

Public and commercial buildings are highlighted in magenta   **Places of interest** are highlighted in blue with a star★

Abbreviations used in the index

Acad	Academy	Comm	Common	Gd	Ground	L	Leisure	Prom	Prom
App	Approach	Cott	Cottage	Gdn	Garden	La	Lane	Rd	Road
Arc	Arcade	Cres	Crescent	Gn	Green	Liby	Library	Recn	Recreation
Ave	Avenue	Cswy	Causeway	Gr	Grove	Mdw	Meadow	Ret	Retail
Bglw	Bungalow	Ct	Court	H	Hall	Meml	Memorial	Sh	Shopping
Bldg	Building	Ctr	Centre	Ho	House	Mkt	Market	Sq	Square
Bsns, Bus	Business	Ctry	Country	Hospl	Hospital	Mus	Museum	St	Street
Bvd	Boulevard	Cty	County	HQ	Headquarters	Orch	Orchard	Sta	Station
Cath	Cathedral	Dr	Drive	Hts	Heights	Pal	Palace	Terr	Terrace
Cir	Circus	Dro	Drove	Ind	Industrial	Par	Parade	TH	Town Hall
Cl	Close	Ed	Education	Inst	Institute	Pas	Passage	Univ	University
Cnr	Corner	Emb	Embankment	Int	International	Pk	Park	Wk, Wlk	Walk
Coll	College	Est	Estate	Intc	Interchange	Pl	Place	Wr	Water
Com	Community	Ex	Exhibition	Junc	Junction	Prec	Precinct	Yd	Yard

Index of localities, towns and villages

Alcester 143 B2; Alderminster 130 D3; Allesley 60 B7; Alveston 121 D3; Ansley 27 A2; Ansty 51 D4; Appleby Magna 3 C4; Ash Green 49 C6; Astley 37 C4; Aston Cantlow 119 F6; Aston Flamville 32 E6; Aston le Walls 134 F5; Aston Magna 140 A6; Astwood Bank 102 C1; Atherstone 18 C4; Austrey 3 A1; Avon Dassett 133 C5; Badby 126 F5; Baddesley Ensor 11 B1; Baginton 77 F2; Balsall Common 74 A7; Banbury 139 E3; Barby 101 B1; Barford 122 B7; Barnacle 51 B6; Barston 57 B1; Barton-on-the-Heath 140 F3; Bascote 115 C2; Baxterley 17 B3; Bearley 120 E7; Beausale 91 C2; Bedworth 39 B1; Bentley Heath 71 E5; Berkswell 58 D3; Bickenhill 44 D1; Bidford-on-Avon 148 C2; Binley Woods 79 C7; Binton 120 A1; Birchley Heath 17 C1; Birdingbury 115 F7; Birmingham 33 D5; Bishops Itchington 124 B4; Bishops Tachbrook 122 E7; Blackdown 105 F6; Bourton on Dunsmore 97 C1; Bradnock's Marsh 57 D3; Bramcote 40 E6; Brandon 79 F5; Braunston 117 E5; Bretford 80 B4; Brinklow 64 C2; Broadwell 116 B4; Broom 148 A4; Broughton 139 E1; Bubbenhall 95 B3; Bulkington 40 B1; Burmington 141 A8; Burton Green 75 C4; Burton Hastings 41 A4

Butlers Marston 131 F5; Catherine de Barnes 56 B6; Catthorpe 68 B1; Chadwick End 90 B7; Charwelton 126 D2; Cherington 141 D7; Cheswick Green 70 E4; Chipping Campden 135 B2; Chipping Warden 134 F3; Church Lawford 81 A3; Church Lench 127 A6; Churchover 67 B3; Claverdon 113 F3; Claybrooke Magna 43 B3; Claybrooke Parva 43 C2; Claydon 134 B5; Cleeve Prior 128 A4; Clifford Chambers 129 F6; Clifton upon Dunsmore 84 A3; Coleshill 33 F6; Combrook 131 E6; Cookhill 118 D5; Corley 48 B7; Coughton 118 F7; Coventry 61 C4; Coventry 151 C1; Cropredy 134 C1; Cubbington 106 D6; Curdworth 23 B6; Darlingscott 136 D5; Daventry 117 F1; Dordon 10 C3; Dorridge 71 E3; Drayton 139 E4; Drayton Bassett 8 B3; Dunchurch 99 B2; Dunnington 127 E8; Earlswood 70 B1; Easenhall 65 C2; Ebrington 135 F3; Epwell 138 D3; Ettington 131 B3; Farnborough 133 F4; Fazeley 8 C4; Fenny Compton 133 D7; Fenny Drayton 20 A3; Fillongley 36 C2; Flecknoe 117 C2; Frankton 97 B1; Furnace End 25 C2; Gaydon 123 E1; Grandborough 116 E5; Great Alne 119 E6; Great Rollright 142 B1; Great Wolford 140 F5; Grendon 11 B2; Halford 137 A8; Hampton Lucy 121 F4; Hampton Magna 114 F4

Hampton-in-Arden 57 B8; Hanwell 139 F6; Harborough Magna 66 A2; Harbury 123 E7; Hartshill 19 A1; Harvington 127 C4; Hatton 114 E6; Hellidon 126 B5; Henley-in-Arden 113 B5; Higham on the Hill 21 A2; Hinckley 31 B8; Hockley Heath 88 D6; Hollywood 69 B8; Honiley 91 D3; Honington 137 A5; Hook Norton 142 D4; Horley 139 D6; Hornton 139 B8; Hurley 16 B2; Ilmington 136 B6; Kenilworth 92 D4; Keresley 48 F5; Kilsby 101 C2; Kineton 132 C6; Kingsbury 15 C3; Kinwarton 143 C3; Knightcote 124 B1; Knowle 72 B6; Ladbroke 124 D5; Lapworth 88 E3; Lawford Heath 98 B4; Lea Marston 24 A4; Leamington Hastings 116 B6; Leek Wootton 104 F7; Lighthorne 123 B2; Lighthorne Heath 123 C2; Lilbourne 84 C3; Little Compton 141 A1; Little Packington 45 C6; Long Compton 141 C3; Long Itchington 115 D4; Long Lawford 82 A2; Long Marston 129 B3; Lower Boddington 134 E7; Lower Brailes 137 F2; Lower Quinton 129 D2; Lower Shuckburgh 116 F1; Lowsonford 113 B6; Loxley 130 F8; Luddington 129 C7; Lutterworth 55 C3; Mappleborough Green 112 B6; Marton 115 C7; Maxstoke 35 A1; Meer End 74 D1; Meriden 46 D1; Mickleton 135 C6; Middleton 8 A1; Minworth 22 C5

Mollington 134 A2; Monks Kirby 53 C1; Moreton Morrell 122 F3; Moreton-in-Marsh 140 B3; Napton on the Hill 125 C8; Nether Whitacre 25 A3; New Arley 37 A4; Newbold-on-Stour 130 E1; Newton 68 A1; Newton Regis 2 B2; North Newington 139 D2; Northend 133 B7; Norton 127 C2; Norton Lindsey 114 C2; Nuneaton 29 B6; Offchurch 111 B4; Offenham 127 D1; Old Arley 26 C1; Orton-on-the-Hill 6 C2; Oxhill 137 F8; Pailton 66 A4; Pebworth 128 F1; Piccadilly 15 C4; Pillerton Hersey 131 E3; Pillerton Priors 131 D2; Polesworth 5 A1; Portway 86 A5; Preston Bagot 113 D5; Princethorpe 96 C1; Priors Hardwick 125 D3; Priors Marston 125 F4; Radford Semele 110 E5; Ratley 133 A2; Redditch 102 C4; Rowington 114 A8; Rowington Green 90 A1; Rowney Green 85 A3; Royal Leamington Spa 109 C5; Rugby 83 A1; Ryton-on-Dunsmore 79 B2; Salford 150 C3; Salford Priors 127 F6; Sambourne 118 D8; Seckington 2 A2; Shawell 68 B3; Shenington 138 F5; Sherbourne 121 F8; Shilton 51 F5; Shipston-on-Stour 149 C3; Shotteswell 139 E8; Shrewley 114 B6; Shustoke 24 C1; Shutford 139 A3; Shuttington 4 C4; Sibford Ferris 142 D7; Sibford Gower 142 D8; Snitterfield 121 B6; Solihull 71 B7; South Littleton 127 F1

Southam 147 A2; Staverton 126 D7; Stockton 147 C4; Stoke Golding 21 B3; Stoneleigh 94 B6; Stratford-upon-Avon 145 A2; Stretton on Dunsmore 97 A3; Stretton on Fosse 136 B1; Stretton under Fosse 65 B4; Studley 112 C2; Sutton Coldfield 13 B3; Swalcliffe 142 F8; Swerford 142 F1; Tamworth 9 B3; Tanworth-In-Arden 87 B2; Temple Grafton 119 E2; Temple Herdewyke 132 E7; Thorpe Constantine 1 C3; Thurlaston 98 C2; Tidbury Green 69 E4; Tiddington 145 C2; Todenham 140 E6; Tredington 136 F6; Twycross 6 C4; Tysoe 138 C7; Ufton 111 C4; Ullenhall 112 D6; Upper Boddington 134 D8; Upper Brailes 137 E2; Upper Quinton 129 D1; Wardington 134 F1; Warmington 133 D2; Warton 5 C2; Warwick 108 E7; Water Orton 23 C4; Welford on Avon 129 A6; Wellesbourne 146 B2; Weston under Wetherley 107 B4; Whatcote 137 D7; Whichford 141 F5; White Stitch 46 C3; Whitnash 110 C3; Wibtoft 43 A2; Wigston Parva 42 C4; Willey 54 C3; Willoughby 117 B6; Wilmcote 120 C4; Wishaw 14 B2; Witherley 19 A4; Withybrook 52 C3; Wolston 80 A2; Wolvey 41 B2; Wood End 10 B1; Wootton Wawen 113 B1; Wroxall 90 E3; Wroxton 139 D5; Wythall 69 B3

1

1st Ave GL56 . . . . .140 B4

2

2nd Ave GL56 . . . . .140 B4

3

3rd Ave GL56 . . . . .140 B3

5

5 Hos The CV23 . . . . .67 B3
5th Ave GL56 . . . . .140 C4

6

6th Ave GL56 . . . . .140 B4

7

7th Ave GL56 . . . . .140 B3

8

8th Ave GL56 . . . . .140 B3

A

Ab Lench Rd WR11 . . . .127 A6
Abberley B77 . . . . .4 B1
Abberton Gr B90 . . . . . . .71 B7
Abberton Way CV4 . . . . . .76 E3
Abbey CE Inf Sch CV11 . .29 B5
Abbey Cl Alcester B49 . .143 A3
Southam CV47 . . . . .147 A1
Abbey Croft B78 . . . . .5 A1
Abbey Ct CV3 . . . . .78 B6
Abbey Est CV2 . . . . .62 F5
Abbey End CV8 . . . . .92 F4
Abbey Gate CV11 . . . . . .29 C4
Abbey Gate Sh Ctr CV11 .29 C4
Abbey Gn CV11 . . . . . . .29 B5
Abbey Green B78 . . . . .5 A1
Abbey Hill CV8 . . . . .92 F5
Abbey La CV47 . . . . . . .147 A2
Abbey Mews B49 . . . . . .143 A2
Abbey Rd CV3 . . . . .78 A6
Abbey St Nuneaton CV11 .29 B5
Rugby CV21 . . . . .83 B2
Abbey The CV8 . . . . .92 F5
Abbey View B78 . . . . . . .11 A4
Abbey Way CV3 . . . . . . .77 F6
Abbeydale Cl CV3 . . . . . .62 F2
Abbeyfields Dr B80 . . . .103 C3
Abbots Cl B93 . . . . .72 A7
Abbots Farm Jun & Inf Schs
CV21 . . . . .83 C1
Abbots Way CV34 . . . . .108 D6
Abbots Wlk CV6 . . . . . . .80 A2
Abbotsbury Cl CV2 . . . . .63 A4
Abbotsford Rd CV11 . . . .29 E1
Abbotsford Sch CV8 . . . .92 F6
Abbotts Gn LE10 . . . . . .31 F5
Abbotts La CV1 . . . . . . .151 A3
Abbotts St CV31 . . . . . .109 F7
Abbotts Way CV21 . . . . .83 C1
Abbotts Wlk CV3 . . . . . .79 C7
Abeles Way CV9 . . . . . . .12 B1
Abelia B77 . . . . .4 A2
Abercorn Rd CV5 . . . . . .60 E2
Aberdeen Cl CV5 . . . . . .60 A5
Aberdeen Rd CV11 . . . . .29 E1
Aberfoyle Rd CV35 . . . .132 D4
Abergavenny Wlk CV3 . . .78 F6
Abingdon Way
Birmingham B35 . . . . . . .22 A3
Nuneaton CV11 . . . . .29 F7
Abu Sultan Rd CV47 . . .132 F5
Acacia Ave CV1 . . . . .61 E1
Acacia Gr CV21 . . . . .83 A2
Acacia Rd Nuneaton CV10 .28 E5
Royal Leamington Spa
CV32 . . . . .105 D1
Achal Ct CV6 . . . . .49 F2
Achilles Cl CV34 . . . . . .109 F2
Achilles Rd CV6 . . . . . . .62 A7
Achray Cotts CV21 . . . . .97 C1
Acorn Cl Bedworth CV12 .49 C8
Stoneleigh CV8 . . . . .94 B7
Acorn Ct CV32 . . . . . . .106 A2
Acorn Dr CV22 . . . . .82 A1
Acorn St CV3 . . . . .78 B8
Acre Cl CV31 . . . . .110 A4
Acre Ditch OX15 . . . . . .142 D8
Acton Ho CV4 . . . . .59 F3
Adam Rd CV6 . . . . .61 F7
Adams St CV21 . . . . .82 C2
Adams Way B49 . . . . . . .143 A3
Adare Dr CV3 . . . . .77 C8
Adcock Dr CV8 . . . . .93 B5
Addenbrooke Rd CV7 . . .49 A6
Adderley St CV1 . . . . . . .61 E4

Addingham Cl **2** CV34 . .104 E1
Addison Cl CV10 . . . . . . .28 A5
Addison Pl B46 . . . . .23 B3
Addison Rd Coventry CV6 .61 A8
Rugby CV22 . . . . .82 B1
Adelaide Ct CV12 . . . . . .39 A2
Adelaide Rd CV31,CV32 .109 E8
Adelaide St CV1 . . . . . . .151 D4
Adkins Croft CV7 . . . . . .36 C2
Adkinson Ave CV22 . . . . .99 B2
Admington Dr CV35 . . . .114 F5
Admington La CV36 . . . .135 E7
Admiral Gdns CV8 . . . . . .93 C6
Admirals Way CV11 . . . . .40 E6
Adrians Ct CV37 . . . . . .145 A2
Agincourt Rd CV3 . . . . . .77 E7
Aikman Gn CV23 . . . . . .116 F5
Ainsbury Rd CV5 . . . . . .76 E8
Ainsdale Cl CV6 . . . . . . .50 B4
Aintree Cl Bedworth CV12 .49 C1
Coventry CV6 . . . . .61 C5
Aintree Dr CV32 . . . . . .106 C3
Aintree Rd CV37 . . . . . .144 B1
Airport Way B26 . . . . . . .44 C3
Ajax Cl CV21 . . . . .83 B3
Akon Ho CV6 . . . . .48 F2
Alan Bray Cl LE10 . . . . . .30 D7
Alan Higgs Way CV4 . . . .75 C8
Alandale Ave CV5 . . . . . .59 E4
Alandale Ct CV5 . . . . . . .49 C8
Alauna Ave B49 . . . . . . .143 B3
Albany Ct CV1 . . . . .61 A2
Albany Rd Coventry CV5 . .61 A1
Stratford-u-A CV37 . . . . .144 A1
Albany Terr CV32 . . . . . .105 E1
Albert Bean Cl CV31 . . .110 A4
Albert Cl B80 . . . . .103 C2
Albert Cres CV2 . . . . . . .49 B3
Albert Rd Allesley CV5 . . .59 A8
Fazeley B78 . . . . .9 A4
Albert Sq CV21 . . . . .83 A2
Albert St Coventry CV1 . . .61 E4
Nuneaton CV10 . . . . .28 E2
Royal Leamington Spa
CV32 . . . . .105 C1
Rugby CV21 . . . . .83 A2
Warwick CV34 . . . . .108 D7
Albion Cotts B46 . . . . . . .23 B3
Albion Ct CV11 . . . . .29 D3
Albion Ind Est CV6 . . . . .61 D7
Albion St CV8 . . . . .93 A5
Albion Terr Broom B50 . .148 B4
Water Orton B46 . . . . . . .23 B3
Albrighton Wlk CV11 . . . .30 A2
Albury Rd B80 . . . . .103 C2
Alcester By-Pass B49 . . .143 A2
Alcester Gram Sch B49 .143 A1
Alcester Heath B49 . . . .118 E6
Alcester High Sch B49 . .143 B3
Alcester Highway B98 . .102 C4
Alcester Hospl B49 . . . .143 A2
Alcester Inf Sch B49 . . .143 A2
Alcester Rd
Hollywood B47 . . . . .69 A8
Portway B48 . . . . .85 F7
Portway B48,B94,B98 . . .86 B4
Stratford-u-A CV37 . . . . .144 B2
Studley B80 . . . . .103 C2
Wootton Wawen B95 . . . .113 A1
Alcester Southern By-Pass
B49 . . . . .143 B1
Alcocks Rd B49 . . . . . . .143 B1
Alcott Cl B93 . . . . .71 F7
Alcott Hall Jun & Inf Sch
B37 . . . . .33 B1
Aldbourne Rd CV1 . . . . . .61 C5
Aldbury Rise CV5 . . . . . .60 C4
Alder Cl B47 . . . . .69 B6
Alder Ct CV9 . . . . .12 B1
Alder Dr B37 . . . . .33 B1
Alder La CV7 . . . . .74 C5
Alder Meadow Cl CV6 . . .49 D4
Alder Rd CV6 . . . . .50 A2
Alderbrooke Dr CV11 . . . .30 A1
Alderhanger La B98 . . . .112 B8
Alderman Callow Sch & Com
Coll CV4 . . . . .76 A6
Alderman Gee Hall CV12 .39 A4
Alderman Harris Prim Sch
CV4 . . . . .75 F7
Alderman Smith Sch
CV10 . . . . .28 D2
Alderman Way CV33 . . . .107 B4
Alderman's Green Com Prim
Sch CV2 . . . . .50 C3
Alderman's Green Ind Est
CV2 . . . . .50 D2
Alderman's Green Rd
CV2 . . . . .50 B3
Alderminster Cl B97 . . . .102 C2
Alderminster Gr CV35 . . .114 F5
Alderminster Rd
Coventry CV5 . . . . .60 A4
Solihull B91 . . . . .71 C8
Aldermoor Farm Prim Sch
CV3 . . . . .78 B8
Aldermoor La CV3 . . . . . .62 A1
Alderney Cl
Bramcote CV11 . . . . .40 F6
Coventry CV6 . . . . .49 B2
Alders Dr B98 . . . . .112 A6
Alders Gr CV34 . . . . . . .108 D4
Alders La CV10 . . . . .28 A7
Alders The CV12 . . . . . . .38 E2
Aldersgate Kingsbury B78 .15 B4
Nuneaton CV11 . . . . .29 C3
Aldershaws B90 . . . . . . .70 A5
Alderton Mews **16** CV31 110 C6

Aldrich Ave CV4 . . . . . . .59 E2
Aldridge Cl B78 . . . . . . .10 C4
Aldridge Rd LE10 . . . . . .31 D6
Aldrin Way CV4 . . . . . . .76 D5
Aldwick Cl CV32 . . . . . .106 A4
Alesworth Dr LE10 . . . . .31 F4
Alex Grierson Cl CV3 . . . .78 E7
Alexander Ct **1** CV34 . .108 F7
Alexander Rd CV12 . . . . .39 C3
Alexandra Ct
Atherstone CV9 . . . . .18 C4
Kenilworth CV8 . . . . .93 A4
15 Rugby CV21 . . . . . . .83 A2
Alexandra Hospl The
B98 . . . . .103 B3
Alexandra Rd
Coventry CV1 . . . . .61 F4
Royal Leamington Spa
CV31 . . . . .110 B6
Rugby CV21 . . . . .83 A2
Alexandra St CV11 . . . . .29 B4
Alexandra Terr CV6 . . . . .49 E2
Alfall Rd CV2 . . . . .62 B5
Alfred Green Cl CV22 . . . .83 A1
Alfred Rd CV1 . . . . .61 F4
Alfreda Ave B47 . . . . . . .69 A8
Alfreton Cl LE10 . . . . . . .31 F5
Alfriston Rd CV3 . . . . . . .77 C4
Alice Arnold Ho **1** CV2 . .50 B4
Alice Cl CV12 . . . . .38 F1
Alice Stevens Sch CV3 . .78 A4
Alicia CV22 . . . . .99 A4
Alison Sq CV6 . . . . .50 B4
All Saints CE Inf Sch
CV12 . . . . .39 C2
All Saints CE Jun Sch
CV34 . . . . .105 A1
All Saints CE Prim Sch
Coventry CV1 . . . . .61 E1
Leek Wootton CV35 . . . .105 A5
Nuneaton CV10 . . . . .29 C1
All Saints Cl CV7 . . . . . .52 C3
All Saints La CV1 . . . . . .61 F3
All Saints Rd
Bedworth CV12 . . . . .38 F1
Warwick CV34 . . . . .109 B8
All Saints Sq CV12 . . . . .39 B3
All Souls RC Prim Sch
CV5 . . . . .60 E2
Allan Rd CV6 . . . . .60 F4
Allans Cl CV23 . . . . .84 A3
Allans Dr CV23 . . . . .84 A3
Allans La CV23 . . . . .84 A3
Allard Ho CV3 . . . . .78 B6
Allard Way CV3 . . . . .78 C7
Allen Cl B80 . . . . .103 C2
Allendale Ave B80 . . . . .103 C2
Allendale Cres B80 . . . .103 C2
Allendale Rd B80 . . . . . .103 C2
Allens Cl CV9 . . . . .17 B4
Allens Orch OX17 . . . . .134 F3
Allerton Cl CV2 . . . . .62 E2
Allesley Croft CV5 . . . . . .60 A6
Allesley Ct CV5 . . . . .60 A6
Allesley Hall Dr CV5 . . . .60 C5
Allesley Hall Prim Sch
CV5 . . . . .60 D3
Allesley Old Rd CV5 . . . .60 C3
Allesley Prim Sch CV5 . .60 A7
Allesley Rd CV21 . . . . . . .82 C3
Alliance Cl CV11 . . . . . . .29 F3
Alliance Way CV2 . . . . . .62 A5
Allibone Cl CV31 . . . . . .110 A4
Allied Cl CV6 . . . . .49 D2
Allimore La B49 . . . . . . .143 A2
Allitt Gr CV8 . . . . .93 B5
Allwood Cl B49 . . . . . . .143 A2
Alma Cl CV11 . . . . .40 F6
Alma St CV1 . . . . .151 D3
Almond Ave
Nuneaton CV10 . . . . .28 C6
Royal Leamington Spa
CV32 . . . . .105 F3
Almond Cl CV23 . . . . . .101 B1
Almond Gr Rugby CV21 . . .82 A2
Warwick CV34 . . . . .105 A1
Almond Tree Ave CV2 . . .50 C2
Almshouses
Bedworth CV12 . . . . .39 B3
Chipping Campden GL55 .135 B2
Dunchurch CV22 . . . . . . .99 B2
Rowington Green CV35 . . .90 A1
Stoneleigh CV8 . . . . .94 C6
Stratford-u-A CV37 . . . . .145 A1
2 Warwick CV34 . . . . .108 E6
Alne Bank Rd B49 . . . . .143 B2
Alne Cl B95 . . . . .113 B4
Alpha Bsns Pk CV2 . . . . .50 D1
Alpha Ho CV2 . . . . .62 A4
Alpine Ct CV8 . . . . .93 A6
Alpine Rise CV3 . . . . . . .77 A5
Alspath La CV5 . . . . .59 F4
Alspath Rd CV7 . . . . .46 C1
Althorpe Dr B93 . . . . . . .71 E3
Althorpe Ho B90 . . . . . .110 A6
Althorpe Ind Est **15**
CV31 . . . . .110 A7
Althorpe St CV31 . . . . . .110 A7
Alton Cl CV2 . . . . .50 D2
Alum Cl CV6 . . . . .61 D8
Alvecote Cotts B79 . . . . . .4 B3
Alverley Rd CV6 . . . . . . .61 C6
Alverstone Rd CV2 . . . . .62 A4
Alverton Cl B77 . . . . .9 B2
Alveston CE Prim Sch
CV37 . . . . .145 C2
Alveston Gr B93 . . . . . . .72 B7
Alveston Grange GL55 . .135 B6

Alveston La CV37 . . . . . .121 D3
Alveston Pl **18** CV32 . . .105 F1
Alveston Rd B47 . . . . . . .69 A7
Alvin Cl CV3 . . . . .62 F1
Alvis Gate OX16 . . . . . .139 F4
Alvis Ret Pk CV5 . . . . . . .61 A3
Alvis Way NN11 . . . . . . .117 F2
Alvis Wlk B36 . . . . .22 F1
Alwyn B77 . . . . .9 C4
Alwyn Rd CV22 . . . . .99 B3
Alwynne Freeman Ct
CV7 . . . . .49 A6
Ambassador Ct CV32 . . .105 F3
Ambassador Rd B26 . . . .44 C4
Amber Bsns Village B77 . .4 A2
Amber Cl B77 . . . . .4 A2
Amber Ct B77 . . . . .4 A2
Amberley Ave CV12 . . . . .40 C2
Ambien Rd CV9 . . . . .18 B4
Ambler Gr CV2 . . . . .62 C3
Ambleside Coventry CV2 . .50 E2
Rugby CV21 . . . . .83 B4
Ambleside Way CV11 . . . .29 E6
Ambrose Cl CV21 . . . . . .83 B3
Amelia Cl CV23 . . . . .40 C3
Amersham Cl CV5 . . . . . .60 B4
Amery Lodge Farm
WR11 . . . . .128 A2
Amherst Rd CV8 . . . . . . .92 E6
Amhurst Bsns Ctr CV34 .108 B7
Amicombe B77 . . . . .4 B1
Amington Heath Com Prim
Sch B77 . . . . .4 A2
Amington Ind Est B77 . . . .4 A2
Amington Rd B90 . . . . . .70 A8
Amos Ave CV10 . . . . .29 B2
Amroth Mews CV31 . . . .110 C6
Amy Cl CV6 . . . . .49 F4
Anchor La
Harvington WR11 . . . . . .127 D3
Harvington WR11 . . . . . .127 E3
Anchorway Rd CV3 . . . . .77 B4
Anderson Ave CV22 . . . .100 A4
Anderson Dr CV31 . . . . .110 A2
Anderton Rd
Bedworth CV12 . . . . .38 C1
Coventry CV2,CV6 . . . . . .50 B4
Andover Ho B35 . . . . . . .22 B3
Andrew Cl CV13 . . . . . . .21 B4
Angel Mews **8** B46 . . . .33 F7
Angela Ave CV2 . . . . . . .50 E1
Anglesey Ave B36 . . . . . .33 B6
Anglesey Cl CV5 . . . . . . .60 B7
Angless Way CV8 . . . . . . .92 F3
Angus Cl Coventry CV5 . . .60 A4
Kenilworth CV8 . . . . .93 C6
Anker Dr CV23 . . . . .82 A3
Anker St CV11 . . . . .29 D3
Anker View B78 . . . . .11 A4
Ankerside B78 . . . . .5 A2
Ann Rd B47 . . . . .69 A3
Anne Cres CV3 . . . . .78 C5
Anne Hathaway's Cott★
CV37 . . . . .144 B1
Annie Osborn Prim Sch
CV2 . . . . .62 D7
Anns La CV23 . . . . .65 B4
Ansell Dr CV6 . . . . .50 A5
Ansell Rd CV34 . . . . . . .108 D7
Ansley Comm CV10 . . . . .28 A7
Ansley La CV7,CV10 . . . .26 C2
Ansley Rd CV10 . . . . . . .27 C2
Anson Cl Rugby CV22 . . . .82 B1
Wellesbourne CV35 . . . . .146 B1
Anson Ct B78 . . . . .9 A4
Anson Way CV2 . . . . .62 F8
Anstey Croft B37 . . . . . . .33 A4
Ansty Rd CV2 . . . . .62 E5
Antelope Gdns CV34 . . .108 C8
Anthony Way CV2 . . . . . .62 C2
Anton Dr B76 . . . . .22 A6
Antony Gardner Cres
CV31 . . . . .110 A4
Antrim Cl CV5 . . . . .60 B7
Antrobus Cl CV35 . . . . .114 C5
Apollo Way CV34 . . . . . .109 D5
Appian Cl B77 . . . . .9 C4
Appian Way B90 . . . . . . .70 D4
Apple Gr CV22 . . . . .82 A1
Apple Pie La CV10 . . . . . .19 A1
Applebee Rd LE10 . . . . . .31 D6
Appleby Cl Banbury OX16 139 F4
Great Alne B49 . . . . .119 D6
Appleby Gr B90 . . . . . . .71 B6
Appleby Hill CV9 . . . . .3 A2
Applecross Cl CV4 . . . . . .75 F6
Appledore Dr CV5 . . . . . .59 F5
Appletree Cl B91 . . . . . . .56 B5
Appletree Cotts CV35 . . .89 F1
Appletree Ind Est OX17 .134 F4
Appletree La
Aston le W NN11 . . . . . .134 F5
Cookhill WR7 . . . . .118 A3
Appletree Rd OX17 . . . .134 F3
Approach The CV31 . . . .109 F6
Apsley Gr B93 . . . . .71 F2
Aqua Ho CV32 . . . . .106 A1
Aragon Cl CV34 . . . . . . .109 D6
Aragon Ho CV3 . . . . . . .77 C8
Arbor Way B37 . . . . .33 C1
Arboretum The CV4 . . . . .75 F6
Arbour Cl Kenilworth CV8 .93 B3
Mickleton GL55 . . . . . . .135 B6
Rugby CV22 . . . . .99 B4
Arbour Tree La B93 . . . . .89 F7
Arbury Ave
Bedworth CV12 . . . . .39 A3

Arbury Ave continued
Coventry CV6 . . . . .49 F2
Arbury Banks OX17 . . . .134 F3
Arbury Cl CV32 . . . . . . .106 A4
Arbury Ct
Henley-in-A B95 . . . . . . .113 B5
Nuneaton CV10 . . . . .28 C3
Arbury Garth CV10 . . . . .28 C3
Arbury Hall Park & Gdns★
CV10 . . . . .38 D7
Arbury Hall Rd B90 . . . . .70 D8
Arbury Rd CV10 . . . . . . .28 D2
Arbury Wlk B76 . . . . .22 D5
Arcade The CV3 . . . . .62 B2
Arch Rd CV2 . . . . .62 E5
Archer Ave NN11 . . . . . .117 C5
Archer Cl B80 . . . . .103 B2
Archer Rd CV8 . . . . .92 E3
Archers Spinney CV21 . .101 A4
Archery Fields CV34 . . . .108 F6
Archery Rd Meriden CV7 .46 B1
Royal Leamington Spa
CV31 . . . . .109 E8
Arches Bsns Ctr CV21 . . .83 B3
Arches Ind Est CV21 . . . .83 B3
Arches Ind Est The CV5 . .61 A3
Arches La CV21 . . . . .83 B3
Arden Ave CV9 . . . . .18 C4
Arden Bldgs B93 . . . . . . .71 F3
Arden Bsns Ctr B49 . . . .143 A3
Arden Cl
Balsall Common CV7 . . . . .74 B7
Drayton OX15 . . . . .139 E4
Henley-in-A B95 . . . . . . .113 B4
Meriden CV7 . . . . .46 C1
Royal Leamington Spa
CV31 . . . . .110 B5
Rugby CV22 . . . . .99 B3
Warwick CV34 . . . . .105 A1
Wilmcote CV37 . . . . .120 C5
Arden Croft B46 . . . . . . .23 F1
Arden Ct Alcester B49 . .143 A3
Binley Woods CV3 . . . . . .79 D6
Hampton-in-A B92 . . . . . .57 A7
Arden Dr Dorridge B93 . . .72 A1
Sutton Coldfield, Falcon Lodge
B75 . . . . .13 B5
Arden Forest Est CV10 . .18 A1
Arden Forest Ind Est
B49 . . . . .143 B3
Arden Forest Inf Sch
CV12 . . . . .40 B3
Arden Hill Inf Sch CV9 . .18 C4
Arden Lawn Sch B95 . . .113 A4
Arden Leys B94 . . . . .86 D2
Arden Meads B94 . . . . . .88 C6
Arden Rd Alcester B49 . .143 A3
Dorridge B93 . . . . .71 F2
Henley-in-A B95 . . . . . . .113 B4
Hollywood B47 . . . . .69 A6
Kenilworth CV8 . . . . .93 B3
Nuneaton CV11 . . . . .30 A1
Tamworth B77 . . . . .9 C3
Arden St Atherstone CV9 .18 C4
Coventry CV5 . . . . .76 F8
Stratford-u-A CV37 . . . . .144 C2
Arden Vale Rd B93 . . . . .72 B7
Ardencote **6** B90 . . . . .70 C8
Ardens Cl B98 . . . . .112 A5
Arderne Dr B37 . . . . .33 A1
Argyle Cl CV21 . . . . .83 B2
Argyle Way **5** CV33 . . .122 F8
Argyll St CV2 . . . . .62 A3
Ariel Way CV22 . . . . .99 B3
Arkle B77 . . . . .9 B2
Arkle Dr CV2 . . . . .62 F7
Arklet Cl CV10 . . . . .28 C5
Arlescote Cl CV35 . . . . .114 F6
Arleston Way B90 . . . . . .70 E8
Arley La CV10 . . . . .27 B2
Arley Mews CV32 . . . . . .105 E1
Arlidge Cres CV8 . . . . . .93 C5
Arlington Ave CV32 . . . .105 F2
Arlington Ct **2** CV32 . . .105 F2
Arlington Mews **5**
CV32 . . . . .105 F2
Arlington Way CV11 . . . . .29 F2
Arlon Ave CV10 . . . . . . .28 D7
Armarna Dr CV5 . . . . . . .59 B8
Armfield St CV6 . . . . . . .62 A8
Armorial Rd CV3 . . . . . . .77 B7
Armour Cl LE10 . . . . . . .31 D5
Armscote Gr CV35 . . . . .114 E6
Armscote Rd
Ilmington CV36 . . . . .136 B6
Tredington CV36 . . . . . . .136 B6
Armscott Rd CV2 . . . . . .62 C6
Armson Rd CV7 . . . . .39 A1
Armstrong Ave CV3 . . . . .62 B1
Armstrong Cl Rugby CV22 82 C1
Whitnash CV31 . . . . .110 A2
Armstrong Dr B36 . . . . . .22 F1
Arna Ho CV3 . . . . .78 B6
Arncliffe Cl CV11 . . . . . .30 A2
Arncliffe Way **4** CV34 . .104 F1
Arne Rd CV2 . . . . .63 A6
Arnhem Cnr CV3 . . . . . . .78 C6
Arnold Ave CV3 . . . . .77 C5
Arnold Cl CV22 . . . . .83 A1
Arnold Lodge Sch CV32 105 F2
Arnold Rd CV13 . . . . .21 B3
Arnold St CV21 . . . . .83 A2
Arnold Villas **17** CV21 . .83 A2
Arnolds La B46 . . . . .34 C2
Arnside Cl CV1 . . . . .151 D4
Arran Cl CV10 . . . . .29 A3

Arran Dr B77 9 C4
Arran Way B36 33 B7
Arras Bvd CV35 108 A7
Arrow Cl B93 72 A6
Arrow Cres B49 143 B3
Arrow End WR11 128 A2
Arrow La WR11 127 F2
Arthingworth Cl CV3 62 E1
Arthur Alford Ho CV12 38 D1
Arthur Rd CV37 145 A2
Arthur St Coventry CV1 151 C4
Kenilworth CV8 93 A5
Artillery Rd CV11 40 F6
Artmeis Dr CV34 109 E5
Arun Way B76 13 A1
Arundel B77 9 B4
Arundel Cl 2 CV34 108 F8
Arundel Pl OX16 139 F3
Arundel Rd
Bulkington CV12 40 C3
Coventry CV3 77 D6
Asbury Rd CV7 74 B5
Ascot Cl Bedworth CV12 39 B4
Coventry CV3 78 C6
Stratford-u-A CV37 144 B1
Ascot Dr B77 9 B2
Ascot Rd CV35 132 D3
Ascot Ride CV32 106 C3
Ascote Way CV47 147 B2
Ascott Hill CV36 142 A5
Ascott Rd CV36 141 F5
Asfare Bsns Pk LE10 31 E1
Ash Cl CV35 114 C5
Ash Ct CV22 99 C4
Ash Dr Kenilworth CV8 93 A4
Nuneaton CV10 28 A8
Ash End House Farm★ B78 14 B8
Ash Gr Arley CV7 26 C1
Ash Green CV7 49 C7
Kingsbury B78 15 B4
Southam CV47 147 A3
Stratford-u-A CV37 144 C3
Tamworth B77 9 C3
Ash Green La CV7 49 D6
Ash Green Sch CV7 49 D6
Ash La Bearley CV37 120 E7
Newton Regis B79 2 C3
Ash Lawn Ho 8 CV31 110 A7
Ash Priors Cl CV4 60 B1
Ash Tree Ave CV4 61 A8
Ash Tree Cl CV35 146 C2
Ash Tree Gr CV7 51 E5
Ash Way NN11 117 D5
Ashborough Dr B91 71 C8
Ashbourne Way B90 70 B8
Ashbridge Rd CV5 60 C4
Ashbrook Cres B91 71 C8
Ashbrook Rise CV10 28 E4
Ashburton Cl LE10 32 A6
Ashburton La OX15 142 D3
Ashburton Rd CV2 62 E8
Ashby Cl CV3 78 F8
Ashby Ct CV11 29 D3
Ashby Rd NN11 117 E5
Ashcombe Dr CV4 59 F3
Ashcroft Cl CV2 63 A8
Ashcroft Way CV2 63 B8
Ashdale Cl CV3 79 E7
Ashdene Gdns CV8 93 B4
Ashdown Cl CV3 78 D8
Ashdown Dr CV10 28 F2
Ashe Rd CV10 28 B3
Ashfield Ave CV4 59 D1
Ashfield Rd CV8 93 B4
Ashford Dr CV12 39 A3
Ashford Gdns CV31 109 F3
Ashford La B94 88 C7
Ashford Rd Hinckley LE10 31 B7
Whitnash CV31 109 F2
Ashfurlong Cl CV7 74 B6
Ashgrove CV36 149 C2
Ashington Gr CV3 78 A5
Ashington Rd CV12 38 C1
Ashlawn Rd CV22 100 B4
Ashlawn Sch CV22 100 C4
Ashlea B78 10 C3
Ashleigh Cl CV23 101 B1
Ashleigh Dr
Nuneaton CV11 29 F1
Tamworth B77 9 C4
Ashley Cres CV34 109 B6
Ashley Way CV7 74 B7
Ashman Ave CV23 82 A3
Ashmead Rd OX17 139 F5
Ashmore Rd CV6 61 B4
Ashmores Cl B97 102 B3
Ashorne Cl Coventry CV2 50 C2
Redditch B98 103 B4
Ashorne Hall Nickelodeon★ CV33 122 F5
Ashorne Hill Management Coll CV33 122 E5
Ashow Cl CV8 93 B4
Ashridge Cl CV11 39 F8
Ashstead Cl B76 22 B6
Ashurst Cl CV6 50 B5
Ashwood Ave CV6 60 F5
Ashwood Dr B37 33 D3
Ashwood Rd CV10 28 E5
Aspbury Croft B36 22 D1
Aspen Cl Alcester B49 143 A3
Coventry CV4 59 D1
Aspen Dr Birmingham B37 44 C8
Coventry CV6 50 C6
Aspen Gr B47 69 B5
Aspens The B78 15 B4
Asplen Ct CV8 93 C4
Aspley Ct CV35 114 F6
Aspley Heath B94 86 D2
Aspley Heath La B94 86 D2
Assheton Cl CV22 99 B4
Aster Cl Hinckley LE10 31 E6
Nuneaton CV11 30 A1
Aster Way LE10 31 D6
Asthill Croft CV3 77 C8
Asthill Gr CV3 77 C8
Astley Ave CV6 49 E2
Astley Cl Redditch B98 103 A4
Royal Leamington Spa CV32 105 D2
Astley La Bedworth CV12 38 C4
Fillongley CV7 37 A2
Nuneaton CV10 28 B1
Astley Wlk CV47 133 A7
Astley's Pl CV21 101 A4
Aston Cantlow Rd CV37, B95 120 B5
Aston Flamville Rd LE10 32 C7
Aston Hill CV37 120 B5
Aston La LE10 32 A6
Aston Pk Ind Est CV11 29 B5
Aston Rd
Chipping Campden GL55 135 B3
Coventry CV5 60 F1
Nuneaton CV11 29 B5
Astwood Bank Fst Sch B96 102 C1
Astwood La B96 102 B1
Atch Lench Rd WR11 127 A6
Atcheson Cl B80 103 C2
Athena Dr CV34 109 E5
Athena Gdns CV6 50 A1
Atherston Pl CV4 76 D6
Atherstone Ind Est CV37 130 C6
Atherstone La CV9 16 C3
Atherstone Rd
Appleby Magna DE12 3 C3
Atherstone CV9 12 B2
Fenny Drayton CV13 20 A3
Furnace End B46 25 C3
Hartshill CV10 19 A1
Hurley CV9 16 B2
Atherstone St B77,B78 9 A4
Atherstone Sta CV9 18 B4
Athol Rd CV2 63 A6
Atholl Cres CV10 28 E2
Atkins Way LE10 31 E7
Atterton La CV9 19 B4
Attleborough Fields Ind Est CV11 29 F3
Attleborough La B46 23 A1
Attleborough Rd CV11 29 D3
Attoxhall Rd CV2 62 E4
Attwood Cres CV2 62 C7
Atworth Cl B98 103 A3
Auckland Dr B36 33 B7
Auden Cl CV10 27 C2
Augusta Pl CV32 109 F8
Augustine Ave B80 103 B2
Augustus Cl B46 23 F1
Augustus Dr B49 143 A2
Augustus Rd CV1 61 F4
Austcliff Cl B97 102 B3
Austcliff Dr B91 71 C8
Austen Cl CV10 27 C3
Austen Ct CV32 106 E5
Austin Cl CV9 18 B4
Austin Croft B36 22 E1
Austin Dr Banbury OX16 139 F4
Coventry CV6 62 A7
Austin Edwards Dr CV34 109 B8
Austin Way NN11 117 F2
Austin's Way OX15 142 E4
Austrey CE Prim Sch CV9 3 A1
Austrey Cl B93 72 A6
Austrey La Austrey B79 3 A3
Newton Regis B79 2 C2
Austrey Rd
Appleby Magna CV9,DE12 3 B3
Warton B79 5 C3
Austwick Cl CV34 104 E1
Auxerre Ave B98 103 A4
Auxerre Ho B98 103 A4
Avebury Cl CV11 29 F2
Aventine Way CV21 82 C4
Avenue Cl B93 72 A3
Avenue Farm CV37 144 C3
Avenue Field Ind Est CV37 144 C2
Avenue Rd
Astwood Bank B96 102 C1
Dorridge B93 72 A3
Kenilworth CV8 92 D6
Nuneaton CV11 29 D2
Royal Leamington Spa CV31 109 F7
Rugby CV21 82 C2
Stratford-u-A CV37 145 A2
Avenue The Coventry CV3 78 A6
Rowington Green CV35 90 A1
Stratford-u-A CV37 144 B3
Avery Ct 5 CV34 108 F7
Aviemore Cl CV10 29 A2
Avill B77 10 A3
Avocet Cl CV2 50 B3
Avon B77 10 A3
Avon Aquatics★ CV37 130 A3
Avon Ave CV35 138 B6
Avon Carrow CV47 133 D4
Avon Cl Barford CV35 122 B8
Bulkington CV12 40 B6
Ettington CV37 131 B3
Avon Cres Alcester B49 143 B3
Avon Cres *continued*
Stratford-u-A CV37 145 B1
Avon Ct Kenilworth CV8 92 F5
Offenham WR11 127 D1
Rugby CV21 83 A2
Avon Dassett Rd CV47 133 D6
Avon Fields CV37 131 B3
Avon Ho CV4 76 C6
Avon Ind Est Rugby CV21 83 B3
Stratford-u-A CV37 144 C2
Avon Mill CV37 145 A2
Avon Rd Coventry CV4 76 B6
Kenilworth CV8 92 E3
Lighthorne Heath CV33 123 D2
Whitnash CV31 110 A3
Avon St Clifton u D CV23 83 C2
Coventry CV2 62 B5
Rugby CV21 83 A2
Warwick CV34 109 A7
Avon Terr CV8 95 B3
Avon Valley Sch The CV21 82 C3
Avon Way CV35 138 B6
Avonbank CV37 145 A2
Avonbank Cl B97 102 B3
Avonbank Dr CV37 129 E8
Avonbank Paddocks CV37 145 A1
Avonbrook Cl CV37 144 B2
Avoncroft WR11 127 D1
Avoncroft Ho B37 33 A2
Avondale Rd Brandon CV8 79 F5
Coventry CV5 77 A8
Royal Leamington Spa CV32 106 C4
Avonfields Cl CV37 121 D3
Avonhurst CV37 145 C2
Avonlea Rise CV32 105 D2
Avonmeadow Cl CV37 144 C1
Avonmere CV21 82 C4
Avonside CV37 145 A1
Avonside Cvn Pk CV37 129 A7
Awson St CV6 61 F6
Axholme Rd CV2 62 E4
Axminster Cl CV11 29 F5
Aylesbury Cl B94 88 C6
Aylesbury Rd B94 88 D7
Aylesdene Ct CV5 76 F8
Aylesford Ct 7 CV31 110 A6
Aylesford Dr B37 44 A7
Aylesford Sch CV34 108 C4
Aylesford St Coventry CV1 61 E4
Royal Leamington Spa CV31 110 A6
Aylstone Cl CV37 129 D2
Aynho Cl CV5 60 A3
Aysgarth Cl CV11 30 A2
Azalea Cl LE10 31 E5
Azalea Dr LE10 31 E6
Azalea Wlk LE10 31 E5

B

Babbacombe Rd CV3 77 D5
Bablake Cl CV6 60 F8
Bablake Jun Sch CV1 151 A4
Bablake Sch CV1 61 B4
Bachelors Bench CV9 18 B4
Back Ends GL55 135 B2
Back Hill OX17 139 E8
Back La Birdingbury CV23 115 F7
Claverdon CV35 114 A6
Claybrooke Magna LE17 43 C3
Cleeve Prior WR11 128 A4
Harborough Magna CV23 66 A2
Henley-in-A B95 113 B5
Long Compton CV36 141 D3
Long Lawford CV23 82 A2
Lower Quinton CV37 129 E2
Meriden CV7 58 E5
Mickleton GL55 135 B6
Pebworth CV37 128 E1
Shustoke B46 24 C1
Sibford Ferris OX15 142 D8
Solihull B90 70 A5
Tysoe CV35 138 B7
Warwick CV34 108 E6
Back St Ilmington CV36 136 B6
Nuneaton CV11 29 C5
Backside La OX15 142 D8
Badbury Cl B80 103 B2
Badbury Gdns B80 103 B2
Badby Leys CV22 100 A4
Badby Sch NN11 126 F6
Baddesley Cl CV31 110 C5
Baddesley Clinton★ B93 89 F4
Badger Brook La B96 102 C1
Badger Cl B90 70 D4
Badger Rd CV3 78 D8
Badgers Cres CV36 149 C4
Badgers Farm La CV35 138 C8
Badgers Field GL55 135 B2
Baffin Cl CV22 82 C1
Baginton Fields Sch CV3 78 B4
Baginton Rd
Birmingham B35 22 B4
Coventry CV3 77 C5
Bagot Way CV34 109 E3
Bagshaw Cl CV8 79 A1
Bailey Ave B77 9 C3
Bailey Rd CV37 129 B1
Bailey's La CV23 82 A2
Bakehouse La
Chadwick End B93 90 B6
Nether Whitacre B46 24 C3
Rugby CV21 82 C2
Shotteswell OX17 139 E8
Baker Ave
Royal Leamington Spa CV31 109 F6
Stratford-u-A CV37 144 B2
Baker Dr CV35 146 B2
Baker St CV6 50 B6
Baker's Hill GL55 135 C5
Bakers Croft CV9 11 B1
Bakers Ct CV9 18 B4
Bakers La Coventry CV5 60 E2
Knowle B93 72 D1
Swalcliffe OX15 142 F8
Bakers Mews B93 90 B6
Bakers Wlk B77 9 C3
Bakewell Cl CV3 78 F8
Balcombe Ct CV22 100 C4
Balcombe Rd CV22 100 B4
Balding Cl CV23 101 B1
Baldwin Croft CV6 50 B1
Baldwins La CV35 138 B6
Balfour Cl LE10 31 E7
Ballantine Rd CV6 61 B6
Ballard Wlk B37 33 A6
Ballards Cl GL55 135 B6
Ballards La CV36 136 B6
Ballingham Cl CV4 60 A2
Balliol Rd Coventry CV2 62 C4
Hinckley LE10 31 F6
Balmoral Ave
Banbury OX16 139 F3
Banbury, Crouch Hill OX16 139 F2
Balmoral Cl CV2 62 E6
Balmoral Ct CV10 28 E6
Balmoral Rd B36 33 A7
Balmoral Way CV32 106 C6
Balsall Common Prim Sch CV7 74 B5
Balsall St B93,CV7 73 D7
Balsall St E CV7 74 B5
Balthazar Cl CV34 109 E4
Bamburgh B77 9 B4
Bamburgh Gr CV32 105 E3
Ban Brook Copse WR11 127 F6
Ban Brook Rd WR11 127 F6
Banbury Rd
Chipping Warden OX17 134 F3
Ettington CV37 131 B3
Kineton CV35 132 C5
Ladbroke CV47 124 D4
Lighthorne Heath CV35 123 C3
Lower Boddington NN11 134 E7
North Newington OX15 139 E2
Shutford OX15 139 A3
Southam CV47 147 A1
Southam CV47 147 A2
Stratford-u-A CV37 130 D7
Swerford OX7 142 E1
Warmington OX17 133 D1
Warwick CV34 109 A3
Banbury St CV35 132 B5
Bancroft Pl CV37 145 A2
Bangley La
Drayton Bassett B78 7 C3
Fazeley B78 8 A4
Bangor Ho B37 33 B4
Banister Way CV36 149 C3
Bank Cl CV35 131 F5
Bank Croft CV31 110 C5
Bank Rd CV9 18 C4
Bank St CV21 83 A2
Bank The
Bidford-on-A B50 148 B2
Bidford-on-A, Marlcliff B50 148 B1
Lighthorne CV35 123 B2
Stoneleigh CV8 94 C6
Bank View CV35 131 F5
Bankfield Dr CV32 105 C1
Banks Rd CV6 61 A5
Bankside Cl CV3 78 A6
Banky Mdw LE10 32 A7
Banner La CV4 59 D2
Banners La B97 102 C3
Banquo App
Royal Leamington Spa CV34 109 F2
Royal Leamington Spa CV34 109 F3
Bantam Gr CV6 49 A3
Bantock Rd CV4 59 E2
Bar Rd CV3 77 E8
Barber Wlk CV35 114 F4
Barbers La B91 56 C6
Barbican Rise CV2 62 E2
Barbourne Cl B91 71 B7
Barbridge Cl CV12 40 C2
Barbridge Rd CV12 40 C3
Barby CE Prim Sch CV23 117 E8
Barby La CV22 101 A2
Barby Rd Kilsby CV23 101 C2
Rugby CV22 100 A4
Barcheston Dr CV35 114 E6
Barcheston Rd B93 72 A4
Barcombe Cl OX16 139 F5
Bardley Dr CV6 61 C6
Bardon View Rd B78 11 A4
Bards Wlk CV37 145 A3
Bardswell Ct CV37 144 C2
Barford App CV31 110 B2
Barford Cl CV3 78 D8
Barford Rd CV8 93 B3
Barford St Peter's CE Prim Sch CV35 122 B7
Barham Cl B90 71 A5
Bari Rd CV35 132 E5
Barker's Butts La CV6 61 A4
Barkers La B47 69 A1
Barkers' Butts La CV6 61 A5
Barkus Cl CV47 147 B2
Barle Gr B36 33 A7
Barley Cl Henley-in-A B95 113 B4
Rugby CV21 101 A4
Sibford Gower OX15 142 D8
Barley Ct CV32 105 F2
Barley Lea Ho CV3 78 B8
Barley Lea The CV3 78 C8
Barlichway B49 143 B2
Barlow Ct B78 15 B3
Barlow Rd CV2 50 D2
Barn Cl
Clifford Chambers CV37 129 F7
Coventry CV5 60 C5
Dordon B78 10 C3
Whitnash CV31 110 B3
Barn End Rd B79 5 C2
Barn La CV23 96 C1
Barnack Ave CV3 77 B5
Barnack Dr CV34 104 E1
Barnacle La CV12 40 C1
Barnard Cl
Birmingham B37 33 D1
Royal Leamington Spa CV32 106 C3
Barnbrook Rd B93 72 A7
Barncroft CV36 141 C3
Barne Cl CV11 40 B7
Barnfield Ave CV5 60 B6
Barnsley Cl CV9 18 B4
Barnstaple Cl CV5 59 F5
Barnwell Cl CV22 99 B2
Baron's Croft CV3 77 E7
Baron's Field Rd CV3 77 E8
Barons Croft CV10 28 C4
Barpool Rd CV10 28 F4
Barr La Brinklow CV23 64 C2
Higham on t H CV13 21 A2
Barr's Hill Sch & Com Coll CV1 151 A4
Barra Croft B35 22 B4
Barrack Cl B75 13 A6
Barrack St CV34 108 E7
Barracks Gn CV35 130 F7
Barracks La CV35 91 C2
Barracks Way CV1 151 B2
Barras Ct CV2 62 A4
Barras Gn CV2 62 A4
Barras La CV1 61 B3
Barrels Pitch GL55 135 B2
Barretts La CV7 74 C6
Barrington Rd CV22 82 B1
Barrow Cl CV2 63 B6
Barrow Rd CV8 92 F4
Barrowfield Ct CV8 92 F4
Barrowfield La CV8 92 F4
Barry Ho CV2 50 D1
Barsby Cl CV9 18 B4
Barston Cl CV6 50 A2
Barston La
Balsall Common CV7 73 D8
Barston B92 57 C1
Catherine de B B91 56 B2
Hampton-in-A B92 56 D3
Bartholomew Ct CV3 78 A6
Bartleet Rd B98 103 C4
Bartlett Cl Coventry CV6 49 E2
2 Warwick CV34 108 F7
Barton Cres CV31 110 C6
Barton Dr B93 72 B4
Barton Fields CV37 129 A6
Barton Rd Bedworth CV12 39 A4
Coventry CV6 49 F2
Long Compton CV36,GL56 141 B4
Nuneaton CV10 29 C1
Rugby CV22 99 B4
Barton's Mdw CV2 62 B6
Barwell Cl Dorridge B93 71 E4
Royal Leamington Spa CV32 105 F3
Basant Cl CV34 109 A7
Bascote Rd CV47 115 C3
Bascote Rise CV47 147 A3
Baseley Way CV6 49 D4
Basford Brook Dr CV6 49 F4
Basildon Wlk 3 CV2 63 A7
Basin Bridge La CV13 21 B2
Bassett Rd CV6 61 A5
Bastyan Ave CV37 129 D2
Bateman Rd B46 23 F1
Bateman's Acre S 1 CV6 61 A4
Bates Cl B76 22 B8
Bates La B94 86 F1
Bates Rd CV5 76 E8
Bath Pl 3 CV31 109 F7
Bath Rd Atherstone CV9 18 C4
Nuneaton CV11 29 C5
Bath St Coventry CV1 151 C4
Royal Leamington Spa CV31 109 F7
Rugby CV21 83 A2
Bathurst Rd CV6 61 A6
Bathway Rd CV3 77 A4
Batsford Cl B98 103 A3
Batsford Rd CV6 60 F4
Battalion Ct CV6 49 A1
Battle Ct CV35 132 B6
Baulk La CV7 58 D1
Bawnmore Ct CV22 99 B4
Bawnmore Inf Sch CV22 99 C4
Bawnmore Pk CV22 99 C4
Bawnmore Rd CV22 99 B4
Baxter Cl CV4 60 A2
Baxter Ct 10 CV31 110 A7
Baxters Gn B90 70 B8

Baxters Rd B90 ....70 B8
Bay Tree Cl CV2 ....50 D1
Bay Tree Farm WR11 ...128 A4
Bayley La CV1 ....151 C2
Bayliss Ave CV6 ....50 A4
Bayton Rd CV7 ....50 B7
Bayton Road Ind Est CV7 50 B8
Bayton Way CV7 ....50 C7
Baywell Cl B90 ....71 A7
Bazzard Rd CV11 ....41 A3
Beacon Cl B49 ....143 B3
Beacon Rd CV6 ....49 D3
Beaconsfield Ave CV22 ..83 A1
Beaconsfield Ct CV11 ...29 D5
Beaconsfield Rd CV2 ....62 B2
Beaconsfield St CV31 ..110 B7
Beaconsfield St W CV31 110 B8
Beake Ave CV6 ....61 B7
Beale Cl Birmingham B35 ..22 A2
10 Bishops Tachbrook CV33 ....122 F8
Beamish Cl CV2 ....63 A6
Beanacre Rd OX15 ....142 D3
Beanfield Ave CV3 ....76 F4
Bear Cl B95 ....113 B5
Bear La B95 ....113 A5
Bear La Cl B78 ....5 A1
Bearcroft Gdns GL55 ...135 C6
Bearley Croft B90 ....70 C8
Bearley Gn CV37 ....120 E7
Bearley Grange CV37 ..120 D7
Bearley Halt B95 ....120 D7
Bearley Rd
Aston Cantlow B95 ....120 A7
Snitterfield CV37 ....121 A7
Beatty Dr CV22 ....82 B1
Beauchamp Ave CV32 ..105 F1
Beauchamp Cl
1 Birmingham B37 ....33 B2
Sutton Coldfield B76 ....22 B7
Beauchamp Ct 1 CV32 .105 F1
Beauchamp Gdns CV34 .109 B6
Beauchamp Hill CV32 ..105 E1
Beauchamp Ind Pk B77 ...9 B4
Beauchamp Rd
Alcester B49 ....143 B3
Kenilworth CV8 ....92 F2
Royal Leamington Spa CV32 ....105 F1
Tamworth B77 ....9 C3
Warwick CV34 ....109 B8
Beaudesert Cl
Henley-in-A B95 ....113 B4
Hollywood B47 ....69 A6
Beaudesert La B95 ....113 B5
Beaudesert Rd
Coventry CV5 ....61 A1
Hollywood B47 ....69 A6
Beaufell Cl CV34 ....104 E1
Beaufort Ave CV32 ....106 C5
Beaufort Cl Hinckley LE10 .31 E4
Wellesbourne CV35 ....146 B1
Beaufort Dr CV3 ....78 F7
Beaulieu Pk CV31 ....110 D6
Beaumaris Cl
Banbury OX16 ....139 F4
Coventry CV5 ....59 F5
Beaumont Ave LE10 ....31 A7
Beaumont Cl CV47 ....133 A7
Beaumont Cres CV6 ....61 A4
Beaumont Ct
9 Coventry CV6 ....61 A4
8 Royal Leamington Spa CV31 ....110 A6
Beaumont Pl CV11 ....29 A4
Beaumont Rd
Keresley CV7 ....49 A6
Nuneaton CV11 ....29 A4
Beausale Croft CV5 ....60 A3
Beausale Dr B93 ....72 C7
Beausale La CV35 ....114 E7
Beck's Cl CV47 ....147 C4
Beck's La CV47 ....147 C4
Beckbury Rd CV2 ....62 F6
Becket Cl GL56 ....140 E7
Beckfoot Cl CV21 ....83 B4
Beckfoot Dr CV2 ....50 F1
Beckford Croft B93 ....71 F3
Becks La CV7 ....47 A5
Beconsfield Cl B93 ....71 F2
Bedale Rd CV35 ....132 D4
Bede Arc CV12 ....39 B3
Bede Rd Bedworth CV12 ..39 A4
Coventry CV6 ....61 B6
Nuneaton CV10 ....28 D3
Bedford Cl OX16 ....139 F4
Bedford Ho B36 ....33 B6
Bedford Pl 5 CV32 ....109 F8
Bedford St Coventry CV1 ..61 A2
Royal Leamington Spa CV32 ....109 F8
Bedlam La CV6 ....49 E2
Bedworth Cl CV12 ....40 B2
Bedworth La CV12 ....38 D4
Bedworth Rd
Bedworth CV12 ....39 F2
Bulkington CV12 ....40 A2
Coventry CV6,CV7 ....50 A5
Bedworth Sta CV12 ....39 C2
Beech Ave B37 ....33 B1
Beech Cl Alcester B49 ...143 B1
Hurley CV9 ....16 B3
Kingsbury B78 ....15 B4
Nuneaton CV10 ....28 A8
Rowington CV35 ....114 A8
Beech Cl *continued*
Southam CV47 ....147 A2
Stratford-u-A CV37 ....145 B1
Beech Cliffe CV34 ....108 F8
Beech Ct
Royal Leamington Spa CV34 ....109 E2
Rugby CV22 ....100 C4
Stratford-u-A CV37 ....145 A1
Beech Dr Kenilworth CV8 ..93 B5
Rugby CV22 ....99 B4
Thurlaston CV23 ....98 C2
Beech Gr Arley CV7 ....26 C1
Warwick CV34 ....105 B1
Beech Hill NN11 ....126 B5
Beech Rd Coventry CV6 ...61 B5
Hollywood B47 ....69 B6
Oxhill CV35 ....137 F8
Beech Tree Ave CV4 ....60 B2
Beecham Ind Est CV37 .130 C5
Beecham Wlk CV37 ....144 B2
Beechcroft Bedworth CV12 38 F1
Long Itchington CV47 ....115 D4
Beechcroft Rd B36 ....22 C1
Beecher's Keep CV8 ....79 F5
Beeches The
Bedworth CV12 ....38 E2
Clifton u D CV23 ....83 C3
Harbury CV33 ....123 E7
Hartshill CV10 ....19 A1
Polesworth B78 ....11 A4
Beeches Wlk CV37 ....145 C2
Beechnut Cl CV4 ....59 D2
Beechtree Pk B50 ....148 C3
Beechwood Ave
Coventry CV5 ....76 F8
Hinckley LE10 ....31 D3
Beechwood Cl B90 ....70 D4
Beechwood Croft CV8 ....92 F2
Beechwood Ct CV5 ....76 F8
Beechwood Rd
Bedworth CV12 ....39 D4
Nuneaton CV10 ....28 D6
Beehive Hill CV8 ....92 E7
Beehive La B76 ....23 C6
Beeston Cl CV3 ....78 F8
Begonia Cl LE10 ....31 E5
Begonia Dr LE10 ....31 E5
Belcony GL56 ....136 C1
Belfry Cl LE10 ....31 D4
Belgrave Dr CV21 ....83 B3
Belgrave Rd Coventry CV2 62 E4
Tamworth B77 ....9 C4
Belgrave Sq CV2 ....62 E4
Belgravia Ct B37 ....33 A5
Bell Brook CV37 ....121 B6
Bell Cl B36 ....33 B6
Bell Ct
Royal Leamington Spa CV32 ....105 F2
Stratford-u-A CV37 ....145 A1
Bell Dr CV7 ....49 E7
Bell Green Rd CV6 ....62 A8
Bell Hill OX15 ....142 D4
Bell La Monks Kirby CV23 ..53 C1
Snitterfield CV37 ....121 B6
Stratford-u-A CV37 ....144 B1
Studley B80 ....103 C2
Bell Mead B80 ....103 C2
Bell St
Claybrooke Magna LE17 ...43 C3
Hornton OX15 ....139 B7
Bell Tower Mews CV32 .105 F3
Bell Wlk CV21 ....101 A4
Bell's La OX15 ....142 D4
Bellairs Ave CV12 ....38 E1
Bellam Rd CV35 ....114 F4
Bellbrooke Cl CV6 ....50 B1
Belle Cotts B94 ....88 D5
Belle Vue CV10 ....28 E3
Belle Vue Terr B92 ....57 A6
Bellemere Rd B92 ....57 B6
Bellfield B94 ....87 A2
Bellingham B77 ....4 B1
Bellington Croft 5 B90 ..71 A6
Bells La OX15 ....137 E3
Bellview Way CV6 ....50 B1
Belmont Ct CV32 ....106 A4
Belmont Dr CV32 ....106 A4
Belmont Mews CV8 ....92 F4
Belmont Rd Coventry CV6 .62 A7
Rugby CV22 ....83 A1
Tamworth B77 ....9 C4
Belton Cl B94 ....88 C5
Belvedere Rd CV5 ....77 A8
Belvoir B77 ....9 B4
Benedict Sq CV2 ....62 C8
Benedictine Rd CV3 ....77 C8
Bengrove Cl B98 ....103 A4
Benn Rd CV12 ....40 B2
Benn St CV22 ....83 B1
Bennet Cl CV13 ....21 B4
Bennett Ct CV8 ....79 F3
Bennett Dr CV34 ....109 C7
Bennett Pl CV36 ....136 B6
Bennett St CV21 ....82 C2
Bennett's Rd CV7 ....48 F4
Bennett's Rd N CV7 ....48 E7
Bennett's Rd S CV6 ....48 F2
Bennfield Rd CV21 ....83 A2
Benson Rd Coventry CV6 ..49 A1
Stratford-u-A CV37 ....145 A2
Benthall Rd CV6 ....49 F2
Bentley Cl Banbury OX16 .139 F4
Royal Leamington Spa CV32 ....106 B3
Bentley Ct Coventry CV6 ..49 C4
Nuneaton CV11 ....29 A4
Bentley Farm Cl B93 ....71 E4
Bentley Heath CE Prim Sch B93 ....71 F5
Bentley Heath Cotts B93 .71 F5
Bentley La B46 ....35 B2
Bentley Rd Bedworth CV7 .39 A1
Nuneaton CV11 ....29 A4
Bentley Way NN11 ....117 F2
Benton Green La CV7 ....58 F2
Bentree The CV3 ....78 B8
Beoley La B98 ....86 B1
Berenska Dr CV32 ....106 A2
Beresford Ave CV6 ....49 E1
Bericote Rd CV32 ....105 E8
Berkeley Cl
Banbury OX16 ....139 F4
Nuneaton CV11 ....29 B3
Redditch B98 ....112 A6
Berkeley Rd CV8 ....92 E6
Berkeley Rd N CV5 ....61 A1
Berkeley Rd S CV5 ....77 A8
Berkett Rd CV6 ....49 B2
Berkshire Cl CV10 ....28 E3
Berkswell CE Prim Sch CV7 ....58 C3
Berkswell Hall CV7 ....58 C3
Berkswell Rd
Coventry CV6 ....50 B2
Meriden CV7 ....58 C7
Berkswell Sta CV7 ....74 C8
Berkswell Windmill★ CV7 ....74 D4
Bermuda Bsns Pk CV10 ..39 A7
Bermuda Ind Est CV10 ...39 B8
Bermuda Rd CV10 ....29 A1
Berners Cl CV4 ....59 E2
Berrills La CV36 ....141 D7
Berrington Rd
Chipping Campden GL55 .135 C2
Nuneaton CV10 ....28 D7
Royal Leamington Spa CV31 ....110 B6
Berrow Cottage Homes B93 ....72 C6
Berry Ave CV36 ....149 C3
Berry Cl CV36 ....149 C3
Berry Hall La B91 ....56 B4
Berry La NN11 ....126 B5
Berry Mdw CV47 ....133 E7
Berry St CV1 ....61 E4
Berryfields CV7 ....36 C2
Berryfields La CV36, CV37 ....136 C7
Berrymound View B47 ...69 C7
Bertie Rd CV8 ....93 A4
Bertie Terr CV32 ....105 E1
Berwick Cl Coventry CV5 ..60 B4
Warwick CV34 ....104 E2
Berwicks La B37 ....33 B1
Berwood Pk B35 ....22 A2
Berwyn Ave CV6 ....49 A1
Berwyn Way CV10 ....28 C4
Besbury Cl B93 ....71 E2
Besford Gr B90 ....71 B6
Best Ave CV8 ....93 C7
Beswick Gdns CV22 ....99 B4
Bettina Cl CV10 ....28 B5
Bettman Cl CV3 ....77 E6
Bettridge Pl CV35 ....146 B2
Beverley Ave CV10 ....28 B4
Beverley Cl
Astwood Bank B96 ....102 C1
Balsall Common CV7 ....74 C7
Beverley Rd CV32 ....105 D1
Beverly Dr CV4 ....76 D2
Bevington Cres CV6 ....60 E5
Bexfield Cl CV5 ....60 A6
Beyer Cl B77 ....4 A1
Biart Pl CV21 ....83 B2
Bicester Sq B35 ....22 B4
Bickenhill Green Ct B92 .44 D1
Bickenhill La
Birmingham B26,B37,B40 ..44 D4
Birmingham B37 ....44 C6
Catherine de B B92 ....56 C6
Bickenhill Parkway B37 .44 D6
Bickenhill Rd B37 ....44 B7
Bickmarsh La B50 ....148 B1
Bickmarsh Lodge Cotts WR11 ....128 D2
Bidavon Ind Est B50 ...148 C3
Biddles Hill B94 ....86 C6
Biddulph Terr CV23 ....97 B1
Bideford Rd CV2 ....62 C7
Bidford on Avon CE Prim Sch B50 ....148 B2
Bidford Rd B50 ....148 B4
Bigbury Cl CV3 ....77 E5
Biggin Cl B35 ....22 A3
Biggin Hall Cres CV3 ....62 B2
Biggin Hall La CV23 ....98 C1
Bignolds Cl OX17 ....134 B4
Bigwood Dr B75 ....13 A5
Bilberry Rd CV2 ....50 D2
Bilbury Cl B97 ....102 B3
Billesden Cl CV3 ....78 E8
Billesley La B48 ....85 E6
Billesley Rd CV37 ....120 C4
Billing Rd CV5 ....60 D3
Billingham Cl B91 ....71 B8
Billinton Cl CV2 ....62 E2
Bills La B90 ....69 F8
Bilton CE Jun Sch CV22 .99 B3
Bilton Grange Sch CV22 .99 C2
Bilton High Sch CV22 ...82 A1
Bilton Ind Est CV3 ....61 F1
Bilton Inf Sch CV22 ....99 B4
Bilton La Dunchurch CV22 .99 B2
Bilton La *continued*
Long Lawford CV22,CV23 ..82 A2
Bilton Rd CV22 ....82 C1
Binley Ave CV3 ....78 F7
Binley Bsns Pk CV3 ....63 A1
Binley Cl B90 ....70 A8
Binley Gr CV3 ....78 F7
Binley Ind Est CV3 ....79 A8
Binley Rd CV2,CV3 ....62 D1
Binley Woods Prim Sch CV3 ....79 E7
Binns Cl CV4 ....75 F8
Binswood Ave CV32 ....105 F2
Binswood Cl CV2 ....50 D2
Binswood End CV33 ....123 E7
Binswood Mans 12 CV32 ....105 F2
Binswood St CV32 ....105 E1
Binton Rd Coventry CV2 ..50 D2
Welford on A CV37 ....129 A7
Bintonhill CV37 ....120 A1
Birbeck Ho B36 ....33 B6
Birch Abbey B49 ....143 A2
Birch Cl Bedworth CV12 ..39 D4
Coventry CV5 ....59 F6
Kingsbury B78 ....15 B4
Birch Coppice Distribution Pk B78 ....10 C2
Birch Croft B37 ....33 C1
Birch Ct CV34 ....109 E2
Birch Dr CV22 ....82 A1
Birch End CV34 ....109 B8
Birch Gr
Balsall Common CV7 ....74 B8
Polesworth B78 ....10 B4
Wellesbourne CV35 ....146 C2
Birches La CV8 ....93 B3
Birches The CV12 ....40 B4
Birchfield Cl CV9 ....10 B1
Birchfield Rd
Coventry CV6 ....60 F8
Stratford-u-A CV37 ....145 A3
Birchgrave Cl CV6 ....62 A7
Birchley Heath Rd CV10 .17 C1
Birchmoor Rd B78 ....10 C4
Birchtree Rd CV10 ....28 C6
Birchway Cl CV32 ....105 C1
Birchwood Ave B78 ....10 C4
Birchwood Prim Sch B78 10 C4
Birchwood Rd CV3 ....79 C7
Birchy Cl B90 ....69 F6
Birchy Leasowes La B90 .69 E5
Bird Grove Ct CV1 ....61 D5
Bird Rd
Lighthorne Heath CV33 ...123 D2
Royal Leamington Spa CV34 ....109 D4
Bird St CV1 ....151 C3
Birdhaven Cl CV33 ....123 D2
Birdhope B77 ....4 B1
Birdingbury La CV23 ...115 E8
Birdingbury Rd
Birdingbury CV23 ....115 F8
Marton CV23 ....115 D7
Birds Bush Prim Sch B77 .9 C4
Birds Bush Rd B77 ....9 C4
Birds La OX15 ....138 D3
Birkdale Cl Coventry CV6 .49 B4
Nuneaton CV11 ....30 A1
Birmingham Bsns Pk B37 ....44 E8
Birmingham Int Airport B40 ....44 B4
Birmingham Int Sta B40 .44 D4
Birmingham Rd
Alcester B49 ....143 A2
Allesley CV5 ....59 E7
Ansley CV10 ....27 A2
Burton Green CV8 ....75 A1
Coleshill B46 ....33 E5
Henley-in-A B95 ....113 B6
Kenilworth CV8 ....92 C8
Little Packington CV7 ....45 E3
Nether Whitacre B46,B76 ..24 B4
Shrewley CV35 ....114 D6
Stoneleigh CV8 ....94 B6
Stratford-u-A CV37 ....144 C3
Studley B80 ....103 C4
Warwick CV34 ....108 B8
Water Orton B46 ....23 A3
Wilmcote CV37,B95 ....120 D6
Wroxall B93,CV35 ....90 D3
Birstall Dr CV21 ....83 B3
Birvell Ct CV12 ....39 D3
Bishop Carpenter CE Prim Sch Ox15 ....139 D2
Bishop St CV1 ....151 B3
Bishop Ullathorne RC Sch CV3 ....76 F4
Bishop Wilson CE Prim Sch B37 ....33 C3
Bishop Wulstan RC Sch CV22 ....83 A1
Bishop's Ct B37 ....44 E8
Bishop's Hill CV35 ....123 B2
Bishop's Itchington Prim Sch CV47 ....124 B4
Bishop's Tachbrook CE Prim Sch CV33 ....122 F8
Bishopgate Bsns Pk CV1 61 D5
Bishopgate Ind Est CV1 .61 D5
Bishops Bowl Lakes Water Sports Ctr CV47 ....124 A5
Bishops Cl
16 Bishops Tachbrook CV33 ....122 F8
Stratford-u-A CV37 ....144 B2
Bishops Cleeve CV9 ....3 A1
Bishops Gate CV47 ....124 B5
Bishops Wlk CV5 ....77 B8
Bishopton Cl CV5 ....60 B3
Bishopton La CV37 ....144 B3
Bishopton Prim Sch CV37 ....144 B2
Bisset Cres 12 CV31 ....110 C6
Bitham Rd CV33 ....123 D3
Bixhill La B46 ....25 A2
Black Bank CV7 ....39 B1
Black Hall La CV7 ....36 B2
Black Horse Hill DE12 ....3 C4
Black Horse Rd CV6 ....50 B6
Black La CV32 ....106 C2
Black Prince Ave CV3 ....77 E6
Black-a-Tree Ct CV10 ...28 F5
Black-A-Tree Rd CV10 ...28 E4
Blackberry Ave B94 ....88 C6
Blackberry Cl CV23 ....83 B4
Blackberry La
Ash Green CV7 ....49 C5
Coventry CV2 ....62 C6
Blackbird Croft B36 ....33 A7
Blackburn Rd CV6 ....49 F3
Blackcat Cl B37 ....33 A3
Blackdown B77 ....4 B1
Blackdown Rd B93 ....72 B6
Blackfirs La B37,B46 ....44 D7
Blackford Cl B95 ....113 B4
Blackford Hill B95 ....113 B4
Blackford Rd B90 ....70 C8
Blackford Way CV35 ....137 F8
Blackgreaves La B76 ....14 F1
Blacklow Rd CV34 ....105 A1
Blackman Way CV21 ....82 C2
Blackshaw Dr CV2 ....62 F6
Blacksmith's La NN11 ...134 F5
Blacksmiths Cl WR11 ...127 F1
Blacksmiths La
Hockley Heath B94 ....88 C6
Mollington OX17 ....134 A2
Northend CV47 ....133 B7
South Littleton WR11 ....127 F1
Blacksmiths Yd CV13 ....21 B4
Blackthorn Cl CV4 ....76 D5
Blackthorn Gr CV11 ....29 F2
Blackthorn Rd CV37 ....145 A3
Blackthorn Way B49 ....143 A3
Blackthorne Rd CV8 ....93 A3
Blackwatch Rd CV6 ....61 C8
Blackwell Rd
Coventry CV6 ....61 E8
Tredington CV36 ....136 F6
Blackwood Ave CV22 ....82 B1
Blackwood Rd B77 ....9 B4
Blacon Way CV37 ....144 B2
Bladon Cl CV11 ....29 F8
Bladon Wlk 6 CV31 ....110 C6
Blair Dr CV12 ....38 D1
Blair Gr B37 ....33 D1
Blake Cl Nuneaton CV10 ..28 A5
Rugby CV22 ....82 B1
Blake's Hill WR11 ....128 B1
Blakelands Ave CV31 ....110 B6
Blakenhurst WR11 ....127 C4
Blandford Ave B36 ....22 E1
Blandford Dr CV2 ....62 F5
Blandford Rd CV32 ....105 C1
Blandford Way CV35 ....108 A7
Blanning Ct B93 ....71 E3
Blaze La B96,B97 ....102 A2
Bleaberry CV21 ....83 B4
Bleachfield St B49 ....143 A2
Blenheim Ave CV6 ....49 C2
Blenheim Cl
Bidford-on-A B50 ....148 B3
Nuneaton CV11 ....29 F2
Blenheim Cres CV31 ....110 C5
Blenheim Way B35 ....22 B2
Blenheim Wlk
Coventry CV6 ....49 B4
Wellesbourne CV35 ....146 B1
Bletchley Dr Coventry CV5 60 B4
Tamworth B77 ....9 B4
Blew Gates OX15 ....137 F2
Blewitt Cl B36 ....22 D2
Blick Rd CV34 ....109 C4
Blind La Berkswell CV7 ...58 D4
Chipping Campden GL55 ..135 A1
Kenilworth CV8 ....75 F1
Tanworth-In-A B94 ....86 D1
Blindpit La B76 ....23 B8
Bliss Cl CV4 ....59 E3
Blockley Rd CV12 ....39 C4
Blockley's Yd 4 LE10 ....31 D8
Blondvil St CV3 ....77 D7
Bloxam Gdns CV22 ....82 C1
Bloxam Pl 6 CV21 ....83 A2
Bloxham Rd OX16 ....139 F1
Blue Cap Rd CV37 ....145 A3
Blue Coat CE Sch CV1 ...61 F1
Blue La CV35 ....130 E6
Blue Lake Rd B93 ....72 B2
Blue Lias Ind Est CV47 .115 F4
Bluebell Cl CV23 ....83 B4
Bluebell Dr
Bedworth CV12 ....38 E2
Birmingham B37 ....33 E2
Bluebell Wlk CV4 ....59 F1
Bluebellwood Cl B76 ....13 A3
Blundells Croft CV37 ...129 A7
Blundells The CV8 ....93 A5
Blyth Ave CV7 ....74 C5
Blyth Cl CV12 ....38 C1
Blyth Ct CV11 ....29 C3
Blythe Cl B97 ....102 B4
Blythe Gate B90 ....70 F3
Blythe Rd Coleshill B46 ...34 A4

Blythe Rd *continued*
Coventry CV1 . . . . .61 E4
Blythe Special Sch B46 . .34 A2
Blythe Valley Pk B90 . . . .70 F2
Boar Croft CV4 . . . . .59 F2
Boat La CV37 . . . . .129 A7
Bockendon Rd CV4 . . . . .75 E5
Boddington Cl CV32 . . . .106 E5
Boddington Rd OX17 . . .134 B5
Bodington Cotts CV37 . .129 D7
Bodmin Rd CV2 . . . . .62 F5
Bodnant Way CV3 . . . . . .93 C6
Bodymoor Heath La B76 .15 A4
Bohun St CV4 . . . . .59 F1
Boleyn Cl CV34 . . . . . . .109 C6
Bolingbroke Dr CV34 . . .109 E3
Bolingbroke Rd CV3 . . . .62 A1
Bolton Cl CV3 . . . . .77 E5
Bolyfant Cl CV31 . . . . . .110 A2
Bond Dr B35 . . . . .22 A3
Bond End CV23 . . . . .53 C2
Bond Gate CV11 . . . . . . .29 C4
Bond St Coventry CV1 . .151 B3
Nuneaton CV11 . . . . .29 C5
Rugby CV21 . . . . .82 C2
Boningale Way B93 . . . . .71 E3
Bonington Dr CV12 . . . . .39 A4
Bonneville Cl CV5 . . . . . .59 B8
Bonniksen Cl 7 CV31 . .109 F5
Bonnington Cl CV21 . . . .84 A1
Boot Hill CV9 . . . . .11 B1
Booths Fields CV6 . . . . .49 E2
Bordesley Ct CV32 . . . . .106 A3
Bordon Hill CV37 . . . . . .144 B1
Bordon Pl CV37 . . . . . . .144 B1
Borough The LE10 . . . . . .31 D8
Borrowdale CV21 . . . . . .83 B4
Borrowdale Cl CV6 . . . . .61 A8
Borrowdale Dr CV32 . . . .105 D2
Borrowell La CV8 . . . . . .92 E4
Borrowell Terr CV8 . . . . .92 E4
Boscobel Rd B90 . . . . . .70 D5
Bosley Cl CV36 . . . . .149 C2
Bostock Cres CV33 . . . . .107 B4
Boston Pl CV6 . . . . .61 D8
Boswell Dr CV2 . . . . .63 A7
Boswell Gr CV34 . . . . . . .104 D1
Boswell Rd CV22 . . . . . . .99 C4
Bosworth Dr B37 . . . . . . .33 A2
Bosworth Wood Prim Sch
B36 . . . . .22 F1
Boteler Cl B49 . . . . .143 A2
Botoner Rd CV1 . . . . .61 F2
Bott Rd CV5 . . . . .76 D8
Bott's La DE12 . . . . .3 C4
Bottom St CV47 . . . . . . .133 B7
Bottrill St CV11 . . . . .29 B5
Botts Green La B46 . . . . .25 B3
Boucher Cl CV37 . . . . . .144 B1
Boughton Leigh Inf Sch
CV21 . . . . .83 B4
Boughton Leigh Jun Sch
CV21 . . . . .83 B4
Boughton Rd CV21 . . . . .83 B3
Boulters La CV9 . . . . .10 B1
Boultons La B97 . . . . . . .102 B3
Boundary Rd CV21,CV22 .83 B1
Boundary Rd E CV37 . . . .129 C2
Boundary Rd N CV37 . . . .129 C2
Boundary Rd W CV37 . . .129 B2
Bourne Brook Cl CV7 . . .36 C2
Bourne Cl CV9 . . . . .12 C1
Bourne End CV47 . . . . . .147 A2
Bourne La OX15 . . . . . . .142 D4
Bourne Rd CV3 . . . . .62 C1
Bourne The OX15 . . . . . .142 D4
Bournebrook CE Prim Sch
CV7 . . . . .36 C2
Bournebrook View CV7 . .26 C1
Bourton Dr CV31 . . . . . . .110 B5
Bourton La CV23 . . . . . . .115 F8
Bourton Rd Frankton CV23 97 B1
Moreton-in-M GL56 . . . . .140 A3
Bouts La WR7,B96 . . . . .118 B5
Bovey Croft B76 . . . . . . .22 A7
Bovingdon Rd B35 . . . . . .22 A3
Bow Ct CV5 . . . . .76 D8
Bow Fell CV21 . . . . .83 B4
Bow La CV7,CV23 . . . . . .53 A2
Bowbrook Ave B90 . . . . . .71 A5
Bowen Rd CV22 . . . . .83 B1
Bowers Croft CV32 . . . . .106 A5
Bowes Lyon Cl GL56 . . . .140 A2
Bowfell Cl CV5 . . . . .60 B4
Bowley's La DE12 . . . . . . .9 E8
Bowling Green Ave B77 . .9 C4
Bowling Green Ct GL56 . .140 A3
Bowling Green La CV7,
CV12 . . . . .49 E8
Bowling Green St CV34 108 D6
Bowls Ct CV5 . . . . .60 F3
Bowman Gn LE10 . . . . . . .31 F6
Bowness Cl CV6 . . . . .61 A8
Bowshot Cl B36 . . . . .22 D1
Box Cl CV31 . . . . .110 B3
Box Rd B37 . . . . .44 C8
Box Trees Rd B93 . . . . . .71 C1
Boxhill The CV3 . . . . .62 B1
Boyce Way CV23 . . . . . . .82 A3
Boyd Cl CV2 . . . . .63 A4
Boyslade Rd LE10 . . . . . .31 F6
Boyslade Rd E LE10 . . . . .31 F5
Bracadale Cl CV3 . . . . . . .63 A2
Bracebridge Cl CV7 . . . . .74 B6
Bracebridge Rd
Atherstone CV9 . . . . .18 B4
Kingsbury B78 . . . . .15 B3

Bracebridge St CV11 . . . .29 B3
Bracken Cl CV22 . . . . . . .82 C1
Bracken Croft 1 B37 . . .33 C3
Bracken Dr Rugby CV22 . .82 C1
Sutton Coldfield B75 . . . . .13 A5
Wolvey LE10 . . . . .41 B1
Brackendale Dr
Barby CV23 . . . . .101 B1
Nuneaton CV10 . . . . .28 F3
Brackenhurst Rd CV6 . . . .61 A7
Bracklesham Way B77 . . .4 A3
Brackley Cl CV6 . . . . .60 F7
Bracknell Wlk 1 CV2 . . .63 A7
Braddock Cl CV3 . . . . .63 A1
Brade Dr CV2 . . . . .63 B7
Bradestone Rd CV11 . . . .29 D1
Bradewell Rd B36 . . . . . . .22 D1
Bradfield Cl CV5 . . . . .60 C5
Bradford Rd 6 CV33 . . . .122 E8
Brading Rd CV10 . . . . . . .29 D6
Bradley Croft CV7 . . . . . .74 B6
Bradmore Cl B91 . . . . . . .71 A8
Bradney Gn CV4 . . . . .75 E7
Bradnick Pl CV4 . . . . .59 F1
Bradnock's Marsh La
B92 . . . . .57 E2
Braemar Cl CV2 . . . . .62 E6
Braemar Rd CV32 . . . . . .106 B4
Braemar Way CV10 . . . . .29 A2
Braeside Croft B37 . . . . . .33 D2
Brafield Leys CV22 . . . . .100 A3
Braggington La CV37 . . . .128 F5
Braggs Farm La B90 . . . .70 A4
Braids Cl CV21 . . . . .83 B2
Brailes CE Prim Sch
OX15 . . . . .137 C2
Brain St B77 . . . . .4 A1
Brakesmead CV31 . . . . . .109 F5
Bramber Cl OX16 . . . . . . .139 F4
Bramble Cl
6 Coleshill B46 . . . . . . .33 F7
Nuneaton CV11 . . . . .29 C2
Bramble St CV1 . . . . .61 E2
Brambles The B76 . . . . . .22 A8
Brambling B77 . . . . .10 A4
Brambling Cl CV23 . . . . . .83 B4
Bramcote Cl CV12 . . . . . .40 D2
Bramcote Hospl CV11 . . .40 E7
Bramdene Ave CV10 . . . .29 D8
Bramley Dr B47 . . . . .69 B6
Bramley Rd CV35 . . . . . .132 E6
Bramley Way B50 . . . . . .148 B3
Brampton Way CV12 . . . .40 B3
Bramshall Dr B93 . . . . . . .71 E3
Bramston Cres CV4 . . . . .59 F1
Bramwell Gdns CV6 . . . . .49 F5
Brancaster Cl B77 . . . . . .4 A3
Brandfield Rd CV6 . . . . . .60 F8
Brandon Ct CV3 . . . . .79 A7
Brandon La CV3,CV8 . . . .79 C5
Brandon Marsh Nature
Reserve★ CV3 . . . . . . .79 A4
Brandon Marsh Visitor Ctr★
CV3 . . . . .79 B4
Brandon Par CV32 . . . . .110 A8
Brandon Rd
Bretford CV8,CV23 . . . . . .80 B3
Coventry CV3 . . . . .79 A4
Hinckley LE10 . . . . .31 B7
Brandon Wood Farm★
CV8 . . . . .79 D5
Branksome Rd CV6 . . . . .60 E6
Bransdale Ave CV6 . . . . .49 D3
Bransford Ave CV4 . . . . . .76 D5
Bransford Rise B91 . . . . . .56 B5
Branstree Dr CV6 . . . . . . .49 D2
Brascote Rd LE10 . . . . . .30 F8
Bratches The GL55 . . . . .135 B3
Brathay Cl CV3 . . . . .77 D6
Braunston CE Prim Sch
NN11 . . . . .117 E5
Braunston Cl B76 . . . . . . .13 A2
Braunston La NN11 . . . . .126 E8
Braunston Pl CV22 . . . . .100 B4
Braunston Rd NN11 . . . . .117 F2
Bray Bank B46 . . . . .25 B2
Bray's La CV2 . . . . .62 A3
Brayford Ave CV3 . . . . . . .77 C6
Brays Cl CV23 . . . . .64 C2
Braytoft Cl CV6 . . . . .49 C2
Brazil St CV4 . . . . .59 E2
Breach La CV35 . . . . .113 F3
Breach Oak La CV7 . . . . . .37 B2
Breaches La B98 . . . . . . .103 B4
Bream B77 . . . . .9 B4
Bream Cl B37 . . . . .33 C2
Brechin Cl LE10 . . . . .31 A8
Bredon Ave CV3 . . . . .78 F8
Bredon Ho B98 . . . . .103 A4
Bredon View B97 . . . . . . .102 B4
Bree's La CV8 . . . . .74 A1
Breeden Dr B76 . . . . .23 B6
Brendan Cl B46 . . . . .34 A3
Brendon B77 . . . . .4 A1
Brendon Way CV10 . . . . .28 A3
Brenfield Dr LE10 . . . . . . .31 A8
Brent B77 . . . . .9 C4
Brentwood Ave CV3 . . . . .77 C3
Brentwood Gdns CV3 . . . .77 C3
Brese Ave CV34 . . . . .104 F1
Bretch Hill OX16 . . . . . . .139 F3
Bretford Rd CV2 . . . . .50 C1
Bretshall Cl B90 . . . . .70 F5
Bretts Cl CV1 . . . . .151 D4
Bretts Hall Est CV10 . . . . .28 A4
Brewer Rd CV12 . . . . .40 D2
Brewers Cl CV3 . . . . .63 A1

Brewery La OX15 . . . . . . .142 C4
Brewery Row GL56 . . . . .140 F1
Brewery St CV37 . . . . . . .144 C2
Brewster Cl CV2 . . . . .62 E2
Briansway CV6 . . . . .49 E3
Briar B77 . . . . .4 A2
Briar Cl Hinckley LE10 . . .31 F6
Royal Leamington Spa
CV32 . . . . .106 B2
Briar Coppice B90 . . . . . .70 D4
Briar Croft CV37 . . . . . . .144 D1
Briar Hill Inf Sch CV31 . .110 B3
Briardene Ave CV12 . . . . .39 B2
Briarmead LE10 . . . . .31 E4
Briars Cl Coventry CV2 . . .62 C2
Long Lawford CV23 . . . . .82 A2
Nuneaton CV11 . . . . .29 E5
Briarwood B90 . . . . .70 D4
Brick Hill OX15 . . . . .142 D3
Brick Hill La CV5 . . . . . . .59 E8
Brick Kiln La
Middleton B78 . . . . .14 D6
Solihull B90,B91 . . . . . . .70 F8
Brick Kiln St LE10 . . . . . .31 C8
Brick Row OX15 . . . . . . .142 F8
Brickall The CV37 . . . . . .129 B3
Brickhill Cl CV36 . . . . . . .149 C3
Brickhill Dr B37 . . . . .33 C2
Brickkiln La CV9 . . . . .16 A2
Brickyard La B80 . . . . . . .103 B2
Bridal Path The CV5 . . . . .60 B6
Bridge Cl CV47 . . . . .147 A2
Bridge End
Southam CV47 . . . . .147 A2
Warwick CV34 . . . . .108 F5
Bridge Foot CV37 . . . . . .145 A1
Bridge Ho CV31 . . . . .110 A8
Bridge La Ladbroke CV47 124 D5
Witherley CV9 . . . . .19 A4
Bridge Meadow Dr B93 . .71 F6
Bridge St Barford CV35 . .122 A7
Coventry CV6 . . . . .62 A7
Fenny Compton CV47 . . .133 D7
Hampton Lucy CV35 . . . .121 F4
Hurley CV9 . . . . .16 B2
Kenilworth CV8 . . . . .92 F5
Kineton CV35 . . . . .132 B5
Nuneaton CV11 . . . . .29 C4
Nuneaton, Chilvers Coton
CV11 . . . . .29 C2
Polesworth B78 . . . . .5 A1
Rugby CV21 . . . . .83 B2
Stratford-u-A CV37 . . . . .145 A1
Warwick CV34 . . . . .109 C8
Wellesbourne CV35 . . . . .146 B2
Bridge Town Prim Sch
CV37 . . . . .145 A1
Bridge View Bagington CV8 77 D3
3 Coleshill B46 . . . . . . .33 F7
Bridgeacre Gdns CV3 . . . .62 F2
Bridgecote CV3 . . . . .78 E6
Bridgeman Rd CV6 . . . . . .61 B4
Bridget St CV22 . . . . .82 C2
Bridgetown Rd CV37 . . . .145 A1
Bridgeway CV37 . . . . . . .145 A2
Bridle Brook La CV5,CV7 .48 A3
Bridle Rd
Lighthorne Heath CV33 . .123 D2
Rugby CV21 . . . . .82 C2
Bridport Cl CV2 . . . . .63 A4
Brierley Rd CV2 . . . . .62 C8
Briggs Cl OX16 . . . . .139 F7
Bright St CV6 . . . . .61 E6
Brightmere Rd CV6 . . . . . .61 B4
Brighton St CV2 . . . . .61 F3
Brightwalton Rd CV3 . . . .77 D7
Brightwell Cres B93 . . . . .71 E3
Brill Cl CV4 . . . . .76 C5
Brindle Ave CV3 . . . . .62 C2
Brindles Alley CV36 . . . . .149 C3
Brindley Dr
Atherstone CV9 . . . . .12 B1
Daventry NN11 . . . . .117 F3
Brindley Paddocks CV1 .151 B4
Brindley Rd Bedworth CV7 50 B8
Hinckley LE10 . . . . .30 E8
Rugby CV21 . . . . .84 A1
Brinklow Cl B98 . . . . .103 B4
Brinklow Rd Coventry CV3 63 A2
Easenhall CV23 . . . . .65 C2
Stretton-on D CV23 . . . . .77 E6
Brisbane Cl CV3 . . . . .78 E6
Brisbane Ct CV12 . . . . . . .39 A4
Briscoe Rd CV6 . . . . .49 D4
Bristol Rd CV5 . . . . .60 F2
Bristol Way CV35 . . . . . .146 B1
Britannia Rd LE10 . . . . . .32 A5
Britannia St CV2 . . . . .61 F3
Briton Rd CV2 . . . . .62 A4
Brittania Sh Ctr 3 LE10 .31 D8
Britten Cl CV11 . . . . .40 A7
Brittons La CV35 . . . . . . .114 C2
Brixfield Way B90 . . . . . . .70 B5
Brixham Cl CV11 . . . . .29 F5
Brixham Dr CV2 . . . . .62 C7
Brixworth Cl CV3 . . . . . . .78 E8
Broad Cl CV33 . . . . .123 F6
Broad Heath Com Prim Sch
CV6 . . . . .61 E6
Broad La Coventry CV5 . . .59 D4
Fillongley CV7 . . . . .36 A2
Tanworth-in-A B94 . . . . . .86 E3
Broad Marston Rd
Mickleton CV37,GL55 . . .135 B7
Pebworth CV37 . . . . .128 F1
Broad Oaks B76 . . . . .13 A1
Broad Park Rd CV2 . . . . . .62 D8
Broad St Brinklow CV23 . .64 C2

Broad St *continued*
Coventry CV6 . . . . .61 E7
Long Compton CV36 . . . .141 C3
Stratford-u-A CV37 . . . . .144 C1
Warwick CV34 . . . . .108 F7
Broad Street Jetty CV6 . .61 E7
Broad Wlk CV37 . . . . . . .144 C1
Broadfern Rd B93 . . . . . . .72 B8
Broadgate CV1 . . . . .151 B3
Broadhaven Cl CV31 . . . .110 C7
Broadlands Cl CV5 . . . . . .60 C2
Broadlee B77 . . . . .4 B1
Broadmead Ct CV5 . . . . . .60 C2
Broadmeadow La CV37 . .144 C3
Broadmere Rise CV5 . . . . .60 A2
Broadmoor La CV36 . . . .141 A6
Broadsword Way LE10 . . .31 D4
Broadwater CV5 . . . . .77 A8
Broadway Coventry CV5 . .61 A1
Cubbington CV32 . . . . . .106 E5
Broadway Mans CV5 . . . . .61 A1
Broadway Rd GL55 . . . . .135 B6
Broadwell Ct CV4 . . . . . . .75 F6
Broadwells Cres CV4 . . . .76 A5
Brockenhurst Way CV6 . . .50 B6
Brockhill La B98 . . . . .85 F2
Brockhurst Ave LE10 . . . .31 D4
Brockhurst Dr CV4 . . . . . .59 D2
Brockhurst La
Monks Kirby CV23 . . . . . .53 C2
Solihull B90 . . . . .70 B5
Sutton Coldfield B75 . . . . .7 A4
Brodick Cl LE10 . . . . .31 A8
Brodick Rd LE10 . . . . .30 F8
Brodick Way CV10 . . . . . .28 A5
Bromage Ave B78 . . . . . . .15 B3
Brome Hall La B94 . . . . . .89 D2
Bromford Way CV37 . . . .144 B2
Bromleigh Dr CV2 . . . . . .62 C2
Bromleigh Villas CV8 . . . .77 F2
Bromley Cl CV8 . . . . .92 E6
Bromsgrove Highway
B98 . . . . .102 C4
Bromsgrove Rd B80 . . . .103 B1
Bromwich Cl CV3 . . . . . . .78 F8
Bromwich Rd CV21 . . . . . .83 C1
Bromyard Ave B76 . . . . . .22 A8
Bronte Nuneaton CV10 . . .27 C3
Rugby CV21 . . . . .83 B2
Bronze Cl CV11 . . . . .39 E8
Brook Ave B77 . . . . .10 A4
Brook Cl Coventry CV1 . . .61 E4
Kingsbury B78 . . . . .15 B3
Shipston-on-S CV36 . . . .149 C3
Brook Cottage B46 . . . . . .25 B2
Brook Cotts CV36 . . . . . .137 A2
Brook Croft B37 . . . . .44 B7
Brook End B78 . . . . .9 A4
Brook End Cl B95 . . . . . .113 A4
Brook End Dr B95 . . . . . .113 A4
Brook Farm Ind Est B94 .70 B2
Brook Green La B92 . . . . .57 A1
Brook La
Moreton Morrell CV35 . . .122 F3
Newbold-on-S CV37 . . . .130 E1
Nuneaton CV10 . . . . .29 C6
Brook Piece Wlk B35 . . . .22 B3
Brook Rd B95 . . . . .119 F6
Brook St Bedworth CV12 . .39 B5
Fenny Compton CV47 . . .133 D7
Warwick CV34 . . . . .108 C6
Wolston CV8 . . . . .80 A2
Brook View CV22 . . . . . . .99 B2
Brook Wlk CV9 . . . . .18 C4
Brookdale
Harvington WR11 . . . . . .127 C4
Hinckley LE10 . . . . .31 B7
Brookdale Rd CV10 . . . . . .29 E7
Brooke Cl CV34 . . . . .108 F5
Brooke Ct 6 CV21 . . . . . .82 C2
Brooke Rd CV8 . . . . .93 B4
Brooke Specl Sch
Rugby CV22 . . . . .82 C1
Rugby CV22 . . . . .99 C4
Brookfield Cl B97 . . . . . .102 B2
Brookfield Dr LE10 . . . . . .41 B2
Brookfield Rd
Cubbington CV32 . . . . . .106 E5
Hinckley LE10 . . . . .31 C6
Brookford Ave CV6 . . . . . .49 A3
Brookhampton Cl B97 . . .102 C2
Brookhurst Ct CV32 . . . .105 D1
Brookhurst Prim Sch
CV32 . . . . .105 C1
Brookhus Farm Rd B76 . .22 A8
Brooklands B37 . . . . .44 A8
Brooklea CV12 . . . . .38 F2
Brookline Dr CV3 . . . . . . .83 C4
Brooklime Rd CV1 . . . . . .61 D6
Brooklyn Rd CV1 . . . . . . .61 D6
Brooks Cl CV23 . . . . .117 B6
Brooks Croft B35 . . . . . . .22 A2
Brooksby Gr B93 . . . . . . .72 A2
Brookshaw Way CV2 . . . .62 F8
Brookside
Cheswick Green B90 . . . . .70 D3
Hinckley LE10 . . . . .31 E7
Hook Norton OX15 . . . . .142 D4
Snitterfield CV37 . . . . . .121 B7
Stretton on D CV23 . . . . .96 C3
Brookside Ave
Coventry CV5 . . . . .60 C3
Kenilworth CV8 . . . . .92 F4
Pailton CV23 . . . . .66 A4
Wellesbourne CV35 . . . . .146 C2
Brookside Cl Rugby CV22 .83 A1
Stratford-u-A CV37 . . . . .144 B2
Brookside Rd CV37 . . . . .144 B2

Brookside Way B77 . . . . . .10 A3
Brookstray Flats CV5 . . . .60 B3
Brookvale Ave CV3 . . . . . .62 E1
Brookvale Rd CV37 . . . . .144 C1
Brookweed B77 . . . . .4 A2
Broom Cl CV22 . . . . .82 C1
Broom La B90 . . . . .70 A6
Broome Croft CV6 . . . . . . .49 B3
Broomey Croft Childrens
Farm★ B76 . . . . .15 A4
Broomfield Ave B78 . . . . . .9 A4
Broomfield Pl CV5 . . . . . . .61 A2
Broomfield Rd CV5 . . . . . .61 A1
Broomfield Rise CV10 . . . .28 F2
Broomybank CV8 . . . . . . .93 B6
Broughton Rd OX15,
OX16 . . . . .139 F2
Browett Rd CV6 . . . . .61 A5
Brown Ave B77 . . . . .9 B4
Brown's Bridge Rd
CV47 . . . . .147 A2
Brown's La Allesley CV5 . .48 C1
Dordon B78 . . . . .11 A3
Browning Ave CV34 . . . . .108 C5
Browning Rd Coventry CV10 28 A5
Browning Rd
Coventry CV2 . . . . .62 C3
Rugby CV21 . . . . .101 A4
Brownley Rd B90 . . . . .70 E2
Brownlow St 6 CV32 . . . .106 A2
Browns La B93 . . . . .71 E6
Browns Rd NN11 . . . . . . .117 F1
Brownshill Ct CV6 . . . . . . .60 F8
Brownshill Green Rd
CV6 . . . . .48 E1
Brownsover Cl B36 . . . . . .22 B1
Brownsover Com Sch
CV23 . . . . .83 B4
Brownsover La CV21 . . . .83 A4
Brownsover Rd
Rugby CV21 . . . . .82 C4
Rugby CV21 . . . . .83 A4
Broxell Cl CV34 . . . . .104 C1
Bruce Rd Bedworth CV7 . .49 F5
Coventry CV6 . . . . .61 B8
Bruce Williams Way
CV22 . . . . .83 A1
Brudenell Cl CV22 . . . . . . .99 A4
Brunel Cl Coventry CV2 . . .61 F3
Daventry NN11 . . . . .117 F2
Whitnash CV31 . . . . .110 B2
Brunel Rd LE10 . . . . .31 C8
Brunel Wlk B78 . . . . .5 A2
Brunes Ct CV21 . . . . .83 B4
Brunswick Cl CV21 . . . . . .83 B3
Brunswick Ct CV31 . . . . .110 A5
Brunswick Rd CV1 . . . . . . .61 E2
Brunswick St CV31 . . . . .110 A5
Bruntingthorpe Way CV3 78 E8
Brunton Cl CV3 . . . . .63 B1
Brutus Dr B46 . . . . .23 E1
Bryan Mews B50 . . . . . . .148 C2
Bryanston Cl CV2 . . . . . . .63 A4
Bryant Rd CV7 . . . . .50 A7
Brympton Rd CV3 . . . . . . .62 C2
Bryn Jones Cl CV3 . . . . . .78 F7
Bryn Rd CV6 . . . . .61 F7
Bryony Cl CV12 . . . . .38 C2
Buccleuch Cl CV22 . . . . . .99 B2
Buchan Cl CV10 . . . . .27 C2
Buchannan Rd CV22 . . . . .82 C1
Buckbury Croft B90 . . . . . .71 B6
Buckden B77 . . . . .4 B1
Buckden 2 CV34 . . . . . . .104 F1
Buckfast Cl CV3 . . . . .77 E5
Buckhold Dr CV5 . . . . .60 B5
Buckingham Cl CV10 . . . . .29 B1
Buckingham Rd CV47 . . . .132 F5
Buckingham Rise CV5 . . . .60 B4
Buckland Rd CV6 . . . . .49 B2
Buckle St WR11,B50 . . . .128 C3
Buckler's Yd CV12 . . . . . . .39 A2
Buckley Ho CV5 . . . . .60 F1
Buckley Rd CV32 . . . . . . .106 C2
Buckminster Dr B93 . . . . .71 F4
Bucknill Cres CV21 . . . . .101 A4
Buckridge La B90 . . . . . . .70 A5
Bucks Hill CV10 . . . . .28 C5
Buckwell La CV23 . . . . . . .84 A3
Budbrooke Cl CV2 . . . . . .50 D2
Budbrooke Ind Est
CV34 . . . . .108 C3
Budbrooke Prim Sch
CV35 . . . . .114 F4
Budbrooke Rd CV34 . . . . .108 B7
Bufferys Cl B91 . . . . .71 B8
Bulkington La CV11 . . . . . .40 A7
Bulkington Rd
Bedworth CV12 . . . . .39 D2
Shilton CV7 . . . . .51 E6
Wolvey LE10 . . . . .41 B2
Bull Ring Harbury CV33 . .123 F6
Nuneaton CV10 . . . . .29 B2
Bull Ring Farm Rd CV33 123 F7
Bull St Nuneaton CV11 . . .29 D2
Southam CV47 . . . . .147 A2
Stratford-u-A CV37 . . . . .144 C1
Bull Yd CV1 . . . . .151 B2
Bull Yd The CV47 . . . . . .147 A2
Bull's Head La CV3 . . . . . .62 B2
Bull's La B76 . . . . .13 E1
Bullaces La LE17 . . . . .68 B2
Bullfield Ave CV4 . . . . .59 E1
Bullfurlong La LE10 . . . . . .31 F4
Bullimore Gr CV8 . . . . . . .93 A2

Bullivents Cl B93 ....71 F5
Bulls Head Yd B49 .....143 A2
Bulwer Rd CV6 ....61 A6
Bulwick Cl CV3 ....63 B1
Bungalows The CV37 ...129 B7
Bunkers Hill NN11 .....126 F5
Burbage Ave CV37 .....144 C3
Burbage CE Inf Sch LE10 32 A5
Burbage CE Jun Sch
LE10 ....31 F6
Burbage Rd LE10 ....32 A7
Burbages La CV6 ....49 D4
Burberry Gr CV4 ....74 A6
Burbury Cl Bedworth CV12 39 C4
Royal Leamington Spa
CV32 ....106 C2
Burbury Ct CV34 ....109 B8
Burford La B49,B80 ....112 C1
Burford Mews 13 CV31 .110 C6
Burford Rd Hollywood B47 69 A6
Stratford-u-A CV37 ......145 B1
Burgage Pl CV11 ....29 C4
Burgage Wlk CV11 .....29 B5
Burges CV1 ....151 B3
Burges Gr CV34 ....104 F1
Burghley Cl CV11 ......29 F2
Burhill Way B37 ....33 B5
Burleigh Cl CV7 ....74 A7
Burlington Ct B78 .....9 A4
Burlington Rd
Coventry CV1 ....61 F4
Nuneaton CV10 ....39 A1
Burman Dr B46 ....34 A3
Burnaby Cl CV10 ....28 A3
Burnaby Rd CV6 ....49 B1
Burnaston Cres B90 ....71 C6
Burnell Cl B50 ....148 B3
Burnett Rd CV33 ....123 D2
Burnham Rd CV3 ....78 A6
Burnham Rise CV11 .....30 A6
Burns Ave CV34 ....108 C5
Burns Cl B97 ....102 B4
Burns Rd Coventry CV2 ..62 B3
Royal Leamington Spa
CV32 ....106 B4
Burns Wlk CV12 ....39 C1
Burnsall Gr CV5 ....76 D8
Burnsall Rd CV5 ....76 D8
Burnside Coventry CV3 ..63 A2
Rugby CV22 ....82 C1
Burnthurst Cres B90 ...71 A7
Burrow Hill La CV7 .....48 D7
Burrows Cl CV31 ....110 B3
Burrows The CV37 .....130 E1
Burton Cl CV5 ....48 C2
Burton Dassett Hills Cntry
Pk★ CV47 ....133 B7
Burton Green CE Prim Sch
CV8 ....75 B3
Burton La CV11 ....40 F7
Burton Rd CV9 ....3 C1
Bury Court La OX17 ....139 E8
Bury Rd CV6 ....59 F3
Bury Rd CV31 ....109 F7
Burycroft Rd OX15 .....142 D3
Buryway La CV36 ....141 C3
Busby Cl CV3 ....78 F7
Busbys Piece CV23 .....53 C2
Bush Cl CV4 ....59 F3
Bush Ct CV2 ....62 B6
Bush Heath La CV33 ....123 F6
Bush Hill La CV23 ......117 B3
Bushbery Ave CV4 ....59 F2
Bushbury Croft B37 .....33 C3
Bushley Cl B98 ....103 A4
Bushley Croft B91 ......71 B8
Bushwood Dr B93 ....72 B3
Bushwood La B94,B95 ...113 C8
Bushy End CV34 ....109 E4
Butcher's La CV5 ....60 C6
Butchers Cl
Bishops Itchington CV47 .124 A4
Brinklow CV23 ....64 C2
Butchers La OX15 ......137 F2
Butchers Rd B92 ....57 A6
Butler Cl CV8 ....93 C7
Butler St B96 ....102 C1
Butlers Cl
Aston le W NN11 ....134 F5
Long Compton CV36 ......141 D3
Butlers Cres CV37 ......39 A1
Butlers End CV35 ....91 C7
Butlers La Grendon CV9 .11 B1
Long Compton CV36 ......141 D3
Butlers Leap CV21 ......83 B3
Butlers Leap Ind Est
CV21 ....83 B2
Butlers Rd CV36,OX7 ...141 E3
Butlin Rd Coventry CV6 ..49 C4
Rugby CV21 ....83 B2
Butt Hill CV47 ....125 C8
Butt La Allesley CV5 ....60 B7
Harbury CV33 ....123 F6
Butter St B49 ....143 B2
Buttermere Rugby CV21 ..83 B4
Tamworth B77 ....10 A4
Buttermere Ave CV11 ...30 A6
Buttermere Cl CV3 ......78 F7
Buttermilk La CV5 ......113 F5
Butterworth Dr CV4 .....76 A6
Butts CV1 ....61 A2
Butts Cl CV9 ....3 A1
Butts La B94 ....87 B2
Butts Rd CV1 ....61 B5

Butts The
Long Compton CV36 .....141 C3
Napton on t H CV47 ....125 C8
Warwick CV34 ....108 E7
Buxton Ave B78 ....9 A4
By Pass Rd B77 ....4 A3
Byfield Pl CV7 ....74 D5
Byfield Rd
Chipping Warden OX17 ..134 F4
Coventry CV6 ....60 E5
Priors Marston CV47 ....125 F4
Byford Cl CV10 ....28 F4
Byford St CV10 ....28 F4
Byford Way B37 ....44 B8
Byron Ave Bedworth CV12 39 D2
Warwick CV34 ....108 C4
Byron Ct B93 ....72 A6
Byron Rd Redditch B97 .102 B4
Stratford-u-A CV37 .....145 B1
Byron St CV1 ....151 A4
Byron Wlk CV47 ....132 F7
Bywater Cl CV3 ....77 B5

C

Cable & Wireless Coll
CV4 ....75 E6
Cadbury Dr B35 ....22 A2
Cadden Dr CV4 ....60 B2
Cadman Cl CV12 ....39 C3
Cadogan Rd B77 ....9 B3
Caen Cl CV35 ....108 A7
Caernarfon Dr CV11 ....29 D3
Caernarvon Way OX16 ..139 F3
Caesar Rd CV8 ....92 E3
Caesar Way B46 ....23 E1
Caister B77 ....4 A3
Caistor Cl B78 ....8 A4
Caithness Cl CV5 ....60 A4
Calcott Ho CV3 ....78 B5
Calcutt Mdw CV47 ......147 B2
Calcutt Way B90 ....70 A6
Caldecote Cl CV10 .....29 C8
Caldecote Hall Dr CV10 .19 C2
Caldecote Rd CV6 ......61 C5
Caldecott Pl CV21 .....83 B1
Caldecott St CV21,CV22 .83 B1
Caldeford Ave B90 .....71 A7
Calder B77 ....4 A1
Coventry CV3 ....77 E7
Calder Dr B76 ....22 A7
Calder Wlk CV31 ....110 C6
Caldon Cl LE10 ....31 B8
Caldwell Ct CV11 ......29 D1
Caldwell Rd CV11 ......29 D1
Calf's La GL55 ....135 B2
Caliban Mews CV34 .....109 E3
Callaways Rd CV36 .....149 C2
Callendar Cl CV11 .....30 A7
Callis Wlk B77 ....9 C3
Callow Hill La B97 .....102 A3
Calmere Cl CV2 ....62 F8
Calpurnia Ave CV34 ....109 E2
Caludon Castle Sch CV2 62 E4
Caludon Lodge CV2 .....62 E5
Caludon Park Ave CV2 ..62 E5
Caludon Rd CV2 ....62 A4
Calvert Cl Coventry CV3 .77 D6
Rugby CV21 ....83 C4
Calvestone Rd CV22 ....99 A4
Camberwell Terr CV31 ..110 A7
Camborne Dr CV11 ......29 F5
Cambourne Rd LE10 .....32 A6
Cambria Cl B90 ....69 E7
Cambrian B77 ....4 A1
Cambridge Ct CV21 .....83 B2
Cambridge Dr
Birmingham B37 ....33 A1
Nuneaton CV10 ....28 E3
Cambridge Gdns CV32 ..106 A1
Cambridge St
Coventry CV1 ....61 E5
Rugby CV21 ....83 B2
Camden Cl GL56 ....140 F3
Camden St CV2 ....62 A4
Camellia Rd 1 CV2 .....50 B2
Camelot Gr CV8 ....93 C5
Cameron Cl Allesley CV5 .60 A7
Royal Leamington Spa
CV32 ....106 A4
Camhouses B77 ....4 A1
Camp Hill Dr CV10 .....28 D7
Camp Hill Prim Sch CV10 28 E6
Camp Hill Rd CV10 .....28 C7
Camp La Henley-in-A B95 113 B6
Warmington OX17 ....133 B2
Campbell Cl CV10 ......28 A4
Campbell St CV21 ......82 C2
Campden Ave CV36 .....135 F5
Campden Cl B97 ....102 B3
Campden Gr CV35 ......114 F6
Campden Lawns CV37 ...130 D3
Campden Pitch CV36 ...136 A6
Campden Rd
Ebrington GL55 ....135 D3
Lower Quinton CV37 ....129 D4
Mickleton GL55 ....135 B4
Shipston-on-S CV36 ....149 B3
Campden St CV36 ......136 A6
Campion Cl CV3 ....77 D6
Campion Gn CV32 ......106 A2
Campion Rd CV32 ......106 A2
Campion Sch & Com Coll
CV31 ....110 C5
Campion Terr CV32 ....106 A1
Campion Way Rugby CV23 83 B4

Campion Way continued
Solihull B90 ....70 A5
Camplea Croft B37 ......33 A2
Campling Cl CV12 ......40 B2
Campriano Dr CV34 ....109 A8
Campton Cl LE10 ....31 E7
Camville CV3 ....63 A2
Canada La CV35 ....114 D1
Canal Rd Coventry CV6 ..61 F8
Hatton CV35 ....114 E5
Canal Way LE10 ....30 F7
Canalside B94 ....89 D3
Canberra Cl CV35 .....146 B1
Canberra Ct 2 CV12 ...38 F2
Canberra Rd CV2 ....50 C4
Canberra Way LE10 .....31 E4
Canford Cl CV3 ....77 C3
Canley Ford CV4,CV5 ...76 E7
Canley Rd CV5 ....76 D8
Canley Sta CV5 ....60 D1
Cannes Cl CV4 ....76 D6
Cannocks La CV4 ....76 D6
Cannon Cl CV4 ....76 F6
Cannon Hill Rd CV4 ....76 D5
Cannon Park District Ctr
CV4 ....76 C6
Cannon Park Prim Sch
CV4 ....76 C6
Cannon Park Rd CV4 ....76 E5
Canon Dr CV7 ....49 D6
Canon Evans CE Inf Sch
CV12 ....39 A2
Canon Hudson Cl CV3 ...78 C6
Canon Maggs CE Jun Sch
CV12 ....39 A2
Canon Young Rd CV31 ..110 B3
Canterbury Cl
Kenilworth CV8 ....93 C3
Studley B80 ....103 B2
Canterbury Dr B37 .....44 A7
Canterbury St CV1 .....151 D3
Canterbury Way CV11 ...30 A8
Cantlow Cl CV5 ....60 A3
Canton La B46 ....24 A3
Canwell Dr B75 ....7 A3
Cape Ind Est CV34 .....108 E7
Cape Rd CV34 ....108 D8
Capmartin Rd CV6 ......61 C7
Captain's Hill B49 ....143 B3
Capulet Cl Coventry CV3 .78 C6
Rugby CV22 ....99 C3
Capulet Dr CV34 ....109 E3
Capulet Ho CV37 ......145 A2
Caradoc B77 ....4 A1
Caradoc Cl CV2 ....62 D7
Caradoc Hall CV2 ......62 D7
Cardale Croft 1 CV3 ...78 F8
Cardiff Cl CV3 ....78 D5
Cardigan Rd CV12 ......38 C1
Cardinal Newman RC Sch &
Com Coll CV6 ....48 F2
Cardinal Wiseman RC Sch
CV2 ....50 E1
Carding Cl CV5 ....59 F4
Carew Cl CV37 ....144 C3
Carey B77 ....10 A3
Carey St CV6 ....62 B8
Cargill Cl CV6 ....49 F5
Carhampton Rd B75 .....13 A5
Carisbrook Rd CV10 ....29 D6
Carisbrooke B77 ....4 A1
Carisbrooke Ave B37 ...33 C2
Carlcroft B77 ....4 A1
Carlton Cl CV12 ....40 B3
Carlton Ct CV5 ....60 F2
Carlton Gdns CV5 ......77 A8
Carlton Ho 8 CV32 ....109 F8
Carlton Rd Coventry CV6 .49 F1
Rugby CV22 ....82 B1
Carlyle Cl CV10 ....27 C3
Carlyon Rd CV9 ....18 C4
Carlyon Rd Ind Est CV9 .18 C4
Carlyon Road Ind Est
CV9 ....12 C1
Carmelite Rd CV1 ......61 E2
Carnbroe Ave CV3 ......78 F7
Carnegie Cl CV3 ....78 B5
Carnoustie B77 ....4 A3
Carnoustie Cl CV11 ....40 C8
Caroline Cl CV11 ......39 F7
Carpenters Cl LE10 ....31 F5
Carrie Ho CV1 ....151 A2
Carraway Head Hill B78 .7 B3
Carsal Cl CV7 ....49 D5
Carson Cl GL56 ....136 C1
Cart's La CV9 ....11 B1
Carter Dr CV35 ....122 A7
Carter Rd CV3 ....78 A8
Carters La CV37 ......145 C2
Carters Leaze CV36 ....140 E5
Carthusian Rd CV3 .....77 C7
Cartmel Cl CV5 ....60 A4
Carvell Cl CV5 ....48 B1
Carver Cl CV2 ....62 E2
Cascade Cl CV3 ....77 E6
Case La CV35 ....114 B8
Casern View B75 ....13 A6
Cash's Bsns Ctr CV1 ...61 D5
Cash's La CV1 ....61 D6
Cashmore Ave CV31 ....109 F5
Cashmore Rd
Bedworth CV12 ....38 E1
Kenilworth CV8 ....93 C4
Casia Gr CV8 ....93 C4
Caspian Way CV2 ....63 A8
Cassandra Cl CV4 ......76 D3
Cassandra Gr CV34 ....109 D4
Castello Dr B36 ....22 D1

Castle Bromwich Bsns Pk
B35 ....22 A1
Castle Cl Coventry CV3 ..77 D6
Fillongley CV7 ....36 C1
Henley-in-A B95 ....113 B4
Warwick CV34 ....108 E6
Castle Cres CV35 ......132 B5
Castle Ct Hinckley LE10 .31 D6
Kenilworth CV8 ....93 A6
Castle Dr Astley CV10 ..37 C4
Coleshill B46 ....33 F5
Castle Gdns GL55 .....135 C2
Castle Gn CV8 ....92 D5
Castle Gr CV8 ....92 E4
Castle Hill Kenilworth CV8 92 E5
Upper Brailes OX15 ....137 E3
Warwick CV34 ....108 E6
Castle Hill La CV35 ...137 E2
Castle La Maxstoke B46 .34 C4
Warwick CV34 ....108 E6
Castle Mews 6 CV34 ...108 E6
Castle Mound CV23 ....101 B1
Castle Mound Way CV23 .67 B1
Castle Nurseries GL55 .135 C2
Castle Place Ind Est
CV1 ....151 D4
Castle Rd Alcester B49 .143 B3
Henley-in-A B95 ....113 B4
Kenilworth CV8 ....92 E5
Kineton CV35 ....132 B6
Nuneaton CV10 ....29 C7
Studley B80 ....103 C2
Tamworth B77 ....9 C3
Castle St
Astwood Bank B96 .....102 C1
Coventry CV1 ....151 D4
Hinckley LE10 ....31 D8
Rugby CV21 ....83 A2
Warwick CV34 ....108 E6
Castle Vale Ind Est B76 22 B3
Castle Vale Sec Sch B35 22 B3
Castle Vale Sports Ctr
B35 ....22 B2
Castle View CV10 ......19 A1
Castleditch La CV4 ....102 C4
Castlegate Mews 4
CV34 ....108 F7
Castlehall B77 ....4 A1
Caswell Rd CV31 ......110 B6
Catbrook GL55 ....135 A1
Catbrook Cl GL55 .....135 B1
Catesby End NN11 .....126 B5
Catesby La B94 ....89 B2
Catesby Rd Coventry CV6 .61 B8
Rugby CV22 ....83 B1
Cathedral Lanes Sh Ctr
CV1 ....151 B3
Catherine de Barnes La
Bickenhill B92 ....44 D1
Catherine de B B92 .....56 C7
Catherine St CV2 ......61 F3
Catherine Ward Hall
CV12 ....39 B5
Catherines Cl B91 .....56 B4
Cathiron La CV23 ......65 B1
Cattell Dr B75 ....13 B5
Cattell Rd CV34 ......108 E7
Cavalier Cl CV11 ......29 E2
Cavans Cl CV3 ....79 A8
Cavans Way CV3 ....79 A8
Cave Cl CV22 ....99 A4
Cavendish Cl B93 ......72 A3
Cavendish Rd CV4 ......59 E2
Caversham Cl CV11 .....30 A7
Cawdon Gr B93 ....71 F3
Cawnpore Rd CV6 ......49 B2
Cawston La CV22 ......99 A3
Cawston Way CV22 .....99 B4
Cawthorne Cl 1 CV1 ...61 E4
Cecil Ct CV31 ....110 A8
Cecil Leonard Knox Cres
CV11 ....40 F6
Cecily Rd CV3 ....77 E7
Cedar Ave CV8 ....79 B1
Cedar Cl Kingsbury B78 .15 B3
Royal Leamington Spa
CV32 ....106 A4
Stratford-u-A CV37 ....145 A2
Cedar Ct Allesley CV5 ..60 A6
Hinckley LE10 ....32 A6
Cedar Dr CV37 ....121 B7
Cedar Gr CV34 ....105 A1
Cedar Ho CV35 ....122 A7
Cedar Rd Mickleton GL55 135 C6
Nuneaton CV10 ....28 D6
Cedar Wlk 6 B37 ......33 B2
Cedar Wood Dr CV7 .....74 B6
Cedars Ave CV6 ....60 F5
Cedars Mews The 3
CV32 ....109 D8
Cedars Rd CV7 ....39 B1
Cedars The CV36 ......149 C3
Cedric Cl CV3 ....78 C5
Celandine CV23 ....83 B4
Celandine Rd CV2 ......50 D2
Celandine Way CV12 ...38 C2
Cemetery La CV10 ......19 A1
Centaur Rd CV5 ....60 F2
Centenary Bsns Ctr CV31 29 E3
Centenary Rd CV4 ......76 D7
Central Ave Coventry CV2 62 A2
Nuneaton CV11 ....29 B5
Royal Leamington Spa
CV31 ....109 F6
Central Bldgs
Coventry CV1 ....151 B1

Central Bldgs continued
16 Rugby CV21 ....83 A2
Central Bvd
Coventry CV6,CV7 ....49 A5
Keresley CV7 ....48 F6
Central City Ind Est CV6 .61 F5
Central Dr CV47 ......124 B4
Central Flats CV3 .....151 B1
Central Park Dr CV23 ..67 B1
Centrovell Ind Est CV11 .29 C2
Centurion Cl B46 ......23 F1
Centurion Pk B77 ......10 A3
Centurion Way B77 .....10 A3
Century Pk B26 ....44 C6
Ceolmund Cres B37 .....33 B2
Chace Ave CV3 ....78 C6
Chace Prim Sch CV3 ....78 C6
Chaceley Cl CV2 ....63 A8
Chadbury Croft 1 B91 ..71 B8
Chadbury Rd WR11 .....127 A1
Chadshunt Cl B36 ......22 D2
Chadstone Cl B90 ......71 B6
Chadwick Cl CV5 ....60 B3
Chadwick La
Chadwick End B93 ....90 B8
Knowle B93 ....73 B2
Chadwick Manor B93 ...73 A1
Chadwick Mews
Chadwick End B93 ....90 B6
Redditch B98 ....103 A4
Chadworth Ave B93 .....71 E3
Chaffinch Dr B36 ......33 B7
Chalfont Cl
Bedworth CV12 ....39 A4
Coventry CV5 ....60 B4
Chalford Way B90 ......70 C8
Challenge Bsns Pk CV1 .61 D5
Challenge Cl CV1 .....151 C4
Chamberlain Cl CV32 ..106 E5
Chamberlain La B49 ...118 D5
Chamberlain Rd CV21 ..101 A4
Chamberlain Wlk 10 B46 33 F7
Chamberlaine St CV12 ..39 B3
Chance Fields CV31 ...110 F6
Chancellors Cl CV4 ....76 D4
Chancery Ct CV10 ......28 A7
Chancery La CV10 ......28 B7
Chanders Rd CV34 .....104 D1
Chandlers Cl CV31 ....109 D7
Chandlers Cl B97 ......102 B4
Chandlers Dr B77 ......4 A3
Chandlers Rd CV31 ....110 A2
Chandos Ct 13 CV32 ...105 F1
Chandos St Coventry CV2 .62 A3
Nuneaton CV11 ....29 A4
Royal Leamington Spa
CV32 ....105 F1
Change Brook Cl CV11 ..29 F8
Chantries The CV1 .....61 E5
Chantry Cl B47 ....69 A7
Chantry Cres B49 .....143 A2
Chantry Heath Cres B93 72 C7
Chantry The CV34 .....105 A1
Chapel Cl
Bidford-on-A B50 ......148 B2
Welford on A CV37 .....129 B6
Chapel Ct B96 ....102 C1
Chapel Dr
Balsall Common CV7 ....74 B8
Wythall B47 ....69 A3
Chapel End OX7 ....142 A2
Chapel Farm Cl CV3 ....78 C6
Chapel Gdns GL56 .....136 C1
Chapel Gn CV47 ....125 C2
Chapel Hill OX7 ....142 F2
Chapel La
Aston Cantlow B95 .....119 F7
Barnacle CV7 ....51 B6
Bidford-on-A B50 ......148 B2
Cropredy OX17 ....134 C1
Lapworth B94 ....89 D7
Mickleton GL55 ....135 B6
Newbold-on-S CV37 ....130 E1
Pillerton Priors CV35 ..131 D2
Ratley OX15 ....133 A2
Ryton-on-D CV8 ....79 B2
Salford OX7 ....150 C3
Shotteswell OX17 ......139 E8
Stratford-u-A CV37 ....145 A1
Ullenhall B95 ....112 E6
Witherley CV9 ....19 B4
Chapel Rd B96 ....102 C1
Chapel Row CV34 ......108 E7
Chapel St
Astwood Bank B96 .....102 C1
Bedworth CV12 ....39 C3
Bishops Itchington CV47 124 A4
Charwelton NN11 ....126 D2
Coventry CV1 ....151 B3
Harbury CV33 ....123 F6
Hook Norton OX15 .....142 D4
Long Lawford CV23 .....82 A2
Nuneaton CV11 ....29 C4
5 Royal Leamington Spa
CV31 ....110 A7
Rugby CV21 ....83 A2
Stratford-u-A CV37 ....145 A1
Warmington OX17 ......133 D2
Warwick CV34 ....108 E7
Welford on A CV37 .....129 B6
Wellesbourne CV35 ....146 B2
Chapel Wlk B50 ....148 B2
Chapelhouse Rd B37 ...33 A1
Chapelon B77 ....4 A1
Chapman Cl CV31 ......110 E5
Chapman Ct CV34 ......109 C8
Chapman Way B49 .....143 B3
Chard Rd CV3 ....78 D8

Charingworth Dr CV35 .114 F5
Chariot Way CV21 .83 A4
Charity Hos The CV23 .67 B3
Charity Rd CV7 .49 A7
Charlbury Mews CV31 .110 C6
Charlecote Cl CV37 .145 C2
Charlecote Croft B90 .70 C8
Charlecote Fields CV35 .146 B2
Charlecote Gdns CV31 .110 D5
Charlecote Pk* CV35 .121 F3
Charlecote Rd
Coventry CV6 .49 A2
Wellesbourne CV35 .146 B2
Wellesbourne, Charlcote CV35 .146 A3
Charlecote Wlk CV11 .39 F8
Charles Ct
Warwick, Budbrooke Ind Est CV34 .108 C7
1 Warwick, Emscote CV34 .109 B8
Charles Eaton Rd CV12 .38 F3
Charles Gardner Rd 6 CV31 .109 F6
Charles Lakin Cl CV7 .51 C5
Charles Rd CV9 .18 C4
Charles St Arley CV7 .37 A4
Coventry CV1 .151 D4
Hurley CV9 .16 B3
Nuneaton CV11 .29 A5
Rugby CV21 .82 C2
Warwick CV34 .109 A8
Charles Warren Cl CV21 .83 A2
Charlesfield Rd CV22 .100 A4
Charlesworth Ave B90 .71 B6
Charlewood Rd CV6 .49 B2
Charlotte St
Royal Leamington Spa CV31 .109 F6
Rugby CV21 .83 A2
Charlton Terr GL56 .140 B3
Charminster Dr CV3 .77 D4
Charnwood Ave CV10 .28 E2
Charnwood Dr CV10 .19 A1
Charnwood Way CV32 .106 C3
Charter App CV34 .108 D5
Charter Ave CV4 .76 B7
Charter Ho CV4 .76 A7
Charter Rd CV22 .100 C4
Charterhouse Rd CV1 .61 E2
Chartley Cl B93 .71 E3
Chartwell Cl CV11 .29 F1
Chartwell Dr B90 .70 D5
Charwelton Dr CV21 .83 C3
Chase Cl CV11 .29 E6
Chase La CV8 .92 B7
Chater Dr B76 .13 A1
Chaters Orch CV47 .115 D4
Chatham Cl CV3 .78 C8
Chatillon Cl CV34 .109 E3
Chatsworth Cl
Cheswick Green B90 .70 E5
Hinckley LE10 .31 F6
Chatsworth Dr CV11 .29 F2
Chatsworth Gdns CV31 .110 D6
Chatsworth Gr CV8 .93 C5
Chatsworth Rise CV3 .77 E6
Chattaway Dr CV7 .74 B6
Chattle Hill B46 .23 E2
Chaucer Dr CV10 .28 A4
Chaucer Rd CV22 .99 C3
Chauntry Pl CV1 .151 C3
Chauson Gr B91 .71 A8
Chaytor Rd B78 .11 A4
Cheadle Cl CV2 .50 A4
Cheam Cl CV6 .50 A1
Cheatle Ct B77 .9 B3
Cheedon Cl B93 .71 E2
Chelmarsh CV6 .61 C6
Chelmsley Ave B46 .33 F6
Chelmsley Circ B37 .33 B3
Chelmsley La B37 .44 A8
Chelmsley Rd B37 .33 C2
Chelmsley Wood Ind Est B37 .33 B4
Chelney Wlk CV3 .63 A1
Chelsea Cl CV11 .29 F7
Chelsey Rd CV2 .62 E8
Cheltenham Cl CV12 .39 B4
Cheltenham Croft CV2 .62 F7
Cheltondale 3 B90 .70 C8
Chelveston Rd CV6 .60 E5
Chelwood Gr CV2 .50 F1
Chenies Cl CV5 .60 B3
Chepstow Cl Coventry CV3 78 C5
Stratford-u-A CV37 .144 C1
Chepstow Gdns OX16 .139 F3
Chequer St CV12 .40 C2
Cheriton Cl CV5 .60 D4
Cherry Blossom Gr CV31 .110 B2
Cherry Cl Coventry CV6 .49 D2
Ettington CV37 .131 A3
Hurley CV9 .16 B2
Offenham WR11 .127 D1
Cherry Fields OX17 .134 C1
Cherry Gr CV22 .99 C4
Cherry La Bearley CV37 .120 E7
Hampton Magna CV35 .114 F4
Cherry Orch
Henley-in-A B95 .113 B5
Kenilworth CV8 .93 A5
Shipston-on-S CV36 .149 C3
Stratford-u-A CV37 .144 C1
Wellesbourne CV35 .146 B2
Cherry Orchard Cl GL55 135 B1
Cherry Orchard Est CV13 20 C2
Cherry Pit La B98 .86 A1
Cherry Rd OX16 .139 F4
Cherry St
Stratford-u-A CV37 .144 C1
Warwick CV34 .108 F7
Cherry Tree Ave CV10 .28 E6
Cherry Tree Cres WR11 .127 F6
Cherry Tree Wlk CV47 .147 A3
Cherry Way CV8 .93 A5
Cherry Wlk B47 .69 B5
Cherrybrook Way CV2 .50 C1
Cherryfield Cl CV10 .19 A1
Cherrywood Cres 3 B91 71 C8
Cherrywood Gr CV5 .59 F5
Cherwell Cl LE10 .31 A8
Cherwell The NN11 .117 F1
Cherwell Way CV23 .82 A2
Chesford Cres
Coventry CV6 .50 B2
Warwick CV34 .105 B1
Chesford Gr CV37 .144 B2
Chesham St CV31 .110 B7
Cheshire Cl CV22 .99 B4
Chesholme Rd CV6 .49 B2
Cheshunt Ho 3 B37 .33 B2
Chesils The CV3 .77 D6
Chessetts Wood Rd B94 .89 C7
Chester Cl B37 .33 A2
Chester Ct 4 B37 .33 D2
Chester Rd
Birmingham, Chelmsley Wood B37 .44 F8
Hampton-in-A B46,B92,CV7 .45 B5
Chester St Coventry CV1 .61 B3
Rugby CV21 .83 B2
Chester Way OX16 .139 F3
Chesterton Cl B97 .102 B2
Chesterton Dr
Nuneaton CV10 .28 A5
Royal Leamington Spa CV31 .110 C5
Chesterton Hill CV35 .123 B4
Chesterton Rd
Coventry CV6 .61 A7
Lighthorne CV35 .123 C3
Chesterwood B47 .69 A6
Chestnut Ave CV8 .92 F3
Chestnut Cl
Ettington CV37 .131 B3
Kingsbury B78 .15 B3
Chestnut Cres CV10 .28 E5
Chestnut Ct Alcester B49 143 B2
Coventry CV3 .78 B8
Royal Leamington Spa CV34 .109 E2
Chestnut Dr CV11 .29 E3
Chestnut Field CV21 .83 A2
Chestnut Gr Coleshill B46 .34 A4
Coventry CV4 .60 A2
Moreton Morrell CV35 .122 E3
Wolston CV8 .80 A2
Chestnut Pl CV47 .147 A3
Chestnut Rd
Astwood Bank B96 .102 C1
Bedworth CV12 .39 D4
Mollington OX17 .134 A2
Chestnut Sch CV1 .151 B1
Chestnut Sq
Royal Leamington Spa CV32 .106 B2
Wellesbourne CV35 .146 B2
Chestnut Tree Ave CV4 .60 A2
Chestnut Wlk
2 Birmingham B37 .33 B2
Henley-in-A B95 .113 A5
Stratford-u-A CV37 .144 C1
Chestnuts The CV12 .38 E2
Cheswick Cl Coventry CV6 62 A7
Redditch B98 .112 A6
Cheswick Green Prim Sch B90 .70 E4
Cheswick Way B90 .70 D4
Cheswood Dr B76 .22 B6
Chetton Ave CV6 .61 C6
Chetwode Cl CV5 .60 B4
Chetwynd Ave B78 .11 A4
Chetwynd Dr CV11 .40 B7
Chetwynd Jun Sch CV11 .40 A7
Cheveral Ave CV6 .61 B6
Cheveral Rd CV12 .39 A3
Cheverel Pl CV11 .29 B2
Cheverel St CV11 .29 B3
Cheviot B77 .4 B1
Cheviot Cl CV10 .28 B3
Cheviot Rise CV32 .106 C3
Cheviot The CV4 .76 D6
Cheviot Way OX16 .139 F5
Cheylesmore CV1 .151 B2
Chichester Cl CV11 .30 A7
Chichester Gr B37 .33 B1
Chichester La CV35 .114 F3
Chicory Dr CV23 .83 B4
Chideock Hill CV3 .77 B6
Chiel Cl CV5 .59 F4
Chigwell Cl B35 .22 A3
Childs Cl CV37 .144 C3
Childs Oak Cl CV7 .74 A6
Chilham Dr B37 .33 C2
Chillaton Rd CV6 .49 B2
Chillingham B77 .9 B4
Chiltern Ct 2 CV6 .61 A5
Chiltern Ho CV5 .59 D4
Chiltern Leys 2 CV6 .61 A4
Chiltern Rd B77 .4 B1
Chilterns The CV5 .60 B4
Chilvers Coton Com Inf Sch CV11 .29 B3
Chilvers Coton Craft Ctr CV11 .29 C2
Chilvers Ct CV11 .29 C4
Chilworth Cl CV11 .39 E8
Chines The CV10 .29 D7
Chingford Rd CV6 .50 A4
Chingley Bank B95 .113 B4
Chipping Campden Sch GL55 .135 B2
Chipping Norton Rd OX15 .142 D4
Chipstone Cl 1 B93 .71 C8
Chiswick Wlk B37 .33 E2
Chivenor Ho 1 B35 .22 A2
Chivenor Jun & Inf Sch B35 .22 A2
Chivington Cl B90 .71 B6
Chorley Way CV6 .61 C6
Choyce Cl CV9 .12 B1
Christ the King RC Inf Sch CV6 .60 F6
Christ the King RC Jun Sch CV6 .60 F7
Christchurch Cl CV10 .28 F1
Christchurch Rd CV6 .61 A5
Christine Ledger Sq 9 CV31 .110 A6
Christopher Hooke Ho CV6 .61 E8
Chub B77 .9 B4
Chudleigh Rd CV2 .62 E7
Church Ave B46 .23 B3
Church Bank
Binton CV37 .129 A8
Temple Grafton B49 .119 E1
Church Cl Arley CV7 .26 C1
Birmingham B37 .33 A6
Bishops Itchington CV47 .124 A4
Drayton Bassett B78 .8 C3
Ebrington GL55 .135 E3
Harborough Magna CV23 .66 A2
Hinckley LE10 .32 A5
Luddington CV37 .129 C7
Nuneaton CV10 .28 B8
Ryton-on-D CV8 .79 B2
Stoke Golding CV13 .21 B4
Wardington OX17 .134 F1
Whitnash CV31 .110 B4
Wolvey LE10 .41 C2
Wood End CV9 .10 B1
Church Cotts B46 .25 B2
Church Ct CV6 .48 F1
Church Down Cl B97 .102 B3
Church Dr Cookhill B49 .118 D5
Kenilworth CV8 .92 F5
Church End
Great Rollright OX7 .142 A2
Radford Semele CV31 .110 E6
Church Farm Ct CV35 .138 C7
Church Farm La GL56 .140 A6
Church Fields NN11 .126 E8
Church Hill Badby NN11 .126 F5
15 Bishops Tachbrook CV33 .122 F8
Coleshill B46 .34 A4
Combrook CV35 .131 E6
Cubbington CV32 .106 E5
Royal Leamington Spa CV32 .109 E8
Stretton on D CV23 .96 C3
Ullenhall B95 .112 E6
Warmington OX17 .133 D2
Wolvey LE10 .41 C2
Church Hill Ct CV35 .123 B2
Church La Alveston CV37 121 D3
Ansley CV10 .27 B1
Arley CV7 .26 C1
Ash Green CV7 .49 E7
Aston Cantlow B95 .119 F6
Austrey CV9 .3 A1
Austrey, No Man's Heath CV9 .3 A3
Barford CV35 .122 B7
Bearley CV37 .120 E7
Berkswell CV7 .58 C3
Bickenhill B92 .44 E2
Claydon OX17 .134 B5
Cookhill B49 .118 D5
Corley CV7 .48 B7
Coventry, Middle Stoke CV2 .62 B3
Coventry, Upper Eastern Green CV5 .59 C5
Cropredy OX17 .134 C1
Cubbington CV32 .106 E5
Curdworth B76 .23 B6
Ettington CV37 .131 A3
Fenny Drayton CV13 .19 C3
Fillongley CV7 .36 C2
Gaydon CV35 .132 E8
Hanwell OX17 .139 F6
Hellidon NN11 .126 B5
Hornton OX15 .139 B7
Kingsbury B78 .15 B3
Lapworth B94 .88 E3
Lea Marston B76 .24 A4
Leek Wootton CV35 .104 F6
Lighthorne CV35 .123 B2
Meriden CV7 .58 E8
Middleton B78 .8 B1
Mollington OX17 .134 A2
Newbold-on-S CV37 .130 E1
Norton WR11 .127 C2
Nuneaton CV10 .29 C7
Oxhill CV35 .137 F8
Radford Semele CV31 .110 E6
Royal Leamington Spa CV32 .106 A3
Shawell LE17 .68 B2
Shotteswell OX17 .139 E8
Shuttington B79 .4 C4
Church La *continued*
Snitterfield CV37 .121 B7
South Littleton WR11 .127 F1
Stoneleigh CV8 .94 C6
Stratford-u-A CV37 .144 B2
Thurlaston CV23 .98 C1
Welford on A CV37 .129 A7
Whatcote CV36 .137 D7
Whitnash CV31 .110 B4
Wigston Parva LE10 .42 C4
Wishaw B76 .14 A2
Church Lawford Bsns Ctr CV23 .81 A3
Church Lees 7 CV33 .122 F8
Church Lench CE Fst Sch WR11 .127 A6
Church Mews CV35 .132 B6
Church Park Cl CV6 .48 F1
Church Path CV35 .114 F3
Church Rd
Astwood Bank B96 .102 C1
Baginton CV8 .77 F2
Braunston NN11 .117 D5
Bubbenhall CV8 .95 B3
Church Lawford CV23 .81 B3
Claverdon CV35 .113 F3
Dordon B78 .11 A3
Gaydon CV35 .132 E8
Grandborough CV23 .116 F5
Ladbroke CV47 .124 D5
Long Itchington CV47 .115 D4
Newbold-on-S CV37 .130 E1
Norton Lindsey CV35 .114 C2
Nuneaton, Chapel End CV10 28 B8
Nuneaton, Stockingford CV10 .28 C3
Pebworth CV37 .128 F1
Ryton-on-D CV8 .79 B2
Shilton CV7 .51 E5
Shustoke B46 .25 A1
Snitterfield CV37 .121 B6
Tamworth B77 .9 B2
Ullenhall B95 .112 D5
Upper Boddington NN11 .134 E8
Warton B79 .5 C2
Wilmcote CV37 .120 C4
Witherley CV9 .19 A4
Church Row CV36 .141 D7
Church St Alcester B49 .143 B2
Appleby Magna DE12 .3 C4
Atherstone CV9 .18 B4
Barford CV35 .122 B7
Bidford-on-A B50 .148 C2
Bulkington CV12 .40 C2
Charwelton NN11 .126 D2
Chipping Campden GL55 .135 B2
Churchover CV23 .67 B3
Clifton u D CV23 .84 A3
Coventry CV1 .151 C4
Fenny Compton CV47 .133 D7
Hampton Lucy CV35 .121 F4
Harbury CV33 .123 F6
Harvington WR11 .127 D3
Hinckley LE10 .32 A5
Marton CV23 .115 C7
Moreton-in-M GL56 .140 A3
Nuneaton CV11 .29 D4
Offenham WR11 .127 D1
Royal Leamington Spa CV31 .110 A7
Rugby CV21 .83 A2
Shipston-on-S CV36 .149 C3
Staverton NN11 .126 D8
Stockton CV47 .147 C4
Stratford-u-A CV37 .144 C1
Studley B80 .103 C2
Warwick CV34 .108 E6
Welford on A CV37 .129 A7
Wellesbourne CV35 .146 B2
Wroxton OX15 .139 D4
Church Terr
Cubbington CV32 .106 E5
Harbury CV33 .123 F7
1 Royal Leamington Spa CV31 .110 A7
Church View
Aston Magna GL56 .140 A6
Tamworth B77 .9 C4
Warton B79 .5 C2
Church Way CV12 .39 B2
Church Wlk Allesley CV5 .60 C6
Atherstone CV9 .18 C4
Barby CV23 .101 B1
Hinckley LE10 .31 D8
Norton WR11 .127 C2
1 Royal Leamington Spa CV31 .109 F7
Rugby CV21,CV22 .83 A1
Rugby, Bilton CV22 .99 B4
Thurlaston CV23 .98 C2
Wellesbourne CV35 .146 B2
Church Wlks CV13 .21 B4
Churchdale Cl CV10 .28 C4
Churchfield CV37 .129 A7
Churchill Ave
Coventry CV6 .61 E8
Kenilworth CV8 .93 A6
Churchill Cl CV37 .131 A4
Churchill Ho 10 CV32 .109 F8
Churchill Par B75 .13 A5
Churchill Rd Rugby CV22 .83 A1
Sutton Coldfield B75 .13 A5
Churchlea OX17 .134 A2
Chylds Ct CV5 .60 A5
Cicero App CV34 .109 E2
Cicester Terr 14 GL56 .140 A3
Cicey La CV11 .41 A4
Cidermill La GL55 .135 B2
Cinder La CV9 .6 A4
Circle The CV10 .28 E4
Circuit The CV37 .129 C8
Circus Ave B37 .33 C2
City Arc CV1 .151 B2
City Coll Coventry CV1 .61 A2
City Coll Coventry (Butts Ctr) CV1 .61 B1
City College Coventry (Tile Hill Ctr) CV4 .59 F1
City Tech Coll The B37 .33 A4
Cladswell Cl B49 .118 D5
Cladswell La B49,B96 .118 C6
Clapham Sq CV31 .110 B7
Clapham St CV31 .110 B6
Clapham Terr CV31 .110 B7
Clapham Terrace Com Prim Sch CV31 .110 B7
Clara St CV2 .62 A2
Clare Cl CV32 .106 C2
Clare Ct CV21 .82 C2
Claremont Cl CV12 .40 B4
Claremont Rd
Royal Leamington Spa CV31 .109 F6
Rugby CV21 .83 B2
Claremont Wlk CV5 .60 C6
Clarence Ct 5 LE10 .31 E8
Clarence Rd Hinckley LE10 31 E8
Rugby CV21 .82 C2
Stratford-u-A CV37 .144 B2
Clarence St
5 Coventry CV1 .61 E4
Nuneaton CV11 .29 A4
Royal Leamington Spa CV31 .110 A6
Clarence Terr 6 CV32 .105 F1
Clarendon Ave CV32 .105 F1
Clarendon Cres CV32 .105 E1
Clarendon Ct 18 CV21 .83 A2
Clarendon Ho LE10 .31 B7
Clarendon Pl CV32 .105 E1
Clarendon Rd
Hinckley LE10 .31 C7
Kenilworth CV8 .93 A3
Clarendon Sq CV32 .105 F1
Clarendon St
Coventry CV5 .60 F1
Royal Leamington Spa CV32 .106 A1
Clarewell Ave B91 .71 B8
Clark Cl CV36 .149 C3
Clark St CV6 .50 A1
Clark Wlk CV37 .131 B4
Clarke Ave GL56 .140 C3
Clarke's Ave CV8 .93 A3
Clarks La CV36 .141 D3
Clarkson Dr CV31 .110 A4
Claverdon Cl B97 .102 B2
Claverdon Prim Sch CV35 .113 F3
Claverdon Rd CV5 .60 B3
Claverdon Sta CV35 .114 A3
Clay Ave CV11 .29 F7
Clay Bank OX15 .142 D4
Clay La Allesley CV5 .47 E3
Coventry CV2 .62 A4
Clay Pit La B90 .70 A5
Claybrook Dr B98 .103 C4
Claybrooke Prim Sch LE17 .43 C2
Claydon Gr CV35 .114 F6
Claydon Rd OX17 .134 C2
Claymore B77 .9 C4
Clayton Rd CV6 .60 E5
Clayton Wlk B35 .22 A2
Cleasby B77 .4 B1
Cleaver Gdns CV10 .29 C6
Cleeve Ct B50 .148 B1
Cleeve Prior CE Fst Sch WR11 .128 A4
Cleeve Rd
Bidford-on-A B50 .148 B1
South Littleton WR11 .127 F2
Cleeves Ave CV34 .109 D6
Clematis B77 .4 A2
Clemens St CV31 .110 A7
Clement St CV11 .29 B3
Clement Way CV22 .99 A4
Clements St CV2 .62 A3
Clennon Rise CV2 .62 D8
Clent Ave B97 .102 B4
Clent Dr CV10 .28 B3
Cleobury La B94 .70 A3
Cleopatra Gr CV34 .109 E4
Clevedon Gn WR11 .128 A1
Cleveland Ct 1 CV32 .105 F2
Cleveland Rd
Bulkington CV12 .40 B3
Coventry CV2 .62 A4
Hinckley LE10 .31 C8
Cleveley Dr CV10 .28 D7
Clews Rd B98 .102 C4
Clifden Gr CV8 .93 C6
Cliff Hall La B78 .9 A1
Cliffe Ct CV32 .105 D1
Cliffe Rd CV32 .105 D1
Cliffe Way CV34 .109 A8
Clifford Bridge Prim Sch CV3 .63 A3
Clifford Bridge Rd CV3 .62 F4
Clifford La CV37 .130 A8
Clifford Mill CV37 .129 F7
Clifford Rd B93 .71 F4
Clifton Cl B98 .103 C4

Clifton Ct **5** CV31 ......110 B7
Clifton La B79 ....1 A2
Clifton Rd Nuneaton CV10 .28 F4
　Rugby CV21 ....83 B2
Clifton St CV1 ....151 D4
Clifton-upon-Dunsmore CE
　Prim Sch CV23 ....83 C3
Clinic Dr CV11 ....29 C3
Clinton Ave
　Kenilworth CV8 ....92 D6
　Warwick CV34 ....108 A7
Clinton La CV8 ....92 D6
Clinton Prim Sch CV8 ....92 E3
Clinton Rd Coleshill B46 .33 F6
　Coventry CV6 ....49 F2
　Solihull B90 ....70 D8
Clinton St **2** CV31 ....110 A7
Clipstone Rd CV6 ....60 E6
Clive Rd CV7 ....74 C5
Cliveden Wlk CV11 ......39 E8
Clock La B92 ....44 D2
Cloister Croft CV2 ....62 F6
Cloister Crofts CV32 ....105 F3
Cloister Way CV32 ......105 F3
Cloisters The
　Atherstone CV9 ....18 C4
　Royal Leamington Spa
　CV32 ....105 F3
　Studley B80 ....103 B2
Clopton Cres B37 ....33 C4
Clopton Ct CV37 ....144 C2
Clopton Rd CV37 ......144 C2
Close The Brandon CV8 ...79 F5
　Chipping Warden OX17 .134 F3
　Cleeve Prior WR11 ....128 A4
　Epwell OX15 ....138 D3
　Halford CV36 ....137 A8
　Hampton Lucy CV35 ...121 F4
　Hollywood B47 ....69 A5
　Kenilworth CV8 ....93 A6
　Lower Quinton CV37 ..129 E2
　Royal Leamington Spa
　CV31 ....110 A5
Closers Bsns Ctr CV11 ..29 D2
Closter Gn CV35 ....132 B6
Cloud Gn CV4 ....76 D5
Cloudsley Bush La LE10 .42 A3
Clovelly Gdns CV2 ......62 C5
Clovelly Rd CV2 ....62 B5
Clovelly Way CV11 ......29 E5
Clover Ave B37 ....33 D2
Clover Cl Rugby CV23 ....83 B4
　Stratford-u-A CV37 ...144 C3
Cloverdale Cl CV6 ....49 B4
Cloweswood La B94 ......86 F8
Clumber Park Rd CV35 .132 D3
Clunes Ave CV11 ....29 E6
Clyde Rd Bulkington CV12 .40 A2
　Dorridge B93 ....72 A2
Co-Operative St CV2 ....50 B3
Coach Ho The CV35 ....131 F7
Coach House Ct CV34 ..149 C3
Coach House Rise B77 ...9 C4
Coal Pit La Willey CV23 ..54 B3
　Wolvey LE10 ....41 B1
Coalpit Fields Rd CV12 .39 C1
Coalpit La CV8 ....80 B1
Coat Of Arms Bridge Rd
　CV3 ....77 A6
Cobbs Rd CV8 ....92 E6
Cobden Ave CV31 ......110 C5
Cobden St CV6 ....61 E5
Cobia B77 ....9 B4
Coburg Ho CV5 ....60 E3
Cockerills Mdw CV21 ...101 A4
Cockermouth Cl CV32 ..105 D2
Cocksfoot Cl CV37 .....144 C3
Cocksparrow St CV34 ..108 D7
Cockspur St B78 ....10 C4
Coffee Pot La CV35 ....114 C6
Colbek Ct CV10 ....27 C2
Colbourne Gr CV32 ....105 D2
Cold Comfort La B49 ..143 A2
Coldfield Dr B98 ....102 C4
Coldicotts Cl GL55 ....135 B2
Coldwells Ct CV22 .....83 A1
Cole Ct B37 ....33 B2
Colebridge Cres B46 ...33 F8
Colebrook Cl
　Alcester B49 ....143 B2
　Coventry CV3 ....62 F2
Coleby Cl CV4 ....75 D7
Coleford Dr B37 ....33 A2
Colehurst Croft B90 ....70 F6
Coleman St CV4 ....59 F3
Colemeadow Rd B46 ...33 F7
Coleridge Cl B97 ......102 B4
Coleridge Rd CV2 ......62 C3
Coleshill CE Prim Sch
　B46 ....33 F6
Coleshill Cl B97 ....102 B3
Coleshill Heath Rd
　Birmingham B37 ....44 C7
　Coleshill B37,B46 ......32 E2
Coleshill Heath Sch B37 .33 C1
Coleshill Ind Est B46 ...23 F2
Coleshill Rd Ansley CV10 .27 B4
　Atherstone CV9 ....18 B3
　Birmingham, Marston Green
　B37 ....44 B8
　Curdworth B76 ....23 C5
　Drayton Bassett B78 ....9 A4
　Furnace End B46 ....25 B2
　Maxstoke B46 ....34 C3
　Nuneaton CV10 ....28 A7

Coleshill Rd continued
　Shustoke B46 ....24 C1
　Water Orton B46 ......23 B2
Coleshill Sch The B46 ..34 A2
Coleshill St
　Atherstone CV9 ....18 B4
　Fazeley B78 ....9 A4
Colesleys The B46 ......34 A3
Coleville Rd B76 ....22 B6
Coley Cl LE10 ....31 D7
Colina Cl CV3 ....78 C5
Colledge Cl CV23 ......64 C2
Colledge Rd CV6 ....49 D1
College Dr CV32 ......105 F2
College La
　Balsall Common CV8 ...73 E1
　Long Compton CV36 ..141 D2
　Stratford-u-A CV37 ...144 C1
College Mews CV37 ...144 C1
College Rd CV23 ......117 C6
College St Nuneaton CV10 .29 C1
　Stratford-u-A CV37 ...144 C1
Collets Brook B75 ....7 A1
Collett B77 ....4 A1
Collett Wlk **2** CV1 ....61 B3
Colliers Way CV7 ....36 C4
Colliery La CV7 ....39 B1
Colliery La N CV7 ......39 B1
Colling Wlk B37 ....33 A5
Collingham La CV47 ...115 E4
Collingwood Ave CV22 .82 B1
Collingwood Rd CV5 ...36 A1
Collins Gr CV4 ....76 D5
Collins Rd CV34 ......109 D5
Collins Way B49 ......143 B2
Colmore Dr B75 ....13 A5
Colony Rd OX15 ......142 D8
Colts Cl LE10 ....31 D4
Columbia Gdns CV12 ...39 E2
Columbine Way CV12 ...38 E1
Colyere Cl CV7 ....49 A6
Combe Fields Rd CV3 ..63 F4
Combroke Gr CV35 ....114 F5
Comet Rd B26 ....44 C4
Commainge Cl CV34 ..108 D7
Commander Cl **12** CV33 122 F8
Commanders Cl CV33 ..123 C3
Commissary Rd B26 ....44 A3
Common La
　Claverdon CV35 ......113 F4
　Corley CV7 ....47 E7
　Kenilworth CV8 ....93 B7
　Mappleborough Green
　B80 ....112 A6
　Polesworth B78 ....11 A4
Common The CV9 ......11 B1
Common Way CV2 ......62 A6
Compass Ct **4** CV1 ...61 B3
Compton Cl CV32 .....106 C2
Compton Croft B37 ....33 D1
Compton Ct
　Long Compton CV36 ..141 C4
　Shipston-on-S CV36 ..149 C3
Compton District Prim Sch
　The CV36 ....141 C3
Compton Hill CV35 ....131 E7
Compton Rd Coventry CV6 49 D2
　Lighthorne Heath CV33 123 D2
Compton Verney★
　CV35 ....131 F7
Comrie Cl CV2 ....62 F6
Comyn St CV32 ....106 B1
Concorde Rd B26 ......44 C4
Conduit Hill GL55 .....135 A1
Coneybury Wlk B76 ....22 D5
Congleton Cl CV6 ......49 E2
Congrave Wlk CV12 ....39 B2
Congreve Cl CV34 ....104 F2
Conifer Cl CV12 ....39 C4
Conifer Gr **3** CV31 ..109 F5
Conifer Paddock CV3 ...62 E1
Conifers The CV8 ......93 B3
Coningsby Cl **3** CV31 110 C6
Coniston B77 ....10 A4
Coniston Cl
　Bulkington CV12 ....40 C3
　Rugby CV21 ....83 B3
Coniston Ct
　Nuneaton CV11 ....29 F7
　2 Royal Leamington Spa
　CV32 ....105 D1
Coniston Dr CV5 ....59 D4
Coniston Grange CV8 ..92 F5
Coniston Rd Coventry CV5 60 F1
　Royal Leamington Spa
　CV32 ....105 D1
Coniston Way CV11 ....29 F7
Conrad Cl CV22 ....99 C3
Conrad Rd CV6 ....61 A7
Constable Cl CV12 .....39 A5
Constable Rd CV21 ....84 A1
Constance Cl CV12 ....49 F8
Constance Dr CV33 ...123 F6
Constance Harris Cl
　CV35 ....146 B2
Constantine La B46 ....23 F1
Consul Rd CV21 ....83 A3
Convent Cl
　Atherstone CV9 ....18 C4
　Kenilworth CV8 ....93 A7
Convent La CV9 ....18 C4
Conway Ave CV4 ....75 D8
Conway Croft B49 ....127 E8
Conway Dr OX16 .....139 F3
Conway Rd
　Birmingham, Fordbridge
　B37 ....33 B3

Conway Rd continued
　Royal Leamington Spa
　CV32 ....109 D8
Conwy Cl CV11 ....29 D3
Cook Cl Knowle B93 ...72 C6
　Rugby CV21 ....83 B4
Cook St CV1 ....151 B3
Cook's Hill OX15 .....139 A3
Cooke Cl Coventry CV6 ..50 A4
　Warwick CV34 ....104 F2
Cooks Cl CV9 ....18 B4
Cooks La Birmingham B37 .33 A4
　Frankton CV23 ....97 B1
　Salford OX7 ....150 C3
Coombe Abbey Ctry Pk★
　CV3 ....63 E3
Coombe Abbey Visitor Ctr★
　CV3 ....63 E4
Coombe Ave CV3 ....78 F7
Coombe Ct CV3 ....63 A2
Coombe Dr CV3 ....79 E7
Coombe Park Rd CV3 ..62 F2
Coombe St CV3 ....62 B2
Cooper St CV11 ....29 D4
Cooper's Way CV47 ...132 F6
Coopers Wlk CV8 ......95 B3
Cope Arnolds Cl CV6 ..49 F4
Cope St CV1 ....151 C3
Copeland CV21 ....83 B4
Copeland Cl B79 ....5 C2
Copland Pl CV4 ....59 E1
Coplow Cl CV7 ....74 A6
Copper Beech Cl CV6 ..49 E1
Copperas St CV2 ....50 B2
Copperfield Rd CV2 ...62 B3
Coppice Cl
　Cheswick Green B90 ...70 C4
　Stratford-u-A CV37 ...145 A3
Coppice Dr Dordon B78 .10 A4
　Polesworth B78 ....10 C4
Coppice La Middleton B78 .7 B1
　Thorpe Constantine B79 .2 A4
Coppice Prim Sch The
　B47 ....69 A6
Coppice Rd CV31 .....110 B2
Coppice The
　Atherstone CV9 ....19 A3
　Coventry CV3 ....78 B8
　Hinckley LE10 ....31 F8
　Nuneaton CV10 ....29 C7
Coppice Way **7** B37 ..33 B2
Coppice Wlk B90 ......70 D4
Copps Rd CV32 ....109 D8
Copse Dr CV5 ....59 B8
Copse The CV7 ....50 A8
Copsewood Ave CV11 ..40 B7
Copsewood Terr CV3 ..62 C2
Copston La LE10 ....42 A3
Copstone Dr B93 ......71 F3
Copt Heath Croft B93 ..72 B8
Copt Heath Dr B93 ....72 A7
Copt Oak Cl CV4 ......75 C6
Copthorne Rd CV6 .....60 F8
Coral Cl Coventry CV5 ..60 C2
Coralin Cl B37 ....33 C2
Corbett Rd B47 ....69 A7
Corbett St CV21 ....83 B2
Corbetts Cl B92 ....57 B7
Corbin Rd B78 ....11 A3
Corbison Cl CV34 ....104 D1
Corbizum Ave B80 ....103 B2
Cord La CV23 ....65 C2
Cordelia Gn CV34 ....109 D4
Cordelia Way CV22 ....99 C3
Corder's La CV36 .....140 A3
Corders Cl **5** GL56 ..140 A3
Corfe Cl CV2 ....62 F5
Corinne Croft B37 .....33 A4
Corinthian Pl CV2 .....62 D6
Coriolanus Sq CV34 ..109 F3
Corley Sch CV7 ....48 B6
Corley View CV7 ....49 C6
Corn Mdws CV12 ......39 C2
Corncrake Dr B36 .....33 A7
Cornel Cl B37 ....44 C8
Cornelius St CV3 ......77 D8
Cornerstone Ho CV1 .151 C4
Cornet's End La CV7 ..58 B6
Cornets End La CV7 ...57 E7
Cornfield Croft B37 ....33 D3
Cornfield The CV3 .....62 C1
Cornflower Dr CV23 ...83 B4
Cornhill Gr CV8 ....93 C5
Cornish Cl CV10 ....27 C4
Cornish Cres CV10 ....29 A2
Cornish Hos GL56 ....140 B3
Cornwall Cl **3** CV34 .108 F8
Cornwall Pl CV32 ....105 D1
Cornwall Rd CV1 ......61 E1
Cornwallis Rd CV22 ...82 B1
Cornwell Cl B98 ......103 A3
Coronation Ave B78 ...5 A1
Coronation Cl GL55 ..135 A2
Coronation Cres B79 ..4 C4
Coronation Ct CV11 ...29 B4
Coronation La OX17 ..139 E8
Coronation Rd
　Church Lawford CV23 ..81 A3
　Coventry CV1 ....61 F4
　Hurley CV9 ....16 B3
Coronel Ave CV6 ......49 E4
Corporation St
　Coventry CV1 ....151 B3
　Nuneaton CV11 ....29 B5
　Rugby CV21 ....83 A2
Corpus Christi RC Sch
　CV3 ....78 D7

Correen B77 ....4 B1
Corsham Rd CV47 ....132 F6
Corston Mews CV31 ..110 C6
Corunna Rd CV34 ....108 C7
Cosford Cl CV32 ......106 B3
Cosford Cres B35 .....22 A3
Cosford La CV21 ......67 A1
Costard Ave CV36 ....149 C3
Costock Cl B37 ....44 B8
Coten End CV34 ......108 F7
Coten End Prim Sch
　CV34 ....109 A7
Cotes Rd LE10 ....31 F5
Cotheridge Cl B90 ....71 C6
Cotman Cl CV12 ......39 A4
Coton Park Dr CV23 ..83 B4
Coton Rd Churchover CV23 67 B2
　Nether Whitacre B46 ..15 B1
　Nuneaton CV11 ....29 C3
　Rugby CV21 ....84 A1
Cotsmore Cl LE56 ....140 B3
Cotswold Bsns Village
　GL56 ....140 B3
Cotswold Cl
　Sibford Ferris OX15 ..142 D8
　Tredington CV36 .....136 F6
Cotswold Cnr OX7 ...142 A2
Cotswold Cres CV10 ..28 B3
Cotswold Dr CV3 ......77 C3
Cotswold Edge GL55 .135 B6
Cotswold Gdns **21** GL56 140 A3
Cottage Cl CV31 ......110 C6
Cottage Farm Ct GL56 136 F6
Cottage Farm Lodge CV6 49 A1
Cottage Farm Rd
　Coventry CV6 ....49 A2
　Tamworth B77 ....9 B4
Cottage La Minworth B76 .22 D6
　Nether Whitacre B46 ..24 B3
　Stratford-u-A CV37 ...144 B1
Cottage Leap CV21 ....83 B3
Cottage Wlk B77 ....9 C3
Cotterell Rd CV21 .....82 C3
Cotterill's Cl CV31 ....110 B3
Cotters Croft CV47 ...133 D7
Cottesbrook Cl CV3 ...62 E1
Cotton Dr CV8 ....93 C6
Cotton Mill Spinney
　CV32 ....106 E6
Cottrells Mews CV34 ..23 B2
Coughton CE Prim Sch
　B49 ....118 F7
Coughton Ct★ B49 ...119 A7
Coughton Dr CV31 ....110 C6
Coughton Fields La B49 143 B4
Coughton La B49 .....118 F7
Council Hos CV5 ......47 D1
Council Hos The OX17 139 F6
Coundon Court Sch & Com
　Coll CV6 ....60 E7
Coundon Gn CV6 ......60 E8
Coundon Prim Sch CV6 .60 E5
Coundon Rd CV1 ......61 B3
Coundon St CV1 .....151 A4
Coundon Wedge Dr CV5 .60 D7
Countess Rd CV11 ....29 A4
Countess's Croft The
　CV3 ....77 D7
Countryside NN11 ....117 D5
Court Cl
　7 Bishops Tachbrook
　CV33 ....122 E8
　Warmington OX17 ...133 D2
Court La WR11 ....127 D1
Court Leet CV3 ....79 D7
Court Leet Rd CV3 ....77 E7
Court of Lady Katherine
　Leveson The B93 .....73 B5
Court St CV31 ....110 A7
Court Way B50 ....148 C3
Court Yard The CV35 ..132 B5
Courtaulds Way CV6 ..61 D6
Courthouse Croft CV8 .93 B4
Courthouse Green Prim Sch
　CV6 ....62 A8
Courtland Ave CV6 ....60 F5
Courtney Cl CV11 .....29 F7
Courtyard The
　Coleshill B46 ....23 F2
　Warwick CV34 ....108 F5
Cove Pl CV2 ....62 C7
Coventry & Warwickshire
　Hospl CV1 ....151 C4
Coventry Airport CV8 ..78 A3
Coventry Bsns Pk CV5 .60 D1
Coventry Canal Basin
　Warehouse CV1 .....151 B4
Coventry Cath Church of St
　Michael★ CV1 ......151 C3
Coventry City FC CV1 ..61 F3
Coventry Council Ho
　CV1 ....151 C3
Coventry Gram Sch CV5 60 A5
Coventry Highway B98 112 A7
Coventry Muslim Sch
　CV6 ....61 E8
Coventry Prep Sch CV3 .77 B8
Coventry Railway Ctr
　CV8 ....78 A3
Coventry Rd Baginton CV8 77 F2
　Barnacle CV7,Bayton CV7 51 A8
　Bedworth, Hawkesbury CV2,
　CV7 ....50 E6
　Bedworth, Springfield CV12 39 B2
　Berkswell CV7 ....58 E3
　Brinklow CV3,CV23 ...64 B2
　Bulkington CV12 ......40 B1
　Church Lawford CV23 ..81 A3

Coventry Rd continued
　Coleshill B46 ....34 A3
　Cubbington CV32 ....106 E7
　Dunchurch CV22,CV23 99 A3
　Hampton-in-A B92 ....45 B3
　Hinckley LE10 ....31 B7
　Hinckley, Sketchley LE10 31 F5
　Kenilworth CV8 ....93 A7
　Kingsbury B78 ....15 C2
　Lutterworth LE17 ......55 C3
　Marton CV23 ....115 C8
　Nuneaton CV10 ....39 C7
　Pailton CV23 ....66 A4
　Solihull B26,B92 ....44 C2
　Southam CV47 ....147 A3
　Stoneleigh CV3,CV3 ..94 C7
　Warwick CV34 ....108 F8
　Wigston Parva LE10 ..32 F1
Coventry Ret Mkt CV1 .151 B2
Coventry Road Exhall
　CV7 ....50 A8
Coventry St Coventry CV2 62 A4
　Nuneaton CV11 ....29 C4
　Southam CV47 ....147 A3
Coventry Sta CV1 .....151 B1
Coventry Toy Mus★
　CV1 ....151 C2
Coventry Univ
　Coventry CV1 ....151 C1
　Coventry CV1 ....151 C1
　Coventry CV1 ....151 D2
Coventry Univ Singer Hall
　CV1 ....151 C3
Coventry Walsgrave Triangle
　(Bsns Pk) CV2 ....63 A8
Coventry Walsgrave Triangle
　Bsns Pk CV2 ....51 A1
Cover Croft B76 ....13 A1
Coverley Pl CV22 .....82 C2
Covers The B80 ......103 C3
Cow La
　Lower Brailes OX15 ..137 F2
　Wood End B78 ....9 C2
Cowan Cl CV22 ....82 B1
Cowdray Cl CV11 .....110 C2
Cowley Cl B36 ....22 F1
Cowley Rd CV2 ....62 D4
Cowley Way CV23 ....101 C1
Cowper Cl CV34 .....104 E1
Cowper Rd LE10 ......31 D6
Cox Cl B50 ....148 C3
Cox Cres CV22 ....99 B2
Cox St CV1 ....151 C3
Cox's Cl CV10 ....29 B3
Cox's La NN11 ....126 B5
Cox's La CV47 ....125 C7
Cox's Orch CV31 .....110 A4
Cozens Cl CV12 ....39 A4
Crabbs Cross La B97 .102 C3
Crabmill Cl B93 ....72 C7
Crabmill La CV6 ......61 F7
Crabtree Gr CV31 ....110 C6
Crackley Cotts CV8 ...93 B8
Crackley Cres CV8 ....93 B8
Crackley La Coventry CV4 75 F3
　Kenilworth CV8 ....93 A7
Craddock Ct CV10 ....28 C7
Craddock Dr CV10 ....28 C7
Craig Cl CV31 ....110 B6
Craig Croft B37 ....33 D2
Craigends Ave CV3 ...78 E6
Crakston Cl CV2 ......62 E2
Crammond Cl LE10 ...31 B8
Cramper's Field CV6 ..61 A3
Cranborne Chase CV3 .63 A5
Crane Cl
　Stratford-u-A CV37 ..144 B3
　Warwick CV34 ....104 D1
Cranebrook Hill B78 ...7 C3
Craner's Rd CV1 ......61 F4
Cranford Rd CV5 ......60 D4
Cranham Cl B97 .....102 A4
Cranmer Gr CV34 ....109 D3
Cranmore Ave B90 ....70 E8
Cranmore Bvd B90 ....70 D8
Cranmore Dr B90 .....70 E8
Cranmore Rd
　Birmingham B36 ......22 E1
　Solihull B90 ....70 D8
Crantock Way CV11 ...29 F4
Cranwell Dr CV35 ....146 B1
Cranwell Rise B78 .....8 A4
Cranwell Way B35 ....22 A3
Crathie Cl CV2 ....62 F6
Craven B77 ....4 A1
Craven Arms Rd CV35 132 D3
Craven Ave CV3 ....79 D7
Craven Ct Coventry CV3 .62 F2
　Southam CV47 ....147 A2
Craven La CV47 ......147 A2
Craven Rd CV21 ....83 B2
Craven St CV5 ....60 F2
Crawford Cl
　Bidford-on-A B50 ....148 B2
　Royal Leamington Spa
　CV32 ....106 B5
Crawshaws Rd B36 ...22 C1
Creampot Cl OX17 ...134 D1
Creampot Cres OX17 134 C1
Creampot La OX17 ...134 C1
Crecy Rd CV3 ....77 E7
Crediton Cl CV11 .....29 F5
Crendon Cl B80 ......103 C3
Crescent Ave CV3 ....62 C2
Crescent CV22 ....99 B4
Crescent The
　Baddesley Ensor CV9 .11 B2
　Bidford-on-A B50 ....148 B5

Crescent The continued
Birmingham, Coleshill Heath
 B37 . . . . **44** E8
 Brinklow CV23 . . . . **64** C2
 Hampton-in-A B92 . . . . . . **57** B7
 Harborough Magna CV23 . . **66** A2
 Keresley CV7 . . . . **48** F6
 Lawford Heath CV23 . . . . **98** B3
 Napton on t H CV47 . . . . **125** C2
 Wellesbourne CV35 . . . . **146** B4
 Wootton Wawen B95 . . . . **120** C7
Cressage Rd CV2 . . . . **63** A6
Cressida Cl CV34 . . . . . **109** F3
Cresswell Cl CV10 . . . . . . **29** C8
Cresswell Ho CV6 . . . . . . **61** B1
Crest Hill WR11 . . . . . . **127** D3
Crest The CV32 . . . . . . **106** D3
Crestwood B77 . . . . **4** A3
Crew La CV8 . . . . **93** E6
Creynolds Cl B90 . . . . . . **70** D3
Creynolds La B90 . . . . . . **70** D4
Crick Rd CV21CV23 . . . . **101** B4
Cricket Cl CV5 . . . . **60** F3
Crigdon B77 . . . . **4** B1
Crimscote Cl B90 . . . . . . **70** F6
Crimscote Sq CV35 . . . . **114** F6
Cringlebrook B77 . . . . **9** A4
Cripplegate CV36 . . . . . **149** C4
Critchley Dr CV22 . . . . . . **99** B2
Crockwell St CV36 . . . . **141** C4
Croft Cl
 6 Bishops Tachbrook
 CV33 . . . . **122** F8
 Stretton on D CV23 . . . . . **96** C3
 Warwick CV34 . . . . **109** C3
 Wolvey LE10 . . . . **41** C2
Croft Field CV47 . . . . . . **125** C7
Croft Fields CV12 . . . . . . **39** B2
Croft Holm GL56 . . . . . . **140** B3
Croft Ind Est B37 . . . . . . **33** D2
Croft Jun Sch CV10 . . . . . **28** F3
Croft La Shrewley CV35 . . **114** C6
 Staverton NN11 . . . . . . **126** D8
 Temple Grafton B49 . . . . **119** E2
Croft Mead CV10 . . . . . . **27** B2
Croft Pool CV12 . . . . **38** F2
Croft Rd Atherstone CV9 . . **12** B1
 Bedworth CV12 . . . . . . **38** F2
 Coventry CV1 . . . . **151** A2
 Leek Wootton CV35 . . . . **105** A7
 Nuneaton CV10 . . . . . . **28** F3
 South Littleton WR11 . . . **127** F2
Croft Sch CV37 . . . . **121** D1
Croft Sch The CV37 . . . . **144** C1
Croft The Bulkington CV12 . **40** B2
 Church Lench WR11 . . . . **127** A4
 Coventry CV6 . . . . **49** F4
 Henley-in-A B95 . . . . . . **113** B4
 Meriden CV7 . . . . **46** C1
 Rugby CV21 . . . . **101** A4
 Warton B79 . . . . **5** C2
Croft's La OX15 . . . . **142** D3
Crofts La B96 . . . . **102** A1
Crofts The B76 . . . . **22** A8
Cromarty Cl CV5 . . . . **60** A5
Cromarty Dr LE10 . . . . . . **21** C1
Cromdale Cl CV10 . . . . . . **28** A3
Cromer Rd CV32 . . . . . . **106** B2
Cromes Wood CV4 . . . . . **59** D1
Crompton Ave B50 . . . . . **148** C3
Crompton Ct CV34 . . . . . **108** D6
Crompton St CV34 . . . . . **108** D6
Cromwell La CV4,CV8 . . . . **75** C6
Cromwell Pl CV33 . . . . . **123** D2
Cromwell Rd CV22 . . . . . . **83** B1
Cromwell St CV6 . . . . . . **61** F6
Crondal Rd CV7 . . . . **50** B7
Crook House Yd CV23 . . . . **64** C2
Crooks La Alcester B49 . . **143** B3
 Studley B80 . . . . **103** B2
Croome Cl CV6 . . . . **60** F4
Cropredy CE Prim Sch
 OX17 . . . . **134** C1
Cropthorne Cl B98 . . . . . **103** A4
Cropthorne Dr B47 . . . . . **69** B7
Crosbie Rd CV5 . . . . **60** E3
Cross Cheaping CV1 . . . . **151** B3
Cross Fields Rd ◆ CV34 **108** F8
Cross La Braunston NN11 . **117** E5
 Cubbington CV32 . . . . . **106** E4
Cross Leys CV36 . . . . . . **136** B6
Cross Point Bsns Pk CV2 . **63** B8
Cross Rd Alcester B49 . . . **143** C2
 Coventry CV6 . . . . **61** F8
 Keresley CV7 . . . . **48** F6
 ◆ Royal Leamington Spa
 CV32 . . . . **105** D1
Cross Road Ind Est CV6 . . **61** F7
Cross St Coventry CV1 . . . **151** C4
 Long Lawford CV23 . . . . . **82** A3
 Nuneaton CV10 . . . . **28** D3
 Royal Leamington Spa
 CV32 . . . . **106** A1
 Rugby CV21 . . . . **83** A2
 9 Warwick CV34 . . . . **108** F7
Cross Wlk B78 . . . . **11** A3
Crossfell B77 . . . . **4** A1
Crossgate Rd B98 . . . . . **103** B4
Crosskirk Rd LE10 . . . . . . **21** C1
Crossland Row LE10 . . . . **32** A6
Crosslands CV35 . . . . . . **146** B1
Crossley Ct CV6 . . . . **61** F7
Crossway Rd CV3 . . . . **77** B4
Crossways LE10 . . . . **31** F5
Crossways Cotts CV7 . . . . **37** C4
Crow Hill CV9 . . . . **11** B1
Crow Thorns CV21 . . . . . . **83** B3
Crowberry La B78 . . . . **8** B1

Crowden Rd B77 . . . . **4** A1
Crowhill Rd CV11 . . . . **30** A1
Crowleys Cl B95 . . . . . . **112** E6
Crowmere Rd CV2 . . . . . . **62** F7
Crown Cl CV33 . . . . **123** F7
Crown Gn CV6 . . . . **49** E2
Crown Ho CV5 . . . . **60** E3
Crown St CV33 . . . . **123** F7
Crown Terr CV31 . . . . . . **109** F7
Crown Way CV32 . . . . . . **106** B3
Crownhill Rd LE10 . . . . . . **31** D4
Croxall Dr B46 . . . . **25** A1
Croxhall St CV12 . . . . **39** C3
Croy Dr B35 . . . . **22** B4
Croydon Cl CV3 . . . . **77** E6
Crummock Cl CV6 . . . . . . **49** D3
Crutchley Way CV31 . . . . **110** A2
Cryersoak Cl B90 . . . . . . **71** B7
Cryfield Grange Rd CV4,
 CV8 . . . . **76** C2
Cryfield Hts CV4 . . . . **76** D2
Cubbington CE Prim Sch
 CV32 . . . . **106** F5
Cubbington Rd
 Coventry CV6 . . . . **50** A2
 Royal Leamington Spa
 CV32 . . . . **106** B3
Cuckoo La CV1 . . . . **151** C3
Culey Wlk B37 . . . . **33** D2
Culpepper Cl CV10 . . . . . . **28** E4
Culverley Cres B93 . . . . . . **71** F6
Culworth Cl
 Royal Leamington Spa
 CV31 . . . . **109** C5
 Rugby CV21 . . . . **83** C4
Culworth Ct Coventry CV6 . **61** E7
 Royal Leamington Spa
 CV31 . . . . **110** A5
Culworth Row CV6 . . . . . . **61** B1
Cumberland Cres CV32 . . **106** C3
Cumberland Dr CV10 . . . . **28** E3
Cumberland Wlk B75 . . . . **13** B5
Cumbernauld Wlk **7**
 CV2 . . . . **63** A7
Cumbria Cl CV1 . . . . **61** A3
Cumming St **14** CV31 . . **110** A7
Cumsey The CV35 . . . . . **114** A5
Cundall Cl CV31 . . . . . . **110** B6
Cunnery The CV8 . . . . **94** A3
Cunningham Way N
 CV22 . . . . **82** B1
Cunningham Way S CV22 . **82** B1
Cup & Saucer OX17 . . . . . **134** C1
Curdworth La B76 . . . . . . **23** A8
Curdworth Prim Sch B76 . **23** C6
Curie Cl CV21 . . . . **83** B2
Curlew Cl B77 . . . . **10** A4
Curlew Cl
 Stratford-u-A CV37 . . . . **144** B2
 Warton B79 . . . . **5** C2
Curlieu Cl CV35 . . . . . . **108** A7
Curlieu La CV35 . . . . . . **114** C2
Curran Cl CV31 . . . . **110** B4
Curriers Cl CV4 . . . . **75** D7
Curtis Rd CV2 . . . . **62** D6
Curzon Ave CV6 . . . . **61** B8
Curzon Cl LE10 . . . . **31** F7
Curzon Gr CV31 . . . . . . **110** C6
Cut Throat La B94 . . . . . . **87** D7
Cuttle Mill La B76 . . . . . . **14** D3
Cuttle Pool La B93 . . . . . . **72** F4
Cutworth Cl B76 . . . . **13** A3
Cygnet Ct CV1 . . . . **151** C4
Cymbeline Way
 Royal Leamington Spa
 CV34 . . . . **109** E4
 Rugby CV22 . . . . **99** B3
Cypress Croft CV3 . . . . . . **78** F8
Cypress La CV31 . . . . . . **110** B3
Cyprus Ave B96 . . . . **102** B1

D

D'aubeny Rd CV4 . . . . **76** C8
Dace B77 . . . . **9** B4
Dadglow Rd CV47 . . . . . **124** B4
Daffern Ave CV7 . . . . **37** A4
Daffern Rd CV7 . . . . **39** A1
Dagtail La B97 . . . . **102** B2
Dahlia Cl LE10 . . . . **31** E6
Daimler Ave OX16 . . . . . **139** F4
Daimler Cl B36 . . . . **22** F1
Daimler Rd CV6 . . . . **61** C5
Daintree Croft CV3 . . . . . . **77** C7
Dairyground The OX15 . . . **139** A3
Dalby Cl CV3 . . . . **78** E8
Dale Ave CV37 . . . . **145** B1
Dale Cl
 Long Itchington CV47 . . . **115** C4
 Warwick CV34 . . . . **109** A8
Dale End CV10 . . . . **28** E5
Dale End Cl LE10 . . . . **31** A7
Dale Meadow Cl CV7 . . . . **74** B6
Dale St
 Royal Leamington Spa
 CV32 . . . . **109** E8
 Rugby CV21 . . . . **83** A2
Dale The B95 . . . . **113** B2
Dalehouse Flats CV8 . . . . **93** B6
Dalehouse La CV8 . . . . . . **93** D7
Dales Inf Sch The B77 . . . **10** A4
Dales Jun Sch B77 . . . . . **10** A4
Daleway Rd CV3 . . . . **77** B4
Dalkeith Ave CV22 . . . . . . **99** B4
Dallington Rd CV6 . . . . . . **60** E6
Dalmahoy Cl CV11 . . . . . . **40** C8
Dalmeny Rd CV4 . . . . **75** D7

Dalton Cl CV23 . . . . **81** A3
Dalton Gdns CV2 . . . . **62** F4
Dalton Rd Bedworth CV12 . **39** A2
 Coventry CV5 . . . . **61** B1
Dalwood Way CV6 . . . . . . **50** B4
Daly Ave CV32 . . . . **114** F3
Dama Rd B78 . . . . **8** C4
Dame Agnes Gr CV6 . . . . . **62** B8
Damson Cl B97 . . . . **102** B3
Damson Ct LE10 . . . . **31** B7
Damson Rd CV35 . . . . . . **114** F3
Danbury Cl B76 . . . . **13** A2
Dane Ct NN11 . . . . **117** E5
Dane Rd CV2 . . . . **62** B4
Danesbury Cres CV31 . . . **110** D6
Daneswood Rd CV3 . . . . . **79** E7
Daniel Ave CV10 . . . . **28** C3
Daniel Rd CV9 . . . . **18** C4
Daniell Rd CV35 . . . . **146** B2
Danvers Cl OX15 . . . . **139** E1
Danvers Rd OX15 . . . . . . **139** E1
Danzey Cl B98 . . . . **103** A3
Danzey Green La B94 . . . . **87** B1
Danzey Green Rd B36 . . . . **22** B1
Danzey Sta B94 . . . . **112** E8
Darfield Ct CV8 . . . . **95** B3
Dark La
 Astwood Bank B96 . . . . **102** B1
 Bedworth CV12 . . . . **38** D1
 Braunston NN11 . . . . . . **117** E5
 Coventry CV1 . . . . **151** B4
 Hollywood B47 . . . . **69** A8
 Polesworth B78 . . . . **10** C4
 Tiddington CV37 . . . . . . **145** C2
 Wroxton OX15 . . . . **139** D4
Darlaston Ct CV7 . . . . **46** D1
Darley Green Rd B93 . . . . **72** B1
Darley Rd LE10 . . . . **31** E6
Darlingscote Rd CV36 . . . **149** B2
Darlston Row CV7 . . . . . . **46** B1
Darnbrook B77 . . . . **4** B1
Darnford Cl CV2 . . . . **62** F7
Darrach Cl CV2 . . . . **50** E1
Dart B77 . . . . **10** A3
Dart Cl LE10 . . . . **31** A8
Dartington Way CV11 . . . . **39** F8
Dartmouth Rd CV2 . . . . . . **62** C5
Dartmouth Sch CV2 . . . . . **62** D5
Darwell Pk B77 . . . . **4** A1
Darwin Cl CV2 . . . . **63** A6
Darwin Ct CV12 . . . . **39** A2
Darwin Gr CV2 . . . . **63** A7
Darwin Ho **3** B37 . . . . **33** C1
Dassett CE Prim Sch The
 CV47 . . . . **133** D7
Dassett Rd B93 . . . . **71** F4
Datchet Cl CV5 . . . . **60** C4
Davenport Dr B35 . . . . . . **22** C3
Davenport Lodge Sch
 CV5 . . . . **77** B8
Davenport Rd CV5 . . . . . . **77** B8
Davenport Terr LE10 . . . . **31** E8
Daventry Rd Barby CV23 . **101** B1
 Coventry CV3 . . . . **77** D7
 Rugby CV22,CV23 . . . . . . **99** C1
 Southam CV47 . . . . **147** B2
 Staverton NN11 . . . . . . **126** D8
 Staverton NN11 . . . . . . **126** E8
Daventry St CV47 . . . . . . **147** A2
David Rd Bedworth CV7 . . . **49** F8
 Coventry CV1 . . . . **61** F2
 Rugby CV22 . . . . **99** B4
Davidson Ave CV31 . . . . . **110** A7
Davies Rd Bedworth CV7 . . **49** F7
 Moreton-in-M GL56 . . . . **140** B3
Davis Cl CV32 . . . . **105** D2
Dawes Cl CV2 . . . . **62** A3
Dawley Cres B37 . . . . **33** B1
Dawley Wlk **9** CV2 . . . . . **63** A7
Dawlish Cl CV11 . . . . **29** E5
Dawlish Dr CV3 . . . . **77** D5
Dawson Cl CV31 . . . . . . **110** A2
Dawson Rd CV3 . . . . **62** A1
Day's La CV1 . . . . **61** F3
Days Cl CV1 . . . . **61** F3
Daytona Dr CV5 . . . . **59** B8
De Havilland Dr **2** B35 . . **22** A2
De Mohun Cres CV36 . . . **141** F5
De Montfort Rd CV8 . . . . . **92** E6
De Montfort Way CV4 . . . . **76** D5
De-Compton Cl CV7 . . . . . **49** A7
De-La-Bere Cres LE10 . . . **32** A6
Deacon Cl CV22 . . . . **83** B1
Deacon St CV11 . . . . **29** C3
Dean St CV2 . . . . **62** A3
Deanbrook Cl B90 . . . . . . **71** A6
Deane Par CV21 . . . . **101** A4
Deane Rd CV21 . . . . **101** A4
Deans Way CV7 . . . . **49** D6
Deanston Croft CV2 . . . . . **50** F1
Deansway CV34 . . . . **104** E1
Deasy Ho CV3 . . . . **78** B5
Deasy Rd CV1 . . . . **151** C1
Debden Cl Dorridge B93 . . **71** E2
 Wellesbourne CV35 . . . . **146** B1
Dee Wlk Birmingham B36 . . **33** A7
 Daventry NN11 . . . . **117** F1
Deedmore Rd CV2 . . . . . . **50** D1
Deedmore Sch CV2 . . . . . **62** C8
Deegan Cl CV2 . . . . **62** A5
Deeley B77 . . . . **4** A1
Deep La B46 . . . . **24** C3
Deepdale B77 . . . . **4** B1
Deepmore Rd CV22 . . . . . **99** B4
Deer Leap The CV8 . . . . . **93** B6
Deerdale Way CV3 . . . . . . **78** F8
Deerhill B77 . . . . **4** A1
Deerhurst Cl GL56 . . . . . **140** F1

Deerhurst Mews CV22 . . . **99** B2
Deerhurst Rd CV6 . . . . . . **49** B2
Deerings Rd CV21 . . . . . **101** A4
Deerpark Dr CV34 . . . . . **108** E8
Dehavilland Cl CV11 . . . . . **29** B5
Delage Cl CV6 . . . . **50** B4
Delamere Cl B36 . . . . **22** D1
Delamere Rd CV12 . . . . . . **38** F2
Delamere Way CV32 . . . . **106** C4
Delaware Rd CV3 . . . . **77** C5
Delf Ho CV21 . . . . **50** D1
Delhi Ave CV6 . . . . **49** D1
Delius St CV4 . . . . **59** E3
Dell Cl CV3 . . . . **78** C5
Dell Ct B95 . . . . **113** B5
Dell Farm Cl B93 . . . . **72** B6
Delmore Way B76 . . . . . . **22** B6
Delphi Cl CV34 . . . . **109** E4
Deltic B77 . . . . **4** A1
Deltic La B77 . . . . **9** C4
Delves Cres CV9 . . . . **10** B1
Dempster Ct CV11 . . . . . . **29** C4
Dempster Rd CV12 . . . . . . **39** A4
Denbigh Cl B98 . . . . **103** A3
Denbigh Cnr B46 . . . . **45** A6
Denbigh Rd CV6 . . . . **60** E5
Denby Bldgs **15** CV32 . . . **109** F8
Denby Cl CV32 . . . . **106** C3
Denby Croft B90 . . . . **71** B6
Dencer Dr CV8 . . . . **93** C4
Dene Cl CV35 . . . . **132** B5
Denegate Cl B76 . . . . **22** B6
Denehurst Way CV10 . . . . **28** F3
Denemoor Ct CV8 . . . . . . **93** B5
Denewood Way CV8 . . . . . **93** C6
Dengate Cl CV7 . . . . **74** B7
Denham Ave CV5 . . . . **60** C4
Denham Ct CV9 . . . . **18** C4
Denis Rd LE10 . . . . **31** D5
Denne Cl CV37 . . . . **145** A1
Dennett Cl CV34 . . . . . . **104** F2
Dennis Rd CV2 . . . . **62** B6
Denshaw Croft CV2 . . . . . **63** A8
Denton Cl CV8 . . . . **92** D6
Denton Croft B93 . . . . . . **71** D3
Denville Rd CV32 . . . . . . **106** A3
Deppers Bridge CV33,
 CV47 . . . . **124** B6
Derby Dr B37 . . . . **33** B2
Derby La CV9 . . . . **18** B4
Dereham Ct CV32 . . . . . . **106** A2
Derek Ave B78 . . . . **11** A3
Dering Cl CV2 . . . . **62** D8
Deronda Cl CV12 . . . . **39** A3
Derry Cl CV8 . . . . **80** A2
Dersingham Dr CV6 . . . . . **50** B2
Derwent Cl Coventry CV5 . . **59** E4
 Royal Leamington Spa
 CV32 . . . . **105** D1
 Rugby CV21 . . . . **83** B3
Derwent Rd
 Bedworth CV12 . . . . **39** A2
 Coventry CV6 . . . . **49** A2
Derwent Way CV11 . . . . . . **29** F6
Desdemona Ave CV34 . . . **109** E4
Despard Rd CV5 . . . . **59** D4
Devereux Cl CV4 . . . . **59** C1
Devitts Cl B90 . . . . **70** F7
Devon Cl CV10 . . . . **28** F3
Devon Gr CV2 . . . . **62** B6
Devon Ox Rd CV23 . . . . . **101** C1
Devonish Cl B49 . . . . **143** B3
Devonshire Terr **3**
 GL56 . . . . **140** A3
Devoran Cl CV7 . . . . **50** B8
Dew Cl CV22 . . . . **99** B2
Dewar Gr CV21 . . . . **83** C1
Dewbury Cl B96 . . . . **102** C1
Dewis Ho **4** CV2 . . . . **50** B1
Dewsbury Ave CV3 . . . . . . **77** B5
Dexter Ct CV9 . . . . **16** B2
Dexter La CV9 . . . . **16** B2
Dexter Way B78 . . . . **10** C4
Dial House La CV5 . . . . . . **59** F4
Diana Dr CV2 . . . . **50** E1
Dickens Cl CV10 . . . . **28** A4
Dickens Heath Rd
 Solihull, Dickens Heath B90 **70** A6
 Solihull, Dickens Heath B90 **70** B6
 Solihull, Tidbury Green B90 **69** F5
Dickens Rd Coventry CV6 . . **61** A8
 Harbury CV33 . . . . **123** C6
 Rugby CV22 . . . . **99** C3
Dickins Rd CV34 . . . . **105** B1
Dickinson Ct CV22 . . . . . . **83** A1
Didcot Cl B97 . . . . **102** B3
Didcot Way DE12 . . . . **3** C1
Diddington La B92,CV7 . . . **45** C1
Didgley Gr B37 . . . . **33** A5
Didsbury Rd CV7 . . . . **39** A1
Digbey Cl CV5 . . . . **60** B6
Digby Cres B46 . . . . **23** B3
Digby Dr B37 . . . . **44** B6
Digby Pl CV7 . . . . **46** C1
Digby Rd B46 . . . . **33** B6
Dighton Cl CV37 . . . . **129** F7
Dilcock Way CV4 . . . . **75** F7
Dillam Cl CV6 . . . . **50** A4
Dillington Ho **8** B37 . . . . **33** B2
Dillon Ct CV11 . . . . **29** B5
Dillotford Ave CV3 . . . . . . **77** D6
Dingle Cl CV6 . . . . **61** A6
Dingle La
 Appleby Magna CV9 . . . . . **3** B3
 Nether Whitacre B46 . . . . **24** C3
Dingle The
 Cheswick Green B90 . . . . **70** D5

Cre – Dra **161**

Dingle The continued
 Nuneaton CV10 . . . . **28** E6
Dingles Way CV37 . . . . . **145** A3
Dingleside Mid Sch
 B98 . . . . **103** A4
Dingley Rd CV12 . . . . **40** B2
Discovery Way CV3 . . . . . . **79** B7
Ditchford Cl B97 . . . . **102** B2
Ditton Cl CV22 . . . . **82** B1
Dixon Cl B35 . . . . **22** A2
Dobbie Rd CV37 . . . . **129** D1
Dobson La CV31 . . . . **110** A4
Dockers Cl CV7 . . . . **74** C7
Doctors Cl B94 . . . . **87** A2
Doctors La B95 . . . . **113** B5
Dodd Ave CV34 . . . . **109** C7
Dodgson Cl CV6 . . . . **50** A4
Dodwell Pk CV37 . . . . . . **129** C8
Dodwell Trad Est CV37 . . **129** C8
Dodwells Bridge Ind Est
 LE10 . . . . **30** E8
Dodwells Rd LE10 . . . . . . **30** E8
Doe Bank La CV1 . . . . **61** A3
Doe Kennel La B90 . . . . . . **70** D7
Dog La
 Fenny Compton CV47 . . . **133** D7
 Napton on t H CV47 . . . . **125** D4
 Nether Whitacre B46 . . . . **25** A4
 Tamworth B77 . . . . **4** A3
Dogberry Cl CV3 . . . . **78** C6
Dogberry Way CV34 . . . . **109** F2
Doglands The CV31 . . . . . **110** B4
Doily Cl OX15 . . . . **142** D4
Dolomite Ave CV5 . . . . . . **60** D1
Donalbain Cl CV34 . . . . . **109** F3
Doncaster Cl CV2 . . . . **62** D7
Done Cerce Cl CV22 . . . . . **99** B2
Donegal Cl CV4 . . . . **76** A7
Dongan Rd CV34 . . . . . . **108** E7
Donibristle Croft B35 . . . . **22** A4
Donnington Ave CV6 . . . . . **60** E5
Donnington Rd B36 . . . . . **149** C4
Donnithorne Ave CV10,
 CV11 . . . . **29** D1
Doone Cl CV2 . . . . **62** E6
Dorado B77 . . . . **9** B4
Dorcas Cl CV11 . . . . **40** C8
Dorchester Ave CV35 . . . **114** F3
Dorchester Gr OX16 . . . . **139** F2
Dorchester Rd LE10 . . . . . **32** B7
Dorchester Way
 Coventry CV2 . . . . **63** A4
 Nuneaton CV11 . . . . **30** A7
Dordon Com Prim Sch
 B78 . . . . **11** A3
Dordon Rd B78 . . . . **10** C4
Doris Rd B46 . . . . **33** F8
Dorlecote Cl CV10 . . . . . . **29** C1
Dorlecote Pl CV10 . . . . . . **39** C8
Dorlecote Rd CV10 . . . . . **39** C8
Dormer Harris Ave CV4 . . . **59** F1
Dormer Ho **18** CV32 . . . . **105** F2
Dormer Pl CV32 . . . . **109** F8
Dormston Cl B91 . . . . **71** C8
Dorney Cl CV5 . . . . **76** E8
Dorothy Powell Way CV2 . . **50** F1
Dorridge Croft B93 . . . . . . **71** F2
Dorridge Jun & Inf Schs
 . . . . **72** A4
Dorridge Rd B93 . . . . **72** A2
Dorridge Sta B93 . . . . **71** F2
Dorset Cl CV10 . . . . **28** F3
Dorset Rd CV1 . . . . **61** C5
Dorsington Cl CV35 . . . . . **114** F6
Dorsington Rd CV37 . . . . **128** E2
Dosthill Prim Sch B77 . . . . **9** B3
Dosthill Rd (Two Gates)
 B77 . . . . **9** B4
Douglas Ho CV1 . . . . **151** D4
Douglas Rd Hollywood B47 . **69** A4
 Rugby CV21 . . . . **83** B3
Doulton Cl CV2 . . . . **50** E1
Dove Cl Bedworth CV12 . . . **38** E3
 Hinckley LE10 . . . . **31** A8
Dovecote Cl CV6 . . . . **60** D5
Dovecotes The CV5 . . . . . **60** B5
Dovedale CV21 . . . . **83** B4
Dovedale Ave CV6 . . . . . . **49** F2
Dovehouse Dr CV35 . . . . **146** B1
Dover Ave OX16 . . . . **139** F3
Dover St CV1 . . . . **151** A3
Doverdale Cl B98 . . . . . . **103** A4
Doverhouse La CV33 . . . . **123** F7
Dovestone B77 . . . . **4** B1
Dovey Dr B76 . . . . **22** A7
Dowler's Hill Cres B98 . . **103** A4
Dowley Croft CV3 . . . . **63** B1
Down End OX15 . . . . **142** D4
Downderry Way CV6 . . . . . **62** A6
Downing Cl B93 . . . . **72** A4
Downing Cres CV12 . . . . . **39** C4
Downing Ho B37 . . . . **33** B1
Downton Cl CV2 . . . . **63** A8
Dowty Ave CV12 . . . . **38** D1
Doyle Dr CV6 . . . . **49** F3
Dr Phillips Sh Ctr The
 CV2 . . . . **50** D1
Drake St CV6 . . . . **61** D7
Drakes Cl B97 . . . . **102** B3
Drakes Cross Par B47 . . . . **69** A5
Draper Cl CV8 . . . . **93** C4
Draper's Fields CV1 . . . . . **151** B4
Drapers Ct CV1 . . . . **151** B4
Drawbridge Rd B90 . . . . . **69** E8

Draycote Water Ctry Pk★
CV23 ....116 C8
Draycott Rd CV2 ....62 C7
Drayton Ave CV37 ......144 B2
Drayton Cl
  Bidford-on-A B50 ......148 B3
  Fenny Drayton CV13 ....19 C3
  Nuneaton CV10 ....28 A8
  Redditch B98 ....103 B4
  Stratford-u-A CV37 ....144 B2
  Warwick CV34 ....104 E2
Drayton Cres CV5 ....59 C5
Drayton Ct Hartshill CV10 .19 A1
Drayton Fields Ind Est
NN11 ....117 F2
Drayton La
  Drayton Bassett B78 .....8 B3
  Fenny Drayton CV13 ....19 C3
Drayton Leys CV22 ......100 A4
Drayton Manor Dr
  Drayton Bassett B78 .....8 C4
  Fazeley B78 ....8 A4
  Stratford-u-A CV37 ....120 C2
Drayton Manor Pk★ B78 .8 C4
Drayton Rd
  Bedworth CV12 ....39 C2
  Solihull B90 ....70 E8
Drayton Sch OX16 ....139 F4
Drayton Way
  Daventry NN11 ....117 F2
  Nuneaton CV10 ....28 C7
Drem Croft B35 ....22 A2
Drew Cres CV8 ....93 A4
Dreyer Cl CV22 ....82 B1
Driftway The CV36 ......149 C3
Drinkwater Cl CV33 ....123 F6
Drinkwater Ho [7] CV1 ..61 B2
Drive The Coleshill B46 ..34 A1
  Coventry CV2 ....62 E3
  Dunchurch CV22 ....99 C2
Drivers La GL56 ....141 A1
Dronfield Rd CV2 ....62 B3
Drovers Way CV47 ......147 B2
Droylsdon Park Rd CV3 ..77 B3
Druid Rd CV2 ....62 B3
Drummond Cl CV6 ....60 F7
Drummond Way B37 ......33 C2
Drury La CV21 ....83 A2
Drybrooks Cl CV7 ....74 B6
Dryden Cl Kenilworth CV8 .92 F1
  Nuneaton CV10 ....27 C3
Dryden Pl CV22 ....82 C2
Dryden Wlk CV22 ....82 C2
Drymen Rd CV35 ....132 D3
Duck La CV37 ....129 B7
Duck Lake DE12 ....3 C4
Dudley Gn CV32 ....106 B2
Dudley Rd CV8 ....92 F2
Dudley Rise LE10 ....31 D6
Dudley St Atherstone CV9 .18 B4
  Coventry CV6 ....50 A1
Dudley Terr CV8 ....94 B6
Duffy Pl CV21 ....101 A4
Dugard Pl CV35 ....122 F1
Dugdale Ave
  Bidford-on-A B50 ......148 B3
  Stratford-u-A CV37 ....145 A3
Dugdale Ct [5] CV31 ....110 A6
Dugdale Rd CV11 ....29 C3
Dugdale Rd CV6 ....61 B6
Dugdale St CV11 ....29 C4
Duggins La CV4,CV7 ......75 B8
Duke Barn Field CV2 .....62 A5
Duke St Coventry CV5 ....60 F2
  Nuneaton CV11 ....29 B4
  Royal Leamington Spa
  CV32 ....106 A1
  [2] Rugby CV21 ....83 A2
Dukes Jetty [8] CV21 ....83 A2
Dukes Rd B78 ....11 A3
Dulverton Ave CV5 ......60 D4
Dulverton Ct CV5 ....60 D4
Dulverton Pl GL56 ......140 B3
Dumble Pit La B48 ....85 F7
Dumphouse La B48 ....85 C5
Dunblane Dr CV32 ......106 C5
Duncan Dr CV22 ....99 B3
Dunchurch Boughton CE Jun
Sch CV22 ....99 B2
Dunchurch Cl CV7 ....74 B7
Dunchurch Hall CV22 ....99 B2
Dunchurch Highway CV5 60 A4
Dunchurch Inf Sch CV22 .99 B2
Dunchurch Rd CV22 ......99 C4
Dunchurch Trad Est
CV23 ....98 B2
Duncombe Gn [12] B46 ...33 F7
Duncroft Ave CV6 ....60 F7
Duncumb Rd B75 ....13 A5
Dunedin B77 ....4 A1
Dunham Croft B93 ....71 D3
Dunhill Ave CV4 ....59 E3
Dunkirk Pl CV3 ....78 F7
Dunley Croft B90 ....70 F6
Dunlop Rd B97 ....102 B3
Dunn's La B78 ....11 A3
Dunnerdale CV21 ....83 B4
Dunnington CE Prim Sch
B49 ....127 C8
Dunnose Cl CV6 ....61 E8
Dunrose Cl CV2 ....62 C7
Dunsmore Ave
  Coventry CV3 ....78 C6
  Rugby CV22 ....99 C2
Dunsmore Heath CV22 ...99 B2

Dunstall Cres [2] CV33 ..122 E8
Dunstall Ho [17] GL56 ...140 A3
Dunstan Croft B90 ....70 C8
Dunster B77 ....9 B4
Dunster Pl CV6 ....49 D3
Dunster Rd B37 ....33 D2
Dunsville Dr CV2 ....62 F8
Dunton Hall Rd B90 .....70 A8
Dunton La B76 ....14 C1
Dunvegan Cl Coventry CV3 63 A2
  Kenilworth CV8 ....93 C4
Duport Rd LE10 ....31 F7
Durbar Ave CV6 ....61 D8
Durham Cl CV7 ....48 F4
Durham Cres CV5 ....60 B7
Durham Croft B37 ....33 B2
Durlston Cl B77 ....4 A3
Durrell Dr CV22 ....99 A4
Dursley La B98 ....112 A6
Dutton Rd CV2 ....50 D3
Duttons Cl CV37 ....121 B7
Duxford Cl Redditch B97 .102 A4
  Wellesbourne CV35 ....146 B1
Dwarris Wlk CV34 ......104 E2
Dyas Rd B47 ....69 A7
Dyce Cl B35 ....22 A4
Dyer's La
  Chipping Campden GL55 .135 A2
  Wolston CV8 ....80 A2
Dyers La B94 ....87 D8
Dyers Rd CV11 ....40 F6
Dymond Rd CV6 ....49 D3
Dysart Cl CV1 ....61 E4
Dyson Cl CV21 ....83 C1
Dyson St CV4 ....59 E3

E

Eacott Cl CV6 ....49 A3
Eadie St CV10 ....28 D4
Eagle Cl CV11 ....40 B8
Eagle Dr B77 ....4 B2
Eagle Gr B36 ....33 A8
Eagle Ho CV1 ....61 D5
Eagle La CV8 ....92 F3
Eagle St Coventry CV1 ...61 D5
  Royal Leamington Spa
  CV31 ....110 A6
Eagle St E CV1 ....61 D5
Ealingham B77 ....4 A1
Earl Place Bsns Pk CV4 ..60 B1
Earl St Bedworth CV12 ...39 C2
  Coventry CV1 ....151 A2
  Royal Leamington Spa
  CV32 ....106 A1
  Rugby CV21 ....83 A1
Earl's Croft The CV3 ....77 D7
Earl's Wlk CV3 ....79 D7
Earles Cl CV47 ....147 C4
Earls Rd CV11 ....29 A5
Earls Rivers Ave CV34 ..109 D3
Earlsdon Ave N CV5 .....60 F1
Earlsdon Ave S CV5 .....77 A8
Earlsdon Bsns Ctr CV5 ..76 F8
Earlsdon Prim Sch CV5 ..61 A1
Earlsdon St CV5 ....76 F8
Earlsmere B94 ....70 B1
Earlswood Comm B94 ....87 A6
Earlswood Rd B93 ......71 D2
Earlswood Sta B94 ......69 D1
Earlswood Trad Est B94 .86 C6
Easedale Cl Coventry CV3 .77 B6
  Nuneaton CV10 ....30 A6
Easenhall Cl B93 ....72 A4
Easenhall Rd CV23 ......66 A1
Easingwold Rd CV35 ...132 D4
East Ave Bedworth CV12 ..39 D2
  Coventry CV2 ....62 C2
East Car Park Rd B40 ...44 F4
East Cl LE10 ....31 D7
East Dene CV32 ....106 A6
East End OX15 ....142 D4
East Gr CV31 ....110 A6
East Green Dr CV37 ....144 B2
East House Dr CV9 ......16 B2
East Side WR11 ....128 A2
East St Coventry CV1 ....61 E3
  Long Compton CV36 ...141 C3
  Moreton-in-M GL56 ....140 A3
  Rugby CV21 ....83 B2
  Tamworth B77 ....9 B3
East Union St CV22 .....83 A1
East Way B92 ....45 B3
Eastboro Ct CV11 ....29 E2
Eastboro Fields CV11 ...30 A4
Eastboro Way CV11 .....29 F2
Eastbourne Cl CV6 ......60 E6
Eastcote La B92 ....56 F4
Eastcotes CV4 ....60 B1
Eastern Green Jun Sch
CV5 ....59 D5
Eastern Green Rd CV5 ..59 F4
Eastern Hill B96 ......102 C1
Eastfield Cl CV37 .....144 C3
Eastfield Pl CV21 ......83 A2
Eastfield Rd
  Nuneaton CV10 ....29 D6
  Royal Leamington Spa
  CV32 ....110 A8
Eastgate OX15 ....139 B8
Eastgate Ct [4] CV34 ...108 E6
Eastgate Mews [3] CV34 108 E6
Eastlands Gr CV5 ....60 E4
Eastlands Pl CV21 ......83 B2
Eastlands Prim Sch CV21 83 B1
Eastlands Rd CV21 .....83 B2
Eastlang Rd CV7 ....36 C2

Eastleigh Ave CV5 ......76 F7
Eastleigh Croft B76 .....22 A7
Eastley Cres CV34 .....108 B8
Eastnor Gr CV31 ....110 B7
Easton Gr B47 ....69 B7
Eastway B40 ....44 F3
Eastwood Cl CV11 .....110 D6
Eastwood Ct B96 ......102 C1
Eastwood Gr CV21 .....101 B4
Easy La CV21 ....82 C2
Eathorpe Cl Coventry CV2 .50 C1
  Redditch B98 ....103 C4
Eaton Cl CV32 ....105 D2
Eaton Ct CV32 ....105 D1
Eaton Rd CV1 ....151 B1
Eaves Green La CV7 .....46 E1
Ebbw Vale Terr CV3 .....77 D7
Eborall Cl CV34 ....104 E2
Eborne Croft CV7 ....74 C8
Ebourne Cl CV8 ....93 A4
Ebrington Gdns B25 ...135 E3
Ebrington Dr CV35 .....114 F5
Ebro Cres CV3 ....62 F1
Ebsdorf Cl B50 ....148 C3
Eburne Prim Sch CV2 ...50 D2
Eburne Rd CV2 ....50 C3
Eccles Cl CV2 ....62 C8
Eckington Cl B98 ......103 A4
Eclipse Rd B49 ....143 A2
Eclipse Trad Est B49 ...143 A2
Ecton Leys CV22 ......100 A4
Edale B77 ....4 A1
Edale Gn LE10 ....31 F6
Edale Way CV6 ....62 A7
Eddens Wood Cl B78 .....8 C3
Eddie Miller Ct CV12 ...39 B2
Eden Cl B80 ....103 B2
Eden Croft CV8 ....93 B4
Eden Ct CV32 ....106 D3
Eden Gr B37 ....33 D1
Eden Rd Coventry CV2 ...63 A8
  Rugby CV21 ....83 C1
Eden St CV6 ....61 F7
Edge Hill CV9 ....10 A1
Edge La B95 ....113 C5
Edgecote Cl CV21 ......83 C1
Edgefield Rd CV2 ......63 A2
Edgehill Ctry Pk★ OX17 133 B3
Edgehill Pl CV4 ....59 C1
Edgehill Rd CV35 .....123 C2
Edgwick Com Prim Sch
CV6 ....61 E8
Edgioake La B96 ......118 C2
Edgwick Park Ind Est
CV6 ....61 F8
Edgwick Rd CV6 ....61 F7
Edinburgh Cl OX16 ....139 F4
Edinburgh Cres CV31 ..109 F6
Edinburgh Rd Hurley CV9 .16 B3
  Nuneaton CV10 ....28 D6
Edinburgh Villas CV8 ...77 F7
Edinburgh Way
  Banbury OX16 ....139 F3
  Long Lawford CV23 ....82 A3
Edingale Rd CV2 ....50 C1
Edison Rd Coleshill B76 ..23 F4
  Lea Marston B46 ......24 A2
Edmondes Cl CV34 .....104 F1
Edmonds Cl CV37 .....129 D1
Edmondscote Rd CV32 .109 D8
Edmondson Cl CV22 ....99 B2
Edmund Rd CV1 ....61 D5
Edmunds Rd OX16 ......139 F4
Edstone Cl B93 ....71 F4
Edward Bailey Cl CV3 ...78 E7
Edward Ct [11] CV34 ....108 E6
Edward Rd Bedworth CV12 39 C3
  Coventry CV6 ....49 A3
  Water Orton B46 ......23 C3
Edward St Coventry CV6 ..61 E5
  Nuneaton CV11 ....29 A3
  Royal Leamington Spa
  CV32 ....105 C1
  Rugby CV21 ....82 C1
  Warwick CV34 ....108 D7
Edward Tyler Rd CV7 ...39 A1
Edwards Ctr [7] LE10 ...31 D8
Edwards Gr CV8 ....93 C5
Edwin Cl CV22 ....99 A4
Edyth Rd CV2 ....62 E4
Edyvean Cl CV22 ....99 C3
Edyvean Walker Ct CV11 29 B5
Egerton Cl CV21 ....82 C3
Eglamour Way CV34 ...109 F3
Egret Wlk CV2 ....50 B3
Eileen Gdns B37 ....33 A4
Elan Cl CV32 ....106 C3
Elborow St [5] CV21 ....83 A2
Elbury Croft B93 ....71 F5
Eld Rd CV6 ....61 E7
Elder Cl Kingsbury B78 ..15 B4
  Rugby CV21 ....82 A1
Elderberry Way CV2 ....62 B6
Eldersfield Gr B91 .....71 B7
Eldorado Cl B80 ....103 B2
Elford Gr B37 ....33 B1
Elgar Cl CV11 ....40 A7
Elgar Rd CV6 ....62 B8
Eliot Cl CV34 ....104 E2
Eliot Ct CV22 ....82 C2
Elizabeth Ave B78 ......5 A1
Elizabeth Ct
  [8] Coventry CV6 ......61 A4
  Warwick CV34 ....109 B6
Elizabeth Rd CV31 ....109 F6
Elizabeth Way
  Kenilworth CV8 ....92 E5
  Long Lawford CV23 ...82 A3

Elkington Croft B90 ....71 A5
Elkington La CV23 .....101 A1
Elkington St CV6 ....61 F8
Ell La CV23 ....64 C2
Ellacombe Rd CV2 ......62 D8
Ellen Badger Com Hospl
CV36 ....137 A4
Ellerbeck B77 ....4 A1
Ellerdene Cl B98 ......102 B4
Ellerman Gdns CV6 .....49 F3
Ellesmere Rd CV12 .....39 A2
Ellice Dr B36 ....33 B7
Elliot Cl B50 ....148 B3
Elliot Ct CV36 ....149 C3
Elliot Dr CV35 ....146 B2
Elliott's Field Ret Pk
CV21 ....83 A3
Elliotts Orch CV35 ....122 A7
Ellis Park Dr CV3 ......63 B3
Ellison Dr OX17 ......139 F5
Elliston Gr CV31 ......110 C6
Ellys Rd CV1 ....61 C5
Elm Bank CV32 ....106 A4
Ilmington CV36 ....136 B6
Pebworth CV37 ....128 F1
Southam CV47 ....147 A2
Elm Ct CV5 ....59 B8
Elm Dr B49 ....143 B2
Elm Gr Arley CV7 ....26 C1
  Balsall Common CV7 ...74 C6
  Ebrington GL55 ....135 F3
  Hurley CV9 ....16 B2
Elm La LE17 ....68 C1
Elm Lodge B92 ....57 A7
Elm Rd
  Royal Leamington Spa
  CV32 ....106 B3
  Shipston-on-S CV36 ..149 C2
  Stratford-u-A CV37 ..144 C3
Elm Row CV47 ....115 F3
Elm Tree Ave CV4 ......60 B2
Elm Tree Cl B78 ....15 B3
Elm Tree Dr LE10 ......31 F8
Elm Tree Rd CV12 .....40 D2
Elm Tree Rise B92 .....57 B6
Elm Way CV10 ....28 A8
Elmbank CV47 ....147 A2
Elmbank Rd CV8 ....92 E6
Elmbridge Dr B90 ......71 B6
Elmdene Cl Hatton CV35 .114 C5
  Wolston CV8 ....80 A2
Elmdene Rd CV8 ....93 B4
Elmdon Ct B37 ....44 B4
Elmdon La
  Birmingham B37 ....44 A6
  Solihull B26 ....44 A3
Elmdon Rd B37 ....44 A5
Elmdon Trad Est B37 ...44 C5
Elmfield Rd CV10 ......29 C7
Elmhurst Cl B97 ......102 B2
Elmhurst Rd CV6 ......50 A4
Elmore Cl Birmingham B37 33 A4
  Coventry CV3 ....78 D8
Elmore Rd CV22 ....82 C1
Elms Ct CV9 ....3 A1
Elms Dr Austrey CV9 .....3 A1
  Rugby CV22 ....100 C4
Elms Paddock The CV23 .83 C3
Elms The Bedworth CV12 .38 E2
  Leek Wootton CV35 ...104 F6
  Stratford-u-A CV37 ...145 A2
Elmsdale Ave CV6 ......49 F2
Elmstone Cl B97 ......102 B3
Elmwood Ave CV6 ......60 F5
Elmwood Cl CV7 ....74 C7
Elmwood Ct CV1 ......151 B4
Elmwood Gr B47 ....69 A6
Elphin Cl CV6 ....49 A4
Elsee Rd CV21 ....83 A2
Elter Cl CV21 ....83 B4
Eltham Rd CV3 ....77 E7
Elton Cl CV32 ....106 C2
Elton Croft B93 ....71 F4
Elva Croft B36 ....22 F1
Elvers Green La B92,B93 .72 C1
Elwy Circ CV7 ....49 C6
Ely Cl Birmingham B37 ..33 B2
  Coventry CV2 ....63 A6
Ely Gdns CV37 ....144 C1
Ely St CV37 ....145 A1
Embassy Wlk CV2 ......62 D8
Emerald Way CV31 ....109 F5
Emerson Rd CV2 ....62 C3
Emery Cl CV2 ....62 E7
Emily Smith Ho [2] CV2 .50 B1
Emmott Dr CV31 ......110 B5
Emperor Way CV21 .....82 C4
Empire Rd CV4 ....59 E2
Emscote Inf Sch CV34 .109 B8
Emscote Lawn Prep Sch
CV34 ....109 A8
Emscote Rd Coventry CV3 .62 C2
  Warwick CV34 ....109 C8
Ena Rd CV1 ....61 D5
Endemere Rd CV6 ......61 D7
Enderby Cl B93 ....71 A5
Endsleigh Gdns CV31 ..110 B6
Enfield Rd Coventry CV2 .62 B3
  Redditch B97 ....102 B3
Engine La B77 ....4 A1
England Cres CV31 ....109 E7
England Ho [9] CV32 ..105 F2
Engleton Rd CV6 ......61 A6
English Martyrs RC Prim Sch
CV21 ....101 A4
Ennerdale Cl CV32 .....83 B4
Ennerdale Cres CV11 ..105 D2

Ennerdale Cres CV11 ...29 F6
Ennerdale La CV2 ......62 F4
Ennersdale Bglws B46 ..23 F1
Ennersdale Cl B46 .....23 F1
Ennersdale Rd B46 .....23 F1
Enright Cl CV32 ......105 E2
Ensign Bsns Ctr CV4 ...75 F6
Ensign Cl CV4 ....59 D1
Ensor Cl CV11 ....30 A6
Ensor Dr B78 ....4 C1
Enterprise Ho B92 .....57 A6
Enville Ct B37 ....33 B1
Epperston Ct CV31 ....109 F7
Epping Way CV32 .....106 B4
Epsom Cl Bedworth CV12 .39 B4
  Redditch B97 ....102 B4
  Tamworth B77 ....9 B2
Epsom Dr CV3 ....78 C6
Epsom Rd
  Royal Leamington Spa
  CV32 ....106 C4
  Rugby CV22 ....82 B1
Epwell Rd Shutford OX15 138 F3
  Tysoe CV35 ....138 B6
Erdington Rd CV9 ......18 B4
Eric Grey Cl CV2 ....62 A5
Erica Ave CV12 ....38 F2
Erica Dr CV31 ....110 B2
Eringden B77 ....4 A1
Erithway Rd CV3 ....77 B4
Ernesford Grange Prim Sch
CV3 ....78 D7
Ernesford Grange Sch & Com
Coll CV3 ....78 D8
Ernest Richards Rd CV12 39 B4
Ernsford Ave CV3 ......62 B1
Ernsford Cl B93 ....71 F2
Errington GL56 ....140 B3
Esher Dr CV3 ....77 F7
Eskdale CV21 ....83 B4
Eskdale Rd LE10 ....31 A7
Eskdale Wlk [5] CV3 ...78 D7
Essen La CV23 ....101 C2
Essex Cl Coventry CV5 ..60 B3
  Kenilworth CV8 ....92 E2
Essex Ct CV34 ....108 E8
Essex Gn CV47 ....132 F7
Essex St CV21 ....83 C2
Esterton Cl CV6 ....49 C2
Ethelfield Rd CV2 .....62 E3
Ethelfleda Rd B77 ......9 C3
Eton Rd CV37 ....145 B1
Etone Com Sch CV11 ...29 D5
Etone Ct CV11 ....29 B5
Ettingham Cross Roads
CV37 ....131 A4
Ettingham Grange CV37 131 A4
Ettingley Cl B98 ......103 A3
Ettington CE Prim Sch
CV37 ....131 B3
Ettington Cl Dorridge B93 71 D2
  Wellesbourne CV35 ...146 B1
Ettington Rd Coventry CV5 60 A3
  Wellesbourne CV35 ...146 B1
Eunal Ct B97 ....102 C3
Europa Way CV34 .....109 D5
Eustace Rd CV12 ....40 D1
Euston Cres CV3 ....78 C6
Euston Pl CV32 ....109 F8
Euston Sq [1] CV32 ...109 F8
Evans Cl Bedworth CV12 .39 C3
  Stratford-u-A CV37 ...144 B1
Evans Gr CV31 ....110 A2
Evans Rd CV22 ....82 B1
Evelyn Ave CV6 ....49 F2
Evenlode Cl CV37 .....145 B1
Evenlode Cres CV6 .....60 F5
Evenlode Gdns GL56 ..140 B3
Everard Cl CV23 ....84 A3
Everard Ct CV11 ....29 E2
Everdon Cl CV22 ......100 C4
Everdon Rd CV6 ....49 B2
Everest Rd CV22 ......99 C4
Everglade Rd CV9 ......10 B1
Everitt Dr B93 ....72 A6
Eversleigh Rd CV6 .....60 E7
Evesham Pl CV37 .....144 C1
Evesham Rd
  Bidford-on-A B50,CV37 .128 E8
  Church Lench WR11 ..127 A6
  Cookhill B49 ....118 C2
  Harvington WR11 .....127 D4
  Redditch, Dagtail End B96,
  B97 ....102 C2
  Redditch, Headless Cross
  B97 ....102 B4
  Salford Priors WR11 ..127 F5
  South Littleton WR11 .127 F3
  Stratford-u-A CV37 ..144 B1
Evesham St B49 ....143 A2
Evesham Wlk CV4 ......76 D5
Evreux Way CV21 ......83 A2
Exbury Way CV11 ......39 E8
Exeter Cl CV3 ....78 D8
Exeter Dr B37 ....44 A8
Exhall Cedars Inf Sch
CV7 ....50 A8
Exhall Cl CV37 ....145 B1
Exhall Gn CV7 ....49 F7
Exhall Grange Sch CV7 .49 C5
Exhall Rd CV7 ....49 A6
Exham Cl CV34 ....104 E1
Exhibition Way B40 ....44 D4
Exis Ct CV11 ....29 E2
Exminster Rd CV3 .....77 C6
Exmoor Dr CV32 ......106 C4
Exmouth Cl CV2 ....62 C7

Exton Cl CV7 .... 49 C6
Eydon Cl CV21 .... 83 C3
Eyffler Cl CV34 .... 108 D7

F

Fabian Cl CV3 .... 78 D7
Fabius Cl LE10 .... 31 C7
Fair Cl CV23 .... 97 B1
Fair Isle Dr CV10 .... 28 F2
Fairbanks Cl CV2 .... 63 A7
Fairbourne Gdns B97 .... 102 B4
Fairbourne Way CV6 .... 60 E8
Faircroft CV8 .... 92 F3
Faircroft Rd B36 .... 22 D1
Fairfax Cl CV35 .... 122 A7
Fairfax Ct 6 CV34 .... 108 F7
Fairfax St CV1 .... 151 C3
Fairfield Ct CV3 .... 78 A7
Fairfield Rise CV7 .... 46 C1
Fairfields Hill B78 .... 10 C4
Fairfields Wlk CV37 .... 144 B2
Fairhurst Dr CV32 .... 105 E3
Fairlands Pk CV4 .... 76 F6
Fairlawn Cl CV32 .... 105 D1
Fairlawns B76 .... 22 A8
Fairmile Cl CV3 .... 78 C8
Fairview Mews 9 B46 .... 33 F7
Fairview Wlk CV6 .... 49 E2
Fairwater Cres B49 .... 143 B2
Fairway Nuneaton CV11 .... 40 B8
Tamworth B77 .... 9 C3
Fairway Ct Rugby CV21 .... 83 B2
Tamworth B77 .... 4 A2
Fairway Rise CV8 .... 93 C6
Fairway The
Banbury OX16 .... 139 F4
Hinckley LE10 .... 31 F7
Fairways B93 .... 72 A8
Fairways Cl CV5 .... 60 A6
Fairways The CV32 .... 105 D2
Falcon B77 .... 10 A3
Falcon Ave CV3 .... 78 F8
Falcon Cl CV11 .... 40 B8
Falcon Cres B50 .... 148 C3
Falcon Ct CV47 .... 147 A2
Falcon Lodge Cres B75 .... 13 A6
Falconers Gn LE10 .... 31 F6
Falcons The B75 .... 13 B5
Falkener Ho CV6 .... 61 E7
Falkland Cl CV4 .... 75 D7
Falkland Pl CV47 .... 133 A7
Falkland Way B36 .... 33 B5
Falkwood Gr B93 .... 71 F6
Fallow Hill CV31 .... 110 C6
Fallowfields CV6 .... 49 C4
Falmouth Cl CV11 .... 30 A5
Falstaff Ave B47 .... 69 A6
Falstaff Cl Nuneaton CV11 .... 30 A1
Sutton Coldfield B76 .... 22 B7
Falstaff Ct
Stratford-u-A CV37 .... 145 A2
Sutton Coldfield B75 .... 13 C5
Falstaff Dr CV22 .... 99 B3
Falstaff Gr CV34 .... 109 E3
Falstaff Rd CV4 .... 59 E1
Fancott Dr CV8 .... 92 F6
Fant Hill OX15 .... 137 E3
Far Gosford St CV1 .... 61 E2
Far Lash LE10 .... 31 F7
Far Moor La B98 .... 112 A6
Far Pool Mdw CV35 .... 113 F3
Faraday Ave Coleshill B76 .... 23 E5
Lea Marston B46 .... 24 A2
Faraday Rd Hinckley LE10 .... 30 E7
Rugby CV22 .... 83 B1
Farber Rd CV2 .... 63 A6
Farcroft Ave CV5 .... 59 D4
Fareham Ave CV22 .... 100 C4
Faringdon B77 .... 4 A1
Farley Ave CV33 .... 123 E6
Farley St CV31 .... 110 B7
Farlow Cl CV6 .... 62 A6
Farm Cl Coventry CV6 .... 49 B3
Harbury CV33 .... 123 E6
Shipston-on-S CV36 .... 149 C3
Farm Gr CV22 .... 83 B1
Farm La Easenhall CV23 .... 65 C2
Grendon CV9 .... 11 C3
South Littleton WR11 .... 127 F1
Farm Rd Hinckley LE10 .... 31 E6
Kenilworth CV8 .... 92 E2
Royal Leamington Spa
CV32 .... 106 B3
Farm St CV33 .... 123 E6
Farm Stile NN11 .... 134 E8
Farm Wlk 2 CV33 .... 122 F8
Farman Rd CV5 .... 61 A2
Farmcote Cl B97 .... 102 B2
Farmcote Lodge CV2 .... 50 B4
Farmcote Rd CV2 .... 50 B4
Farmer Ward Rd CV8 .... 93 A3
Farmhouse Way B90 .... 71 B7
Farmside CV3 .... 78 D5
Farmstead The CV3 .... 78 B8
Farnborough Dr B90 .... 70 F6
Farnborough Hall*
OX17 .... 133 F4
Farnborough Rd B35 .... 22 B3
Farndale Ave CV6 .... 49 D3
Farndon Ave B37 .... 44 B7
Farndon Cl CV12 .... 40 B3
Farnworth Gr B36 .... 22 E1
Farr Dr CV4 .... 60 B2
Farren Rd CV2 .... 62 E5
Farriers Ct CV23 .... 65 B4
Farriers Way
Hinckley LE10 .... 31 F6
Nuneaton CV11 .... 29 F2
Farrington Cl CV35 .... 146 B1
Farrington Ct CV35 .... 146 B1
Farther Sand Cl CV35 .... 121 F4
Farthing La B76 .... 23 C6
Farvale Rd B76 .... 22 C6
Faseman Ave CV4 .... 59 F3
Fasson Cl B77 .... 9 B4
Faulconbridge Ave CV5 .... 59 E4
Faulconbridge Way
CV34 .... 109 E3
Faultlands Cl CV11 .... 39 F8
Fawley Cl CV3 .... 78 C6
Fawsley Leys CV22 .... 100 A4
Faygate Cl CV3 .... 62 F3
Fearnings Cotts B97 .... 102 B3
Featherbed La
Bascote CV47 .... 115 B1
Cherington CV36 .... 141 D7
Coventry CV4 .... 76 A5
Redditch B97 .... 102 B3
Rugby CV21 .... 84 A1
Wilmcote CV37 .... 120 D5
Withybrook CV7 .... 52 C3
Featherston Dr LE10 .... 31 E6
Featherstone Cl CV10 .... 29 C2
Feckenham Rd
Astwood Bank B96 .... 102 C1
Redditch, Headless Cross
B97 .... 102 B4
Redditch, Hunt End B97 .... 102 B2
Feilding Cl CV2 .... 63 A6
Feilding Way CV10 .... 28 A5
Felgate Cl B90 .... 71 A6
Fell Gr CV32 .... 106 C3
Fell Mill La CV36 .... 137 A3
Fell's La CV47 .... 125 C8
Fellmore Gr CV31 .... 110 D7
Fellows Way CV21 .... 100 C4
Felspar Rd B77 .... 4 A2
Felstead Cl B77 .... 9 B2
Felton Cl CV2 .... 50 E1
Fen End Rd CV8 .... 73 E4
Fencote Ave B37 .... 33 A4
Fenn Lanes CV13 .... 20 B4
Fennell Ho 10 CV1 .... 61 B2
Fennis Cl B93 .... 71 F3
Fenny Compton Rd
OX17 .... 134 B5
Fenside Ave CV3 .... 77 D4
Fentham Cl B92 .... 57 B6
Fentham Gn B92 .... 57 A7
Fentham Rd B92 .... 57 A6
Fenton Rd B47 .... 69 A7
Fenwick Cl B49 .... 143 B3
Fenwick Dr CV21 .... 101 A4
Ferguson Cl CV37 .... 131 B3
Fern Cl Coventry CV2 .... 50 C2
Rugby CV23 .... 83 B4
Salford Priors WR11 .... 127 D6
Fern Dale Rd CV7 .... 73 F6
Fern Gr CV12 .... 38 E2
Fern Hill Way LE10 .... 41 B2
Ferncumbe CE Prim Sch The
CV35 .... 114 D6
Ferndale Cl CV11 .... 29 E5
Ferndale Ct B46 .... 34 A3
Ferndale Dr CV8 .... 93 A2
Ferndale Mews B46 .... 34 A3
Ferndale Rd
Banbury OX16 .... 139 F4
Binley Woods CV3 .... 79 D7
Coleshill B46 .... 34 A3
Ferndown Cl CV4 .... 60 A3
Ferndown Ct CV22 .... 82 C1
Ferndown Rd CV22 .... 82 C1
Ferndown Terr CV22 .... 82 C1
Fernhill Cl CV8 .... 92 E6
Fernhill Dr CV32 .... 106 B1
Fernhill La CV7,CV8 .... 73 F5
Fernwood Cl B98 .... 103 A3
Ferrers Cl CV4 .... 59 F2
Ferrieres Cl CV22 .... 99 B2
Ferry La CV37 .... 121 D3
Fetherston Cres CV8 .... 79 B1
Fetherston Ct 4 CV31 .... 109 F6
Fiddlers Gn B92 .... 57 A7
Field Barn Rd CV35 .... 108 A7
Field Cl Harbury CV33 .... 123 F8
Kenilworth CV8 .... 93 B5
Warwick CV34 .... 109 B7
Field Ct CV2 .... 62 D7
Field Gate La CV47 .... 133 E7
Field Head La CV34 .... 109 B6
Field Ho CV8 .... 92 F5
Field La B91 .... 56 A5
Field March CV3 .... 78 E5
Field View Binton CV37 .... 120 A1
Braunston NN11 .... 117 E5
Whitnash CV31 .... 110 B3
Field View Cl CV7 .... 50 A8
Field Way B94 .... 88 C6
Fieldfare Cl CV21,CV23 .... 83 B4
Fieldfare Croft B36 .... 33 A8
Fieldgate La
Kenilworth CV8 .... 92 F6
Whitnash CV31 .... 110 B2
Fieldgate Lawn CV8 .... 92 F6
Fieldhouse Cl B95 .... 113 B4
Fielding Cl CV9 .... 12 B1
Fields Ct CV34 .... 108 F8
Fields Park Dr B49 .... 143 B2
Fieldside La CV3 .... 62 F3
Fieldways Cl B47 .... 69 A7
Fife Rd CV5 .... 60 F2
Fife St CV11 .... 29 A4
Fifield Cl CV11 .... 29 D2
Fighting Cl CV35 .... 132 B6
Fillingham Cl B37 .... 33 D1
Fillongley Rd
Maxstoke B46,CV7 .... 35 B2
Meriden CV7 .... 46 E3
Filton Croft B35 .... 22 A4
Finch Cl CV6 .... 49 C2
Finch Croft CV7 .... 74 B7
Finch La WR11 .... 127 D3
Findley Cl CV9 .... 18 C3
Findon Cl CV12 .... 40 C3
Fineacre La CV8,CV23 .... 96 B3
Finford Croft CV7 .... 74 B6
Fingal Cl CV3 .... 78 C6
Fingest Cl CV5 .... 60 B4
Finham Cres CV8 .... 93 B6
Finham Flats CV8 .... 93 B6
Finham Gr CV3 .... 77 C3
Finham Green Rd CV3 .... 77 B3
Finham Park Sch CV3 .... 77 A4
Finham Prim Sch CV3 .... 77 B3
Finham Rd CV8 .... 93 B6
Finings Ct 7 CV32 .... 105 F2
Finlay Ct CV1 .... 151 C1
Finmere CV21 .... 83 B3
Finnemore Cl CV3 .... 77 B5
Finwood Rd CV35 .... 113 F8
Fir Gr CV4 .... 60 A2
Fir Tree Ave CV4 .... 60 B2
Fir Tree Gr CV11 .... 39 D8
Fircroft B78 .... 15 B4
Fircroft Ho B37 .... 33 A2
Fire Safety Engineering Coll
GL56 .... 140 C3
Fire Station Rd B26 .... 44 C5
Firethorn Cres CV31 .... 110 A2
Firleigh Dr CV12 .... 40 D2
Firs Dr CV22 .... 82 C1
Firs The Bedworth CV12 .... 38 E2
Coventry CV5 .... 77 B8
Kingsbury B78 .... 15 B4
Lower Quinton CV37 .... 129 E2
Meriden CV7 .... 46 B1
Wroxton OX15 .... 139 D4
First Ave
Birmingham, Tyburn B76 .... 22 A5
Coventry CV3 .... 62 C1
First Exhibition Ave B40 .... 44 D4
Firth Ave GL56 .... 140 C3
Firtree Cl OX16 .... 139 F5
Firtree La CV7 .... 37 A4
Fisher Ave CV22 .... 100 C4
Fisher Rd
Bishops Itchington CV47 .... 124 A4
Coventry CV6 .... 61 E8
Fisher's Ct CV34 .... 108 D4
Fishers Cl CV23 .... 101 C1
Fishers Dr B90 .... 69 F5
Fishponds Rd CV8 .... 92 E3
Fishpool La CV7 .... 45 B5
Fitton St CV11 .... 29 B3
Fitzalan Cl CV23 .... 81 A3
Fitzroy Cl CV2 .... 63 B6
Five Lane Ends LE10 .... 41 C3
Five Ways CV35 .... 90 F1
Five Ways Rd CV35 .... 114 C7
Fivefield Rd CV7 .... 48 E5
Fladbury Cl B98 .... 103 A4
Flamboro' Cl CV3 .... 78 F8
Flamville Rd LE10 .... 32 B5
Flats La CV9 .... 3 A1
Flaunden Cl CV5 .... 60 B4
Flavel Cres CV31 .... 109 F7
Flavel Ct CV9 .... 3 A1
Flax Cl B47 .... 69 A5
Flaxley Cl B98 .... 112 A6
Flecknoe Cl B36 .... 22 C1
Flecknose St CV3 .... 78 C6
Fleet Cres CV21 .... 83 C1
Fleet Ho CV1 .... 151 B2
Fleet St CV1 .... 151 B3
Fleming Rd LE10 .... 30 F7
Fletchamstead Highway
CV5 .... 76 D7
Fletcher Gr B93 .... 72 B4
Fletcher Rd LE10 .... 31 E7
Fletchers Way CV35 .... 146 B2
Fletchworth Gate CV5 .... 76 D8
Fleur de-lys Ct CV34 .... 109 B8
Flint Cl CV9 .... 12 C1
Florence Cl
Atherstone CV9 .... 12 B1
Bedworth CV12 .... 49 F8
Florian Way LE10 .... 21 C1
Flower Rd CV37 .... 144 C3
Flowerdale Dr CV2 .... 62 B6
Floyd Gr CV7 .... 74 C7
Flude Rd CV7 .... 49 C6
Flying Fields Rd CV47 .... 147 B2
Flynt Ave CV5 .... 60 B6
Foldyard Cl B76 .... 22 A8
Foleshill CE Prim Sch
CV6 .... 50 A2
Foleshill Rd CV1,CV6 .... 61 D6
Folkland Gn CV6 .... 61 A7
Folly Ct OX15 .... 142 E8
Folly La
Baddesley Ensor CV9 .... 17 B4
Napton on t H CV47 .... 125 B7
Folly The B97 .... 102 B4
Fontmell Cl CV2 .... 63 A4
Ford Cotts CV33 .... 106 F2
Ford La CV37 .... 113 F1
Ford St Coventry CV1 .... 151 C3
Nuneaton CV10 .... 28 E4
Fordbridge Inf Sch B37 .... 33 A5
Fordbridge Rd B37 .... 33 A5
Forde Hall La B94,B95 .... 112 D7
Fordham Ave CV37 .... 145 A2
Fordington Pl CV35 .... 132 B6
Fordrift The B37 .... 44 A6
Fordrough The B90 .... 69 C7
Fords Rd B90 .... 69 E7
Fordwell Cl CV5 .... 60 F3
Foredraught B80 .... 103 C2
Foregate St B96 .... 102 C1
Foreland Way CV6 .... 49 A3
Forest Ct Coventry CV5 .... 60 A4
Dorridge B93 .... 71 F3
Forest Oak Specl Sch
B36 .... 22 E1
Forest Rd Dorridge B93 .... 71 F3
Hinckley LE10 .... 31 F8
Forest View B97 .... 102 C3
Forest Way Hollywood B47 .... 69 B6
Nuneaton CV10 .... 28 E2
Forester's Rd CV3 .... 77 E6
Foresters Pl CV21 .... 101 A4
Forfield Pl CV31 .... 110 A7
Forfield Rd CV6 .... 60 E5
Forge Croft B76 .... 22 B6
Forge La B76 .... 22 B5
Forge Rd Kenilworth CV8 .... 93 A6
Shustoke B46 .... 25 A1
Forge Way CV6 .... 49 C3
Forknell Ave CV2 .... 62 C5
Fornside Cl CV21 .... 83 B4
Forrest Rd CV8 .... 92 E4
Forresters Cl LE10 .... 31 F6
Forresters Rd LE10 .... 31 F6
Forryan Rd LE10 .... 31 F7
Forshaw Heath La B94 .... 86 A7
Forshaw Heath Rd B94 .... 69 C1
Forth Dr B37 .... 33 B4
Forties B77 .... 9 C4
Forum Dr CV21 .... 83 A3
Forum Rd B40 .... 44 E3
Forward Rd B26 .... 44 A3
Fosberry Cl CV34 .... 109 B8
Fossdale Rd B77 .... 10 A4
Fosse Cotts CV23 .... 80 C4
Fosse Cres CV23 .... 96 C2
Fosse Way
Ettington CV35,CV37 .... 131 C5
Harbury CV33 .... 123 C7
Moreton Morrell CV35 .... 123 A3
Shipston-on-S CV36,GL56 .... 149 A3
Stretton u F CV23 .... 65 A4
Tredington CV36,GL56 .... 136 E4
Ufton CV31,CV33 .... 111 B3
Wolvey CV23 .... 42 C1
Fosseway Ave GL56 .... 140 A2
Fosseway Cl GL56 .... 140 A2
Fosseway Cres CV36 .... 136 F6
Fosseway Dr GL56 .... 140 A2
Fosseway Gdns LE17 .... 43 C3
Fosseway Rd CV3 .... 77 B4
Foster Ave B80 .... 103 C2
Foster Rd CV6 .... 61 B7
Fosterd Rd CV21 .... 82 C3
Founder Cl CV4 .... 76 A8
Foundry Ct 4 CV37 .... 144 C2
Fountain Gdns CV35 .... 146 B2
Fountain Way CV37 .... 145 A1
Four Ashes Rd B93 .... 71 E4
Four Crosses CV23 .... 117 C6
Four Oaks Cl B98 .... 102 B4
Four Pounds Ave CV5 .... 60 F3
Fourfields Way CV7 .... 37 A4
Fourways CV9 .... 18 C4
Fow Oak CV4 .... 59 C2
Fowey Cl B76 .... 22 A7
Fowler Rd Coventry CV6 .... 61 B4
Sutton Coldfield B75 .... 13 B5
Fox Ave CV10 .... 29 D7
Fox Cl Harbury CV33 .... 123 F6
Rugby CV21 .... 84 A1
Fox Hill Rd B75 .... 7 A1
Fox Hollies Rd B76 .... 13 B2
Fox's Covert CV13 .... 19 C3
Foxbury Dr B93 .... 72 B3
Foxcote Cl B90 .... 70 D8
Foxcote Dr B90 .... 70 D8
Foxcote Hill CV36 .... 136 B6
Foxcovert La CV13 .... 21 A4
Foxdale Wlk 8 CV31 .... 110 C6
Foxes La CV37 .... 120 C5
Foxes Mdw B76 .... 22 A8
Foxes Way
Balsall Common CV7 .... 74 B6
Warwick CV34 .... 108 D4
Foxfield CV23 .... 66 A4
Foxford Cl B36 .... 22 D1
Foxford Cres CV2 .... 50 B4
Foxford Sch & Com Arts Coll
CV6 .... 50 A5
Foxglove B77 .... 4 A2
Foxglove Cl
Bedworth CV12 .... 38 E1
Coventry CV6 .... 49 C2
Rugby CV23 .... 83 C4
Foxhills Cl CV11 .... 30 C1
Foxholes La B97 .... 102 A3
Foxland Cl
Birmingham B37 .... 33 D2
Cheswick Green B90 .... 70 D4
Foxley Dr B91 .... 56 B5
Foxon's Barn Rd CV21 .... 83 B3
Foxtail Cl CV37 .... 144 B3
Foxton Rd CV3 .... 62 E1
Foxwood Rd B78 .... 10 C4
Framlingham Gr CV8 .... 93 C6
Frampton Cl B37 .... 33 D3
Frampton Wlk CV2 .... 62 F4
Frances Ave CV34 .... 109 A7
Frances Cres CV12 .... 39 A3
Frances Havergal Cl 2
CV31 .... 109 F6
Frances Rd Baginton CV8 .... 77 F3
Harbury CV33 .... 123 F6
Francis Cl B78 .... 5 A1
Francis Dr CV22 .... 99 A4
Francis Gibbs Gdns
CV31 .... 110 A4
Francis St CV6 .... 61 E7
Franciscan Rd CV3 .... 77 D8
Frank St CV11 .... 29 B3
Frank Walsh Ho CV1 .... 151 C4
Frankholmes Dr B90 .... 71 A6
Frankland Rd CV6 .... 50 A1
Franklin Ct CV11 .... 29 D1
Franklin Gr CV4 .... 59 E1
Franklin Rd
Nuneaton CV11 .... 29 D1
Whitnash CV31 .... 110 A3
Frankpledge Rd CV3 .... 77 E7
Frankton Ave CV3 .... 77 C5
Frankton Cl B98 .... 103 C4
Frankton La CV23 .... 97 A3
Frankton Rd CV23 .... 97 C1
Frankwell Dr CV2 .... 50 E1
Fraser Cl CV10 .... 28 B6
Fraser Rd CV6 .... 49 A1
Frasers Way CV37 .... 129 B6
Fred Lee Gr CV3 .... 77 D4
Frederick Bird Prim Sch
CV2 .... 61 F5
Frederick Early Ho B98 .... 103 A4
Frederick Neal Ave CV5 .... 59 D4
Frederick Press Way 5
CV21 .... 82 C2
Frederick Rd CV7 .... 37 A4
Frederick St CV21 .... 82 C2
Freeboard La CV8,CV23 .... 96 C4
Freeburn Cswy CV4 .... 76 C7
Freehold St CV1 .... 61 F4
Freeman Cl CV10 .... 28 D4
Freeman St CV6 .... 61 F6
Freeman's La LE10 .... 32 A5
Freemans Cl CV32 .... 105 E2
Freemantle Rd CV22 .... 82 B1
Freer St CV11 .... 29 E2
Freesland Rise CV10 .... 28 B6
Frensham Cl B37 .... 33 C2
Frensham Dr CV10 .... 28 B5
Freshfield Cl CV5 .... 48 C1
Freshwater Gr 1 CV31 .... 110 C6
Freswick Cl LE10 .... 21 C1
Fretton Cl CV6 .... 61 F7
Frevill Rd CV6 .... 62 B8
Friar's Gate CV9 .... 18 B4
Friars Cl CV3 .... 79 E7
Friars La OX15 .... 137 F2
Friars St CV34 .... 108 D6
Friars Wlk B37 .... 33 D2
Friars' Rd CV1 .... 151 B2
Friary Ave B90 .... 71 A6
Friary Cl CV35 .... 114 F3
Friary Rd CV9 .... 12 B1
Friary St CV11 .... 29 B5
Friday Cl B50 .... 148 B3
Friday Furlong B50 .... 148 B3
Friday La B92 .... 56 D4
Friday St
Lower Quinton CV37 .... 129 E2
Pebworth CV37 .... 128 F1
Frilsham Way CV5 .... 60 B4
Frisby Ct CV11 .... 29 E2
Frisby Rd CV4 .... 59 E2
Friswell Dr CV6 .... 61 F8
Friswell Ho 2 CV2 .... 62 D8
Friz Hill CV35 .... 131 D8
Frobisher Rd
Coventry CV3 .... 77 C5
Rugby CV22 .... 82 B1
Frog La
Balsall Common CV7 .... 74 A5
Ilmington CV36 .... 136 A6
Upper Boddington NN11 .... 134 E8
Welford on A CV37 .... 129 B6
Froglands La WR11 .... 128 A4
Frogmere Cl CV5 .... 60 C6
Frogmore La CV8 .... 73 F2
Frogmore Rd CV37 .... 121 B6
Frolesworth La LE17 .... 43 C4
Front St Ilmington CV36 .... 136 B6
Pebworth CV37 .... 128 E1
Frost Rd CV35 .... 146 B2
Froxmere Cl B91 .... 71 C8
Fryer Ave CV32 .... 105 E3
Frythe Cl CV8 .... 93 C6
Fuchsia Cl 3 CV2 .... 50 B2
Fulbrook La CV35 .... 121 F8
Fulbrook Rd CV2 .... 50 C2
Fulford Dr B76 .... 22 B5
Fulford Hall Rd B90,B94 .... 69 D3
Fullbrook Cl B90 .... 71 A5
Fuller Pl CV35 .... 122 F3
Fullers Cl CV6 .... 60 F7
Fullwood Cl CV2 .... 50 E2
Fulwell Mews B37 .... 44 B8
Furlong Mdw CV36 .... 149 C2
Furlong Rd CV1 .... 151 C1
Furnace Cl CV12 .... 39 D3
Furnace Rd CV12 .... 39 D4
Furness Cl CV21 .... 83 B4
Furrow Cl CV21 .... 83 B2
Furrows The CV47 .... 147 B3
Furze Hill Rd CV36 .... 149 C2

Furze La
Chipping Campden GL55 . .**135** C4
Redditch B98 . . . .**112** A6
Fylde Ho CV2 . . . .**62** D4
Fynford Rd CV6 . . . .**61** B5

G

Gables Cl CV22 . . . .**99** B4
Gables The B78 . . . .**5** A1
Gabor Cl CV21 . . . .**83** B3
Gadsby Ct CV11 . . . .**29** E3
Gadsby St CV11 . . . .**29** E3
Gadshill CV34 . . . .**109** E4
Gainford Rise CV3 . . . .**63** A3
Gainsborough Cres
Knowle B93 . . . .**72** A6
Rugby CV21 . . . .**84** A1
Gainsborough Dr
Bedworth CV12 . . . .**39** A4
Fazeley B78 . . . .**8** A4
Royal Leamington Spa
CV31 . . . .**110** D6
Gainsborough Rd CV37 .**144** B3
Gainsborough Terr
GL55 . . . .**135** A1
Gainsborough Trad Est
CV47 . . . .**147** A2
Galena Cl B77 . . . .**4** A1
Galey's Rd CV3 . . . .**77** D8
Gallagher Bsns Pk CV6 . .**49** E5
Gallagher Rd CV12 . . . . . .**39** A2
Gallagher Ret Pk CV6 . . .**61** F8
Galley Common Inf Sch
CV10 . . . .**27** C3
Galliards The CV4 . . . . . .**76** D4
Galliers Cl B77 . . . .**9** C3
Gallows Hill CV34 . . . . . .**109** B4
Galmington Dr CV3 . . . . .**77** B6
Gannaway Rd CV35 . . . . .**114** B3
Garden Cl Hinckley LE10 .**31** D6
Knowle B93 . . . .**71** F6
Mickleton GL55 . . . .**135** B6
Garden Ct
Warwick, Emscote CV34 . .**109** C8
Warwick, Packmores CV34 **108** F7
Garden Flats CV5 . . . .**59** D5
Garden Gr CV12 . . . .**49** F8
Garden Terr CV35 . . . . . .**146** B2
Gardenia Dr CV5 . . . .**60** B6
Gardens The
Kenilworth CV8 . . . .**93** A3
Radford Semele CV31 . . . .**110** E5
Rugby CV22 . . . .**99** B4
Thurlaston CV23 . . . .**98** C2
Gardner Ho 8 CV1 . . . . . .**61** B2
Gardner Way CV8 . . . .**93** A2
Garlands Croft CV7 . . . . .**49** A6
Garlick Dr CV8 . . . .**93** C6
Garnette Cl CV10 . . . .**28** B5
Garrard Cl WR11 . . . .**127** F6
Garratt Cl CV23 . . . .**82** A3
Garrett St CV11 . . . .**29** E2
Garrick Cl CV5 . . . .**59** C4
Garrick Way CV37 . . . . . .**144** C1
Garrigill B77 . . . .**4** A1
Garth Cres CV3 . . . .**78** D8
Garth Ho CV3 . . . .**78** D8
Garton Cl DE12 . . . .**3** C4
Garway Cl CV32 . . . .**105** F4
Garyth Williams Cl CV22 .**99** C4
Gas House La B49 . . . . . .**143** B2
Gas St
Royal Leamington Spa
CV31 . . . .**109** F7
Rugby CV21 . . . .**83** A2
Gate Farm Dr CV23 . . . . .**53** C2
Gate La Dorridge B93 . . . .**71** C3
Nether Whitacre B46 . . . . .**24** C3
Gatehouse CV31 . . . .**109** D7
Gatehouse Cl CV21 . . . . .**101** A4
Gatehouse La CV12 . . . . . .**39** A2
Gateley Cl B98 . . . .**112** A6
Gateside Rd CV6 . . . .**49** E2
Gatwick Rd B35 . . . .**22** B4
Gaulby Wlk CV3 . . . .**63** A1
Gaveston Cl 7 CV34 . . . .**108** F8
Gaveston Rd Coventry CV6 **60** F6
Royal Leamington Spa
CV32 . . . .**105** C1
Gaydon Cl CV6 . . . .**62** A8
Gaydon Rd CV47 . . . .**124** A3
Gayer St CV6 . . . .**50** A1
Gayhurst Cl CV3 . . . .**78** E8
Gayle B77 . . . .**4** A1
Gaza Cl CV4 . . . .**60** A1
Gazelle Cl CV1 . . . .**151** D3
Geeson Cl B35 . . . .**22** B4
Gentian Way CV23 . . . . . .**83** C4
Gentlemans La B94 . . . . .**112** E7
Geoffery Cl CV2 . . . .**62** B5
Geoffrey Cl B76 . . . .**22** B7
George Birch Cl CV23 . . . .**64** C2
George Eliot Ave CV12 . . .**39** D2
George Eliot Com Sch
CV11 . . . .**29** D1
George Eliot Hospl CV10 .**29** D4
George Eliot Rd CV1 . . . . .**61** D5
George Eliot Sch CV11 . . .**39** D8
George Eliot St CV11 . . . .**29** C2
George Fentham Prim Sch
B92 . . . .**57** B6
George Fox La CV13 . . . . .**20** A3

George Hodgkinson Cl
CV4 . . . .**59** F3
George La GL55 . . . .**135** B1
George Marston Rd CV3 . .**62** E1
George Park Cl Ansty CV7 **51** D3
Coventry CV2 . . . .**50** C1
George Poole Ho 6 CV1 .**61** B2
George Rd
Warwick CV34 . . . .**109** A8
Water Orton B46 . . . .**23** C3
George Robertson Cl
CV3 . . . .**78** E7
George St Arley CV7 . . . . .**37** A4
Coventry CV1 . . . .**61** E5
Hinckley LE10 . . . .**31** D8
Nuneaton CV11 . . . .**29** E2
Royal Leamington Spa
CV31 . . . .**110** A7
Rugby CV21 . . . .**82** C2
Stockton CV47 . . . .**115** F3
George Street Ringway
CV12 . . . .**39** B3
George's Elm La B50 . . . .**148** C4
Georgian Cl B49 . . . .**143** A2
Gerandria Ct CV22 . . . . . .**100** C4
Gerard Ave CV4 . . . .**76** B8
Gerard Rd Alcester B49 . .**143** B2
Rugby CV22 . . . .**99** A4
Gerrard St 1 CV34 . . . . .**108** E6
Gerrards Rd CV36 . . . . . .**149** C3
Gibbet Hill Rd CV4 . . . . . .**76** B3
Gibbet La LE17 . . . .**68** A3
Gibbons Cl CV4 . . . .**59** F2
Gibbs Cl CV2 . . . .**63** B6
Gibbs Cl CV37 . . . .**145** B6
Gibbs La WR11 . . . .**127** D1
Gibson Cres CV12 . . . .**39** A2
Gibson Dr CV21 . . . .**84** A1
Gielgud Way CV2 . . . .**63** B8
Giffard Way CV34 . . . . . .**104** E1
Gifford Rd CV33 . . . .**123** D3
Gifford Wlk CV37 . . . .**144** B2
Gigg La B76 . . . .**14** B3
Gilberry Cl B93 . . . .**72** A4
Gilbert Ave CV22 . . . .**82** B1
Gilbert Cl 3 Coventry CV1 **61** E3
Stratford-u-A CV37 . . . . . .**144** C3
Gilberts Rugby Football
Mus★ CV21 . . . .**83** A2
Giles Cl CV6 . . . .**49** C2
Gilfil Rd CV10 . . . .**29** B1
Gilkes La CV35 . . . .**137** F8
Gillet Cl CV11 . . . .**29** B3
Gillett's La OX15 . . . .**137** E2
Gillians Wlk CV2 . . . .**63** A8
Gillows Croft B90 . . . .**71** A4
Gilquart Way CV1 . . . . . .**151** C1
Gilson Dr B46 . . . .**33** D8
Gilson Rd B46 . . . .**33** E8
Gilson Way B37 . . . .**33** A5
Gingko Wlk 2 CV31 . . . .**109** F5
Gipsy Cl CV7 . . . .**74** B5
Gipsy La
Balsall Common CV7 . . . . .**74** C5
Nuneaton CV10,CV11 . . . .**39** D7
Wolvey LE10 . . . .**41** C4
Girdlers Cl CV3 . . . .**77** B5
Girtin Cl CV12 . . . .**39** A4
Girvan Gr CV32 . . . .**106** C5
Gisburn Cl CV34 . . . .**104** F1
Givens Ho 9 CV1 . . . .**61** B2
Glade The CV5 . . . .**59** F3
Gladiator Way CV21 . . . . .**82** C4
Gladstone Rd B93 . . . .**72** A2
Gladstone St CV21 . . . . . .**82** C2
Gladstone Terr LE10 . . . . .**31** E8
Glaisdale Ave CV6 . . . .**49** E3
Glamis Pl OX16 . . . .**139** F3
Glamorgan Cl CV3 . . . .**78** D5
Glaramara Cl CV21 . . . . . .**83** B4
Glascote Heath Prim Sch
B77 . . . .**4** A1
Glascote La B77 . . . .**9** C4
Glasshouse La
Kenilworth CV8 . . . .**93** D4
Tanworth-in-A B94 . . . . . .**88** F6
Glaston Dr B91 . . . .**71** A8
Gleave Rd CV31 . . . .**110** A3
Glebe Ave CV12 . . . .**38** E1
Glebe Cl Bidford-on-A B50 **148** B2
Coventry CV4 . . . .**76** A7
Stockton CV47 . . . .**147** C4
Glebe Cotts WR11 . . . . . .**127** D3
Glebe Cres Kenilworth CV8 **93** A3
Rugby CV21 . . . .**82** C2
Glebe Ct CV31 . . . .**110** A3
Glebe Est CV37 . . . .**120** B5
Glebe Farm (Mus)★
CV37 . . . .**120** C5
Glebe Farm Ind Est CV21 **82** C4
Glebe Farm Rd CV21 . . . .**82** C4
Glebe Fields B76 . . . .**23** B6
Glebe Fold GL55 . . . .**135** B2
Glebe La Nuneaton CV11 . .**29** F6
Staverton NN11 . . . .**126** E8
Glebe Pl CV31 . . . .**110** B7
Glebe Rd Claverdon CV35 .**113** F3
Hinckley LE10 . . . .**31** F8
Nuneaton CV11 . . . .**29** D4
Southam CV47 . . . .**147** A3
Stratford-u-A CV37 . . . . . .**144** B2
Glebe Rise CV9 . . . .**3** A1
Glebe The Corley CV7 . . . . .**48** C7
Hook Norton OX15 . . . . . .**142** D4
Wootton Wawen B95 . . . . .**113** B2
Glebe Way CV7 . . . .**74** A7
Glebefarm Gr CV3 . . . .**62** F3
Gleeson Dr CV34 . . . .**104** E1

Glen Cl CV36 . . . .**149** C3
Glenbarr Cl LE10 . . . .**31** A8
Glenbarr Dr LE10 . . . .**31** A8
Glencoe Rd CV3 . . . .**62** B1
Glendale Ave CV8 . . . .**93** A6
Glendale Ct B77 . . . .**10** A3
Glendale Inf Sch CV10 . . .**28** F2
Glendale Way CV4 . . . .**59** C2
Glendon Gdns CV12 . . . . .**40** C3
Glendon Way
Dorridge B93 . . . .**71** D3
Dorridge B93 . . . .**71** E3
Glendower CV37 . . . .**145** A2
Glendower App CV34 . . . .**109** E3
Glendower Ave CV5 . . . . . .**60** D3
Gleneagles B77 . . . .**4** A3
Gleneagles Cl
Hinckley LE10 . . . .**31** D4
Nuneaton CV11 . . . .**30** A1
Gleneagles Rd CV2 . . . . . .**62** E6
Glenfern Gdns CV8 . . . . . .**78** E2
Glenfield Ave CV10 . . . . . .**29** D7
Glenfield Cl
Redditch B97 . . . .**102** B3
2 Solihull B91 . . . .**71** C8
Glenhurst Rd B95 . . . .**113** A4
Glenmore Dr CV6 . . . .**49** F5
Glenmount Ave CV6 . . . . . .**49** F5
Glenn St CV6 . . . .**49** D3
Glenridding Cl CV6 . . . . . .**49** F5
Glenrosa Wlk CV4 . . . .**76** A7
Glenroy Cl CV2 . . . .**62** E6
Glentworth Ave CV6 . . . . .**49** A2
Glentworth Dr B76 . . . .**13** A2
Glenville Ave CV9 . . . .**10** B1
Glenwood Dr B90 . . . .**70** D4
Glenwood Gdns CV12 . . . .**39** A5
Gloster Dr CV8 . . . .**92** F6
Gloster Gdns CV35 . . . . . .**146** B4
Gloucester Cl CV11 . . . . . .**30** A7
Gloucester La GL55 . . . . .**135** B6
Gloucester St
Coventry CV1 . . . .**61** B3
3 Royal Leamington Spa
CV31 . . . .**110** A7
Gloucester Way B37 . . . . .**33** A1
Glover Cl CV34 . . . .**108** B4
Glover Rd B75 . . . .**13** A5
Glover St CV3 . . . .**77** D8
Glover's Cl CV9 . . . .**18** C4
Glovers Cl CV7 . . . .**46** C1
Godfrey Cl CV31 . . . .**110** E5
Godiva Pl CV1 . . . .**151** D3
Godiva Trad Est CV6 . . . . .**61** F8
Godsons La CV47 . . . .**125** C8
Gofton B77 . . . .**10** A4
Gold Ave CV22 . . . .**99** A4
Gold Cl CV11 . . . .**39** E8
Goldacre Cl CV31 . . . .**109** F4
Goldcrest B77 . . . .**10** A3
Goldcrest Croft B36 . . . . .**33** A8
Golden Acres La CV3 . . . . .**78** F7
Golden End Dr B93 . . . . . .**72** D6
Goldicote Bsns Pk CV37 .**130** E6
Goldicote Mews CV37 . . .**130** E6
Goldicote Rd CV35 . . . . . .**130** E6
Goldsborough B77 . . . .**4** A1
Goldsmith Ave
Rugby CV22 . . . .**99** C3
Warwick CV34 . . . .**108** C5
Goldthorn Cl CV5 . . . .**59** D4
Golf Dr CV11 . . . .**30** B1
Golf La CV31 . . . .**110** B2
Good Shepherd RC Sch
CV6 . . . .**49** F1
Goodacre Cl CV23 . . . .**84** A3
Goode Cl CV34 . . . .**108** C7
Goode Croft CV4 . . . .**59** F2
Goodere Ave B78 . . . .**11** A4
Goodere Dr B78 . . . .**5** A1
Goodeve Wlk B75 . . . .**13** B5
Goodfellow St CV32 . . . . .**105** C1
Goodman Way CV4 . . . . . .**59** C1
Goodway Ct 7 CV34 . . . .**108** F7
Goodway Ho 5 CV32 . . . .**109** D8
Goodwood Cl
Coventry CV3 . . . .**78** C6
Stratford-u-A CV37 . . . . . .**129** A6
Goodyers End La CV12 . . .**49** D8
Goodyers End Prim Sch
CV12 . . . .**49** E8
Goose La CV37 . . . .**129** D1
Goosehills Rd LE10 . . . . . .**31** E5
Gorcott Hill B98 . . . .**112** B7
Gorcott La B90 . . . .**70** A5
Gordon Cl CV12 . . . .**39** C4
Gordon Rd CV37 . . . .**129** C2
Gordon St Coventry CV1 . .**61** B2
Royal Leamington Spa
CV31 . . . .**110** A7
Goring Rd CV2 . . . .**62** A4
Gorse Cl CV22 . . . .**82** C1
Gorse Farm Rd CV11 . . . . .**40** B8
Gorse La B95 . . . .**113** A4
Gorse Lea CV47 . . . .**147** A3
Gorseway CV5 . . . .**60** C3
Gorsey Cl B96 . . . .**118** C8
Gorsey La Coleshill B46 . . .**23** F2
Wythall B47 . . . .**69** A3
Gorsey Way B46 . . . .**23** E2
Gorsy Bank Rd B77 . . . .**9** C3
Gorsy Way CV10 . . . .**28** D5
Gorton Croft CV7 . . . .**74** B7
Gosford Ind Est CV1 . . . . .**61** F2
Gosford Park Prim Sch
CV1 . . . .**61** F2
Gosford St CV1 . . . .**151** D2
Gospel Oak Rd CV37 . . . .**120** F5

Gospel Oak Rd CV6 . . . . . .**49** B4
Gosport Rd CV6 . . . .**61** E8
Gossett La CV8 . . . .**79** F7
Gould Cl NN11 . . . .**117** D5
Gould Rd CV35 . . . .**108** A7
Governor's Ct CV34 . . . . .**108** D8
Grace Rd CV5 . . . .**59** A8
Grafton Cl B98 . . . .**103** A4
Grafton Ct CV4 . . . .**76** B7
Grafton La B50 . . . .**148** B5
Grafton St CV1 . . . .**61** F2
Graham Cl CV6 . . . .**50** B1
Graham Rd CV21 . . . .**83** B2
Graham St CV11 . . . .**29** C5
Granary Mus of Bygones★
OX17 . . . .**134** B4
Granborough Cl CV3 . . . . .**78** F8
Granborough Ct CV32 . . .**106** A3
Granbrook La GL55 . . . . . .**135** C7
Granby Cl LE10 . . . .**31** C7
Granby Rd Hinckley LE10 . .**31** C7
Honington CV36 . . . .**137** A5
Nuneaton CV10 . . . .**28** F3
Grand Depot Rd CV11 . . . .**40** F6
Grandborough Fields Rd
CV23 . . . .**116** E5
Grange Ave
Coventry, Binley CV3 . . . . .**78** F7
Coventry, Finham CV3 . . . .**77** C3
Kenilworth CV8 . . . .**92** E7
Grange Cl Nuneaton CV10 .**28** C7
Ratley OX15 . . . .**132** F2
Southam CV47 . . . .**147** A3
Tamworth B77 . . . .**9** B4
Warwick CV34 . . . .**109** C8
Grange Dr LE10 . . . .**31** E5
Grange Farm Dr CV47 . . .**147** C4
Grange Farm Prim Sch
CV3 . . . .**77** B5
Grange Gdns CV35 . . . . . .**146** B2
Grange La
Harvington WR11 . . . .**127** D3
Sibford Ferris OX15 . . . . .**142** E8
Grange Mews The 1
CV32 . . . .**105** C1
Grange Pk CV37 . . . .**145** A2
Grange PRU The CV6 . . . .**48** E1
Grange Rd
Balsall Common CV7 . . . . .**73** F7
Bearley CV37 . . . .**120** E7
Bidford-on-A B50 . . . .**148** C2
Coventry CV6 . . . .**50** B5
Dorridge B93 . . . .**71** E2
Hartshill CV10 . . . .**19** B1
Royal Leamington Spa
CV32 . . . .**106** B3
Rugby CV21 . . . .**82** C3
Tanworth-in-A B94 . . . . . .**88** E8
Grange The
Cubbington CV32 . . . .**106** F5
Moreton-in-M GL56 . . . . .**140** A3
Royal Leamington Spa
CV32 . . . .**106** B3
Royal Leamington Spa, Myton
CV34 . . . .**109** C7
Grange Wlk CV6 . . . .**50** B5
Grangehurst Prim Sch
CV6 . . . .**50** B4
Grangemouth Rd CV6 . . . .**61** B7
Grangers La B98 . . . .**102** C3
Granhill Cl B98 . . . .**103** A4
Granleigh Ct CV32 . . . . . .**106** E5
Granoe Cl CV3 . . . .**78** E8
Grant Rd Bedworth CV7 . . .**39** A1
Coventry CV3 . . . .**62** B2
Grantham St CV2 . . . .**61** F3
Grantley Dr B37 . . . .**33** B3
Grants Cl CV47 . . . .**133** D7
Granvile Rd CV35 . . . .**146** B2
Granville Ct CV36 . . . .**149** C3
Granville Gdns LE10 . . . . .**31** C8
Granville Rd Dorridge B93 .**72** A2
Hinckley LE10 . . . .**31** C8
Granville St CV32 . . . .**106** A2
Grapes Cl CV6 . . . .**61** B5
Grasmere Ave CV3 . . . .**76** F6
Grasmere Cl CV21 . . . .**83** B3
Grasmere Cres CV11 . . . . .**29** F7
Grasmere Ct CV37 . . . . . .**145** A2
Grasmere Rd CV12 . . . . . .**39** B2
Grasscroft Dr CV3 . . . .**77** E6
Grassholme B77 . . . .**10** A4
Grassington Ave CV34 . . .**104** F1
Grassington Dr CV11 . . . . .**30** A2
Gratton Ct CV3 . . . .**76** F6
Gravel Hill CV4 . . . .**59** F1
Gravel The B76 . . . .**14** B2
Gray's La 18 GL56 . . . . . .**140** A3
Graylands The CV3 . . . . . .**77** C4
Grayling B77 . . . .**9** B3
Grayling Wlk B37 . . . .**33** C3
Grays Orch CV23 . . . .**98** C3
Grayswood Ave CV5 . . . . . .**60** D4
Grazier Ave B77 . . . .**9** B4
Great Alne Prim Sch
B49 . . . .**119** D6
Great Balance CV23 . . . . . .**64** C3
Great Borne CV21 . . . .**83** B4
Great Central Walk Nature
Trail★ CV22 . . . .**100** B3
Great Central Way CV21 . .**83** B3
Great Pinley Barns
CV35 . . . .**114** C3
Great Rollright CE Prim Sch
OX7 . . . .**142** A2
Great William St CV37 . . .**145** A2
Greatheed Rd CV32 . . . . .**105** E2
Greaves Cl CV34 . . . .**109** C7

Greaves The B76 . . . .**22** F6
Greaves Way The CV47 . .**124** B4
Green Cl
Long Lawford CV23 . . . . . .**81** C2
Studley B80 . . . .**103** C2
Whitnash CV31 . . . .**110** B4
Wythall B47 . . . .**69** A3
Green Ct CV21 . . . .**83** B2
Green End CV47 . . . .**115** D4
Green Farm End CV35 . . .**132** B6
Green Field The CV3 . . . . .**78** B8
Green Gables B47 . . . .**69** A7
Green Gates B95 . . . .**113** B5
Green La Arley CV10 . . . . .**26** C4
Balsall Common CV7 . . . . .**74** B7
Brinklow CV23 . . . .**64** B2
Church Lawford CV23 . . . . .**81** B3
Coleshill B46 . . . .**33** F5
Corley CV7 . . . .**47** D6
Coventry CV3 . . . .**77** B4
Grendon CV9 . . . .**11** C2
Middleton B78 . . . .**14** B6
Nuneaton CV10 . . . .**28** C7
Oxhill CV35 . . . .**137** F8
Polesworth B77,B78 . . . . .**10** B4
Redditch B97 . . . .**102** A4
Shipston-on-S CV36 . . . . .**149** C3
Shrewley CV35 . . . .**114** C6
Studley B80 . . . .**103** A3
Swalcliffe OX15 . . . .**139** A1
Warwick CV34 . . . .**108** F8
Wibtoft LE17 . . . .**43** A2
Wolvey LE10 . . . .**42** B3
Green Lane Cl CV36 . . . . .**149** C3
Green The Austrey CV9 . . . .**3** A1
Barby CV23 . . . .**101** B1
Braunston NN11 . . . .**117** E5
Chipping Campden GL55 . .**135** B1
Claverdon CV35 . . . .**113** F4
Cleeve Prior WR11 . . . . . .**128** A4
Dordon B78 . . . .**10** B2
Great Rollright OX7 . . . . .**142** A2
Great Wolford CV36 . . . . .**140** E5
Hellidon NN11 . . . .**126** B5
Hook Norton OX15 . . . . . .**142** D4
Hornton OX15 . . . .**139** B7
Kingsbury B78 . . . .**15** B3
Lighthorne CV35 . . . .**123** B2
Little Compton CV36 . . . .**141** A6
Long Itchington CV47 . . . .**115** D4
9 Moreton-in-M GL56 . . .**140** A3
Nuneaton CV11 . . . .**29** C2
Orton-on-t-H CV9 . . . .**6** B2
Priors Marston CV47 . . . .**125** E4
Ratley CV35 . . . .**132** F3
Rugby CV22 . . . .**99** B4
Seckington B79 . . . .**2** A2
Shawell LE17 . . . .**68** B3
Shrewley CV35 . . . .**114** C6
Shustoke B46 . . . .**24** C1
Snitterfield CV37 . . . .**121** B6
Stoke Golding CV13 . . . . .**21** C4
Stoneleigh CV8 . . . .**94** C6
Swalcliffe OX15 . . . .**142** F8
Tamworth B77 . . . .**4** A3
Tanworth-In-A B94 . . . . . .**87** A2
Green's Cl CV23 . . . .**67** B3
Greenacre Cl B77 . . . .**4** A3
Greenacres B76 . . . .**22** A8
Greenacres Prim Sch B77 .**4** A3
Greendale Cl CV9 . . . .**18** C4
Greendale Rd
Atherstone CV9 . . . .**18** C4
Coventry CV5 . . . .**60** D3
Greenfield Ave CV7 . . . . . .**74** A7
Greenfields Cl CV36 . . . . .**149** C3
Greenfinch Cl B36 . . . .**33** A7
Greenfinch Rd B36 . . . .**33** A7
Greenheart B77 . . . .**4** A4
Greenhill Cl B77 . . . .**9** B3
Greenhill Rd Rugby CV22 . .**82** C1
Stoke Golding CV13 . . . . .**21** B4
Greenhill St CV37 . . . .**144** C2
Greenland Ave CV5 . . . . . .**59** F5
Greenland Ct CV5 . . . .**59** F5
Greenlands Ave B98 . . . . .**103** A4
Greenlands Dr B98 . . . . . .**102** C4
Greenlands Rd B37 . . . . . .**33** C1
Greenlea B77 . . . .**10** A4
Greenleaf Cl CV5 . . . .**60** A3
Greenmoor Rd
Hinckley LE10 . . . .**31** D5
Nuneaton CV10 . . . .**29** A3
Greenodd Dr CV6 . . . .**49** F5
Greens Rd CV6 . . . .**49** A1
Greens Yd CV12 . . . .**39** C3
Greenside B90 . . . .**70** D4
Greenside Cl CV11 . . . .**30** C1
Greensleeves Cl CV6 . . . . .**49** B2
Greensward Cl CV8 . . . . . .**93** B6
Greensward The
Coventry CV3 . . . .**63** A2
Wardington OX17 . . . .**134** F1
Greenswood CV37 . . . . . .**120** E7
Greenway
Braunston NN11 . . . .**117** D5
Nuneaton CV11 . . . .**40** B8
Polesworth B78 . . . .**5** A2
Warwick CV34 . . . .**104** F1
Greenway Cl CV36 . . . . . .**149** C3
Greenway Nature Trail The★
CV37 . . . .**129** C5
Greenway Rd CV36 . . . . . .**149** C3
Greenway The B37 . . . .**44** C6
Greenways Ct CV36 . . . . .**149** C3
Greenways The CV32 . . . .**106** B3

Greenwood Cl CV23 .....82 A3
Greenwood Ct
  Nuneaton CV11 .....29 E3
  Royal Leamington Spa
  CV32 ....106 B1
Greenwood Rd CV13 ...21 C4
Greenwood Sq **5** B2 ...33 B2
Greenwood Way B37 ...33 B5
Gregory Ave CV3 .....77 A6
Gregory Hood Rd CV3 ..77 E4
Grenden Hall Rd CV35 .132 D3
Grendon Cl CV4 .....59 C1
Grendon Dr CV21 .....83 C4
Grendon Rd B78 .....11 A4
Grenfell Cl CV31 .....110 D6
Grenville Ave CV2 .....62 B3
Grenville Cl CV22 .....82 B1
Gresham Ave CV32 ....106 B2
Gresham Pl CV32 .....106 B2
Gresham Rd CV10 .....39 B8
Gresham St CV2 .....62 A2
Greswold Cl CV4 .....59 F1
Greswoldes The CV31 .110 F6
Gretna Rd CV3 ....76 F4
Grevel La GL55 .....135 B2
Greville Rd Alcester B49 .143 A3
  Kenilworth CV8 .....92 F4
  Warwick CV34 .....105 B1
Greville Smith Ave
  CV31 ....110 B4
Grewcock Cl LE17 .....43 C3
Grey Mill Cl B90 .....70 B2
Grey Tree Cres B93 ...71 E3
Grey's Rd B80 .....103 C2
Greycoat Rd CV6 .....49 A2
Greyfriars Ct CV6 .....61 A4
Greyfriars La CV1 .....151 B2
Greyfriars Rd CV1 ....151 B2
Greygoose La GL56 ...150 A3
Greyhurst Croft **5** B91 .71 B8
Greyrick Ct GL55 .....135 B6
Greys Cl OX16 .....139 F3
Griff La Nuneaton CV10 .39 A6
  Nuneaton CV10 .....39 B6
Griff Specl Sch The CV10 39 B8
Griffin Rd CV34 .....109 C7
Griffiths Ho CV21 .....83 B4
Griggs Cl GL55 .....135 B2
Grimshaw Villas B93 ...72 D8
Grimston Cl CV3 .....63 A2
Grindle Rd CV6 .....49 F4
Grindley Ho **5** CV1 ...61 B2
Grindsbrook B77 .....10 A4
Grizebeck Dr CV5 .....60 A5
Grizedale CV21 .....83 B4
Grosvenor Cres LE10 ..32 A6
Grosvenor Ct **2** CV32 .105 F1
Grosvenor Ho CV1 ....151 A2
Grosvenor Rd
  Coventry CV1 .....151 A1
  Royal Leamington Spa
  CV31 ....110 A5
  Rugby CV21 ....83 B2
Grouse Cl CV37 .....144 B3
Grove Croft CV35 .....114 F3
Grove Ct CV5 ....77 B8
Grove Fields CV10 .....29 D8
Grove La Keresley CV7 ..48 F7
  Lapworth B94 .....88 F4
  Wishaw B76 ....13 F2
Grove Pk
  Hampton Magna CV35 .114 F3
  Hinckley LE10 .....32 A6
Grove Pl Nuneaton CV10 .28 D3
  2 Royal Leamington Spa
  CV31 ....110 A6
Grove Rd Ansty CV7 ...51 D3
  Atherstone CV9 .....18 B4
  Dorridge B93 ......72 B3
  Hinckley LE10 .....32 A6
  Nuneaton CV10 .....28 D3
  Stratford-u-A CV37 ...144 C1
Grove St Coventry CV1 .151 C4
  Royal Leamington Spa
  CV32 ....109 E8
Grove The Bedworth CV12 .39 C3
  Coleshill B46 ....33 F4
  Hampton-in-A B92 ...45 A1
  Hinckley LE10 .....31 C8
  Moreton-in-M GL56 ..140 B3
  Studley B80 ....103 B2
Grovefield Cres CV7 ...74 C8
Grovehurst Pk CV8 ....94 B2
Grovelands Ind Est CV7 .50 A6
Grump St CV36 .....136 B6
Guardhouse Rd CV6 ...61 B8
Guernsey Dr B36 .....33 B6
Guild Cotts The **12** CV34 108 E6
Guild Rd
  Aston Cantlow B95 ...119 F6
  Coventry CV6 ....61 D7
Guild St CV37 .....145 A2
Guildford Ct CV6 .....61 D7
Guillemard Ct B37 ....33 B1
Guilsborough Rd CV3 ..78 E8
Guinness Cl B98 .....102 B4
Gulistan Ct **6** CV32 ..105 E1
Gulistan Rd CV32 .....105 E1
Gullet The B78 ....4 C1
Gullicote La OX17 ....139 F6
Gulliman's Way CV31 ..110 D2
Gulliver's Cl OX15 ....139 D6
Gulson Hospl CV1 ....151 D2
Gulson Rd CV1 ....61 E2
Gun Hill CV7 ....37 A4
Gun Hill Inf Sch CV7 ..37 A4
Gun La CV2 ....62 A5

Gundry Cl CV31 .....110 A7
Gunn Ct B49 ....119 E6
Gunn End CV36 .....149 C4
Gunner Gr B75 ....13 A6
Gunnery Terr **3** CV32 .105 D1
Gunnings Rd B49 .....143 B2
Gunton Ave CV3 .....78 C6
Guphill Ave CV5 .....60 D2
Guphill La CV5 ....60 D3
Gurnard B77 ....9 B3
Gurney Cl CV4 ....59 E3
Gutteridge Ave CV6 ...49 A2
Guy Pl E **11** CV32 ...105 F1
Guy Pl W **10** CV32 ..105 F1
Guy Rd CV8 ....92 F2
Guy St
  Royal Leamington Spa
  CV32 ....105 F1
  Warwick CV34 .....108 F7
Guy's Cl CV34 .....109 A8
Guy's Cliffe Ave CV32 .105 D2
Guy's Cliffe Rd CV32 ..109 E8
Guy's Cliffe Terr CV34 .108 F7
Guy's Cross Park Rd
  CV34 ....108 F8
Gypsy La Atherstone CV9 .12 B1
  Dordon B78 ....11 A2
  Kenilworth CV8 .....92 F2
  Water Orton B46 .....23 D2

H

Hack La CV36 .....141 C5
Hackwell St CV47 .....125 C8
Haddon End CV3 .....77 E6
Haddon Rd CV32 .....106 B2
Haddon St CV6 ....62 A8
Hadfield Cl CV23 .....84 A3
Hadfield Way B37 ....33 A4
Hadleigh Croft B76 ...22 A6
Hadleigh Rd CV3 .....77 C4
Hadley Cl B47 ....69 A5
Hadleys Croft B78 ....15 B3
Hadrian Cl CV32 .....106 B4
Hadrian Dr B46 ....23 F1
Hadrians Cl B77 ....9 B4
Hadrians Way CV21 ...82 C4
Hadrians Wlk B49 ....143 A2
Halberd Cl LE10 .....31 D5
Haldale B77 ....4 B1
Hales Cl CV37 .....121 B7
Hales Park Ind Est CV6 .49 E4
Hales St CV1 .....151 C3
Halford Gr CV35 .....114 F5
Halford La CV6 ....49 A2
Halford Lodge CV6 ...49 A2
Halford Rd
  Ettington CV37 .....131 A3
  Stratford-u-A CV37 ...144 C1
  Whatcote CV36 .....137 C7
Halfpenny Field Wlk B35 22 A3
Halfway La CV22 .....99 A2
Halifax Cl Allesley CV5 ..60 A7
  Wellesbourne CV35 ...146 A1
Hall Brook Rd CV6 ...49 A4
Hall Cl CV8 ....94 B6
Hall Cl The CV22 .....99 B1
Hall Dr Baginton CV8 ..77 E3
  Birmingham B37 .....44 A7
  Stoke Golding CV13 ..21 C4
Hall End CV11 ....29 D2
Hall End Pl CV11 .....29 D2
Hall Gr CV23 ....64 C2
Hall Green Rd CV2,CV6 .50 B2
Hall La Coventry CV2 ..62 F6
  Harbury CV33 .....123 F7
  Witherley CV9 .....19 A4
  Wolvey LE10 ....41 B2
Hall Rd Hinckley LE10 ..31 D5
  Royal Leamington Spa
  CV32 ....105 F1
  Wolvey LE10 ....41 B2
Hall Wlk B46 ....33 F4
Hall's Cl CV31 .....110 B3
Hallam Rd CV6 ....49 B2
Hallams Cl CV8 ....79 F5
Hallcroft Way B93 ....72 A6
Hallfields CV31 .....110 E5
Hallway Dr CV7 ....51 E6
Halstead Gr B91 .....71 A8
Haltonlea B77 ....10 A4
Hamar Way B37 .....33 B1
Hambridge Rd CV47 ..124 C3
Hames La B79 ....2 B2
Hamilton Cl CV12 ....38 C1
Hamilton Ct
  Coventry CV1 .....151 B4
  Nuneaton CV10 .....28 D4
Hamilton Dr B80 .....103 B2
Hamilton Rd Coventry CV2 62 A3
  Radford Semele CV31 .110 E5
  Redditch B97 ....102 B4
  Tiddington CV37 .....145 C2
Hamilton Terr CV32 ..109 F8
Hamlet Cl Nuneaton CV11 .30 B1
  Rugby CV22 ....99 B3
Hamlet The
  Bidford-on-A B50 ....148 B1
  Leek Wootton CV35 ..105 A7
Hammersley St CV12 ..38 E1
Hammerton Way CV35 .146 B1
Hammond Bsns Ctr CV11 29 E3
Hammond Cl CV11 ....29 E3
Hammond Gn CV35 ...146 B2
Hammond Rd CV2 ....61 F4
Hammonds Terr CV8 ..92 D5

Hampden Cl OX16 ....139 F3
Hampden Ct CV47 ....133 A7
Hampden Way CV22 ...99 B4
Hampdon Way CV35 ..146 B1
Hampshire Cl CV3 ....78 F8
Hampstead Norreys Rd
  CV35 ....132 C4
Hampton Ave CV10 ...28 A4
Hampton Cl Coventry CV6 .61 F6
  Redditch B98 .....103 A4
Hampton Croft CV35 ..114 F2
Hampton Ct B92 .....57 B6
Hampton Gr CV32 ....106 B1
Hampton Grange CV7 .46 B1
Hampton La Meriden CV7 .57 E8
  Solihull B91 ....56 B5
Hampton Lucy CE Prim Sch
  CV35 ....121 F4
Hampton Rd Coventry CV6 61 F6
  Knowle B93 ....72 C8
  Warwick CV34 .....108 B5
Hampton St CV34 ....108 D6
Hampton-in-Arden Sta
  B92 ....57 B7
Hams La B76 ....23 F6
Hanbury Cl CV35 .....132 B6
Hanbury Rd
  Bedworth CV12 .....39 C4
  Dorridge B93 ....71 F4
Hancock Gn CV4 .....75 F8
Hancox Cl CV33 .....107 B4
Handcross Gr CV3 ....77 A5
Handley Gr CV34 .....104 D1
Handley's Cl CV8 .....79 A1
Hands Paddock CV37 .130 E1
Hanford Cl CV6 ....61 E6
Hanger Rd B26 ......44 A3
Hangmans La B79 .....2 A1
Hanley Ct B49 .....143 B2
Hanlith B77 ....10 A4
Hanover Ct Hinckley LE10 .31 E6
  Redditch B98 .....102 B4
Hanover Gdns
  8 Royal Leamington Spa
  CV32 ....106 A1
  Rugby CV21 ....83 A2
Hanover Glebe CV11 ..29 C2
Hans Cl CV2 ....61 F4
Hansell Dr B93 ....71 E2
Hanson Ave CV36 ....149 C3
Hanson Ct **2** LE10 ..31 D8
Hanson Way CV6 .....50 A4
Hanson's Bridge Rd B24 .22 A4
Hanwell Cl B76 ....22 A7
Hanwell Ct OX17 .....139 F6
Hanwood Cl CV5 .....59 D4
Hanworth Cl CV32 ....106 C2
Hanworth Rd CV34 ...108 D8
Harbet Dr B40 ....44 E4
Harborough Cotts B94 .89 D3
Harborough Dr B36 ...22 D1
Harborough Rd
  Coventry CV6 ....49 B2
  Rugby CV21,CV23 ....82 B4
Harbour Cl B50 .....148 B2
Harbury CE Prim Sch
  CV33 ....123 F6
Harbury Cl B76 ....22 B6
Harbury La Harbury CV33 123 B7
  Royal Leamington Spa
  CV33,CV34 ....109 C2
Harbury Rd CV47 ....124 C6
Harby Cl B37 ....44 B8
Harcourt Cl CV3 .....78 E5
Harcourt CV23 .....111 C8
Harcourt Gdns CV11 ..29 C3
Hardingwood La CV7 ..35 C2
Hardwick Cl CV5 .....60 A4
Hardwick La B80 .....112 B3
Hardwick Pk OX16 ...139 F5
Hardwick Rd CV47 ...125 E4
Hardwyn Cl CV3 .....63 A1
Hardy Cl Nuneaton CV10 .29 B2
  Rugby CV22 ....82 B1
Hardy Rd CV6 ....61 A8
Hare & Hounds La CV10 .29 A2
Harebell B77 ....4 A2
Harebell Way CV23 ...83 B4
Harebell Wlk **1** B37 ..33 D2
Harefield Ho CV2 .....62 B3
Harefield La CV12 ....38 F8
Harefield Rd Coventry CV2 62 B3
  Nuneaton CV11 .....29 A4
Haresfield B90 ....70 A5
Hareway La CV35 ....122 C7
Harewood Rd CV5 ....60 C2
Harger Ct CV8 ....92 F4
Harger Mews CV8 ....92 F4
Hargrave Cl Coventry CV3 63 A1
  Grandborough CV23 .116 F5
  Water Orton B46 .....23 B3
Harington Rd CV6 ....61 A5
Harlech Cl Banbury OX16 139 F4
  Kenilworth CV8 .....93 C5
Harley St CV2 ....62 A3
Harlow Wlk **8** CV2 ..63 A7
Harmar Cl CV34 .....104 D1
Harmer Cl CV2 ....63 A7
Harmony Ct CV10 ....29 B2
Harnall Cl B95 ....70 E7
Harnall Ind Est CV1 ..151 C4
Harnall La CV1 .....151 C4
Harnall La E CV1 ....61 E4
Harnall La W CV1 ....151 C4
Harnall Row Coventry CV1 61 E3
  Coventry CV1 ....61 E3
Harold Cox Pl CV22 ..99 C3
Harold Rd CV2 ....62 D2

Harold St CV11 ....29 C3
Harpenden Dr CV5 ....60 A5
Harper Rd CV1 ....61 E2
Harpers La CV9 ....19 A4
Harrier Parkway LE17 ..55 B4
Harrington Ct CV3 ....62 F2
Harrington Way CV10 .39 A7
Harriott Dr CV34 .....109 D4
Harris CE High Sch CV22 82 C1
Harris Cl B95 ....113 B4
Harris Dr CV22 ....99 C4
Harris Mews B95 ....113 B4
Harris Rd Coventry CV3 .62 B2
  Warwick CV34 .....108 C8
Harrison Cl CV21 ....101 A4
Harrison Cres CV12 ...39 A2
Harrison Rd B97 .....102 B4
Harrison Way CV31 ..109 F5
Harrow Cl CV6 ....50 A4
Harrow Rd CV31 .....110 B3
Harrowbrook Ind Est
  LE10 ....30 E7
Harrowbrook Rd LE10 .30 E7
Harry Caplan Ho CV5 .60 B6
Harry Edwards Ho **2**
  CV2 ....62 D8
Harry Rose Rd CV2 ...62 E3
Harry Salt Ho CV1 ...151 D3
Harry Stanley Ho CV6 .62 A8
Harry Taylor Fst Sch
  B97 ....102 C3
Harry Truslove Cl CV6 .61 A7
Harry Weston Rd CV3 .63 A1
Hart Cl CV21 ....83 B1
Hartington Cl B93 ....71 E3
Hartington Cres CV5 ..61 F1
Hartington Gn LE10 ..31 E6
Hartland Ave CV2 ....62 B5
Hartlebury Cl B93 ....71 F3
Hartlepool Rd CV1 ...151 D4
Hartley Gdns CV47 ..147 A2
Hartleyburn B77 .....10 A4
Hartridge Wlk CV5 ...60 B4
Hartshill Hayes Ctry Pk★
  CV10 ....18 C1
Hartshill Hayes Ctry Pk
  Woodland★ CV10 ...19 A1
Hartshill Hayes Visitors Ctr★
  CV10 ....18 C1
Hartshill Sch CV10 ...28 B8
Harvard Cl CV35 .....146 B1
Harvest Hill Cl **7** CV31 .110 C6
Harvest Hill La CV5,CV7 .47 C4
Harvesters Cl CV3 ....63 A2
Harvey Cl CV5 ....60 A7
Harvington CE Fst Sch
  WR11 ....127 D4
Harvington Dr B90 ...71 B6
Harvington Way B76 ..22 A8
Harwood Dr B77 ......9 B2
Harwood Gr **1** B90 ..70 C8
Haselbech Rd CV3 ....62 F1
Haselbury Cnr CV10 ..28 F1
Haseley Bsns Ctr CV35 .114 D7
Haseley Cl CV31 .....110 B5
Haseley Rd CV2 .....50 C1
Haselor Cl B49 .....143 B2
Haselor Sch B49 ....119 D4
Hasilwood Sq CV3 ...62 B2
Haslucks Green Rd B90 .69 F7
Hassall Cl **9** CV33 ..122 F8
Hastang Fields CV31 ..110 C5
Hastings Cl
  Banbury OX16 .....139 F3
  Tamworth B77 ....9 C3
Hastings High Sch LE10 .31 F7
Hastings Rd
  Banbury OX16 .....139 F4
  Coventry CV2 ....62 A4
  Wellesbourne CV35 ..146 B2
Haswell Cl CV22 .....83 B1
Hatchford Wlk B37 ...33 B1
Hathaway Cl
  Balsall Common CV7 ..74 B7
  South Littleton WR11 .127 F1
Hathaway Dr
  Nuneaton CV11 .....30 A1
  Warwick CV34 .....104 E2
Hathaway Green La
  CV37 ....144 C3
Hathaway Hamlet CV37 .144 B1
Hathaway La CV37 ...144 B1
Hathaway Rd CV4 ....59 D1
Hatherden Dr B76 ....13 A2
Hatherell Rd CV31 ...110 E5
Hatters Dr CV9 ....12 B1
Hatton Bank La CV37 .121 D5
Hatton Cl CV35 .....114 E5
Hatton Ctry World★
  CV35 ....114 D5
Hatton Sta CV35 .....114 D5
Hatton Terr CV35 .....114 F5
Haunch La B76 ....24 A1
Haunchwood Park Dr
  CV10 ....27 C2
Haunchwood Park Ind Est
  CV10 ....27 C2
Haunchwood Rd CV10 .28 D4
Havendale Cl CV6 ....61 B5
Hawbridge Cl B90 ....71 B6
Hawfinch B77 ....10 A3
Hawk Cl CV11 ....40 B8
Hawke's Dr CV34 ....109 D4
Hawkes Dr CV34 .....109 D4
Hawkes Mill La CV5 ..48 B2
Hawkesbury Fields Sch
  CV2 ....50 C3

Hawkesbury La CV2 ...50 D5
Hawkeshead CV21 ....83 B4
Hawkeswell La B46 ...34 A2
Hawkesworth Dr CV8 .93 A6
Hawkinge Dr B35 ....22 A4
Hawkins Cl CV22 .....82 C1
Hawkins Rd CV5 .....61 A2
Hawkshead Dr B93 ...71 F6
Hawkside B77 ....10 A4
Hawkswood Dr CV7 ..74 B7
Hawksworth **1** CV1 ..61 F2
Hawlands CV21 .....83 B3
Hawley Rd LE10 .....31 D7
Hawnby Gr B76 ......13 A4
Hawthorn Ave CV9 ...16 B3
Hawthorn Cl B49 ....143 A3
Hawthorn Cres LE10 ..31 E4
Hawthorn Ct CV4 ....59 E1
Hawthorn La CV4 ....59 E1
Hawthorn Rd CV31 ..109 F6
Hawthorn Terr CV23 .66 A2
Hawthorn Way
  Nuneaton CV10 .....28 A8
  Rugby CV22 ....82 A1
  Shipston-on-S CV36 ..149 C2
Hawthorne Ave CV7 ..37 A4
Hawthorne Cl CV8 ....80 A2
Hawthorne Dr B47 ...69 B6
Hawthorne Terr CV10 .28 F5
Hawthorns The B78 ...15 B4
Hay La Coventry CV1 ..151 C2
  Solihull B90 ....71 A6
Hay Mdw CV36 .....149 C3
Hay Pool OX17 .....133 F5
Hay Wood La B93,CV35 .90 A3
Haybarn The B76 ....22 A8
Haydock Cl Coventry CV6 .50 B4
  Stratford-u-A CV37 ..144 C1
  Tamworth B77 ....9 B2
Haydon Cl Dorridge B93 .71 F2
  Studley B80 ....103 C3
Haydon Way B49 ....118 F8
Haydons Cl GL55 .....135 B2
Haye La B80 ....112 A5
Hayes Cl CV21 ....83 B4
Hayes Green Rd CV12 .49 F8
Hayes La CV7 ....50 A8
Hayes Rd CV10 ......28 A8
Hayle Ave CV34 .....104 F1
Hayle Cl CV11 ....30 A5
Haynes Way CV21 ....82 C4
Haynestone Rd CV6 ..60 E6
Hays La B78 ....31 B7
Haysum's Cl GL55 ...135 B1
Hayton Gn CV4 ......75 F8
Haytor Rise CV2 .....62 C7
Hayward Cl CV35 ....114 F3
Hayward's Gn CV6 ...61 A7
Hayway La CV23 ....116 B4
Hazel Cl Nuneaton CV10 .28 A8
  Royal Leamington Spa
  CV32 ....106 A2
Hazel Croft
  Birmingham, Chelmsley Wood
  B37 ....33 B1
  Braunston NN11 .....117 E5
Hazel Dr B47 ....69 A7
Hazel Gr Bedworth CV12 .39 D3
  Hockley Heath B94 ...88 C6
Hazel Rd Coventry CV6 .50 B1
  Nuneaton CV10 .....28 A8
Hazelcroft B78 ....15 B4
Hazelgarth B77 ......10 A4
Hazelhead St Georges (Ind
  Est) CV1 ....61 F2
Hazell Way CV10 .....29 A1
Hazeltree Gr B93 ....71 E3
Hazelwood Cl CV22 ..99 A2
Hazlemere Cl CV5 ....60 B4
Headborough Rd CV2 .62 A5
Headington Ave CV6 ..49 A2
Headland Cl CV37 ...129 A6
Headland Rd CV37 ..129 A6
Headland Rise CV37 .129 A6
Headlands The CV5 ..60 D4
Headley Ct B97 .....102 B4
Healey Cl CV21 ......83 B4
Healey Ct CV34 .....108 F7
Health Centre Rd CV4 .76 C6
Heanley La CV9 .....16 B3
Hearsall Com Prim Sch
  CV5 ....60 F2
Hearsall Comm CV5 ..60 F2
Hearsall Ct CV5 .....60 F2
Hearsall Golf Course
  CV5 ....76 E7
Hearsall La CV5 .....60 F2
Heart of England Sch
  CV7 ....74 C6
Heart of England Way
  CV11 ....29 F3
Heath Ave CV12 .....38 E1
Heath Cres CV2 ......62 A6
Heath End La CV37 ..121 D7
Heath End Rd CV10 ..28 F2
Heath Farm La CV35 .123 C2
Heath Green Way CV4 .75 F6
Heath La CV23 ......64 C1
Heath Rd Bedworth CV12 .39 B2
  Coventry CV2 ....62 A4
  Hollywood B47 .....69 A7
Heath Terr Beausale CV35 .91 C2
  Royal Leamington Spa
  CV32 ....105 E1
Heath The CV22 .....99 B2

Heath Way CV22 . . . . . . .100 B4
Heathcote Cl B77 . . . . .10 A4
Heathcote Ct CV6 . . . . . . .61 C4
Heathcote Ind Est CV34 109 D4
Heathcote La
  Royal Leamington Spa
  CV34 . . . . .109 D4
  Warwick CV34 . . . . .109 A5
Heathcote Rd CV31 . . . . .110 A4
Heathcote St CV6 . . . . . . .61 A7
Heathcote Way CV34 . . . .109 D4
Heather Cl
  Birmingham B36 . . . . . . .33 A8
  Nuneaton CV10 . . . . .28 F3
  Rugby CV22 . . . . .82 C1
  Southam CV47 . . . . .147 A3
  Stratford-u-A CV37 . . . .144 B2
Heather Ct CV9 . . . . .12 B1
Heather Dr CV12 . . . . .38 E2
Heather Rd
  Binley Woods CV3 . . . . . .79 D7
  Coventry CV2 . . . . .50 C2
Heathfield Cl B93 . . . . . . .72 A5
Heathfield Rd
  Coventry CV5 . . . . .60 C1
  Norton WR11 . . . . .127 B2
Heathfields Inf Sch B77 . .9 C3
Heathgreen Cl B37 . . . . . .33 D3
Heathley La B78 . . . . .8 C3
Hebden B77 . . . . .10 A4
Hebden Ave CV34 . . . . . .104 F1
Hebden Way CV11 . . . . . . .30 A2
Heber Dr CV33 . . . . .123 E6
Heckley Rd CV7 . . . . .50 A7
Heddle Gr CV6 . . . . .62 B8
Hedgefield Way CV4 . . . . .75 F8
Hedgerow Wlk CV6 . . . . . .49 B4
Hedgerows The
  Nuneaton CV10 . . . . .28 F6
  Tamworth B77 . . . . .9 C4
Hedges Cl CV47 . . . . .124 B7
Hedgetree Croft B37 . . . .33 C2
Hedging La B77 . . . . .9 C3
Hedging La Ind Est B77 . .9 C3
Hedingham Gr B37 . . . . . .33 D2
Hedley Croft B35 . . . . .22 B4
Heemstede La CV32 . . . .106 A2
Heera Cl CV6 . . . . .61 D8
Hele Rd CV3 . . . . .77 D6
Helen St CV6 . . . . .61 F6
Helena Cl CV10 . . . . .28 F3
Hellidon Cl CV32 . . . . . . .106 A4
Hellidon Rd CV47 . . . . . .125 F4
Helmdon Cl CV21 . . . . . . .83 D3
Helmsdale Rd CV32 . . . .106 B5
Helmswood Dr B37 . . . . . .44 C8
Helston Cl CV11 . . . . .30 A5
Helvellyn Way CV21 . . . . .83 B4
Hemdale CV11 . . . . .30 A1
Heming Rd B98 . . . . .103 C4
Hemingford Rd CV2 . . . . .63 A8
Hemingford Croft B37 . . .44 A7
Hemlingford Rd
  Kingsbury B78 . . . . .15 B2
  Sutton Coldfield B76 . . . .22 A6
Hemmings Cl CV31 . . . . .110 E5
Hemmings Mill CV35 . . . .122 A4
Hemsby Cl CV4 . . . . .76 A7
Hemsworth Dr CV12 . . . . .40 B2
Hen La CV6 . . . . .49 D3
Henbrook La OX15 . . . . .137 E2
Hendre Cl CV5 . . . . .60 D2
Henley Cl CV11 . . . . .29 F8
Henley Coll CV2 . . . . .62 C8
Henley Ct CV2 . . . . .62 D7
Henley Mill La CV2 . . . . . .62 C7
Henley Park Ind Est CV2 .62 E7
Henley Rd
  Claverdon CV35 . . . . . . .113 E4
  Coventry CV2 . . . . .62 D7
  Lowsonford B95 . . . . . . .113 D6
  Norton Lindsey CV35 . . .114 D3
  Royal Leamington Spa
  CV31 . . . . .110 B5
Henley St Alcester B49 . .143 B2
  Stratford-u-A CV37 . . . .145 A2
Henley Wlk CV2 . . . . .62 D8
Henley-in-Arden High Sch
  B95 . . . . .113 B4
Henley-in-Arden Prim Sch
  B95 . . . . .113 B4
Henley-in-Arden Sta
  B95 . . . . .113 A4
Henleydale **4** B90 . . . . . .70 C8
Henrietta St CV6 . . . . .61 E5
Henry Boteler Rd CV4 . . .76 B7
Henry Hinde Inf Sch
  CV22 . . . . .82 B1
Henry Hinde Jun Sch
  CV22 . . . . .82 A1
Henry St Coventry CV1 . .151 B3
  Kenilworth CV8 . . . . .93 A5
  Nuneaton CV11 . . . . .29 C2
  Rugby CV21 . . . . .83 A2
Henry Tanday Ct **4**
  CV32 . . . . .105 E1
Hensborough B90 . . . . . . .70 A5
Henson Rd CV12 . . . . .38 E1
Henwood La B91 . . . . .56 B4
Henwoods Ct CV36 . . . . .149 C4
Hepworth Rd CV3 . . . . . . .63 B1
Herald Ave CV5 . . . . .60 D1
Herald Bsns Pk CV3 . . . . .78 F7
Herald Rd B26 . . . . .44 C4
Herald Way Coventry CV3 .79 A7

Herald Way continued
  Hinckley LE10 . . . . .31 D4
Heralds Ct **6** CV34 . . . .109 B8
Herbert Art Gall & Mus★
  CV1 . . . . .151 C2
Herbert Fowler Jun Sch
  CV7 . . . . .26 C1
Herbert St CV10 . . . . .28 E3
Herbert's La CV8 . . . . .93 A5
Hercules Ho B35 . . . . .22 B3
Herdwycke Cl CV47 . . . . .147 B2
Hereford Cl CV10 . . . . . . .28 E4
Hereford Rd CV11 . . . . . . .40 F6
Hereward Coll CV4 . . . . . .59 F1
Herford Way LE10 . . . . . . .31 F6
Heritage Ct CV4 . . . . .76 D3
Heritage Dr CV6 . . . . .50 C6
Heritage Motor Ctr★
  CV35 . . . . .123 D1
Hermes Cl CV34 . . . . . . .109 E5
Hermes Cres CV2 . . . . . . .62 E6
Hermes Rd B26 . . . . .44 C4
Hermit's Croft CV3 . . . . . .77 D8
Hermitage Cl LE17 . . . . . .68 C1
Hermitage Dr B76 . . . . . . .13 A4
Hermitage Rd CV2 . . . . . .62 D4
Hermitage Way CV8 . . . . .93 A3
Heron Cl Alcester B49 . . .143 A3
  Cheswick Green B90 . . . .70 D4
Heron Ho CV3 . . . . .62 B2
Heron La CV37 . . . . .144 B3
Heron Way CV37 . . . . . . .130 E1
Heronbank CV4 . . . . .59 C2
Herrick Rd CV2 . . . . .62 D3
Herring Rd CV9 . . . . .18 C4
Hertford Pl CV1 . . . . .151 A2
Hertford Rd Alcester B49 143 B3
  Stratford-u-A CV37 . . . .144 C1
Hertford St CV1 . . . . .151 B2
Hertford Way B93 . . . . . . .72 B4
Hesleden B77 . . . . .10 A4
Heslop Cl CV3 . . . . .78 F8
Hetton Cl **1** CV34 . . . . .104 F1
Hewitt Ave CV6 . . . . .61 B4
Hexby Cl CV2 . . . . .63 A6
Hexworthy Ave CV3 . . . . .77 B5
Heybrook Cl CV2 . . . . .62 C7
Heycroft CV4 . . . . .76 A4
Heydons Terr OX17 . . . . .133 F4
Heyford Cl CV2 . . . . .50 D3
Heyford Gr B91 . . . . .71 C8
Heyford Leys CV22 . . . . . .99 C3
Heyford Way B35 . . . . . . .22 B5
Heyville Croft CV8 . . . . . . .93 C3
Heywood Cl CV6 . . . . .62 A7
Hibberd Cr CV8 . . . . .92 F4
Hibbert Cl CV22 . . . . .83 A1
Hickman Rd CV10 . . . . . . .27 C3
Hicks Cl CV34 . . . . .104 E2
Hidcote Ave B76 . . . . .22 A8
Hidcote Cl Nuneaton CV11 .39 F8
  Royal Leamington Spa
  CV31 . . . . .110 C5
Hidcote Gr B37 . . . . .44 A7
Hidcote Manor Gdn★
  GL55 . . . . .135 D5
Hidcote Rd
  Ebrington GL55 . . . . . . .135 D3
  Kenilworth CV8 . . . . .93 C6
High Ash Cl CV7 . . . . .49 F7
High Beech CV5 . . . . .60 A6
High Brink Rd B46 . . . . . . .33 F7
High Cross La CV35 . . . . .113 F6
High Cross Rd LE17 . . . . .43 B3
High La OX15 . . . . .137 E5
High Mdw OX15 . . . . .138 D1
High Meadow Inf Sch
  B46 . . . . .33 F8
High Park Cl CV5 . . . . .59 F3
High St Alcester B49 . . . .143 A2
  Astwood Bank B96 . . . . .102 C1
  Barford B35 . . . . .122 B8
  Bedworth CV12 . . . . .39 B2
  Bidford-on-A B50 . . . . . .148 C2
  Bidford-on-A, Broom B50 148 A4
  Bishops Itchington CV47 .124 A4
  Braunston NN11 . . . . . .117 D5
  Charwelton NN11 . . . . . .126 D2
  Chipping Campden GL55 .135 B2
  Coleshill B46 . . . . .33 F7
  Coventry CV1 . . . . .151 C2
  Coventry, Keresley CV6 . .48 F1
  Cropredy OX17 . . . . . . .134 C1
  Cubbington CV32 . . . . . .106 E5
  Fenny Compton CV47 . . .133 D7
  Great Rollright OX7 . . . .142 A2
  Hampton-in-A B92 . . . . . .57 A7
  Harbury CV33 . . . . .123 F6
  Henley-in-A B95 . . . . . . .113 B5
  Hook Norton OX15 . . . . .142 D4
  Hurley CV9 . . . . .16 B3
  Kenilworth CV8 . . . . .92 E5
  Knowle B93 . . . . .72 C6
  Lower Brailes OX15 . . . .137 F2
  Marton CV23 . . . . .115 C7
  Mickleton GL55 . . . . . . .135 C6
  Moreton-in-M GL56 . . . .140 A3
  Napton on t H CV47 . . . .125 C7
  Nuneaton CV11 . . . . .29 B4
  Polesworth B78 . . . . .5 A1
  Ratley OX15 . . . . .133 A2
  Royal Leamington Spa
  CV31 . . . . .110 A7
  Rugby CV21 . . . . .83 A2
  Rugby, Hillmorton CV21 .101 A4
  Ryton-on-D CV8 . . . . .79 B1
  Shipston-on-S CV36 . . . .149 C3
  Shutford OX15 . . . . .139 A3

High St continued
  Southam CV47 . . . . .147 A2
  Stockton CV47 . . . . .147 C4
  Stoke Golding CV13 . . . . .21 B4
  Stratford-u-A CV37 . . . .145 A1
  Studley B80 . . . . .103 C2
  Tamworth B77 . . . . .9 B3
  Warwick CV34 . . . . .108 E6
  Welford on A CV37 . . . . .129 A7
High Trees Cl B98 . . . . . .102 C4
High Trees Rd B93 . . . . . .72 A7
High View Dr CV7 . . . . . . .49 C7
High View Rd CV32 . . . . .106 C5
Higham La Nuneaton CV11 29 E7
  Stoke Golding CV13 . . . . .21 B3
  Stoke Golding, Wykin LE10 .21 C2
Higham Lane Sch CV10 . .29 D6
Higham on the Hill CE Prim
  Sch CV13 . . . . .21 A2
Higham Way LE10 . . . . . . .31 E7
Higham Way Ho LE10 . . .31 E7
Highbury Gn CV10 . . . . . . .28 C7
Highclere Gdns OX16 . . .139 F3
Highcliffe Rd B77 . . . . .9 B4
Highcroft CV35 . . . . .113 F3
Highcroft Cres CV32 . . . .105 C1
Highdown Cres **3** B90 . .71 A6
Highdown Rd CV31 . . . . .110 B6
Highfield Hatton CV35 . . .114 F6
  Meriden CV7 . . . . .46 C1
Highfield Ave
  Redditch B97 . . . . .102 B4
  Tamworth B77 . . . . .4 A3
Highfield Cl
  Kenilworth CV8 . . . . .92 E4
  Snitterfield CV37 . . . . . .121 B7
Highfield La CV7 . . . . .37 B1
Highfield Rd Coventry CV2 61 F4
  Nuneaton CV11 . . . . .29 E2
  Redditch B97 . . . . .102 B4
  Stratford-u-A CV37 . . . .144 C3
  Studley B80 . . . . .103 B2
Highfield Terr CV32 . . . . .105 D1
Highgrove Coventry CV4 . .75 F5
  Rugby CV22 . . . . .99 B4
Highland Rd Coventry CV5 60 F1
  Kenilworth CV8 . . . . .93 C7
  Royal Leamington Spa
  CV32 . . . . .106 B4
Highland Way B98 . . . . . .103 A4
Highlands OX16 . . . . .139 F5
Highlands Cl CV34 . . . . . .109 A8
Highlands Ct B90 . . . . . . .70 A8
Highlands Rd B90 . . . . . . .70 F8
Highview CV9 . . . . .16 B2
Highwaymans Croft CV4 .76 D5
Hijaz Coll CV11 . . . . .21 B1
Hiker Gr **3** B37 . . . . .33 D2
Hilary Bevins Cl CV13 . . .20 C2
Hilary Dr B76 . . . . .13 A3
Hilary Rd Coventry CV4 . .76 E6
  Nuneaton CV10 . . . . .28 F5
Hill Cl Northend CV47 . . .133 B7
  Royal Leamington Spa
  CV32 . . . . .106 A4
Hill Cres CV23 . . . . .96 C3
Hill Crest CV32 . . . . .106 E5
Hill Crest Farm Cl B79 . . .5 C2
Hill Crest Hospl B98 . . . .103 B3
Hill Farm Ave CV11 . . . . . .30 B1
Hill Farm Prim Sch CV6 .61 B7
Hill Fray Dr CV3 . . . . .78 A5
Hill Ho CV37 . . . . .145 A2
Hill La Sutton Coldfield B75 .7 A1
  Upper Brailes OX15 . . . .137 E3
  Upper Quinton CV37 . . .129 D1
Hill Rd
  Grandborough CV23 . . . .116 E6
  Keresley CV7 . . . . .48 F6
  Lower Boddington NN11 .134 E7
Hill Rise OX7 . . . . .142 A2
Hill Row NN11 . . . . .117 E4
Hill Side Coventry CV2 . . .62 A6
  Kingsbury B78 . . . . .15 B2
Hill St Bedworth CV12 . . .39 B5
  Coventry CV1 . . . . .151 A3
  Hinckley LE10 . . . . .31 E8
  Nuneaton CV10 . . . . .28 D4
  Royal Leamington Spa
  CV32 . . . . .106 A1
  Rugby CV21 . . . . .83 A2
  Warwick CV34 . . . . .109 B8
Hill The CV37 . . . . .145 A2
Hill Top
  Baddesley Ensor CV9 . . . .11 A1
  Coventry CV1 . . . . .151 C3
Hill View CV47 . . . . .124 A4
Hill View Cl GL55 . . . . . . .135 C7
Hill View Rd B50 . . . . . . .148 C3
Hill Wootton Rd CV32,
  CV35 . . . . .105 C6
Hillary Rd CV22 . . . . .99 C4
Hillborough La B50 . . . . .128 E3
Hillcrest Pk B47 . . . . .85 F8
Hillcrest Rd
  Nuneaton CV10 . . . . .28 E5
  Polesworth B78 . . . . .11 A4
Hillfield Mews **3** B91 . .71 B8
Hillfield Rd Rugby CV22 . .82 B1
  Solihull B91 . . . . .71 B8
Hillfields Ho **1** CV1 . . . .61 E3
Hillhurst Gr B36 . . . . .22 D1
Hilliard Cl CV12 . . . . .39 B4
Hillman Gr B36 . . . . .22 F1
Hillman Ho CV1 . . . . .151 B3
Hillman Way CV37 . . . . . .131 B3
Hillmorton La
  Clifton u D CV23 . . . . . . .84 A2

Hillmorton La continued
  Lilbourne CV23 . . . . .84 C3
Hillmorton Prim Sch
  CV21 . . . . .101 A4
Hillmorton Rd
  Coventry CV2 . . . . .50 C1
  Knowle B93 . . . . .72 A5
  Rugby CV22 . . . . .83 B1
Hillrise LE10 . . . . .31 F8
Hillside Appleby Magna DE12 .3 C4
  Harbury CV33 . . . . .123 E7
  Napton on t H CV47 . . . .125 C8
  Nuneaton CV10 . . . . .28 A8
Hillside Croft CV47 . . . . .125 C8
Hillside Dr CV10 . . . . .28 C7
Hillside N CV2 . . . . .62 B4
Hillside Rd Hinckley LE10 .31 D6
  Stratford-u-A CV37 . . . .144 B2
Hilltop Cl Honiley CV8 . . . .90 E8
  Southam CV47 . . . . .147 A3
Hillwood Ave B90 . . . . . . .71 A6
Hillyard Rd CV47 . . . . . . .147 A3
Hilmore Way B77 . . . . .9 C4
Hilton Ave CV10 . . . . .28 B6
Hilton Ct CV5 . . . . .60 F7
Himbleton Croft **1** B90 . .71 A6
Himley Rd CV12 . . . . .38 D2
Himley Rise CV8 . . . . .70 E4
Hinckley & District Hospl
  LE10 . . . . .31 C8
Hinckley Bsns Pk LE10 . .30 F8
Hinckley La CV13 . . . . . . .21 B2
Hinckley Rd
  Ansty CV2,CV7 . . . . .51 C2
  Aston Flamville LE10 . . . .32 D7
  Aston Flamville LE9 . . . . .32 D8
  Burton Hastings CV11 . . . .31 A1
  Coventry CV2 . . . . .63 A8
  Hinckley LE10 . . . . .32 A6
  Nuneaton CV11 . . . . .29 E5
  Stoke Golding CV13 . . . . .21 C4
  Wolvey LE10 . . . . .41 C4
Hinckley Sta LE10 . . . . . . .31 D7
Hind Cl CV34 . . . . .104 F2
Hinde Cl CV21 . . . . .83 B4
Hindlip Cl B98 . . . . .112 A6
Hintons Coppice B93 . . . .71 E6
Hipsley Cl B36 . . . . .22 C1
Hipsley La CV9 . . . . .16 C3
Hipswell Highway CV2 . . .62 B2
Hipton Hill WR11 . . . . . . .127 B3
Hiron Croft CV3 . . . . .77 C8
Hiron The CV3 . . . . .77 C8
Hiron Way CV34 . . . . .108 B7
Hirst Cl CV23 . . . . .82 A3
Hitchman Ct CV31 . . . . . .110 A5
Hitchman Mews CV31 . . .110 A5
Hitchman Rd CV31 . . . . .110 A5
Hithersand Cl CV35 . . . .121 F4
Hitherside B90 . . . . .70 B5
HM Prison Rye Hill
  CV23 . . . . .100 B1
HM Young Offender
  Institution CV23 . . . . . . .100 B1
Hoarestone Ave CV11 . . .40 A7
Hob La
  Balsall Common CV7 . . . .74 E4
  Burton Green CV8 . . . . . .75 A3
  Knowle B92 . . . . .73 A8
Hobbins The CV36 . . . . . .149 C3
Hobley Cl CV22 . . . . .99 B4
Hockett St CV3 . . . . .77 D8
Hocking Rd CV2 . . . . .62 E4
Hockley Cl CV23 . . . . .116 F5
Hockley Ct B94 . . . . .88 C7
Hockley Heath Prim Sch
  B94 . . . . .88 C6
Hockley La Coventry CV5 . .59 D5
  Ettington CV37 . . . . .131 B3
Hockley Rd
  Shrewley CV35 . . . . .114 C6
  Tamworth B77 . . . . .9 C3
Hoden La WR11 . . . . .128 B3
Hodge La B77 . . . . .4 A3
Hodgett's La
  Berkswell CV7 . . . . .74 F7
  Coventry CV7,CV8 . . . . . .75 A6
Hodgson Rd CV37 . . . . . .144 C3
Hodnell Cl B36 . . . . .22 C1
Hodnell Dr CV47 . . . . . . .147 B2
Hodnet Cl CV8 . . . . .93 B5
Hogarth Cl CV12 . . . . .39 A4
Hogarth Rd CV37 . . . . . .144 B1
Hogg End OX17 . . . . .134 F3
Hoggrills End La B46 . . . .25 A2
Holbeche Cres CV7 . . . . . .39 A1
Holbeche Rd Knowle B93 .72 A7
  Sutton Coldfield B75 . . . .13 B5
Holbein Cl CV12 . . . . .39 A4
Holborn Ave CV6 . . . . .49 C2
Holbrook Ave CV21 . . . . . .83 A2
Holbrook Gr B37 . . . . .33 B1
Holbrook La CV6 . . . . .49 D2
Holbrook Park Est CV6 . . .61 D8
Holbrook Prim Sch CV6 . .49 E1
Holbrook Rd
  Long Lawford CV23 . . . . . .82 A3
  Stratford-u-A CV37 . . . .144 B2
Holbrook Way CV6 . . . . . .49 D1
Holcot Leys CV22 . . . . . .100 A4
Holder Cl B50 . . . . .148 B3
Hole House La B94 . . . . . .88 F1
Holioak Dr CV34 . . . . . . .109 B6
Holland Ave B93 . . . . .72 B8
Holland Cl B50 . . . . .148 B2
Holland Croft B76 . . . . . . .15 A1
Holland Mdw CV37 . . . . .129 A6

Holland Rd CV6 . . . . .61 A6
Hollberry Cl B98 . . . . . . .112 A6
Hollick Cres CV7 . . . . .37 A4
Hollicombe Terr CV2 . . . . .62 D8
Hollies Rd B78 . . . . .11 A4
Hollies The CV23 . . . . . . .67 C1
Hollin Brow Cl B93 . . . . . .72 B3
Hollings Gr B91 . . . . .71 B8
Hollington Way B90 . . . . .71 C7
Hollinwell Cl CV11 . . . . . .40 C8
Hollis La CV8 . . . . .92 E8
Hollis Rd CV3 . . . . .62 A2
Hollow Cres CV6 . . . . .61 B5
Hollow Way CV47 . . . . . .125 C8
Holloway Field CV6 . . . . . .61 A6
Holloway Hill OX15 . . . . .138 A1
Holloway La OX15 . . . . . .138 A1
Holloway The
  Mollington OX17 . . . . . .134 A2
  Priors Marston CV47 . . .125 E4
  Warwick CV34 . . . . .108 D6
Hollowell Way CV21 . . . . .83 B4
Hollows The CV11 . . . . . . .29 F1
Holly Bank CV5 . . . . .77 A8
Holly Bank Est CV9 . . . . . .3 A1
Holly Cl LE10 . . . . .31 E5
Holly Dr Hollywood B47 . .69 B7
  Hurley CV9 . . . . .16 B2
  Ryton-on-D CV8 . . . . .79 B1
Holly Farm Bsns Pk CV8 .91 B7
Holly Gr
  Church Lawford CV23 . . . .81 A3
  Coventry CV4 . . . . .60 B2
Holly La Atherstone CV9 . .12 B1
  Balsall Common CV7 . . . .74 B3
  Portway B48 . . . . .85 F5
  Wishaw B76 . . . . .13 F1
Holly Lane Ind Est CV9 . .12 B1
Holly Lodge CV35 . . . . . .146 B2
Holly Lodge Wlk B37 . . . .33 A2
Holly Orch CV37 . . . . . . .145 A2
Holly Rd CV36 . . . . .149 C2
Holly St CV32 . . . . .105 F1
Holly Stitches Rd CV10 . .28 E6
Holly Tree Wlk LE17 . . . . .43 C3
Holly Wlk Baginton CV8 . .77 E2
  Nuneaton CV11 . . . . .29 F2
  Royal Leamington Spa
  CV32 . . . . .106 A1
  Stratford-u-A CV37 . . . .144 B2
Hollyberry Ave B91 . . . . . .71 A8
Hollybush La
  Coventry CV6 . . . . .50 A4
  Priors Marston CV47 . . .125 E4
Hollybush Rd OX15 . . . . .142 D4
Hollyfast La CV7 . . . . .48 C4
Hollyfast Prim Sch CV6 . .60 E6
Hollyfast Rd CV6 . . . . .60 E6
Hollyhurst Bedworth CV12 38 F1
  Water Orton B46 . . . . . . .23 C2
Hollyhurst Gr B90 . . . . . . .70 B8
Hollyland B46 . . . . .24 C1
Hollywell Rd B93 . . . . .72 A5
Hollywood Gdns B47 . . . .69 A8
Hollywood La B47 . . . . . . .69 B7
Holman Way CV11 . . . . . . .29 D3
Holmcroft CV2 . . . . .62 F8
Holme Cl CV21 . . . . .83 B3
Holme Way CV23 . . . . . . .101 B1
Holmes Ct CV8 . . . . .92 F5
Holmes Dr CV5 . . . . .59 D5
Holmes Rd CV31 . . . . . . .110 B3
Holmewood Cl CV8 . . . . . .93 B5
Holmewood Ct CV8 . . . . . .93 B5
Holmfield Rd CV2 . . . . . . .62 B3
Holmsdale Rd CV6 . . . . . .61 E7
Holroyd Ho CV4 . . . . .59 F2
Holsworthy Cl CV11 . . . . .29 E5
Holt Ave CV33 . . . . .122 E8
Holt Gdns B80 . . . . .103 C1
Holt Leys CV47 . . . . .147 B2
Holt Rd Hinckley LE10 . . . .31 E6
  Studley B80 . . . . .103 C1
Holt The Mollington OX17 .133 F2
  Royal Leamington Spa
  CV32 . . . . .106 B3
Holte Rd CV9 . . . . .18 B4
Holtom St CV37 . . . . .144 C1
Holwich B77 . . . . .10 A4
Holy Cross Ct CV2 . . . . . .62 A4
Holy Cross Prim Sch B76 13 A3
Holy Family RC Prim Sch
  CV6 . . . . .49 B3
Holyhead Rd CV5 . . . . . . .60 E5
Holyoak Cl Bedworth CV12 38 F1
  Rugby CV22 . . . . .99 B4
Holyoke Gr CV31 . . . . . . .110 B2
Holyrood Ct CV10 . . . . . . .28 D5
Holywell Cl CV4 . . . . .59 D1
Holywell Rd CV47 . . . . . .147 A2
Home Cl Bubbenhall CV8 . .95 B3
  Staverton NN11 . . . . . . .126 E8
Home Farm CV35 . . . . . .104 F6
Home Farm Cl
  Pailton CV23 . . . . .66 A4
  Witherley CV9 . . . . .19 A4
Home Farm Cotts CV8 . . .94 A3
Home Farm Cres CV31 . .110 B3
Home Furlong CV35 . . . .146 B1
Home Mdw CV35 . . . . . . .113 F3
Home Park Rd CV11 . . . . .29 C3
Homefield La CV22 . . . . . .99 C2
Homefield Pre-Prep Sch
  CV22 . . . . .99 C2
Homer Cl CV34 . . . . .109 E5
Homestalls Mdw CV35 . .131 D2
Homeward Way CV3 . . . . .63 A1
Honeybourne Cl CV5 . . . .60 B3

Honeybourne Rd B50 . . . .148 C2
Honeyfield Rd CV1 . . . . . .61 D5
Honeysuckle Cl CV23 . . . .83 B4
Honeysuckle Dr CV2 . . . .50 B2
Honiley Ct CV2 . . . . .50 D1
Honiley Rd Honiley CV8 . . .91 B6
　Meer End CV8 . . . . .74 A1
Honiley Way CV2 . . . . . . .50 D1
Honington Hall★ CV36 .137 A5
Honiton Rd CV2 . . . . .62 C5
Honiwell Cl CV33 . . . . . .123 E6
Hoo La GL55 . . . . .135 A2
Hood St CV1 . . . . .61 E3
Hood's Way CV22 . . . . . . .82 B1
Hook Norton Brewery★
　OX15 . . . . .142 C4
Hook Norton CE Sch
　OX15 . . . . .142 D4
Hook Norton Rd
　Great Rollright OX7 . . . .142 A2
　Sibford Ferris OX15 . . . .142 D8
Hoopers La B96 . . . . . . .102 C1
Hope Aldridge Bsns Ctr
　CV10 . . . . .29 C6
Hope Cl CV7 . . . . .49 A7
Hope St CV1 . . . . .61 B2
Hopedale Cl CV2 . . . . . . .62 E3
Hopkins Field CV37 . . . .129 B3
Hopkins Prec The B49 . .143 B2
Hopkins Rd CV6 . . . . .61 A4
Hopkins Way CV35 . . . . .146 B3
Hopper's La CV35 . . . . . .146 B2
Hopton Cl CV5 . . . . .60 A4
Hopton Crofts CV32 . . . .105 C2
Horley Path Rd OX15 . . .139 D5
Hornbeam B77 . . . . .4 A2
Hornbeam Dr CV4 . . . . . .59 D1
Hornbeam Gr CV31 . . . .110 C6
Hornchurch Cl CV1 . . . . .151 B1
Horndean Cl CV6 . . . . . . .61 E8
Horne Cl CV21 . . . . .101 A4
Horninghold Cl CV3 . . . . .78 E8
Hornsey Cl CV2 . . . . .62 E7
Hornton Prim Sch OX15 139 B7
Horse Shoe Rd CV6 . . . . .50 A4
Horsefair CV36 . . . . .149 C3
Horsefair The 8 LE10 . . .31 D8
Horsepool LE10 . . . . .32 A5
Horsewell CV47 . . . . . . .147 A2
Horsfall Rd B75 . . . . .13 A5
Horsford Rd CV3 . . . . . . .77 E6
Horsham Cl OX16 . . . . . .139 F5
Horton Cl B49 . . . . .143 B3
Horton Cres CV22 . . . . . .83 A1
Horton Gr B90 . . . . .71 A5
Hosiery St CV12 . . . . .39 C2
Hoskyn Cl CV21 . . . . . . .100 C4
Hospital La CV12 . . . . . . .38 B1
Hospital of St Cross
　CV22 . . . . .83 A1
Hospital Rd GL56 . . . . . .140 A3
Hotchkiss Cl CV35 . . . . .146 B1
Hotchkiss Way CV3 . . . . .79 A7
Hothorpe Cl CV3 . . . . . . .62 C7
Houldsworth Cres CV6 . . .49 C4
Houndsfield Cl B47 . . . . .69 C6
Houndsfield Farm B47 . . .69 B5
Houndsfield Gr B47 . . . . .69 A5
Houndsfield La B47 . . . . .69 C6
Houston CV21 . . . . .83 B3
Houting B77 . . . . .9 B3
Hove Ave CV5 . . . . .59 E4
Hovelands Cl CV2 . . . . . .62 C8
Howard Cl
　Bidford-on-A B50 . . . . .148 B2
　Coventry CV5 . . . . .59 E4
　Dunchurch CV22 . . . . . . .99 B2
Howard Rd
　Nuneaton CV10 . . . . .29 A3
　Redditch B98 . . . . .103 B4
Howard St CV1 . . . . .151 C4
Howard Wlk CV31 . . . . . .109 D6
Howat Rd CV7 . . . . .48 F7
Howcombe La CV47 . . . .125 C7
Howcotte Gn CV4 . . . . . . .75 E8
Howe Green La CV7,CV10 37 B2
Howells Cl CV12 . . . . .38 D1
Howes Com Prim Sch
　CV3 . . . . .77 E5
Howes Croft B35 . . . . . . .22 A2
Howes La CV3 . . . . .77 D3
Howkins Rd CV21 . . . . . .83 B3
Howlette Rd CV4 . . . . . . .59 E2
Hoylake B77 . . . . .4 A2
Hoylake Cl CV11 . . . . . . .30 B1
Huckson Rd CV47 . . . . . .124 B4
Huddesford Dr CV7 . . . . .74 C8
Hudson Ave B46 . . . . . . .33 F6
Hudson Rd CV22 . . . . . . .82 C1
Huggins Cl CV7 . . . . .74 C7
Hugh Rd CV3 . . . . .62 A2
Hughes Cl
　Harvington WR11 . . . . . .127 B8
　Warwick CV34 . . . . .104 D2
　Whitnash CV31 . . . . .110 A2
Hughes Hill CV35 . . . . . .114 B6
Hughes La WR11 . . . . . .127 D4
Hughes The CV34 . . . . . .108 E6
Hulme Cl CV3 . . . . .63 B1
Humber Ave Coventry CV1 61 F1
　Coventry CV3 . . . . .61 F2
　Sutton Coldfield B76 . . . .22 A7
Humber Cl NN11 . . . . . . .117 F2
Humber Gr B36 . . . . .22 F1
Humber Rd CV3 . . . . .78 A8
Humber Wlk OX16 . . . . .139 F4
Humberstone Rd 4 CV6 .61 A5

Humphrey Burton's Rd
　CV3 . . . . .77 C8
Humphrey-Davy Rd
　CV12 . . . . .49 D8
Humphris St CV34 . . . . .109 B8
Hungerfield Rd B36 . . . . .22 C1
Hunningham Gr 6 B91 . . .71 B8
Hunscote La CV35 . . . . .121 F1
Hunt Cl CV35 . . . . .114 F3
Hunt End La B97 . . . . . . .102 B3
Hunt Hall La CV37 . . . . .129 A6
Hunt La CV9 . . . . .19 A4
Hunt Paddocks CV8 . . . . .92 E1
Hunt Terr CV4 . . . . .76 B7
Hunter Bvd LE17 . . . . . . .55 A3
Hunter St CV21 . . . . .83 B2
Hunter Terr CV5 . . . . . . .76 B3
Hunters Cl CV3 . . . . .63 A2
Hunters La
　Fenny Drayton CV13 . . . . .20 A3
　Rugby CV21 . . . . .83 A3
Hunters Lane Ind Est
　CV21 . . . . .83 A3
Hunters Pk CV9 . . . . .11 B1
Hunters Wlk CV9 . . . . . . .19 A4
Huntingdon Rd CV5 . . . . .77 A8
Huntingdon Way CV10 . . .28 E3
Huntington Ct CV35 . . . .146 C2
Hunts Rd CV37 . . . . .145 B1
Hurdlers La CV37 . . . . . .121 B6
Hurlbutt Rd CV34 . . . . . .109 C4
Hurley Cl CV32 . . . . .106 A2
Hurley Comm CV9 . . . . . .16 B3
Hurley La B46 . . . . .25 B3
Hurley Prim Sch CV9 . . . .16 B2
Hurn Way CV6 . . . . .50 B4
Hurricane Way 3 B35 . . .22 A2
Hurst Green Rd
　Bentley Heath B93 . . . . . .71 F4
　Minworth B76 . . . . .22 D6
Hurst Rd Bedworth CV12 . .39 B3
　Coventry CV6 . . . . .50 A4
　Hinckley LE10 . . . . .31 D8
　Southam CV47 . . . . .147 A2
Hurst The B47 . . . . .69 A6
Hurst Wlk CV6 . . . . .50 A4
Husbandmans Cl CV3 . . .149 C3
Hyacinth Way LE10 . . . . .31 D5
Hyde Cl CV2 . . . . .109 E8
Hyde Rd Coventry CV2 . . .62 E4
　Kenilworth CV8 . . . . .93 A5
Hydes La LE10 . . . . .30 E4
Hypericum Gdns CV2 . . . .62 C4

I

Ibex Cl CV3 . . . . .62 F1
Ibstock Rd CV6 . . . . .50 A5
Icknield Cl B50 . . . . .148 C2
Icknield Ct B50 . . . . .148 C2
Icknield Row B49 . . . . . .143 A2
Icknield St
　Bidford-on-A B50 . . . . . .148 C2
　Rowney Green B48 . . . . . .85 B6
Icknield Street Dr B98 . .103 B4
Iden Rd CV1 . . . . .61 E4
Idlicote Rd CV36 . . . . . . .137 B8
Ilam Pk CV8 . . . . .93 C5
Ilex Ct CV34 . . . . .109 A7
Ilford Cl CV12 . . . . .39 A3
Ilford Ct CV3 . . . . .79 D7
Ilford Dr CV3 . . . . .77 B5
Ilfracombe Gr CV3 . . . . . .77 A5
Iliffe Ho LE10 . . . . .31 B7
Illshaw Cl B98 . . . . .112 A6
Illshaw Heath Rd B90,
　B94 . . . . .70 D2
Ilmer Cl CV21 . . . . .83 C4
Ilmington CE Prim Sch
　CV36 . . . . .136 A6
Ilmington Cl Coventry CV3 77 B5
　Hatton CV35 . . . . .114 E6
Ilmington Rd
　Ilmington CV36,CV37 . . .136 D7
　Tredington CV36 . . . . . .136 E6
Ilminster Cl LE10 . . . . . . .32 B7
Imogen Gdns CV34 . . . .109 E3
Imperial Rise B46 . . . . . .23 E2
Inca Cl CV3 . . . . .78 F8
Inchbrook Rd CV8 . . . . . .93 C7
Inchford Ave CV34 . . . . .104 E2
Inchford Cl CV11 . . . . . . .29 E1
Infantry Pl B75 . . . . .13 A6
Ingle Ct CV31 . . . . .109 E7
Ingleton Cl CV11 . . . . . . .30 A2
Inglewood Cl CV32 . . . . .106 A3
Ingon La CV37 . . . . .121 B5
Ingram Cl CV36 . . . . . . .140 E5
Ingram Pit La B77 . . . . . . .4 A3
Ingram Rd CV5 . . . . .76 D8
Innage Cl CV31 . . . . .110 B8
Innage Park Small Ind Units
　CV9 . . . . .12 B1
Innage Terr CV9 . . . . .18 B4
Innage The B47 . . . . .69 A5
Innis Rd CV5 . . . . .76 E8
Innisfree House Sch B47 69 C4
Innsworth Dr B35 . . . . . .22 A4
Instone Rd CV6 . . . . .49 A1
Inveraray Cl CV8 . . . . . . .93 C4
Inverlea Cl GL55 . . . . . .135 B6
Inverness Cl CV5 . . . . . . .60 A4
Invicta Rd CV3 . . . . .78 F8
Ipsley Fst Sch B98 . . . . .102 C4
Ipswich Wlk B37 . . . . . . .33 B2
Irelands La B94,B95 . . . .113 D7
Ireton Cl CV4 . . . . .59 C1

Iris Cl LE10 . . . . .31 E5
Ironmonger Row CV1 . . .151 B3
Ironstone Hollow OX15 .142 E4
Irving Rd CV1 . . . . .61 E2
Isambard Dr CV6 . . . . . . .49 F5
Isis Gr B36 . . . . .33 A8
Islington Cres CV9 . . . . . .10 B1
Ivanhoe Ave CV11 . . . . . .29 E1
Ivor Rd Atherstone CV9 . . .18 C4
　Coventry CV6 . . . . .49 F2
Ivy Cl CV13 . . . . .21 B4
Ivy Farm La CV4 . . . . . . .76 D6
Ivy Gr CV10 . . . . .28 D6
Ivy La Ettington CV37 . . .131 A3
　Harbury CV33 . . . . .123 F6
　Mollington OX17 . . . . . .134 A2
　Shutford OX15 . . . . .139 A3
Ivy Lodge Cl B37 . . . . . . .44 A7
Ivy St CV21 . . . . .84 B5
Ivybridge Rd CV3 . . . . . . .77 D6
Ivycroft Rd B79 . . . . .5 C3
Ivyhouse Wlk B77 . . . . . . .9 C3
Izod's Cl GL55 . . . . .135 A1

J

Jack Cade Way CV34 . . .109 E4
Jack O'Watton Bsns Pk
　B46 . . . . .23 D3
Jack Thomson Croft
　WR11 . . . . .127 F6
Jackdaw Dr B36 . . . . .33 A8
Jacker's Rd CV2 . . . . .50 B4
Jacklin Dr CV3 . . . . .77 C4
Jacknell Rd LE10 . . . . . . .30 D8
Jackson Cl
　Hampton Magna CV35 . . .114 F3
　Keresley CV7 . . . . .49 A5
Jackson Gr CV8 . . . . .93 C4
Jackson La CV47 . . . . . . .125 C2
Jackson Rd Coventry CV6 .49 D1
　Rugby CV21 . . . . .84 A1
Jackson Wlk B35 . . . . . . .22 A2
Jacksons Mdw B35 . . . . .148 B3
Jacksons Orch CV37 . . . .129 B3
Jackwood Gn CV12 . . . . .49 C8
Jacob Dr CV4 . . . . .76 D6
Jacobean La B93 . . . . . . .56 B1
Jacox Cres CV8 . . . . .93 C5
Jacquard Cl CV3 . . . . . . .77 D4
Jacquard Ho 3 CV1 . . . . .61 E4
Jade Cl CV1 . . . . .151 D4
James Ct 14 Rugby CV21 .83 A2
　Warwick CV34 . . . . .108 E4
James Dawson Dr CV5 . . .59 B8
James Diskin Ct CV11 . . .29 E2
James Galloway Cl CV3 . .78 E7
James Green Rd CV4 . . . .59 F2
James Ho CV2 . . . . .62 C8
James Rd B46 . . . . .33 F6
James St Arley CV7 . . . . .37 A4
　Nuneaton CV11 . . . . .29 A5
　Rugby CV21 . . . . .83 A2
James Watt Cl NN11 . . .117 F2
Jamescroft CV3 . . . . .78 E6
Jameson Ct 22 GL56 . . .140 A3
Jaques Cl B46 . . . . .23 B2
Jardine Cres CV4 . . . . . . .59 F2
Jasmine Gr Coventry CV3 .78 C5
　Royal Leamington Spa
　CV32 . . . . .106 A2
Jasmine Rd B77 . . . . .4 A2
Javelin Ho B35 . . . . .22 C3
Jays Cl B98 . . . . .112 A6
Jean St CV9 . . . . .11 B1
Jedburgh Gr CV3 . . . . . . .77 A4
Jeff's Cl OX15 . . . . .137 F2
Jeffrey Cl CV12 . . . . .49 D8
Jeffrey Woods Cross CV1 61 F4
Jeffs Cl B98 . . . . .138 B6
Jeliff St CV4 . . . . .59 F2
Jenkins Ave CV5 . . . . . . .59 F4
Jenkins Rd CV21 . . . . . . .84 A1
Jenner St CV1 . . . . .151 C4
Jenton Rd CV31 . . . . . . .110 B6
Jephcott Cl B49 . . . . . . .143 A2
Jephcott Ho 2 CV1 . . . . .61 E4
Jephson Ct CV2 . . . . .50 C4
Jephson Pl 3 CV31 . . . . .110 B7
Jersey Croft B36 . . . . . . .33 B6
Jervis Rd B77 . . . . .9 C3
Jesmond Rd CV1 . . . . . . .61 E4
Jesson Rd B75 . . . . .13 A5
Jill La B96 . . . . .103 A1
Jim Forrest Cl 4 CV3 . . .78 F8
Joan of Arc Ho CV3 . . . . .77 E6
Joan Ward St CV3 . . . . . .77 D8
Joan's Cl CV31 . . . . .110 C6
Job's La CV4 . . . . .60 A2
Jodrell St CV11 . . . . .29 B6
Joe O'Brien Cl CV3 . . . . .78 C6
Joe Williams Cl 7 CV3 . .78 F8
John Grace St CV3 . . . . . .77 D8
John Gulson Prim Sch
　CV1 . . . . .61 D5
John Knight Rd CV12 . . . .39 B5
John McGuire Cres CV3 . .78 E7
John Nash Sq CV8 . . . . . .92 F3
John Nichols St LE10 . . . .31 B7
John O'Gaunt Rd CV8 . . .92 E3
John of Gaunt Ho CV3 . . .77 E6
John Rous Ave CV4 . . . . .76 B7
John Shelton Com Prim Sch
　CV6 . . . . .49 D4
John Shelton Dr CV6 . . . .49 D4
John Simpson Cl CV8 . . . .80 A7

John Sinclair Ho CV1 . . .151 B4
John St Bedworth CV12 . . .39 A2
　Nuneaton, Coton CV11 . . .29 C2
　Nuneaton, Stockingford
　CV10 . . . . .28 E3
　Royal Leamington Spa
　CV32 . . . . .109 F8
　Stratford-u-A CV37 . . . .145 A2
John Taylor Way CV3 . . .122 E3
John Tofts Ho CV1 . . . . .151 B4
John's Cl LE10 . . . . .31 D5
Johndory B77 . . . . .9 B3
Johns Cl B80 . . . . .103 B2
Johnson Ave CV22 . . . . . .82 C1
Johnson Pl B95 . . . . .113 B5
Johnson Rd
　Bedworth CV12 . . . . .39 C3
　Coventry CV6 . . . . .62 A8
Johnson St CV9 . . . . .10 B1
Jolyffe Park Rd CV37 . . .145 A2
Jon Baker Ct LE10 . . . . . .31 E8
Jonathan Rd CV2 . . . . . . .62 F8
Jones Rd CV7 . . . . .39 A1
Jones Wood Cl B76 . . . . .22 A7
Jonkel Ave B77 . . . . .10 A3
Jordan Cl CV8 . . . . .93 B2
Jordan Well CV1 . . . . . . .151 C2
Jordans Cl B97 . . . . .102 B3
Jordans The CV5 . . . . . . .60 C4
Joseph Cash Prim Sch
　CV6 . . . . .61 C7
Joseph Creighton Cl CV3 78 E7
Joseph Halpin Ho 3
　CV1 . . . . .151 C4
Joseph Latham Ho 3
　CV2 . . . . .50 B1
Joseph Luckman Rd
　CV12 . . . . .39 B4
Joseph Way CV37 . . . . . .144 C3
Jourdain Pk CV34 . . . . . .109 E3
Joyce Pool CV34 . . . . . . .108 E7
Joyce Way CV22 . . . . . . .99 A4
Jubilee Ave
　Lower Shuckburgh NN11 .116 E1
　Redditch B97 . . . . .102 B4
Jubilee Cl
　Bidford-on-A B50 . . . . . .148 C3
　Chipping Campden GL55 .135 A2
Jubilee Cres CV6 . . . . . . .61 B7
Jubilee Ct B78 . . . . .15 B3
Jubilee St CV21 . . . . .82 C2
Jubilee Terr CV12 . . . . . .39 B4
Judd Cl CV12 . . . . .38 F3
Judds La CV6 . . . . .49 E4
Judge Cl CV23 . . . . .82 A3
Judith Way CV22 . . . . . . .99 A4
Juggins La B94 . . . . .86 B7
Julian Cl CV2 . . . . .62 F8
Juliet Cl CV11 . . . . .30 A1
Juliet Dr
　Royal Leamington Spa
　CV34 . . . . .109 F3
　Rugby CV22 . . . . .99 B3
Julius Dr B46 . . . . .23 F1
Junction One Ret Pk
　CV21 . . . . .83 A3
Junction St CV1 . . . . . . .151 A2
Junewood Cl CV21 . . . . . .83 B4
Juniper B77 . . . . .4 A2
Juniper Cl CV12 . . . . .38 E2
Juniper Dr Coventry CV5 . .59 F5
　Sutton Coldfield B76 . . . .22 A7
Juno Dr CV31 . . . . .109 F5
Jury St CV34 . . . . .108 E6
Justice Cl CV31 . . . . .110 A4
Justins Ave CV37 . . . . . .144 C3

K

Kalfs Dr CV22 . . . . .99 A4
Kanzan Rd CV2 . . . . .50 B4
Kareen Gr CV3 . . . . .79 C7
Karen Cl CV10 . . . . .28 E7
Karlingford Cl CV5 . . . . . .76 D8
Kathleen Ave CV12 . . . . .38 E1
Katrine Cl CV10 . . . . .28 C5
Kay Cl CV21 . . . . .83 B4
Kaysbrook Dr CV23 . . . . .97 A3
Keats Cl CV10 . . . . .28 A4
Keats Ho B97 . . . . .102 B4
Keats Rd Coventry CV2 . . .62 D2
　Stratford-u-A CV37 . . . .145 A1
Keble Ho B37 . . . . .33 A2
Keble Rd GL56 . . . . .140 A2
Kebull Gn CV4 . . . . .75 E8
Keele Ho B37 . . . . .33 B4
Keeling Rd CV8 . . . . .93 B5
Keenan Dr CV12 . . . . . . .38 D1
Keepers Cl B46 . . . . .34 A2
Keepers Wlk CV12 . . . . . .38 D1
Keetley Cl CV36 . . . . . . .149 C2
Kegworth Cl CV6 . . . . . . .50 A4
Keir Cl CV32 . . . . .106 A2
Keith Rd CV32 . . . . .106 B4
Kele Rd CV4 . . . . .76 A7
Kelmscote Rd CV6 . . . . . .60 F8
Kelsey Cl CV11 . . . . .29 E3
Kelsey La CV7 . . . . .74 D5
Kelsey's Cl CV8 . . . . .79 F3
Kelsull Croft B37 . . . . . . .33 A2
Kelvin Ave CV2 . . . . .62 D5
Kelvin Rd CV32 . . . . .106 C5
Kelway CV3 . . . . .63 A2
Kelways CV3 . . . . .63 A2
Kem St CV11 . . . . .29 E2
Kemble Dr B35 . . . . .22 A3
Kemerton Way B90 . . . . .70 F6

Hon – Kil 167

Kemp Cl CV34 . . . . .109 A7
Kempley Ave CV2 . . . . . .62 C2
Kemps Green Rd
　Balsall Common CV7 . . . .74 B6
　Tanworth-in-A B94 . . . . .88 A1
Kempsey Cl B98 . . . . . . .103 A4
Kempsford Cl B98 . . . . . .102 C3
Kempton Cl CV37 . . . . . .129 F8
Kempton Cres CV32 . . . .106 C4
Kempton Dr B77 . . . . .9 B2
Kendal Ave Coleshill B46 . .33 F7
　Royal Leamington Spa
　CV32 . . . . .105 C2
Kendal Cl Nuneaton CV11 .30 A6
　Redditch B98 . . . . .112 A6
Kendal Rise CV5 . . . . . . .60 C5
Kendall Ave CV37 . . . . . .145 A2
Kenderine Montessori Sch
　CV5 . . . . .77 A8
Kendon Ave CV6 . . . . . . .60 E6
Kendrick Cl CV6 . . . . .50 A5
Kenelm Ct CV3 . . . . .78 C5
Kenhill Rd OX15 . . . . . . .138 F5
Kenilcourt CV8 . . . . .92 D6
Kenilworth Castle★ CV8 .92 D5
Kenilworth Ct B97 . . . . .102 B3
Kenilworth Ct CV3 . . . . . .77 B3
Kenilworth Dr CV11 . . . . .29 B3
Kenilworth Hall Mews
　CV8 . . . . .92 F5
Kenilworth Rd
　Balsall Common CV7,CV8 .74 D4
　Coventry CV4 . . . . .76 E3
　Cubbington CV32 . . . . . .106 C6
　Hampton-in-A B92 . . . . . .57 E5
　Kenilworth CV8 . . . . .93 C8
　Knowle B93 . . . . .72 E5
　Lighthorne Heath CV33 . .123 D2
　Meriden CV7 . . . . .45 D1
　Royal Leamington Spa
　CV32 . . . . .105 E5
Kenilworth Sch CV8 . . . . .93 C5
Kenilworth Sch Castle Hall
　Sixth Form CV8 . . . . . . .92 F2
Kenilworth St 16 CV32 . .105 F1
Kenilworth Way OX16 . . .139 F3
Kennan Ave CV31 . . . . . .109 F6
Kennedy Dr CV22 . . . . . .82 B1
Kennedy Sq 3 CV32 . . . .106 A1
Kennel La CV9 . . . . .19 A4
Kennet Cl CV2 . . . . .62 C8
Kenning Cl CV47 . . . . . . .115 C4
Kenpas Highway CV3 . . . .77 A5
Kenrick Croft 4 B35 . . . .22 A2
Kensington Ct
　Coventry CV5 . . . . .61 A1
　Nuneaton CV10 . . . . .28 C6
Kensington Rd CV5 . . . . .61 A1
Kent Cl CV3 . . . . .77 E6
Kent Rd CV47 . . . . .132 F5
Kent The CV21 . . . . .84 F1
Kenthurst Cl CV5 . . . . . . .59 C4
Kentmere Cl CV5 . . . . . . .50 E2
Kents La CV37 . . . . .131 A4
Kenway B47 . . . . .69 A7
Kenwyn Gn CV7 . . . . .50 B8
Keppel Cl CV22 . . . . .82 B1
Keppel St CV1 . . . . .61 E5
Keresley Brook Rd CV6 . .49 A2
Keresley Cl CV6 . . . . .49 A2
Keresley Grange Prim Sch
　CV6 . . . . .48 F1
Keresley Green Rd CV6 . .48 F1
Keresley Newland Prim Sch
　CV7 . . . . .48 F7
Keresley Rd CV6 . . . . . . .61 B8
Kerns Terr CV37 . . . . . . .145 A2
Kerr Way GL56 . . . . .140 C3
Kerria Ctr B77 . . . . .4 A2
Kerria Rd B77 . . . . .4 A2
Kerrls Way CV3 . . . . .63 A1
Kerry's Ho 4 CV1 . . . . . .61 B2
Kerswell Dr B90 . . . . .71 A5
Kestral Ho B35 . . . . .22 C3
Kestrel B77 . . . . .10 A3
Kestrel Cl Hinckley LE10 . .31 F6
　Stratford-u-A CV37 . . . .145 A3
Kestrel Croft 2 CV3 . . . .78 F8
Keswick Cl CV11 . . . . . . .30 A6
Keswick Dr CV21 . . . . . . .83 B4
Keswick Gn CV32 . . . . . .105 D1
Keswick Wlk CV2 . . . . . . .62 F4
Kettlebrook Rd B90 . . . . .71 C6
Kettlewell Cl CV34 . . . . .104 E1
Keviliok St CV3 . . . . .77 D6
Kew Cl CV8 . . . . .93 C5
Kew Ho CV4 . . . . .59 F3
Kew Rd CV21 . . . . .83 A2
Keys Dr CV22 . . . . .82 B1
Keys Hill CV9 . . . . .11 B1
Keys La CV47 . . . . .125 C4
Keyte Rd CV36 . . . . .136 B6
Keytes Acre GL55 . . . . . .135 C3
Keytes La CV35 . . . . . . .122 B7
Kiblers La CV35 . . . . . . .131 A3
Kielder Dr CV10 . . . . .28 E2
Kiftsgate Court Gdns★
　GL55 . . . . .135 C6
Kilburn Dr CV5 . . . . .60 F3
Kilby Gn LE10 . . . . .31 F6
Kilby Gr CV31 . . . . .110 C5
Kilbye Cl B77 . . . . .9 C3
Kildale Cl CV1 . . . . .151 D3
Kilderkin Ct CV1 . . . . . . .151 B1
Kildwick Way 5 CV34 . . .104 E1

Killworth Rd CV21 .....**101** A4
Kiln Cl Nuneaton CV10 ....**28** E3
Royal Leamington Spa
  CV32 ....**106** A1
  Studley B80 ....**103** B2
Kiln La B90 ....**70** A5
Kiln Way Polesworth B78 ....**4** C1
  Shilton CV7 ....**51** E7
Kilnsey Gr CV34 ....**104** E1
Kilsby Gr B91 ....**71** C8
Kilsby La CV23 ....**101** B4
Kilsby Rd CV23 ....**101** B1
Kilworth Ho **7** CV32 ....**105** F1
Kimbell Cl CV47 ....**124** B1
Kimberley B77 ....**9** C4
Kimberley Cl CV5 ....**59** F4
Kimberley Rd
  Baginton CV8 ....**77** F2
  Bedworth CV12 ....**39** C4
  Rugby CV21 ....**83** A2
Kimberley Wlk B76 ......**22** D6
Kimble Cl CV5 ....**60** B4
Kimmond Ct **17** CV32 ...**105** F1
Kinchford Cl B91 ....**71** B8
Kineton CE Prim Sch
  CV35 ....**132** B6
Kineton High Sch CV35 .**132** C6
Kineton La B94 ....**71** A1
Kineton Rd Coventry CV2 ..**62** C6
  Kenilworth CV8 ....**93** C4
  Southam CV47 ....**147** A2
  Wellesbourne CV35 ....**146** C1
Kineton Road Ind Est
  CV47 ....**147** A2
King Edward Rd
  Coventry CV1 ....**61** F4
  Nuneaton CV11 ....**29** D4
  Rugby CV21 ....**83** A2
King Edward VI Coll
  CV11 ....**29** D4
King Edward VI Sch
  CV37 ....**145** A1
King George's Ave
  Bedworth CV12 ....**39** B5
  Coventry CV6 ....**49** F2
King George's Ct CV23 ...**82** A3
King George's Way LE10 ..**31** B7
King Henry VIII Sch
  CV3 ....**151** A1
King John's La CV35 ....**132** E2
King John's Rd CV35 ...**132** B6
King Richard St CV2 .....**61** F3
King St Bedworth CV12 ....**39** C2
Royal Leamington Spa
  CV32 ....**106** A1
  Rugby CV21 ....**83** A2
King William St CV1 .....**61** E4
King's Ct CV11 ....**29** B4
King's High Sch for Girls The
  CV34 ....**108** E7
King's Hill La CV8 ....**77** B2
King's La Broom B50 ....**148** A3
  Newton Regis B79 ....**2** B3
  Norton WR11 ....**127** B2
  Snitterfield CV37 ......**121** B6
  Stratford-u-A CV37 ....**144** C4
Kingcomb La GL55 ......**135** A2
Kingfield Rd CV1,CV6 ....**61** D7
Kingfisher B77 ....**10** A3
Kingfisher Ave CV10 .....**28** C5
Kingfisher Dr B36 ....**33** A8
Kingfisher Prim Sch B36 **33** A8
Kingfisher Way B49 .....**143** A3
Kingham Cl B98 ....**112** A6
Kingham Hill Sch OX7 ..**150** A1
Kingland Dr CV32 ......**105** C1
Kingley Ave B49 ....**143** B3
Kings Ave CV9 ....**18** C4
Kings Coughton La B49 **143** A3
Kings Gdns CV12 ....**39** C2
Kings Gr CV2 ....**62** B3
Kings Mdw CV10 ....**28** C5
Kings Newnham La CV23 **80** C4
Kings Newnham Rd CV23 **81** A3
Kings Park Dr CV3 ....**63** B1
Kingsbridge Rd CV10 ....**29** D6
Kingsbrook Dr B91 ......**71** B8
Kingsbury Bsns Pk B76 ..**22** E6
Kingsbury Cl B76 ....**22** D5
Kingsbury Comp Sch
  B78 ....**15** B3
Kingsbury Inf Sch B78 ...**15** B3
Kingsbury Jun Sch B78 ..**15** B3
Kingsbury Rd
  Coventry CV6 ....**60** E5
  Curdworth B76 ....**23** B7
  Kingsbury B76 ....**15** A1
  Minworth B76 ....**22** D5
  Sutton Coldfield B35,B76 ..**22** B5
Kingsbury Water Park Visitor
  Ctr★ B76 ....**15** A3
Kingsbury Water Pk★
  B76 ....**15** A3
Kingscote Gr CV3 ....**77** A4
Kingscote Rd B93 ....**71** E2
Kingsfield Ind Est CV1 ...**61** C6
Kingsford Cl B36 ....**22** D1
Kingsgate Ho B37 ....**33** C2
Kingsholm Cl CV3 ....**63** B1
Kingshurst CV31 ....**110** E6
Kingshurst Inf Sch B37 ..**33** A6
Kingshurst Jun Sch B37 .**33** A6
Kingsland Ave CV5 ......**60** F2
Kingsland Dr B93 ....**71** E4
Kingsleigh Dr B36 ......**22** B1

Kingsley Ave CV21 ......**83** C1
Kingsley Coll B98 ......**103** B3
Kingsley Cres CV12 .....**40** B3
Kingsley Ct CV3 ....**79** D6
Kingsley Orch CV21 .....**83** C1
Kingsley Prep Sch B93 ..**72** A4
Kingsley Rd **11** CV33 ..**122** F8
Kingsley Sch The CV32 .**105** F1
Kingsley Terr CV2 ....**62** E8
Kingsley Wlk CV2 ....**62** F7
Kingsmead Mews CV3 ...**78** D6
Kingston La CV35 ......**113** E3
Kingston Mews CV31 ...**110** C6
Kingston Rd CV5 ....**60** E2
  Kingsbury B78 ....**15** B3
  Lighthorne Heath CV33 .**123** D2
  Nuneaton CV11 ....**29** B4
Royal Leamington Spa
  CV31 ....**109** F6
  Rugby CV22 ....**83** A3
Kingsway Com Prim Sch
  CV31 ....**109** F6
Kingsway Ho CV12 ......**39** C2
Kingswood Ave CV7 .....**48** B8
Kingswood Cl
  Coventry CV6 ....**49** D1
  Lapworth B94 ....**89** E5
Kingswood Cotts B94 ...**89** D3
Kingswood Gdns CV10 ..**28** B4
Kingswood Rd CV10 .....**28** B4
Kington Rise CV35 .....**113** E2
Kinman Way CV21 ....**83** B3
Kinross Cl CV10 ....**28** F2
Kinross Rd CV32 ....**106** B4
Kinross Way LE10 ....**21** C1
Kinsall Gn B77 ....**10** B3
Kinsham Dr B91 ....**71** B8
Kintyre The CV2 ....**63** B7
Kinver Cl CV2 ....**50** E1
Kinver Croft B76 ....**22** A8
Kinwalsey La CV7 ....**46** F6
Kinwarton Dovecote★
  B49 ....**143** C3
Kinwarton Farm Rd B49 **143** B3
Kinwarton Rd B49 .....**143** B2
Kinwarton Workshops
  B49 ....**143** B3
Kipling Ave CV34 ......**108** C4
Kipling Cl CV10 ....**28** A5
Kipling Rd Coventry CV6 ..**61** A8
  Stratford-u-A CV37 ...**130** A8
Kirby Ave CV34 ....**104** F1
Kirby Cl Brandon CV8 ....**79** F5
  Coventry CV1 ....**61** D6
Kirby Cnr CV4 ....**76** B5
Kirby La CV7 ....**52** C3
Kirby Corner Rd CV4 ....**76** B6
Kirby Rd CV5 ....**60** F2
Kirigushi Rd CV35 .....**132** E5
Kirkby Cl CV3 ....**83** C3
Kirkby Rd CV21 ....**83** C1
Kirkdale Ave CV6 ....**49** D3
Kirkland Way B78 ....**8** A4
Kirkstone CV21 ....**83** B4
Kirkstone Rd CV12 ......**39** A2
Kirkstone Wlk CV11 .....**30** A6
Kirkwall CV47 ....**147** A2
Kirtland Cl CV9 ....**3** A1
Kirton Cl Coventry CV6 ...**48** F1
  Whitnash CV31 ....**110** B3
Kissing Tree La CV37 ...**121** D3
Kitchener Rd
  Coventry CV6 ....**61** E8
  Long Marston CV37 ...**129** C2
Kitebrook Cl B90 ....**71** A7
Kites Cl CV34 ....**104** E4
Kites Nest La CV35 ....**114** E8
Kittermaster Rd CV7 ....**46** C1
Kitwood Ave B78 ....**10** C3
Kixley La B93 ....**72** C6
Klevedon Cl CV11 ....**30** A1
Knebley Cres CV10 ......**29** C1
Knibbs Sh Ctr The CV34 **108** E7
Knight Ave CV1 ....**61** E1
Knight Ct B75 ....**13** C5
Knightcote Dr
Royal Leamington Spa
  CV32 ....**109** E4
  Solihull B91 ....**71** B8
Knightley Cl CV32 .....**106** E5
Knightlow Ave CV3 ......**78** C6
Knightlow CE Prim Sch
  CV23 ....**96** C4
Knightlow Cl CV8 ....**93** C3
Knightlow Way CV33 ...**123** F6
Knights Cl LE10 ....**31** D4
Knights Ct LE10 ....**30** E8
Knights La CV37 ......**145** C2
Knights Templar Way
  CV4 ....**60** A1
Knightsbridge Ave CV12 .**39** C4
Knob Hill CV23 ....**96** C3
Knoll Croft
  Cheswick Green B90 ...**70** D4
  Coventry CV3 ....**77** C6
Knoll Dr Coventry CV3 ....**77** C6
  Warwick CV34 ....**104** E1
Knottesford Cl B80 ....**103** B2
Knowlands Rd B90 .....**70** A7
Knowle CE Prim Sch B93 **72** C6
Knowle Hill Hurley CV9 ..**16** B6
  Kenilworth CV8 ....**93** C6
Knowle Rd B92 ....**56** C2
Knowle Wood Rd B93 ...**72** B3
Knowles Ave CV10 ......**28** C4
Knox Cres CV11 ....**29** F8
Kranji Rd CV47 ....**132** F5

Kurtus B77 ....**9** B3
Kwikform Bldg CV6 .....**49** E4
Kyetts Cnr OX17 ......**134** C1
Kynner Way CV3 ....**79** B8
Kyter La B36 ....**22** B1

L

Laburnum Ave
  Coventry CV6 ....**60** F5
  Kenilworth CV8 ....**93** A4
Laburnum Cl
  Bedworth CV12 ....**38** E2
  Hollywood B47 ....**69** A5
  Kingsbury B78 ....**15** B3
Laburnum Dr
  Sutton Coldfield B76 ....**13** A3
  Whitnash CV31 ....**110** B3
Laburnum Gr
  Nuneaton CV10 ....**28** D6
  Rugby CV22 ....**99** C4
  Warwick CV34 ....**105** B1
Lacell Cl CV34 ....**104** E1
Ladbroke By-Pass
  CV47 ....**124** D5
Ladbroke Hall CV47 ...**124** D5
Ladbroke Pk CV34 .....**104** E1
Ladbroke Rd CV47 ....**124** B4
Ladbrook Cl B98 ......**102** C4
Ladbrook Rd CV5 ....**60** A4
Lady Byron La
  Knowle, Copt Heath B93 ..**56** A1
  Knowle, Tilehouse Green
  B93 ....**71** F8
Lady Grey Ave CV35 ...**113** E3
Lady Katherine Leveson CE
  Sch B93 ....**73** B5
Lady La Coventry CV6 ....**49** F4
  Earlswood B90,B94 .....**70** B3
  Kenilworth CV8 ....**92** F4
Lady Warwick Ave CV12 .**39** D2
Ladycroft CV32 ....**106** E5
Ladyfields Way CV6 .....**49** B4
Ladygrove Cl B98 .....**103** A4
Ladymead Dr CV6 ......**49** B2
Ladysmock CV23 ....**83** B4
Laertes Gr CV34 ......**109** F2
Laggan Cl CV10 ....**28** C5
Lair The B78 ....**10** C4
Lake View Rd CV5 ......**60** F4
Lakeland Dr B77 ....**10** A4
Lakeland Ho CV34 ....**109** A7
Lakes Halt The B94 .....**86** F8
Lakeside CV12 ....**39** A2
Lakeside Dr B90 ....**70** F7
Lakin Ct CV34 ....**108** F3
Lakin Dr CV47 ....**124** A4
Lakin Ho CV34 ....**108** F3
Lakin Rd CV34 ....**108** F3
Lamb St CV1 ....**151** B3
Lambert Cl B50 ....**148** B3
Lambert Ct Barford CV35 **122** A7
  Warwick CV34 ....**108** D6
Lambert Sch CV37 ....**145** A3
Lambeth Cl
  Birmingham B37 ....**33** B4
  Coventry CV2 ....**62** E7
Lambourn Cres CV31 ..**110** C6
Lambourne Cl
  Bidford-on-A B50 .....**148** B3
  Coventry CV5 ....**60** A4
Lamerton Cl CV2 ....**62** C6
Lamintone Dr CV32 ...**105** D2
Lammas Croft CV31 ...**110** A3
Lammas Ct
  Warwick CV34 ....**108** D6
  Wolston CV8 ....**80** A2
Lammas Ho **6** CV6 ....**61** A4
Lammas Rd CV6 ....**60** F4
Lammas Wlk CV34 ....**108** D7
Lamorna Cl CV11 ....**29** F4
Lamp La CV7 ....**36** C3
Lampitts Gn OX15 ....**139** D4
Lamprey CV3 ....**9** B3
Lancaster Cl
  Atherstone CV9 ....**12** C1
  Wellesbourne CV35 ...**146** B1
Lancaster Dr B35 ......**22** B2
Lancaster Pl CV8 ......**92** E2
Lancaster Rd
  Hinckley LE10 ....**31** D8
  Rugby CV21 ....**83** A2
Lance Cl LE10 ....**31** D5
Lanchester Dr OX16 ..**139** F4
Lanchester Rd CV6 .....**61** B6
Lanchester Way
  Birmingham B36 ....**22** F1
  Daventry NN11 ....**117** F2
Lancia Cl CV6 ....**50** B4
Lancing Rd CV12 ....**40** C2
Land La B37 ....**44** A7
Landor Ho CV31 ....**110** A2
Landor Rd Knowle B93 ...**72** A6
  Redditch B98 ....**103** A4
  Warwick CV34 ....**108** D8
  Whitnash CV31 ....**110** A3
Landrail Wlk B36 ....**33** A8
Landsdowne Pl CV21 ...**83** B1
Landseer Cl CV21 ......**84** A1
Lane Croft B76 ....**22** A8
Lane The
  Burmington CV36 ....**137** A1
  Little Compton CV36 ..**141** A6
Laneside CV3 ....**78** E6
Lanfear Ct LE10 ....**31** C7
Langbank Ave CV3 .....**78** D7

Langbay Ct CV2 ....**62** F6
Langcliffe Ave CV34 ...**104** F1
Langcomb Rd B90 ......**70** A8
Langdale Ave CV6 ......**49** D3
Langdale Cl
Royal Leamington Spa
  CV32 ....**106** D3
  Rugby CV21 ....**83** B4
Langdale Ct B77 ....**4** A3
Langdale Dr CV11 ......**30** A6
Langdale Rd LE10 ......**31** A8
Langfield Rd B75 ....**72** A7
Langlands The CV35 ..**121** F4
Langley Croft CV4 ......**60** A2
Langley Dr B35 ....**22** A1
Langley Hall Dr B75 ....**13** B5
Langley Hall Rd B75 ....**13** B5
Langley Heath Dr B76 ..**13** A3
Langley Rd
  Claverdon CV35 ......**113** E3
  Whitnash CV31 ....**110** A4
Langley Specl Sch B75 .**13** A6
Langley Wlk B37 ....**33** D2
Langlodge Rd CV6 ......**49** B2
Langnor Rd CV2 ....**62** C6
Langton Cl
  Birmingham B36 ....**33** B6
  Coventry CV3 ....**78** E8
Langton Rd CV21,CV22 ..**83** C1
Langwood Cl CV4 ....**76** B8
Lankett The CV47 .....**133** D7
Lansbury Cl CV2 ....**62** E7
Lansdowne Cir CV32 ..**106** A1
Lansdowne Cl CV12 ....**39** A3
Lansdowne Cres
  6 Royal Leamington Spa
  CV32 ....**106** A1
  Studley B80 ....**103** B2
  Tamworth B77 ....**9** B4
Lansdowne Rd
  2 Royal Leamington Spa
  CV32 ....**106** A1
  Studley B80 ....**103** B2
Lansdowne St
  Coventry CV2 ....**61** F3
Royal Leamington Spa
  CV32 ....**106** A1
Lant Cl CV7 ....**75** B7
Lapwing B77 ....**10** A3
Lapwing Dr B92 ....**57** B7
Lapworth CE Prim Sch
  B94 ....**89** D3
Lapworth Cl B98 ......**102** C4
Lapworth Oaks B94 ....**89** D3
Lapworth Rd CV2 ......**50** C1
Lapworth St B94 ....**89** B2
Lapworth Sta B94 .....**89** D4
Larch Cl Alcester B49 ..**143** A3
  Rugby CV22 ....**82** A1
  Stratford-u-A CV37 ...**145** A2
Larch Croft B37 ....**33** B2
Larch Gr CV34 ....**105** A1
Larch Tree Ave CV4 ....**60** A2
Larches The
  Bedworth CV12 ....**50** B8
  Kingsbury B78 ....**15** B4
Larchfields CV8 ....**80** A2
Larchwood Rd CV7 .....**39** B1
Larkfield Way CV5 ......**60** A6
Larkin Cl CV12 ....**40** B3
Larkin Gr CV2 ....**62** F6
Larkspur Rugby CV23 ....**83** B4
  Tamworth B77 ....**9** B4
Larkspur Ct CV12 ......**49** C8
Latham Rd CV5 ....**61** A3
Latimer Cl CV8 ....**92** F2
Latymer Cl B76 ....**22** A7
Lauderdale Ave CV6 ....**49** D3
Lauderdale Cl CV23 ....**82** A2
Launce Gr CV34 ......**109** F2
Launceston Dr CV11 ...**29** F4
Laundry Cotts CV35 ....**90** E4
Laurel Ave B78 ....**11** A4
Laurel Cl CV2 ....**50** E2
Laurel Ct CV5 ....**76** C6
Laurel Dr Nuneaton CV10 .**28** A7
  Stockton CV47 ....**147** C4
Laurel Fields LE17 .....**43** C3
Laurel Gdns CV22 ......**99** C4
Laurels Cres CV7 ......**74** C6
Laurels The
  Bedworth CV12 ....**38** E2
  Kingsbury B78 ....**15** B4
Lavender Ave CV6 ......**60** F5
Lavender Cl CV23 ......**83** C4
Lavender Hall La CV7 ...**58** C2
Lavenham Cl CV11 .....**40** C8
Lawford Cl CV3 ....**62** E7
Lawford Heath Ind Est
  CV23 ....**98** B4
Lawford Heath La CV23 .**98** B3
Lawford La CV22 ....**82** A1
Lawford Rd
Royal Leamington Spa
  CV31 ....**110** B5
  Rugby CV21,CV22,CV23 ..**82** C2
Lawley Cl CV4 ....**75** D8
Lawns The Bedworth CV12 **38** C2
  Hinckley LE10 ....**31** E8
Lawnsdale Cl B46 ......**33** F7
Lawnswood Hinckley LE10 **31** A8
  Sutton Coldfield B76 ...**22** A8
Lawrence Dr B76 ....**22** D6
Lawrence Gdns CV8 ....**93** C6
Lawrence Mackie Gdns
  CV35 ....**146** C2

Lawrence Rd
  Bedworth CV7 ....**50** A8
  Rugby CV21 ....**83** B2
Lawrence Saunders Rd
  CV6 ....**61** B5
Lawrence Sheriff Sch
  CV21 ....**83** A2
Lawrence Sherriff St
  CV22 ....**83** A1
Lawson Ave CV37 ....**145** C2
Lawton Cl LE10 ....**30** F8
Laxford Cl LE10 ....**21** C1
Laxton Way OX17 ....**139** F5
Lay Gdns CV31 ....**110** C5
Le Hanche Cl CV7 ......**49** A7
Lea Cl Alcester B49 ...**143** B3
  Stratford-u-A CV37 ...**144** A2
Lea Cres CV21 ....**82** B3
Lea Croft Rd B97 .....**102** B3
Lea Green La B47 ......**69** C5
Lea Wlk CV8 ....**79** B1
Leacrest Rd CV6 ....**49** A2
Leaf Ct CV3 ....**77** D4
Leaf La Coventry CV3 ...**77** E5
  Coventry CV3 ....**77** F6
Leafield Cl CV2 ....**62** F8
Leagh Cl CV8 ....**93** B7
Lealholme Ct CV5 ......**76** F8
Leam Cl CV11 ....**29** F1
Leam Gn CV4 ....**76** D5
Leam Rd
  Lighthorne Heath CV33 .**123** D2
Royal Leamington Spa
  CV31 ....**109** D7
Leam St CV31 ....**110** B7
Leam Terr CV31 ......**110** B8
Leam The NN11 ......**117** F1
Leamington Hastings CE Inf
  Sch CV23 ....**116** B6
Leamington Hastings Rd
  CV23 ....**115** F7
Leamington Rd
  Coventry CV3 ....**77** C6
  Kenilworth CV8 ....**93** B2
  Long Itchington CV47 .**115** C4
  Princethorpe CV23 .....**96** B1
  Ryton-on-D CV8 ....**96** A4
  Southam CV47 ....**124** C8
Leamington Spa Art Gallery
  & Mus★ CV32 ......**109** F8
Leamington Spa Sta
  CV31 ....**109** F7
Lear Gr CV34 ....**109** E4
Leas Cl CV12 ....**39** A3
Leasowe's Ave CV3 .....**76** F4
Leasows The
  Chipping Campden GL55 .**135** A1
  Mickleton GL55 ......**135** C6
Leather St CV47 ......**115** D4
Leathermill La CV10 ...**19** B2
Leaward Cl CV10 ....**28** C2
Ledbrook Rd CV32 ....**106** E5
Ledbury Rd CV31 .....**110** C6
Ledbury Way B76 ......**22** A8
Ledwell B90 ....**70** A5
Lee Cl CV34 ....**104** E2
Lee Rd Hollywood B47 ...**69** A7
Royal Leamington Spa
  CV31 ....**109** E6
Lee The CV5 ....**60** C4
Leeder Cl CV6 ....**49** C2
Leeming Cl CV4 ....**76** C6
Leicester Cres CV9 .....**12** C1
Leicester Cswy CV1 ....**61** D5
Leicester Ct CV12 ......**40** C2
Leicester La
  Cubbington CV32 ......**94** E1
Royal Leamington Spa
  CV32 ....**106** C6
Leicester Rd
  Bedworth CV12 ....**39** B4
  Nuneaton CV11 ....**29** D5
  Rugby CV21 ....**83** A4
  Shilton CV7 ....**51** F6
Leicester Row CV1 ....**151** B4
Leicester St
  Bedworth CV12 ....**39** B3
  Bulkington CV12 ....**40** C2
Royal Leamington Spa
  CV32 ....**106** A1
Leigh Ave CV3 ....**77** C3
Leigh CE Prim Sch CV4 .**75** D8
Leigh Cres CV47 .....**115** D3
Leigh Rd Rugby CV21 ...**82** C4
  Sutton Coldfield B75 ...**13** B5
Leigh St **4** CV1 ......**61** E4
Leighton Cl Coventry CV4 **76** D2
Royal Leamington Spa
  CV32 ....**106** C4
Leisure Wlk B77 ....**9** C3
Lennon Cl CV21 ......**101** B4
Lennox Cl CV3 ....**78** E6
Lenton's La CV2 ....**50** E4
Leofric St CV6 ....**61** A5
Leonard Parkins Ho
  CV12 ....**40** D2
Leontes Mdws CV34 ..**109** E3
Leopold Rd CV1 ....**61** F4
Lesingham Dr CV4 .....**59** E1
Lestock Cl CV22 ....**82** B1
Letchlade Cl CV2 ......**62** C8
Level The OX15 ......**138** F5
Leven Cl LE10 ....**31** B8
Leven Croft B76 ....**22** A7
Leven Way CV2 ....**63** A8
Lever Rd CV21 ....**84** A1
Leveson Cres CV7 .....**74** B6
Levett Rd B77 ....**4** A3

Levy Cl CV21 82 C2
Lewis Ct CV9 18 C3
Lewis Rd Coventry CV1 61 D5
Radford Semele CV31 110 F5
Lexington Ct CV11 29 B5
Leyburn Cl Coventry CV6 49 E2
Nuneaton CV11 30 A2
3 Warwick CV34 104 F1
Leycester Cl CV33 123 E7
Leycester Ct 14 CV34 108 E6
Leycester Pl 13 CV34 108 E6
Leycester Rd CV8 93 A2
Leyes La CV8 93 C5
Leyes The CV23 68 A1
Leyfields Cres CV34 108 D4
Leyland Rd
Bulkington CV12 40 B2
Coventry CV5 60 D4
Nuneaton CV11 29 E1
Leyland Specl Sch CV11 29 E1
Leymere Cl CV7 46 C1
Leys Cl Northend CV47 133 B7
Wroxton OX15 139 D4
Leys La CV7 46 C1
Leys Rd Harvington WR11 127 B5
Rugby CV21 101 B4
Leys The
Bidford-on-A B50 148 C3
Halford CV36 137 A8
Salford OX7 150 C3
Upper Boddington NN11 134 E8
Leysbourne GL55 135 B2
Leysfield WR11 127 C4
Leyside CV3 78 E5
Leysmill Cl LE10 21 C1
Libbards Gate 4 B91 71 C8
Libbards Way B91 71 B8
Liberty Rd B77 9 C3
Liberty Way CV11 29 F3
Library Cl LE10 32 A5
Library Rd CV4 76 B5
Lichen Gn CV4 76 D5
Lichfield Cl Arley CV7 37 A4
Nuneaton CV11 30 A7
Lichfield Cotts B78 15 B3
Lichfield Rd Coventry CV3 77 D8
Water Orton B46,B76 23 D4
Wishaw B76,B78 14 B3
Lichfield St B78 9 A4
Liecester Rd LE10 41 C3
Lifford Way CV3 79 A7
Light Hall Sch B90 70 B8
Light La CV1 151 B4
Lighthorne Heath Prim Sch
CV33 123 C2
Lighthorne Rd CV35 132 B6
Lightoak Cl B97 102 B3
Lightwood Cl B93 72 B8
Lilac Ave CV6 60 F5
Lilac Cl LE10 31 E6
Lilac Dr CV22 82 A1
Lilac Gr CV34 105 A1
Lilac Rd CV12 39 D5
Lilacvale Way CV4 76 D5
Lilbourne Rd CV23 84 B3
Lilley Cl CV6 49 C2
Lilley Green Rd B48 85 D5
Lillington Ave CV32 105 F2
Lillington Cl
Royal Leamington Spa
CV32 106 A3
Sutton Coldfield B75 13 A4
Lillington Prim Sch
CV32 106 B3
Lillington Rd
Coventry CV2 50 D1
Royal Leamington Spa
CV32 106 A3
Solihull B90 70 B8
Limbrick Ave CV4 60 A1
Limbrick Wood Prim Sch
CV4 59 F3
Lime Ave CV32 106 A4
Lime Cl B47 69 A5
Lime Gr
Birmingham, Chemsley Wood
B37 33 B1
Coventry CV4 60 B2
Hurley CV9 16 A2
Kenilworth CV8 93 A4
Nuneaton CV10 28 E5
Lime Kiln B78 11 A4
Lime Rd CV47 147 A3
Lime Tree Ave
Coventry CV4 60 A2
Rugby CV22 99 A4
Limekiln La B94 70 D1
Limes Ave CV37 144 B1
Limes Coppice CV10 27 C4
Limes The Bedworth CV12 38 E2
Tiddington CV37 145 C2
Limestone Hall La CV23 81 A2
Linaker Rd CV3 78 C5
Lincoln Ave CV10 28 B7
Lincoln Cl Warwick CV34 104 E1
Wellesbourne CV35 146 B1
Lincoln Ct CV32 110 A8
Lincoln Gr B37 33 A1
Lincoln St CV1 151 C4
Lincroft Cres CV5 60 E4
Lindale CV21 83 B4
Linden Ave CV35 146 C2
Linden Cl CV34 104 E2
Linden Lea CV12 39 B3
Lindera B77 4 A2
Lindfield The CV3 78 C8
Lindhurst Dr B94 88 C6
Lindisfarne Dr CV8 93 C4
Lindley Rd Bedworth CV12 38 D2
Coventry CV3 62 B2
Lindridge Cl B98 112 A6
Lindridge Dr B76 22 D6
Lindridge Rd B75,B76 13 B6
Lindsay Wlk CV47 132 F7
Lindsey Cres CV8 93 A1
Lineholt Cl B98 103 A3
Linen St CV34 108 D6
Linford Wlk CV2 50 F1
Lingard Rd B75 13 A5
Lingfield Cres CV37 129 F8
Lingfield Ct CV6 50 B4
Lingwood Dr CV10 28 F3
Links Rd CV6 61 B8
Linkway CV31 109 E6
Linley Rd CV47 147 A3
Linnell Rd CV21 83 C1
Linnet Cl CV3 78 D5
Linstock Way CV6 50 B4
Linthouse Wlk B77 9 C3
Lintly B77 10 A4
Linwood Dr CV2 50 F1
Lion Fields Ave CV5 60 B6
Liskeard Cl CV11 30 A5
Liskeard Rd CV35 132 D3
Lisle Ct 4 CV31 110 A6
Lisle Gdns 4 CV33 122 F8
Lismore Croft CV2 63 B7
Lister Rd CV9 12 C1
Lister St CV11 29 D3
Little Acre B97 102 B3
Little Back La NN11 126 B5
Little Brum CV9 11 B1
Little Church St
1 Coventry CV1 151 C4
Rugby CV21 83 A2
Little Cryfield CV4 76 C2
Little Duke St CV11 29 B4
Little Elborow St CV21 83 A2
Little Farm CV3 78 D5
Little Field CV2 62 A5
Little Forge Rd B98 103 B4
Little Gr CV22 83 B1
Little Heath Ind Est CV6 50 A2
Little Heath Prim Sch
CV6 49 F1
Little Lawford La CV21,
CV23 82 A4
Little London La CV23 68 A1
Little Park St CV1 151 C2
Little Pennington St 3
CV21 82 C2
Little Pittern CV35 132 B6
Little Pk CV47 147 A2
Little South St CV1 61 E3
Little Woods B97 102 C3
Littlemead Rd B90 69 E8
Littleshaw Croft B47 69 C4
Littleshaw La B47 69 C4
Littlethorpe CV3 78 D6
Littleton Cl
Kenilworth CV8 93 A7
Sutton Coldfield B76 13 A2
Littleton Croft 6 B91 71 C8
Littletons CE Fst Sch The
WR11 127 F1
Littlewood Cl 2 B91 71 B8
Littlewood Gn B80 103 B2
Littleworth
Chipping Campden GL55 135 A2
Henley-in-A B95 113 B4
Litton B77 4 B1
Liveridge Cl B93 71 F6
Liveridge Hill B95 113 B7
Livery St CV32 109 F8
Livingstone Ave CV23 81 C2
Livingstone Rd CV6 61 E7
Liza Ct CV21 83 B4
Llewellyn Rd CV31 110 A6
Lloyd Cl
Hampton Magna CV35 114 F3
Norton WR11 127 C2
Nuneaton CV11 29 D2
Lloyd Cres CV2 62 E3
Lloyd Rd CV21 83 B3
Loach Dr CV2 50 B4
Lobelia Cl LE10 31 E5
Lochmore Cl LE10 31 A8
Lochmore Dr LE10 31 A8
Lochmore Way LE10 31 A8
Lochsong Cl B77 9 B2
Lock Cl CV37 145 A2
Lock La CV34 108 D8
Locke Cl CV6 49 A1
Lockhart Cl CV8 93 A4
Lockheed Cl 8 CV31 109 F5
Lockhurst La CV6 61 D7
Locking Croft B35 22 B3
Locks The
Royal Leamington Spa
CV31 109 D7
Rugby CV21 84 A1
Loder Cl CV4 59 F3
Lodge Cl Atherstone CV9 19 A3
Hinckley LE10 32 A5
Lodge Cres CV34 108 D4
Lodge Croft B93 72 B6
Lodge Green La CV7 46 F2
Lodge Green La N CV7 46 E3
Lodge Rd Coventry CV3 62 B1
Knowle B93 72 B6
Rugby CV21 83 A2
Stratford-u-A CV37 144 C2
Logan Rd CV2 62 E7
Lole Cl CV6 50 A4
Lollard Croft CV3 77 D8
Lomita Cres B77 9 B4
Lomond Cl LE10 31 B8
Lomond Way CV10 28 C5
Lomsey Cl CV4 60 A1
London End NN11 134 E8
London Rd
Coventry, Cheylesmore CV3 77 E7
Coventry, Willenhall CV3 78 B5
Hinckley LE10 31 E8
Middleton B75,B78 13 D7
Moreton-in-M GL56 140 B3
Ryton-on-D CV8 79 B1
Shipston-on-S CV36 149 C2
Sutton Coldfield B75 7 A2
Willoughby CV23 117 C6
London Road Terr GL56 140 B3
Long Brook La CV7,CV8 73 E5
Long Close Ave CV5 60 B6
Long Close Wlk 1 B35 22 A3
Long Furlong CV22 100 A4
Long Hyde Rd WR11 127 F1
Long Itchington CE Prim Sch
CV47 115 E3
Long La CV5,CV7 48 D2
Long Lawford Prim Sch
CV23 82 A3
Long Leys Croft B46 23 B2
Long Leys Ct B46 23 B2
Long Marston Rd
Mickleton CV37,GL55 135 B8
Pebworth CV37 128 F2
Welford on A CV37 129 B5
Long Shoot The CV11 30 C6
Long St Atherstone CV9 18 B4
Bulkington CV12 40 D2
Dordon B78 11 A3
Longborough Cl B97 102 A3
Longcroft Cl B35 22 A2
Longdon Cl B98 103 A4
Longdon Croft B93 72 A8
Longdon Rd B93 72 A6
Longdown La CV23 117 D7
Longfellow Ave CV34 108 C4
Longfellow Cl B97 102 B4
Longfellow Rd CV2 62 C3
Longfield Ho CV6 62 A8
Longfield Rd CV31 110 B6
Longford Cl
Bidford-on-A B50 148 C3
Dorridge B93 72 B3
Longford Park Prim Sch
CV6 50 A3
Longford Rd
Bedworth CV7 50 A6
Coventry CV6 50 A4
Longford Sq CV6 50 A4
Longhope Cl B98 112 A6
Longleat Dr B90 70 E5
Longleat Gr 17 CV31 110 C6
Longley Ave B76 22 D5
Longrood Rd CV22 99 B3
Longstone Cl B90 71 B6
Longville Ct CV3 78 A6
Longwood Cl CV4 75 F6
Lonscale Dr CV3 77 B5
Lonsdale Rd CV32 106 B4
Lord Lytton Ave CV2 62 D2
Lord St CV5 60 F2
Lords La B80 103 C1
Lorenzo Cl CV3 78 D6
Lossiemouth Rd LE10 21 C1
Lothersdale B77 10 B4
Loudon Ave CV6 61 A5
Loudon Gate CV11 29 F1
Loughshaw B77 4 B1
Louisa Ward Cl CV23 115 C7
Love La LE10 32 A6
Love Lyne B97 102 A3
Loveday Cl CV9 12 B1
Loveday Dr CV32 105 E2
Lovelace Ave B91 71 D8
Lovell Cl CV7 50 A8
Lovell Rd CV12 39 A3
Loverock Cres CV21 83 C1
Lovetts Cl LE10 30 F8
Low Rd WR11 127 A6
Lowbrook La B90 69 D4
Lowdham B77 4 B1
Lowe Rd CV6 49 A2
Lower Ave CV31 109 F7
Lower Cape CV34 108 D8
Lower Cladswell La
B49 118 C5
Lower Eastern Green La
CV5 59 F4
Lower End Bubbenhall CV8 95 B3
Salford OX7 150 C2
Shutford OX15 139 A3
Lower Farm La OX17 133 F2
Lower Ford St CV1 151 D3
Lower Grinsty La B97 102 A4
Lower High St GL55 135 A2
Lower Hillmorton Rd
CV21 83 B1
Lower Holyhead Rd
CV1 151 A3
Lower House La CV9 11 A2
Lower Ladyes Hills CV8 93 A6
Lower Leam St CV31 110 B7
Lower Prec CV1 151 B3
Lower Rd CV7 51 C6
Lower St Rugby CV21 101 A4
Willoughby CV23 117 B6
Lower Villiers St 1
CV32 106 A1
Lowes Ave CV34 104 E1
Lowes La CV35 146 B1
Loweswater Cl CV11 30 A6
Loweswater Rd CV3 62 E1
Lowforce B77 4 B1
Lowry Cl CV12 39 A4
Lowther St CV2 61 F4
Loxley CE Com Prim Sch
CV35 130 F7
Loxley Cl Coventry CV2 50 D2
Wellesbourne CV35 146 B1
Loxley Ct CV2 50 D2
Loxley Fields CV35 130 F7
Loxley Rd Alveston CV37 121 D1
Stratford-u-A CV37 145 B1
Loxley Way CV32 106 A2
Lucas Ct
Royal Leamington Spa
CV32 109 D8
Rugby CV21 83 A2
Lucas Ho CV32 105 F2
Lucas Rd LE10 31 D6
Luce Cl B35 22 B4
Lucerne Cl CV2 50 C3
Lucian Cl CV2 63 B7
Luddington Rd CV37 129 E8
Ludford Cl Ansley CV10 27 A2
Stratford-u-A CV37 144 B2
Ludford Rd CV10 28 C6
Ludgate Cl B46 23 B3
Ludlow Cl CV37 33 C2
Ludlow Dr OX16 139 F4
Ludlow Rd CV5 61 A2
Ludlow's La CV35 114 C7
Ludworth Ave B37 44 B8
Luff Cl CV3 78 B8
Lugtrout La B91 56 A6
Lulworth Pk CV8 93 C6
Lumley Gr B37 33 D2
Lumsden Cl CV2 62 F8
Lunar Cl CV4 76 D5
Lundy View B36 33 B6
Lunn Ave CV8 92 E3
Lunn Poly Ho 3 CV32 105 F1
Lunt The* CV8 77 E3
Lupin Cl LE10 31 D5
Lupton Ave CV3 77 C7
Luscombe Rd CV2 62 E8
Luther Way CV5 59 F4
Lutterworth Rd
Brinklow CV23 64 C2
Churchover CV23 67 B3
Coventry CV2 62 C5
Hinckley LE10 32 C3
Nuneaton CV11 40 C8
Pailton CV23 54 B1
Shawell LE17 68 B3
Wolvey LE10 41 C3
Luxor La CV5 59 B8
Lychgate Cl LE10 32 A5
Lychgate La LE10 32 C5
Lydd Croft B35 22 B4
Lydford Cl CV2 62 C7
Lydgate Ct Bedworth CV12 39 A4
Nuneaton CV11 29 C3
Lydgate Rd CV6 61 B5
Lydstep Gr CV31 110 C7
Lye Green Rd CV35 113 F4
Lyecroft Ave B37 33 D2
Lymesy St CV3 77 D7
Lymington Cl CV6 61 D8
Lymington Dr CV6 50 B6
Lymore Croft CV2 63 A8
Lynbrook Cl B47 69 A7
Lynbrook Rd CV5 76 D8
Lynch The Nuneaton CV11 29 D2
Polesworth B78 4 C1
Lynchgate Ct CV4 76 C6
Lynchgate Ho CV4 76 C6
Lynchgate Rd CV4 76 C6
Lyndale B77 9 C3
Lyndale Cl CV5 60 C3
Lyndale Rd CV5 60 C3
Lyndhurst Cl Coventry CV6 50 B6
Hinckley LE10 32 A7
Lyndhurst Croft CV5 59 C4
Lyndhurst Rd CV21 83 C1
Lyndon Croft B37 44 B7
Lyndon Ct CV32 109 E8
Lyne Ho 1 CV2 62 D8
Lyneham Gdns B76 22 B6
Lyng Cl CV5 60 A4
Lyng Hall Sch CV2 62 C6
Lynmouth Cl CV11 29 E5
Lynmouth Rd CV2 62 E8
Lynton Cl CV34 104 E1
Lynton Rd CV6 49 F1
Lynwood Wlk 10 CV31 110 C6
Lysander Cl CV35 146 B1
Lysander Ct CV37 145 A1
Lyster Cl CV34 108 B8
Lythall Cl CV31 110 F5
Lythalls La CV6 49 E2
Lythalls Lane Ind Est CV6 49 E1
Lytham B77 4 B3
Lytham Cl B76 22 B6
Lytham Rd CV22 82 C1
Lyttelton Rd CV34 108 E8
Lyttleton Cl CV3 63 A1

M

M40 Distribution Pk
CV35 146 A1
Macadam Cl NN11 117 F3
Macaulay Rd
Coventry CV2 62 D4
Rugby CV22 99 C4
Macbeth App CV34 109 D4
Macbeth Cl CV22 99 C3
Macdonald Rd CV2 62 D3
Macefield Cl CV2 50 D2
Mackenzie Cl CV5 60 A7
Mackley Way CV33 123 E6
Madam's Hill Rd B90 70 D7
Madden Pl CV22 82 B1
Madeira Croft CV5 60 E2
Madrona B77 4 A2
Maffey Ct CV22 83 A1
Magdalen Cl CV37 129 D2
Magdalen Rd CV23 117 C6
Magna Pk LE17 55 B3
Magnet La CV22 99 B4
Magnolia B77 4 A2
Magnolia Cl CV3 77 B5
Magnus B77 9 C3
Magpie Ho CV5 59 D5
Magpie La CV7 73 E6
Maguire Ind Est CV4 75 F8
Magyar Cres CV11 40 A8
Maidavale Cres CV3 77 C4
Maidenhair Dr CV23 83 B4
Maidenhead Cl CV37 145 A2
Maidenhead Rd CV37 145 A2
Maidwell Dr B90 70 E8
Main Rd Ansty CV7 51 D3
Austrey CV9 3 A1
Baxterley CV9 17 A4
Binton CV37 120 A1
Broughton OX15 139 E1
Claybrooke Magna LE17 43 C3
Kilsby CV23 101 C2
Lower Quinton CV37 129 E2
Meriden CV7 58 D8
Newton Regis B79 2 B1
Main St Aston le W NN11 134 F5
Badby NN11 126 F5
Birdingbury CV23 115 F7
Bourton on D CV23 97 C1
Burmington CV36 141 A8
Church Lench WR11 127 A6
Claydon OX17 134 B5
Cleeve Prior WR11 128 A4
Clifton u D CV23 83 C3
Easenhall CV23 65 C2
Frankton CV23 97 B1
Grandborough CV23 116 F6
Hanwell OX17 139 F6
Harborough Magna CV23 66 A2
Higham on t H CV13 21 A2
Long Compton CV36,OX7 141 C3
Long Lawford CV23 82 A3
Mollington OX17 134 A2
Monks Kirby CV23 53 C2
Newton CV23 68 A1
North Newington OX15 139 D2
Norton Lindsey CV35 114 C2
Offenham WR11 127 D1
Orton-on-t-H CV9 6 B2
Oxhill CV35 137 F8
Rugby CV22 99 B4
Rugby, Newbold on Avon
CV21 82 B4
Shawell LE17 68 B3
Sibford Gower OX15 142 D8
South Littleton WR11 127 F1
Stoke Golding CV13 21 B4
Stretton u F CV23 65 A4
Thurlaston CV23 98 C2
Tiddington CV37 145 C2
Tysoe CV35 138 B7
Willey CV23 54 C3
Willoughby CV23 117 C6
Withybrook CV7 52 C3
Wolston CV8 80 A2
Wroxton OX15 139 D4
Makepeace Ave CV34 104 F1
Malam Cl CV4 60 A1
Maldens The CV36 149 C3
Malham Cl CV11 30 A2
Malham Rd Tamworth B77 4 B1
Warwick CV34 104 F1
Malins The CV34 109 B6
Mallaby Cl B90 70 A8
Mallard Ave CV10 28 C6
Mallard Cl CV37 144 B3
Mallard Dr LE10 31 A7
Mallard Rd B80 103 C2
Mallender Dr B93 71 F6
Mallerin Croft CV10 28 B5
Mallory Dr CV34 108 D7
Mallory Rd
Bishops Tachbrook CV33 122 E8
Lighthorne Heath CV33 123 D2
Mallory Way CV6 49 E4
Mallow Way CV23 83 B4
Malmesbury Rd CV6 49 A3
Malt House Cl
Broom B50 148 B4
Northend CV47 133 B7
Malt House La
Church Lench WR11 127 A6
Northend CV47 133 B7
Malthouse Cl Ansley CV10 27 A2
Harvington WR11 127 D3
Malthouse La
Earlswood B94 86 E7
Kenilworth CV8 92 E6
Long Compton CV36 141 C3
Shutford OX15 139 A3
Malthouse Row B37 44 A8
Maltings Ct 2 CV37 144 C2
Maltings The
Nuneaton CV11 29 E5
Royal Leamington Spa
CV32 105 F2

Maltings The continued
Studley B80 ....103 B2
Maltmill La B49 ......143 B2
Malvern Ave
Nuneaton CV10 ....28 B3
Rugby CV22 ....83 B1
Malvern Dr B76 ......22 A8
Malvern Ho CV5 .....59 D4
Malvern Rd
Balsall Common CV7 ...74 C6
Coventry CV5 ....60 F4
Redditch B97 ....102 B4
Manby Rd B35 ....22 A4
Mancetter Rd
Atherstone CV9 ....19 A3
Nuneaton CV10 ....28 D7
Manchester Ct 4 GL56 .140 A3
Mandarin Cl LE10 ....31 A6
Mander Gr CV34 ......108 C4
Manderley Cl CV5 ....59 C5
Mandrake Cl CV6 .....49 D4
Manfield Ave CV2 ....63 A7
Mann's Cl CV8 ....96 A4
Manning Wlk 3 CV21 ..83 A2
Mannings Cl OX15 ....142 D8
Manor Barns CV36 ...136 B6
Manor Cl
Charwelton NN11 ......126 D2
Grendon CV9 ....11 A1
Hinckley LE10 ....31 C5
Manor Court Ave CV11 .29 B5
Manor Court Mews CV11 29 A5
Manor Court Rd CV11 ..29 A5
Manor Ct
Cleeve Prior WR11 ....128 A4
Dorridge B93 ....71 F2
Ettington CV37 ....131 A3
Fenny Compton CV47 ..133 D7
Kenilworth CV8 ....93 A6
Royal Leamington Spa
CV31 ....109 F7
Manor Dr
Stretton on D CV23 ....96 C3
Ullenhall B80 ....112 D4
Wilmcote CV37 ....120 C4
Manor Est CV8 ....79 F3
Manor Farm WR11 ...127 F1
Manor Farm Cl CV23 ..101 B1
Manor Farm Cotts CV37 129 C7
Manor Farm Craft Ctr★
B94 ....69 F2
Manor Farm Rd CV36 ..136 F6
Manor Gn CV37 ....145 B1
Manor Hall Mews CV3 .78 D6
Manor House Cl
Aston Flamville LE10 ...32 E6
Rugby CV21 ....82 B4
Manor House Dr CV1 ..151 B2
Manor House La
Astwood Bank B96 .....102 C2
Water Orton B46 ....23 B3
Manor La Claverdon CV35 114 A4
Clifton u D CV23 ....84 A3
Ettington CV37 ....131 A3
Honiley CV8,CV35 ......91 A5
Kineton CV35 ....132 B5
Shipston-on-S CV36 ...149 C3
Wroxall CV35 ....90 F4
Manor Mews B80 .....103 C2
Manor Orch
Harbury CV33 ....123 E6
Horley OX15 ....139 D4
Manor Park Com Sch
CV11 ....29 A5
Manor Park Prim Sch
CV3 ....77 D7
Manor Park Rd CV11 ..29 A5
Manor Pk Claydon OX17 .134 B5
Harvington WR11 ......127 D3
Manor Prim Sch B78 ..8 C3
Manor Rd Atherstone CV9 .18 C3
Bishops Itchington CV47 .124 A4
Claybrooke Magna LE17 .43 B3
Coventry CV1 ....151 B1
Dorridge B93 ....71 F3
Harbury CV33 ....123 F6
Kenilworth CV8 ....92 F6
Loxley CV35 ....130 F7
Royal Leamington Spa
CV32 ....106 B3
Rugby CV22 ....83 A2
South Littleton WR11 ..127 F1
Staverton NN11 ....126 D8
Stockton CV47 ....147 C4
Stratford-u-A CV37 ....145 B1
Studley B80 ....103 C2
Wythall B47 ....69 A3
Manor Ind Est CV9 ...18 C4
Manor Terr CV37 .....93 A6
Manor View CV8 ......79 F3
Manor Way LE10 .....31 D5
Mansard Ct B46 ......34 A4
Manse Cl CV7 ....39 A1
Manse Gdns B80 .....103 C2
Mansel St CV6 ....61 E8
Mansell Rd B97 ......102 B4
Mansell St CV37 .....144 C2
Mansfield Ho B37 ....33 D3
Mansion Ho Flats CV5 .132 B5
Mansion St 1 LE10 ..31 D8
Mansions CV47 ......124 A4
Mansley Bsns Ctr The
CV37 ....144 B3
Manston Dr CV35 ....146 B1
Manta Rd B77 ....9 B3

Mantilla Dr CV3 ....77 B5
Manton Croft B93 .....71 E3
Mantua CV37 ....145 A2
Maple Ave CV7 ....39 B1
Maple Cl LE10 ....31 E5
Maple Dr B78 ....15 B4
Maple Gr Rugby CV21 ..83 A2
Stratford-u-A CV37 ....144 C3
Warwick CV34 ....105 A1
Maple Leaf Dr B37 ...44 B8
Maple Rd Nuneaton CV10 .28 E5
Royal Leamington Spa
CV31 ....109 F6
Maple Rise B77 ....4 A2
Maple Wlk 4 B37 ....33 B2
Maplebeck Cl CV5 ....61 A3
Maples The CV12 .....38 E2
Mapleton Rd CV6 .....60 F8
Maplewood B76 ......22 A8
Mapperley Cl CV2 ....63 A8
Mappleborough Green CE
Prim Sch B98 ....112 A5
Marble Alley B80 .....103 C2
March Cl CV22 ....83 A1
March Rd
Mollington OX17 ......133 F2
Warmington OX17 .....133 E2
March Way CV3 ......78 D7
Marchant Rd LE10 ....31 C8
Marchfont Cl CV11 ...30 A1
Marcos Dr B36 ....22 F1
Marcroft Pl CV31 .....110 D6
Mardol Cl CV2 ....62 D7
Marfield Cl B76 ......22 A6
Margaret Ave CV12 ...39 B3
Margaret Cl CV33 ....123 F6
Margaret Rd CV9 .....18 C4
Margeson Cl CV2 .....62 E2
Margetts Cl CV8 .....92 F4
Marie Brock Cl CV4 ..60 B1
Marie Cl CV9 ....19 A4
Marie Corelli Sch CV37 .144 B2
Marigold Dr LE10 ....31 E5
Marina Cl CV4 ....75 E7
Marion Rd CV6 ....61 D7
Mark Antony Dr CV34 .109 D4
Mark Cnr Baginton CV8 .77 F2
7 Royal Leamington Spa
CV31 ....109 F6
Market End Cl CV12 ..38 C2
Market Hill CV47 .....147 A2
Market Mall 4 CV21 ..83 A2
Market Pl Alcester B49 .143 A2
Hinckley LE10 ....31 D8
Nuneaton CV11 ....29 C4
Rugby CV21 ....83 A2
Shipston-on-S CV36 ...149 C3
Warwick CV34 ....108 E6
Market Sq CV35 .....132 B6
Market St Atherstone CV9 .18 B4
Polesworth B78 ....5 A1
Rugby CV21 ....83 A2
Warwick CV34 ....108 D6
Market Way CV1 .....151 B2
Markham Dr CV31 ....110 B3
Marks Mews 7 CV34 ..108 E6
Marlborough Cl LE10 ..32 B7
Tamworth B77 ....9 B2
Marlborough Ct B75 ..13 A4
Marlborough Dr CV31 .110 D5
Marlborough Rd
Coventry CV2 ....62 A3
Nuneaton CV11 ....29 B3
Rugby CV22 ....99 C4
Marlborough Way B77 .9 C4
Marlcroft CV3 ....78 E5
Marleigh Rd B50 .....148 B3
Marlene Croft B37 ...33 C1
Marler Rd CV4 ....75 F7
Marlin B77 ....9 B3
Marlissa Dr CV6 .....49 E2
Marloes Wlk CV31 ...110 C6
Marlow Cl CV5 ....60 B4
Marlow Rd CV9 ......16 B3
Marlowe Cl
Banbury OX16 ....139 F3
Nuneaton CV10 ....27 C3
Marlston Wlk CV5 ....60 B4
Marlwood Cl CV6 .....49 E4
Marne Cl CV34 ....109 A8
Marner Cres CV6 ....61 B5
Marner Rd Bedworth CV12 39 A3
Nuneaton CV10 ....29 B1
Marnhull Cl CV2 .....62 F4
Marram Ct CV37 .....144 C2
Marrick B77 ....4 B1
Marriners La CV5 ....60 B5
Marriott Rd
Bedworth CV12 ....38 D2
Coventry CV6 ....61 A4
Marsdale Dr CV10 ...28 C3
Marsett B77 ....10 B4
Marsh Cl WR11 ......127 D4
Marsh Ct 1 GL56 ....140 A3
Marsh Ho CV2 ....63 A7
Marsh La
Bradnock's Marsh B92 .57 D5
Curdworth B76 ....23 D5
Hampton-in-A B92 ....57 B6
Water Orton B46 ......23 C3
Marsh Rd CV37 ......120 B5
Marshall Ave CV36 ..149 C3
Marshall Lake Rd B90 .70 D8
Marshall Rd CV7 .....49 F8
Marshalls Cl OX15 ...138 F5
Marsham Cl CV34 ....109 B8
Marshbrook Cl CV2 ..50 E3
Marshdale Ave CV6 ..49 E3
Marshfield B90 ....70 B5

Marshfield Dr CV4 ...76 D2
Marston Ave CV33 ...123 D2
Marston Cl CV32 .....106 B2
Marston Dr B37 ......33 A5
Marston Green Jun & Inf
Schs B37 ....44 A7
Marston Hill CV47 ....125 F4
Marston La
Bedworth CV12 ....39 D5
Nuneaton CV10 ....39 E8
Wishaw B76 ....14 E1
Marten Cl CV35 ......108 A4
Martin Cl Coventry CV5 .59 E4
Stratford-u-A CV37 ....145 A3
Martin La CV22 ......99 B4
Martindale Rd CV7 ...50 C8
Martinique Sq CV34 ..108 D6
Martins Dr CV9 ......12 C1
Martins Rd CV12 ....38 E1
Martlesham Sq B35 ..22 A4
Martley B98 ....103 A4
Martley Croft B91 ...71 B8
Marton Rd
Birdingbury CV23 .....115 E7
Long Itchington CV47 ..115 D5
Martyrs' Cl The CV3 ..77 D8
Marwood Cl CV11 ....39 E7
Mary Arden's Ho★
CV37 ....120 C5
Mary Herbert St CV3 .77 D7
Mary Slessor St CV3 .78 D7
Marystow Cl CV5 ....60 B8
Marywell Cl LE10 ....21 C1
Masefield Ave CV34 ..108 C4
Masefield Rd CV37 ..145 A1
Maseley Ct CV37 ....129 D2
Mason Ave CV32 ....106 C3
Mason Cl
Bidford-on-A B50 .....148 C3
Redditch B97 ....102 B4
Mason Ct LE10 ....31 B8
Mason La B94 ....69 F1
Mason Rd Coventry CV6 .49 F1
Redditch B97 ....102 B4
Masons Cl CV37 .....120 C5
Masons Rd CV37 ....144 B2
Masons Way CV37 ...144 B2
Masser Rd CV6 ......49 D4
Massey Sham Ave GL56 140 C3
Master's Yd CV23 ....115 F7
Masters Rd CV31 ....110 A4
Mathe Croft CV31 ...110 C5
Matlock Cl CV21 .....83 B4
Matlock Rd CV1 .....61 D6
Matterson Rd CV6 ...61 A5
Matthews Cl CV37 ...145 A2
Maud Rd B46 ....23 D3
Maudslay Rd CV5 ...60 E2
Maureen Cl CV4 .....59 C1
Maurice Mead Ct 12
CV31 ....110 A6
Mavor Dr CV12 ......38 D1
Mawby's La DE12 ...3 C4
Mawnan Cl CV7 .....50 B8
Max Rd CV6 ....60 F5
Maxstoke Cl Meriden CV7 .46 B1
Tamworth B77 ....9 B2
Maxstoke Croft B90 ..70 C8
Maxstoke Ct B46 ....34 A2
Maxstoke Gdns CV31 .109 F6
Maxstoke La Coleshill B46 34 A3
Meriden CV7 ....46 B2
May Farm Cl B47 ....69 A6
May La Ebrington GL55 ..135 E2
Hollywood B47 ....69 A7
Rugby CV22 ....82 B1
May St CV6 ....61 E8
May's Hill B95 ....113 A4
Mayama Rd B78 .....8 C4
Maybird Ctr CV37 ...144 C2
Maybird Rd
Stratford-u-A CV37 ....144 C2
Sutton Coldfield B76 ..22 A5
Maycock Rd CV6 ....61 D7
Mayfair Dr
Drayton Bassett B78 ..9 A4
Nuneaton CV10 ....27 C2
Mayfield B77 ....10 B4
Mayfield Ave CV37 ...145 A2
Mayfield Cl
Bedworth CV12 ....39 B3
9 Royal Leamington Spa
CV31 ....110 C6
Mayfield Ct CV37 ....145 A2
Mayfield Dr
Henley-in-A B95 ......113 A5
Kenilworth CV8 ....93 C4
Mayfield Rd Coventry CV5 .61 A1
Nuneaton CV11 ....29 E2
Southam CV47 ....147 A3
Mayflower Dr CV2 ...62 E2
Mayhurst Cl B47 ....69 C6
Mayhurst Rd B47 ...69 B6
Maynard Ave
Bedworth CV12 ....49 D8
Warwick CV34 ....109 A7
Mayne Cl CV35 ......114 F3
Mayo Dr CV8 ....93 A4
Mayo Rd CV36 ......149 C4
Mayor's Croft CV4 ...76 B7
Maypole La CV9 .....11 B1
Maypole Rd B79 .....5 C2
Mayswood Rd B95 ..113 A3
Maythorn Ave B76 ..22 A6
Maythorn Gr 4 B91 ..71 B8
Maytree Cl B37 ....33 A2

Mc Kinnell Cres CV21 ..83 C1
McDonnell Dr CV6 ...49 F6
McMahon Rd CV12 ..49 E8
Mead Cl 15 GL56 .....140 A3
Mead The OX17 .....133 F2
Meadfoot Rd CV3 ....78 E6
Meadow Cl Ansty CV7 .51 D3
Hockley Heath B94 ....88 C6
Kingsbury B78 ....15 B3
Lighthorne CV35 ......123 B4
Royal Leamington Spa
CV32 ....106 C4
Stratford-u-A CV37 ....144 B2
Stretton on D CV23 ....97 A3
Wolvey LE10 ....41 B2
Meadow Croft Arley CV7 .26 C1
Wythall B47 ....69 A3
Meadow Crofts CV47 ..124 B5
Meadow Ct CV11 ....29 B4
Meadow Dr
Hampton-in-A B92 ....57 B7
Hinckley LE10 ....32 A7
Meadow Gdns CV9 ..17 B4
Meadow Green Prim Sch
B47 ....69 A3
Meadow Ho 5 CV1 ..61 B3
Meadow La B94 .....89 D3
Meadow Lea CV37 ..144 B2
Meadow Pleck La B90 .70 A6
Meadow Rd Alcester B49 143 A3
Coventry CV6 ....49 B4
Henley-in-A B95 ......113 B4
Hurley CV9 ....16 B3
Nuneaton CV10 ....28 A8
Rugby CV21 ....82 C3
Southam CV47 ....147 A3
Wolston CV8 ....80 A2
Wythall B47 ....69 A3
Meadow Rise
Balsall Common CV7 ...74 C7
Ullenhall B95 ....112 E6
Meadow St
Atherstone CV9 ....18 B4
Coventry CV1 ....151 A2
Nuneaton CV11 ....29 B5
Meadow Sweet Rd
CV37 ....144 C3
Meadow View WR11 .127 F6
Meadow Way
Fenny Compton CV47 ..133 E7
Harborough Magna CV23 66 A2
Meadowcroft Cl CV4 .75 F8
Meadows Sch The CV4 .59 E3
Meadows The
Bidford-on-A B50 .....148 B3
Hinckley LE10 ....32 A7
Leek Wootton CV35 ...105 A7
Meadowside CV11 ...40 B8
Meadowsweet CV23 ..83 B4
Meadway CV2 ....62 B6
Meadway N CV2 .....62 B6
Meadway The
Hinckley LE10 ....31 F7
Redditch B97 ....102 B4
Mearse La WR7 .....118 B5
Medhurst Cl CV22 ...99 B2
Medina Rd CV6 ......49 E1
Medland Ave CV3 ...76 F5
Medley Gr CV31 .....109 D3
Meer End Rd CV8 ...74 D1
Meer St CV37 ....145 A2
Meerhill Ave B90 ....71 A6
Meeting House La CV7 .74 C6
Meeting La B49 .....143 B2
Meir Rd B98 ....103 B4
Melbourne Cl CV11 ..39 E8
Melbourne Ct 3 CV12 .38 F2
Melbourne Rd CV5 ..61 A2
Meldrum Ct CV47 ...132 F7
Meldrum Rd CV10 ...28 D4
Melfort Cl Coventry CV3 .62 F2
Nuneaton CV10 ....28 C5
Melksham Sq B35 ...22 A3
Mellish Ct CV22 .....82 C1
Mellish Rd CV22 ....82 C1
Mellor Rd CV21 .....101 A4
Mellowdew Rd CV2 ..62 C4
Mellowship Rd CV5 ..59 D5
Mellwaters B77 ......10 B4
Melmerby B77 ....10 B4
Melrose Ave CV12 ..49 D8
Melrose Cl LE10 .....31 B8
Melton Rd CV32 .....106 B4
Melville Cl Bedworth CV12 50 A8
Rugby CV22 ....82 C1
Melville Rd CV1 ......61 A3
Memorial Rd CV47 ..133 D7
Menai Wlk B37 ......33 B4
Mendip Dr CV10 ....28 B3
Mendip Way B77 ....4 B1
Meon Cl CV37 ....129 D1
Meon Rd GL55 ......135 C2
Mercer Ave Coventry CV2 .62 A5
Water Orton B46 .....23 A3
Mercer Ct 4 CV22 ..100 C4
Mercers Mdw CV7 ..49 A6
Merchants Ct 5 CV32 .106 A1
Mercia Ave CV8 .....92 F4
Mercia Bsns Village CV4 .75 F6
Mercia Ho CV1 ......151 B3
Mercia Way CV34 ...109 B7
Mercian Pk B77 .....4 A2
Mercian Way B77 ...4 B2
Mercot Cl B98 ....103 A3
Mercury Ct B77 .....4 A2
Mere Ave B35 ....22 B3
Mere La LE10 ....42 B2

Meredith Rd CV2 ....62 D2
Merestone Cl CV47 ..147 A3
Merevale Ave
Hinckley LE10 ....31 C7
Nuneaton CV11 ....29 A4
Merevale Cl Hinckley LE10 31 C7
Redditch B98 ....103 B4
Merevale Ct CV11 ...29 A4
Merevale La CV9 ....17 C4
Merevale Rd CV9 ...12 B1
Merevale View CV9 .18 B4
Merganser B77 .....10 A3
Meriden Bsns Pk CV5 .59 B8
Meriden CE Prim Sch
CV7 ....46 C1
Meriden Cl B98 ......112 A6
Meriden Dr B37 .....33 A6
Meriden Hill CV7 ....58 E8
Meriden Rd Berkswell CV7 58 C4
Fillongley CV7 ....36 B1
Hampton-in-A B92 ....57 C7
Meriden St CV1 .....61 B3
Merlin Ave CV10 ....28 B6
Merlin Cl Birmingham B35 .22 A3
Rugby CV21,CV23 ....83 B4
Tamworth B77 ....10 A3
Merrick Ct LE10 .....31 F5
Merrifield Gdns LE10 .31 E5
Merrington Cl 5 B91 .71 C8
Merrivale Rd CV5 ...60 E3
Merryfields Way CV2 .50 F1
Mersey Rd CV12 ....40 A3
Merstone Specl Sch B37 33 A1
Merttens Dr CV22 ...82 C1
Merynton Ave CV4 ..76 E5
Meschines St CV3 ..77 D6
Metalloys Ind Est B76 .22 B5
Metcalfe Cl OX15 ...139 E4
Metchley Croft B90 ..70 F6
Mews Rd CV32 ......109 D8
Mews The Atherstone CV9 18 B4
Bedworth CV12 ....39 B2
Kenilworth CV8 ....92 E3
Rugby CV21 ....84 A1
Wootton Wawen B95 ..113 B2
Mica Cl B77 ....4 A2
Michael Blanning Gdns
B93 ....71 E3
Michael Drayton Jun Sch
CV10 ....28 A8
Michaelmas Rd CV3 .151 B1
Michel Ho CV1 ......151 C4
Michell Cl CV3 ......78 B8
Mickle Mdw B46 ....23 B3
Micklehill Dr B90 ....70 B8
Mickleton B77 ....10 B4
Mickleton Cl B98 ....102 C4
Mickleton Dr CV35 ..114 F5
Mickleton Prim Sch
GL55 ....135 B6
Mickleton Rd
Coventry CV5 ....77 A8
Ilmington CV36 ....136 A7
Middelburg Cl CV11 ..30 A1
Middle Bickenhill La B92 45 A4
Middle Hill OX15 ....142 D4
Middle La
Nether Whitacre B46 ..24 C3
Shotteswell OX17 .....139 E8
Wroxton OX15 ....139 B4
Middle Lock La CV35 .114 E5
Middle Rd CV33 .....123 D4
Middle Ride CV3 ....78 E5
Middle St Ilmington CV36 136 B4
Tredington CV37 .....136 E7
Middleborough Rd CV1 151 B4
Middlecotes CV4 ....60 B1
Middlefield Ave B93 ..72 B4
Middlefield Dr CV3 ..63 B1
Middlefield La CV37 ..130 E1
Middlefield Pl CV3 ...63 A1
Middlemarch Bsns Pk
CV3 ....78 C2
Middlemarch Rd
Coventry CV6 ....61 C7
Nuneaton CV10 ....29 B1
Middlemarch Sch CV10 .29 B1
Middlemore Cl B80 ..103 B2
Middlesmoor B77 ...10 B4
Middleton Cl CV35 ..138 B4
Middleton Hall★ B78 .8 C1
Middleton La B78 ...13 F6
Middletown
Moreton Morrell CV35 .122 F3
Studley B80 ....103 B1
Middletown La B96 ..103 B1
Midland Air Mus★ CV8 .78 B3
Midland Oak Trad Est
CV6 ....49 E2
Midland Rd Coventry CV6 .61 E5
Nuneaton CV11 ....29 A5
Midland Trad Est CV21 .83 A3
Midpoint Park Ind Est
B76 ....22 C5
Milburn B77 ....10 B4
Milburn Hill Rd CV4 ..76 B6
Milby Ct CV11 ....29 C3
Milby Dr CV11 ......30 A7
Milby Prim Sch CV11 .29 F8
Milcote Cl B98 ......103 A4
Milcote Manor Cotts
CV37 ....129 C6
Milcote Rd CV37 ....129 C6
Mildmay Cl CV37 ...144 C1
Mile End B94 ....87 C2
Mile La CV1 ....151 C1
Mile Tree La CV2 ...50 F7
Milebush Ave B36 ...22 D1

Mil – New 171

Miles Mdw Coventry CV6 ..50 B1
Newbold-on-S CV37 .....130 E1
Milestone Dr CV22 .....99 C4
Milestone Ho 2 CV1 ....61 B2
Milestone Rd CV37 .....130 B8
Milfoil Cl LE10 ....30 F7
Milford Cl Allesley CV5 ...60 B6
Redditch B97 ....102 B3
Milford Ct CV31 ....110 A8
Milford Gr B90 ....71 C7
Milford St CV10 ....29 B2
Milking La B95 ....113 B4
Mill Bank B46 ....25 B2
Mill Bank Mews CV8 ....93 B6
Mill Cl Braunston NN11 ..117 D5
Broom B50 ....148 A4
Coventry CV2 ....50 B3
Hollywood B47 ....69 A7
Norton Lindsey CV35 ....114 C2
Nuneaton CV11 ....29 F1
Southam CV47 ....147 A3
Wolston CV8 ....79 F3
Mill Cotts B50 ....148 A4
Mill Cres Kineton CV35 ..132 B6
Kingsbury B78 ....15 B2
Southam CV47 ....147 A3
Mill Ct CV36 ....149 C3
Mill End CV8 ....93 A6
Mill Farm Cl CV22 ....99 B2
Mill Field CV37 ....128 F2
Mill Hill CV8 ....77 D3
Mill House Cl CV32 ....109 C8
Mill House Dr CV32 ....109 C8
Mill House Terr CV32 ...109 C8
Mill La Alcester B49 .....143 A1
Aston Cantlow B49,B95 ...119 F6
Atherstone CV9 ....19 A3
Barford CV35 ....122 A7
Bentley Heath B93 ....71 F4
Bramcote CV11 ....40 F8
Broom B50 ....148 A4
Bulkington CV12 ....40 A3
Chipping Warden OX17 ...134 F3
Cleeve Prior WR11 ......128 A4
Clifton u D CV23 ....83 C3
Coventry CV3 ....62 F2
Cubbington CV32 ....106 F5
Drayton OX15 ....139 E4
Earlswood B94 ....86 B8
Fazeley B78 ....9 A4
Fenny Compton CV47 ....133 D7
Fillongley CV7 ....36 B3
Great Alne B49 ....119 E6
Halford CV36 ....136 F8
Harbury CV33 ....123 F7
Kineton CV35 ....132 B6
Lapworth B94 ....89 C4
Lowsonford, Finwood
CV35 ....113 E7
Lowsonford, Turner's Green
CV35 ....113 F8
Mickleton GL55 ....135 B6
Newbold-on-S CV37 .....130 F1
Shrewley CV35 ....114 C6
Stratford-u-A CV37 ......145 A1
Tredington CV36 ....136 F6
Welford on A CV37 ......129 A7
Wolvey LE10 ....41 C3
Wythall B47,B94 ....69 B1
Mill Pleck B80 ....103 C2
Mill Pool La B93 ....89 A8
Mill Race La CV6 ....50 B3
Mill Race View CV9 ......12 B1
Mill Rd
Napton on t H CV47 .....125 C8
Royal Leamington Spa
CV31 ....110 A8
Rugby CV21 ....83 B3
Southam CV47 ....147 A3
Mill Row LE10 ....41 C3
Mill St Bedworth CV12 ....39 B3
Coventry CV1 ....151 A3
Harbury CV33 ....123 E7
Kineton CV35 ....132 B6
Nuneaton CV11 ....29 C4
Royal Leamington Spa
CV31 ....110 A7
Shipston-on-S CV36 .....149 C3
Warwick CV34 ....108 F6
Mill Terr CV12 ....39 B5
Mill Wlk CV11 ....29 C4
Millais Cl CV12 ....39 A4
Millbank CV34 ....105 B1
Millbeck CV21 ....83 B4
Millennium Way CV8 .....79 F3
Miller's Bank B50 ......148 A4
Millers Cl Dunchurch CV22 99 A2
Lower Boddington NN11 ..134 E6
Welford on A CV37 ......129 B6
Millers Dale Cl CV21 ....83 B4
Millers Gn LE10 ....31 F6
Millers La Hornton OX15 .139 B8
Monks Kirby CV23 ....53 B2
Millers Rd CV34 ....108 E8
Millers Wharf B78 ....5 A1
Millfield CV31 ....110 A8
Millfield Cl CV37 ....129 D2
Millfield Prim Sch B78 .....9 A4
Millfields Ave CV21 .....100 C4
Millholme Cl CV47 .....147 B2
Millhouse Cl CV6 ....61 F7
Milliners Ct CV9 ....18 B4
Millison Gr B90 ....71 A7
Mills La OX15 ....139 D4
Millway Dr 1 CV33 .....122 F8
Milner Cl CV12 ....40 E2
Milner Cres CV2 ....50 E1
Milner Dr B79 ....4 C4
Milrose Way CV4 ....75 F8
Milton Ave CV34 ....108 C5
Milton Cl Bedworth CV12 .39 D1
Bentley Heath B93 ....71 F4
Redditch B97 ....102 B4
Milton Rd B93 ....71 F4
Milton St CV2 ....62 A4
Milverton Cres 1 CV32 .105 E1
Milverton Cres W 3
CV32 ....105 E1
Milverton Ct CV32 ......109 E8
Milverton Hill CV32 ....109 E8
Milverton House Prep Sch
CV11 ....29 D3
Milverton Lodge 2
CV32 ....105 E1
Milverton Prim Sch
CV32 ....105 E1
Milverton Rd
Coventry CV2 ....50 D2
Knowle B93 ....72 C5
Milverton Terr CV32 ....109 E8
Miners Wlk B78 ....4 C1
Minerva Mews B49 .....143 A2
Minions Cl CV9 ....18 B4
Miniva Dr B76 ....13 A2
Minster Cl
Hampton Magna CV35 ....114 F3
Knowle B93 ....72 B8
Minster Rd CV1 ....61 B3
Minton Rd CV2 ....50 E1
Minworth Ind Pk B76 ....22 B5
Minworth Jun & Inf Sch
B76 ....22 D5
Minworth Rd B46 ....23 A3
Mira Dr CV10 ....20 B2
Miranda Cl CV3 ....78 D7
Miranda Dr CV34 ....109 E2
Mistral Cl LE10 ....31 F8
Mitcheldean Cl B98 ....102 C4
Mitchell Ave CV4 ....76 A7
Mitchell Ho Coventry CV4 .76 A7
Warwick CV34 ....108 E7
Mitchell Rd CV12 ....39 C2
Mitchison Cl CV23 ......117 E8
Mitford Villas GL56 .....140 A3
Moat Ave CV3 ....76 F5
Moat Cl Bubbenhall CV8 ...95 B3
Thurlaston CV23 ....98 C1
Moat Croft
Birmingham B37 ....33 A2
Sutton Coldfield B76 ......22 B7
Moat Dr B78 ....8 C3
Moat Farm Dr
Bedworth CV12 ....49 C8
Rugby CV21 ....101 A4
Moat Farm La B95 ......112 E6
Moat Gn CV35 ....108 A1
Moat House Ct B80 ....103 C4
Moat House La
Coventry CV4 ....76 C7
Shustoke B46 ....25 A1
Moat La LE10 ....41 C3
Mobbs La OX15 ....142 D4
Mockley Wood Rd B93 ...72 B7
Modbury Cl CV3 ....77 D5
Model Village The
CV47 ....115 D3
Molesworth Ave CV3 .....62 A1
Mollington Gr CV35 ....114 F6
Mollington La OX17 ....133 D2
Mollington Rd
Claydon OX17 ....134 B4
Whitnash CV31 ....110 A3
Momus Bvd CV2 ....62 C2
Moncrieff Dr CV31 ......110 C5
Monk's Croft The CV3 ....77 C7
Monks Cl CV22 ....99 A4
Monks Dr B80 ....103 B2
Monks Field Cl CV4 ......60 A1
Monks Kirby La CV23 ....53 C3
Monks Rd
Binley Woods CV3 ....79 C7
Coventry CV1 ....61 F2
Monks Way CV34 ....108 D6
Monkspath B90 ....71 A6
Monkspath Bsns Pk B90 .70 F8
Monkspath Cl B90 ....70 D7
Monkspath Hall Rd B90 ..71 B7
Monkspath Jun & Inf Sch
B90 ....71 B6
Monkswood Cres CV2 ...62 D8
Monmouth Cl
Coventry CV5 ....60 B3
Kenilworth CV8 ....92 F6
Monmouth Gdns CV10 ...28 E3
Monnington Ho CV8 ......93 B7
Montague Ho CV37 ....145 A2
Montague Rd Rugby CV22 99 B3
Warwick CV34 ....109 A8
Montague's Cnr CV37 ..129 A6
Montalt Rd CV3 ....77 E7
Montana Wlk CV10 ......28 E3
Montfort Rd B46 ....33 F5
Montgomery Ave CV35 .114 F3
Montgomery Cl
Coventry CV3 ....78 C4
Stratford-u-A CV37 .....144 C1
Montgomery Dr CV22 ....82 B1
Montgomery Rd CV31 ..109 F4
Montilo La CV23 ....66 B3
Montjoy Cl CV3 ....78 D7
Montley B77 ....10 B4
Montpelier Ho CV8 ....92 F5
Montpellier Cl CV3 ....77 C6
Montrose Ave CV32 ....106 B5
Montrose Dr
Birmingham B35 ....22 A4
Montrose Dr *continued*
Nuneaton CV10 ....28 F3
Montrose Rd CV22 ....83 A1
Montsford Cl B93 ....71 F6
Monument Way CV37 ..145 A3
Monwode Lea La B46 ....26 A2
Moor Farm Cl CV23 ......96 C3
Moor La
Tamworth, Amington B79 ...4 A3
Willoughby CV23 ....117 B6
Moor Rd CV10 ....28 A8
Moor St CV5 ....60 F1
Moor The B76 ....22 A8
Moor Wood Farm★ CV10 18 C1
Moorbrooke CV10 ....28 A7
Moorcroft Cl
Nuneaton CV11 ....30 B1
Redditch B97 ....102 A3
Moorcroft Gdns B97 ...102 A3
Moore Cl
Appleby Magna DE12 ....3 C4
Coventry CV6 ....50 A5
Warwick CV34 ....104 E2
Moore Wlk CV34 ....109 C7
Moorend Ave B37 ....33 B2
Moorfield Ave B93 ....71 F6
Moorfield Rd B49 ....143 A2
Moorfield The CV3 ....78 B8
Moorhill Rd CV31 ....110 A3
Moorhills Croft B90 ......70 B8
Moorings The CV31 .....109 D7
Moorlands Ave CV8 ....92 F3
Moorlands Lodge CV8 ...92 F3
Moorpark Cl CV11 ....40 C8
Moorwood Cres CV10 ...28 A8
Moorwood La
Nuneaton CV10 ....27 C4
Nuneaton CV10 ....28 A7
Morar Cl B35 ....22 C4
Moray Cl LE10 ....31 A8
Mordaunt Rd CV35 .....146 C2
Moreall Mdws CV4 ....76 D3
Moreland Croft B76 ......22 B6
Moreton Cl CV37 ....145 B1
Moreton Morrell La
CV35 ....123 B2
Moreton-in-Marsh District
Hospl GL56 ....140 A3
Moreton-in-Marsh Sta
GL56 ....140 A3
Morfa Gdns CV6 ....60 D5
Morgan Cl Arley CV7 .....36 C4
Banbury OX16 ....139 F4
Norton Lindsey CV35 ....114 C2
Studley B80 ....103 C1
Morgan Gr B36 ....22 F1
Morgans Rd CV5 ....59 C4
Morgrove Ave B93 ....71 F6
Morland Cl CV12 ....40 D2
Morland Rd CV6 ....49 C2
Morningside CV5 ....77 B8
Mornington Ct B46 ....34 A4
Morpeth B77 ....9 B4
Morrell St CV32 ....105 F1
Morris Ave CV2 ....62 D4
Morris Cl CV21 ....82 C3
Morris Croft B36 ....22 F1
Morris Dr Banbury OX16 .139 F4
Nuneaton CV11 ....29 D1
Whitnash CV31 ....110 B2
Morris Hill B78 ....11 A4
Morris Rd NN11 ....117 F2
Morse Rd CV31 ....110 B3
Morson Cres CV21 ....83 C1
Morston B77 ....9 B2
Mortimer Rd CV8 ....92 F2
Morton Cl CV6 ....49 A1
Morton Gdns CV21 ....83 B1
Morton La B97 ....102 A4
Morton Morrell CE Prim Sch
CV35 ....122 F2
Morton St CV32 ....105 F1
Morville Cl B93 ....71 D3
Mosedale
Moreton-in-M GL56 .....140 B3
Rugby CV21 ....83 B4
Moseley Ave CV6 ....61 A4
Moseley Prim Sch CV6 ...61 A4
Moseley Rd CV8 ....93 B3
Moss Cl CV22 ....82 C1
Moss Gr CV8 ....93 B7
Moss La
Mappleborough Green
B98 ....112 A8
Newbold-on-S CV37 .....130 E1
Moss St 12 CV31 ....110 A7
Mossdale B77 ....10 B4
Mossdale Cl CV6 ....61 B6
Mossdale Cres CV10 .....28 F2
Mossop Ct CV37 ....144 C2
Mosspaul Cl CV32 .....105 D2
Mottistone Cl CV3 ....77 D6
Motts Way B46 ....34 A3
Moultrie Rd CV21,CV22 ...83 A2
Mount Cres CV37 ....144 B2
Mount Dr CV12 ....39 A3
Mount Field Ct CV1 ....151 D4
Mount Gdns CV5 ....77 B8
Mount Nod Prim Sch
CV5 ....60 A3
Mount Nod Way CV5 .....60 B3
Mount Pleasant
Bishops Itchington CV47 ..124 A4
Stockton CV47 ....147 C4
Stratford-u-A CV37 .....144 B2
Tamworth B77 ....9 B4
Mount Pleasant Cl
CV47 ....147 C4
Mount Pleasant Cotts
CV2 ....63 A7
Mount Pleasant La B95 .112 E6
Mount Pleasant Rd CV12 39 A3
Mount Pleasant Terr
CV10 ....28 F6
Mount Rd
Henley-in-A B95 ....113 B4
Hinckley LE10 ....31 D8
Mount St Coventry CV5 ....60 F2
Nuneaton CV11 ....29 B4
Mount Street Pas CV11 ..29 B4
Mount The Coventry CV3 ..77 E8
Curdworth B76 ....23 C6
Mountbatten Ave CV8 ....93 C3
Mountbatten Cl CV37 ..144 B1
Mountford Cl CV35 .....146 C2
Mountford Rise CV35 ...123 B2
Mowbray St CV2 ....61 F3
Mowe Croft B37 ....44 B7
Mows Hill Rd B94,B95 ..113 A8
Moxhull Rd B37 ....33 A5
Moyeady Ave CV22 .....100 C4
Moyle Cres CV5 ....59 D4
Much Park St CV1 ......151 C2
Muirfield B77 ....4 B3
Muirfield Cl CV11 ....40 C8
Mulberry Cl CV32 ......106 A2
Mulberry Ct CV37 ......145 A2
Mulberry Dr 5 CV34 ....108 C8
Mulberry Rd Coventry CV6 62 A7
Rugby CV22 ....82 A1
Mulberry St CV37 ......145 A2
Mulberry Tree Ctr The
CV37 ....145 A2
Mulberry Way CV10 .....28 A8
Mull Croft B36 ....33 B7
Mullard Dr CV31 ....110 B3
Mullensgrove Rd B37 ....33 A5
Mulliner St CV6 ....61 F5
Mulliners Cl 2 B37 ....33 D2
Muntz Cres B94 ....88 C6
Murcott Ct CV31 ....110 A3
Murcott Rd E CV31 .....110 A3
Murcott Rd W CV31 .....110 A3
Murray Rd Coventry CV6 ..61 A7
Rugby CV21 ....83 A2
Murrayfield Way CV3 ....63 B1
Murrayian Cl CV21 ....83 A2
Murton B77 ....10 B4
Mus of British Road
Transport★ CV1 ....151 B3
Musborough Cl B36 ......22 C1
Museum of Arms & Armour★
CV37 ....145 A1
Myatt Rd WR11 ....127 D1
Myatt's Field WR11 ....127 D4
Myers Rd CV21 ....101 B4
Mylgrove CV3 ....77 D3
Mynors Cres B47 ....69 A6
Myrtle Gr CV5 ....60 F1
Mythe La CV9 ....19 A4
Mythe View CV9 ....12 C1
Myton Cres CV34 ....109 C6
Myton Crofts CV31 .....109 D7
Myton Gdns CV34 ......109 A6
Myton La CV34 ....109 C6
Myton Rd CV31,CV34 ...109 B6
Myton Sch CV34 ....108 B6
Mytton Rd B46 ....22 F3

N

Nailcote Ave CV4 ....75 C8
Nailcote La CV7 ....75 A7
Nailer Cl CV21 ....83 B3
Nailsworth Rd B93 ....71 D2
Nairn Cl CV10 ....29 A2
Napier St CV1 ....61 E3
Naples Rd CV35 ....132 E5
Napton Dr CV32 ....106 A2
Napton Gn CV5 ....60 A3
Napton Rd CV47 ....147 C4
Napton Rise CV47 ......147 B2
Narberth Way CV2 ....62 F8
Nares Cl CV22 ....82 C1
Narrow La
Lowsonford B95,CV35 ....113 F6
Stratford-u-A CV37 .....144 C1
Narrows The 1 LE10 .....31 E8
Naseby Cl CV3 ....78 F8
Naseby Rd CV22 ....83 B1
Nash Croft B37 ....44 B8
Nash's La GL55 ....135 E3
Nashes The CV37 ....129 F7
Nathaniel Newton Inf Sch
CV10 ....28 B8
National Agricultural Ctr★
CV8 ....94 A4
National Distribution Pk
B46 ....24 A3
National Ex Ctr B40 ......44 E4
National Herb Ctr★
OX17 ....133 D1
National Motorcycle Mus
The★ B92 ....45 A2
Naul's Mill Ho CV1 .....151 B4
Navigation Way CV6 .....62 A8
Naysmyth Rd NN11 .....117 F3
Neal Ct CV2 ....63 A8
Neale Ave CV5 ....60 A6
Neale Cl CV12 ....40 C1
Neale's Cl CV33 ....123 F7
Nebsworth La CV36 .....135 F5
Needhill Cl B93 ....71 F6
Needle Cl B80 ....103 C2
Needlers End La CV7 ....74 A7
Neilston St 13 CV31 .....110 A7
Nellands Cl CV36 ....136 B6
Nelson Ave CV34 ....109 A8
Nelson Cl CV37 ....131 A4
Nelson La CV34 ....109 A8
Nelson St 7 CV1 ....61 E4
Nelson Way CV22 ....82 B1
Nemesia B77 ....4 A2
Nene Cl CV3 ....78 D7
Nene Side Cl NN11 .....126 F6
Nene Wlk NN11 ....117 F1
Nesfield Gr B92 ....57 B7
Nesscliffe Rd CV47 .....132 F5
Netherfield B98 ....103 A4
Nethermill Rd 1 CV6 ....61 A5
Nethersole CE Prim Sch The
B78 ....5 A1
Nethersole St B78 ....5 A1
Netherwood La B93 ......90 A7
Netting St OX15 ....142 D4
Nevada Way B37 ....33 C1
Nevill Cl CV31 ....109 F6
Neville Ct 5 CV34 ......108 E6
Neville Gr CV34 ....104 F1
Neville Rd
Birmingham, Castle Bromwich
B36 ....22 E1
Solihull B90 ....69 F8
Neville Wlk B35 ....22 A2
New Ash Dr CV5 ....59 F5
New Bldgs CV1 ....151 C3
New Broad St CV37 ....144 C1
New Brook St 3 CV32 ..109 E8
New Century Pk CV3 .....62 C2
New Century Way CV11 ..29 B4
New Cl CV35 ....114 F3
New Cotts CV37 ....144 C1
New End Rd B46 ....35 A2
New Gate Ct CV1 ......151 C2
New Hall Jun & Inf Sch
B75 ....13 A5
New Inn La WR11 ......127 D5
New Leasow B76 ....22 A7
New Mill La B78 ....9 A4
New Park Cotts OX15 ..137 F2
New Place & Nash's Ho
(Mus)★ CV37 ....145 A1
New Rd
Alderminster CV37 ......130 D3
Appleby Magna DE12 ....3 C4
Ash Green CV7 ....49 B6
Astwood Bank B96 ......118 C8
Coventry CV6 ....48 F1
Ebrington GL55 ....135 E3
Henley-in-A B95 ....113 A4
Hinckley LE10 ....32 A6
Hollywood B47 ....69 A8
Lowsonford CV35 ....113 E6
7 Moreton-in-M GL56 ....140 A3
Norton Lindsey CV35 ....114 C2
Pebworth CV37 ....128 F1
Ratley OX15 ....133 A2
Shotteswell OX17 ....139 E8
Shuttington B79 ....1 B1
Studley B80 ....103 C2
Tamworth B77 ....9 C4
Temple Grafton B49 .....119 E1
Temple Herdewyke CV47 .133 A6
Water Orton B46 ....23 B3
New Row B78 ....8 C3
New St
Baddesley Ensor CV9 ......11 B1
Bedworth CV12 ....39 C2
Bulkington CV12 ....40 D2
Cubbington CV32 ....106 E5
Dordon B78 ....11 A3
Fazeley B78 ....9 A4
Kenilworth CV8 ....92 F6
Napton on t H CV47 .....125 C7
Polesworth B78 ....10 C4
Royal Leamington Spa
CV31 ....110 A7
Rugby CV22 ....82 C2
Shipston-on-S CV36 .....149 C3
Stratford-u-A CV37 ......144 C1
Tiddington CV37 ....145 C2
Warwick CV34 ....108 E6
New Union St CV1 ......151 B2
Newall Cl CV23 ....83 C3
Newbold & Tredington CE
Prim Sch
Newbold-on-S CV37 .....130 E1
Tredington CV36 ....136 F6
Newbold Cl
Bentley Heath B93 ....71 F5
Coventry CV3 ....62 F1
Newbold Comyn Pk★
CV32 ....110 D8
Newbold Lawn CV32 ...110 A8
Newbold Pl
Royal Leamington Spa
CV32 ....110 A8
Wellesbourne CV35 .....146 C2
Newbold Quarry Ctry Pk★
CV21 ....82 C3
Newbold Rd Rugby CV21 ..82 C3
Wellesbourne CV35 .....146 C3
Newbold Revel Coll CV23 65 B3
Newbold Riverside Prim Sch
CV21 ....82 C3
Newbold St CV32 ....110 A8
Newbold Terr CV32 ....110 A8
Newbold Terr E CV32 ...110 B8
Newborough Cl CV9 ....3 A1
Newburgh Cres CV34 ...108 E8

Newburgh Prim Sch
CV34 ....108 C4
Newbury Cl 4 CV31 ...110 C6
Newbury Dr CV37 ....144 C1
Newby Cl CV3 ....77 E6
Newby Gr B37 ....33 B5
Newcastle Croft B35 ...22 C3
Newcombe Cl CV22 ....99 B2
Newcombe Rd CV5 .....61 A1
Newcomen Cl CV12 ....49 D8
Newcomen Rd CV12 ...38 D1
Newdegate Pl CV11 ....29 C4
Newdegate St CV11 ....29 C4
Newdigate CV31 ....110 C5
Newdigate Cl CV12 ....39 A4
Newdigate Prim Sch
CV12 ....38 C1
Newdigate Rd
  Bedworth CV12 ....39 A3
  Coventry CV6 ....61 F6
  Sutton Coldfield B75 ...13 A5
Newent Cl B98 ....112 A6
Newey Ave CV12 ....49 D8
Newey Dr CV8 ....93 A2
Newey Rd CV2 ....62 D4
Newfield Ave CV8 .....93 B3
Newfield Rd CV1 ......61 C5
Newgale Wlk CV31 ....110 C7
Newhall Rd CV2 ....62 D7
Newham Gn CV10 ......28 C7
Newhaven Cl CV6 ......60 E6
Newhouse Croft CV7 ...74 B6
Newing Ct WR11 ......127 D4
Newington Cl CV6 .....60 D6
Newington Rd B37 .....44 B8
Newland Cl B98 ....103 A4
Newland La CV7 ....49 B7
Newland Rd Coventry CV1 61 D5
  Royal Leamington Spa
  CV32 ....106 C3
Newland St CV22 ......82 C2
Newlands Cl CV3 ......61 F2
Newlands La B37 ......44 A6
Newlands Rd
  Baddesley Ensor CV9 ...11 B1
  Bentley Heath B93 .....71 A4
Newlands The B80 ....103 B2
Newlyn Cl CV11 ....29 F4
Newman Cl CV12 ......39 B4
Newmarket Cl
  Coventry CV6 ....50 B4
  Stratford-u-A CV37 ...129 F8
Newmarsh Rd B76 .....22 B6
Newnham Ho B36 ......33 B5
Newnham La B95 .....120 D7
Newnham Rd
  Coventry CV1 ....61 F5
  Royal Leamington Spa
  CV32 ....106 B3
Newport Cl B97 ....102 A3
Newport Dr B49 ......143 A2
Newport Rd CV6 ....49 D1
Newquay Cl CV11 .....29 F5
Newscut La OX17 .....134 C1
Newsholme Cl 1 CV34 104 E1
Newstead Ave LE10 ...31 D4
Newstead Cl CV11 .....29 F2
Newstead Dr CV47 ....147 A2
Newstead Way CV3 ....63 B1
Newton Cl Coventry CV2 .62 F7
  Hartshill CV10 ....19 A1
  Redditch B98 ....103 A3
Newton La Newton CV23 .68 A2
  Newton Regis B79,CV9 ...2 C1
  Seckington B79 ....2 A2
Newton Manor La CV21,
  CV23 ....83 B4
Newton Rd Hinckley LE10 .30 E7
  Knowle B93 ....72 B7
  Newton CV23 ....84 A4
Newton Regis CE Prim Sch
  B79 ....2 B2
Newtown Bldgs CV12 ..39 B3
Newtown Rd
  Bedworth CV12 ....39 A2
  Nuneaton CV11 ....29 C5
Nibbits La NN11 .....117 E5
Nicholas Chamberlaine Comp
  Sch CV12 ....39 D3
Nicholas Cl CV12 .....39 C3
Nicholls St CV2 ....61 F4
Nicholson Cl CV34 ...104 F1
Nickson Rd CV4 ....59 E1
Nightingale B77 ....10 A3
Nightingale Ave B36 ..33 A8
Nightingale Cl
  Atherstone CV9 ....12 C1
  Great Alne B49 ....119 D6
Nightingale Ct CV31 ..110 B8
Nightingale La
  Cleeve Prior WR11 ....128 A4
  Coventry CV5 ....76 E7
Nimbus B77 ....9 B2
Nine Days La B98 ....103 A3
Nineacres Dr B37 .....33 A3
Ninefoot La B77 ....9 C4
Ninian Pk B77 ....9 B3
Ninian Way B77 ....9 C3
Niton Rd CV10 ....29 D6
Niven Cl CV5 ....60 A6
No Man's Heath La CV9 .3 A2
Noble Cl CV34 ....108 D5
Noble Dr CV22 ....99 A4
Nod Rise CV5 ....60 B3
Node Hill Cl B80 .....103 B2

Noel Ct
  Chipping Campden GL55 .135 B2
  Redditch B97 ....102 B4
Nolan Cl CV6 ....49 D4
Nook The CV11 ....29 E2
Norcombe Gr B90 .....71 A5
Nordic Drift CV2 ......63 A6
Norfolk Cl LE10 ....31 D4
Norfolk Cres CV10 ....28 E4
Norfolk St Coventry CV1 61 B3
  Royal Leamington Spa
  CV32 ....106 A1
Norfolk Terr CV4 ......76 B7
Norluck Ct CV36 .....149 C3
Norman Ashman Coppice
  CV3 ....79 C7
Norman Ave Coventry CV2 .50 F1
  Nuneaton CV11 ....29 B4
Norman Place Rd CV6 ..60 F7
Norman Rd CV21 ......82 C3
Normandy Mdws CV31 .110 A2
Normandy Cl CV35 ...108 A7
Normandy Way LE10 ...21 C1
North Ave Bedworth CV12 .39 D2
  Birmingham B40 ....44 F5
  Coventry CV2 ....62 A3
North Brook Rd CV6 ...60 D8
North Circular Rd GL56 140 C4
  Cubbington CV32 .....106 E5
  Hinckley LE10 ....31 E6
North Leamington Com Sch
  & Arts Coll CV32 ...105 F4
North Leamington Com Sch
  & Arts Coll (Sixth Form)
  CV32 ....105 F2
North Rd CV23 ....83 C3
North St Atherstone CV9 .18 C4
  Coventry CV2 ....62 B5
  Kilsby CV23 ....101 C2
  Marton CV23 ....115 C7
  Nuneaton CV10 ....28 F3
  Rugby CV21 ....83 A2
North View CV2 ....51 A1
North Villiers St CV32 .106 A1
North Warwickshire &
  Hinkley Coll
  Hinckley LE10 ....31 F8
  Nuneaton CV11 ....29 E6
North Warwickshire &
  Hinkley Coll (Atherstone
  Coll) CV9 ....18 C4
Northampton La CV22 ..99 B2
Northbourne Dr CV11 ..39 F7
Northcote Rd CV22 ....82 C1
Northcote St 7 CV31 ..110 B7
Northcote Wlk CV9 ....12 B1
Northend Rd CV47 ....133 C7
Northey Rd CV6 ....61 D8
Northfield Rd
  Coventry CV1 ....61 F2
  Hinckley LE10 ....31 C1
  Southam CV47 ....147 A2
Northgate CV34 ......108 E7
Northgate St CV34 ...108 E7
Northlands Prim Sch
  CV21 ....83 A2
Northolt Dr B35 ....22 B3
Northside Cl B98 .....102 C4
Northumberland Ave
  CV10 ....28 F3
Northumberland Rd
  Coventry CV1 ....61 A3
  Royal Leamington Spa
  CV32 ....105 E2
Northvale Cl CV8 ......93 B6
Northway Birmingham B40 .44 F5
  Royal Leamington Spa
  CV31 ....110 A5
  Rugby CV21 ....83 A2
Norton Curlieu La CV35 114 C3
Norton Dr CV34 ......104 E2
Norton Grange CV5 ....60 C6
Norton Green La B93 ..72 C2
Norton Hill CV9 ....3 B1
Norton Hill Dr CV5 ....62 E6
Norton La B47,B90,B94 ..69 E3
Norton Lea CV35 .....114 C2
Norton Leys CV22 .....99 C3
Norton Rd B46 ....33 F8
Norton St CV1 ....151 C4
Norton View GL55 ....135 B6
Nortons Cl CV47 .....133 B7
Norval Cres WR11 ....127 D1
Norwich Cl CV11 ......30 A8
Norwich Dr CV3 ....77 B5
Norwood Gr CV2 ....50 E2
Norwood Ho 11 CV32 ..105 F2
Nova Croft CV5 ....59 C4
Nuffield Ho B36 ....33 A8
Nuffield Rd Coventry CV6 .62 E4
  Hinckley LE10 ....30 E7
Nugent Gr B90 ....70 D3
Nuneaton Borough Football
  Club CV11 ....29 A4
Nuneaton La CV13 .....20 C1
Nuneaton Mus & Art Gal*
  CV11 ....29 C3
Nuneaton Rd
  Bedworth CV12 ....39 B4
  Bulkington CV12 ....40 B4
  Fillongley CV7 ....36 C2
  Furnace End B46,CV10 .26 B3
  Hartshill CV10 ....19 A1
  Nuneaton CV10 ....19 A1
  Nuneaton Sta CV11 ...29 C5
Nunts La CV6 ....49 B3
Nunts Park Ave CV6 ...49 B4

Nunwood La CV23 .....96 A1
Nursery Cl
  Mickleton GL55 ......135 C7
  Moreton-in-M GL56 ...140 A4
Nursery Gdns B90 ....69 E8
Nursery Hill Prim Sch
  CV10 ....27 C4
Nursery La CV31 .....110 A5
Nursery Rd Ansley CV10 .27 C4
  Atherstone CV9 ....18 C4
Nutbrook Ave CV4 ....59 E2
Nuthurst B75 ....13 B4
Nuthurst Cres CV10 ...27 B4
Nuthurst Gr B93 ......71 E3
Nuthurst Grange Rd B94 88 C4
Nuthurst La CV10 .....27 B1
Nuthurst Rd B94 ....88 C4
Nutt's La LE10 ....31 A7
Nymet B77 ....9 C4

O

Oak Ave CV7 ....26 C1
Oak Cl Baginton CV8 ...77 F2
  Bedworth CV12 ....39 C4
  Hinckley LE10 ....31 E5
Oak Ct Coventry CV5 ...77 F7
  Royal Leamington Spa
  CV34 ....109 E2
Oak Dr CV10 ....28 A8
Oak Farm Cl B76 ......22 A7
Oak Farm Craft Ctr* B78 .8 A3
Oak Field Gdns CV8 ...18 C4
Oak La Allesley CV5 ...47 E1
  Barston B92 ....57 B1
Oak Leigh CV33 ......123 D2
Oak Rd CV37 ....145 C2
Oak Rise B46 ....33 F5
Oak St CV22 ....83 A1
Oak Tree Ave CV3 .....77 A6
Oak Tree Cl
  Bentley Heath B93 ....71 E4
  Royal Leamington Spa
  CV32 ....106 A2
Oak Tree Ct CV32 ....106 A2
Oak Tree La Cookhill B49 118 D5
  Hollywood B47 ....69 B6
  Sambourne B96 ......103 A1
Oak Tree Rd Coventry CV3 .79 A7
  Harvington WR11 ....127 C4
Oak Trees B47 ....69 A7
Oak Way CV4 ....59 D2
Oakdale Rd CV3 ....79 C7
Oakdene Cl CV35 ....113 F3
Oakdene Cres
  Hatton CV35 ....114 C5
  Nuneaton CV10 ....29 D7
Oakdene Ct CV37 ....144 C2
Oakenhayes Cres B76 ..22 C5
Oakey Cl CV6 ....49 F4
Oakfield Ho CV3 ....63 A1
Oakfield Jun Sch CV9 ..18 C4
Oakfield Prim Sch CV22 .82 C1
Oakfield Rd Coventry CV6 .60 F5
  Rugby CV22 ....82 C1
Oakfields Way B91 ....56 B5
Oakford Dr CV5 ....59 F6
Oakhall Dr B93 ....71 F4
Oakham Cl B98 ....103 A3
Oakham Cres CV12 ....40 D2
Oakham La NN11 .....126 D8
Oakham Rd GL56 .....141 A1
Oakington Ho B35 .....22 A3
Oaklands B76 ....23 B5
Oaklands Croft B76 ...22 B7
Oaklands Ct B46 ......93 A4
Oaklands The
  Birmingham B37 ......44 A7
  Coventry CV4 ....60 A2
Oakleigh Rd CV37 ....144 C3
Oakley CV8 ....73 F1
Oakley Ct CV12 ....38 D1
Oakley Wood Rd CV33 .122 F7
Oakmoor Rd CV6 ......50 A4
Oakridge Rd CV32 ...106 C4
Oakroyd Cres CV10 ...28 D7
Oaks Pl CV6 ....50 A3
Oaks Prec CV8 ....92 E3
Oaks Rd CV8 ....92 E2
Oaks The Bedworth CV12 .38 F2
  Royal Leamington Spa
  CV32 ....109 D8
  Sutton Coldfield B75 ...13 A3
Oakthorpe Dr B37 .....33 A5
Oaktree Cl Bearley CV37 120 D7
  Kingsbury B78 ....15 B3
  Moreton Morrell CV35 .122 E3
Oaktree Farm Mobile Homes
  Pk B94 ....86 B2
Oakwood Cl CV9 ....11 B1
Oakwood Gr CV34 ....105 A1
Oakwood Rd B47 ......69 A6
Oakworth Cl CV2 ......62 F8
Oaston Rd CV11 ....29 D4
Oatlands Cl CV6 ......49 C4
Oban Dr CV10 ....29 A2
Oban Rd Coventry CV6 ..49 F5
  Hinckley LE10 ....31 A7
Oberon Cl Nuneaton CV11 .30 A1
  Royal Leamington Spa
  CV34 ....109 E4
  Rugby CV22 ....99 B3
Occupation Rd CV2 ....62 C3
Oddfellows' Terr 12
  GL56 ....140 A3
Oddicombe Croft CV3 ..77 D5
Odingsel Dr CV47 ....115 C4

Odstone Dr LE10 ......30 F8
Offa Dr CV8 ....93 A4
Offa Rd CV31 ....110 B5
Offchurch La CV31 ...110 F6
Offchurch Rd CV33 ...110 F6
Offchurch Rd CV32 ..106 E4
Offenham CE Fst Sch
  WR11 ....127 D1
Ogley Dr B75 ....13 A5
Okeford Way CV10 ....29 A1
Okehampton Rd CV3 ...77 E5
Okement Gr CV23 .....82 A3
Oken Cl CV34 ....108 D7
Oken Rd CV34 ....108 D8
Olaf Pl CV2 ....63 A7
Old Bowling Gn The
  CV36 ....149 C3
Old Brewery Cl CV36 ..137 A4
Old Budbrooke Rd
  CV35 ....108 A8
Old Church Rd
  Coventry CV6 ....50 A1
  Water Orton B46 ....23 B3
Old Courtyard The
  CV33 ....107 B4
Old Crown Mews CV7 ..50 D5
Old Damson La B92 ....44 A2
Old Dickens Heath Rd
  B90 ....70 A5
Old Farm La B46 ......25 A3
Old Farm Rd CV3 ......18 C3
Old Ford Ave CV47 ...147 A3
Old Forge Bsns Ctr B98 103 B4
Old Forge Dr B98 ....103 B4
Old Forge Rd
  Fenny Drayton CV13 ...20 A3
  Great Rollright OX7 ..142 A2
Old Gated Rd The CV33,
  CV35 ....123 C4
Old Gram School Mews
  GL55 ....135 B2
Old Green La CV8 ......73 C1
Old Hall Ct B79 ....2 B1
Old Hedging La B77 ....9 B3
Old Hinckley Rd CV10 ..29 D5
Old Holly La CV9 ......12 B2
Old House La CV7 .....48 A7
Old Kingsbury Rd B76 ..22 C5
Old La B48 ....85 D4
Old Langley Hall B75 ...13 C4
Old Leicester Rd CV21 ..83 A4
Old Manor Cl B78 ......8 C3
Old Manor Gdns GL55 .135 C6
Old Meeting Yd CV12 ..39 B3
Old Mill Ave CV4 ......76 D5
Old Mill Rd B46 ....33 F4
Old Milverton CV32 ..105 A8
Old Milverton La CV32 105 E5
Old Milverton Rd CV32 105 C2
Old Orchard The
  Birdingbury CV23 ....115 F7
  Ebrington GL55 ......135 E3
Old Penn's Yd CV12 ...39 B3
Old Rd
  Bishops Itchington CV47 124 B4
  Braunston NN11 .....117 E4
  Meriden CV7 ....46 E1
  Ratley OX15 ....132 F2
  Shipston-on-S CV36 ..149 C3
  Southam CV47 ....147 A2
Old Rectory Cl CV23 ...67 B3
Old Rectory Gdn B49 .143 A2
Old Rectory The CV37 130 A6
Old Red Lion Ct CV37 .145 A2
Old School Cl WR11 ..127 D1
Old School End OX15 ..142 D4
Old School La
  Hampton Magna CV35 .114 F3
  Lighthorne CV35 .....123 C2
  Wilmcote CV37 ......120 C4
Old School Mews CV32 106 B3
Old School The CV36 ..149 C3
Old School Yd The B77 ..4 A3
Old Snitterfield Rd
  CV37 ....120 E7
Old Sq CV1 ....108 E6
Old Sq The CV37 .....144 B1
Old Station Rd B92 ....57 A8
Old Stone Yd CV32 ...105 E1
Old Town
  24 Moreton-in-M GL56 .140 A3
  Stratford-u-A CV37 ...145 A1
Old Town Mews CV37 .144 C1
Old Tramway Wlk CV37 145 A1
Old Tree La CV35 .....138 B6
Old Vicarage Gdns B80 103 C4
Old Walled Gdn The
  CV35 ....131 E7
Old Warwick Rd
  Lapworth B94,CV35 ...89 D3
  Rowington CV35 .....114 A7
  Royal Leamington Spa
  CV31 ....109 E7
Old Waste La CV7 ......74 E6
Old Winnings Rd CV7 ..48 F6
Oldany Way CV10 .....28 F2
Oldberrow Cl 4 B90 ..71 A6
Oldborough Dr CV35 ..130 E8
Oldbury Rd Hartshill CV10 18 C1
  Nuneaton CV10 ....28 A1
Oldbury View CV10 ....19 A1
Oldbutt Rd CV36 .....149 C3
Oldfield Rd CV5 ....60 E3
Oldham Ave CV2 ......62 E4
Oldham Way CV23 .....82 A2
Oldington Gr B91 ......71 B8
Oldwich La E Honiley CV8 .90 E8
  Knowle CV8 ....73 D1
Oldwich La W B93 .....90 C8

Olive Ave CV2 ....62 D5
Oliver St Coventry CV6 ..61 F6
  Rugby CV21 ....82 C2
Olivers Lock CV37 ....145 A2
Olivier Way CV2 ....63 B8
Olney Rd CV35 ....132 D3
Olton Ave CV5 ....59 E4
Olton Cl CV11 ....41 A4
Olton Pl CV11 ....28 F4
Olympus Ave CV34 ...109 D5
Olympus Cl CV5 ....59 B8
Omar Rd CV2 ....62 D2
Ombersley Cl B98 ....103 B4
Omega Pl 11 CV21 ....83 A2
Onley La CV22 ....100 B3
Onley Terr CV4 ....76 C7
Onslow Croft CV32 ...105 F2
Openfield Croft B46 ...23 C2
Ophelia Dr CV34 .....109 E3
Oratory Dr CV3 ....78 C6
Orchard Cl Austrey CV9 ..3 A1
  Badby NN11 ....126 F6
  Bidford-on-A B50 ....148 B2
  Bishops Itchington CV47 124 B4
  Bubbenhall CV8 ....95 B3
  Coleshill B46 ....33 F7
  Curdworth B76 ....23 B7
  Hinckley LE10 ....32 A5
  Hurley CV9 ....16 B2
  Lower Brailes OX15 ..137 F2
  Mickleton GL55 ......135 C7
  Nuneaton CV10 ....28 B7
  Polesworth B78 ....5 A2
  Salford OX7 ....150 C2
  Shipston-on-S CV36 ..149 C3
  Tamworth B77 ....9 B3
  Welford on A CV37 ..129 B6
  Witherley CV9 ....19 A4
  Wolvey LE10 ....41 B2
Orchard Cres CV3 .....77 C8
Orchard Ct Atherstone CV9 18 B4
  Coventry CV3 ....63 A1
  Lower Quinton CV37 .129 D2
Orchard Dr Alcester B49 .143 A2
  Coventry CV5 ....59 C4
Orchard Gr
  Astwood Bank B96 ...118 C8
  Stockton CV47 ......147 C4
Orchard Ho CV6 ......50 A4
Orchard La CV8 ....93 C3
Orchard Meadow Wlk
  B35 ....22 B3
Orchard Piece OX17 ..134 A2
Orchard Pl
  Clifford Chambers CV37 .129 F7
  Harvington WR11 ....127 C4
  Redditch B80 ....103 C4
Orchard Rd
  Hockley Heath B94 ....88 C6
  Hook Norton OX15 ..142 D4
  Orchard Ret Pk CV3 ...78 D4
Orchard Rise CV9 ......11 B1
Orchard St Bedworth CV12 39 B4
  Hinckley LE10 ....31 E8
  Nuneaton CV11 ....29 D4
Orchard The
  Baxterley CV9 ....17 B4
  Lower Quinton CV37 .129 D2
  Marton CV23 ....115 C7
  Staverton NN11 .....126 D8
  Upper Boddington NN11 134 E8
  Whatcote CV37 ......137 E7
Orchard View OX17 ..134 C1
Orchard Way
  Hollywood B47 ....69 A8
  Long Itchington CV47 .115 C4
  Nuneaton CV10 ....28 C6
  Rugby CV22 ....99 B4
  Southam CV47 ....147 A3
  Stratford-u-A CV37 ..144 C1
  Stretton on D CV23 ...96 C3
  Studley B80 ....103 C1
Orchards The
  Astwood Bank B96 ..102 B1
  Cheswick Green B90 ...70 D4
  Hollywood B47 ....69 A7
  Newton CV23 ....68 A1
Orchid Way CV23 ......83 B4
Ordnance Rd CV6 ......61 E5
Orford Cl CV35 ....146 C2
Orford Rise CV10 .....27 C2
Oriel Gr GL56 ....140 A2
Oriel Ho B37 ....33 A3
Orion Cres CV2 ....50 E2
Orkney Cl CV10 ....29 A2
Orkney Croft B36 ......33 B7
Orkney Dr B77 ....9 C4
Orlando Cl CV22 ......99 B3
Orlescote Rd CV4 ......76 E6
Orpington Dr CV6 ......49 D4
Orrian Cl CV37 ....144 C3
Orsino Cl CV34 ....109 E2
Orson Leys CV22 ......99 C4
Orton Ave B76 ....22 A6
Orton Cl B46 ....23 A3
Orton Hill CV9 ....6 B3
Orton La Austrey CV9 ....6 B3
  Orton-on-t-H CV9 ......6 C1
  Twycross CV9 ....3 C1
Orton Rd Coventry CV6 ..49 D4
  Warton B79 ....5 C2
Orton Way B35 ....22 C2
Orwell Cl Clifton u D CV23 84 A3
  Nuneaton CV10 ....28 A5
Orwell Ct CV1 ....151 C4
Orwell Rd CV1 ....61 F1
Osbaston Cl CV5 ......59 E4
Osborne Rd CV31 ....110 A4

Osborne Rd CV5 ....77 A8
Osbourne Croft B90 .....70 D5
Oslo Gdns CV2 ....63 A7
Osney Cl OX15 ....142 A1
Osprey B77 ....10 A3
Osprey Cl Coventry CV2 ..63 B6
Nuneaton CV11 ......40 B8
Ossetts Hole La CV35 .113 E4
Oswald Rd CV32 .....109 D8
Oswald Way CV32 .....82 B2
Oswestry Cl B97 .....102 B4
Oswin Gr CV2 ....62 C4
Othello Ave CV34 .....109 F3
Othello Cl CV22 ......99 B3
Otter Cl B98 ....112 A6
Otters Rest CV31 .....110 C5
Ottery B77 ....10 A3
Our Lady & St Teresa's RC
Prim Sch CV6 ....106 D5
Our Lady of the Angels RC Inf
Sch CV11 ....29 C3
Our Lady of the Assumption
RC Prim Sch CV4 .....59 E1
Our Lady of the Wayside RC
Prim Sch B90 ....70 C8
Our Lady's RC Prim Sch
Alcester B49 ....143 A3
Princethorpe CV23 ....96 B1
Ousterne La CV7 ......36 B2
Outermarch Rd CV6 ....61 C7
Outlands Dr LE10 .....21 C1
Outwood Cl B98 ......102 C4
Outwoods Cl CV9 ......18 B4
Oval Rd CV22 ....100 B4
Overbare Cl B94 ......87 A1
Overberry Cl CV2 .....50 D2
Overberry Orch 5 CV33 122 E8
Overdale B96 ....102 C1
Overdale Rd CV5 ......60 C3
Overell Gr CV32 ......105 D2
Overslade Cres CV6 ....60 E8
Overslade Manor Dr
CV22 ....99 C4
Oversley Rd B76 ......22 A6
Overstone Rd CV7 .....52 C3
Overton Dr B46 ......23 C3
Overtons Cl CV31 .....110 F5
Overwoods Rd B77 ....10 A3
Owen Sq CV9 ....18 B4
Owen St CV9 ....18 B4
Owenford Rd CV6 .....61 C7
Owl End La NN11 .....134 E7
Owl End Way NN11 ....134 E7
Owlets End B50 ......148 C2
Ox Cl CV2 ....62 A6
Ox Leys Rd B75,B76 ...13 D3
Oxendon Way CV3 .....78 E8
Oxford Cl CV11 ......29 F8
Oxford Pl 12 CV32 ....105 F1
Oxford Rd Marton CV23 .115 D7
Princethorpe CV8,CV23 .96 B2
Ryton-on-D CV8 ......78 F1
Oxford Row 14 CV32 ...105 F1
Oxford St Coventry CV1 ..61 E3
Moreton-in-M GL56 ...140 A3
Royal Leamington Spa
CV32 ....105 F1
Rugby CV21 ....83 B2
Southam CV47 ......147 A2
Oxford Way CV35 .....146 A1
Oxhayes Cl CV7 ......74 C6
Oxhill Bridle Rd CV35 .131 E3
Oxhill Rd CV35 ......138 B6
Oxley Dr CV3 ....77 C3
Oxstall Cl B76 ......22 D5
Oxway Cl CV36 ......149 C3

P

Packington Ave CV5 ....60 B6
Packington La
Coleshill B46 ....34 A1
Little Packington CV7 ..45 C6
Maxstoke B46 ......35 A1
White Stitch CV7 .....46 A3
Packmore St CV34 ....108 F8
Packmores B90 ......70 A5
Packsaddle Hill CV35 ..145 C4
Packwood Ave CV21 ...101 B4
Packwood Cl
Bentley Heath B93 ....71 E4
Nuneaton CV11 ......39 F8
Royal Leamington Spa
CV31 ....110 C5
Packwood Cotts B93 ...71 F1
Packwood Gn CV5 .....60 A3
Packwood Ho* B94 ....89 A5
Packwood La B94 .....89 A4
Packwood Mews 5
CV34 ....109 B8
Packwood Rd B94 .....89 A7
Paddiford Pl CV10 ....28 C3
Paddock Cl
Bidford-on-A B50 ....148 B3
Napton on t H CV47 ..125 C8
Paddock Dr B93 ......72 A2
Paddock La Redditch B98 102 C4
Stratford-u-A CV37 ..144 C1
Paddock The
Claybrooke Magna LE17 .43 C3
Lower Boddington NN11 .134 E7
Newton CV23 ....68 A1
Paddocks Cl
Polesworth B78 ......4 C1

Paddocks Cl continued
Wolston CV8 ....80 A2
Paddocks The
Bulkington CV12 .....40 B3
Kenilworth CV8 ......93 B5
Mollington OX17 ....133 F2
Norton WR11 ....127 B2
Stretton on D CV23 ...96 C3
Warwick CV34 ......108 F7
Paddox Cl CV22 ......100 C4
Paddox Prim Sch
Rugby CV22 ....100 B4
Rugby CV22 ....100 B4
Padgate Cl B35 ......22 B3
Padmore Ct CV31 .....110 B6
Padstow Cl CV11 .....29 F5
Padstow Rd CV4 ......75 C8
Padua CV37 ....145 A2
Page Rd CV4 ....75 E7
Pages La OX15 ......139 B7
Paget Ct CV2 ....50 D2
Paget's La CV8 ......95 B3
Painswick Cl B98 ....102 C3
Pake's Croft 3 CV6 ...61 A5
Palefield Rd B90 .....70 F6
Palermo Ave CV3 .....77 E6
Pallett Dr CV11 ......29 C7
Palm Tree Ave CV2 ....50 C2
Palmer La CV1 ......151 B3
Palmer Rd CV31 .....110 B4
Palmer's Cl CV21 ....101 A4
Palmers Leys CV35 ...132 B6
Palmerston Rd CV5 ....76 F8
Pampas Cl CV37 .....144 C3
Pancras Cl CV2 ......50 E1
Pandora Rd CV2 .....62 E7
Pangbourne Cl CV11 ...29 F8
Pangbourne Rd CV2 ...62 C8
Pangfield Pk CV5 .....60 C4
Pantolf Pl CV21 ......82 C4
Papenham Gn CV4 ....76 A8
Parade CV32 ....109 F8
Parade The
Birmingham B37 .....33 A5
6 Hinckley LE10 .....31 D8
Nuneaton CV11 ......29 C3
Paradise Ho 4 CV6 ...61 F7
Paradise St
Coventry CV1 ....151 C1
Rugby CV21 ....83 B2
Warwick CV34 ......108 F8
Paradise Way CV2 ....51 B1
Paradise Works CV6 ...61 F7
Paragon Way CV7 ....50 B8
Parbrook Cl CV4 .....75 E8
Parbury B77 ....9 B3
Parisienne Ho CV5 ....60 E2
Park Ave Coleshill B46 .33 F6
Coventry CV6 ....49 C3
Nuneaton CV11 ......29 E3
Polesworth B78 ......11 A4
Studley B80 ....103 C2
Park Cl
Avon Dassett CV47 ...133 C4
Claverdon CV35 .....113 F3
Hanwell OX17 ......139 F6
Hook Norton OX15 ...142 D3
Kenilworth CV8 ......93 B5
Wilmcote CV37 ......120 C4
Park Croft B47 ......69 A5
Park Ct Allesley CV5 ..60 B6
Stratford-u-A CV37 ..144 C2
Park Dr Claverdon CV35 113 F3
Royal Leamington Spa
CV31 ....109 E7
Park Farm Cl CV22 ....82 B1
Park Farm Ind Est B98 103 B4
Park Gates CV33 ....111 A4
Park Gr B46 ....23 C2
Park Hall Cres B36 ...22 C1
Park Hall Mews WR11 .127 E6
Park Hall Sch B36 ...22 E1
Park Hill
Hook Norton OX15 ...142 D4
Kenilworth CV8 ......93 B5
Park Hill Jun Sch CV8 .93 C5
Park Hill La Allesley CV5 60 A6
Coventry CV5 ....60 A5
Park Hill Prim Sch CV5 .60 A4
Park La Astley CV10 ...37 B3
Berkswell CV7 ......58 B2
Birmingham, Castle Vale
B35 ....22 C4
Great Alne B49 .....119 D6
Harbury CV33 ......123 F6
Ilmington CV36 .....135 F7
Lower Quinton CV37 ..129 D2
Lower Shuckburgh NN11 116 F1
North Newington OX15 139 E2
Nuneaton CV10 ......27 C2
Snitterfield CV37 ....121 C6
Southam CV47 ......147 A2
Swalcliffe OX15 .....142 F8
Park Lane Prim Sch
CV10 ....27 C2
Park Paling The CV3 ...77 E7
Park Piece CV35 .....132 B6
Park Rd
Baddesley Ensor CV9 ..11 A1
Bedworth CV12 .....39 B2
Chipping Campden GL55 135 A1
Coleshill B46 ....33 F6
Coventry CV1 ....151 B1
Hinckley LE10 ......31 E8

Park Rd continued
Hook Norton OX15 ...142 D4
Kenilworth CV8 ......93 A6
Polesworth B78 ......11 A4
Royal Leamington Spa
CV32 ....106 A4
Rugby CV21 ....83 A2
Stratford-u-A CV37 ..144 C2
Tamworth B77 ......9 B3
Park Sq B37 ....44 D8
Park St Coventry CV6 ..61 E7
Nuneaton CV11 ......29 D3
Royal Leamington Spa
CV32 ....105 F1
Park The OX15 ......137 F3
Park View Cookhill B96 118 F3
Coventry CV3 ....62 A2
Hockley Heath B94 ...88 C6
Park View CV7 ......50 A8
Park Wood La CV4 ....75 D7
Parkend B77 ....83 B4
Parkers La CV7 ......140 A3
Parkes St CV34 .....108 D7
Parkfield B93 ....72 A1
Parkfield Cl B97 .....9 B4
Parkfield Cres B77 ...9 B4
Parkfield Ct 11 B46 ...33 F7
Parkfield Dr
Birmingham B36 .....22 C1
Kenilworth CV8 ......93 B5
Parkfield Rd Coleshill B46 33 F6
Keresley CV7 ....49 A6
Rugby CV21 ....82 C3
Parkfields CV47 .....147 A2
Parkgate Prim Sch CV6 49 B3
Parkgate Rd CV6 .....49 C3
Parkhill Dr CV5 ......60 A5
Parkinson Dr CV9 ....12 C1
Parkland Cl CV6 .....49 C3
Parklands Ave CV32 ..106 C4
Parkside CV1 ....151 C2
Parkside CV LE10 ....31 E8
Parkstone Rd CV6 ....49 F2
Parkview CV5 ....151 A1
Parkville Cl CV6 .....49 A3
Parkville Highway CV6 .49 B3
Parkway CV2 ....63 B8
Parkwood Ct CV8 ....93 B5
Parmington Cl B97 ...102 A4
Parmiter Ho CV32 ....105 F2
Parnell Cl CV21 .....82 C2
Parolles Cl CV34 ....109 E3
Parr Cl CV34 ....109 D6
Parrotts Gr CV2 .....50 D5
Parry Rd CV2 ....62 C7
Parson St B77 ......9 C4
Parson's La LE10 .....31 F8
Parson's Nook CV2 ...62 A5
Parsonage Cl CV33 ...122 F8
Parsons Cl CV36 ....149 C3
Parsons Hollow B77 ..9 C4
Parsons Rd NN11 ....117 F3
Partridge Cl
Birmingham B37 .....33 D3
Charwelton NN11 ....126 D3
Partridge Croft CV6 ...50 A1
Partridge La B97 ....102 A4
Partridge Rd CV37 ...144 B2
Patch La B98 ....102 C3
Paterson Ct B93 .....72 C6
Patience Gr CV34 ....109 F3
Patricia Cl CV4 .....59 C1
Pattens Rd CV34 ....105 B1
Patterdale CV21 .....83 B4
Patterton Dr B76 ....22 A7
Pattison Coll CV3 ....62 A2
Paul Stacy Ho CV1 ...151 D4
Pauline Ave CV6 .....50 B2
Pavilion The B77 ....4 A2
Pavilion Way CV5 ....60 F3
Paxmead Cl CV6 .....49 A2
Paxton Rd CV6 ......61 A4
Payne Cl CV32 ......106 A2
Payne's La CV1 ......61 F3
Paynell Cl CV6 ......49 B2
Paynes La CV2 ......82 B2
Payton St CV37 .....145 A2
Peace Wlk B37 ......33 B1
Peacock Ave CV2 ....50 F1
Peacock Cl CV35 ....146 B2
Peacock La CV35 ....138 C7
Peacocks The CV34 ..108 B2
Peake Ave CV11 .....29 E7
Pear Tree Ave
Kingsbury B78 ......15 B3
Nuneaton CV10 .....28 E6
Pear Tree Cl
Chipping Campden GL55 135 B1
4 Coventry CV2 .....50 B2
Shuttington B79 .....4 C4
Pear Tree Way CV22 ..82 A1
Pearl Hyde Ho 4 CV1 151 C4
Pearl Hyde Prim Sch
CV2 ....63 A5
Pearmans Croft B47 ..69 A6
Pears Cl CV8 ....92 F5
Pearson Ave CV6 ....50 B2
Peart Dr B80 ....103 B2
Peartrees CV47 .....133 B7
Peat Cl CV22 ....82 C1
Pebble Cl B77 ......4 A2
Pebble Island Way
CV31 ....110 C6
Pebblebrook Way CV12 39 C1
Pebworth Ave B90 ...71 B6
Pebworth Cl CV5 .....60 B3
Pebworth Dr CV35 ...114 F6
Pebworth Fst Sch CV37 128 F1

Peddimore La B76 ....22 C7
Pedmore Cl B98 ....103 A4
Peel Cl Coventry CV6 ..61 C6
Drayton Bassett B78 ...8 C3
Hampton-in-A B92 ...57 B6
Peel Ct B78 ....61 C6
Peel La CV6 ....61 F5
Peel Rd CV34 ......108 E8
Peel St CV6 ....61 E6
Pegasus Prim Sch B35 .22 A2
Pegmill Cl CV3 ......77 F8
Pelham La B49 ......119 D5
Pembridge Rd B93 ...71 E3
Pembroke Cl
Bedworth CV12 .....38 C1
1 Warwick CV34 ...108 F8
Pembroke Ct 8 CV32 .108 F8
Pembroke Gdns CV35 146 B1
Pembroke Way CV11 ..29 D3
Pembrook Rd CV6 ....49 C4
Pembury Ave CV6 ....50 A3
Penarth Gr CV3 .....78 F7
Pencraig Cl CV8 .....93 C5
Pendenis Cl CV6 .....62 A8
Penderel Ct CV6 .....49 C3
Pendicke Ct CV47 ...147 A2
Pendicke St CV47 ...147 A2
Pendigo Way
Birmingham B40 .....44 E3
Birmingham B40 .....44 F4
Pendine Ct 4 CV32 ..109 D8
Pendred Rd CV22 ....82 C2
Pendrell Cl B37 .....33 A3
Penelope Cl CV33 ...123 F6
Penfold Cl 3 CV33 ..122 F8
Penmire Cl CV9 .....11 B2
Penn Ho CV4 ....59 F1
Penn La
Tanworth-In-A B94 ...86 C4
Wibtoft LE17 ......43 B1
Pennant Rd LE10 ....31 D5
Pennine Way
Nuneaton CV10 .....28 B3
Tamworth B77 ......10 A4
Pennington Mews 4
CV21 ....82 C2
Pennington St 1 CV21 .82 C2
Pennington Way CV6 ..61 E8
Penns Cl CV32 ......106 E5
Penns La B46 ....33 F7
Penny Park La CV6 ...49 A3
Pennyford La B95 ....113 B1
Pennymoor Rd B77 ...10 A4
Pennystone Cl CV31 ..110 D6
Penrhyn Cl OX16 ....139 F4
Penrith Cl Coventry CV6 49 C2
Royal Leamington Spa
CV32 ....105 C2
Penrith Gr B37 ......33 C2
Penrose Cl CV4 .....76 A7
Penryhn Cl CV8 .....93 C5
Penryn Cl CV11 .....30 A5
Pensham Croft B90 ...71 A6
Penshurst Way CV11 ..39 F8
Pensilva Way 2 CV1 ..61 E4
Pentire Cl CV11 .....29 C5
Penzance Way CV11 ..30 A5
Pepper La CV1 ......151 B2
Pepys Cnr CV4 ......59 E3
Perch Ave B37 ......33 A3
Perchfoot Cl CV1 ....151 C1
Percival Dr CV33 ...123 F6
Percival Rd CV22 ...100 B4
Percy Cres CV8 .....92 E2
Percy Rd Kenilworth CV8 92 E2
Warwick CV34 ......108 E8
Percy St Coventry CV1 151 A3
Stratford-u-A CV37 ..145 A2
Percy Terr 5 CV32 ...105 D1
Peregrine Dr CV5 ....60 A5
Perimeter Rd
Birmingham B40 .....44 D4
Birmingham B40 .....44 E4
Periwinkle Cotts WR11 127 F6
Perkins Cl Hornton OX15 139 B8
Salford Priors WR11 ..127 E6
Perkins Gr CV21 ....83 C1
Permian Cl CV21 ....83 B3
Perry Mill La B95 ...112 F6
Perryfields Cl B98 ...102 C3
Perryford Dr B91 ....71 C8
Perryman Dr B78 ....15 C4
Perrymill La B96 ....103 A1
Peter Hall La CV7,CV23 64 A3
Peterbrook Cl B98 ...102 C4
Peterbrook Rd B90 ...69 E8
Peterlee Wlk 6 CV2 ..63 A7
Peters Wlk CV6 .....50 A4
Petitor Cres CV2 ....50 C1
Peto Gr CV34 ......109 F2
Pettiford La B95 ....113 C3
Pettiphers Farm CV37 129 A3
Pettiver Cres CV21 ...83 C1
Pettyfields Cl B93 ...72 A5
Peveril Dr CV3 ......77 B5
Peyto Cl CV6 ....49 C2
Pheasant Cl
Bedworth CV12 .....38 D1
Stratford-u-A CV37 ..144 B2
Pheasant Croft B36 ..33 A8
Pheasant La B98 ....102 C4
Pheasant Oak CV4 ...59 C2
Philip Ct
1 Royal Leamington Spa
CV31 ....109 F1

Philip Ct continued
10 Rugby CV21 ......83 A2
Phillip Docker Ct CV12 .40 B2
Phillippes Rd 6 CV34 .104 F1
Phipps Ave CV21 .....83 C1
Phoenix Bsns Pk LE10 .30 E8
Phoenix Ho CV1 .....151 C4
Phoenix Pk Ind Est CV7 50 B7
Phoenix Way CV6 ....49 E3
Piccadilly B78 ......9 C1
Piccadilly Cl B37 ....33 C1
Piccadilly Cres B78 ...9 C1
Pickard Cl CV21 ....83 C4
Pickard St CV34 ....109 A4
Pickford Cl CV11 ....30 A1
Pickford Grange La CV5 59 C7
Pickford Green La CV5 .59 C7
Pickford Way CV5 ...60 B6
Picton Croft 6 B37 ..33 D2
Piers Cl CV34 ......108 F8
Pike Cl LE10 ....31 D5
Pike Dr B37 ....33 C3
Pikehorne Croft B36 ..22 D2
Pikers La CV7 ......48 A3
Pilgrims Gate LE10 ...32 A6
Pilgrims La CV23 ....67 C1
Pilkington Rd CV5 ...76 D8
Pill La GL56 ....140 F1
Pilling Cl CV2 ......62 F8
Pimlico La CV37 ....121 D2
Pinbury Croft B37 ...33 B1
Pinchester Cl GL56 ..141 A1
Pinders Ct 13 CV21 ..83 A2
Pinders La CV21 ....83 A2
Pine Cl Stoke Golding CV13 21 C4
Stratford-u-A CV37 ..144 B1
Pine Ct Coventry CV5 .59 C4
Royal Leamington Spa
CV32 ....106 B3
Pine Gr CV21 ......84 A1
Pine Sq B37 ....33 B2
Pine Tree Ave CV4 ...60 A2
Pine Tree Cres CV47 .147 B3
Pine Tree Ct CV12 ...39 C4
Pine Tree Rd CV12 ...39 D4
Pineham Ave CV33 ..123 F6
Pinehurst CV32 .....2 C2
Pines The Bedworth CV12 38 E2
Cheswick Green B90 ..70 D5
Coventry CV4 ....75 D7
Pinewood Ave CV9 ...10 B1
Pinewood Dr CV3 ....79 C7
Pinewood Gr CV5 ....77 B8
Pinfold Gn NN11 ....126 F6
Pinfold St CV21 .....82 C2
Pingle Ct CV11 .....29 D2
Pink Green La B98 ...112 A8
Pinley Fields CV3 ...78 B8
Pinner's Croft CV2 ...62 A5
Pinnock Pl CV4 .....59 F1
Pinwall La CV9 ......12 C2
Pioneer Ho
Birmingham B35 .....22 C3
Coventry CV1 ....151 D4
Pipe La CV9 ....6 B2
Piper's End LE10 ....41 B2
Piper's La CV8 ......93 A5
Pipers La CV10 .....27 C5
Pipers Rd B98 ......103 B4
Pipewell Cl CV22 ...82 B1
Pippin Cl B50 ......148 B3
Pirie Cl CV33 ......123 F6
Pit Hill CV8 ....95 B3
Pitt La B92 ....44 D2
Pittons La CV23 ....101 A3
Pittway Ave CV36 ...149 C3
Pixhall Wlk B35 ....22 B3
Plain Rd The OX15 ..139 A3
Plane Gr B37 ....33 B1
Plank La B46 ....23 A3
Plantagenet Dr CV22 .99 C3
Plantagenet Pk CV34 109 E3
Plantation The OX17 .134 C1
Planter Cl CV4 .....59 A4
Plants Brook Rd B76 ..22 A6
Plants Hill Cres CV4 ..59 E1
Plato Cl CV4 ....109 E5
Pleasant Way CV32 ..106 A4
Pleck Cl B50 ....148 B2
Pleck The B50 .....148 B2
Plexfield Rd CV22 ...82 B1
Pleydell Cl CV3 .....78 C5
Plomer Cl CV22 ....99 B4
Plot Rd OX15 ......139 A3
Plott La CV23 ......96 C3
Plough Hill Rd CV10 ..28 A6
Plough La CV47 ....124 A4
Ploughmans Holt CV47 147 A3
Plover Cl Alcester B49 143 A3
Stratford-u-A CV37 ..144 B3
Plowden Cl NN11 ...134 F5
Plowman St CV21 ...82 C2
Plymouth Cl CV2 ....62 C7
Plymouth Pl CV31 ...110 A7
Poins Cl CV34 ......109 F3
Poitiers Rd CV3 .....77 D6
Polesworth High Sch
B78 ....10 C4
Polesworth Sta B78 ..5 A2
Polperro Dr CV5 ....60 A5
Pomeroy Cl CV4 ....75 D7
Pond Farm Mews CV5 59 C5
Pondthorpe CV3 ....78 E6
Pontrilas Rd CV35 ...132 D4
Pontypool Ave CV3 ..78 F6

Pool Bank St CV11 .....**29** B4
Pool Cl
  Little Compton GL56 ...**140** F1
  Rugby CV22 ....**99** B4
  Welford on A CV37 ....**129** B6
Pool Close Cotts GL56 .**140** F1
Pool End CV93 ....**71** F6
Pool Mdw B76 ....**22** A8
Pool Rd Nuneaton CV10 ..**28** F5
  Studley B80 ....**103** C2
Pool Road Bsns Ctr CV10 **28** F5
Poole Rd CV6 ....**61** A6
Pooley Fields Heritage Ctr★
  B78 ....**4** C2
Pooley La B78 ....**4** C1
Pooley View B78 ....**5** A1
Poolgate CV35 ....**138** B6
Poolhead La
  Earlswood B94 ....**86** C7
  Tanworth-In-A B94 ....**86** E5
Poolside Gdns CV3 ......**77** A5
Pope St CV22 ....**82** C2
Popes La B96 ....**102** C1
Poplar Ave Bedworth CV12 **39** D2
  Birmingham, Coleshill Heath
    B37 ....**44** C8
Poplar Cl Alcester B49 ..**143** B2
  Knightcote CV47 ......**124** C4
Poplar Gr Rugby CV21 ...**83** A2
  Ryton-on-D CV8 ....**79** B1
Poplar Ho CV12 ....**39** D2
Poplar Rd
  Bishops Itchington CV47 .**124** B4
  Coventry CV5 ....**60** F1
  Dorridge B93 ....**71** F3
  Napton on t H CV47 ...**125** C8
Poplar Trees B47 ....**69** A6
Poplar Way WR11 ....**127** D4
Poplars Cl GL55 ....**135** B4
Poplars La B96 ....**102** A1
Poplars The
  Bidford-on-A B50 ......**148** C3
  Nuneaton CV10 ....**28** D3
Poplars Trad Est B80 ...**103** B3
Poppy Dr CV23 ....**83** C4
Poppyfield Ct CV4 ....**76** D3
Porchester Cl CV3 ....**63** A2
Porlock Cl CV3 ....**77** E5
Porter Cl CV4 ....**75** E8
Portia Cl CV11 ....**30** A1
Portia Way CV34 ....**109** E3
Portland Ct ⑨ CV32 ....**109** F8
Portland Dr CV10 ....**28** C4
Portland Pl CV21 ....**83** B1
Portland Pl E CV32 .....**109** F8
Portland Pl W ⑤ CV32 .**109** E8
Portland Rd CV21 ....**83** B1
Portland St CV32 ....**109** F8
Portleys La B78 ....**8** B2
Portmanteau Mews B94 .**88** C6
Portree Ave CV3 ....**62** F2
Portsea Cl CV3 ....**77** D6
Portway Cl Coventry CV4 .**75** E8
  Royal Leamington Spa
    CV31 ....**110** D6
Portwrinkle Ave CV6 ....**62** A6
Poseidon Way CV34 .....**109** F4
Post House Gdns CV23 ..**66** A4
Post Office La
  Lighthorne CV35 ......**123** B2
  Stockton CV47 ....**147** C4
  Witherley CV9 ....**19** A4
Post Office Rd CV8 ......**11** B1
Post Office Wlk B96 ....**102** C1
Post Office Yd CV23 .....**64** C2
Postbridge Rd CV3 ......**77** D5
Postle Cl CV23 ....**101** C1
Potters Cl CV23 ....**64** C2
Potters Green Prim Sch
  CV2 ....**50** E2
Potters Green Rd CV2 ...**50** E1
Potters La
  Darlingscott CV36 ....**136** D5
  Polesworth B78 ....**11** A4
Potters Rd CV12 ....**38** E1
Potton Cl CV3 ....**78** E6
Potts Cl CV8 ....**93** C4
Poultney Rd CV6 ....**61** A6
Pound Cl Berkswell CV7 ..**58** D3
  Lapworth B94 ....**89** B3
  Shipston-on-S CV36 ..**149** C3
Pound Field B95 ....**113** B2
Pound House La
  Tanworth-in-A B94 .....**87** F4
  Tanworth-in-A B94 .....**88** A4
Pound La Badby NN11 ...**126** F6
  Coleshill B46 ....**34** A2
  Furnace End B46 ......**25** B2
  Mickleton GL55 ....**135** B6
  Royal Leamington Spa
    CV32 ....**106** A3
  Sibford Gower OX15 ..**138** D1
Pound The OX15 ....**139** D2
Pound Way CV47 ....**147** D2
Powell Cl ⑰ CV33 ......**122** F8
Powell Rd CV2 ....**62** A4
Powell Way CV11 ....**29** C4
Powers Ct ④ CV32 .....**105** F1
Powis Gr CV8 ....**93** C5
Powys Gr OX16 ....**139** F4
Poyser Rd CV10 ....**39** C8
Pratts La B80 ....**112** A4
Prebend The CV47 ......**133** B7
Precinct The CV1 ....**151** B3
Precision Way B49 .....**143** B3

Prentice Cl CV23 ....**82** A3
Prescelly Cl CV10 ....**28** B3
Prescelly Ct CV10 ....**28** B3
Prescott Ave OX16 .....**139** F3
President Kennedy Sch &
  Com Coll CV6 ....**49** B4
Prestbury Cl B98 ....**112** A6
Preston Cl CV4 ....**75** F7
Preston Fields La B95 ..**113** D6
Preston La CV37 ....**130** A4
Prestwick Rd B35 ....**22** B4
Pretorian Way CV21 .....**83** A4
Priam Cir CV34 ....**109** F3
Price Rd CV32 ....**106** E5
Pridmore Rd CV6 ....**61** D7
Priest Meadow Cl B96 ..**102** B1
Priestfield Rd B97 ......**102** C3
Priesthills Rd LE10 ....**31** D8
Primley Ave B77 ....**9** C3
Primrose Cl CV23 ....**83** C4
Primrose Ct GL56 ......**140** A3
Primrose Dr
  Bedworth CV12 ....**38** E1
  Hinckley LE10 ....**31** E5
Primrose Hill CV34 .....**104** E2
Primrose Hill St CV1 ...**151** C4
Primrose La
  Alcester B49 ....**143** B1
  Solihull B90 ....**70** A5
Primsland Cl B90 ....**71** C7
Prince Harry Rd B95 ...**113** D6
Prince of Wales Rd CV5 .**60** E3
Prince Regent Ct ③
  CV31 ....**109** F6
Prince William Cl CV6 ...**60** E6
Prince's Ave CV11 ....**29** B3
Prince's Dr CV31 ....**109** D7
Prince's Rd B78 ....**5** A1
Prince's St Nuneaton CV11 **29** C3
  Royal Leamington Spa
    CV32 ....**106** B1
Princes Cl CV3 ....**78** B8
Princes Ct ① CV21 .....**83** A2
Princes Dr Coventry CV3 ..**50** B1
  Kenilworth CV8 ....**93** B7
Princes Rd CV9 ....**16** B3
Princes St CV21 ....**83** A2
Princess Rd
  Atherstone CV9 ....**18** C4
  Hinckley LE10 ....**31** E8
Princess St CV6 ....**61** F7
Princethorpe Coll CV8 ...**96** B2
Princethorpe Way CV3 ..**78** E8
Printers Pl CV37 ....**144** C2
Prior Deram Wlk CV4 ...**76** C7
Priors Cl CV7 ....**74** B6
Priors Ct CV47 ....**125** E4
Priors Field Prim Sch
  CV8 ....**92** D7
Priors Grange WR11 ...**127** F6
Priors Harnall CV1 .....**151** C4
Priors Marston Rd
  NN11 ....**126** B5
Priors Mdw CV47 ......**147** B2
Priors The CV12 ....**39** C2
Priorsfield Rd
  ④ Coventry CV6 ......**61** A4
  Kenilworth CV8 ....**92** D6
Priorsfield Rd N ③ CV6 .**61** A4
Priorsfield Rd S CV6 ....**61** A4
Priory Cl Coleshill B46 ...**34** A3
  Lapworth B94 ....**89** D5
Priory Croft CV8 ....**93** A4
Priory Ct Coventry CV5 ..**61** A1
  Nuneaton CV11 ....**29** A4
  Solihull B91 ....**71** B7
  Studley B80 ....**103** C3
Priory Ho CV8 ....**92** F4
Priory La CV35 ....**131** D2
Priory Mews CV34 ......**108** E7
Priory Rd Alcester B49 ..**143** A2
  Kenilworth CV8 ....**93** A4
  Warwick CV34 ....**108** E7
  Wolston CV8 ....**80** A2
Priory Row CV1 ....**151** C3
Priory Sq B80 ....**103** C3
Priory St Coventry CV1 ..**151** C3
  Nuneaton CV10 ....**28** D3
  Royal Leamington Spa
    CV31 ....**109** F6
Priory Terr CV31 ....**110** A7
Priory Visitors Ctr★
  CV1 ....**151** C3
Priory Wlk Atherstone CV9 **18** C3
  ⑧ Warwick CV34 ....**108** F7
Privet Rd CV2 ....**50** B2
Proffitt Ave CV6 ....**50** A1
Progress Cl CV3 ....**79** A7
Progress Way CV3 ....**79** A8
Projects Dr CV21 ....**83** B3
Prospect Rd CV31 ......**110** B5
Prospect Way
  Daventry NN11 ....**117** F2
  Rugby CV21 ....**83** B3
Prospero Dr CV34 ......**109** E3
Prossers Wlk B46 ....**33** F7
Providence St CV5 ....**76** F8
Provost Williams CE Prim
  Sch CV8 ....**79** A1
Ptarmigan Pl CV11 ......**29** F2
Puckering's La ⑪ CV34 **108** E6
Pudding Bag La CV23 ...**98** C1
Pudlicott La GL55 ......**135** E1
Pughe's Cl LE10 ....**32** A6
Pullman Cl B77 ....**4** A1
Puma Way CV1 ....**151** C1
Pump La CV7 ....**36** B2
Purbrook B77 ....**9** C4

Purcell Ave CV11 ....**40** A7
Purcell Cl CV32 ....**110** A8
Purcell Rd CV6 ....**62** B8
Purefoy Rd CV3 ....**77** D8
Purley Chase La CV9 ....**18** B2
Purley Way CV9 ....**18** C3
Purlieu La CV8 ....**92** D5
Purnells Way B93 ....**72** A5
Purser Dr CV34 ....**108** A1
Purton Cl B49 ....**143** B3
Purton Mews CV31 .....**110** C6
Putney Wlk B37 ....**33** B3
Pye Ct CV23 ....**117** B6
Pyeharps Rd LE10 ....**31** E5
Pyt Pk CV5 ....**60** D4
Pytchley Rd CV22 ....**83** B1
Pytman Dr B76 ....**22** A7

Q

Quadrangle The B90 ....**70** E8
Quadrant The
  Coventry CV1 ....**151** B2
  Nuneaton CV11 ....**29** E3
Quail La CV37 ....**144** B2
Quaker Cl CV13 ....**20** A3
Quantock Dr CV10 ....**28** B3
Quarry Berry La DE12 ....**2** C4
Quarry Cl
  Leek Wootton CV35 ...**104** F7
  Rugby CV21 ....**82** C3
Quarry Fields CV35 ....**104** F7
Quarry La Atherstone CV9 .**19** A3
  Cleeve Prior WR11 ...**128** A4
  Nuneaton CV11 ....**29** F1
  Rowington Green CV35 ..**90** C1
Quarry Rd CV8 ....**92** E6
Quarry St CV32 ....**109** C8
Quarry Yd CV10 ....**28** C4
Quarryfield La CV1 .....**151** C1
Quarrywood Gr CV2 ......**62** A4
Queen Eleanors Dr B93 .**72** B8
Queen Elizabeth Rd
  CV10 ....**28** D5
Queen Elizabeth Sch
  CV9 ....**18** C4
Queen Isabel's Ave CV3 .**77** D8
Queen Margaret's Rd
  CV4 ....**76** C8
Queen Mary's Rd
  Bedworth CV12 ....**39** C5
  Coventry CV6 ....**61** E8
Queen Philippa St CV3 .**77** D6
Queen St
  Astwood Bank B96 ...**102** C1
  Bedworth CV12 ....**39** C2
  Coventry CV1 ....**151** C4
  Cubbington CV32 .....**106** C5
  Hook Norton OX15 ...**142** D4
  Royal Leamington Spa
    CV32 ....**106** A1
  Rugby CV21 ....**83** A2
Queen Victoria Rd
  Coventry CV1 ....**151** B2
  Coventry CV1 ....**151** A2
Queen Victoria St CV21 .**83** B2
Queen's Cl CV3 ....**92** F3
Queen's Cres OX15 ....**139** E4
Queen's Dr CV35 ....**90** A1
Queen's Park Ct ③ LE10 **31** E8
Queen's Park Flats ②
  LE10 ....**31** E8
Queen's Park Terr ④
  LE10 ....**31** E8
Queen's Rd
  Atherstone CV9 ....**18** C4
  Coventry CV1 ....**151** A2
  Hinckley LE10 ....**31** E8
  Kenilworth CV8 ....**92** F3
  Nuneaton CV11 ....**29** B4
Queen's Sq CV34 ......**108** D5
Queens Arc CV11 ....**29** C4
Queens Ave CV36 ......**149** C3
Queens CE Jun Sch CV11 **29** A4
Queens Cl Harbury CV33 **123** F6
  Shipston-on-S CV36 ..**149** C3
Queens Ct CV11 ....**29** A4
Queens Dr CV31 ....**110** A7
Queens Rd Bretford CV23 **80** C4
  Tredington CV36 .....**136** F6
Queens St CV36 ....**136** F8
Queens Way Dordon B78 .**10** C3
  Hurley CV9 ....**16** B2
Queensferry Cl CV22 ....**99** B4
Queensland Ave CV5 ....**60** F2
Queenspark CV31 ......**109** E6
Queensway
  Bidford-on-A B50 .....**148** B3
  Nuneaton CV10 ....**29** E6
  Royal Leamington Spa
    CV31 ....**109** E6
Queensway Trad Est
  CV31 ....**109** E6
Queenswood Cl CV7 ....**48** D4
Quillets Cl CV6 ....**50** A1
Quince B77 ....**4** A2
Quince Tree Sch B77 .....**4** A2
Quiney's Leys CV37 ....**129** A7
Quiney's Rd CV37 ......**144** B1
Quinn Cl CV3 ....**78** B7
Quinney's Ct B50 ......**148** B2
Quinney's La B50 ......**148** C3
Quinneys La B98 ....**103** A3
Quinton Cl CV35 ....**114** E6
Quinton Flats CV3 ....**77** D7
Quinton Grange CV37 ..**129** E1

Quinton Par CV3 ....**77** D7
Quinton Pk CV3 ....**77** D7
Quinton Prim Sch CV37 **129** D2
Quinton Rd CV1 ....**151** C1
Quintondale ⑤ B90 ....**70** C8
Quorn Way CV3 ....**78** E7

R

Race Leys Inf Sch CV12 .**39** B3
Race Leys Jun Sch CV12 .**39** B3
Racemeadow Prim Sch
  CV9 ....**12** C1
Racemeadow Rd CV9 ....**12** C1
Radbourne Cl CV47 ....**147** B2
Radbourne La CV47 ....**124** E5
Radbrook Way CV31 ....**110** D6
Radburn Cl GL56 ....**140** B3
Radcliffe Gdns ⑥ CV31 **110** A6
Radcliffe Rd CV5 ....**76** F8
Radford Circ ⑤ CV6 ....**61** A4
Radford Cl CV9 ....**12** C1
Radford Hall CV31 ......**110** E6
Radford Ho CV6 ....**61** A7
Radford Prim Sch CV6 ..**61** B5
Radford Rd
  Coventry CV1,CV6 .....**61** B5
  Royal Leamington Spa
    CV31 ....**110** C2
Radford Semele CE Prim Sch
  CV31 ....**110** E5
Radley Dr CV10 ....**29** A1
Radlow Cres B37 ....**44** B8
Radnor Dr CV10 ....**28** B2
Radnor Wlk CV2 ....**62** F8
Radway Ind Est B90 .....**70** E7
Radway Rd B90 ....**70** E8
Raglan Cl CV11 ....**29** D4
Raglan Ct ⑦ CV1 ....**61** E3
Raglan Gr CV8 ....**93** B5
Raglan St CV1 ....**151** D4
Raglan Way B37 ....**33** D1
Ragley Cl B93 ....**72** B7
Ragley Hall★ B96 ......**118** F2
Ragley Mill La B49 .....**143** A2
Ragley Rd WR11 ....**127** D4
Ragley Way CV11 ....**29** F2
Railway Cl B80 ....**103** B2
Railway Cres CV36 ....**149** C4
Railway Mews B49 .....**143** A2
Railway St CV23 ....**82** A2
Railway Terr
  Atherstone CV9 ....**18** B4
  Bedworth CV12 ....**39** C2
  Rugby CV21 ....**83** A2
Rainbow Fields CV36 ..**149** C3
Rainsbrook Ave CV22 ..**100** C4
Rainsbrook Cl CV47 ...**147** B2
Rainsbrook Dr
  Nuneaton CV11 ....**30** A1
  Solihull B90 ....**70** F6
Rainsbrook Secure Training
  Ctr CV23 ....**100** B1
Rainsbrook Valley Rly★
  CV22 ....**100** B3
Rainscar B77 ....**10** A4
Rainsford Cl CV37 ......**129** F7
Raison Ave CV11 ....**29** F8
Raleigh Rd CV2 ....**62** B2
Ralph Cres B78 ....**15** B3
Ralph Rd CV6 ....**60** F5
Ramp Rd B26 ....**44** C5
Ramsay Cres CV5 ....**60** B7
Ramsden Ave CV10 ......**28** D6
Ramsden Ct CV10 ....**28** C7
Ramsden Rd CV9 ....**19** A4
Ramsey Rd CV31 ....**110** B7
Ramshill La B94 ....**112** B7
Ran-tan The B97 ....**102** C3
Ranby Rd CV2 ....**61** F4
Randall Rd CV8 ....**92** F3
Randle Rd CV10 ....**28** D4
Randle St CV6 ....**61** B5
Randolph Cl ⑪ CV31 ..**110** C6
Ranelagh St CV31 .....**110** A6
Ranelagh Terr CV31 ...**109** F6
Range Meadow Cl CV32 **105** C3
Range Way B78 ....**15** B3
Rangemoor CV3 ....**78** D6
Rangeworthy Cl B97 ...**102** B4
Rankine Cl CV21 ....**82** B4
Rannoch Cl LE10 ....**31** B8
Rannoch Dr CV10 ....**28** C5
Rannock Cl CV3 ....**62** F2
Ransom Rd CV6 ....**61** E8
Ranulf Croft CV3 ....**77** C7
Ranulf St CV3 ....**77** C7
Raphael Cl CV5 ....**60** C3
Rashwood Cl B94 ....**88** B6
Ratcliffe Ct CV10 ....**28** C4
Ratcliffe La CV9 ....**12** C2
Ratcliffe Rd
  Atherstone CV9 ....**12** C1
  Hinckley LE10 ....**31** F6
Ratcliffe St CV9 ....**18** B4
Rathbone Cl Keresley CV7 **49** A6
  Rugby CV21 ....**101** A4
Rathlin Croft B36 ....**33** B6
Ratliffe Rd CV22 ....**99** C4
Rattlecombe Rd OX15 ..**138** E5
Raveloe Dr CV11 ....**29** D1
Raven Cragg Rd CV5 ....**76** E8
Raven Way CV11 ....**29** F2
Ravenglass CV21 ....**83** A4
Ravensdale Ave CV32 ..**105** C2

Ravensdale Prim Sch
  CV2 ....**62** D4
Ravensdale Rd CV2 .....**62** D3
Ravenshaw La B91 ....**56** A4
Ravenshaw Way B91 ....**56** A3
Ravensholt CV4 ....**76** D6
Ravensthorpe Cl CV3 ...**78** E8
Ravenstone B77 ....**10** A4
Ravenswood Hill B46 ....**33** F7
Rawlins Croft B35 ....**22** C3
Rawlinson Rd CV32 ....**106** B2
Rawn View CV9 ....**18** C3
Rawnsley Dr CV8 ....**93** C6
Raygill B77 ....**10** A4
Raymond Cl CV6 ....**49** F5
Raynor Cres CV12 ....**38** D1
Raynsford Wlk CV34 ...**104** D1
Raywoods The CV10 .....**28** F3
Read St CV1 ....**61** E3
Reading Ave CV11 ....**29** F7
Reading Cl CV2 ....**50** B3
Readings The CV47 ....**133** E7
Reardon Ct CV34 ......**104** E1
Recreation Rd CV6 ......**50** A3
Rectory Cl Allesley CV5 ..**60** C6
  Barby CV23 ....**101** B1
  Bedworth CV7 ....**39** A1
  Drayton Bassett B78 ....**8** C3
  Harvington WR11 ....**127** D3
  Stockton CV47 ....**147** C4
  Warmington OX17 ...**133** D2
  Whitnash CV31 ....**110** B4
Rectory Dr CV7 ....**39** A1
Rectory Gdns OX15 ....**139** E4
Rectory La Allesley CV5 ..**60** C6
  Barby CV23 ....**101** B1
  Lower Brailes OX15 ..**137** F2
  Whatcote CV36 ......**137** D7
Rectory Rd Arley CV7 ....**26** C1
  Hook Norton OX15 ...**142** D4
  Sutton Coldfield B75 ...**13** A6
Red Deeps CV11 ....**39** D8
Red Hill CV35 ....**131** B8
Red Hill Cl B80 ....**103** C3
Red La Astley CV10 ......**37** C4
  Burton Green CV8 .....**75** C2
  Coventry CV6 ....**61** F5
  Kenilworth CV8 ....**92** D8
Red Lion Cl CV47 ......**147** C4
Red Lion St OX17 ......**134** C1
Red Lodge Dr CV22 .....**99** C4
Red Rd CV35 ....**132** B5
Red Wing Wlk B36 ......**33** A8
Redcap Croft CV6 ....**49** D4
Redcar Cl CV32 ....**106** C4
Redcar Rd CV1 ....**61** E5
Reddicap Heath Rd B75 .**13** A4
Reddings The B47 ......**69** A5
Redditch Rd B80 ....**103** B3
Redditch Wlk ④ CV2 ...**63** A7
Redesdale Ave CV6 .....**60** F5
Redesdale Mews ⑥
  GL56 ....**140** A3
Redesdale Pl GL56 ....**140** A2
Redfern Ave CV8 ....**93** A6
Redgrave Cl CV2 ....**63** B8
Redhill Bank CV37 .....**130** B3
Redhill Cl CV35 ....**146** B1
Redhouse Cl B93 ....**71** E4
Redlake B77 ....**9** C4
Redland Cl CV2 ....**50** E2
Redland La CV8 ....**79** A2
Redland Rd CV31 ......**110** B5
Redlands Cres CV37 ...**144** B3
Redliff Ave B36 ....**22** D1
Redmoor Way B76 ....**22** D6
Redruth Cl Coventry CV6 .**62** A4
  Nuneaton CV11 ....**30** A4
Redthorne Gr CV8 ....**93** B8
Redwing B77 ....**10** A3
Redwing Cl CV37 ......**144** B3
Redwood Croft CV11 ....**29** A1
Redwood Dr B78 ....**15** B4
Reed Sq B35 ....**22** B4
Rees Dr CV3 ....**77** D4
Reeve Dr CV8 ....**93** A4
Reeves Rd LE10 ....**31** F6
Reg Hadden Ct CV10 ....**29** D6
Regal Cl B77 ....**9** B4
Regal Ct CV9 ....**18** C4
Regal Rd CV37 ....**144** C2
Regal Road Trad Est
  CV37 ....**144** C2
Regan Ct B75 ....**13** C5
Regency Arc ⑥ CV32 ..**109** F8
Regency Cl CV10 ....**29** D6
Regency Ct CV5 ....**76** F8
Regency Dr Alcester B49 **143** A3
  Coventry CV3 ....**76** F5
  Kenilworth CV8 ....**92** F3
Regency Ho CV32 ......**110** A8
Regency Mews CV32 ...**110** A8
Regent Ct ⑤ LE10 ....**31** E8
Regent Gr CV32 ....**109** F8
Regent Pl
  ④ Royal Leamington Spa
    CV31 ....**110** A7
  Rugby CV21 ....**83** A2
Regent St Bedworth CV12 **39** C4
  Coventry CV1 ....**151** A2
  Hinckley LE10 ....**31** D8
  Nuneaton CV11 ....**29** D5
  Royal Leamington Spa
    CV32 ....**109** F8
  Rugby CV21 ....**83** A2
Regiment Ct CV6 ....**49** A1

Regina Cres CV2 ....63 A7
Regis Wlk CV2 ....62 F7
Reignier Pl CV34 ....109 F2
Reindeer Rd B78 ....8 C4
Relay Dr B77 ....10 B4
Relton Mews CV6 ....61 F6
Rembrandt Cl CV5 ....60 C3
Remburn Gdns CV34 ....108 F8
Remembrance Rd CV3 ....78 D6
Renfrew Sq B35 ....22 B4
Renfrew Wlk CV4 ....76 A8
Renison Rd CV12 ....38 E1
Renolds Cl CV4 ....60 C2
Renown Ave CV4 ....60 C1
Repington Ave CV9 ....12 B1
Repington Rd N B77 ....4 A3
Repington Rd S B77 ....4 A3
Repington Way B75 ....13 B5
Repton Dr CV6 ....50 B2
Reservoir Dr B46 ....24 C1
Reservoir Rd CV21 ....83 B3
Retreat St B96 ....102 C1
Revel CE Prim Sch The CV23 ....53 C1
Rex Cl CV4 ....75 D8
Reynolds Cl CV21 ....84 A1
Reynolds Rd CV12 ....39 A4
Rhoose Croft B35 ....22 B3
Rhyl Rd CV11 ....40 F6
Ribble Cl CV12 ....40 B2
Ribble Rd CV3 ....61 F2
Ribblesdale B77 ....10 A4
Ribbonbrook CV11 ....29 D3
Ribbonfields CV11 ....29 D3
Rich Cl CV34 ....109 B7
Richard Joy Cl CV6 ....49 C2
Richard Lee Prim Sch CV2 ....62 E3
Richards Cl CV8 ....92 F5
Richards Gr CV31 ....110 A5
Richardson Cl CV34 ....104 F1
Richardson Way CV2 ....63 B8
Richman Gdns OX16 ....139 F4
Richmond Ct 6 CV31 ....110 B7
Richmond Ho 2 B37 ....33 C1
Richmond Rd
Atherstone CV9 ....18 B4
Hollywood B47 ....69 C7
Nuneaton CV11 ....29 A4
Rugby CV21 ....83 B1
Richmond St CV2 ....62 A3
Richmond Way 2 B37 ....33 C3
Rickard Cl B93 ....71 E6
Rickyard Cl B78 ....5 A1
Rickyard The OX15 ....139 A3
Riddell Cl B49 ....143 B2
Riddings Gdns B78 ....11 A4
Riddings Hill CV7 ....74 C8
Riddings La CV9 ....11 B2
Riddings The
Coventry CV5 ....76 E7
Grendon CV9 ....11 B1
Sutton Coldfield B76 ....22 B8
Riddon Dr LE10 ....31 B8
Ridewell Gr CV31 ....110 A1
Ridge Ct CV5 ....60 A6
Ridge Dr CV21 ....83 B2
Ridge La CV10 ....18 A1
Ridgeley Cl CV34 ....104 E2
Ridgethorpe CV3 ....78 E6
Ridgeway Ave CV3 ....77 C6
Ridgeway Cl B80 ....103 C1
Ridgeway Mid Sch B96 ....118 C8
Ridgeway Sch CV34 ....105 A1
Ridgeway The
Astwood Bank B96 ....118 D6
Barby CV23 ....117 F8
Hinckley LE10 ....31 D6
Warwick CV34 ....105 A1
Ridgeway Trad Est B96 ....102 C1
Ridgewood Cl CV32 ....105 C1
Ridgewood Rise B77 ....4 A3
Ridgley Rd CV4 ....75 E8
Ridgway The CV37 ....120 C3
Ridley La B46 ....25 A3
Ridsdale Cl WR11 ....127 F6
Rigby Cl CV34 ....109 D4
Rigdale Cl CV2 ....62 E2
Riley Cl Daventry NN11 ....117 F2
Kenilworth CV8 ....93 D4
Riley Ct CV21 ....83 B2
Riley Dr Banbury OX16 ....139 F4
Birmingham B36 ....23 A1
Riley Sq CV2 ....50 B1
Rimell Cl CV37 ....130 E1
Ringway Hill Cross CV1 ....151 A3
Ringway Queens CV1 ....151 A2
Ringway Rudge CV1 ....151 A2
Ringway St Johns CV1 ....151 C2
Ringway St Nicholas CV1 ....151 B3
Ringway St Patricks CV1 ....151 B1
Ringway Swanswell CV1 ....151 C3
Ringway Whitefriars CV1 ....151 C3
Ringwood Highway CV2 ....50 E2
Rinhill Gr CV31 ....110 D6
Riplingham 3 CV32 ....105 F2
Ripon Cl CV5 ....60 B8
Risborough Cl CV5 ....60 C3
Risdale Cl CV32 ....105 D2
Rise The B37 ....44 A7
Rising La
Chadwick End B93 ....90 B5
Lapworth B94,B93 ....89 F5
Rising Rd B94 ....89 C5
River Cl Bedworth CV12 ....38 F1
Royal Leamington Spa CV32 ....109 D8
River Ct 3 CV1 ....61 B3
River Dr CV9 ....12 B1
River House Specl Sch B95 ....113 B4
River Way CV36 ....137 A4
River Wlk CV2 ....50 C2
Riverbank Gdns CV37 ....145 A1
Riverford Croft CV4 ....76 D4
Rivermead CV11 ....29 A4
Rivermead Ct B50 ....148 B2
Rivermead Dr CV37 ....145 C2
Riversdale 6 CV32 ....109 E8
Riversdale Rd CV9 ....19 A4
Riverside Alcester B49 ....143 B2
Studley B80 ....103 C2
Witherley CV9 ....19 A4
Riverside Cl CV3 ....78 A7
Riverside Ct 1 B46 ....33 F7
Riverside Gdns B95 ....113 B4
Riverside Ind Est B78 ....9 A4
Riversleigh Rd CV32 ....105 C1
Riversley Rd CV11 ....29 C3
Ro-Oak Rd CV6 ....60 F5
Roach B77 ....9 B3
Roach Cl B37 ....33 C3
Roanne Ringway CV11 ....29 B4
Robbins Ct 5 CV22 ....100 C4
Robert Cl CV3 ....78 C4
Robert Cramb Ave CV4 ....75 F8
Robert Hill Cl CV21 ....84 A1
Robert Rd CV7 ....49 F8
Roberts Cl CV23 ....96 C3
Roberts La WR11 ....127 F1
Robertson Cl CV23 ....84 A3
Robey's La B78 ....4 B2
Robin Cl Birmingham B36 ....33 A8
Tamworth B77 ....9 B4
Robin Hood Rd CV3 ....78 C6
Robina Cl CV32 ....106 B2
Robinia B77 ....4 A2
Robins Cl OX7 ....142 A2
Robins Gr CV34 ....108 C4
Robins Way CV10 ....28 A3
Robinson Rd CV12 ....49 D8
Robinson Way LE10 ....31 F4
Robinson's Way B76 ....22 D5
Robotham Cl CV21 ....82 C3
Rocheberie Way CV22 ....99 C4
Rochester Cl
Nuneaton CV11 ....29 B3
Redditch B97 ....102 B4
Rochester Rd CV5 ....76 E8
Rochford Cl B76 ....22 A8
Rochford Ct
Royal Leamington Spa CV31 ....109 E7
Solihull B90 ....71 A6
Rock Cl Coventry CV6 ....50 B1
Nuneaton CV10 ....27 C2
Rock La CV7 ....48 C7
Rock Mill La CV32 ....109 C8
Rocken End CV6 ....61 D8
Rockford Cl B98 ....102 C3
Rockingham Cl B93 ....71 D2
Rockingham Dr CV11 ....39 F7
Rocky La CV8 ....93 D2
Rodborough Rd B93 ....71 E3
Rodhouse Cl CV4 ....59 D1
Rodney Cl CV22 ....82 B1
Rodway Dr CV5 ....59 D4
Rodyard Way CV1 ....151 C1
Roe Cl CV34 ....108 F8
Roebuck Pk B49 ....143 A3
Rofs Croft B78 ....5 A1
Rogers La CV37 ....131 A3
Rogers Way CV34 ....108 B4
Rokeby Ct CV22 ....99 C4
Rokeby Inf Sch CV22 ....100 A4
Rokeby Jun Sch CV22 ....100 A4
Rokeby St CV21 ....83 B2
Rolan Dr B90 ....69 E8
Roland Ave CV6 ....49 C3
Roland Mount CV6 ....49 C3
Rollason Cl CV6 ....61 C8
Rollason Rd CV6 ....61 B8
Rollason's Yd CV6 ....50 A3
Rolling Stones GL55 ....135 B2
Rollright Stones★ OX7 ....141 D1
Rolph Ct GL56 ....140 A2
Roman Cl LE17 ....43 C3
Roman Ct B77 ....9 C4
Roman Pk B46 ....23 F1
Roman Rd CV2 ....62 B3
Roman Row CV36 ....141 F5
Roman Way Alcester B49 ....143 A2
Coleshill B46 ....23 F2
Coventry CV3 ....77 D3
Dordon B78 ....11 A3
Halford CV36 ....136 F8
Rugby CV21 ....83 A4
Southam CV47 ....147 B2
Romeo Arbour CV34 ....109 E3
Romford Rd CV6 ....49 B2
Romilly Cl B76 ....13 A4
Romney B77 ....9 C4
Romney Rd OX16 ....139 F5
Romsey Ave CV10 ....29 D8
Romsley Rd CV6 ....61 C6
Ronald Gr B36 ....22 D1
Rookery Cl CV13 ....20 A4
Rookery La Coventry CV6 ....49 B4
Ettington CV37 ....131 A3
Newbold-on-S CV37 ....130 E1
Preston Bagot B95 ....113 E5
Rookery The
Birchley Heath CV10 ....17 C1
Nuneaton CV10 ....27 C3
Rookes Ct 1 CV37 ....144 C2
Rooks Nest CV23 ....64 C2
Roosevelt Dr CV4 ....59 E2
Rope Way OX15 ....142 D3
Roper Cl CV21 ....101 A4
Ropewalk B49 ....143 A2
Rosaville Cres CV5 ....60 A6
Rose Ave Coventry CV6 ....60 F5
Henley-in-A B95 ....113 B5
Rose Cottage Flats CV5 ....59 D5
Rose Croft CV8 ....92 E6
Rose Ct CV7 ....74 B8
Rose Hill CV9 ....18 C4
Rose La
Napton on t H CV47 ....125 C7
Nuneaton CV11 ....29 C3
Rose Rd B46 ....33 F8
Roseberry Ave CV2 ....50 C1
Rosebery Rd B77 ....9 B2
Rosebriars B90 ....69 E7
Rosefield Pl 4 CV32 ....109 F8
Rosefield St CV32 ....110 A8
Rosefield Wlk 3 CV32 ....109 F8
Rosegreen Cl CV3 ....77 E6
Rosehall Cl B98 ....102 C3
Rosehip Dr CV2 ....62 B6
Roseland Rd CV8 ....92 F3
Roselands Ave CV2 ....62 D8
Rosemary Cl CV4 ....59 E3
Rosemary Hill CV8 ....92 F5
Rosemary Mews CV8 ....92 F5
Rosemary Way LE10 ....31 B7
Rosemount Cl CV2 ....62 E7
Rosemullion Cl CV7 ....50 B8
Roses La OX7 ....150 C3
Roseway CV13 ....21 B4
Rosewood CV11 ....29 F1
Rosewood Ave CV22 ....100 A4
Rosewood Cl LE10 ....31 F6
Rosewood Cres CV32 ....106 B2
Ross Cl CV5 ....60 A5
Ross Ct CV21 ....83 B2
Ross Way CV11 ....40 B7
Rossendale Way CV10 ....28 E2
Rosslyn Ave CV6 ....60 E6
Rosslyn Rd B76 ....22 A6
Roston Dr LE10 ....31 A8
Rothay B77 ....9 C4
Rother Rd OX16 ....139 F5
Rother St CV37 ....144 C1
Rotherby Gr B37 ....44 B7
Rotherfield Cl CV31 ....110 B7
Rotherham Rd CV6 ....49 C2
Rotherhams Hill CV9 ....17 B4
Rotherhams Oak La B94 ....87 F7
Rotherwick Ct CV36 ....149 C3
Rothesay Ave CV4 ....60 B2
Rothesay Cl CV10 ....29 A2
Rothley Dr CV21 ....83 C4
Rothwell Rd CV34 ....104 C1
Rough Coppice Wlk B35 ....22 A2
Rough Farm Ind Est CV37 ....130 C5
Rough Hill Dr B98 ....102 C3
Rough The B97 ....102 B4
Roughknowles Rd CV4 ....75 D6
Rouncil La CV8 ....104 C8
Round Ave CV23 ....82 A3
Round Cl B90 ....70 A6
Round Close Rd OX15 ....142 D4
Round House Rd CV3 ....78 B8
Round Moor Wlk B35 ....22 A3
Round Oak Sch The CV32 ....106 A3
Round St 2 CV21 ....82 C2
Roundhill Rd OX17 ....134 A2
Rounds Gdns CV21 ....82 C2
Rounds Hill CV8 ....92 E2
Rouse La CV35 ....137 F8
Rover Dr B36 ....22 F1
Rover Rd CV1 ....151 B2
Row The CV7 ....51 D3
Rowan Cl
Binley Woods CV3 ....79 D7
Hollywood B47 ....69 B5
Kingsbury B78 ....15 B3
Stratford-u-A CV37 ....144 C3
Rowan Dr Rugby CV22 ....82 A1
6 Warwick CV34 ....108 F8
Rowan Gdns B78 ....11 A4
Rowan Gr CV2 ....50 E2
Rowan Rd CV10 ....28 C6
Rowan Way
Birmingham, Chelmsley Wood B37 ....33 C1
Nuneaton CV10 ....28 A8
Rowans The
Bedworth CV12 ....38 E2
Harvington WR11 ....127 D4
Rowborough Cl
Astwood Bank B96 ....102 C1
Hatton CV35 ....114 F5
Rowbrook Cl B90 ....69 E8
Rowcroft Rd CV2 ....63 A6
Rowington Cl CV6 ....60 D5
Rowington Gn CV35 ....89 F1
Rowland Ave
Polesworth B78 ....5 A2
Studley B80 ....103 C2
Rowland Ct CV7 ....26 C1
Rowland St CV21 ....82 C2
Rowland Way CV9 ....12 B1
Rowley Cres CV37 ....145 A2
Rowley Dr CV3 ....78 B4
Rowley La CV3 ....78 D3
Rowley Rd
Coventry CV3,CV8 ....78 B3
Whitnash CV31 ....110 A2
Rowley's Green La CV6 ....49 E4
Rowleys Green Lane Ind Est CV6 ....49 E4
Rowse Cl CV21 ....83 B4
Rowthorn Dr B90 ....71 A6
Roxburgh Croft CV32 ....106 C6
Roxburgh Rd CV11 ....29 E1
Royal Cres CV3 ....78 C5
Royal Ct LE10 ....31 D7
Royal Leamington Spa Rehabilitation Hospl CV34 ....109 E4
Royal Oak Ind Est NN11 ....117 F2
Royal Oak La CV7,CV12 ....49 C7
Royal Oak Terr GL55 ....135 A1
Royal Oak Way N NN11 ....117 F2
Royal Oak Way S NN11 ....117 F2
Royal Oak Yd CV12 ....39 B4
Royal Priors 15 CV32 ....105 F1
Royal Shakespeare Theatre★ CV37 ....145 A1
Royston Cl CV3 ....63 A3
Rubens Cl CV5 ....60 C3
Rudgard Rd CV6 ....50 A4
Rufford Cl Alcester B49 ....143 B3
Hinckley LE10 ....31 D3
Rugby Coll CV21 ....83 B1
Rugby High Sch CV22 ....99 B3
Rugby La CV23 ....97 A3
Rugby Rd Barby CV23 ....101 B1
Binley Woods CV3 ....79 D8
Brinklow CV23 ....64 C2
Bulkington CV12 ....40 D2
Church Lawford CV23 ....81 B3
Clifton u D CV23 ....83 C3
Cubbington CV32 ....106 E6
Dunchurch CV22 ....99 B2
Easenhall CV23 ....65 C2
Harborough Magna CV23 ....66 A1
Hinckley LE10 ....31 D6
Kilsby CV21,CV23 ....101 C3
Lilbourne CV23 ....84 C3
Long Lawford CV23 ....82 A2
Pailton CV23 ....66 A4
Princethorpe CV23 ....96 C1
Royal Leamington Spa CV32 ....105 D1
Shawell LE17 ....68 A4
Stockton CV47 ....115 F3
Rugby Sch CV22 ....83 A1
Rugby Sta CV21 ....83 B2
Ruislip Cl B35 ....22 A4
Rumbush La
Earlswood B90,B94 ....69 F3
Solihull B90 ....70 A5
Rumer Cl CV37 ....129 B4
Runcorn Cl
Birmingham B37 ....33 C4
Redditch B98 ....102 C4
Runcorn Wlk 10 CV2 ....63 A7
Runneymede Gdns CV10 ....28 F3
Runnymede Dr CV7 ....74 C5
Rupert Brooke Rd CV22 ....99 C4
Rupert Kettle Dr CV47 ....124 B4
Rupert Rd CV6 ....61 B8
Rush La B77,B78 ....9 B2
Rushbrook La B94 ....86 D3
Rushbrook Rd CV37 ....145 B1
Rushford Cl B90 ....71 A7
Rushleigh Rd B90 ....69 E8
Rushmoor Dr CV5 ....60 F3
Rushmore St CV31 ....110 B7
Rushmore Terr 9 CV31 ....110 B7
Rushock Cl B98 ....103 B4
Rushton Cl CV7 ....74 C7
Rushwick Gr B90 ....71 A6
Rusina Ct CV31 ....109 F6
Ruskin Cl Coventry CV6 ....60 D6
Nuneaton CV10 ....28 A5
Rugby CV22 ....99 C3
Russell Ave CV22 ....99 B2
Russell Cl CV47 ....115 D4
Russell Ct 7 CV31 ....110 A7
Russell St Coventry CV1 ....151 C4
Royal Leamington Spa CV32 ....105 F1
Russell St N 2 CV1 ....151 C4
Russell Terr CV31 ....110 A7
Russelsheim Way CV22 ....83 A1
Russet Gr CV4 ....76 D3
Rutherford Glen CV11 ....29 F1
Rutherford Way NN11 ....117 F3
Rutherglen Ave CV3 ....78 A6
Rutland Ave Hinckley LE10 ....31 C7
Nuneaton CV10 ....28 F4
Rutland Croft 3 CV3 ....78 F8
Rydal B77 ....10 A4
Rydal Ave CV11 ....30 A6
Rydal Cl Allesley CV5 ....60 B8
Hinckley LE10 ....30 F7
Rugby CV21 ....83 B3
Ryde Ave CV10 ....29 D7
Ryder Cl CV35 ....114 F3
Ryder Row CV7 ....37 A4
Ryders Hill Cres CV10 ....28 C7
Rye Cl Banbury OX16 ....139 F5
Stratford-u-A CV37 ....144 C3
Rye Croft B47 ....69 A5
Rye Fields 1 CV33 ....122 E8
Rye Grass Wlk B35 ....22 B3
Rye Hill CV5 ....60 A6
Rye Piece Ringway CV12 ....39 C3
Ryeclose Croft B37 ....33 D3
Ryefield La B76 ....14 B2
Ryegrass La B97 ....102 B3
Ryelands The CV23 ....98 B4
Ryhope Cl CV12 ....38 C1
Ryknild St B49 ....143 A3
Ryland Cl CV31 ....110 C6
Ryland Rd CV35 ....122 B8
Ryland St CV37 ....144 C1
Rylston Ave CV6 ....49 A1
Rylstone Way 4 CV34 ....104 E1
Ryon Hill CV37 ....145 C4
Ryton B77 ....9 C4
Ryton Cl CV4 ....76 B8
Ryton Organic Gdns★ CV8 ....79 E1
Ryton Pools Ctry Pk★ CV8 ....95 C3
Ryton Pools Visitor Ctr★ CV8 ....95 C3

S

Sabin Cl CV47 ....115 C4
Sabin Dr CV33 ....107 B4
Sackville Cl CV37 ....144 B2
Sackville Ct OX17 ....139 F6
Sackville Ho 1 CV1 ....151 D4
Sacred Heart RC Prim Sch CV2 ....62 A3
Saddington Rd CV3 ....78 E8
Saddlebow La CV35, CV37 ....114 B2
Saddlers Cl LE10 ....31 F6
Saddleton St CV35 ....138 C7
Sadler Cl CV37 ....144 C3
Sadler Gdns CV12 ....39 C2
Sadler Rd CV6 ....61 A8
Sadlers Ave CV36 ....149 C3
Sadlers Cl CV36 ....149 C3
Sadlers Mdw B46 ....26 A1
Sadlerswell La B94 ....88 B6
Saffron B77 ....4 A2
Saffron Cl CV23 ....83 C4
Saffron Mdw CV37 ....144 C1
Saffron Wlk CV37 ....144 C1
Saint's Peter & Paul RC Prim Sch CV2 ....62 F7
Saintbury Cl CV37 ....145 B1
Saintbury Dr B91 ....71 C8
Saints Way CV10 ....29 D5
St Agatha's Rd CV2 ....62 A3
St Agnes Cl B80 ....103 B2
St Agnes La CV1 ....151 B3
St Agnes Way CV11 ....29 F4
St Albans Cl CV32 ....105 C2
St Andrew's CE Inf Sch CV5 ....59 C5
St Andrew's Cres CV37 ....144 C1
St Andrew's Ct CV21 ....83 A2
St Andrew's Rd
Coventry CV5 ....76 F8
Royal Leamington Spa CV32 ....106 B5
St Andrews B77 ....4 A2
St Andrews Benn CE Fst Sch CV21 ....83 B2
St Andrews Benn CE Prim Sch CV21 ....83 B2
St Andrews Cres CV22 ....100 A4
St Andrews Dr CV11 ....30 B1
St Ann's Cl CV31 ....110 C7
St Ann's Rd CV2 ....62 A3
St Anne's RC Prim Sch
Birmingham B37 ....33 A2
Coventry CV3 ....78 C6
Nuneaton CV10 ....28 D7
St Anne's Rd CV22 ....82 C1
St Annes Gr B93 ....72 A6
St Anthony's RC Prim Sch CV31 ....110 C7
St Antony's RC Prim Sch B37 ....33 A5
St Asaphs Ave B80 ....103 B2
St Athan Croft B35 ....22 B3
St Augustine's RC Prim Sch CV6 ....61 A7
St Augustine's RC Prim Sch CV8 ....92 E7
St Augustine's RC Sch B97 ....102 B3
St Augustine's Wlk CV6 ....61 A7
St Austell Cl CV11 ....30 A5
St Austell Rd CV2 ....62 E3
St Bartholemews Cl CV3 ....63 A2
St Bartholomew's CE Prim Sch CV3 ....78 E7
St Benedict's RC High Sch B49 ....143 B2
St Benedict's RC Prim Sch
Atherstone CV9 ....18 C4
Coventry CV1 ....61 E4
St Benedicts Cl CV9 ....18 B4
St Bernards Wlk CV3 ....78 D6
St Blaise Ave B46 ....23 C2
St Bride's Cl CV31 ....110 C6
St Catherine's LE10 ....31 F7
St Catherine's Cl CV3 ....78 B8
St Catherine's Cres CV34 ....109 F3
St Catherine's Lodge 7 CV6 ....61 A4
St Catherine's RC Prim Sch GL55 ....135 A2
St Chads Mews B94 ....89 D3

St Chads Rd
3 Bishops Tachbrook
  CV33 ....122 E8
Studley B80 ....103 B2
St Christian's Croft CV3 .77 E8
St Christian's Rd CV3 ...77 E8
St Christopher Prim Sch
  CV5 ....60 D4
St Christopher's Cl
  CV34 ....108 D8
St Clements Ct CV2 ....62 D8
St Columba's Cl CV1 ..151 B4
St David's Cl CV31 ....110 C7
St David's Ct GL56 ....140 A3
St David's Prim Sch
  GL56 ....140 A3
St Davids Orch CV3 ....78 F7
St Davids Way CV10 ...39 A6
St Davids Wlk CV37 ...130 E1
St Denis View CV23 ....66 A4
St Edith's Cl CV23 ....53 C2
St Edith's Cn 3 CV34 ..109 B8
St Edith's Ho 2 CV34 ..109 B8
St Editha's Ct B78 .....5 A1
St Edithas Rd B78 .....11 A4
St Edmonds Rd CV9 ....16 B3
St Edward's RC Prim Sch
  B46 ....34 A2
St Edwards Ct GL56 ...140 A2
St Edwin's Cl WR11 ...127 B2
St Elizabeth's RC Prim Sch
  CV6 ....61 E7
St Elizabeth's Rd CV6 ..61 E7
St Faith's CE Jun Sch
  B49 ....143 B3
St Faith's Rd B49 .....143 B3
St Francis RC Prim Sch
  CV12 ....39 C3
St Fremund Way CV31 ..110 C5
St George & Teresa RC
  Prim Sch B93 ....72 A4
St George's Cl
  19 Moreton-in-M GL56 ..140 A3
  Stratford-u-A CV37 ...144 B2
St George's Rd
  Atherstone CV9 ....12 C1
  Coventry CV1 ....61 F2
  Royal Leamington Spa
  CV31 ....109 F6
  Solihull B90 ....70 D8
St Georges Ave CV22 ...99 C4
St Georges Way CV10 ...39 B8
St Gerard's (Warwickshire)
  Orthopaedic Hospl B46 .34 A3
St Gerard's RC Prim Sch
  B35 ....22 B4
St Giles Jun Sch CV7 ...49 F8
St Giles Rd Coventry CV7 .49 D6
  Gaydon CV35 ....132 E8
St Govan's Cl 2 CV31 ..110 C6
St Gregory's RC Prim Sch
  CV2 ....62 E3
St Gregory's RC Prim Sch
  CV37 ....145 A2
St Gregory's Rd CV37 ..145 A2
St Helen's Rd CV31 ....110 A5
St Helen's Way CV5 ....60 B8
St Helena Rd B78 ......11 A4
St Ives Cl CV2 ....62 E3
St Ives Way CV11 ......29 F5
St James & Ebrington CE
  Prim Sch GL55 ....135 B1
St James CE Jun Sch
  CV12 ....40 C2
St James CE Mid Sch
  CV12 ....40 C2
St James CE Prim Sch
  CV47 ....147 A3
St James Cl WR11 .....127 D3
St James Cres CV47 ...147 A3
St James Ct Coventry CV3 .78 E6
  Moreton-in-M GL56 ...140 A2
St James Gdns CV12 ....40 C2
St James Meadow Rd
  CV32 ....105 C2
St James Rd CV47 .....147 A3
St James' Ave CV35 ...146 C2
St James' La CV3 ......78 D6
St James's Cl LE10 .....31 D5
St John Fisher RC Prim Sch
  CV2 ....62 D5
St John the Baptist RC Prim
  Sch B36 ....33 B7
St John the Divine CE Prim
  Sch CV3 ....78 C5
St John Vianney RC Prim Sch
  CV5 ....60 B3
St John's Ave CV8 .....93 A3
St John's CE Prim Sch
  CV5 ....60 C4
St John's Cl
  Cherington CV36 .....141 D7
  Henley-in-A B95 .....113 A4
St John's Ct 3 CV34 ...108 F7
St John's Flats CV8 ....93 A3
St John's La CV23 ......82 A1
St John's Mus* CV34 ..108 F7
St John's Prim Sch CV8 .92 F2
St John's Rd
  Cherington CV36 .....141 D7
  Royal Leamington Spa
  CV31 ....110 A6
St John's St
  Coventry CV1 ....151 C2

St John's St continued
  Kenilworth CV8 ....93 A3
St John's Terr 18 CV31 .110 A6
St Johns CV34 ....108 F7
St Johns Ave CV22 ....100 C4
St Johns Cl Knowle B93 .72 B6
  Stratford-u-A CV37 ...144 C1
St Johns Rd CV10 ......27 C4
St Johns Way B93 ......72 C6
St Joseph's B96 ....118 D8
St Joseph's RC Jun Sch
  CV11 ....29 C3
St Joseph's RC Prim Sch
  Banbury OX16 ....139 F3
  Whitnash CV31 ....110 A3
St Joseph's Sch CV8 ....93 B7
St Jude's Cres CV3 .....78 D7
St Judes Ave B80 ......103 B2
St Laurence Ave CV34 ..108 D5
St Laurence Cl CV35 ...114 A8
St Laurence Way B50 ..148 B3
St Lawrence CE Prim Sch
  CV47 ....125 C7
St Lawrence Cl
  Knowle B93 ....72 B5
  Napton on t H CV47 ..125 C8
St Lawrence Rd CV47 ...27 A2
St Lawrence's Rd CV6 ...49 F1
St Leonard's Wlk CV8 ...79 A1
St Leonards Cl
  Birmingham B37 ......44 A7
  Dordon B78 ....11 A3
St Leonards View B78 ...10 C4
St Luke's Rd CV6 ......49 D3
St Lukes Way CV10 .....28 C4
St Margaret Rd
  Coventry CV1 ....61 F2
  Stoke Golding CV13 ...21 C4
St Margaret's CE Jun Sch
  CV31 ....110 B3
St Margaret's CE Prim Sch
  CV13 ....21 B4
St Margaret's Ho CV31 .110 B3
St Margaret's Rd CV31 .110 B5
St Marie's RC Inf Sch
  CV22 ....83 A1
St Marie's RC Jun Sch
  CV22 ....82 C1
St Mark's Annexe (Coventry &
  Warwickshire Hospl)
  CV1 ....151 C4
St Mark's Ave CV22 ....99 B4
St Mark's Cl
  Gaydon CV35 ....132 E8
  Ullenhall B95 ....112 E6
St Mark's Mews CV35 ..105 C1
St Mark's Rd CV32 ....105 D1
St Marks Cl CV10 ......28 C4
St Martin's LE10 ....31 E6
St Martin's Cl CV37 ...144 C1
St Martin's RC High Sch
  CV13 ....21 C4
St Martin's Rd CV3 .....77 C2
St Martins Ave B80 ....103 B2
St Mary St CV1 ....151 C2
St Mary's CE Prim Sch
  LE10 ....31 D8
St Mary's Cl
  Priors Hardwick CV47 .125 D3
  Southam CV47 ....147 B3
  Ullenhall B95 ....112 E6
  Warwick CV34 ....108 D8
St Mary's Cres CV31 ...110 B7
St Mary's Ct CV11 .....29 B5
St Mary's Immaculate RC
  Prim Sch CV31 ....108 E8
St Mary's La OX7 ......142 F7
St Mary's Prim Sch
  Aston le W NN11 .....134 F5
  Coventry CV2 ....61 F3
  Henley-in-A B95 .....113 B4
  Southam CV47 ....147 B2
  Studley B80 ....103 C2
St Mary's Rd
  Alcester B49 ....143 B2
  Atherstone CV9 ......18 C4
  Fillongley CV7 ....36 C2
  Hinckley LE10 ....31 D8
  Nuneaton CV11 ....29 B5
  Royal Leamington Spa
  CV31 ....110 B7
  Stratford-u-A CV37 ...145 A2
St Mary's Terr CV31 ...110 B7
St Marys Acre CV37 ...120 E7
St Marys Gr B79 ....2 B2
St Matthew's Bloxam CE Prim
  Sch CV22 ....82 C1
St Matthews Cl WR11 ..127 E6
St Matthews St 7 CV21 .83 A2
St Mawgen Cl B35 ......22 C4
St Michael's CE Prim Sch
  CV12 ....39 D3
St Michael's Cl Arley CV7 .37 A4
  Bishops Itchington CV47 .124 A4
  Claverdon CV35 ......113 F3
  South Littleton WR11 .127 F1
  Weston u W CV33 ....107 B4
St Michael's Cres CV47 ..147 C4
St Michael's Dr DE12 ...3 C4
St Michael's Hospl
  CV34 ....108 D8
St Michael's Rd
  Claverdon CV35 ......113 F3
  Coventry CV2 ....62 A3
  Warwick CV34 ....108 D8
St Michael's Way CV10 ..28 C4
St Michaels Cl
  Atherstone CV9 ....12 C1

St Michaels Cl continued
  Ufton CV33 ....111 C1
  Wood End CV9 ....10 B1
St Milburgh Cl WR11 ...127 D1
St Nicholas Ave CV8 ....92 F3
St Nicholas CE Prim Sch
  CV8 ....92 F5
St Nicholas Church St
  CV34 ....108 F6
St Nicholas Cl
  Alcester B49 ....143 B2
  Austrey CV9 ....3 A1
  Coventry CV1 ....61 C5
St Nicholas Ct
  3 Coventry, Edgwick CV6 .61 F7
  Coventry, Radford CV6 .61 B6
St Nicholas Est CV9 ....11 B1
St Nicholas Rd
  Henley-in-A B95 .....113 B4
  Radford Semele CV31 .110 F5
St Nicholas St CV1 ....151 B4
St Nicholas Terr CV31 ..110 E4
St Nicholas Wlk B76 ....23 B6
St Nicolas CE Prim Sch
  CV11 ....110 E4
St Nicolas Park Dr CV11 .29 F7
St Nicolas Rd CV11 .....29 D5
St Osburg's RC Prim Sch
  CV1 ....151 A3
St Osburg's Rd CV2 .....62 A3
St Oswalds CE Prim Sch
  CV22 ....82 B2
St Patrick's CE Prim Sch
  B94 ....70 C2
St Patrick's RC Prim Sch
  Birmingham B37 ......33 C2
  Coventry CV2 ....50 D1
St Patrick's Rd CV1 ....151 B1
St Patricks RC Prim Sch
  CV31 ....109 F6
St Paul's CE Prim Sch
  Nuneaton CV10 ....28 C3
  Royal Leamington Spa
  CV32 ....106 B1
St Paul's Cl CV34 ......108 D6
St Paul's Cres 5 B46 ...33 F7
St Paul's Ct B77 ....9 B2
St Paul's Rd Coventry CV6 .61 E6
  Nuneaton CV10 ....28 D3
St Paul's Sq 4 CV32 ...106 A1
St Paul's Terr CV34 ....108 D6
St Pauls Ct
  Moreton-in-M GL56 ...140 A2
  Water Orton B46 ......23 B3
St Peter's Ave CV9 .....19 A4
St Peter's Cl
  Redditch B97 ....102 C3
  Water Orton B46 ......23 B2
  Witherley CV9 ....19 A4
St Peter's Ct CV1 ......151 D4
St Peter's Dr CV10 .....27 C2
St Peter's Pl B78 ....15 B3
St Peter's RC Prim Sch
  CV32 ....109 F8
St Peter's Rd
  7 Royal Leamington Spa
  CV32 ....109 F8
  Rugby CV21 ....83 B2
  Wellesbourne CV35 ..146 B2
St Peters Ct GL56 ......140 A2
St Peters La B92 ....44 D1
St Peters Rd
  Atherstone CV9 ....19 A4
  Kineton CV35 ....132 B6
St Swithin's Dr CV37 ...129 D2
St Thomas Cl CV10 .....28 D3
St Thomas More RC Fst Sch
  B98 ....103 A4
St Thomas More RC Prim Sch
  CV3 ....77 D5
St Thomas More RC Sch
  CV10 ....29 A3
St Thomas' Rd CV6 .....50 A3
St Thomas's Ct 18 CV1 .61 B2
St Thomas's Ho 12 CV1 .61 B2
St Wulstan Way CV47 ..147 B3
Salcombe Cl Coventry CV3 .78 D6
  Nuneaton CV11 ....29 F5
Salem Rd LE10 ....31 F5
Salford Coventry CV2 ....62 A5
  Redditch B98 ....103 C3
Salford Priors CE Prim Sch
  WR11 ....127 F6
Salford Rd B50 ....148 B2
Salisbury Ave CV3 ......77 C6
Salisbury Cl CV8 ....79 F3
Salisbury Dr
  Nuneaton CV10 ....28 B7
  Water Orton B46 ......23 C3
Salisbury Rd LE10 ......32 B7
Salt La CV1 ....151 B2
Salt Way B96 ....118 B7
Salt Way La OX15 ......137 F2
Salter St B94 ....70 C2
Salters La B95 ....120 C7
Saltisford CV34 ....108 D7
Saltisford Gdns CV34 ..108 C8
Salts La B78 ....8 C3
Sam Gault Cl CV3 ......78 E7
Sambourne La
  Astwood Bank B96 ...102 C1
  Coughton B49,B96 ...118 E7
  Sambourne B96 ......103 A1
Sambourne Pk B96 ....118 D8
Sammons Way CV4 .....59 D1
Sampson Cl CV2 ....62 C8
Samuel Hayward Ho 5
  CV2 ....50 B1

Samuel Vale Ho CV1 ...151 B4
Sanby Cl CV12 ....39 A4
Sanctus Dr CV37 ......144 C1
Sanctus Rd CV37 ......144 C1
Sanctus St CV37 ......144 C1
Sand Barn La CV37 ....121 D6
Sanda Croft B36 ....33 B6
Sandbarn Cl B90 ....70 F6
Sandel Cl CV37 ....144 C1
Sanders Cl Atherstone CV9 .12 C1
  Braunston NN11 ......117 D5
Sanders Ct CV34 ......109 C8
Sanders Rd Bedworth CV6 .50 B6
  Salford Priors WR11 ..127 F6
Sandfield B90 ....70 B8
Sandfield La CV37 ......130 E1
Sandfield Rd CV37 .....144 C1
Sandfine Rd OX15 .....139 D1
Sandford Cl CV2 ....50 C5
Sandford Gn OX16 .....139 F4
Sandford Way CV22 ....99 B2
Sandgate Cres CV2 .....62 E2
Sandhills Cres B91 .....71 B8
Sandhurst Gr CV6 ......61 B5
Sandilands Cl CV2 ......62 E4
Sandon Rd CV11 ....29 B5
Sandown Ave CV6 ......49 F2
Sandown Cl
  Royal Leamington Spa
  CV32 ....106 C4
  Stratford-u-A CV37 ...144 B1
Sandown Rd CV21 ......83 B2
Sandpiper B77 ....10 A3
Sandpiper Cl
  Newton CV23 ....67 B1
  Stratford-u-A CV37 ...144 B3
Sandpiper Rd CV2 .....50 B3
Sandpits Cl Curdworth B76 .23 B6
  Tysoe CV35 ....138 B6
Sandpits La CV6 ....48 F2
Sandpits Rd CV35 ......138 B7
Sandpits The CV12 .....40 C2
Sandringham Cl CV4 ....75 F5
Sandringham Ct CV10 ...28 F6
Sandwick Cl CV3 ....78 F8
Sandy La Blackdown CV32 .105 F6
  Coventry CV1 ....61 C5
  Furnace End B46 ......25 C2
  Marton CV23 ....115 D7
  Monks Kirby CV23 ....53 C2
  Newton Regis B79 .....2 B3
  Royal Leamington Spa
  CV32 ....105 D4
  Rugby CV21 ....99 A4
Sandy Lane Bsns Pk CV1 .61 C5
Sandy Way Barford CV35 .122 B7
  Tamworth B77 ....4 C2
Sandy Way La B78 ......11 B4
Sandythorpe CV3 ....78 E6
Sankey Gr GL56 ....140 A2
Santos Cl CV3 ....78 F8
Sapcote Gr CV2 ....50 B4
Sapcote Rd LE10 ....32 B7
Saplings The B76 ....22 A8
Sapphire Dr CV31 ......109 F5
Sapphire Gate CV2 .....62 C2
Saracen Dr
  Balsall Common CV7 ..73 E6
  Sutton Coldfield B75 ..13 A6
Sargeaunt St CV31 .....109 F7
Sark Dr B36 ....33 B6
Satchwell Ct 18 CV32 ..109 F8
Satchwell Wlk 14 CV32 .109 F8
Saumur Way CV34 ......109 C6
Saunders Ave CV12 .....39 B2
Saunders Ho 10 CV32 ..105 F2
Saunton Cl CV5 ....60 B8
Saunton Rd CV22 ......82 C1
Savages Cl CV33 ......122 F8
Savernake Rd CV35 ....132 C4
Saville Gr CV8 ....93 C5
Sawbridge Rd CV23 ....116 F5
Saxon Cl
  Binley Woods CV3 .....79 D7
  Polesworth B78 ....4 C1
  Rugby CV22 ....99 A4
  Stratford-u-A CV37 ...145 B1
  Studley B80 ....103 C3
  Tamworth B77 ....9 C3
Saxon Ct B50 ....148 B2
Saxon Mdws CV32 .....105 C2
Saxon Rd CV2 ....62 B4
Saxon Wood Rd B90 ....70 D5
Saxonfields B50 ....148 B2
Scafell CV21 ....83 B4
Scafell Cl CV5 ....60 A4
Scammerton B77 ....10 A4
Scar Bank CV34 ....104 E1
Scarborough Way CV4 ..75 F7
Scarman Rd CV4 ....76 B5
Schofield Rd B37 ....33 A5
Scholars Cl CV37 ......144 C1
Scholars La CV37 ......144 C1
Scholfield Rd CV7 ......49 A6
School Ave WR11 ......127 F6
School Bell Mews CV8 ..94 B6
School Cl Birmingham B37 .33 A6
  Braunston NN11 ......117 E5
  Coventry CV3 ....61 D1
  Great Alne B49 ......119 D6
  Hinckley LE10 ....32 A6
  Long Compton CV36 ..141 C3
School Cotts CV35 ......90 F3
School Croft CV35 ......91 C2
School Dr B47 ....69 A4
School Gdns CV21 .....84 A1
School Hill
  Mollington OX17 .....133 F2

School Hill continued
  Napton on t H CV47 ..125 C8
  Nuneaton CV10 ....28 A8
  Offchurch CV33 ......111 A4
  Wootton Wawen B95 ..113 A3
School House La CV2 ....63 A6
School La Badby NN11 ..126 F6
  Bearley CV37 ....120 E7
  Bedworth CV7 ....49 F7
  Kenilworth CV8 ....92 F5
  Ladbroke CV47 ......124 D5
  Lea Marston B76 ......24 A4
  Lower Brailes OX15 ..137 F2
  North Newington OX15 .139 E2
  Nuneaton CV10 ....27 C3
  Priors Marston CV47 ..125 E4
  Radford Semele CV31 .110 E5
  Shuttington B79 ....4 C4
  South Littleton WR11 .127 F1
  Stretton on D CV23 ...96 C3
  Tamworth B77 ....9 B3
  Tiddington CV37 .....145 C2
  Warmington OX17 ....133 D2
  Weston u W CV33 ....107 C3
  Wolvey LE10 ....41 C2
  Wroxall CV35 ....90 E4
School Rd Alcester B49 ..143 A2
  Bulkington CV12 ......40 C2
  Great Alne B49 ......119 D6
  Henley-in-A B95 .....113 B4
  Hockley Heath B94 ....88 B7
  Pebworth CV37 ......128 F1
  Salford Priors WR11 ..127 F6
  Snitterfield CV37 ....121 B6
  Wellesbourne CV35 ..146 C2
School St
  Church Lawford CV23 ..81 A3
  Churchover CV23 ......67 B3
  Dunchurch CV22 ......99 B2
  Long Lawford CV23 ...82 A2
  Rugby CV21 ....84 A1
  Southam CV47 ....147 B2
  Stockton CV47 ......147 C4
  Wolston CV8 ....80 A2
School Wlk CV11 ....29 E2
Scotchill The CV6 ......49 A1
Scotland End OX15 ....142 D4
Scots Cl CV22 ....99 B4
Scots La CV6 ....60 F6
Scott Ave CV35 ....29 D8
Scott Cl B50 ....148 B3
Scott Rd Kenilworth CV8 .92 E2
  Redditch B97 ....102 B4
  Royal Leamington Spa
  CV31 ....110 B6
Seabroke Ave CV22 .....82 C2
Seafield La B48 ....85 E4
Seaford Cl CV6 ....50 B4
Seagrave Rd CV1 ......151 D1
Sealand Dr CV12 ....39 A3
Sear Hills Cl CV7 ....74 B6
Seathwaite CV21 ....83 B4
Seaton B77 ....9 C4
Seaton Cl Hinckley LE10 .32 B7
  Nuneaton CV11 ....29 F5
Sebastian Cl CV3 ....78 B5
Second Ave CV3 ....62 C1
Second Exhibition Ave
  B40 ....44 D4
Sedgemere Gr CV7 .....74 C5
Sedgemoor Rd CV3 .....78 B5
Sedlescombe Lodge
  CV22 ....99 C4
Sedlescombe Pk CV22 ...99 C4
Seed Field Croft CV3 ....77 E7
Seekings The CV31 ....110 B3
Seeney La B76 ....15 A1
Seeswood Cl CV10 .....28 C2
Sefton Rd Coventry CV4 ..76 E6
  Tamworth B77 ....9 B2
Seggs La B49 ....143 A2
Segrave Cl CV35 ......132 B6
Selborne Rd CV22 ......99 B4
Selby Way CV10 ....28 B5
Selina Dix Ho CV1 .....151 C4
Selsdon Cl B47 ....69 C5
Selsey Cl CV3 ....78 C4
Selside CV21 ....83 B4
Selworthy Rd CV6 ......49 E3
Selwyn Cl CV35 ....146 B2
Selwyn Ho B37 ....33 D3
Semele Cl CV31 ....110 E5
Seneschal Rd CV3 ......77 C7
Sennen Cl CV11 ....30 A5
Sentry Way B75 ....13 A6
Sephton Dr CV6 ....50 C6
Servite Ho 2 Coleshill B46 .33 F7
  Kenilworth CV8 ....92 F3
Sett The CV35 ....137 F8
Seven Acre Cl 4 CV33 .122 E8
Seven Meadows Rd
  CV37 ....144 C1
Seven Stars Ind Est CV3 .78 B7
Severn Ave LE10 ....31 A8
Severn Cl CV32 ....106 C3
Severn Rd Bulkington CV12 .40 A3
  Coventry CV1 ....61 F1
Sevincott Cl CV37 .....144 B2
Sevington Cl B91 ....71 C8
Sewall Ct CV6 ....62 A8
Sewall Highway CV2 ....62 B6
Seymour Cl Coventry CV3 .78 C5
  Hampton Magna CV35 .114 F3
Seymour Gate GL55 ...135 B2
Seymour Gr CV34 .....109 D6
Seymour Ho CV3 ....77 C8
Seymour Rd
  Alcester B49 ....143 B3

Seymour Rd continued
Nuneaton CV11 . . . .**29** D3
Rugby CV21 . . . .**83** B3
Stratford-u-A CV37 . . . . . .**144** B1
Shackleton Dr LE10 . . . . . .**31** E4
Shackleton Way LE17 . . . . .**55** B3
Shadow Brook La B92 . . . . .**56** E7
Shadowbrook Rd CV6 . . . . .**61** A5
Shaft La CV7 . . . .**47** A4
Shaftesbury Ave CV7 . . . . . .**49** A7
Shaftesbury Rd CV5 . . . . . .**76** F8
Shakells Cl B97 . . . .**102** C2
Shakers La CV47 . . . .**115** C5
Shakesfield Cl CV36 . . . . . .**136** F6
Shakespeare Ave
Bedworth CV12 . . . .**39** D2
Warwick CV34 . . . .**108** C3
Shakespeare Ct CV37 . . . . .**145** A2
Shakespeare Ctr Mus The★
CV37 . . . .**145** A2
Shakespeare Dr CV11 . . . . . .**30** A1
Shakespeare Gdns CV22 . . .**99** C4
Shakespeare La WR11 . . . .**127** D3
Shakespeare Rd B90 . . . . . .**70** D8
Shakespeare St
Coventry CV2 . . . .**62** B4
Stratford-u-A CV37 . . . . . .**145** A2
Shakespeare's Grave★
CV37 . . . .**145** A1
Shakespeares Birthplace
Mus★ CV37 . . . .**145** A2
Shakleton Rd CV5 . . . .**61** A2
Shanes Castle Rd CV35 . . .**132** D3
Shanklin Dr CV10 . . . .**29** D6
Shanklin Rd CV3 . . . .**78** B4
Shannon B77 . . . .**9** C4
Shap Fell CV21 . . . .**83** B4
Sharnford Rd LE10 . . . .**32** F6
Sharp Cl CV6 . . . .**49** C2
Sharpe Cl CV34 . . . .**108** E8
Sharpe St B77 . . . .**4** A1
Sharpless Rd LE10 . . . .**31** F7
Sharpley Ct CV2 . . . .**63** A8
Sharratt Rd CV12 . . . .**39** C4
Sharry La CV37 . . . .**129** C1
Shaw's La CV35 . . . .**114** C8
Shawberry Ave B35 . . . .**22** B4
Shawbury La B46 . . . .**35** B4
Shawbury Village B46 . . . . .**35** C3
Shawe Ave CV10 . . . .**29** C7
Shawell Rd LE17 . . . .**68** B4
Shawfield B47 . . . .**69** A5
Shawhurst Croft B47 . . . . . .**69** A7
Shawhurst Gdns B47 . . . . . .**69** B7
Shawhurst La B47 . . . .**69** A6
Shearings The OX15 . . . . . .**142** D4
Sheen Ho CV2 . . . .**62** D8
Sheep Dip La CV23 . . . .**96** C1
Sheep St
Chipping Campden GL55 . . .**135** A1
Rugby CV21 . . . .**83** A2
Shipston-on-S CV36 . . . . . .**149** C3
Stratford-u-A CV37 . . . . . .**145** A1
Sheepclose Dr B37 . . . .**33** A3
Sheepcote Cl CV32 . . . . . .**106** A1
Sheepy La CV9 . . . .**6** C2
Sheepy Rd Atherstone CV9 .**12** B1
Atherstone, Pinwall CV9 . . .**12** C3
Shefford Rd CV35 . . . .**132** D3
Shelbourne Rd CV37 . . . . .**144** A2
Sheldon Gr CV34 . . . .**104** F2
Sheldon Rd B98 . . . .**103** A4
Sheldrake Cl CV3 . . . .**63** A4
Shelfield Cl Coventry CV5 . .**60** B3
Hockley Heath B94 . . . .**88** C6
Shelley Ave CV34 . . . .**108** C4
Shelley Cl Bedworth CV12 . .**39** D1
Redditch B97 . . . .**102** B4
Shelley Rd Coventry CV2 . . .**62** C3
Stratford-u-A CV37 . . . . . .**145** A1
Shellon Cl CV3 . . . .**78** F8
Shelly Cres B90 . . . .**71** B6
Shelly La B90 . . . .**71** B6
Shelton Sq CV1 . . . .**151** B2
Shelton St B77 . . . .**9** C4
Shelwick Gr B93 . . . .**71** F4
Shenington CE Prim Sch
OX15 . . . .**138** F5
Shenstone Ave CV22 . . . . . .**83** C1
Shenstone Dr CV7 . . . .**74** A6
Shenton Cl CV13 . . . .**21** C4
Sheperds Hill CV47 . . . . . .**147** B2
Shepherd Cl Coventry CV4 . .**59** F3
Long Itchington CV47 . . . . .**115** C3
Shepherd Pl CV35 . . . .**132** B5
Shepherd St CV23 . . . .**115** C2
Shepherds Cl OX15 . . . . . .**142** D8
Shepperton Bsns Pk
CV11 . . . .**29** C1
Shepperton Ct CV11 . . . . . .**29** C1
Shepperton St CV11 . . . . . .**29** C2
Sheppey Dr B36 . . . .**33** B5
Sherard Croft B36 . . . .**33** B6
Sherborne Rd LE10 . . . .**32** B7
Sherborne B46 . . . .**34** C4
Sherbourne Ave CV10 . . . . .**28** B4
Sherbourne Cres CV5 . . . . .**60** E4
Sherbourne Cres CV1 . . . . .**151** B1
Sherbourne Fields Sch
CV6 . . . .**60** D5
Sherbourne St CV1 . . . .**61** A2
Sherbrooke Ave B77 . . . .**9** C3
Sherdmore Croft B90 . . . . . .**70** F6
Sheridan Cl CV22 . . . .**99** C4
Sheridan Dr CV10 . . . .**27** C4
Sheridan Wlk B35 . . . .**22** A3
Sheriff Ave CV4 . . . .**76** B7
Sheriff Rd CV21 . . . .**83** B2

Sheriffs Orch CV1 . . . .**151** B2
Sheringham Cl CV11 . . . . . .**29** F2
Sherington Ave CV5 . . . . . .**60** C4
Sherlock Rd CV5 . . . .**60** D3
Sherwell Dr B49 . . . .**143** A2
Sherwood Cl CV9 . . . .**10** B1
Sherwood Jones Cl CV6 . . .**61** B6
Sherwood Rd CV13 . . . .**21** C4
Sherwood Wlk CV32 . . . . .**106** C4
Shetland Ave B77 . . . .**9** C4
Shetland Cl CV5 . . . .**60** A4
Shetland Dr CV10 . . . .**29** A2
Shetland Wlk B36 . . . .**33** B6
Shevlock Way CV6 . . . .**62** A6
Shillingstone Cl CV2 . . . . . .**63** A4
Shillingstone Dr
Nuneaton CV10 . . . .**28** F1
Nuneaton CV10 . . . .**29** A1
Shilton Cl B90 . . . .**70** F6
Shilton Ind Est CV7 . . . .**51** E7
Shilton La
Barnacle CV2,CV7 . . . .**51** B4
Bulkington CV12 . . . .**40** D1
Coventry CV2 . . . .**50** C4
Shilton CV7,CV12 . . . .**51** D8
Shinehill La WR11 . . . .**128** A1
Shipston High Sch
CV36 . . . .**149** C3
Shipston Rd
Alderminster CV37 . . . .**130** B5
Coventry CV2 . . . .**62** C6
Long Compton CV36,OX7 . .**141** C4
Tysoe CV35 . . . .**138** B6
Shipton-on-Stour Prim Sch
CV36 . . . .**149** C3
Shire Cl CV6 . . . .**50** B1
Shirebrook Cl CV2 . . . .**50** D2
Shires Gate Ret Pk
CV31 . . . .**109** E6
Shires Gate Trad Est
CV31 . . . .**109** E6
Shires Ret Pk CV34 . . . . . .**109** D6
Shires The CV23 . . . .**81** A3
Shirland Rd B37 . . . .**33** A1
Shirlett Cl CV2 . . . .**50** B4
Shirley La CV7 . . . .**59** A5
Shirley Rd CV2 . . . .**63** A7
Shirley Trad Est B90 . . . . . .**70** F8
Shirleydale 2 B90 . . . .**70** C8
Shirrall Dr B75,B78 . . . .**7** C2
Shopping Ctr The CV31 . . .**110** B5
Shopping Prec The
CV34 . . . .**105** A1
Shorncliffe Rd CV6 . . . .**60** E6
Short Acres CV35 . . . .**132** C6
Short La CV47 . . . .**115** C4
Short St Coventry CV1 . . . .**151** C2
Nuneaton CV10 . . . .**28** D4
Shortfield Cl CV7 . . . .**74** B7
Shortland Cl B93 . . . .**72** A7
Shortlands CV7 . . . .**49** D6
Shortley Rd CV3 . . . .**77** F8
Shortwoods The B78 . . . . . .**11** A3
Shottery CV37 . . . .**144** B1
Shottery Cl CV5 . . . .**60** B3
Shottery Rd CV37 . . . .**144** C1
Shottery St Andrew's CE Prim
Sch CV37 . . . .**144** B1
Shotteswell Rd B90 . . . .**70** B8
Shoulderway La CV36 . . . . .**149** C1
Showell La CV7 . . . .**47** A1
Shrewley Comm CV35 . . . .**114** B6
Shrubberies The CV4 . . . . . .**76** E4
Shrubland St CV31 . . . .**110** A6
Shrubland Street Com Prim
Sch CV31 . . . .**110** A6
Shuckburgh Cres
Bourton on D CV23 . . . .**97** C1
Rugby CV22 . . . .**100** B4
Shuckburgh Gr 4 CV32 . . .**106** A2
Shuckburgh Rd
Napton on t H CV47 . . . . . .**125** D3
Priors Marston CV47 . . . . .**125** E4
Shulman's Wlk CV2 . . . .**62** D7
Shultern La CV4 . . . .**76** D6
Shuna Croft CV2 . . . .**63** B7
Shustoke CE Prim Sch
B46 . . . .**25** A1
Shustoke Resr★ B46 . . . . . .**24** C2
Shutford Rd
North Newington OX15 . . .**139** D2
Shutford OX15 . . . .**139** B1
Shutt La B94 . . . .**70** B1
Shuttington Rd B79 . . . .**4** A3
Shuttle St CV6 . . . .**62** B8
Shuttleworth Rd CV23 . . . . .**83** C3
Shylock Gr CV34 . . . .**109** E2
Sibford Gower Prim Sch
OX15 . . . .**142** D8
Sibford Rd
Hook Norton OX15 . . . . . .**142** D4
Shutford OX15 . . . .**138** F2
Sibford Sch OX15 . . . .**142** D8
Sibree Rd CV3 . . . .**78** B4
Sibton Cl CV2 . . . .**50** C1
Sidbury Gr B93 . . . .**71** E3
Sidbury Rd CV6 . . . .**61** C6
Siddaway Ho CV21 . . . .**83** B4
Siddeley Ave
Coventry CV3 . . . .**62** B1
Kenilworth CV8 . . . .**92** E1
Siddeley Way NN11 . . . .**117** F2
Sidelands Rd CV37 . . . .**144** B2
Sidenhill Cl B90 . . . .**70** B8
Sidings The CV21 . . . .**83** B2
Sidmouth Cl Coventry CV2 . .**62** C7
Nuneaton CV11 . . . .**29** F5
Sidney Rd CV22 . . . .**100** B4

Sidney Stringer Com Tech
Coll CV1 . . . .**151** C3
Signal Hayes Rd B76 . . . . . .**13** A2
Signal Rd CV36 . . . .**149** C4
Signal Wlk B77 . . . .**4** A1
Silica Rd B77 . . . .**4** A1
Silken Ct CV11 . . . .**29** B4
Silksby St CV3 . . . .**77** D8
Silver Birch Ave CV12 . . . . .**38** E2
Silver Birch Dr B47 . . . .**69** B6
Silver Birch Gr 5 CV31 . . .**109** F5
Silver Link Rd B77 . . . .**4** A1
Silver St Coventry CV1 . . . .**151** B3
Newton CV23 . . . .**68** A1
Wroxton OX15 . . . .**139** D4
Silver Trees Dr CV12 . . . . . .**40** B4
Silver Wlk CV10 . . . .**28** F3
Silverbirch Cl CV10 . . . .**28** A7
Silverdale Cl CV2 . . . .**50** B4
Silverstone Dr CV6 . . . .**49** E5
Silverton Rd CV6 . . . .**61** C7
Simmonds Way CV9 . . . . . .**12** B1
Simmons Cl B78 . . . .**8** A1
Simmons Ct CV35 . . . .**146** B2
Simms La B47 . . . .**69** A5
Simon Cl CV11 . . . .**29** D2
Simon Ct CV7 . . . .**50** A8
Simon Rd B47 . . . .**69** A7
Simon Stone St CV6 . . . . . .**61** F8
Simpkins Cl CV33 . . . .**107** B4
Simpson Rd CV36 . . . .**149** C3
Sinclair Ave OX16 . . . .**139** F4
Sinclair Dr CV6 . . . .**50** C4
Singer Cl CV3 . . . .**62** B8
Singer Croft B36 . . . .**22** F1
Sir Frank Whittle Bsns Ctr
CV21 . . . .**83** B3
Sir Frank Whittle Prim Sch
CV2 . . . .**62** F8
Sir Henry Parkes Prim Sch
CV4 . . . .**76** C8
Sir Henry Parkes Rd CV5 . .**76** D7
Sir John Moore CE Prim Sch
DE12 . . . .**3** C4
Sir Thomas White's Rd
CV5 . . . .**60** F2
Sir William Lyons Rd
CV4 . . . .**76** C6
Sir Winston Churchill Pl
CV3 . . . .**79** C7
Siskin Cl CV23 . . . .**83** B4
Siskin Dr CV3 . . . .**78** C4
Siskin Parkway E CV3 . . . . .**78** C1
Siskin Parkway W CV3 . . . . .**78** C2
Sitwell Ave CV47 . . . .**115** D3
Sixteen Acres La B50 . . . .**148** C1
Skelwith Rise CV11 . . . .**30** A6
Sketchley Hall Gdns
LE10 . . . .**31** C5
Sketchley Hill Prim Sch
LE10 . . . .**31** E5
Sketchley La LE10 . . . .**31** C5
Sketchley La Ind Est
LE10 . . . .**31** B5
Sketchley Manor La
LE10 . . . .**31** D5
Sketchley Mdws LE10 . . . . .**31** C4
Sketchley Meadows Bsns Pk
LE10 . . . .**31** C4
Sketchley Old Village
LE10 . . . .**31** C5
Sketchley Rd LE10 . . . .**31** E5
Skiddaw CV21 . . . .**83** B4
Skidmore Ave B77 . . . .**9** B3
Skilts Sch B98 . . . .**112** B6
Skipton Gdns CV2 . . . .**62** B6
Skipton Lodge CV2 . . . .**62** B6
Skipwith Cl CV3 . . . .**78** E7
Skipworth Rd CV3 . . . .**63** A1
Sky Blue Way CV1 . . . .**61** E3
Skydome The CV1 . . . .**151** A2
Skye Cl Birmingham B36 . . .**33** B6
Nuneaton CV10 . . . .**28** F2
Tamworth B77 . . . .**9** C4
Slack's Ave CV9 . . . .**18** B4
Slade Cl CV11 . . . .**40** C8
Slade Gr B93 . . . .**71** F6
Slade Hill CV35 . . . .**114** F4
Slade La
Sutton Coldfield B75 . . . .**7** A2
Tamworth B77 . . . .**9** B2
Slade Mdw CV31 . . . .**110** C5
Slade Rd Rugby CV21,CV22 .**83** B1
Sutton Coldfield B75 . . . .**7** A2
Slade The OX17,CV47 . . . .**133** E6
Slateley Cres B90 . . . .**70** F6
Slater Rd B93 . . . .**71** F4
Sleath's Yd CV12 . . . .**39** B3
Sledmere Cl CV2 . . . .**50** B3
Sleets Yd CV12 . . . .**39** A2
Slimbridge Cl
Redditch B97 . . . .**102** C3
2 Solihull B90 . . . .**71** A6
Slingates Rd CV37 . . . .**145** A2
Slingsby B77 . . . .**9** B4
Slingsby Cl CV11 . . . .**29** F2
Slough The B97 . . . .**103** A4
Slowley Hill CV7 . . . .**26** A1
Small Brook Bsns Ctr
B50 . . . .**148** C3
Small Ho OX15 . . . .**142** D8
Small La B94 . . . .**86** E6
Smalley Pl CV8 . . . .**92** F4
Smarts La CV35 . . . .**138** B6
Smarts Rd CV12 . . . .**38** F1
Smeaton La CV23 . . . .**64** C3
Smercote Cl CV12 . . . .**38** D1
Smite CV23 . . . .**53** C2

Smith St Bedworth CV12 . . .**38** E1
Coventry CV6 . . . .**61** F5
2 Royal Leamington Spa
CV31 . . . .**109** F7
Warwick CV34 . . . .**108** F7
Wood End CV9 . . . .**10** B1
Smith's Cl CV37 . . . .**121** B6
Smith's Way B49 . . . .**143** B3
Smithford Way CV1 . . . . . .**151** B3
Smiths Cl B50 . . . .**148** C3
Smiths La B93 . . . .**71** E7
Smiths Orch CV21 . . . .**83** B2
Smiths Way B46 . . . .**23** A3
Smiths Wood Sch B36 . . . . .**33** A6
Smithy La
Aston Flamville LE9 . . . .**32** C8
Church Lawford CV23 . . . . .**81** B3
Tamworth B77 . . . .**9** C4
Smithy Rd CV9 . . . .**17** B3
Smockington La LE10 . . . . .**42** A4
Smorrall La CV12 . . . .**38** C2
Smythe Gr CV34 . . . .**104** E1
Snape Rd CV2 . . . .**62** F5
Snarestone Rd DE12 . . . .**3** C4
Sniterfield La CV37 . . . .**121** C7
Sniterfield La CV37 . . . .**114** C1
Sniterfield Prim Sch
CV37 . . . .**121** B6
Sniterfield Rd CV37 . . . . . .**120** E7
Sniterfield St CV35 . . . .**121** F4
Snowdon Cl CV10 . . . .**28** B3
Snowdrop Cl CV12 . . . .**38** E1
Snowford Hill CV33,
CV47 . . . .**115** A5
Snowhill Cl CV11 . . . .**39** F8
Snows Drive Hill B90 . . . . . .**70** D5
Snowshill Cl CV11 . . . .**39** F8
Snuff La OX17 . . . .**139** C3
Soar Way LE10 . . . .**31** A8
Soden Cl CV3 . . . .**78** D6
Soden's Ave CV8 . . . .**79** A1
Solent Dr CV2 . . . .**50** F1
Solihull Coll Chelmsley
Campus B37 . . . .**33** C4
Solihull Parkway B37 . . . . . .**44** E8
Solihull Rd B92 . . . .**56** E6
Solihull Ret Pk B90 . . . .**70** C8
Solway Cl CV31 . . . .**110** C6
Somerby Dr B91 . . . .**71** A8
Somerly Cl CV3 . . . .**78** F8
Somers Pl 4 CV32 . . . .**109** E8
Somers Rd Keresley CV7 . . .**49** A6
Meriden CV7 . . . .**45** F1
Rugby CV22 . . . .**82** B2
Somerset Dr CV10 . . . .**28** E4
Somerset Rd CV1 . . . .**61** C5
Somerton Dr B37 . . . .**44** B7
Somerville Ho B37 . . . .**33** D3
Sommerville Rd CV2 . . . . . .**62** C4
Soot La OX17 . . . .**133** D2
Sopwith Croft B35 . . . .**22** A2
Sorbus B77 . . . .**4** A3
Sorrel B77 . . . .**4** A3
Sorrel Cl CV4 . . . .**75** E8
Sorrel Dr Kingsbury B78 . . . .**15** B4
Rugby CV23 . . . .**83** B4
Sorrell Pl CV10 . . . .**39** D8
Sorrell Rd CV10 . . . .**39** D8
South Ave CV2 . . . .**62** A2
South Car Park Rd B40 . . . .**44** E3
South Cl NN11 . . . .**117** E5
South Dr B46 . . . .**33** E6
South End OX7 . . . .**142** A2
South Green Dr CV37 . . . . .**144** B2
South Lynn Gdns CV36 . . . .**149** C3
South Par CV33 . . . .**123** B4
South Rd CV23 . . . .**84** A3
South Ridge CV5 . . . .**60** B4
South St Atherstone CV9 . . .**18** A4
Coventry CV1 . . . .**61** E3
Rugby CV21 . . . .**83** B2
South Terr CV31 . . . .**110** B3
South View Kingsbury B78 . . .**15** B4
Warwick CV34 . . . .**108** A6
South View Rd
Long Lawford CV23 . . . .**81** C2
Royal Leamington Spa
CV32 . . . .**106** C5
South Way B40 . . . .**44** F3
Southam Cl CV4 . . . .**75** E7
Southam Coll CV47 . . . . . .**147** A3
Southam Cres CV33 . . . . . .**123** D2
Southam Dr CV47 . . . .**147** A1
Southam Prim Sch
CV47 . . . .**147** A3
Southam Rd
Dunchurch CV22 . . . .**99** A1
Kineton CV35 . . . .**132** B6
Ladbroke CV47 . . . .**124** D6
Long Itchington CV47 . . . . .**115** D3
Mollington OX17 . . . .**134** A2
Priors Marston CV47 . . . . .**125** E4
Southam CV33,CV47 . . . . .**124** B8
Ufton CV33,CV47 . . . .**115** A1
Ufton, Radford Hill CV33,
CV47 . . . .**111** B2
Southam St CV35 . . . .**132** B6
Southbank Ct CV8 . . . .**92** F4
Southbank Rd
Coventry CV6 . . . .**60** E5
Kenilworth CV8 . . . .**92** F4
Southborough Terr 1
CV31 . . . .**110** A6
Southbrook Rd CV22 . . . . . .**83** A1
Southcott Way CV2 . . . .**50** F1
Southern La CV37 . . . .**145** A1
Southey Cl B91 . . . .**71** B8
Southey Rd CV22 . . . .**99** C4
Southfield Cl CV10 . . . .**29** D5

Southfield Dr CV8 . . . .**93** A6
Southfield Rd
Hinckley LE10 . . . .**31** E7
Rugby CV22 . . . .**83** B1
Southam CV47 . . . .**147** A1
Southfields CV32 . . . .**106** A3
Southfields Cl B46 . . . .**34** A2
Southfields Prim Sch
CV1 . . . .**61** E3
Southlands
Atherstone CV9 . . . .**18** C4
8 Royal Leamington Spa
CV31 . . . .**110** B7
Southlea Ave CV31 . . . .**109** E6
Southlea Cl CV31 . . . .**109** E6
Southleigh Ave CV5 . . . .**76** F7
Southmead Gdns B80 . . . .**103** C2
Southport Cl CV3 . . . .**78** B5
Southrop Rd OX15 . . . .**142** D3
Southway CV31 . . . .**110** A5
Sovereign Cl CV8 . . . .**92** F1
Sovereign Dr CV47 . . . .**147** A2
Sovereign Rd CV5 . . . .**61** A2
Sovereign Row CV5 . . . .**61** A2
Sowe Valley Prim Sch
CV3 . . . .**78** D7
Spa View CV31 . . . .**110** B4
Sparkbrook St CV1 . . . .**61** F3
Sparkbrook Workshops
CV1 . . . .**61** F3
Sparrow Cock La B93 . . . . .**73** C1
Sparrowdale Specl Sch
CV9 . . . .**11** B2
Sparta Cl CV21 . . . .**83** A3
Spartan Cl CV34 . . . .**109** E4
Speedway La CV8 . . . .**79** F7
Speedwell Dr CV7 . . . .**74** A6
Speedwell La CV9 . . . .**11** A1
Speedwll Cl CV23 . . . .**83** C4
Spencer Ave CV5 . . . .**61** A1
Spencer Cl CV5 . . . .**151** A1
Spencer St CV31 . . . .**109** F7
Spencer Yd CV31 . . . .**109** F7
Spencer's La CV7 . . . .**58** E1
Spernal Ash B49 . . . .**103** C3
Spernal La
Great Alne B80 . . . .**119** C7
Studley B80 . . . .**112** A1
Spetchley Cl B97 . . . .**102** B3
Sphinx Dr CV3 . . . .**62** B1
Spicer Pl CV22 . . . .**82** B1
Spiers Cl B93 . . . .**72** A6
Spiers Ct B50 . . . .**148** B3
Spilsbury Cl CV32 . . . .**105** E2
Spilsbury Croft B91 . . . .**71** A8
Spindle La B90 . . . .**70** A6
Spindle St CV1 . . . .**61** D6
Spindles The LE10 . . . .**31** F5
Spinners Bridge CV36 . . . .**149** C3
Spinney Cl Arley CV7 . . . . . .**36** C4
Binley Woods CV3 . . . .**79** E7
Lighthorne CV35 . . . .**123** B3
Polesworth B78 . . . .**10** C4
Spinney Dr B90 . . . .**70** D4
Spinney Hill
Braunston NN11 . . . .**117** E5
Warwick CV34 . . . .**105** A4
Spinney La CV10 . . . .**28** C4
Spinney Rd LE10 . . . .**31** C6
Spinney The
Atherstone CV9 . . . .**19** A4
Bishops Itchington CV47 . .**124** B4
Coventry CV4 . . . .**76** D3
Long Lawford CV23 . . . .**82** A3
Royal Leamington Spa
CV32 . . . .**105** D1
Solihull B91 . . . .**71** C8
Wythall B47 . . . .**69** B4
Spire Bank CV47 . . . .**147** A2
Spires The CV10 . . . .**28** C4
Spitfire Way 5 B35 . . . .**22** A2
Spon End CV1,CV5 . . . .**61** A3
Spon Gate Ho CV1 . . . .**61** A3
Spon Gate Prim Sch CV1 . **61** A3
Spon La CV9 . . . .**11** C3
Spon St CV1 . . . .**151** A3
Spottiswood Cl CV22 . . . . . .**99** A4
Spring Cl 6 Coventry CV1 . .**61** E3
Ettington CV37 . . . .**131** A3
Spring Coppice Dr B93 . . . .**72** A3
Spring Ct CV8 . . . .**95** B3
Spring Hill Arley CV7 . . . . . .**36** C4
Bubbenhall CV8 . . . .**95** B3
Combrook CV35 . . . .**131** F7
Spring Hill Rd CV10 . . . . . .**28** C6
Spring La
Combrook CV35 . . . .**131** E6
Hockley Heath B94 . . . .**88** B5
Lapworth B94 . . . .**88** D3
Radford Semele CV31 . . . .**110** E5
Spring Pool CV34 . . . .**108** E7
Spring Rd Barnacle CV7 . . . .**51** B6
Coventry CV6 . . . .**49** F1
Spring St CV21 . . . .**83** A2
Springbrook La B36 . . . .**22** C1
Springbrook La B94 . . . .**87** A7
Springdale Ct CV11 . . . .**29** D3
Springfield OX17 . . . .**139** F6
Springfield Cl CV36 . . . . . .**149** C3
Springfield Cres
Bedworth CV12 . . . .**39** B2
Sutton Coldfield B76 . . . . . .**13** A4
Springfield Ct B75 . . . .**13** C5
Springfield Gr CV47 . . . . . .**147** A3

Springfield House Specl Sch
B93 .73 A5
Springfield Pl CV1 .151 C4
Springfield Rd
Coventry CV1 .151 C4
Hinckley LE10 .31 D7
Nuneaton CV11 .29 E2
Shipston-on-S CV36 .149 C2
Sutton Coldfield B75,B76 .13 A4
Tamworth B77 .9 B4
Springfields B46 .33 F5
Springfields Rd B49 .143 A3
Springhill CV10 .28 A8
Springhill Ind Pk CV7 .36 C4
Springs Cres CV47 .147 A3
Springside B98 .103 B4
Springwell Rd CV31 .110 D6
Spruce B77 .4 A2
Spruce Gr 4 CV31 .109 F5
Spruce Rd 5 CV2 .50 B2
Squadron Cl B35 .22 C4
Square La CV7 .37 A1
Square The
Clifford Chambers CV37 .129 F7
Coventry CV2 .63 A7
Dunchurch CV22 .99 B2
Ettington CV37 .131 A3
Fazeley B78 .9 A4
Kenilworth CV8 .92 F4
Long Itchington CV47 .115 D4
Nuneaton CV11 .29 E2
Stockton CV47 .147 C4
Swalcliffe OX15 .142 F8
Tysoe CV35 .138 B7
Wolvey LE10 .41 B2
Wootton Wawen B95 .113 A3
Squire Pl CV47 .133 D7
Squires Croft
Coventry CV2 .50 F1
Sutton Coldfield B76 .13 A2
Squires Gate Wlk 3 B35 22 A3
Squires Gn LE10 .31 F6
Squires Rd CV23 .96 C3
Squires Way CV4 .76 D6
Squirhill Pl 1 CV31 .110 B7
Squirrel Hollow B76 .13 A2
Sring La CV8 .93 A5
Stable Wlk CV11 .29 F2
Stableford Cl B97 .102 B4
Stables The Berkswell CV7 58 C4
Hinckley LE10 .31 D5
Royal Leamington Spa
CV32 .105 C1
Stacey Ct CV22 .99 B3
Stadium Cl CV6 .49 D2
Stafford Cl CV12 .40 C2
Stafford St CV9 .18 B4
Staines Cl CV11 .29 F7
Stainforth Cl CV11 .30 A2
Stainsby Croft B90 .71 B5
Staircase La CV5 .60 C7
Stamford Ave CV3 .77 C6
Stamford Gdns CV32 .105 E1
Stanbrook Rd B90 .71 A5
Stand St CV34 .108 D5
Standard Ave CV4 .60 B1
Standedge B77 .10 A4
Standish Cl CV2 .62 E2
Standlake Mews 14
CV31 .110 C6
Stanford Cl B97 .102 A3
Stanier Ave CV1 .61 B4
Stanley Ct CV31 .110 C7
Stanley Rd Atherstone CV9 18 B4
Coventry CV5 .76 F8
Nuneaton CV11 .29 A5
Rugby CV21,CV22 .83 C1
Stannells Cl CV37 .129 E8
Stansfield Gr CV8 .93 D4
Stanton Bridge Prim Sch
CV6 .61 F6
Stanton Rd CV31 .110 C6
Stanton Wlk CV34 .104 D1
Stanway Rd CV5 .77 A8
Stapenhall Rd B90 .71 A5
Staple Hill Ho CV35 .122 D2
Stapledon Gn CV47 .132 F7
Staples Cl CV12 .40 C3
Stapleton Cl Studley B80 103 B2
Sutton Coldfield B76 .22 B6
Stapleton Dr B37 .33 A4
Stapleton La CV13 .21 C4
Stapleton Rd B80 .103 B2
Star Cnr CV23 .101 B1
Star Ind Pk CV2 .62 F5
Star La CV35 .114 A4
Starbold Cres B93 .72 B5
Starbold Ct B93 .72 A6
Starbold Rd CV47 .124 A4
Starcross Cl CV2 .62 C7
Stare Gn CV4 .76 D5
Stareton Cl CV4 .76 E6
Starkey Croft B37 .33 D2
Starley Ct CV3 .79 A7
Starley Pk CV7 .50 B8
Starley Rd CV1 .151 A2
Starley Way B37 .44 C6
Starmer Pl CV35 .114 D6
Startin Cl CV7 .49 F7
Station App Dorridge B93 .71 F2
Royal Leamington Spa
CV31 .109 F7
Station Ave Coventry CV4 .75 D8
Warwick CV34 .108 F8
Station Bldgs B46 .23 B3
Station Dr B94 .69 D1
Station La B94 .89 D3
Station Link Rd B26 .44 D4
Station Rd Alcester B49 .143 A2
Arley CV7 .36 B4
Balsall Common CV7 .74 B7
Birmingham, Marston Green
B37 .44 A8
Bishops Itchington CV47 .124 A4
Chipping Campden GL55 .135 C2
Claverdon CV35 .114 A3
Clifton u D CV23 .83 C3
Coleshill B46 .23 F1
Cropredy OX17 .134 C1
Fenny Compton CV47 .133 E7
Hampton-in-A B92 .57 B7
Harvington WR11 .127 D3
Hatton CV35 .114 C5
Henley-in-A B95 .113 A5
Higham on t H CV13 .20 C2
Hinckley LE10 .31 D8
Hook Norton OX15 .142 E4
Kenilworth CV8 .92 F4
Knowle B93 .72 B4
Lapworth B94 .89 D4
Long Marston CV37 .129 C2
8 Moreton-in-M GL56 .140 A3
Polesworth B78 .5 A1
Salford Priors WR11 .127 F6
Shipston-on-S CV36 .149 C3
Shustoke B46 .24 B2
Stockton CV47 .116 A3
Stoke Golding CV13 .21 B4
Stratford-u-A CV37 .144 C2
Studley B80 .103 B2
Warwick CV34 .108 F7
Wilmcote CV37 .120 C5
Wythall B47 .69 B3
Station Sq CV1 .151 B1
Station St CV9 .18 B4
Station St E CV6 .61 E7
Station St W CV6 .61 E7
Station Street W Bsns Pk
CV6 .61 D7
Staunton Rd CV31 .110 A5
Staveley Way CV21 .83 B3
Staverton CE Prim Sch
NN11 .126 E8
Staverton Cl CV5 .60 A3
Staverton Leys CV22 .100 A4
Staverton Rd NN11 .126 F8
Staverton Sports Ctr
NN11 .117 F1
Steeds Ct CV35 .122 A7
Steele St CV22 .82 C2
Steels La CV36 .141 D7
Steeping Rd CV23 .82 A3
Steeplefield Rd CV6 .61 A5
Steeples The CV23 .116 F5
Stefen Way NN11 .126 F8
Stella Croft B37 .33 C2
Stennels Cl CV6 .60 F8
Stephen St CV21 .82 C2
Stephens Rd B76 .13 A4
Stephenson Cl
Daventry NN11 .117 F2
Royal Leamington Spa
CV32 .105 C1
Tamworth B77 .4 A1
Stephenson Ct CV23 .101 C1
Stephenson Dr B37 .33 B2
Stephenson Rd
Bedworth CV7 .50 C7
Hinckley LE10 .30 E7
Stepney Rd CV2 .62 A4
Steppes Piece B50 .148 B3
Stepping Stones B50 .148 B3
Stepping Stones Rd CV5 .60 F4
Sterling Pk LE10 .30 C8
Sterling Way CV11 .39 E8
Stevenage Wlk 2 CV2 .63 A7
Stevens Ho CV1 .151 C4
Stevenson Rd CV6 .61 A8
Stewart Cl CV4 .60 D2
Stewart Ct CV7 .37 A4
Stewart St CV11 .29 C3
Stidfall Gr CV31 .110 D6
Stileman Cl CV37 .129 D2
Stiper's Hill B78 .5 A1
Stirling Ave CV32 .106 B6
Stirling Cl CV3 .78 F8
Stirling Ct OX16 .139 F3
Stirling Rd B90 .70 E8
Stivichall Croft CV3 .77 B6
Stivichall Prim Sch CV3 .77 A6
Stocking La OX15 .138 E5
Stocking Mdw CV23 .53 C2
Stockingford Inf & Jun Sch
CV10 .28 D3
Stockley Rd CV6 .50 C6
Stocks Ct CV22 .99 B4
Stocks La CV23 .98 C2
Stockton Cl
Birmingham B76 .22 C5
Knowle B93 .72 B4
Stockton Gr 2 CV32 .106 A2
Stockton Prim Sch
CV47 .147 C4
Stockton Rd
Coventry CV1 .151 D4
Long Itchington CV47 .115 E3
Stockwell La NN11 .126 B5
Stockwells GL56 .140 A3
Stoke Gn CV3 .62 A2
Stoke Heath Prim Sch
CV2 .62 A6
Stoke La
Stoke Golding LE10 .21 C4
Stoke La *continued*
Stoke Golding, Wykin LE10 .21 C2
Stoke Park Com Coll
CV2 .62 B4
Stoke Park Mews CV2 .62 A3
Stoke Prim Sch CV2 .62 A4
Stoke Rd
Fenny Drayton CV13 .20 C4
Stoke Golding CV13 .21 C3
Stoke Row CV2 .62 A4
Stokesay Cl CV11 .29 B3
Stone Ave B75 .13 A5
Stone Bridge GL56 .140 D7
Stone Cross B46 .23 B3
Stone Ct OX7 .142 A2
Stone Mdw CV7 .49 A6
Stone Pits Mdw CV37 .120 C5
Stonebow Ave B91 .71 B8
Stonebridge Highway
CV3 .77 E4
Stonebridge Rd
Coleshill B46 .33 F5
Lighthorne Heath CV33 .123 C3
Little Packington B46 .45 A7
Long Itchington CV47 .115 B4
Stonebridge Trad Est
CV3 .78 B4
Stonebrook Way CV6 .49 F3
Stonebury Ave CV5 .59 E4
Stonefarn Ct 16 GL56 .140 A3
Stonefield Cl CV2 .63 A8
Stonehall Rd CV22 .99 A4
Stonehaven Dr CV3 .77 C3
Stonehill Croft B90 .70 F6
Stonehill Wlk B77 .9 C3
Stonehills CV21 .83 B4
Stonehouse Cl CV32 .106 D5
Stonehouse La CV3 .78 C4
Stoneleigh Ave CV8 .93 A6
Stoneleigh Cl
Hartshill CV10 .19 A1
Redditch B98 .102 C3
Stoneleigh CV8 .94 B6
Stoneleigh Ct CV11 .29 C3
Stoneleigh Deer Park Bsns
Village CV8 .94 D4
Stoneleigh Gdns CV11 .29 C3
Stoneleigh Rd
Blackdown CV32 .106 A7
Coventry CV4 .76 E2
Kenilworth CV8 .93 A6
Stoneleigh CV8 .94 B3
Stonely Rd CV13 .21 B3
Stonepits La B97 .102 B2
Stoneton Cl CV47 .147 B2
Stoneton Cres CV7 .74 A6
Stoneway NN11 .126 F5
Stoneway Gr CV31 .110 D6
Stonewell Cres CV11 .40 B8
Stoney Ct CV3 .79 A7
Stoney La CV35 .114 C6
Stoney Rd
Coventry CV1,CV3 .151 B1
Nuneaton CV10,CV11 .29 B6
Stoney Stanton Rd CV1,
CV6 .61 E5
Stoneydelph Prim Sch
B77 .4 A1
Stoneymoor Dr B36 .22 D1
Stoneywood Rd CV2 .62 F8
Stonleigh Ave CV5 .76 F7
Stonydelph La B77 .10 A4
Stonyway Rd B35 .22 B4
Storrage La B48 .85 A3
Stour B77 .10 A3
Stour Ct CV36 .149 C3
Stour View CV36 .137 A8
Stourton Cl B93 .72 B7
Stow Rd GL56 .140 A2
Stowe Dr CV47 .147 A2
Stowe Pl CV4 .59 C1
Strachey Ave CV32 .105 E2
Straight Mile CV23 .98 A2
Stratford Ave CV9 .18 B4
Stratford Butterfly Farm*
CV37 .145 A1
Stratford Coll CV37 .144 C2
Stratford Rd
Alcester B49 .143 B2
Bidford-on-A B50 .128 D7
Dorridge B94 .71 B3
Drayton OX15,OX16 .139 E4
Hampton Lucy CV35&CV37 121 E4
Harvington WR11 .127 D3
Henley-in-A B95 .113 A3
Ilmington CV36 .136 B7
Lighthorne Heath CV33 .123 D2
Loxley CV35 .130 F8
Mickleton GL55 .135 B7
Newbold-on-S CV37 .130 E1
Shenington OX15 .138 F7
Shipston-on-S CV36 .149 C3
Solihull B90 .70 D7
Tanworth-in-A, Hockley Heath
B94 .88 C5
Temple Grafton B49 .119 E3
Warwick CV34 .108 C3
Wellesbourne CV35 .146 A2
Wroxton OX15 .139 B5
Stratford St Coventry CV2 .62 A4
Nuneaton CV11 .29 C4
Stratford-upon-Avon Gram
Sch For Girls CV37 .144 B1
Stratford-upon-Avon High
Sch CV37 .144 C2
Stratford-upon-Avon Hospl
CV37 .144 C2
Stratford-upon-Avon Prim
Sch CV37 .144 C1
Stratford-upon-Avon
Racecourse CV37 .129 E8
Stratford-upon-Avon Shire
Horse Ctr* CV37 .129 F7
Stratford-upon-Avon Sta
CV37 .144 C2
Strath Cl CV21 .101 A4
Strathearn Rd CV32 .105 E1
Strathmore Ave CV1 .61 E1
Strathmore Rd LE10 .31 A7
Strawberry Fields CV7 .46 B1
Strawberry Wlk CV2 .50 D2
Streamside Cl CV5 .60 A8
Stretton Ave CV3 .78 C6
Stretton Cl LE10 .31 D6
Stretton Cres CV31 .110 B5
Stretton Ct Hinckley LE10 .31 D3
Rugby CV21 .83 B4
Stretton Rd
Nuneaton CV10 .29 A3
Solihull B90 .70 B8
Wolston CV8 .80 A1
Stroma Way CV10 .28 F2
Strutt Rd LE10 .32 A5
Stuart Cl CV34 .108 D5
Stuart Ct Coventry CV6 .62 A8
7 Royal Leamington Spa
CV32 .105 E1
Stuart Gdns CV47 .132 F7
Stubbs Cl CV12 .39 A4
Stubbs Gr CV2 .62 B5
Stud Farm Cl OX17 .134 F1
Studland Ave CV21 .83 C1
Studland Gn CV2 .63 A4
Studley Com Inf Sch
B80 .103 C2
Studley High Sch B80 .103 C2
Studley Rd B98 .103 A4
Studley St Mary's CE Jun Sch
B80 .103 C2
Sturley Cl CV8 .93 B6
Sturminster Cl CV2 .63 A4
Styles Cl
Hampton Magna CV35 .114 F4
Royal Leamington Spa
CV31 .110 A7
Styvechale Ave CV5 .77 A8
Sudbury Cl CV32 .106 C3
Sudeley B77 .9 B4
Sudeley Cl B36 .22 B1
Sudeley Rd CV10 .39 C8
Suffolk Cl Bedworth CV12 .39 A3
Coventry CV5 .60 B3
Nuneaton CV10 .28 E3
Suffolk St CV32 .106 A1
Sugarswell La OX15 .138 D7
Sulgrave Cl CV2 .62 E7
Sullivan Ct CV6 .62 B7
Sullivan Rd CV6 .62 B7
Sumburgh Croft B35 .22 A3
Summer La B76 .22 D6
Summerhouse Cl B97 .102 A3
Summerton Rd CV31 .110 A3
Sumner Cl CV35 .114 F3
Sumner Rd B46 .34 A3
Sun Rising Hill OX15 .132 D1
Sun St CV21 .83 B2
Sunart Way CV10 .28 C5
Sunbeam Cl
Birmingham B36 .22 F1
Rugby CV21 .83 B2
Sunbridge Terr CV21 .83 B2
Sunbury Rd CV3 .78 C5
Suncliffe Dr CV8 .93 A2
Sunderland Pl CV35 .146 B1
Sundew St CV2 .50 D2
Sundorne Cl CV5 .60 A4
Sunningdale B77 .4 B3
Sunningdale Ave
Coventry CV6 .49 D2
Kenilworth CV8 .93 B4
Sunningdale Cl CV11 .30 A1
Sunnybank Ave CV3 .78 B5
Sunnydale Cres LE10 .31 A7
Sunnydale Rd LE10 .30 F7
Sunnyhill LE10 .31 F7
Sunnyhill S LE10 .31 F6
Sunnyside B95 .119 F7
Sunnyside Cl
Balsall Common CV7 .74 C7
Coventry CV5 .60 F3
Sunnyside Ct CV10 .28 F3
Sunnyside La CV7 .74 C7
Sunset Cl B78 .11 A4
Sunset Dr CV37 .129 C8
Sunshine Cl CV8 .93 A2
Sunway Gr CV3 .77 B6
Surrey Cl Hinckley LE10 .31 E4
Nuneaton CV10 .28 E3
Surrey Ct CV34 .108 E8
Sussex Cl CV10 .28 E3
Sussex Ct CV34 .108 E8
Sussex Rd CV5 .60 F4
Sutcliffe Ave CV37 .130 D3
Sutcliffe Dr CV33 .123 E6
Sutherland Ave CV5 .60 A4
Sutherland Cl CV34 .104 E1
Sutherland Dr CV12 .39 A4
Sutton Ave CV5 .59 D4
Sutton Cl NN11 .134 F6
Sutton Ho CV22 .82 B1
Sutton La OX15 .137 E1
Sutton Pk CV10 .28 B7
Sutton Rd B78 .8 A4
Sutton Sq B76 .22 E6
Sutton Stop CV6 .50 B5
Swadling St CV31 .109 F6
Swain Crofts CV31 .110 B6
Swains Gn LE10 .31 F6
Swalcliffe Park Sch Trust
OX15 .142 F8
Swale Rd B76 .13 A1
Swaledale CV4 .76 D6
Swallow Ave B36 .33 A8
Swallow Cl CV37 .145 A3
Swallow Ct CV12 .49 C8
Swallow Rd CV6 .49 C1
Swallowdean Rd CV6 .60 E8
Swallows Ind Est The
B90 .70 E8
Swallows' Mdw B90 .70 D8
Swan Cl GL56 .140 A3
Swan Ct CV37 .145 A1
Swan La CV2 .61 F4
Swan St Alcester B49 .143 A2
Royal Leamington Spa
CV32 .106 A1
Warwick CV34 .108 E6
Swan's Nest CV37 .145 A1
Swanage Gn CV2 .63 A4
Swancroft B95 .113 A5
Swancroft Rd CV2 .62 A5
Swanfold CV37 .120 C5
Swans Cl CV37 .120 C5
Swanswell St CV1 .151 C4
Swanswood Gr 3 B37 .33 C3
Sweet Knowle Farm Cotts
CV37 .130 A2
Swerford Rd OX15,OX7 .142 D3
Swift Cl Birmingham B36 .33 A8
Kenilworth CV8 .93 A2
Swift Point CV21 .66 C1
Swift Rd CV37 .145 A3
Swift Valley Ind Est CV21 82 C4
Swift's Cnr CV3 .77 E8
Swillington Rd CV6 .61 B5
Swinburne Ave CV2 .62 D2
Swinburne Cl CV10 .28 A5
Swinburne Rd B97 .102 B4
Swindale B77 .10 A4
Swindale Croft CV3 .78 F8
Swinford Gr B93 .71 E3
Swinford Rd Shawell LE17 .68 B3
Shawell LE17 .68 C4
Swiss Lodge Dr B78 .8 C4
Sycamore B77 .9 C4
Sycamore Ave B78 .11 A4
Sycamore Cl
Hinckley LE10 .31 E5
Sibford Gower OX15 .142 D8
Stockton CV47 .147 C4
Stratford-u-A CV37 .144 C3
Wellesbourne CV35 .146 C2
Sycamore Cres Arley CV7 .37 A4
Birmingham B37 .44 A8
Sycamore Ct Allesley CV5 .59 F7
Kineton CV35 .132 B5
Sycamore Dr B47 .69 B6
Sycamore Gr Rugby CV21 .83 A2
Southam CV47 .147 A3
Warwick CV34 .105 A1
Sycamore Rd
Coventry CV2 .50 B2
Kingsbury B78 .15 B4
Nuneaton CV10 .28 D6
Sycamores The CV12 .38 E2
Sydenham Dr CV31 .110 B6
Sydenham Ind Est CV31 110 B6
Sydenham Prim Sch
CV31 .110 C6
Sydnall Fields CV6 .49 F4
Sydnall Rd CV6 .49 F4
Sydney Ct 1 CV12 .38 F2
Sykesmoor B77 .10 A4
Sylvan Dr CV3 .76 F6
Synkere Cl CV7 .49 A6
Sywell Leys CV22 .99 C3

T

Table Oak La CV8 .74 B1
Tachbrook Cl CV2 .50 C2
Tachbrook Link CV34 .109 E4
Tachbrook Park Dr
CV34 .109 E5
Tachbrook Rd CV31 .109 F4
Tachbrook St CV31 .110 A6
Tackford Cl B36 .22 D1
Tackford Rd CV6 .62 A8
Tackley Cl B90 .70 B8
Tailor's La CV37 .129 D1
Tainters Hill CV8 .93 A6
Talbot Cl OX16 .139 F4
Talbot Ct
Royal Leamington Spa
CV32 .106 A1
Wellesbourne CV35 .146 C2
Talbot Rd CV37 .145 A2
Talisman Cl CV8 .92 F3
Talisman Sq CV8 .92 F4
Talland Ave CV6 .62 A6
Tallants Cl CV6 .62 A8
Tallants Rd CV6 .62 A8
Talton Cl B90 .71 A5
Tamar Cl CV23 .82 A3
Tamar Dr B76 .22 B7
Tamar Rd Bulkington CV12 .40 B2
Tamworth B77 .10 A3
Tame Bank B78 .15 B3
Tame Ct B78 .9 A4
Tame Valley Bsns Ctr B77 .9 C3
Tame Valley Ind Est B77 .9 C4
Tame Way LE10 .31 A8

Tameside Dr B35 ... 22 A1
Tamworth Bsns Ctr B77 ... 4 A2
Tamworth Bsns Pk B77 ... 4 A2
Tamworth Rd Corley CV7 ... 37 A1
Fillongley CV7 ... 36 B3
Keresley CV6,CV7 ... 48 D5
Kingsbury B78 ... 15 B4
Polesworth B78 ... 4 C1
Sutton Coldfield B75 ... 7 A1
Tamworth B77 ... 9 B4
Wood End CV9 ... 10 B1
Tamworth Rd (Amington) B77 ... 4 A3
Tamworth Rd (Dosthill) B77 ... 9 B3
Tancred Cl CV31 ... 109 F5
Tandra Cl CV34 ... 109 D3
Tangmere Dr B35 ... 22 A3
Tanhill B77 ... 10 A4
Tankards Hill GL56,GL55 ... 136 B1
Tanners Ctyd CV34 ... 108 D5
Tanners Green La B47, B94 ... 69 B2
Tanners' La CV4,CV7 ... 59 B1
Tannery Cl CV9 ... 18 C4
Tannery Ct CV8 ... 92 F4
Tannery The CV36 ... 149 C3
Tanser Ct CV22 ... 99 B2
Tansley Cl B93 ... 71 F4
Tanwood Cl
Redditch B97 ... 102 A3
Solihull B91 ... 71 B8
Tanworth La
Henley-in-A B95 ... 113 A7
Redditch B98 ... 112 B8
Solihull B90 ... 70 C5
Tanworth-in-Arden CE Prim Sch B94 ... 87 A2
Tanyard Cl CV4 ... 59 D1
Tapcon Way CV2 ... 62 F5
Tappinger Gr CV8 ... 93 C5
Tapster La B94 ... 88 F2
Tara Ct CV2 ... 62 B4
Tarlington Rd CV6 ... 60 E6
Tarn Cl CV12 ... 39 A2
Tarquin Cl CV3 ... 78 D7
Tarragon Cl CV2 ... 50 D1
Tarrant B77 ... 9 C4
Tarrant Wlk CV2 ... 63 A5
Tatchbrook Ct 5 CV31 ... 109 F6
Tatnall Gr CV34 ... 108 E8
Tattle Bank CV47 ... 147 A2
Taunton Way CV6 ... 49 A2
Tavern La CV37 ... 144 B1
Taverners La CV9 ... 18 B4
Tavistock St CV32 ... 105 F1
Tavistock Way CV11 ... 29 E5
Tavistock Wlk CV2 ... 62 C7
Tay Croft B37 ... 33 C4
Tay Rd CV6 ... 61 B6
Taylor Ave CV32 ... 106 B2
Taylor Cl CV8 ... 93 B6
Taylor Ct CV34 ... 108 D7
Tea Gdn The CV12 ... 49 E8
Teachers Cl CV6 ... 61 A5
Teal Bsns Ctr LE10 ... 30 D7
Teal Cl CV37 ... 144 B3
Teal Dr LE10 ... 31 A6
Teal Rd B80 ... 103 C2
Teasel Cl CV23 ... 83 B4
Ted Pitts La CV5 ... 48 B2
Teign B77 ... 10 A3
Telegraph St CV36 ... 149 C3
Telephone Rd CV3 ... 62 C2
Telfer Rd CV6 ... 61 B7
Telford Ave CV32 ... 106 B5
Telford Rd CV7 ... 50 C8
TelfordInf & Jun Sch CV32 ... 106 C5
Templar Ave CV4 ... 60 A1
Templar Ct CV11 ... 29 C3
Templars Prim Sch CV4 ... 60 A1
Templars The CV34 ... 108 F5
Templars' Fields CV4 ... 76 B7
Temple Ave CV7 ... 73 F6
Temple Ct Coleshill B46 ... 23 F1
Rugby CV22 ... 83 B1
Temple End CV33 ... 123 E6
Temple Gr CV34 ... 108 D5
Temple Grafton CE Prim Sch B49 ... 119 E1
Temple Herdewyke Prim Sch CV47 ... 133 A7
Temple Hill LE10 ... 41 C3
Temple La B93 ... 73 A4
Temple Rd B93 ... 72 A3
Temple St CV21,CV22 ... 83 B1
Temple Way B46 ... 23 F1
Templeton Cl B93 ... 72 A3
Ten Acres B49 ... 143 B2
Tenby Cl CV12 ... 38 C1
Tenby Ct CV32 ... 109 E8
Teneriffe Rd CV6 ... 49 F1
Tenlons Rd CV10 ... 28 F2
Tennant Cl CV21,CV22 ... 83 C1
Tennant St CV11 ... 29 E3
Tennyson Ave Rugby CV22 ... 99 C4
Warwick CV34 ... 108 C4
Tennyson Cl CV8 ... 93 C4
Tennyson Rd
Coventry CV2 ... 62 C3
Redditch B97 ... 102 B4
Stratford-u-A CV37 ... 130 A8
Ternhill Ho 4 B35 ... 22 A3
Terrace Rd CV9 ... 18 B4
Terrace The CV35 ... 122 F2
Terrett Ct CV37 ... 145 A1
Terry Ave CV32 ... 105 C1
Terry Rd CV1 ... 61 F1
Tewkesbury Dr CV12 ... 39 C3
Thackeray Cl
Lower Quinton CV37 ... 129 D2
Nuneaton CV10 ... 28 A4
Rugby CV22 ... 99 C4
Thackhall St CV2 ... 61 F4
Thame Cl B80 ... 103 C2
Thames Cl CV12 ... 40 A3
Thames Rd NN11 ... 117 F1
Thamley Rd CV6 ... 61 A4
Thatchers Cl OX15 ... 138 D3
Thatchings The CV22 ... 99 B2
Theatre Ct CV34 ... 108 D6
Theatre St CV34 ... 108 D7
Thebes Cl CV5 ... 59 B8
Theddingworth Cl CV3 ... 78 E8
Thickthorn Cl CV8 ... 93 B2
Thickthorn Mews CV8 ... 93 B2
Thickthorn Orchs CV8 ... 93 B2
Thimble End Rd B76 ... 13 A1
Thimbler Rd CV4 ... 76 C7
Third Exhibition Ave B40 ... 44 D4
Thirlestane Cl CV8 ... 93 C6
Thirlmere CV21 ... 83 B4
Thirlmere Ave CV11 ... 29 F6
Thirlmere Cl CV4 ... 59 E3
Thirlmere Rd
Bedworth CV12 ... 39 A2
Hinckley LE10 ... 31 A7
Thirsk Rd CV3 ... 77 C5
Thistle Way CV23 ... 83 B4
Thistlewood Gr B93 ... 90 B6
Thistley Field E CV6 ... 61 A7
Thistley Field N CV6 ... 61 A7
Thistley Field S CV6 ... 60 F6
Thistley Field W CV6 ... 60 F7
Thomas Jolyffe Prim Sch CV37 ... 145 A3
Thomas King Ho 6 CV1 ... 61 E4
Thomas Landsdail St CV3 ... 77 D8
Thomas Lane St CV6 ... 50 A1
Thomas Naul Croft CV4 ... 59 F3
Thomas Sharp St CV4 ... 76 A7
Thomas St Bedworth CV12 ... 39 A2
Royal Leamington Spa CV32 ... 106 A1
Thomas Way CV23 ... 82 A3
Thomas Wlk B35 ... 22 B3
Thompson's Rd CV7 ... 48 F6
Thomson Cl CV21 ... 83 A3
Thorn Cl CV21 ... 83 B3
Thorn Stile Cl CV32 ... 106 E6
Thorn Way CV47 ... 115 D4
Thornbury Rise OX16 ... 139 F3
Thornby Ave
Kenilworth CV8 ... 93 B3
Tamworth B77 ... 9 C4
Thorncliffe Cl B97 ... 102 A3
Thorncliffe Way CV10 ... 27 C4
Thorney Rd CV2 ... 62 B6
Thornfield Ave CV13 ... 21 C4
Thornfield Way LE10 ... 31 E8
Thorngrove Ave 7 B91 ... 71 C8
Thornhill Dr CV11 ... 40 C8
Thornhill Rd CV1 ... 61 D5
Thornley Cl CV31 ... 110 F5
Thornley Gr B76 ... 22 C6
Thorns Com Inf Sch CV8 ... 93 B4
Thornton Cl Coventry CV5 ... 59 C4
Warwick CV34 ... 104 F1
Thornton Rd B90 ... 70 F6
Thorntons La CV47 ... 125 C7
Thorntons Way CV10 ... 28 A3
Thornycroft Rd LE10 ... 31 E8
Thorpe Rd OX17 ... 134 F1
Threadneedle St CV1 ... 61 D6
Three Acres La B90 ... 69 F6
Three Cocks La WR11 ... 127 D1
Three Corner Cl B90 ... 69 E8
Three Cornered Cl CV32 ... 106 E6
Three Oaks Rd B47 ... 69 B4
Three Pots Rd LE10 ... 31 E4
Three Shires Jct CV6 ... 49 E1
Three Spires Ave CV6 ... 61 A6
Three Spires Ind Est CV6 ... 50 A5
Three Spires Sch CV6 ... 60 D6
Throckmorton Cl CV35 ... 114 C8
Throckmorton Rd
Alcester B49 ... 143 B2
Redditch B98 ... 103 A4
Thurlestone Rd CV6 ... 60 F8
Thurlow Cl CV9 ... 12 B1
Thurne B77 ... 9 C4
Thurnmill Rd CV23 ... 82 B2
Thursfield Rd CV32 ... 106 B3
Tibberton Cl B91 ... 71 A8
Tibbetts Cl B49 ... 143 B2
Tibbits Ct 8 CV34 ... 108 E6
Tiber Cl CV5 ... 59 F4
Tiber Way CV21 ... 82 C4
Tiberius Cl B46 ... 23 F1
Tidbury Cl B97 ... 102 B3
Tidbury Green Sch B90 ... 69 E4
Tiddington Cl B36 ... 22 B1
Tiddington Ct CV37 ... 145 C2
Tiddington Rd CV37 ... 145 B2
Tideswell Cl CV3 ... 63 A1
Tidmarsh Cl CV7 ... 74 A6
Tidmarsh Rd CV35 ... 105 A7
Tidmington Cl CV35 ... 114 F5
Tile Gr B37 ... 33 A5
Tile Hill La
Coventry, Allesley CV4,CV5 ... 60 D2
Coventry, Tile Hill CV4 ... 60 B1
Tile Hill Sta CV4 ... 75 D8
Tile Hill Wood Sch & Language Coll CV4 ... 59 D2
Tilehouse Green La B93 ... 71 F6
Tilehurst Dr CV4 ... 59 D1
Tilemans La CV36 ... 149 C4
Tilesford Cl B90 ... 71 A6
Tilewood Ave CV5 ... 59 F4
Tilia Rd B77 ... 4 A3
Tilton Rd LE10 ... 31 E6
Timber Ct CV22 ... 83 B1
Timberlake Cl B90 ... 71 B6
Timon View CV34 ... 109 E3
Timothy Gr CV4 ... 60 B1
Timothy's Bridge Rd CV37 ... 144 B2
Timsa Rd CV35 ... 132 E5
Tink-A-Tank CV34 ... 108 E6
Tinker's Cl 23 GL56 ... 140 A3
Tinkers Green Rd B77 ... 10 A3
Tinkers La Earlswood B94 ... 87 E7
Lapworth B94 ... 88 E1
Mollington OX17 ... 133 F2
Tintagel Cl CV3 ... 78 D5
Tintagel Gr CV8 ... 93 B4
Tintagel Way CV11 ... 30 A5
Tintern Way CV12 ... 39 C3
Tipper's Hill La CV7 ... 36 C3
Tippett Cl CV11 ... 40 A7
Tipping's Hill B97 ... 102 B3
Tisdale Rise CV8 ... 93 B6
Titan Bsns Ctr CV34 ... 109 E4
Tite La OX15 ... 142 D4
Tithe Barn Cl CV35 ... 114 F4
Tithe Barn La B94 ... 87 C6
Tithe Cl CV13 ... 21 B3
Tithe Ct WR11 ... 127 F2
Titheway WR11 ... 127 F2
Tithings The OX15 ... 142 F8
Tiverton Dr CV11 ... 29 F5
Tiverton Gr CV2 ... 62 D5
Tiverton Rd CV2 ... 62 D5
Tiverton Sch CV6 ... 60 D5
Tiveycourt Rd CV6 ... 50 A3
Tocil Croft CV4 ... 76 D4
Todenham Way CV35 ... 114 F6
Toft Hill CV23 ... 99 A1
Tokchong Rd CV35 ... 132 E5
Toler Rd CV11 ... 29 B5
Toll Gate Cl CV37 ... 144 A2
Toll Gate Rd CV47 ... 147 A3
Tollard Cl CV2 ... 62 F5
Tolson Ave B78 ... 9 A4
Tolson Cl B77 ... 9 B3
Tom Brown St CV21 ... 83 B2
Tom Ellis Ct CV7 ... 50 A8
Tom Henderson Cl CV3 ... 78 F7
Tom Hill B94 ... 87 B3
Tom Ward Cl CV3 ... 78 E7
Tom Williams Way B77 ... 9 B4
Tomkinson Rd CV10 ... 28 F4
Tomlinson Rd B36 ... 22 D1
Tommy's Turn La OX15 ... 137 E1
Tompson Cl NN11 ... 117 E5
Toms Town La B80 ... 103 C2
Tomson Ave CV6 ... 61 B4
Tomwell Cl CV47 ... 147 A3
Tonbridge Rd CV3 ... 78 A6
Top Rd CV7,CV12 ... 51 B7
Top St Appleby Magna DE12 ... 3 C4
Northend CV47 ... 133 B7
Topcliffe Sch B35 ... 22 A3
Topp's Dr CV12 ... 38 E1
Topp's Heath CV12 ... 38 E1
Torbay Rd CV5 ... 60 C4
Torcastle Cl CV6 ... 61 F7
Torcross Ave CV2 ... 62 C6
Torpoint Cl CV2 ... 62 C7
Torrance Rd CV21 ... 82 C2
Torridge B77 ... 10 A3
Torrington Ave CV4 ... 75 E8
Torside B77 ... 10 A4
Torwood Cl CV4 ... 75 F6
Totnes Cl CV2 ... 62 C7
Touchstone Rd CV34 ... 109 F2
Tove Ct CV23 ... 82 A3
Towbury Cl B98 ... 102 C3
Tower Cl
Bidford-on-A B50 ... 148 C3
Stratford-u-A CV37 ... 145 A3
Tower Croft
Bidford-on-A B50 ... 148 C3
Birmingham B37 ... 33 B4
Tower Hill B50 ... 148 C3
Tower Rd Bedworth CV12 ... 39 B2
Rugby CV22 ... 83 B1
Tower St Coventry CV1 ... 151 B3
16 Royal Leamington Spa CV31 ... 110 A7
Tower View Cres CV10 ... 28 B3
Towers Cl CV8 ... 92 F2
Town Fields Cl CV5 ... 60 B7
Town Ground CV35 ... 131 F5
Town Yd CV23 ... 64 C2
Townesend Cl CV34 ... 104 F1
Townhill OX15 ... 133 A2
Townsend Cl
Binton CV37 ... 120 A1
Newton Regis B79 ... 2 B2
Townsend Croft CV3 ... 77 C7
Townsend Dr CV11 ... 29 F3
Townsend La
Long Lawford CV23 ... 82 A2
Upper Boddington NN11 ... 134 E8
Townsend Rd
Coventry CV3 ... 77 C8
Rugby CV21 ... 83 B2
Tiddington CV37 ... 145 C2
Townsends Cl CV11 ... 31 A1
Trafalgar Ct B50 ... 148 B2
Trafalgar Ho 3 CV1 ... 61 B2
Trafford Cl CV9 ... 12 B1
Trafford Dr CV10 ... 28 C6
Trafford Lodge 4 CV31 ... 110 B7
Traitor's Ford La OX15, CV36,OX7 ... 142 B6
Trajan Hill B46 ... 23 F1
Travellers Way B37 ... 33 D3
Tredington Cl B98 ... 103 A4
Tredington Pk CV35 ... 114 F6
Tredington Rd CV5 ... 59 F4
Treedale Cl CV4 ... 75 D8
Trefoil B77 ... 4 A3
Treforest Rd CV3 ... 78 C8
Tregaron CV37 ... 145 A2
Tregorrick Rd CV7 ... 50 A8
Tregullan Rd CV7 ... 50 B8
Trehern Cl B93 ... 72 A5
Treherne Rd CV6 ... 61 B8
Trelawney Rd CV7 ... 50 A7
Tremelline Way CV7 ... 36 C4
Trenance Rd CV7 ... 50 A8
Trench La B49 ... 143 C2
Treneere Rd CV7 ... 50 B8
Trensale Ave CV6 ... 60 F4
Trent Rd Birmingham B26 ... 44 C4
Bulkington CV12 ... 40 A2
Hinckley LE10 ... 31 A8
Nuneaton CV11 ... 29 D5
Trent Wlk NN11 ... 117 F1
Trentham Cl CV11 ... 39 F8
Trentham Gdns CV8 ... 93 C5
Trentham Rd
Coventry CV1 ... 61 F4
Hartshill CV10 ... 19 A1
Tresillian Rd CV7 ... 50 B8
Tressel Croft CV34 ... 109 E2
Trevelyan Cl
Claverdon CV35 ... 113 F3
Stratford-u-A CV37 ... 144 B2
Trevelyan Cres CV37 ... 144 B2
Trevelyan Ho 1 B37 ... 33 C1
Treviscoe Cl CV7 ... 50 A7
Trevor Cl CV4 ... 75 D8
Trevor White Dr CV22 ... 83 A1
Trevose Ave CV7 ... 50 B8
Trewint Cl CV7 ... 50 A8
Triangle The CV5 ... 60 B4
Tribune Trad Est CV21 ... 83 A3
Trident Bsns Pk CV11 ... 29 D3
Trimpley Cl B93 ... 71 E3
Trinculo Gr CV34 ... 109 F2
Trinity Churchyard CV1 ... 151 B3
Trinity Cl Banbury OX16 ... 139 F4
Stratford-u-A CV37 ... 145 A1
Warton B79 ... 5 C2
Trinity Ct Hinckley LE10 ... 31 C8
Rugby CV21 ... 83 A2
Trinity La CV1 ... 151 B3
Trinity RC Sch The CV34 ... 109 C6
Trinity RC Tech Coll CV32 ... 105 D2
Trinity Rd B78 ... 15 C4
Trinity St Coventry CV1 ... 151 B3
Royal Leamington Spa CV32 ... 105 F1
Stratford-u-A CV37 ... 145 A1
Trinity Vicarage Rd LE10 ... 31 C8
Trinity Wlk CV11 ... 29 E3
Triton Pk CV21 ... 82 C4
Triumph Cl CV2 ... 62 E3
Triumph Wlk B36 ... 23 A1
Troon B77 ... 4 B2
Troon Way LE10 ... 31 D4
Trossachs Rd CV5 ... 59 F3
Troubridge Wlk CV22 ... 82 B1
Troughton Cres CV6 ... 61 A5
Troutbeck Ave CV32 ... 105 C2
Troutbeck Rd CV5 ... 59 F4
Troy Ind Est B96 ... 103 A2
Troyes Cl CV3 ... 77 E7
Trueman Cl CV34 ... 108 E8
Truemans Heath La B47, B90 ... 69 C7
Truggist La CV7 ... 74 E8
Trundalls La B90 ... 70 A5
Truro Cl CV11 ... 29 F5
Truro Wlk B37 ... 33 B2
Trussell Way CV22 ... 99 A4
Trust Cotts B49 ... 118 D8
Trusteel Hos CV23 ... 67 B3
Tryan Rd CV10 ... 28 E4
Tuckwell Cl CV47 ... 147 C4
Tudman Cl B76 ... 22 A7
Tudor Ave CV5 ... 59 F4
Tudor Cl CV7 ... 74 A6
Tudor Cres CV9 ... 12 B1
Tudor Ct Coventry CV7 ... 49 E7
Warwick CV34 ... 108 D5
Tudor La CV47 ... 147 A2
Tudor Rd CV10 ... 28 C6
Tuer The WR11 ... 127 A6
Tulip Tree Ave CV8 ... 93 B5
Tulip Tree Ct CV8 ... 93 B4
Tulip Wlk B37 ... 44 C8
Tulliver Cl CV12 ... 39 B3
Tulliver Rd CV10 ... 29 C1
Tulliver St CV6 ... 61 B5
Tunnel Rd CV10 ... 27 B2
Turchil Rd CV22 ... 99 A4
Turchill Dr B76 ... 22 B8
Turlands Cl CV2 ... 63 A7
Turnberry B77 ... 4 B3
Turnberry Dr CV11 ... 40 C8
Turner Cl Bedworth CV12 ... 39 A4
Turner Cl *continued*
Rugby CV21 ... 101 A4
Warwick CV34 ... 108 B4
Turner Rd CV5 ... 60 D3
Turnhouse Rd B35 ... 22 B4
Turnpike Cl
Balsall Common CV7 ... 74 B7
13 Moreton-in-M GL56 ... 140 A3
Turnpike Dr B46 ... 23 C2
Turnstone Cl CV23 ... 83 B4
Turpin Ct CV31 ... 109 F6
Turpin Ho CV21 ... 83 B4
Turton Way CV8 ... 93 C4
Turville Cl LE10 ... 31 F5
Tutbury B77 ... 9 B4
Tutbury Ave CV4 ... 76 E6
Tutehill B77 ... 10 A4
Tutnall Dr B94 ... 88 B6
Tuttle Hill CV10 ... 28 F6
Tuttle Hill Ind Est CV10 ... 28 E7
Twenty One Oaks CV9 ... 17 C3
Twickenham Way CV3 ... 63 B1
Two Gates Com Prim Sch B77 ... 9 B4
Two Gates Ind Est B77 ... 9 B4
Twycross La CV9 ... 6 C3
Twycross Rd LE10 ... 31 F6
Twycross Wlk CV34 ... 104 D1
Twycross Zoo★ CV9 ... 3 C1
Twyford Ctry Ctr★ WR11 ... 127 C1
Tybalt Cl Coventry CV3 ... 78 C5
Royal Leamington Spa CV34 ... 109 D4
Tyler St CV37 ... 145 A2
Tylers Gr B90 ... 70 F6
Tylney Cl CV3 ... 63 B2
Tyne Cl B37 ... 33 C4
Tyne Rd NN11 ... 126 F8
Tynemouth Cl CV2 ... 50 D5
Tynward Cl CV3 ... 77 B5
Tysoe CE Prim Sch CV35 ... 138 C7
Tysoe Cl B94 ... 88 C6
Tysoe Croft CV3 ... 78 F8
Tysoe Rd Kineton CV35 ... 132 B4
Oxhill CV35 ... 137 F8
Tyte End OX7 ... 142 A2
Tythe Barn Cotts WR11 ... 127 B2
Tythebarn La B90 ... 69 F6
Tything Rd B49 ... 143 B3

U

Ufton Croft CV5 ... 60 A3
Ufton Cross Rds CV33 ... 124 A8
Ufton Fields CV33 ... 123 F8
Ufton Hill CV33 ... 111 C1
Ullapool Cl B97 ... 102 B3
Ullenhall La B95 ... 112 D6
Ullenhall Rd Knowle B93 ... 72 A6
Ullenhall B95 ... 112 E5
Ullenhall St B95 ... 112 E6
Ullswater B77 ... 10 A4
Ullswater Ave
Nuneaton CV11 ... 29 F6
Royal Leamington Spa CV32 ... 105 C2
Ullswater Rd
Bedworth CV12 ... 39 A2
Coventry CV3 ... 62 E1
Ulverscroft Rd CV3 ... 77 D7
Ulverston CV21 ... 83 B4
Umberslade Children's Farm★ B94 ... 87 C2
Umberslade Rd
Earlswood B94 ... 87 C7
Tanworth-In-A B94 ... 87 E3
Underhill Cl Coventry CV3 ... 77 D3
Redditch B98 ... 102 C3
Underpass The B40 ... 44 E4
Underwood Cl B97 ... 102 A4
Unicorn Ave CV5 ... 59 E4
Unicorn La CV5 ... 59 F4
Union Bldgs CV1 ... 151 B2
Union Pl CV6 ... 49 F4
Union Rd CV32 ... 105 E1
Union St Rugby CV22 ... 83 A1
Stratford-u-A CV37 ... 145 A2
Unity Ho CV1 ... 151 C4
Univ of Birmingham (The Shakespeare Inst) CV37 ... 144 C1
Univ of Warick (Gibbet Hill) CV4 ... 76 D3
Univ of Warwick CV4 ... 76 C4
Univ of Warwick (Westwood) CV4 ... 76 B6
Univ of Warwick Science Pk CV4 ... 76 B6
University Farm 10 GL56 ... 140 A3
University Rd CV4 ... 76 C5
Upavon Cl B35 ... 22 A4
Uplands CV2 ... 62 A5
Upleadon Cl B97 ... 102 A3
Upper Abbey St CV11 ... 29 B5
Upper Cape CV34 ... 108 D8
Upper Crossgate Rd B98 ... 103 B4
Upper Eastern Green La CV5 ... 59 E5
Upper Farm Mdw CV35 ... 123 E1
Upper Grove St 8 CV32 ... 105 E1

Upper Hill St
Coventry CV1 ....151 A3
Royal Leamington Spa
CV32 ....106 A1
Upper Holly Wlk CV32 .106 A1
Upper Ladyes Hills CV8 .93 A6
Upper Pk CV3 ....78 C8
Upper Ride CV3 ....78 D5
Upper Rosemary Hill CV8 92 F5
Upper Spon St CV1 ......61 A3
Upper Spring La CV8 ....92 F7
Upper Well St CV1 ......151 B3
Upper York St CV1 ......61 B2
Upperfield Way CV3 .....63 A1
Upton CV11 ....39 F8
Upton Ho★ OX15 ....138 E8
Upton La CV13 ....21 A4
Upton Rd CV22 ....82 B2
Utrillo Cl CV5 ....60 C3
Uxbridge Ave CV3 ....62 C2

V

Valanders La CV36 .....136 B6
Vale Cl CV21 ....101 A4
Vale The CV3 ....78 C8
Vale View CV10 ....28 E4
Valencia Croft B35 ....22 B4
Valentine Cl CV37 ......129 F8
Valiant Cl LE10 ....31 E4
Vallet Ave B49 ....143 A3
Valletta Way CV35 .....146 B1
Valley Cl B97 ....102 A3
Valley Dr
Harborough Magna CV21 ..67 A1
Rugby CV21 ....83 A4
Valley La Lapworth B94 ...89 F7
Tamworth B77 ....9 C4
Valley Rd Coventry CV2 ...62 A6
Earlswood B94 ....70 A1
Nuneaton CV10 ....27 C2
Radford Semele CV31 .....110 C4
Royal Leamington Spa
CV32 ....106 C3
Valley The CV31 ....110 C4
Van Dyke Cl CV5 ....60 C3
Vanguard B77 ....9 B3
Vanguard Ave CV5 ....60 C1
Vanguard Rd B26 ....44 C4
Vardon Dr CV3 ....77 D4
Vauxhall Cl 4 CV1 ....61 E3
Vauxhall Cres B36 ....22 F1
Vauxhall La B49 ....119 D1
Vauxhall St CV1 ....61 E3
Vaynor Dr B97 ....102 A4
Vaynor Fst Sch The B97 102 B4
Veasey Cl CV11 ....29 E3
Vecqueray St CV1 ....61 E2
Ventnor Cl CV2 ....62 E3
Ventnor St CV10 ....29 D6
Venture Ct LE10 ....30 E8
Verbena Cl CV2 ....50 B1
Verden Ave CV34 ....108 B4
Verdon Pl CV35 ....122 B8
Verdun Cl CV31 ....110 B2
Vere Rd CV21 ....83 C1
Vermont Gr CV31 ....110 D6
Verney Cl
Butlers Marston CV35 ....131 F4
Lighthorne CV35 ....123 B2
Verney Dr CV37 ....144 C3
Verney Gdns CV37 ......144 C3
Verney Rd CV33 ....123 C3
Vernon Ave CV22 ....100 C4
Vernon Cl 5 Coventry CV1 61 E3
Royal Leamington Spa
CV32 ....105 E3
Vernon Ct 9 CV1 ....61 E4
Vernons Cl CV10 ....28 F4
Vernons La CV10,CV11 ...28 F4
Verona CV37 ....145 A2
Verona Cl CV11 ....30 A1
Vesey Cl B46 ....23 B2
Vicarage Cl
Atherstone CV9 ....18 C4
Dordon B78 ....10 C1
Vicarage Cotts GL55 ....135 B2
Vicarage Field CV34 ....109 B8
Vicarage Gdns OX17 ....134 C1
Vicarage Hill
Badby NN11 ....126 F5
Clifton u D CV21,CV23 ....83 C3
Middleton B78 ....8 A1
Tanworth-In-A B94 ....86 F3
Vicarage La Coventry CV7 .49 D7
Dunchurch CV22 ....99 B2
Harbury CV33 ....123 F6
Long Compton CV36 ......141 C3
Priors Marston CV47 .....125 F4
Warwick CV35 ....108 A1
Water Orton B46 ....23 B2
Vicarage Rd
Cheswick Green B90,B94 ..70 C3
Flecknoe CV23 ....117 B2
Napton on t H CV47 .....125 C8
Royal Leamington Spa
CV32 ....106 B3
Rugby CV22 ....82 C2
Stoneleigh CV8 ....94 B6
Tanworth-in-A B94 ....88 F7
Vicarage Rise 8 CV33 .122 F8
Vicarage St CV11 ....29 C4
Victor Hodges Ho CV47 147 A2
Victoria Ave CV21 ....82 C2

Victoria Bsns Ctr 11
CV31 ....110 A7
Victoria Cl CV37 ....145 A2
Victoria Ct CV5 ....60 D4
Victoria Dr B78 ....9 A4
Victoria Mews
Coventry CV3 ....62 E2
Warwick CV34 ....108 D7
Victoria Rd
Atherstone CV9 ....18 C3
Bidford-on-A B50 ....148 B3
Hinckley LE10 ....31 F5
Nuneaton CV10 ....28 B8
Royal Leamington Spa
CV31 ....109 E8
Victoria St Coventry CV1 151 D4
Nuneaton CV11 ....29 C4
Royal Leamington Spa
CV31 ....109 E8
Rugby CV21 ....82 C2
Warwick CV34 ....108 D7
Victoria Terr
Royal Leamington Spa
CV31 ....109 F7
Stockton CV47 ....147 C4
Victoria Way B50 ....148 B3
Victory Rd CV6 ....49 E1
Victory Terr B78 ....9 A4
Vienna Ho CV5 ....60 E2
Viking B77 ....9 B4
Viking Rd B26 ....44 C3
Vilia Cl LE10 ....31 F4
Villa Cl CV12 ....40 C2
Villa Cres CV12 ....40 C1
Villa Rd CV6 ....61 B6
Village Hall Yd CV37 ...115 D4
Village Mews CV22 ....99 B4
Village Rd OX17 ....133 D2
Village St WR11 ....127 D4
Villebon Way CV31 ......110 A2
Villiers Rd CV8 ....93 B5
Villiers St Coventry CV2 .62 A3
Nuneaton CV11 ....29 B3
Royal Leamington Spa
CV32 ....106 A1
Vincent Ave CV37 ....145 A1
Vincent Ct CV37 ....145 A1
Vincent St Coventry CV1 .61 B2
Royal Leamington Spa
CV32 ....106 A1
Vincent Wyles Ho CV2 ..62 E3
Vine Ct CV34 ....108 F8
Vine La CV34 ....108 F8
Vine St CV1 ....151 C3
Vinecote Rd CV6 ....49 F4
Vinery Ct CV37 ....144 C1
Vineyard The LE17 ....43 C3
Violet Cl Coventry CV2 ...50 C3
Rugby CV23 ....83 C4
Virginia Pl CV10 ....28 E3
Virginia Rd CV1 ....61 E3
Viscount Cl
Birmingham B35 ....22 A2
Royal Leamington Spa
CV31 ....109 F6
Vittle Dr CV34 ....108 D7
Vodena Ct 5 CV32 ......105 E1
Vogue Cl CV1 ....151 D3
Vulcan Ho B35 ....22 C3
Vulcan Way LE17 ....55 B4

W

Wackrill Dr CV32 ....106 C3
Wadburn B90 ....70 A5
Wade Ave CV3 ....77 B5
Wade Gr CV34 ....104 E2
Wade La CV33 ....123 D2
Wadebridge Dr CV11 .....29 F5
Wadham Ho B37 ....33 D3
Wadleys Cl B50 ....148 B3
Waggoner's La B78 ....7 C4
Waggoners Cl CV8 ....95 B3
Wagstaffe Cl CV33 ......123 E6
Wain Cl B49 ....143 A3
Wainbody Ave N CV3 .....77 A6
Wainbody Ave S CV3 .....76 F5
Wainbody Wood Sch
CV4 ....76 D2
Wainrigg B77 ....10 A4
Wake Gr CV34 ....108 B5
Wakefield Cl Coventry CV3 78 F7
Hurley CV9 ....16 A2
Wakefield Gr B46 ....23 B3
Wakeford Rd CV10 ....18 A2
Wakehurst Cl CV11 ....39 F8
Wakelin Rd B90 ....70 B7
Walcot Gn B93 ....72 A2
Waldron Cl CV37 ....145 A2
Walford Gr CV34 ....104 F1
Walford Pl CV22 ....100 C4
Walkers Orch CV8 ....94 B6
Walkers Rd CV37 ....145 A2
Walkers Way
Bedworth CV12 ....38 F1
Coleshill B46 ....34 A3
Kenilworth CV8 ....92 F2
Walkwood CE Mid Sch
B97 ....102 B4
Walkwood Cres B97 .....102 B3
Walkwood Rd B97 ....102 B3
Wall Ave B46 ....33 F5
Wall Hill Rd CV5,CV7 .....48 B3
Wallace Ho CV34 ....108 D7
Wallace Rd CV6 ....61 A8
Waller Cl CV35 ....104 F7

Waller St CV32 ....106 A2
Wallingford Ave CV11 ....29 F7
Wallsgrove Cl CV32 .....106 B3
Wallwin Ct CV34 ....108 D6
Walmer Way B37 ....33 C3
Walmley Ash La B76 .....22 C6
Walmley Ash Rd B76 .....22 A7
Walnut Cl Birmingham B37 33 B1
Braunston NN11 ....117 E5
Harvington WR11 ....127 D3
Nuneaton, Camp Hill CV10 .28 E6
Nuneaton, Hartshill CV10 .28 B8
Walnut Croft CV9 ....17 B4
Walnut Dr CV32 ....106 B3
Walnut Gdns OX17 ......134 B5
Walnut St CV2 ....50 B2
Walnut Tree Cl CV8 ......93 A3
Walnut Way CV22 ....82 A1
Walsal End La B92 ....56 F3
Walsall St CV4 ....76 B7
Walsgrave CE Prim Sch
CV2 ....63 A6
Walsgrave Gdns 5 CV2 ..63 A7
Walsgrave Hospl CV2 .....62 F5
Walsgrave Rd CV2 ....62 B3
Walsgrave Ret Pk CV2 ...63 B7
Walsh La CV7 ....46 E2
Walsingham Dr CV10 .....39 A7
Walter Scott Rd CV12 ....39 C1
Waltham Cres CV10 ......28 B5
Walton Cl Coventry CV3 ..78 E7
Nuneaton CV11 ....40 A7
Walton Fields CV35 .....132 C5
Walton Rd
Hampton Lucy CV35 ......121 F4
Wellesbourne CV35 ......146 C1
Walton W ay CV35 ......146 B1
Wandsbeck B77 ....9 C4
Wanley Rd CV3 ....77 D6
Wansfell Cl CV4 ....76 A7
Wantage Rd B46 ....23 E1
Wappenbury Cl CV2 ......50 E2
Wappenbury Rd CV2 .....50 D2
Wapping La B98 ....112 A7
Ward Gr CV34 ....109 C7
Warden Rd CV6 ....61 B6
Wardens Ave The CV5 ....60 B6
Wardens The CV5 ....93 C5
Wardour Dr B37 ....33 C2
Ware Orch CV23 ....101 B1
Ware Rd CV23 ....101 B1
Wareham Gn CV2 ....63 A5
Waring Way CV22 ....99 B2
Warings Green Rd B94 ...70 D1
Warkworth Cl OX16 .....139 F4
Warmington Cl CV3 ......78 E8
Warmington Gr CV34 ....108 B8
Warmington Rd B47 ......69 A6
Warmwell Cl CV2 ....62 F4
Warneford Mews 9
CV31 ....110 A7
Warneford Pl 20 GL56 ..140 A3
Warner Cl CV34 ....104 D1
Warner Row 2 CV6 ....61 F7
Warren Cl
Royal Leamington Spa
CV32 ....106 A3
Ryton-on-D CV8 ....79 A1
Warren Dr B93 ....72 A3
Warren Field CV8 ....79 A1
Warren Gn CV4 ....75 F7
Warren Rd CV22 ....83 B1
Warrington Cl B76 ....13 A1
Warton Cl CV8 ....93 C4
Warton La Austrey CV9 ...3 A1
Orton-on-t-H CV9 ....6 B2
Warton B79 ....5 C4
**Warton Nethersole's CE Prim
Sch** B79 ....5 C2
Warwick Ave CV5 ....77 A8
Warwick By-Pass
Warwick, Hampton Magna
CV34,CV35 ....108 A5
Warwick, Heathcote CV34 109 A1
Warwick Castle★ CV34 .108 E6
Warwick Cl B80 ....103 B4
Warwick Cres CV37 .....145 A2
Warwick Ct
5 Birmingham, Chelmsley Wood
B37 ....33 D2
Coventry CV3 ....151 B1
Stratford-u-A CV37 ......145 A2
Warwick Dr CV9 ....12 B1
Warwick Gdns CV10 ......28 E4
Warwick Gn CV12 ....40 C1
Warwick Highway
Mappleborough Green
B80 ....112 A5
Redditch B98 ....102 C4
Warwick Hospl CV34 ....108 E8
Warwick House Ind Pk
CV47 ....147 A1
Warwick La CV1 ....151 B2
Warwick Mews CV37 ....145 A2
Warwick New Rd CV32 ..109 C8
Warwick Parkway CV35 108 A7
Warwick Pl
Royal Leamington Spa
CV32 ....105 E1
Shipston-on-S CV36 .....149 C3
Southam CV47 ....147 A2
Warwick Rd
Chadwick End B93 ....90 A7
Coventry CV3 ....151 B1
Ettington CV37 ....131 A4
Hanwell OX16,OX17 .....139 F5

Warwick Rd continued
Henley-in-A B95 ....113 C4
Kenilworth CV8 ....93 A1
Kineton CV35 ....132 B6
Knowle B93 ....72 D3
Leek Wootton CV35 ......104 F7
Norton Lindsey CV35 ....114 C2
Sherbourne CV35 ....121 E7
Snitterfield CV37 ....121 C5
Southam CV47 ....147 A2
Stratford-u-A CV37 .....145 B3
Upper Boddington NN11 .134 E8
Wellesbourne CV35 .....146 B2
Wolston CV8 ....80 A2
Warwick Row CV1 ....151 B2
Warwick Sch CV34 ......109 A6
Warwick Sch Coventry CV5 .60 C1
Royal Leamington Spa
CV32 ....105 F1
Rugby CV21 ....83 A1
Southam CV47 ....147 A2
Warwick Sta CV34 ......108 F7
Warwick Tech Pk CV34 109 B5
Warwick Terr CV32 .....105 E1
Warwicks The CV35 ....114 F3
Warwickshire Coll
CV32 ....109 D8
**Warwickshire Coll (Moreton
Morrell Ctr)** CV35 .....122 E2
Warwickshire Coll of Ag
CV11 ....29 E6
Warwickshire Mus★
CV34 ....108 E6
**Warwickshire Nuffield Hospl
The** CV32 ....105 E5
Wasdale Cl CV32 ....105 C2
Washbourne Rd CV31 ...110 A3
Washbrook La CV5 ....48 A1
Washbrook Pl CV36 .....136 B6
Washford Dr B98 ....103 B4
Washford Ind Est B98 ..103 C4
Washford La B98 ....103 B4
Wasperton Cl 6 CV3 .....78 F8
Wasperton La CV35 .....122 C7
Waste La
Baddesley Ensor CV9 .....11 C1
Balsall Common CV7 ......74 F5
Coventry CV6 ....48 C1
Watch Cl CV1 ....151 A3
Watchbury Cl B36 ....22 C1
Watchmaker Ct CV1 .....151 A2
Watcombe Rd CV2 ....62 E8
Water Orton La B76 .....22 E4
Water Orton Prim Sch
B46 ....23 B2
Water Orton Rd B36 .....22 E1
Water Orton Sta B46 ....23 A3
Watercall Ave CV3 ....77 C6
Waterdale B90 ....70 D5
Waterfall Cl CV7 ....46 C1
Waterfield Gdns CV31 ..110 C2
Waterfield Way LE10 .....31 C5
Watergall Cl CV47 ......147 B2
Waterloo Ave B37 ....33 B4
Waterloo Cl
Stratford-u-A CV37 .....130 B8
Wellesbourne CV35 .....146 B1
Waterloo Cres B50 .....148 C3
Waterloo Ct CV34 ......109 A8
Waterloo Dr CV37 ......145 A1
Waterloo Ind Est
Bidford-on-A B50 ....148 C3
Birmingham B37 ....33 B5
Waterloo Pk B50 ....148 C3
Waterloo Pl 5 CV32 ....105 F1
Waterloo Rd
Bidford-on-A B50 ....148 C3
Hinckley LE10 ....31 D4
Waterloo St
8 Coventry CV1 ....61 E4
Royal Leamington Spa
CV31 ....110 B7
Waterman Rd CV6 ....61 F6
Watersbridge Gdns CV10 29 C1
Waterside Coventry CV6 ..50 C6
Polesworth B78 ....5 A1
Royal Leamington Spa
CV31 ....109 D7
Stratford-u-A CV37 .....145 A1
Waterside Ct B24 ....22 A5
Waterside Ct CV31 .....110 B6
Waterside Dr CV21 ....83 B3
Watersmeet Gr CV2 ......62 B6
Watersmeet Ho B78 ......9 A4
Watersmeet Rd CV2 ......62 B6
Waterson Croft B37 ......33 D3
Watery La
Cheswick Green B90 ......70 D4
Corley CV7 ....47 D5
Coventry CV6 ....49 A4
Hook Norton OX15 ......142 D4
Keresley CV7 ....48 F4
Kineton CV35 ....132 C2
Knowle B93 ....72 E4
Pillerton Hersey CV35 ..131 E3
Portway B48 ....85 D7
Shipston-on-S CV36 .....149 C3
Shustoke B46 ....24 B1
Ullenhall B95 ....112 E6
Warwick CV35 ....108 A1
Wathen Rd
Royal Leamington Spa
CV32 ....106 A2
Warwick CV34 ....108 E8
Watling Cl LE10 ....31 C4
Watling Cres CV23 ....68 B1
Watling Ct CV11 ....29 C3
Watling Dr LE10 ....31 C4

Watling Rd CV8 ....93 B6
Watling St Atherstone CV9 19 A4
Dordon B77,B78 ....10 B3
Hinckley CV11,LE10 ......30 C8
Watson Cl 3 CV34 ......104 E1
Watson Rd CV5 ....60 D2
Watson Way CV7 ....74 C8
Wattisham Sq B35 ....22 A4
Watton Gn B35 ....22 A3
Watton La B46 ....23 D2
Watton's La CV47 ......147 A2
Watts La CV21 ....101 A4
Watts Rd B80 ....103 C1
Waugh Cl B37 ....33 B2
Wavebeck Ct CV23 ....82 A3
Waveley Rd CV1 ....61 A3
Wavendon Cl CV2 ....50 F1
Waveney B77 ....9 C4
Waveney Cl LE10 ....31 A8
Wavere Ct CV21 ....83 B4
Waverley Ave CV11 ......29 C1
Waverley Rd
Kenilworth CV8 ....93 A4
Royal Leamington Spa
CV31 ....110 B6
Rugby CV21 ....84 A1
Waverley Sq CV11 ....29 F1
Waverton Ave B79 ....5 C2
Waverton Mews 15
CV31 ....110 C6
Wavytree Cl CV34 ......108 D7
Wawensmere Rd B95 ...113 A2
Wayside B37 ....44 A8
Weale Gr CV34 ....104 F2
Weatheroak Rd B49 ....143 B2
Weaver Ave B76 ....13 A1
Weaver Dr CV23 ....82 B2
Weavers Cl Redditch B97 102 B2
Shipston-on-S CV36 .....149 C3
Weavers Cotts CV36 ....141 C3
Weavers Hill B97 ....102 B2
Weavers Row OX15 .....139 A3
Weavers Wlk CV6 ....62 B8
Webb Dr CV23 ....83 B4
Webb Ellis Ind Pk CV21 .83 A2
Webb Ellis Rd CV22 .....82 C1
Webb St CV10 ....28 D3
Webster Ave CV8 ....93 B5
Webster Steet CV6 ....61 E7
Webster Way B76 ....22 B8
Weddington Ctry Wlk
Higham on t H CV10 ......20 B1
★ Nuneaton CV10 ....29 B8
Weddington La CV10 .....20 A2
Weddington Prim Sch
CV10 ....29 D7
Weddington Rd CV10 ....29 C7
Weddington Terr CV10 ...29 D5
Wedge-Woods CV5 ......76 F8
Wedgewood Cl CV2 ......62 E8
Wedgewood Ho B37 .....33 B4
Wedgnock Gn CV34 .....108 D8
Wedgnock Ind Est CV34 104 C1
Wedgnock La CV34 .....104 C1
Wedon Cl CV4 ....75 E7
Weigh Bridge Ct GL55 .135 B2
Weilerswist Dr CV31 ....109 F4
Welbeck Ave LE10 ....31 D4
Welchman Pl CV35 .....138 C6
Welcombe Ct CV37 .....145 A2
**Welcombe Hills Ctry Pk (Nat
Res)**★ CV37 ....145 A4
Welcombe Rd CV37 .....145 A2
Welcome St CV9 ....18 C4
Welford Cl B98 ....102 C3
Welford Gr CV35 ....114 C6
Welford Pl CV6 ....61 D7
Welford Rd
Bidford-on-A B50,CV37 .128 D6
Long Marston CV37 ......129 B4
Rugby CV21 ....83 B2
Tamworth B77 ....9 B3
Welford-on-Avon Prim Sch
CV37 ....129 A6
Welgarth Ave CV6 ....60 F6
Welham Croft B90 ....71 A6
Well Bank OX15 ....142 D4
Well Cl B97 ....102 C3
Well La
Shenington OX15 ....138 F5
Staverton NN11 ....126 D8
Tanworth-In-A B94 ....87 A1
Well Spring Cl CV9 ......18 C4
Well St CV1 ....151 B2
Welland Cl
Long Lawford CV23 ....82 B3
Water Orton B46 ....23 B2
Welland Rd CV1 ....61 F1
Welland Way B76 ....22 A7
Wellesbourne CE Prim Sch
CV35 ....146 C1
Wellesbourne Gr CV37 .144 C1
Wellesbourne Rd
Alveston CV37 ....121 D3
Barford CV35 ....122 B7
Coventry CV5 ....60 A3
Lighthorne CV35 ....123 B2
Loxley CV35 ....130 F8
Wellesbourne Water Mill★
CV35 ....146 C1
Wellfield Cl CV7 ....74 D5
Wellington Cl CV35 ....146 B1
Wellington Dr CV37 ....145 B1
Wellington Gdns 1 CV1 .61 B2
Wellington Parkway
LE17 ....55 B3
Wellington Rd
Moreton-in-M GL56 .....140 B3

Wellington Rd *continued*
Royal Leamington Spa CV32 106 C2
Wellington St CV1 151 D4
Wellington Terr GL56 140 B3
Wellington Way 2 B35 22 A3
Wellmeadow Gr B92 57 A7
Wells Cl CV10 27 C2
Wells Ct CV3 77 F7
Wells St CV21 83 A2
Wells Wlk B37 33 A1
Welsh Cl CV34 104 E2
Welsh Rd
Aston le W NN11 134 F6
Bascote CV47 115 B2
Coventry CV2 62 B4
Cubbington CV33 106 F2
Lower Boddington NN11 134 E7
Napton on t H CV47 125 C5
Offchurch CV33 111 C4
Welsh Rd E CV47 147 B1
Welsh Rd W CV47 147 A3
Welton Cl B76 13 A2
Welton Pl CV22 100 B4
Welton Rd
Braunston NN11 117 E5
Warwick CV34 104 D1
Wembrook Cl CV11 29 D2
Wembrook Ho CV11 29 E2
Wembrook Prim Sch CV11 29 C2
Wendiburgh St CV4 76 B7
Wendover Rise CV5 60 C4
Wenlock Way CV10 28 B3
Wensum Cl LE10 31 B8
Wentworth Dr
Coventry CV6 49 B4
Nuneaton CV11 30 A1
Wentworth Rd
Royal Leamington Spa CV31 110 D6
Rugby CV22 82 C1
Wesley Rd CV21 101 A4
Wessenden B77 10 A4
Wessex Cl CV12 39 A4
Wessex Ct B79 4 C4
Wessons Rd B50 148 C3
West Ave Bedworth CV12 39 D2
Coventry CV2 62 A2
Keresley CV7 49 A5
West Cl LE10 31 D7
West End
Cleeve Prior WR11 128 A4
Hornton OX15 139 B7
West End Ct CV34 108 D6
West Green Dr CV37 144 A2
West Leyes CV21 83 A2
West of St Laurence CV35 114 A8
West Orchards Sh Ctr CV1 151 B3
West Park Cl CV37 144 A2
West Ridge CV5 60 A5
West Rock CV34 108 D7
West Side WR11 128 A2
West Side Bsns Ctr CV4 75 F8
West St Coventry CV1 61 E3
Long Lawford CV23 82 A2
17 Royal Leamington Spa CV31 110 A7
Shipston-on-S CV36 149 C3
Shutford OX15 139 A3
Stratford-u-A CV37 144 C1
Warwick CV34 108 D5
West View Rd
Royal Leamington Spa CV32 106 C5
Rugby CV22 82 C1
Westbourne Gr CV22 82 C1
Westbrook Ct CV5 60 A4
Westbury Ct Coventry CV2 62 A3
Warwick CV34 109 A7
Westbury Rd
Coventry CV5 60 D5
Nuneaton CV10 28 D3
Westcliff Dr CV34 104 E2
Westcliffe Dr CV3 77 B5
Westcotes CV4 60 B1
Westend Terr GL55 135 A2
Westerham Cl B93 71 F6
Western Dr LE17 43 C3
Western Hill Cl B96 102 C1
Western Rd CV37 144 C2
Western Road Ind Est CV37 144 C2
Westfield Barns CV47 125 E4
Westfield Cl Dorridge B93 71 F2
Nuneaton CV10 29 D5
Stratford-u-A CV37 144 C3
Westfield Cres CV35 146 B2
Westfield Ct LE10 31 C7
Westfield Ho B36 33 A7
Westfield Jun & Inf Schs LE10 31 B7
Westfield Rd
Hinckley LE10 31 B7
Rugby CV22 82 C1
Southam CV47 147 A2
Westgate Cl CV34 108 D6
Westgate Ho 10 CV34 108 E6
Westgate Prim Sch CV34 108 D6
Westgate Rd CV21 83 C1
Westgrove Ave 6 B90 71 A6
Westgrove Terr 1 CV32 109 D8
Westham Ho B37 33 B4
Westham La CV35 122 A7
Westhill Rd
Blackdown CV32 106 A6
Coventry CV6 60 F6
Westholme Rd B50 148 B3
Westlea Rd CV31 109 E6
Westleigh Ave CV5 76 F7
Westmead Ave B80 103 C2
Westmede Ctr CV5 60 C4
Westminster Dr
Hinckley LE10 31 F4
Nuneaton CV10 28 B7
Westminster Rd CV1 151 A1
Westmorland Ave CV10 28 E4
Westmorland Rd CV2 62 F4
Weston Cl Dorridge B93 72 A2
Dunchurch CV22 99 B2
5 Royal Leamington Spa CV31 110 C6
Warwick CV34 108 F7
Weston Ct
Long Compton CV36 141 D3
Rugby CV21 83 B2
Weston Hall Stables CV12 40 A3
Weston La
Bubbenhall CV8,CV33 95 A2
Bulkington CV12 40 B3
Weston St CV1 151 C4
Westonbirt Cl CV8 93 C6
Westway CV21 83 A2
Westwood Bsns Pk CV4 75 F6
Westwood Cl CV10 28 E3
Westwood Cres CV9 18 B4
Westwood Heath Rd CV4 75 E6
Westwood Rd
Atherstone CV9 18 B4
Coventry CV5 61 A1
Rugby CV22 100 C4
Westwood Way CV4 76 A6
Wetherby Way CV37 144 C1
Wetherell Way CV21 83 B4
Wexford Rd CV2 50 D1
Weymouth Cl CV3 78 D5
Whaley's Croft CV6 61 B8
Wharf Ind Est The CV23 65 A4
Wharf La B94 88 D4
Wharf Lodge CV31 109 D7
Wharf Rd Coventry CV6 61 F5
Stratford-u-A CV37 144 C2
Wharf St CV34 109 A8
Wharf The CV37 120 C5
Wharrage Rd B49 143 B2
Wharrington Cl B98 103 A4
Wharrington Hill B98 103 A4
Whatcote Rd CV35 137 F8
Whateley Ct CV11 29 B4
Whateley Hall Cl B93 72 C7
Whateley Hall Rd B93 72 B7
Whateley La B77,B78 9 C2
Whateley Villas CV9 10 A1
Whateley's Dr CV8 93 A5
Wheat St CV11 29 D4
Wheatcroft Dr B37 33 C1
Wheate Croft CV4 59 F2
Wheaten Cl B37 33 D3
Wheatfield Cl B36 33 A7
Wheatfield Ct GL55 135 B6
Wheatfield Rd CV22 82 B1
Wheathill Cl CV32 105 E2
Wheatley Grange B46 33 F6
Wheatmoor Rd B75 13 A6
Wheatsheaf La B94 113 C8
Wheelbarrow La CV35 114 A3
Wheeler Cl B93 90 B7
Wheeley Moor Rd B37 33 A5
Wheelwright Ct 3 CV37 144 C2
Wheelwright La CV6,CV7 49 C4
Wheelwright Lane Prim Sch CV7 49 D5
Wheler Rd CV3 78 A7
Whernside CV21 83 B4
Whetstone Dr CV21 83 C4
Whichcote Ave CV7 46 C1
Whiley Cl CV23 83 C3
Whimbrel Cl CV23 83 B4
Whitacre Rd Knowle B93 72 B7
Nuneaton CV11 29 E4
3 Royal Leamington Spa CV32 106 A2
Whitacre Rd Ind Est CV11 29 E4
Whitaker Rd CV5 60 C3
Whitburn Rd CV12 38 C1
Whitchurch Cl B98 102 C3
Whitchurch Way CV4 75 F8
White Beam Rd B37 44 D8
White Friars La CV1 151 C2
White Friars St CV1 151 C2
White Hart La CV33 111 C1
White Horse Hill CV37 121 B6
White House Hill B95 120 B7
White Rose Ho 4 CV32 105 F2
White St CV1 151 C3
Whitebeam Cl CV4 59 D1
Whitefield Cl CV4 75 D6
Whitehall Cl CV10 19 A1
Whitehall Rd CV21 83 A1
Whitehead Dr
Kenilworth CV8 93 C7
Minworth B76 22 D6
Wellesbourne CV35 146 C2
Whitehead Gr CV7 74 B7
Whitehorn Dr CV32 106 B2
Whitehorse Cl CV6 50 B6
Whitehouse Cres CV10 28 D3
Whitehouse Rd B78 11 A3
Whitelaw Cres CV5 60 C6
Whitemoor Dr B90 71 A7
Whitemoor Hill Rd B96 118 D8
Whitemoor Rd CV8 93 B5
Whitemoors Cl CV13 21 C4
Whitemoors Rd CV13 21 C4
Whitepits La B48 85 F4
Whitepump La B95 112 E7
Whites Row CV8 93 A3
Whiteside Cl CV3 78 F8
Whiteslade Cl B93 72 A7
Whitestitch La CV7 46 C3
Whitestone Inf Sch CV11 40 A8
Whitestone Rd CV11 40 B7
Whiteway OX17 133 F2
Whitfield Cl CV37 145 C2
Whitford Dr B90 71 C7
Whiting B77 9 B4
Whitley Abbey Com Sch CV3 77 F5
Whitley Abbey Prim Sch CV3 78 A6
Whitley Ct CV3 77 F7
Whitley Rd B95 113 B4
Whitley Village CV3 77 F7
Whitlocks End Halt B90 69 E7
Whitmore Park Prim Sch CV6 49 A1
Whitmore Park Rd CV6 49 D3
Whitmore Rd CV31 110 A3
Whitnash Cl CV7 74 A6
Whitnash Gr CV2 62 D5
Whitnash Prim Sch CV31 110 A4
Whitnash Rd CV31 110 B4
Whittington Cl 4 CV34 109 B8
Whittington La CV9 12 A1
Whittle Cl Coventry CV3 78 F8
Daventry NN11 117 F3
Rugby CV22 99 B4
Whittle Ct 9 CV32 106 A1
Whittle Rd LE10 30 E7
Whittleford Gr B36 22 C1
Whittleford Rd CV10 28 C4
Whittons Cl OX15 142 D4
Whitwell Dr B90 71 A6
Whitworth Ave
Coventry CV3 62 B1
Hinckley LE10 30 F7
Whitworth Cl CV35 146 B1
Whoberley Ave CV5 60 D2
Whoberley Hall Prim Sch CV5 60 C3
Wickham Cl CV6 48 F2
Wickham Ct CV32 106 B3
Wickham Rd B80 103 C2
Wickmans Dr CV4 59 C2
Wiclif Way CV10 28 B3
Widdecombe Cl CV2 62 D7
Widdrington Rd CV1 61 C5
Widney Cl B93 71 F5
Widney La B91 71 B8
Widney Manor Rd B91 71 D7
Widney Manor Sta B91 71 C8
Widney Rd B93 71 F5
Wigford Rd B77 9 B3
Wiggins Hill Rd B76 22 F7
Wight Croft B36 33 B6
Wigston Hill CV9 17 B3
Wigston Rd Coventry CV2 50 F1
Rugby CV21 84 A1
Wike La B96 118 E8
Wilcox Cl CV47 124 A4
Wilcox Leys CV35 122 F2
Wild Goose La B98 103 B4
Wildcroft Rd CV5 60 C3
Wildey Rd CV12 38 D2
Wildmoor Cl CV2 50 B4
Wilford Gr B76 22 B6
Wilkes Way B50 148 B3
Wilkins Cl CV35 122 A7
Wilkinson Way B46 25 A1
Willday Dr CV9 12 B1
Willenhall La CV3 78 F7
Willenhall Wood Prim Sch CV3 78 D6
Willes Ct 2 CV31 110 B7
Willes Rd CV31,CV32 110 A8
Willes Terr CV31 110 B8
Willett Gdns CV35 146 B2
Willett Ho CV35 146 B2
William Arnold Cl CV2 62 A4
William Batchelor Ho CV1 151 B4
William Beesley Cres CV11 40 E6
William Bree Rd CV5 59 C5
William Bristow Rd CV3 77 E7
William Cl OX16 139 F4
William Cree Cl CV8 79 F3
William Groubb Cl CV3 78 D7
William Iliffe St LE10 31 B7
William Malcolm Ho CV2 62 E3
William McCool Cl CV3 78 F7
William McKee Cl CV3 78 E7
William Morris Cty Prim Sch OX16 139 F4
William Sheriden Ho CV2 62 E3
William St Bedworth CV12 39 D2
Nuneaton CV11 29 E3
Royal Leamington Spa CV32 110 A8
Rugby CV21 83 A2
William Tarver Cl CV34 109 A7
William Thomson Ho 2 CV1 151 D4
Williams Rd CV31 110 E4
Willicote Pastures CV37 129 D4
Willington St CV11 29 B5
Willis Croft B79 5 C2
Willis Gr CV12 39 C3
Willoughby Ave CV8 92 E3
Willoughby Cl
Alcester B49 143 A3
Coventry CV3 78 E8
Willoughby Pl CV22 100 B4
Willow Bank CV37 129 A7
Willow Bank Rd B93 71 F6
Willow Brook Rd CV8 80 A2
Willow Cl Alcester B49 143 A1
Bedworth CV12 39 B5
Hinckley LE10 31 E5
Kingsbury B78 15 B4
Nuneaton CV10 28 A7
Whitnash CV31 110 B2
Willow Ctyd CV2 62 D7
Willow Dr
Cheswick Green B90 70 D4
Wellesbourne CV35 146 C2
Willow End GL56 141 A1
Willow Gdns CV47 147 A2
Willow Gr CV4 60 B2
Willow La CV22 83 B1
Willow Meer CV8 93 B5
Willow Park Ind Est CV13 21 B4
Willow Rd CV10 28 F5
Willow Sheets Mdw CV32 106 E6
Willow Tree Gdns CV21 101 A4
Willow Way
Birmingham B37 33 B1
Studley B49 103 C1
Willowbank Rd LE10 31 C7
Willowdale LE10 31 A7
Willowfields Rd CV11 30 A1
Willowherb Cl 5 CV3 78 F8
Willowherb Way B90 70 A5
Willows CE Prim Sch The CV37 144 C1
Willows N CV37 144 C2
Willows The
Atherstone CV9 12 C1
Bedworth CV12 38 E2
Hollywood B47 69 A6
Stratford-u-A CV37 144 C1
Wilmcote CE Prim Sch CV37 120 C4
Wilmcote Gn CV5 60 A3
Wilmcote La B95 120 A5
Wilmcote Sta CV37 120 C5
Wilmhurst Rd CV34 108 C8
Wilmot Ave B46 33 F6
Wilmot Cl CV7 74 B8
Wilnecote Gr CV31 110 B5
Wilnecote High Sch B77 9 C3
Wilnecote Jun Sch B77 9 C4
Wilnecote La B77 9 C4
Wilnecote Sta B77 9 B4
Wilson Cl CV22 82 B1
Wilson Dr B75 13 A5
Wilson Gn CV3 62 F1
Wilson Gr CV8 93 C4
Wilson's La CV6 49 F6
Wilsons La CV7 50 A6
Wilsons Rd B93 72 C6
Wilton Rd CV7 74 B5
Wiltshire Cl
Bedworth CV12 39 A3
Coventry CV5 60 B3
Wimborne Dr CV2 63 A4
Wimbourne Cl CV10 28 B5
Wimbourne Rd B76 13 A4
Wimpstone La CV37 130 B4
Winceby Pl CV4 59 D1
Winchat Cl CV3 62 F1
Winchcombe Rd B49 143 B2
Winchelsea Cl OX16 139 F5
Winchester Ave CV10 29 C7
Winchester Ct CV22 99 B2
Winchester Dr
Birmingham B37 33 A2
Hinckley LE10 32 B7
Winchester St CV1 61 E3
Wincott Cl CV37 145 B1
Windermere B77 10 A4
Windermere Ave
Coventry, Binley CV3 62 E1
Coventry, Upper Eastern Green CV5 59 E4
Nuneaton CV11 29 F6
Windermere Cl CV21 83 B4
Windermere Dr CV32 105 D2
Winderton Ave CV35 114 E5
Winding House La CV6, CV7 49 C4
Windmill Ave 4 B46 33 F7
Windmill Cl
Ilmington CV36 136 B6
Kenilworth CV8 93 A6
Warton B79 5 C2
Windmill Croft CV32 106 D5
Windmill Ct CV6 50 A3
Windmill Dr B97 102 B3
Windmill Gdns
Redditch B97 102 A3
Staverton NN11 126 E8
Windmill Hill
Bidford-on-A B50 128 E8
Royal Leamington Spa CV32 106 D5
Windmill Hill The CV5 60 A7
Windmill Ind Est CV5 59 F7
Windmill La Astley CV10 37 C3
Windmill La *continued*
Austrey CV9 3 A1
Balsall Common CV7 74 D4
Baxterley CV9 17 B3
Corley CV7 47 D6
Dorridge B93 71 F1
Dunchurch CV22 99 A2
Ladbroke CV47 124 D6
Ladbroke CV47 124 E5
Staverton NN11 126 E8
Tanworth-in-A B94 89 A8
Windmill Rd
Atherstone CV9 12 B1
Bedworth CV7 50 A8
Coventry CV6 50 A3
Nuneaton CV10 28 D7
Royal Leamington Spa CV31 109 F5
Windmill Way
Southam CV47 147 A3
Tysoe CV35 138 B6
Windridge Cl CV3 78 C6
Windrush Cl B97 102 B3
Windrush Dr LE10 31 A8
Windrush Rd B47 69 B7
Windrush Way CV23 82 A3
Windsor Ct Coventry CV4 60 B2
Hinckley LE10 32 A5
Nuneaton CV10 28 E6
11 Royal Leamington Spa CV32 109 F8
Windsor Gdns CV10 28 E4
Windsor Pl 8 CV32 105 F1
Windsor Rd B78 5 A2
Windsor St Coventry CV1 61 B2
Hinckley LE10 32 A5
Nuneaton CV11 29 B4
Royal Leamington Spa CV32 109 F8
Rugby CV21 83 B2
Stratford-u-A CV37 144 C2
Windward Way B36 33 B6
Windy Arbor Jun & Inf Sch B37 33 D2
Windy Arbour CV8 93 B4
Windyridge Rd B76 22 A6
Winfield Rd CV11 29 B5
Winfield St CV21 83 B2
Wingfield Rd B46 33 F5
Wingfield Way CV6 49 A2
Wingrave Cl CV5 60 A6
Winifred Ave CV5 61 A1
Winnallthorpe CV3 78 E6
Winsford Ave CV5 60 B4
Winsford Cl CV7 74 A6
Winsford Ct CV5 60 C4
Winsham Wlk CV3 77 D3
Winslow Cl Coventry CV5 60 B3
Royal Leamington Spa CV32 105 C1
Winslow Ho 11 CV1 61 B2
Winspear Cl CV7 46 B1
Winster Ave B93 71 E4
Winster Cl CV7 49 A7
Winston Ave CV2 62 D8
Winston Cl Coventry CV2 62 D8
Stratford-u-A CV37 144 B1
Winston Dr OX17 139 F5
Winterdene CV7 74 B7
Winterton Rd CV12 40 C2
Winthorpe Dr B91 71 C8
Winton Gr B76 22 A6
Winwick Pl CV22 99 B4
Winyates Rd CV33 123 D2
Wise Gr Rugby CV21 83 C1
Warwick CV34 104 E2
Wise St CV31 109 F7
Wise Terr CV31 109 F7
Wishaw Cl B98 103 A4
Wishaw La Curdworth B76 23 A7
Middleton B78 14 C6
Minworth B76 22 E7
Wisley Gr CV8 93 C5
Wistaria Cl 2 CV2 50 B2
Witham The NN11 117 F1
Witherley CE Prim Sch CV9 19 A4
Witherley Rd
Atherstone CV9 18 C4
Witherley CV9 19 A3
Withington Gr B93 71 E4
Withum Cl B76 13 A1
Withy Hill Rd B75 13 B8
Withybrook Cl CV2 50 D2
Withybrook La CV7 51 F5
Withybrook Rd
Bulkington CV12 40 D2
Solihull B90 70 B8
Withycombe Dr OX16 139 F3
Witnell Rd CV6 61 C6
Wixford Rd B49,B50 119 B1
Woburn Cl CV31 110 C6
Woburn Dr CV10 29 A2
Wolds End Cl GL55 135 B2
Wolds La LE10 41 C2
Wolfe Rd CV4 75 F8
Wolford Rd GL56 140 D6
Wolfstan Dr CV47 115 D4
Wolseley Cl B36 23 A1
Wolsey Rd CV22 99 B3
Wolston Bsns Pk CV8 80 A2
Wolston La CV8 79 E2
Wolston St Margaret's CE Prim Sch CV8 80 A2

Wolverton Prim Sch
CV35 . . . .**114** B2
Wolverton Rd
Birmingham, Marston Green
B37 . . . .**44** B7
Coventry CV5 . . . .**60** A3
Norton Lindsey CV35 . . . . .**114** C2
Snitterfield CV37 . . . .**121** B7
Wolvey CE Prim Sch
LE10 . . . .**41** B2
Wolvey CE Prim Sch (annexe)
CV7 . . . .**51** E5
Wolvey Rd
Bulkington CV12 . . . .**40** E2
Hinckley LE10 . . . .**31** E4
Wood Cl B46 . . . .**33** F7
Wood Croft B47 . . . .**69** B6
Wood Ct CV2 . . . .**62** D7
Wood End La
Fillongley CV7 . . . .**37** A2
Tanworth-In-A B94 . . . . . .**86** F5
Wood End Prim Sch
Coventry CV2 . . . .**50** D1
Wood End CV9 . . . .**10** B1
Wood End Sta B94 . . . .**86** F4
Wood Hill Rise CV6 . . . .**49** D2
Wood La Arley CV7 . . . .**26** B1
Aston Cantlow B49,B95 . . .**119** F5
Astwood Bank B96 . . . . . .**118** C6
Birmingham, Marston Green
B37 . . . .**44** A8
Cherington CV36 . . . .**141** D7
Earlswood B94 . . . .**69** E1
Hampton-in-A B92 . . . . . .**56** F2
Higham on t H CV13 . . . . .**20** C2
Shilton CV7 . . . .**51** D5
Nuneaton CV10 . . . .**28** A8
Wood St Bedworth CV12 . . .**39** B5
Nuneaton CV10 . . . .**28** F4
Royal Leamington Spa
CV32 . . . .**110** A8
Rugby CV21 . . . .**83** A2
Southam CV47 . . . .**147** A2
Stratford-u-A CV37 . . . . . .**145** A1
Wood End CV9 . . . .**10** B1
Wood Terr B96 . . . .**118** D8
Woodbank LE10 . . . .**32** A7
Woodberrow La B97 . . . . . .**102** B3
Woodberry Dr B76 . . . .**13** A2
Woodbine Cotts 2
CV32 . . . .**109** E8
Woodbine St 1 CV32 . . . .**109** E8
Woodbine Wlk B37 . . . .**33** D2
Woodbridge Ct CV21 . . . . . .**83** A2
Woodbridge Pk CV9 . . . . . .**16** B2
Woodbrook Ho 9 B37 . . .**33** B2
Woodburn CV5 . . . .**60** B4
Woodbury Cl B97 . . . .**102** A3
Woodby La LE17 . . . .**55** C4
Woodchester Rd B93 . . . . . .**71** E2
Woodclose Ave CV6 . . . .**60** F6
Woodclose Rd B37 . . . .**33** A3
Woodcot Park Dr CV37 . . . .**120** B5
Woodcote Ave
Kenilworth CV8 . . . .**92** D6
Nuneaton CV11 . . . .**29** F8

Woodcote Dr
Dorridge B93 . . . .**72** B2
Leek Wootton CV35 . . . . .**104** F7
Woodcote La CV8,CV35 . . .**104** F7
Woodcote Rd
Royal Leamington Spa
CV32 . . . .**105** F3
Warwick CV34 . . . .**108** F8
Woodcraft Cl CV4 . . . .**60** A2
Woodend Croft CV4 . . . . . .**75** E8
Woodfield Rd
Coventry CV5 . . . .**76** E8
Hinckley LE10 . . . .**31** C6
Woodford Cl
Ash Green CV7 . . . .**49** D5
Nuneaton CV10 . . . .**28** D4
Woodford La CV9,CV10 . . . .**19** B2
Woodgate Rd LE10 . . . .**32** A8
Woodgreen Cl B97 . . . . . .**102** A4
Woodhall Cl CV11 . . . .**30** A2
Woodhams Rd CV3 . . . .**78** C3
Woodhouse Cl CV3 . . . .**78** E8
Woodhouse High Sch B77 **4** A2
Woodhouse La B77 . . . .**4** A3
Woodhouse St CV34 . . . . .**108** D6
Woodington Rd B75 . . . . . .**13** B5
Woodland Ave
Claybrooke Magna LE17 . . .**43** C3
Coventry CV5 . . . .**76** F7
Hinckley LE10 . . . .**32** A7
Woodland Rd
Kenilworth CV8 . . . .**93** B7
Tamworth B77 . . . .**4** A2
Woodland Way B78 . . . .**10** C4
Woodlands Ave B46 . . . . . .**23** B2
Woodlands Cl B78 . . . .**11** A3
Woodlands Ct
Binley Woods CV3 . . . .**79** D7
Coventry CV5 . . . .**77** A8
Woodlands Farm Rd B24 **22** A4
Woodlands Inf Sch B90 . . .**70** B8
Woodlands Jun & Inf Sch
B36 . . . .**33** B6
Woodlands La
Bedworth CV12 . . . .**38** E4
Solihull B90 . . . .**70** B8
Woodlands Rd
Bedworth CV12 . . . .**38** F3
Binley Woods CV3 . . . .**79** D7
Stratford-u-A CV37 . . . . . .**144** C3
Woodlands Sch The
CV5 . . . .**59** D3
Woodlands Terr B78 . . . .**11** A3
Woodlands The
Nuneaton CV10 . . . .**28** A8
Staverton NN11 . . . .**126** D8
Sutton Coldfield B75 . . . . .**13** A6
Wood End CV9 . . . .**10** B1
Woodlands Way B37 . . . . . .**33** D3
Woodleigh Rd CV4 . . . .**75** F5
Woodloes Ave N CV34 . . .**104** F2
Woodloes Ave S CV34 . . . .**104** F1
Woodloes Inf Sch CV34 . . .**104** E1
Woodloes Jun Sch
CV34 . . . .**104** E1
Woodloes La CV34,CV35 . . .**104** F2
Woodloes Rd B90 . . . .**70** B7
Woodman Ct CV37 . . . . . .**144** C2
Woodmill Mdw CV8 . . . . . .**93** B6
Woodpecker Gr B36 . . . . .**33** A7

Woodridge Ave CV5 . . . . . .**60** A6
Woodroffe Wlk CV6 . . . . . .**50** A4
Woodrow Cres B93 . . . .**72** A5
Woodrow Ctr B98 . . . .**103** A4
Woodrow Dr B98 . . . .**103** A3
Woodrow Fst Sch B98 . . . .**103** A4
Woodrow N B98 . . . .**103** A4
Woodrow S B98 . . . .**103** A4
Woodrow Wlk B98 . . . .**103** A4
Woodrush Dr B47 . . . .**69** A5
Woodrush High Sch The
B47 . . . .**69** A6
Woods Piece
Coventry CV7 . . . .**49** A6
Keresley CV7 . . . .**48** F6
Woodshires Rd CV6 . . . . . .**49** F5
Woodsia Cl CV23 . . . .**83** B4
Woodside Arley CV7 . . . . . .**26** B1
Grendon CV9 . . . .**11** B1
Woodside Ave N CV3 . . . . .**76** F6
Woodside Ave S CV3 . . . . .**76** F5
Woodside Bsns Pk CV21 . .**83** A2
Woodside Cl CV9 . . . .**10** B1
Woodside Cres B93 . . . .**72** B4
Woodside Pk CV21 . . . .**83** A3
Woodstock Cl LE10 . . . .**32** A5
Woodstock Cres B93 . . . . . .**71** F3
Woodstock Rd
Coventry CV3 . . . .**77** D7
Nuneaton CV11 . . . .**29** E1
Woodston Gr B91 . . . .**71** C8
Woodville Rd CV34 . . . . . .**108** E8
Woodward Cl CV31 . . . . . .**110** A2
Woodward Ct CV37 . . . . . .**121** B6
Woodway CV35 . . . .**114** F3
Woodway Ave CV35 . . . . . .**114** F3
Woodway Cl CV2 . . . .**62** F8
Woodway La
Claybrooke Parva LE17 . . . .**43** B2
Coventry CV2 . . . .**50** F1
Woodway Park Sch & Com
Coll CV2 . . . .**50** F1
Woodway Rd OX15 . . . . . .**142** D8
Woodway Wlk CV2 . . . .**62** E8
Woolaston Rd B98 . . . .**103** B4
Woolgrove St CV6 . . . .**50** A3
Wooll St 5 CV21 . . . .**83** A2
Woolpack The 9 CV34 . . .**108** E6
Woolpack Way CV9 . . . .**18** A4
Woolscott Rd CV23 . . . . . .**117** B6
Woolwich Rd CV11 . . . .**40** F6
Wootton Cl CV37 . . . .**145** B1
Wootton Ct Coventry CV2 .**62** D7
6 Royal Leamington Spa
CV32 . . . .**105** F2
Wootton Green La CV7 . .**74** A8
Wootton Hall B95 . . . .**113** B2
Wootton La CV7 . . . .**57** E1
Wootton St CV12 . . . .**39** D3
Wootton Wawen CE Prim Sch
B95 . . . .**113** A2
Wootton Wawen Sta
B95 . . . .**113** A2
Worcester Cl CV5 . . . .**60** B7
Worcester Ct CV6 . . . .**50** B4
Worcester Ho B36 . . . .**33** A8
Worcester Pl CV36 . . . . . .**149** C3
Worcester Rd CV8 . . . .**93** B3
Worcester St CV21 . . . .**83** A2
Worcester Wlk B37 . . . . . .**33** A1

Wordsworth Ave
Redditch B97 . . . .**102** B4
Warwick CV34 . . . .**108** D5
Wordsworth Dr CV8 . . . . . .**93** C4
Wordsworth Rd
Bedworth CV12 . . . .**39** D1
Coventry CV2 . . . .**62** C4
Rugby CV22 . . . .**99** C3
Workhouse La LE10 . . . . . .**32** A4
Works Rd B26 . . . .**44** A3
World of Shakespeare
(Mus)★ CV37 . . . .**145** A1
Worsdell Cl CV1 . . . .**61** B4
Worsfold Cl CV5 . . . .**60** A7
Worthy Down Wlk B35 . . .**22** B3
Wr Twr La CV8 . . . .**92** F6
Wren Cl DE12 . . . .**3** C4
Wren St CV2 . . . .**61** F3
Wren's Nest Cl B90 . . . . . .**70** A5
Wrenbury Dr CV6 . . . .**50** A4
Wright Cl B78 . . . .**15** B3
Wright St CV1 . . . .**61** E4
Wrigsham St CV3 . . . .**77** D8
Wroxall Dr CV3 . . . .**78** D5
Wroxton CE Prim Sch
OX15 . . . .**139** D4
Wroxton Coll OX15 . . . . . .**139** D4
Wroxton Ct OX15 . . . .**139** D4
Wyatt Cl CV12 . . . .**39** B3
Wyatt Ho CV2 . . . .**62** D7
Wyatt Rd B75 . . . .**13** B5
Wych Elm Dr 6 CV31 . . .**109** F5
Wych-Elm Cl CV22 . . . .**82** A1
Wychbold Cl B97 . . . .**102** A4
Wychbury B76 . . . .**13** A1
Wychwood Ave
Coventry CV3 . . . .**77** C3
Knowle B93 . . . .**72** B8
Wychwood Cl 14 CV33 . . .**122** F8
Wychwood Dr B97 . . . .**102** B3
Wycliffe Gr CV2 . . . .**62** B5
Wycliffe Rd W CV2 . . . .**62** C5
Wye Cl Bulkington CV12 . . .**40** B2
Hinckley LE10 . . . .**31** A8
Royal Leamington Spa
CV32 . . . .**106** C3
Sutton Coldfield B76 . . . . .**22** A7
Wyke Rd CV2 . . . .**62** C4
Wykeham Ho CV21 . . . .**83** B4
Wykeley Rd CV2 . . . .**62** C4
Wyken Ave CV2 . . . .**62** D5
Wyken Cl B93 . . . .**71** E2
Wyken Croft CV2 . . . .**62** D6
Wyken Croft Nature Pk★
CV2 . . . .**62** D6
Wyken Croft Prim Sch
CV2 . . . .**62** E5
Wyken Grange Rd CV2 . . . .**62** C5
Wyken Way CV2 . . . .**62** B5
Wykham La OX15,OX16 . . .**139** F1
Wykin La CV13 . . . .**21** C3
Wyld Cl CV5 . . . .**60** B5
Wyley Rd CV6 . . . .**61** B5
Wynbrook Gr B90 . . . .**71** A6
Wyncote Cl CV8 . . . .**93** A4
Wyndshiels B46 . . . .**34** A3
Wynter Rd CV22 . . . .**82** B2
Wyre La CV37 . . . .**129** B3
Wythall Sta B47 . . . .**69** C4
Wythburn Way CV21 . . . . .**83** B4

Wythwood Gr B47 . . . .**69** C6
Wythwood Rd B47 . . . .**69** C6
Wyver Cres CV2 . . . .**62** C3
Wyvern Cl CV35 . . . .**146** B1

Y

Yardley Chase Rd CV35 .**132** D4
Yardley Cl CV34 . . . .**104** F2
Yardley St CV1 . . . .**61** E4
Yarmouth Gn CV4 . . . .**75** E8
Yarn Cl B47 . . . .**69** A5
Yarningale Cl B98 . . . .**102** C3
Yarningale La CV35 . . . . . .**113** C5
Yarningale Rd CV3 . . . .**78** D5
Yarningdale 7 B90 . . . . . .**70** C8
Yarranton Cl CV37 . . . . . .**144** C3
Yarrow Cl CV23 . . . .**83** B4
Yates Ave CV21 . . . .**82** C3
Yatesbury Ave B35 . . . .**22** A3
Yelverton Rd CV6 . . . .**61** D8
Yeomanry Cl 10 CV34 . . .**108** F7
Yew Cl CV3 . . . .**62** C1
Yew Tree Cl B94 . . . .**89** D3
Yew Tree Ct Austrey CV9 . . .**3** A1
1 Royal Leamington Spa
CV31 . . . .**109** F5
Yew Tree Gdns B95 . . . . . .**113** A4
Yew Tree Hill CV23 . . . .**64** C2
Yew Tree La B94 . . . .**113** D8
Yew Trees The B95 . . . . . .**113** B4
Yew Wlk B37 . . . .**33** B2
Yewdale Cres CV2 . . . .**50** E1
Yewdale Ct CV2 . . . .**50** F1
Yews The CV12 . . . .**38** E2
York Ave Atherstone CV9 . . .**12** C1
Bedworth CV12 . . . .**39** D2
York Cl Coventry CV3 . . . . .**78** C5
Studley B80 . . . .**103** B2
York Rd CV31 . . . .**109** F8
York St Coventry CV1 . . . . .**61** B2
Nuneaton CV11 . . . .**29** A4
Rugby CV21 . . . .**82** C2
Yorkminster Dr B37 . . . . . .**33** D3
Yorksand Rd B78 . . . .**8** C4
Young Cl CV34 . . . .**108** B5
Yule Rd CV2 . . . .**62** D5
Yvonne Rd B97 . . . .**102** B4

Z

Zorrina Cl CV10 . . . .**28** B5

Name and Address	Telephone	Page	Grid reference

Street Atlases from Philip's

Philip's publish an extensive range of regional and local street atlases which are ideal for motoring, business and leisure use. They are widely used by the emergency services and local authorities throughout Britain.

Key features include:

◆ Superb county-wide mapping at an extra-large scale of 3½ inches to 1 mile, or 2½ inches to 1 mile in pocket editions

◆ Complete urban and rural coverage, detailing every named street in town and country

◆ Each atlas available in three handy formats – hardback, spiral, pocket paperback

'The mapping is very clear... great in scope and value'

★★★★ BEST BUY   AUTO EXPRESS

1 Bedfordshire
2 Berkshire
3 Birmingham and West Midlands
4 Bristol and Bath
5 Buckinghamshire
6 Cambridgeshire
7 Cardiff, Swansea and The Valleys
8 Cheshire
9 Derbyshire
10 Dorset
11 County Durham and Teesside
12 Edinburgh and East Central Scotland
13 North Essex
14 South Essex
15 Glasgow and West Central Scotland
16 Gloucestershire
17 North Hampshire
18 South Hampshire
19 Hertfordshire
20 East Kent
21 West Kent
22 Lancashire
23 Leicestershire and Rutland
24 London
25 Greater Manchester
26 Merseyside
27 Northamptonshire
28 Nottinghamshire
29 Oxfordshire
30 Staffordshire
31 Surrey
32 East Sussex
33 West Sussex
34 Tyne and Wear and Northumberland
35 Warwickshire
36 Wiltshire and Swindon
37 East Yorkshire and Northern Lincolnshire
38 North Yorkshire
39 South Yorkshire
40 West Yorkshire

How to order

The Philip's range of street atlases is available from good retailers or directly from the publisher by phoning 01903 828503